OLD SPANISH READINGS

*Selected on the basis of critically
edited texts*

EDITED, WITH INTRODUCTION, NOTES

AND VOCABULARY, BY

J. D. M. FORD

HARVARD UNIVERSITY

INTER-
NATIONAL
MODERN
LANGUAGE
SERIES

GINN AND COMPANY

GINN AND COMPANY

BOSTON · NEW YORK · CHICAGO · LONDON
ATLANTA · DALLAS · COLUMBUS · SAN FRANCISCO

PREFACE

This book is intended to facilitate the study of the development of the Spanish language in the earlier period of its history. As scholars know, it is unfortunately the case that many of the Old Spanish monuments have been published by editors who modernized their aspect. For scientific purposes their editions are, of course, very unsatisfactory. Therefore, in the present instance, care has been taken to print selections from editions which do not deform the historical conditions of the language. In the Introduction the more elementary matters of Spanish phonology are treated. The Notes are concerned with both linguistic and literary subjects. The Vocabulary has been made as complete as possible, and, in the discussion of certain points, supplements the Notes. Much yet remains to be done in the way of verifying the etyma of Spanish words; the Vocabulary calls attention to a few of the doubtful cases.

J. D. M. F.

CONTENTS

CORRECTIONS FOR THE INTRODUCTION

P. vii, l. 6 : "northeastern" should be "northern."

P. xi, l. 34 : Add *sento* > *siento*.

P. xiv, l. 29 : Add "the final *i* later became *e*."

" l. 30 : Read *vēnī* > *vini* > *vine* ; *fēcī* > *fizi* > *fize*, mod. *hice*.

P. xv, l. 13 : *peu* should be *peur*.

" l. 24 : *coxum should be *cǫxum.

P. xvi, l. 16 : Omit *stŏrea . . . estera*.

P. xviii, l. 2 : Add " (see (5) (b) for *ǒ* before palatal *n*) : "

P. xx, l. 27 : *ŭnd(ĕ)cim* should be **ŭnd(ĕ)cim*.

P. xxiii, l. 12 : *ascondĕre should be *ascondḗre.

" ll. 25–26 : Omit *serviendum . . . sirviendo*.

P. xxiv, l. 26 : For "dissimilate to" read "become."

P. xxvii, l. 9 : In the parenthesis add, after *u*, " or *r*."

P. xxviii, l. 6 : The second *s* should be *š*.

" l. 9 : After *jabón* add the parenthesis " (possibly from O. Sp. *enxabonar*)."

P. xxix, l. 6 : After *fiel* add the parenthesis " (gall)."

P. xxx, l. 16 : "Latin" should be "Classic Latin."

P. xxxi, l. 2 : For "must" read "may."

P. xxxiii, l. 30 : For *ŭbi* > **ob(e)* read *ŭbi* > **oƀ(e)*.

P. xxxiv, l. 27 : *realem* should be *regalem*.

P. xxxvi, l. 33 : Put a period at the end of the line.

" l. 34 : *fŏrtĭa* should be *Fŏrtĭa*.

P. xxxvii, ll. 28–29 : "preceding" should be "following."

" ll. 34–35 : Omit *raphanum . . . rábano*.

P. xxxviii, l. 3 : *h*'s should be *f*'s.

" l. 11 : *arcu* should be *arco*.

P. xxxix, l. 30 : *derectum* should be *directum*.

P. xl, l. 7 : Put a colon after "sound" and add *axem* > *ajše* > O. Sp. *exe* > *eje* ; V. L. *cǫxum > *coxo* > *cojo*.

" l. 30 : Omit from "written" to the end of the line.

P. xli, l. 23 : *enteiro should be *entejro.

INTRODUCTION

Spanish is one of the Romance languages spoken in the Iberian peninsula. It is the speech of the larger and more central part of the region; in the western part we find Portuguese (with its dialect Galician, once much used for literary purposes), and in the eastern part Catalan (closely allied to Provençal). The Basques, who occupy the northeastern part of the territory, have a language of their own, with features quite unlike those of the general Indo-European group; it is thought by some scholars to derive from the ancient Iberian. Through colonial expansion Spanish has become the language of many millions of civilized beings in the New World: Mexico, Central America, Cuba, Porto Rico, and by far the greater part of South America (with the notable exceptions of Brazil and the Guianas), all own its sway. It was once much spoken in Texas and California; it still survives in New Mexico and sporadically in the neighboring districts. In the Philippines it has long been the official language, but has not displaced the native dialects; in the Canaries it has been firmly intrenched for over four centuries. The Spanish Jews, when expelled from Spain, carried the language with them, and they maintain it still in the places occupied by them in Turkey and elsewhere. Through colonial and general trading operations it has fixed itself in still other portions of the globe. On the whole, about twenty million persons speak Spanish in Spain and no less than forty million in foreign parts. As a medium of literary expression Spanish dates back to the 12th century.

In the Spanish of Spain there are discernible three chief dialects: Leonese-Asturian, Navarro-Aragonese, and Castilian. Andalusian does not differ radically enough from Castilian to oblige us to regard it as a separate dialect. Of these dialects, Castilian alone has attained to real literary importance; it is therefore the form of the language that we are now undertaking to study, and it may be said that for the natives of all parts of Spain — and even of all the Spanish-speaking world — *el castellano* means 'Spanish.'

Spanish is one of the several modern spoken forms of Latin that we call the Romance languages. It does not represent in its essence the highly refined and somewhat artificial written Latin known to us as the classic speech of Vergil, Cicero, and the many writers of ancient Rome. On the contrary it perpetuates the Vulgar Latin, the spoken language of the masses in Italy and, in particular, of the Latin soldiers and colonists whom the Roman conquest brought to Spain and who settled there. This Vulgar Latin of everyday use, no less ancient than the classic form of the language, differed from the latter in not a few respects: morphologically it was simpler, disregarding as it did many of the flexional variations of the written Classic Latin; phonologically it differed also in no slight degree; and these differences are well reflected in the Romance languages. Written records of Vulgar Latin are scanty; inscriptions and the testimony of the Roman grammarians furnish us with some material, but it is mainly through a comparative study of the Romance languages that we have arrived at a knowledge of its forms. Of the Iberian and Celtic speeches already used in Spain before the advent of the Romans we need take little cognizance. So complete was the Romanization of the territory that they absolutely disappeared, barring some very few and doubtful survivals in the lexicon. The basis of the Spanish lexicon is Vulgar Latin, with certain accretions from Classic Latin, Germanic, Arabic, French, and Italian, and, in a less degree, from the Indian and other languages. In its phonology, morphology, and syntax, Spanish simply modifies or develops purely Latin features.

In the Notes and Vocabulary questions of morphology and syntax arising out of our texts have been given the notice that seemed necessary in this little manual. For the morphology and syntax of Spanish, reference may be had in general to the works of several authoritative scholars. The more important are these : G. Baist, *Die spanische Sprache*, in Gröber's *Grundriss der romanischen Philologie*, 2d ed., I. 878 ff. ; R. Menéndez Pidal, *Manual Elemental de Gramática Histórica Española*, 2d ed., Madrid, 1905 ; A. Zauner, *Altspanisches Elementarbuch*, Heidelberg, 1908 ; id., *Romanische Sprachwissenschaft*, 2d ed., Leipzig, 1905 ; F. Hanssen, *Spanische Grammatik*, Halle, 1910 ; F. Diez, *Grammatik der romanischen Sprachen*, 3d ed., 1870–1872 (see also the French translation) ; W. Meyer-Lübke, *Grammatik der romanischen Sprachen*, Leipzig, 1890 *et seq.* ; Bello-Cuervo, *Gramática de la Lengua Castellana*. A good and full etymological dictionary of Spanish has not appeared as yet ; we can resort only to Diez's *Etymologisches Wörterbuch der romanischen Sprachen*, 5th ed., Bonn, 1887, and to G. Körting's *Latein-Romanisches Wörterbuch*, 3d ed., Paderborn, 1907, both of which leave a great deal to be desired. Valuable information respecting the Arabic element in Spanish may be gained from Dozy and Engelmann's *Glossaire des mots espagnols et portugais dérivés de l'arabe*, 2d ed., Leyden, 1869. This work is not definitive, however, and its lacunæ have not been filled up by Eguílaz, Pedro de Alcalá, Simonet, or the others who have treated of the subject. In what follows of our Introduction we shall deal with the more elementary matters of Spanish phonology ; more complete information will be found in the various works just mentioned.

PHONOLOGY

I. Vowels

The ordinary vowels and diphthongs of Classic Latin had in Vulgar Latin these counterparts :

Cl. L.	ā ă	æ ĕ	ē œ ĭ	ī	ŏ	ō ŭ	ū	au
V. L.	a	ę	ẹ	i̦	ǫ	ọ	u̦	au

In Vulgar Latin, qualitative distinctions of open and close vowel took the place of the Classic Latin distinctions of quantity, long and short. The dot under a vowel indicates the close pronunciation; the hook marks an open pronunciation. For the development of the Vulgar Latin vowels into Spanish we have to consider separately the history of the accented and the unaccented syllables, and we shall confine our examples in general to the popular words as distinguished from the learned words.

1. Accented Vowels

When the influence of contiguous sounds did not interfere, the Vulgar Latin accented vowels listed above usually developed as follows in Spanish:

V. L.	a	ę	e	i	ǫ	o au	u
Sp.	a	ie	e	i	ue	o	u

It is seen that the open vowels diphthongized, and this diphthongization, contrary to the process followed in French and Italian, is carried out when the Vulgar Latin vowel is in a protected syllable as well as when it stands in a free syllable. When dealing with the individual Vulgar Latin vowels we shall consider the checking or modifying influences of the contiguous sounds. The Vulgar Latin oblique case, as denoted ordinarily by the accusative (whose -m was not pronounced except in monosyllables), became the norm for the development into Spanish.

(1) *a*. (a) V. L. *a*, representing both the *ā* and the *ă* of Classic Latin, ordinarily maintained itself under the accent in Spanish:

āla > ala; pắter, patrem > padre; pars, partem > parte.

(b) An *i* (*y*) immediately following it, or attracted to it from the next syllable, could close the *a* to *e*. Hence a diphthong *ei* (*ey*), which simplified to *e* in Castilian:

laicus, laicum > lego; basium > beso; sartago, sartăgĭnem > after loss of intervocalic *g* (*e, i*), *sartén*.

As often happens, dialectal Spanish and the sister language, Portuguese, show the intermediate stage: cf. Ptg. *leigo*; Leonese *beiso*, Ptg. *beijo*.

The following *dį, gį* (both *y* in V.L.), and *į* might simply remain as *y* and leave the *a* unaffected:

radĭum > rayo; V.L. **plagĭa > playa*; *Malum > Mayo*.

(c) A palatal consonant following the *a* may vocalize and produce an *į* (*y*), which then induces the same result, *e*:

factum > O. Sp. *fecho*, mod. *hecho*, cf. Ptg. *feito*; *axis, axem,* i.e. V. L. *acse(m) > O.* Sp. *exe*, mod. *eje*, cf. Ptg. *eixo*.

(d) A *u* following, whether one already forming a diphthong with the *a* in Classic Latin (*causa*), or one forming such a diphthong in V.L. (L. *amavit*, V.L. *amaut*, found in inscriptions), or one attracted from a following syllable (*sapui > *saupi*), or one developed out of a following *l* before a consonant (*alter, alterum > *autro*), likewise reacted upon the *a*, as the *a* in its turn did upon the *u*. The result was *o* in Castilian. One of the intermediate stages was the diphthong *ou*, still found in Leonese and in (northern) Portuguese:

causa > cosa, cf. Ptg. and Leonese *cousa*; *amavit, amaut > amó*, cf. Ptg. and Leonese *amou*; *sapui > *saupi > O.* Sp. *sope*, mod. *supe*, cf. Ptg. *soube*; *alt(ĕ)rum > *autro > otro*, cf. Ptg. *outro*.

(2) V.L. *ę* for L. *ĕ* and *ae*.

(a) If not checked by adjacent sounds, V.L. *ę* under the accent became in Castilian the diphthong *ie*. It has not yet been definitively ascertained whether the accent fell originally on the *i* or the *e* of the diphthong; most of the conditions resulting in Castilian are met by the theory that already in O. Sp. the accent rested on the *e*, some are not so easily satisfied thereby. Examples of the unchecked development:

pĕtra > piedra; *tĕnet > tiene*; *caelum > cielo*; *caecum > ciego*. sento > siento

(b) A palatal element following the V.L. *ę* may close it to *ẹ* and prevent the diphthongization; sometimes this palatal element remains, and again it is carried over to the *ẹ* and absorbed in it:

> *supĕrbḭa* > *soberbia*; *matĕrḭa* > *madera*, cf. Ptg. *madeira*; *sĕdĕat*, V.L. **sẹyat* > *sea*.

The palatalizing force may be the result of the vocalization of a following consonant:

> *lĕctum* > **leẹḭto* (i.e. *ẹ* + palatal *y* + a *t* infected with the palatalizing force of the *y* and approximating to *tš* or *ch*) > *lecho*, cf. Ptg. *leito*; *integer*, *ĭntĕgrum*, V.L. *intẹgrum* > *entero*, cf. Ptg. *inteiro*.

Here it is to be noticed that, although the closing seems to have occurred in *spĕcŭlum* > **speclum* > *espejo*, it has not in *vĕtŭlum* > V.L. *vẹclum* > *viejo*. The V.L. *veclum* is attested by the *Appendix Probi*, and therefore, belonging to the pre-Romance period, would seem early enough to develop even as *speculum* did. While the palatal *ḭ* thus produced has usually been absorbed in the *ẹ*, it has remained in

> *sĕx*, i.e. *sẹcs* > *seis*; *pĕcten*, *pĕctĭnem* > *peine*.

(c) Sometimes the diphthong *ie* was regularly developed and then a secondary *ḭ* (*y*), occasioned by the loss of an intervening consonant, changed it to *i*:

> *tĕpĭdum* > **tiebido* > *tḭebḭo*, and this by the double palatalizing force > *tibio*.

In like manner a following palatal *l* changed *ie* through *ḭeḭ* to *i*:

> *sĕlla* > O. Sp. *siella* > mod. *silla*; diminutive suffix *-ĕllum* > O. Sp. *-iello* > mod. *-illo*.

A preceding *l* has taken up the *ḭ* of *ie* and been palatalized by it, at a rather recent date, in

> *lĕvat* > O. Sp. *lieva* (as opposed to *lĕvare* > O. Sp. *levar*) > mod. *lleva*.

The diphthong was thus simplified to *e* wherever it appeared, and then the *ll* was generalized: hence *llevar*, etc.

(d) In hiatus the *ie* became *i*:

> *Dĕus > Dieos > Díos > Diós* (with a later shift of accent); *mĕum > mieo* (still Leonese) *> mío*.

Also after the O. Sp. palatal sibilant *dž*, the *i* of the diphthong has been absorbed in the case of *mulĭĕrem*, V. L. *muliérem > O. Sp. mugier > mod. mujer.*

(e) Not well explained as yet are the cases in which O. Sp. *ie* before *s* + a consonant changed to *i*. Examples:

> *vĕspera > viespera > mod. víspera* (note that the retention of the unaccented penult *e* is not wholly popular); *vĕspa > aviespa* (with an *a-* probably due to the analogy of *abeja < apĭcula) > mod. avispa*; *prĕssa > priessa > mod. priesa* and *prisa.*

It is possible that by the act of raising the tongue and narrowing the air chamber in the mouth — an act necessary for the production of *sp* and *st* — the *e* of *ie* was raised and closed to *i*, and the resulting combination was then reduced to *i*.

(3) V. L. *ẹ* from L. *ē, ĭ, oe.*

(a) Except when subjected to the further closing influence of some following sound, V. L. *ẹ* remained in Castilian:

> *sēta > seda; plēnum > lleno; cĭbum > cebo; bĭbit > bebe; poena > pena; foedum > feo.*

(b) A palatal element of the following syllable may close the *ẹ* to *i*. Usually this palatalizing element (*i*) remains in the Spanish word and is constantly exercising its force:

> *cērĕum > cirio; vĭtreum > vidrio.*

A secondary *i* due to the loss of an intervening consonant produces the same effect and also remains:

> *lĭmpĭdum > limpio.*

(c) Where the palatalizing element is one that does not remain in Spanish, generally the *ę* persists. The *i* (and *ę = i̭*), if it follow the *ę* directly, is absorbed by it; if it be separated by another consonant, its force appears to be consumed in the palatalization of that consonant. So, too, an *i* evolved out of a palatal consonant does not affect the *ę*.

> *corrĭgĭa*, V.L. *corręja (*correya*) > *correa*; *dĭssĭdĭum*, V.L. *desseyo > *deseo*; *vĭtĭum* > *vezo*; *tristĭtĭa* > *tristeza* (and so in the many abstracts in *-itia* > *-eza*); *consĭlĭum* > *consejo*; *cĭlĭum*, ntr. pl. *cĭlĭa* > *ceja*; *parĭcŭlum* (through *pariclum) > *parejo* (and so in all the diminutives in *-ĭcŭlum*); *rēgula* > *reja*; *tēctum* > *techo*; *strĭctum* > *estrecho*; *sĭgnʋm* > *seño*; *lĭgnum* > *leño*.

In cases such as *tiñe* < *tĭngit*, *riñe* < V.L. *rĭngit, the *i* may be due to the analogy of other verbs with *e* in the infinitive stem and *i* under the accent in the stem-stressed forms. In *tiña* < *tĭnĕa* we may see the influence of *tiñe*.

(d) A following *ṷ* (*w*) does not appear to have closed the *ę* to *i* with any regularity. As opposed to O. Sp. *mingua* < V.L. *mĭnuat, L. *mĭnŭit*, we have the mod. *mengua*; and so, also, *lĭngua* has given *lengua*.

(e) In hiatus the V.L. *ę* became *i*:

> *vĭa* > *via*; *-ęa* (the impf. indic. ending, which arose in V.L. by dissimilation in such verbs as *habēbam* > *habęa, *debēbam* > *debęa) > *-ía*.

(f) Final unaccented *ī* reacted upon the accented *ę* and closed it to *i*: *Final i latin became e*

> *vēnī* > *vine*; *fēcī* > O. Sp. *fize*, mod. *hice*.
> *vēnī > vini > vine; fēcī > fizi > fize mod. hice*

(4) V.L. *i* for L. *ī*.
    V.L. *i* remains in Spanish:

> *fīcum* > *higo*; *lis*, *lītem* > *lid*.

(5) V. L. *ǫ* for L. *ŏ*.

    (a) V. L. *ǫ* under the accent, if no checking influence pre-
vailed, gave in Castilian the diphthong *ue*, an earlier
stage of which was *uo*, still found in dialects as well
as in the sister language, Italian. The Castilian *ue* has
been found as early as the 10th century, but it has
been argued (cf. Menéndez Pidal, *Gramática del Cid*,
p. 143) that the 12th century *Poema del Cid* still has
uó in rhyme. However this may be, Castilian had *ue*
as the regular sound from the 13th century on, and
uo appearing sporadically in the MSS. can then be only
dialectal. Perhaps the *e* of *ue* had from the beginning
the very open value (like that of French *eu* in *peur*)
which it now has. Examples:

fŏcum > fuego; *mors, mŏrtem > muerte*; *bŏnum > bueno.*

The passage of *uo* to *ue*, where there was no antecedent *ŏ*, is seen in *quōmodo*, V. L. **quomo* > O. Sp.
cuemo beside O. Sp. *como* (the proclitic and unaccented
form), mod. *como.*

    (b) In general a following palatal, whatever its source, will
close the V. L. *ǫ* to *ọ* and prevent the diphthongization in Castilian:

hŏdĭe, V. L. **hǫye > hoy*; *pŏdĭum > poyo*; *nox, nŏctem > noche*;
V. L. **cǫxum* (cf. L. *coxo*) > O. Sp. *coxo* (i.e. *cošo* with palatal *s*), mod. *cojo*; *fŏlĭum*, ntr. pl. *fŏlĭa > hoja*; *ŏcŭlum > ojo.*

In cases like O. Sp. *fuerça*, mod. *fuerza < fŏrtĭa*, the
force of the *i̯* was consumed in the assibilation of the
t and there remained no permanent palatal sound as
there did in *poyo*, *noche*, O. Sp. *coxo*, O. Sp. *ojo*, or we
may see here the analogy of *fuerte*. Apparently the palatal did not prevent the diphthongization in the combinations with *n*; cf.

lŏnge > lueñe (but there is the possible influence of *luengo*);
Saxŏnĭa > Sansueña; *Gascŏnĭa > O. Sp. *Gascueña*, mod.

Gascuña (but cf. *Gasconna* in our texts, **41** 4) ; *sŏmnĭum* >
sueño (but there is the influence of L. *sŏmnum*, in which
the nasals may not have palatalized early enough to prevent
the diphthongization).

(c) In certain cases the *ue* was developed in O. Sp. and later
reduced to *e*. In some instances there is no clear
reason for this change. If a labial combination of
consonants preceded or followed the *ue*, the reduction
might be due to dissimilation of the labial *u̯*. Again, if
the *ue* was in the same syllable with a foregoing group
of two consonants, its disappearance might be due to
the desire to soften a harsh combination of three consonants, since the *u̯* is itself a consonantal *u*. Examples :

frons, *frŏntem* > O. Sp. *fruente*, mod. *frente* ; *flŏccum* > O. Sp.
flueco, mod. *fleco* ; *cŏlŭbra*, V. L. *cŏlŏbra*, O. Sp. *culuebra*,
mod. *culebra* ; *stŏrea* > O. Sp. *estuera*, mod. *estera*.)

If the word containing the *ue* passed into a proclitic unaccented position, through being compounded with
another word, the *ue* seems to have been reduced to *e* :

hŏstem antīquam > O. Sp. (*h*)*uest antigua*, mod. *estantigua* ; *pŏst*
+ *aurĭculum* > *puestorejo*, mod. *pestorejo* ; *pŏst* + *coccĕu* >
puescueço, mod. *pescuezo*.

(d) Some words developed in a double form. Their syntactical function explains the difference in development.
If accented (and then they were generally used in a
stronger and more literal sense), they had the diphthong ; if thrown into a proclitic unaccented position,
they did not diphthongize. Examples :

dŏmĭnum > *dueño* ' master,' ' owner,' but *don* (and this may be
L. *dŏmĭne*) if it is proclitic to a name (*Don Juan*, etc.) ;
comes, *cŏmĭtem* > O. Sp. *cuende*, but *conde* when it stood before a name (*Conde Fernán González*) ; later on *conde* was
generalized in use and displaced *cuende* ;
pons, *pŏntem* > *puente*, in the ordinary use as a noun, but
ponte in combinations forming place names (*Pontevedra* ;
but dialectal circumstances should be considered here) ;

fons, fŏntem > fuente, as a common noun, but *fonte* in place names (*Fontefrida = Fuentefría, Fuenfría*, in the ballads); *homo, hŏmĭnem >* O. Sp. *uemne* in independent use as a noun, but O. Sp. *omne* (whence mod. *hombre*) in unaccented pronominal use like that of French *on* and in apparent proclitic use in phrases such as *omnes de Burgos =* O. Sp. *Burgeses* (cf. Baist, in Gröber's *Grundriss d. roman. Philol.* I, 2d ed., p. 889). *Omne* became very early the general form in all uses. For *mons, mŏntem*, the rather common appearance of the word in place names also gave currency to the undiphthongized form (cf. *Montealegre, Montefrío*, etc.).

The theory that the nasal adjacent to the *ǫ* in all these words closed it has not received full approbation.

(6) V. L. *ǫ* for L. *ō* and *ŭ*, and *au*.

(a) If unaffected by an adjacent closing force, the V. L. *ǫ* remained as *o* in Castilian :

> *vōtum*, pl. *vōta > boda* ; *hōra > hora* ; *lŭtum > lodo* ; *mŭsca > mosca*.

(b) The V. L. diphthong *au*, corresponding to the L. *au*, likewise gave *o* in Castilian, as did also the secondary *au* due to the vocalization of a consonant or the attraction to the *a* of a *u* of the following syllable ; cf. (1) (d). Apparently the *u* of the *au* — a semiconsonant in value — maintained itself long enough to prevent the following consonant from receiving the intervocalic treatment, and hence that consonant, if voiceless, did not voice :

> *aurum > oro* ; *cautum > coto* ; *talpa > topo* (with change of gender) ; *sapuit >* O. Sp. *sopo*.

Where the *au* remains in Castilian, it is of late or learned development :

> *causa > causa* ; *captivum > cautivo* (cf. O. Sp. *cativo*) ; *actum > auto* (with apparently back or velar pronunciation of the *c*, which therefore vocalized as *u* and not as *i*).

(c) A palatalizing element preceding or following, whether primary or secondary (*i* derived from *l* or *c* before *t* ;

the palatal factor in *ñ* from *gn*, or *nᵢ*; etc.), closed the *ǫ* to *u*: (see (5)(b) for ŏ before palatal n):

- *jŭgum* > *yugo*;
- *cōgĭtō* (rather than V. L. **cŏgito*, required for French), V. L. **cǫyito*, **cǫyeto* > *cuido*;
- *fŭgĭo*, V. L. **foyo* > *huyo* (from this and other forms in which an *ᵢ* closed the *o* to *u*, the *u* passed to all the rest of the verb; hence O. Sp. *foir, foido* < V. L. **fŭgīre*, **fŭgītum* became mod. *huir, huído*);
- *trŭcta* > **trujᵢa* > *trucha*;
- *mŭltum* > **mujᵢo* (cf. Ptg. *muito*) > *mucho* (the diphthong remains in *muy*, a proclitic reduction of **mujᵢo*);
- *vultur, vŭltŭrem* > **vultre* > *buitre* (the *ᵢ* remains because it was not consumed in a palatalization of the *t*; before another consonant the *t* could not be palatalized);
- *pŭgnum* > *puño*;
- *cŭneum* > *cuño* (*mn* > *nn* palatalized too late to produce any effect: *autŭmnum* > *otoño*);
- *rŭbĕum* > *rubio*; *plŭvĭa* > *lluvia*; *tŭrbĭdum* > **tǫrbᵢo* > *turbio*; *pŭnctum* > **pǫnto* (the *ñ* became *n* before the consonant) > *punto*.

The combinations *cl*, *lᵢ*, *tᵢ* did not affect the *ǫ*; their palatal force did not go beyond the reaction upon the *l* and *t*:

genŭc(ŭ)lum, L. *genĭculum* > *hinojo* (and in general the diminutive suffix *-ŭc(ŭ)lum* gave *-ojo*); *cŭscŏlĭum* > *coscojo*; *pŭtĕum* > *pozo*.

(d) A situation not yet well understood has arisen when the *ᵢ* has been attracted from a following syllable to the V. L. *ǫ*. The result appears to be *ue* instead of the *ui* that we might expect; cf. *vŭltŭrem* > *buitre*:

cĭcōnĭa > *cigüeña*; V. L. **rĭsōnĕum* > *risueño*; V. L. **vītōnĕum* > *vidueño*, but also *viduño* and *veduño*.

The form *viduño* (cf. also *terruño*, etc.) might be thus explained: **vītōnĕum* > **vidonᵢo* > **vidoᵢño* > **viduᵢño*, and, with absorption of the *ᵢ* by the *ñ*, *viduño*. For the result *-ueño* we have to suppose an opening of the epenthetic *i* to *e*, which seems rather unnatural,

and yet appears to have happened also for the suffix
-ōrĭum > *-uero* (**co-opertōrĭa* > *cobertuera*, mod. *cobertera*; see the Vocab.), and in *augŭrĭum* > *agüero* (cf.
note to **4** 17 and the Vocab. s.v. *verguença*). Or was
the process *ói* > *óe* > *oé* > *ué*? Portuguese and
Leonese show the *oi* stage: *agoiro*, etc. Perhaps the
whole matter is largely one of suffix interchange. In
the case of *fŭĭt* > *fué* (with shift of accent from *fúe*),
it is usually assumed that the hiatus produced the
closing of *ǫ* > *u*; cf. O.Sp. *foe* and *fo*. But we must
bear in mind the possible analogical force of *fŭī* >
O. Sp. *fúi, fúe, fu*, mod. *fuí*; and then, too, the closing
might have occurred first in *fuéron*, O. Sp. *fuesse*, etc.

(7) V. L. *ų* for L. *ū* remains in Castilian:

mūtum > *mudo*; *fūmum* > *humo*.

2. Unaccented Vowels

The history of the unaccented vowels varies according as to
whether they are initial (i.e. either begin the word or stand in
the first syllable), medial, or final. In the initial position they
are more likely to maintain themselves; in the medial and final
positions they often disappear. As *e* and *ę* both became *e*, and
ǫ and *ǫ* both became *o* in Castilian, when not accented, we have
but five vowels, *a, e, i, ǫ* and *ų*, to deal with (besides the V. L.
au which became *ǫ* in Castilian). In the final position these
were reduced to three, *a, e,* and *o,* inasmuch as *i* there opened
to *e* at an early stage of O. Sp. and *ų* from L. *ū* hardly existed
in V. L., at least in really popular words.

a. Final Position

(1) *a.* V. L. *a* remains:

amīca > *amiga*; *amat* > *ama*.

Any closing of the *a* to *e* is rather due to analogical influence or dialectal development: this is probably the

case for the impf. indic. ending *-ia* etc. > O. Sp. *-ie*, and the poss. adjs. *mie, tue, sue.* Cf. the Notes, pp. 119 ff., and the Vocab. s.v. *mi, tu, su.*

(2) *e.* (a) V.L. *e, ę,* and *i* all became *e* and this dropped in O. Sp. if the preceding consonant was one that could stand at the end of a word. Thus, after *d* (from L. intervocalic *t* and often written *t* in the final position in O. Sp., as it was there unvoiced), *l, n, r, s,* and *z* (for both *z* and *ç,* as the latter was not written in the final position), the *e* disappeared:

> *rete* > *red* ; *civitātem* > *ciudad* (also *çibdat* in O. Sp.) ; *vīlem* > *vil* ; *panem* > *pan* ; *mare* > *mar* ; *mensem,* V.L. *mese > *mes* ; *vĭcem* > *vez* ; *pĭscem* > *pez.*

In verb forms the modern language has restored the *e* where O. Sp. occasionally lost it ; *valet* > O. Sp. *val,* mod. *vale* ; *dīcĭt* > O. Sp. *diz,* mod. *dice* ; *fēcī* > O. Sp. *fizi, fize* and *fiz,* mod. *hice.*

So, too, the modern language has restored the *e* often lost in O. Sp. in cases of enclisis : cf. *manol = mano + le,* **16** 174 ; *not = no(n) + te,* **21** 24 ; *aquis = aqui + se,* **17** 1085 ; etc. The loss of the *e* often superinduced further phonetic changes in O. Sp. ; thus the *Cid* shows the forms *nimbla = ni + me + la* and *did el cauallo = di te el c.* ; etc.

(b) After a consonant combination, and after *b, v, ll, rr,* and *x* (i.e. *š,* the mod. *j*), the *e* remained as a vowel of support:

> *hom(ĭ)nem* > *hombre* ; *ŭnd(ĕ)cim* > O. Sp. *onze,* mod. *once* ; *amab(ĭ)lem* > *amable* ; *trabem* > *trabe* ; *bibĭt* > *bebe* ; *habŭi* > O. Sp. *ovi, ove,* mod. *hube* ; *clavem* > *llave* ; *fŏllem* > *fuelle* ; *tŭrrem* > *torre* ; *axem* > O. Sp. *exe,* mod. *eje.*

While in O. Sp. the *e* sometimes dropped after a consonant combination, the modern language regularly writes it : *pueent = puent,* **16** 150 ; *noch* (*= notš*), **15** 137 ; etc. ; the *e* occasionally dropped, too, after one of the consonantal sounds just mentioned : the *Cid*

has *nuef* = *nueve* (the *v* unvoiced in the final position),
off = *ove* < *habŭī* ; etc.

(c) Final *e* in hiatus may become *y* (*i̯*):

rĕgem, V. L. *reye > *reę* > *rey* ; *bŏvem*, V. L. *bŏem > *buee* > *buey*.

(3) *o*. The *o* of V. L. remained in Castilian :

ŭmo > *amo* ; *amīcŭm* > *amigo*.

The loss of the *o*, or the appearance of some other
vowel instead of it, is to be explained as due to some
syntactical reason (proclisis, etc.), or to analogy, or to
some other cause ; the phenomenon cannot be phonological. Thus *un* for *uno*, *buen* for *bueno*, etc. are all
due to proclitic use.

b. Medial Position

(1) The unaccented penult of words accented on the antepenult. ~~Post-tonic~~

(a) After the accent the unaccented vowel of the penult
dropped, unless it was *a* or the resulting combination
of consonants was impossible :

comĭtem > O. Sp. *cuende* and *conde*; *lĕpŏrem* > *liebre*; *cŏmpŭtum*
> *cuento*.

In some cases the loss had occurred already in V.L., as
is shown by the failure of the voiceless intervocalic
consonant to voice :

pŏsitum, V. L. *pŏstum* > *puesto* ; *rĕputo*, V. L. *rĕpto > *rieto*.

(b) But *a* maintained itself :

anas, *anătem* > *ánade* ; *raphănum* > *rábano* ; *orphănum* >
huérfano.

(c) Again, to prevent the juxtaposition of consonants that
could not be pronounced together, the vowel remained :

lacrĭma > *lágrima* (but we expect *lagrema) ; *hospes*, *hŏspĭtem*
> *huésped*.

But most words of this class seem to be at least half-
learned : e.g., *ángel*, *césped*, etc.

(d) Some words in *-ĭdus* lost the intervocalic *d* early and the penult *i* remained as *i* in a word now accented on the penult:

tepĭdum > *tibio*; *sucĭdum* > O. Sp. *suzio*, mod. *sucio*.

In others, however, the *i* went first:

nĭtĭdum > *neto*.

(2) The unaccented vowel between the secondary and the chief accent.

(a) With the exception of *a*, a vowel between the secondary and the chief accent might drop, if the adjacent consonants permitted:

malĕdīco > *maldigo*; *comĭtātum* > *condado*; *catēnātum* > O.Sp. *cañado*, mod. *candado*; *septimana* > O. Sp. *sedmana*, mod. *semana*.

(b) But *a* remained:

paradīsum > *paraíso*; *calamĕllum* > *caramillo*.

(c) If the surrounding consonants could not come together, the vowel remained:

tempestas, *tèmpestãtem* > *tempestad* (but perhaps this is half-learned); *multitudo*, *mùltĭtũdinem* > *muchedumbre* (but this is perhaps only a formation on *mucho*).

(d) In the verb system analogy often explains the retention of the vowel:

adjūto > *ayudo*, and therefore *ayudar* < *adjutãre* (cf. Fr. *aider*, Ital. *aitare*).

c. Initial Position

(1) *a*. (a) Unless affected by a following palatal or labial sound, *a* remained:

caballum > *caballo*.

(b) Under the influence of a following *i̯* or *u̯*, the *a* was affected as it was under the accent:

> *mansio, mansĭōnem*, V. L. *masıonem > *maison > *mesón* ; V. L. **vaṛiọ́la* > *vaịruela > O. Sp. *veṛuela*, and, through the closing force of the *u̯*, > *viruela* ; *maxilla* > O. Sp. *mexilla*, mod. *mejilla* ; *jactare* > *echar* ; *autŭmnum* > *otoño* ; *sapuĭmus* > O. Sp. *sopimʌs*, mod. *supimos* ; *altarĭum* > *otero* (with change of sense).

(c) Assimilation, dissimilation, the interchange of real or seeming prefixes, etc. will explain other cases of alteration of the *a*:

> *abscondĕre*, V. L. **ascondĕ́re* > O. Sp. *asconder*, whence, under the influence of the prefix *ex-*, Sp. *es-*, *esconder* ; V. L. *anĕthŭlum > *anedlo > O. Sp. *aneldo*, whence by assimilation *eneldo*.

(2) *e*. (a) The *e* remains unless closed by an *i̯* or a *u̯* of the accented syllable following:

> *lēgālem* (under the influence of *ley*) > *leal* ; *lĕntĭcula* > *lenteja* ; *praeco, praecōnem* > *pregón* ; V. L. **sĭmĭli̯are* > *semejar*.

(b) The closing of the *e* to *i* by the *i̯* of the following accented syllable is, like that of *o* to *u* under the same conditions, a marked feature of Spanish. It is especially prominent in the verb system:

> *semĕntem* > *simiente* ; *pre(he)nsionem* > *presi̯on* > *prisión* ; *servĭāmus* > *sirvamos* ; *servīvĕrunt* > *servi̯eron* > *sirvieron* ; *servi̯ĕndum* > *servi̯endo* > *sirviendo*.

(c) The closing by *u̯* is less common:

> *aequalem* > O. Sp. *egu̯al* > *igual* ; V. L. *mĭnŭāre > O. Sp. *minguar* beside *menguar* (only the latter has survived) ; O. Sp. *veruela* > mod. *viruela*.

(d) Other changes in initial *e* are to be regarded as due to especial circumstances, such as the obscuring force of adjacent *r*, borrowing from foreign languages, etc.:

> *vervactum* > *barbecho* (possibly *e* > *a* under the influence of the *r*) ; *silvaticum* > *salvaje* (through O. Fr. *salvage*).

(3) *i*. (a) The *i* usually remained:

> *titio, tĭtĭōnem* > *tizón*; *rīpārĭa* > *ribera*.

(b) But by dissimilation from a following accented *i*, it may become *e*:

> *vīcīnum* > **vizino* (cf. Ptg. *vizinho*) > O. Sp. *vezino*, mod. *vecino*; *dīcĕre*, V. L. **dīcīre* > *dizir* > O. Sp. *dezir*, mod. *decir*; *rīdēre*, V. L. **rīdīre* > O. Sp. *riir*, mod. *reir*.

(4) *o*. (a) Unless closed by some preceding or following force, the *o* (including Sp. *o* from V. L. *au*) maintained itself:

> *nōmĭnāre* > *nombrar*; *fŭgĕre*, V. L. **fŭgīre* > O. Sp. *foir* (the *u* of mod. *huir*, etc., is due to the analogy of *fŭgio* > *huyo*, etc.); *cŏrōna* > *corona*; *aurĭcŭla* > *oreja*.

(b) The change of *o* to *u* as the result of a preceding palatal seems to have occurred in

> V. L. **jŏcāre* > O. Sp. *jogar*, mod. *jugar*.

There are cases like mod. *lugar* for O. Sp. *logar*, *logal* < *lŏcāle*, and mod. *pulgar* < *pŏllĭcāre*, which are not readily explained. Vulgar wit may have connected the latter word with *pūlex*, V. L. **pūlica*, Sp. *pulga*.

(c) A following *i* or *u̯* closed the *o* to *u*:

> *mŭlĭĕrem* > O. Sp. *mugier*, mod. *mujer*; *cŏgnātum* > *cuñado*; *dŏrmīvērunt* > *dormi̯eron* > *durmieron*; *dŏrmĭāmus* > *durmamos*; *dŏrmĭĕndum* > *durmiendo*.

(d) By dissimilation from accented *o*, an initial *o*, especially if obscured by an adjacent *r*, may ~~dissimilate to~~ become *e*:

> *formōsum* > *hermoso*; *rotŭndum* > **rodondo* > *redondo*; F. *horloge* > **rolož* (*ž* = Fr. *j* or *g* before *e*) > O. Sp. *relox*, mod. *reloj*.

(5) *u*. The V. L. *u̯* maintained itself in Spanish:

> *mūtāre* > *mudar*; V. L. **pūrĭtĭa* > *pureza*.

II. CONSONANTS

The fate of the Latin consonants in Spanish was dependent upon their position as initial, medial, or final. In the initial position they maintained themselves to a considerable degree; in the medial position they underwent certain changes necessary to adapt them to the surrounding vocalic conditions (the voiceless consonants voiced, some of the voiced disappeared, etc.); and in the final position, as a result of a weakening in their enunciation, they tended to vanish.

a. Final Consonants

Since for substantives it is the oblique (accusative) case which is the basis of development for the Romance word, many consonants apparently final in Latin were not so in the V. L. sources of our Spanish words. Even for neuter nouns we often have to suppose an oblique stem; thus, L. *mel* has not a final *l* from our point of view; we start with a V. L. **melle*, whence Sp. *miel*. It is chiefly in the parts of speech not substantival that we can accept a Classic Latin final consonant as final for our purposes.

(1) *s*, *n*, *r*. These remain in Spanish.

    (a) *s* remains chiefly as the sign of the plural in substantives and as a flexional sign in verbs:

> *causas* > *cosas*; *amas* > *amas*. Cf. also *mĭnus* > *menos*; *magis*, V. L. *max* (i.e. *macs*) > *mas*; *sex* (i.e. *secs*) > *seis*.

    (b) *n* was final in but a few words:

> *ĭn* > *en*; *non* > *non*. (From this came *no*, through a development in syntactical relation: *non* + *me* (enclitic) > O. Sp. *nom(e)*; *non* + *lo* (enclitic) > O. Sp. *nolo*; *non* + *se* (enclitic) > O. Sp. *nos(e)*. A redivision led to *no me*, *no lo*, etc.)

    (c) A sure V. L. case of final *r* is difficult to find. We doubtless must assume a V. L. *por* (L. *pro*, but *por-* in composition), whence Sp. *por*. Instead of L. *quattuor* and *semper* we must postulate V. L. **quáttoro*, **sémpere*.

(2) *t, nt, st*. These are chiefly important in connection with the inflection of the verb.

(a) Final *t* disappeared:

> *amat > ama*; *stat > está*; *aut > ó*.

Final *nt > n*:

> *amant > aman*; *sŭnt > son.*

Final *st > s*:

> *est > es*; *pŏst > pues* and unaccented *pos* (*en pos de*).

While *caput* could give Sp. *cabo*, we should still postulate a V.L. **capum*, in view of V.L. **capĭcia > O. Sp. cabeça*, mod. *cabeza*.

(3) *m*. (a) In an unaccented final syllable *m* dropped:

> *fīlĭum > hijo*; *amīcum > amigo*.

(b) In monosyllables, i.e. in the accented syllable, *m > n*:

> *quĕm > quien*; *cŭm > con*; *tam > tan* (but this may be *tantum > tanto > tant > tan* in proclitic use).

L. *sŭm* should have given *son*, but the influence of the 1 sg. forms in *o* (*do*, *sto*, etc.) and a desire to differentiate the form from *sŭnt > son* produced the O. Sp. *so*, whence mod. *soy*.

(4) *l*. There is no certain case of *l* in an accented syllable; it appears to have been lost in the single case of an unaccented syllable:

> V.L. **ĭnsémŭl* (cf. *ĭnsĭmŭl* and *sĕmel*) *> O. Sp. ensiemo*.

(5) *d*. Final *d* was lost:

> *ad > a*; *quĭd > que*; *alĭd > *ale > O. Sp. al* (still in use in the Golden Age).

(6) *c*. Final *c* was lost:

> *dīc > di*; *nec > *ne > ni*; *hīc > O. Sp. y* 'there' (this is preserved in *hay*); *eccum*, V.L. **accu + hīc > aquí*.

b. Initial Consonants

(1) The simple stop consonants, whether labial stops, *p*, *b*, or dental stops, *t*, *d*, or guttural (velar) stops, *c* (before *a*, *o*, *u*), *g* (before *a*, *o*, *u*), remained :

> *pater, patrem > padre*; *bibit > bebe*; *tectum > techo*; *dentem > diente*; *colorem > color*; *gula > gola*.

Before *r* also these remained :

> *probar, tratar, crecer, grano, dragón, bruno.*

In a few cases the initial L. *c* (before *a*, *o*, *u*) appears in Sp. as *g* :

> *cattum > gato* ; *crēta > greda.*

This phenomenon is due to a weak enunciation of the *c*, which was thus confused with the voiced sound *g*; a similar change had occurred for certain Greek words passing into Latin, as, κυβερνᾶν *> gubernare.*

In the O. Sp. period the initial *b* from L. *b* seems to have remained the stop sound as did the intervocalic *b* from L. *p* ; later on these *b*'s became confused, as they are now, with the spirant labial derived from initial L. *v* and intervocalic L. *b* and *v*. In energetic pronunciation or after a word or syllable ending in a nasal the stop sound is heard : ¡*basta* !, *un banco* (= *um banco*), *convidar* (= *combidar*), *investire > embestir.* In *d* the explosive quality is now usually slight ; the sound is in great measure a spirant one.

(2) There also were preserved in Spanish the Latin initial *l* (lateral fricative), *r* (tongue-trilled fricative), *m* and *n* (labial and dental nasals), *s* (sibilant), and *v* (labial fricative or spirant) :

> *lectum > lecho*; *rota > rueda*; *multum > mucho* ; *novum > nuevo* ; *seta > seda* ; *vanum > vano.*

The initial *r* was more strongly trilled than the intervocalic or final *r* or the *r* after most consonants ; hence the scribes often wrote it as *rr* or *R* to indicate its specific value. After *n* they sometimes wrote it in the same way, *onrra = honra*.

The initial *v* (usually written *u*) had probably already in O. Sp. the modern bilabial spirant value.

Moorish mispronunciation of *s* as *š* (written O. Sp. *x*) has produced certain variations, especially in geographical names which the Moors had to use : *(possibly from O. Sp. xabonar)*

sapo, sapōnem > O. Sp. *xabon*, mod. *jabón*; *Salonem* > O. Sp. *Xalon*, mod. *Jalón*.

(3) L. *h*, meaning nothing in real pronunciation in Latin, was valueless in V. L. and also in Spanish; the scribes generally did not write it in O. Sp. (cf. *aver* < *habere*). Etymological considerations have restored the initial *h* frequently in modern spelling.

(4) In popular pronunciation the L. *f* became a Spanish aspirate before a vowel sound; it remained as *f*, i.e. as a labio-dental spirant, before the diphthong *ue* and in combination with *r* :

fabulare > O. Sp. *fablar*, mod. *hablar*; *fel, felle-* > O. Sp. *fiel*, mod. *hiel*; *filium* > O. Sp. *fijo*, mod. *hijo*; *folia* > O. Sp. *foja*, mod. *hoja*; V. L. *fugio* > O. Sp. *fuyo*, mod. *huyo*.

The O. Sp. spelling with *f* in such cases as those just mentioned is only traditional; the sound had certainly become that of a strong aspirate (English *h* in *hat*, etc.). This is evidenced by the spelling in the *Cid* of *fonta*, *fardida*, etc., derived from the French *honte, hardie*, etc., with an aspirated *h* of Germanic origin. O. Sp. had no specific sign at hand to render accurately the aspirate value, and simply kept the sign denoting the sound which had changed to the aspiration.

The labio-dental value remained in such words as

fŏrtem > *fuerte*; *frŏntem* > O. Sp. *fruente*, mod. *frente*.

For *f* before *l* (the only other consonant combination that it could form), see below.

The many cases of *f* before a vowel (except *ue*) in modern Spanish are due to learned influence, which early began to restore it. The aspirate which was really developed in O. Sp. in such instances as *fablar*, *fiel*, *fijo*, *foja*, and *fuyo* began to be represented by *h* at the end of the Middle Ages. This still denoted the aspiration in the 15th and 16th centuries. The aspiration disappeared in Castilian in the 16th century, but the spelling with *h* remains. As a result we have an *h* in modern Spanish which represents an unpronounced L. *h*, and another which takes the place of an O. Sp. aspirate derived from L. *f* and now silent; both of these modern *h*'s mean nothing in sound in modern Castilian, except that before *ue* (*huerto* < *hŏrtum*) a slight aspiration may be made. The written *f* of modern Castilian stands for a voiceless labio-dental spirant like the English *f*, unless, perchance, it have also a voiceless labial spirant value, comparable to the voiced labial spirant sound of *b* and *v*.

(5) While the guttural (velar) *c* and *g* generally maintained themselves in Spanish, the palatal *c* and *g*, i.e. *c* and *g* before the front vowels *e* and *i*, underwent certain changes. Already in the V.L. period this *g* had become *y* (*i̯*) and was equivalent in the initial position to L. *j* and *di̯* which also meant *y* in V.L.

(6) In the unaccented syllable the V.L. *y* disappeared before *e*, *i*:

> *germanum* > *i̯ermano* > *ermano*, now written *hermano* (with inorganic *h*); *jactare* > **i̯echar* > *echar*.

In the accented syllable and in popular treatment it remained as *y* before *e*, *i*, and also before *a*, *u*:

> *gy̆psum* > *yeso*; *jacet* > *yace*; *jam* > *ya*; *jugum* > *yugo* (but cf. the many cases of mod. *j* = χ); *deō(r)sum* > O. Sp. *yuso* (cf. mod. *ayuso*).

Before *ĕ* of course the *y* had a double reason for remaining

> *gĕnĕrum* > **yi̯enro* > **yi̯erno* > *yerno*; *gĕmma* > **yi̯ema* > *yema*; *gĕlum* > **yi̯elo* > O.Sp. *yelo* (now written *hielo*).

(7) In many cases the V.L. *y* before *a* or a back vowel (*o, u*) seems to have become O.Sp. *j* (*dž*), whence the modern velar *j* (*χ*); this occurred before the accented or unaccented vowel:

> *jam magis* > *jamás*; *di̯ŭrnata* > *jornada* (but this word is late and is probably a loan-word; cf. Ital. *giornata*, Fr. *journée*, etc.); *Jŏvis* > *jueves*; *jŏcum* > *juego*; *jŭncum* > *junco*; *jŭvĕnem* > *joven*; *justum* > *justo*; *judicium* > *juicio*, etc.

Some of the words of this last category are certainly learned, others may be loan-words. Before the *u̯e* the *dž* may have developed phonologically.

(8) Before *e* (*ae, oe*) and *i* the *c* had perhaps begun to assibilate already in the late _{classic} Latin period; in O.Sp. it became the voiceless dental sibilant *ts*, written *ç*:

> *cēra* > *çera*; *cĕntum* > *çiento*; *caelum* > *çielo*; *coena* > *çena*; *cīvitātem* > *çibdad, çiudad*.

The scribes wrote the cedilla pretty constantly in such cases, although it really became unnecessary in O.Sp. since the sibilant value was the only one possessed by the *c* before *e, i*. The retention was due to the appearance of the cedilla for the sibilant value in *ça, ço, çu*. In the 16th century the *ts* sound began to be lisped in Castilian, because the tongue, in the enunciation of it, was advanced onto the teeth or into the interdental position; hence the modern voiceless *th* sound. In Andalusian and colonial Spanish the sound is that of *s*.

(9) The combinations *pl, fl, cl* became palatalized *ĺ*, which is now written *ll* as a result of the fact that L. *ll* also palatalized. In the early O.Sp. period the scribes often wrote single *l* for the palatalized sound. In the case of *cl* the palatalizing force is evident; in the case of *pl* and *fl* we may assume an intermediate stage of assimilation to double *l*; but the *l* itself ~~must~~ ^{may} have had some palatal quality of its own in the original combination; cf. Ital. *piano*, *fiamma*, from *planum* and *flamma*. Examples:

planum > llano; *piorare > llorar*; *plenum > lleno*; *flamma > llama*; *clamare > llamar*; *clavem > llave*.

(10) But there are many exceptions to the rule that *pl*, *fl*, *cl* palatalized to *ll*. Some of them are certainly due to learned influence and to the fact that the words were borrowed at a relatively late period:

planta > planta; *placĭtum > plazo*; *flaccum > flaco*; *flos*, *flōrem > flor*; *clarum > claro*.

In the case of *fl* it is likely that the palatalized *l* (*ll*) developed in certain cases and later became the simple *l*:

flaccĭdum > lacio; *Flammŭla > Lambla*, *Lambra* (proper name in the epic *Siete Infantes de Lara*), beside *Llambla*.

(11) In thoroughly popular use, the initial combination *gl* seems to have passed beyond the stage *ll* (palatalized *l*) to that of simple *l*:

V. L. **glirōnem* (L. *glis*) *> lirón* (but cf. also Fr. *liron*); *glattīre > latir*; V. L. **glandinem* (L. *glans, glandis*) *> landre*.

The words retaining the *gl* in Spanish are learned or half-learned.

(12) The combination *bl* appears to have remained:

Germanic *blank- > blanco*; *blĭtum > bledo*.

If *lastimar* is to be connected with *blasphemare*, we seem to have one more case of initial palatalization leading to simplification to *l*; but this is doubtful.

(13) The initial combination *qu* maintained itself as *cu* before accented *a*:

quando > cuando; *qualem > cual*; *quattuor*, V. L. **quattŏro > cuatro*.

In the sentence-stressed position the *u̯* remained also before *o* in

quomodo, V. L. **quomo* > O. Sp. *cuemo*.

But the modern form of this word, *como*, is due to the atonic development.

(14) In the unaccented position before *a* and *o*, the *qu* lost its labial *u̯* element and became *k* (*c*):

quattuordecim > *catorce*; V. L. **quomo* (not accented in the sentence) > *como*.

(15) Before *e*, *i*, the *qu* regularly lost its labial *u̯* element:

qui > O. Sp. *qui* (pronounced *ki*; the *u* is silent after *q* before *e*, *i*); *quĕm* > *quien*; *quindecim* > *quince*; *quaero*, V. L. **quɛro* > *quiero*.

Quinque had already lost the *u̯* in V. L. and become **cinque*, whence *cinco* (for the analogical *o* cf. *ocho*, etc.).

(16) Every Latin word beginning with *s* + a consonant has an *e* (originally *i* in the oldest Spanish) prefixed:

statum > *estado*; *scribo* > *escribo*.

c. Medial Consonants

(1) In the intervocalic position the voiceless stops, *p*, *t*, *c* (*a*, *o*, *u*) voiced to *b*, *d*, *g* if single; if double they remained voiceless but simplified:

sapĕre, V. L. **sapēre* > *saber*; *vita* > *vida*; *pacat* > *paga*; *cĭppum* > *cepo*; *cattum* > *gato*; *vacca* > *vaca*.

The L. *pt* and *ps* became *tt* and *ss*; the *tt* simplified to *t*, but the *ss* remained as voiceless *s* in O. Sp.:

captare > *catar*; *ipse* > O. Sp. *esse* > *ese*.

If followed by *r*, the voiceless stops also voiced:

capra > *cabra*; *matrem* > *madre*; *sacratum* > *sagrado*.

Intervocalic and before *a*, the combination *qu* voiced to *gu̯*:

aqua > *agua*; *aequalem* > *igual*.

Before the other vowels the *q* (*k*) voiced to *g*, but the *u̯* was lost. Graphically the *u* has remained before *e*, *i* :

aliquot > *algo* ; *sequor*, V. L. *sequo > *sigo* ; *sequi*, V. L. *sequĭre > *seguir* ; *aliquem* > *alguien*.

For the combinations *pl*, *cl*, etc. see below. In modern Castilian the *b* from *p* is a bilabial spirant indistinguishable from *v* and the *b* corresponding to L. *b*. After *m* or *n*, however, the sound of both *b* and *v* is that of the labial stop *b*. The modern *d*, from whatsoever source, has acquired a spirant value ; in popular pronunciation and, to a certain degree, even in refined pronunciation it tends to disappear in the medial and final positions :

amado > *amao* (or *amau̯*) ; *ciudad* > *ciudá* ; *usted* > *usté*.

In the 2 pl. endings in verbs it vanished long ago :

amatis > O. Sp. *amades* > *amáis* ; *amate vos* > *amad* (*v*)*os* > *amaos*.

Where *i̯* or *u̯* (i.e. a semiconsonant) followed the voiceless stop, the voicing did not occur :

sapiat > *sepa* ; *sapui* > O. Sp. *sope* > mod. *supe*.

(2) Between vowels the Latin voiced consonants *b*, *d*, and *g* either maintained themselves (with some modification in sound for *b* and *d*) or tended to disappear.

The L. *b* became the bilabial spirant and as such was equal in value to the Sp. result from L. intervocalic *v* ; in O. Sp. the spelling with *v* (*u*) was the usual one :

probare > O. Sp. *provar*, mod. *probar* (with etymological *b*) ; *bĭbĕre*, V. L. *bĭbēre > O. Sp. *bever*, mod. *beber* ; *nŏvum* > *nuevo*.

While L. *v* disappeared after L. *ĭ*, L. *b* remained as a bilabial spirant. However, after a preceding labial (rounded) vowel (*o*, *u*) the *b* could disappear :

rīvum > *río* ; *ŭbi* > *ob(*e*) and this, in proclitic position before a word beginning with a consonant, could become *ou, whence O. Sp. *o*, still found in poetical *do* from *de ŭbi* ; *sŭbŭndare > *sondar* ; *sŭbŭmbrarium > *sombrero*. (In cases like these last where a labial vowel both follows and precedes, the complete assimilation of the labial consonant does not seem unnatural.)

In some instances the *b* seems to have been lost before a following labial vowel:

sabūcum > saúco; *sabŭrra > sorra*.

For *buey* we appeal to V.L. **bŏem* (cf. L. gen. pl. *boum*) instead of *bovem*.

In a number of words of undoubtedly popular development, the intervocalic *d* has vanished; it should have been easy for it to do so since even the secondary *d* from L. *t* could be lost under certain conditions:

sedēre > O. Sp. seer, mod. *ser*; *pĕdem > pie*; *vĭdet > O.Sp. vee*, mod. *ve*; *ridere*, V.L. **ridīre > reir*; *fĭdem > fe*; *limpĭdum > limpio*; *audīre > oir*; *foedum > feo*; etc.

The reasons for the retention of the *d* in such words as *sudar, sudor, nido, nudo, crudo* are not clear. Cf. Ptg. *suar, ninho* (for *nĩo*), *nu, cru*. A learned influence or some especial circumstances must be appealed to for an explanation.

Before *e, i,* the L. *g* was already *y* in V.L.; it disappeared in Spanish:

rēgem > V.L. *reye > reę > rey; *sĭgĭllum > O.Sp. seello*, mod. *sello*; *regīna > reina*.

Before the other vowels, the intervocalic *g* remained:

negare > negar; *plaga > llaga*; *Augŭstum*, V.L. **Agustum > agosto*; *augurium*, V.L. **agurium > agüero*.

Leal for L. *legalem* and *real* for ~~realem~~ +eqalem would appear to be reformed on *ley* and *rey*, whence *leyal, reyal*, whose *y* regularly disappeared after the *e* in Castilian. Certain verb forms seem to present difficulties; the *g* seems lost before *a, o* in *liar, lio* (*lĭgare*), *rumiar, rumio* (*rumĭgare*), *humear* (*fumĭgare*), *lidiar* (*litĭgare*). One wonders whether the loss of the *g* did not commence in them with the forms of the verb whose ending began with *e*:

ligent > lien, etc.

(3) The nasals and so-called liquids remain :

> *ramum > ramo* ; *lana > lana* ; *pĭlum > pelo* ; *parare > parar.*

While *mm* merely simplified to *m*, *nn* and *ll* palatalized (although, seemingly, not in the earliest O. Sp. period, since they did not prevent the diphthongization of preceding *ĕ* and *ŏ*) and *rr* remained as a reënforced *r*, trilled as forcibly as the initial *r* :

> *flamma > llama* ; *annum > año* ; *callem > calle* ; *fŏllem > fuelle* ; *pĕllem > *pielle > piel* ; *carrum > carro.*

In words of late adoption from Latin or some other language (e.g. French), *nn* and *ll* were occasionally rendered as *nd*, *ld* :

> Fr. *pennon > pendón* ; *cella > celda.*

(4) The Latin voiceless sibilant *s* became voiced, i.e. equivalent to the English *z*, in Castilian ; this voiced sound (regularly written *s* in O. Sp.) again unvoiced in the 16th century :

> *usum >* O. Sp. *uso (s =* Eng. *z)*, mod. *uso (s =* Eng. *ss).*

The Latin voiceless *ss* remained voiceless *ss* in O. Sp. and is now written *s* :

> *amavĭssem, amassem >* O. Sp. *amasse*, mod. *amase* ; *prĕssa >* O. Sp. *priessa*, mod. *priesa, prisa.*

The intervocalic O. Sp. *ss* sometimes resulted from the assimilation of another consonant preceding the *s* :

> *ĭpse >* O. Sp. *esse*, mod. *ese* ; *ŭrsum >* O. Sp. *osso*, mod. *oso.*

The combination *ns* in popular use was reduced to *s* in V. L., and therefore a voiced sound must have resulted in O. Sp. :

> *menses > meses* ; *pensare >* V. L. **pęsare >* O. Sp. and mod. *pesar.*

(5) O. Sp., and to a certain degree already V. L., developed new sibilant sounds from Latin stop sounds which through their juxtaposition with front or palatal vowels

assibilated. The assibilation of L. *c* before *e, i,* and of L. *ty, cy* (*ty̆, cy̆*), must have been developed early in the Middle Ages if not already in Late Latin.

(a) Intervocalic *c* (*e, i*) and *ty̆* produced in O. Sp. a voiced dental sibilant *dz* written *z*. In the 16th century this unvoiced to *ts* and therefore was confused with the voiceless O. Sp. *ç* from L. *c* (*e, i*) after a consonant, L. *ty* and *cy* after a consonant, and L. intervocalic *cy*; by the end of that century the interdental pronunciation (lisping), i.e. the voiceless *th* of modern Spanish, had been established in Castilian:

> *facĕre,* V. L. **facēre* > O. Sp. *fazer,* mod. *hacer; vĭces* > O. Sp. *vezes,* mod. *veces; vacīvum* > O. Sp. *vazio,* mod. *vacío; ratiōnem* > O. Sp. and mod. *razón; pŭtĕum* > O. Sp. and mod. *pozo;* abstract suffix *-ĭtĭa* > O. Sp. and mod. *-eza.*

Before *e* it seems that *cy* (*cy̆*) early became *c* and also voiced in O. Sp.:

> *acies* > O. Sp. *azes; facĭĕndum,* or V. L. **facĕndum* > O. Sp. *faziendo,* mod. *haciendo.*

(b) After a consonant, *c* (*e, i*), *ty,* and *cy* became *ts,* written *ç* in O. Sp. This voiceless dental sibilant became confused with the unvoiced result of the corresponding *z* (*dz*), in the 16th century, and both have become the modern interdental *th,* now written *c* before *e, i,* and *z* otherwise. Examples:

> *vincĕre,* V. L. **vĭncēre* > O. Sp. *vençer,* mod. *vencer; cognoscere,* V. L. **conoscēre* > O. Sp. *conoçer,* mod. *conocer; merces, mercēdem* > O. Sp. *merçed,* mod. *merced; piscem* > O. Sp. and mod. *pez.* In the final position the scribes wrote only *z* for both the *ts* and the *dz* sound; both meant *ts,* since the voiced *dz* unvoiced in the final position. Note that *s* disappeared regularly in Spanish before *ç = ts:* so also *crescĕre,* V. L. **crescēre* > *creçer; pisces* > O. Sp. *peçes,* mod. *peces; fŏrtĭa* > O. Sp. *fuerça,* mod. *fuerza; martĭum* > O. Sp. *março,* mod. *marzo; calcea* > O. Sp. *calça,* mod. *calza; lancea* > O. Sp. *lança,* mod. *lanza.*

(c) In really popular treatment it is likely that intervocalic *cy* also gave voiceless O. Sp. *ç* :

> V. L. **capĭcĭa* (from V. L. **capum* for *caput*) > O. Sp. *cabeça*, mod. *cabeza* ; V. L. **coracĭōnem* (based on V. L. **corem* for L. *cor, cordis*) > O. Sp. *coraçon*, mod. *corazón*.

Still, intervocalic *cy* seems to have yielded a real *z* (voiced *dz*) in O. Sp. in quite a number of cases. These are chiefly instances of forms having the suffixes *-ĭcĭum, -ĭcĭam* (as in O. Sp. *ceniza*) ; *-ĭcĭum, -ĭcĭam* (as in O. Sp. *corteza*) ; *-acĕum, -acĕam,* and *-acĭum, -acĭam* (as in O. Sp. *fogaza* < **focaceam*) ; and *-ūcĕum, -ūcĕam,* and *-ūcĭum, -ūcĭam* (as in O. Sp. *fiuza* < *fiducia* and *lechuza* < **lactucea*). These cases are not old, and learned or analogical influences may explain their O. Sp. *z* instead of *ç*.

(d) Where the sound *ts* entered before a consonant in O. Sp. (as in later O. Sp. it did before a consonant plus *a* or *o* in inceptive verbs), the scribes denoted it by *z* (not by *ç*), just as they also wrote *z* in the final position for an indubitable *ts* :

> O. Sp. *meresco* > *mereçco* (through the analogy of *mereçes, mereçe,* etc.) and written regularly *merezco* ; *ad + sat(i)s* > O. Sp. *assaz,* mod. *asaz.*

(6) In Classic Latin of course *f* was hardly to be found in the intervocalic position ; in composition (derivatives, etc.), however, it did acquire the intervocalic relation, and then, when developed in Spanish, it became the spirant *b, v,* and might even, undergoing attraction into a ~~pre-ceeding~~ following syllable, become *u* :

> *profectum* > *provecho* ; suffix *-ifĭcare* > **-ivegar* > **-iugar* > *-iguar* (*ad-pacificare* > *apaciguar*).

In learned acceptation the *ph* of Greek origin was equivalent to L. *f,* and also voiced :

> *Stephanum* > O. Sp. *Estevan,* mod. *Esteban* ; *raphanum* (ῥάφανος) > O. Sp. *ravano,* mod. *rábano.* omit

If, in the Latin derivative, the *f* was still felt as initial, it did not voice:

defensa > *dehesa* (i.e. the *f* was lost like other initial *f*'s. Cf., however, the more popular development of the same word to *devesa*).

d. *Consonant Combinations in the Medial Positions*

We have already considered the doubled consonants and some of the combinations of which *y* is the second element. There are several other groupings.

(1) *r*, *l*, *m*, *n*, *s* before another consonant may remain equally unaffected with that consonant:

pŏrta > *puerta*; *arcum* > *arco*; *altum* > *alto*; *falsum* > *falso*; *tempu-* > *tiempo*; *mantum* > *manto*; *fungum* > *hongo*; *musca* > *mosca*.

But in popular pronunciation *rs* > *ss*, mod. *s*:

ursum > O. Sp. *osso*, mod. *oso*.

After *r*, and also after *n* (in a few cases), *g* followed by *e*, *i*, seems to have become the voiced dental palatal sibilant *dž* (English *j* in *jam*, etc.), which then lost its palatalization and became *dz* (written *z*) in O. Sp.:

spargĕre, V.L. **spargīre*, O. Sp. *esparzir*, mod. *esparcir*; V.L. **singellum* (for *singulum*) > O. Sp. *senziello*, mod. *sencillo*.

But, in general, *ng* before *e* became *ñ*.

The combinations *ns*, *nf* were popularly reduced to *s*, *f* (with compensative lengthening, i.e. closing, of the preceding vowel) in V.L.:

mensa > *mesa*; *ĭnfans*, *ĭnfantem* > O. Sp. *ifante*.

When followed by *b*, an *m* had a tendency to assimilate that consonant, whence *mm* and then *m*:

lŭmbum > *lomo*; *palŭmba* > *paloma*; *ambos* > O. Sp. *amos*, mod. *ambos*.

The combination *mn* in certain cases, whether the combination was original in Latin or only secondary (i.e. found in V.L.), gave by assimilation *nn*, whence in later O. Sp. palatalized *ñ* :

damnum > daño ; *dŏmĭnum*, V. L. **dǫmnum > dueño.*

But the secondary *mn* also proceeded otherwise ; it dissimilated the second nasal to *r*, and the vocal organs, in the passage from *m* to *r*, produced a labial stop *b* :

nomen, nom(ĭ)ne > nombre ; *homo, homĭnem >* O. Sp. *omne, omre > hombre.*

Mpt > mt > nt :

comp(ŭ)tare > contar ; *assumptum > asunto.*

The story of the development of *l* before a consonant is one not too well understood. Sometimes the *l* has vocalized to *u* (especially before a voiceless consonant), as in *talpa > topo* ; *alt(ĕ)rum > otro* ; *saltum > soto* ; again the *l* has remained, as in *altum > alto* (cf. *altarĭum > otero*) ; and yet again, after *u* it has palatalized and changed the following voiceless dental stop *t* to the voiceless dental palatal sibilant *tš*, written *ch* :

multum > mucho ; *cultellum > cuchillo.*

The intermediate stage of *i̯* is shown in *buitre < vŭltŭrem* and in *muy*, which represents a proclitic development of *mŭltum* (*mŭltum bŏnum > mui̯to bueno > *mui̯t* [with loss of the palatalization before another consonant] *bueno*, >, by assimilation of the *t*, *mui̯*, i.e. *muy*, *bueno*).

There are many cases of the retention of *l*, especially before a voiced stop, or before a spirant or a sibilant.

(2) In the combination *ct*, the palatal *c* vocalized to *i̯* and reacted both on the preceding vowel, which it closed, and the following *t*, which it palatalized to *tš*, written *ch* :

factum > O. Sp. *fecho*, mod. *hecho* ; *dĭrectum > derecho.*

For the three consonants *nct* the result was *nt* in Spanish, but the palatal *c* has exercised its closing force upon a preceding vowel :

V. L. **pŭnctum > punto.*

The L. $x = cs$ developed through palatal i (which affected a preceding vowel) + palatal s ($š$, written x in O. Sp.) to modern j, a velar spirant which came into existence by the end of the 16th century; a recession in the mouth of the place of articulation from the palatal to the velar position would necessarily produce the modern Castilian sound:- *axem > aišе > O.Sp. exe > eje; VL coxum > coxo > cojo*

The effect of a preceding palatal element in a consonant combination is seen also in *gn*, which became palatalized *ñ*:

lĭgnum > leño.

Although learned pronunciation keeps the *gn*, e.g. *dignum > digno*, the people at large simplify it to *n*, *dino*.

(3) There were several combinations of consonants with a following *l* or *r*: *pl, bl, fl, cl* (*tl*), *gl, pr, br, fr, tr, dr, cr, gr*. In many cases these were secondary combinations, arising in V. L. through the loss of an intervening vowel.

Intervocalic *pl > bl*:

dŭplare > doblar; *pŏp(ŭ)lum > pueblo*.

After a consonant the *pl > ch*:

amplum (if not *amplium) *> ancho*.

Fl apparently occurred in *ffl*, which seems to have simplified to *fl*, whence palatalized *ll*:

*afflare > *faflare > O. Sp. fallar*, mod. *hallar*; *sufflare > sollar*.

After a different consonant the *fl* seems to have acted like *pl*:

inflare > hinchar.

Intervocalic *bl* remains:

fab(ŭ)lare > hablar; *neb(ŭ)lam > niebla*.

Intervocalic *cl* and *gl* became palatalized *ľ*, which became wholly a palatal *y* and then developed further to the O. Sp. *dž* (written *j* and also *g* (if before *e*, *i*):) omit

oc(ŭ)lum > ojo (Ptg. *olho* shows the intermediate stage of *ľ*); *reg(ŭ)la > reja* (cf. Ptg. *relha*).

The combination *lị* between vowels likewise palatalized and became O. Sp. *j, g (e, i)*, i.e. *dž*, a voiced dental plus a voiced palatal sibilant:

alĭum > ajo ; *cĭlĭa > ceja.*

In V.L. the secondary combination *tl* became *cl*, which acted like the other *cl*:

vetŭlum > veclum > viejo.

After a consonant the *cl* produced the voiceless *ch* (i.e. *tš*, the voiceless sound corresponding to voiced *dž*):

masculum > macho (*tš* absorbed the preceding *s*).

In the combination *ngl*, the nasal triumphed:

ung(ŭ)la > *uñła > *uñya > uña.

Intervocalic *pr* and *fr* > *br*:

aprīre > abrir; *capra > cabra*; *Afrĭcum > ábrego.*

Intervocalic *br* remained:

fĭbra > hebra.

Intervocalic *cr* voiced to *gr*:

sacratum > sagrado; *lacrima > lágrima.*

Intervocalic *tr* voiced to *dr*:

patrem > padre; *latrōnem > ladrón.*

Intervocalic *gr* seems to have vocalized the *g* and been reduced to *r* in really popular treatment:

intégrum > *enteiro (cf. Ptg. *inteiro*) *> entero*; *pigritia > pereza.* Therefore, in *nĭgrum > negro* we have a learned treatment.

Intervocalic *dr* was reduced to *r* in

quadraginta > cuarenta; *cathédra > cadera.* Therefore *cuadro < quadrum* and *yedra < hĕdĕra* do not seem wholly popular.

(4) A number of consonants formed combinations with the following semiconsonant *ị*.

Intervocalic *dy* and *gy* became *y* in V.L. and had the same history as L. *j*; the *y* was lost after *e*, *i*, otherwise it remained:

> *radĭum* > *rayo*; *exagĭum?* > *ensayo*; *majorem* > *mayor*; *sedĕat* > *sea*; *corrigĭa* > *correa*.

The cases of a supposed development of *dy* to *z* or *ç* are open to question; the etyma may not be correct, the words may be loan-words, etc.: this is so for *gozo*, *berza* (O. Sp. *berça*), *vergüenza* (O. Sp. *verguença*), said to come from *gaudium*, **virdia*, *verecundia*, etc.

For *ty* and *cy*, which assibilated, see p. xxxvi.

It would seem that *sty* and *scy* were able to produce a palatal sibilant *š* written *x*:

> *angustia* > O. Sp. *congoxa* (with change of seeming prefix) > *congoja*; *fascia* > O. Sp. *faxa*, mod. *faja*.

But compare V.L. **ūstium* > O. Sp. *uço*.

For intervocalic *ly* which became *j*, see p. xli.

After a consonant the *ly*, like *cl*, produced voiceless *ch*:

> *cochlĕāre* > *cuchara*.

Ny became palatalized *ñ*:

> *cuneum* > *cuño*.

In *py*, *sy*, and *ry* the *y* was attracted to the preceding syllable, and the *p* remained voiceless:

> *sapiat* > *sepa*; *caseum* > *queso*; *corium* > *cuero*.

My, *by*, and *vy* remain:

> *vindemia* > *vendimia*; *labium* > *labio*; *pluvia* > *lluvia*.

Instead of *fovea* we probably have to suppose a V.L. **fodĭa* (cf. *fodere*) as the source of *hoya*.

(5) The diphthong *au* of V.L. seems to have retained its *u* as a semiconsonant late enough to prevent the voicing of an adjacent voiceless stop:

> *cautum* > *coto*; *paucum* > *poco*.

So did also the *u* which was attracted to the *a* of a preceding syllable :

capui > **caupe* > O. Sp. *cope*, mod. *cupe.*

Cf., however, O. Sp. *yogo* < *jacuit* and *plogo* < *placuit.*
In spite of the *ụ* the *s* seems to have voiced, as O. Sp.
writes regularly *s* and not *ss* in such cases as

ausare > *osar, causa* > *cosa,* etc.

For the many other problems arising in connection with the
consonantal system we cannot stop here; Baist in the
Grunariss, l.c., Menéndez Pidal, and Hanssen have
taken them up.

CORRECTIONS FOR THE TEXT

P. 4, l. 19 : Omit " non."
  "   l. 20 : Omit " non."
P. 38, stz. 366, l. 3 : " tolosanos " should be " tolosanas."

OLD SPANISH READINGS

I

DOCUMENTS OF THE CHURCH OF VALPUESTA

(From the *Chartes de l'Église de Valpuesta*, published by L. Barrau-Dihigo in the *Revue hispanique*, VII. 273 ff.)

No. I. DECEMBER 21, 804

Sub Christi nomine et diuino imperio. Ego Ihoannes episcopus sic ueni in locum que uocitant Ualle Conposita et inueni ibi eglesia deserta uocabulo Sancte Marie Uirginis et feci ibi fita sub regimine Domino Adefonso principe Obetau, et construxi uel confirmabi ipsam eglesia in ipso loco et feci ibi presuras 5 cum meos gasalianes mecum comorantes : id [est] illorum terminum de Meuma usque collatu de Pineto et per sum Penna usque ad Uilla Alta : et de alia parte de illo moiare usque ad Cancellata et exinde ad Sancti Emeteri et Celedoni. . . .

No. XV. FEBRUARY 18, 935

In Dei nomine. Ego Gutier tibi emtori meo Didacus epis- 10 copo, placui, nobi adque conueni ut uindere tibi et ad tuos gasalianes uinea in Liciniana de limite ad limite integrata, iusta limite de Munio, et accepi de te pretio, id est quatuor bobes et canape et plumazo et sabana et bracas et adtorralinia, et nicil in te non remansit de ipso pretio aput te ; ita de odie 15 die de iuri meo in dominio tuo abeas ipsa uinea confirmata

perpetim abiturim. Quo si ego Gutier aut filiis meis uel aliquis
de aliqua parte, iam dicto te Didacus episcopo aut posteritas
tua, ad iudicio proferre temptaberi, abeas ad me ipso pretio in
duplo, et si noster mercatus firmes . . . Facta cartula uindi-
5 cionis XII kalendas martias, era DCCCCLXXIII, regnante
Domino Ranemiri et comite Fredenando Gundesalbiz in
Lantarone. Munnio scripsit.

No. LII. July 26, 1039

In Dei nomine. Ego Gundesaluo presbiter sic tradidi mea
conparatione de terris, de uineis, que conparaui in uilla que
10 dicitur Elcetu, pro remedio anime mee, ad atrio Sancte Marie
Uirginis in transitu meo uel ad confratres meos uel ad episcopo
Domino Ato prenominatu Malguelo, in caput de monte, latus
uinga de Munnio Beilaz. . . . Ego Gundesaluo, sapiente meos
confratres, conparaui illas, et si aliquis homo istum meum
15 factum uel confirmatum disrumpere uoluerit, reges, comes,
ifançones, aut iudex, sagone aut aliquis ex m[eis propinquis],
inprimis excomunicatus [fiat] a corpus Christi et de fide
sancta cahtolica et maledictus fiat. . . .

No. LXVI. 1065

In Dei nomine. Ego Obiecco et usor mea Domna Maiore,
20 spontaneas nostras uoluntantes, pro remedio anime nostre, ad
atrium Sancte Marie Uirginis, abbate Domino Munio, trado
terra in loco que uocita in Pobalias, iusta terra de regula, circa
karraria, et una uinea in Uallelio, iusta uinea de illo potro, que
est uinea de regula, et de alia pars de Fruela de Orbone, in
25 perpetum abituri ; sedeat ipsa terra uel ipsa uinea confirmata
abbate et tota conllatione qui ibi sunt in ipsa regula. Et quiquid disrupere uoluerit, iermanis aut coniermanis aut neptis
[a]ut aliquis de alia parte, libra auri (*sic*) et excomunicatus
permaneat ad fide Christi. . . .

II

OLD SPANISH GLOSSES

950-1000 more probably.

(In a MS. of the 11th century, originally of the monastery of Santo
Domingo de Silos at Burgos in Old Castile, now in the British Museum,
Add. 30853. The glosses — also of the 11th century — are in the nature
of marginal and interlinear interpretations of the Latin terms of a
Penitential contained in the MS. The greater number of them have
been published by J. Priebsch in the *Zeitschrift für romanische Philologie*, XIX. 1 ff., whence the following are reprinted.)

 5 deuenerit : non aflaret
 8 proditum : aflatu fueret

 9 conburatur : kematu siegat
11 abluantur : labatu siegat

16 ignorans : qui non sapiendo   5
26 si ignorans : si non sapet
29 ignorantem : non sapiendo
119 ignorans : non sapiento
286 ignorans : non sapiendo

20 caste : munda mientre   *chaste : pure*   10
91 adgrabans : grabe mientre
116 uiolenter : fuertemientre(za)

25 inbalidis : debiles, aflitos
27 fiat : siegat
28 in periurium : et ficieret mentiru   15
31 periuratusset : ke se periuret super so cosa
42 ad homicidium faciendum : por fere ke faciat omiciero
46 prebent : ministrent, sierben
49 strages : occisiones, matatas
54 interficere : matare   20
74 negant : occidunt, mata[n]
82 extingunt : matan

mente > miente {mente}   mente — intrusion of
false analysis gives this result
dum interim > ×domentre > de mentre > mentre
*   miente*
*   mientras*

85 interficiat : matare
53 interitu : muerte
92 puniuntur : muertos fuerent
182 usque infinem : ata que mueran
5   56 deducantur : lieben adduitos, leuatos
57 uexatus : focato fueret
61 per poculum : ueuetura de la ierba
65 esse : sedere
233 esse : ke iet, ke son
10   237 deesse : ke iet menos
76 absente : luenge stando
79 quod : por ke
81 ⎰
185 ⎱ hii : estos
15   93 inici : por iactare
96 negat : non quisieret dare
100 auguria : agueros
111 nunquam : alquantre
112 accedant : non aplekan
20   208 accedat : non aplekat
122 conplexu : constrinitu brazaret
124 femora : campas
125 propris : sos
138 quot : quantos
25   146 uti : ke aiat usuale lege
188 habeat : aiat
153 raptores : elos predatores
223 abitum : ela similia
274 cadabera : elos cuerpos
30   35 incendii : de lo incentitu
88 hostili : de lo aduersario gentile
105 in collectiones : enas collituras
200 in cogitatione polluti : ena pullutione

44 sed casu occiderit : eno periculo, *etc*.

222 in saltatione : ena sota

161 prius : anzes

166 semel : una uece

167 fuerit lapsus : kadutu fuere   5

187 si se ipsum : so caput

191 noberce : matastra

192 consobrina : cusina

193 abunculi : tio

194 màtertere : tia   10

243 materteram : tia

211 nec audeat : non siegat osatu

214 ad nubtias : alas uotas

216 saltare : sotare

224 monstruose : qui tingen lures faces   15

234 emersise : ke cadiot

240 quamuis : macare ke siegat

244 secum retinere uoluerit : consico kisieret tenere

260 suffocato : mortizino

272 accipiter : acetore   20

295 ferre : leuare

III

AUTO DE LOS REYES MAGOS

(From the edition of R. Menéndez Pidal in the *Revista de Archivos, Bibliotecas y Museos*, Madrid, 1900)

ESCENA I
(CASPAR, SOLO)

Dios criador, qual marauila
no se qual es achesta strela !
Agora primas la e ueida,
poco timpo a que es nacida.
5 Nacido es el Criador
que es de la gentes senior?
Non es uerdad non se que digo,
todo esto non uale uno figo ;
otra nocte me lo catare,
10 si es uertad, bine lo sabre. (*pausa*)
Bine es uertad lo que io digo?
en todo, en todo lo prohio.
Non pudet seer otra sennal?
Achesto es i non es al ;
15 nacido es Dios, por uer, de fembra
in achest mes de december.
Ala ire o que fure, aoralo e,
por Dios de todos lo terne.

(BALTASAR, SOLO)

Esta strela non se dond uinet,
20 quin la trae o quin la tine.
Porque es achesta sennal?

en mos dias on ui atal.
Certas nacido es en tirra
aquel qui en pace i en guera
senior a a seer da oriente   25
de todos hata in occidente.
Por tres noches me lo uere
i mas de uero lo sabre. (*pausa*)
En todo, en todo es nacido ?
non se si algo e ueido.   30
ire, lo aorare,
i pregare i rogare.

(MELCHIOR, SOLO)

Ual, Criador, atal facinda
fu nunquas alguandre falada
o en escriptura trubada?   35
Tal estrela non es in celo,
desto so io bono strelero ;
bine lo ueo sines escarno
que uno omne es nacido de carne,
que es senior de todo el mundo,   40
asi cumo el cilo es redondo ;
de todas gentes senior sera
i todo seglo iugara.
Es ? non es ?
cudo que uerdad es.   45
Ueer lo e otra uegada,
si es uertad o si es nada. (*pausa*)
Nacido es el Criador
de todas las gentes maior ;
bine lo [u]eo que es uerdad,   50
ire ala, par caridad.

ESCENA II
(CASPAR Á BALTASAR)

Dios uos salue, senior; sodes uos strelero?
dezidme la uertad, de uos sabelo quiro
[Vedes tal marauila?]
55   [nacida] es una strela.

(BALTASAR)

Nacido es el Criador,
que de las gentes es senior.
Ire, lo aorare.

(CASPAR)

Io otrosi rogar lo e.

(MELCHIOR Á LOS OTROS DOS)

60   Seniores, a qual tirra, o que[redes] andar?
queredes ir conmigo al Criador rogar?
Auedes lo ueido? io lo uo [aor]ar.

(CASPAR)

Nos imos otrosi, sil podremos falar.
Andemos tras el strela, ueremos el logar.

(MELCHIOR)

65   Cumo podremos prouar si es homne mortal
o si es rei de terra o si celestrial?

(BALTASAR)

Queredes bine saber cumo lo sabremos?
oro, mira i acenso a el ofrecremos:
si fure rei de terra, el oro quera;

si fure omne mortal, la mira tomara ;   70
si rei celestrial, estos dos dexara,
tomara el encenso quel pertenecera.

(CASPAR Y MELCHIOR)

Andemos i asi lo fagamos.

ESCENA III

(CASPAR Y LOS OTROS DOS REYES Á HERODES)

Salue te el Criador, Dios te curie de mal,
un poco te dizeremos, non te queremos al,   75
Dios te de longa uita i te curie de mal ;
imos in romeria aquel rei adorar
que es nacido in tirra, nol podemos fallar.

(HERODES)

Que decides, o ides ? a quin ides buscar ?
de qual terra uenides, o queredes andar ?   80
Decid me uostros nombres, no m' los querades celar.

(CASPAR)

A mi dizen Caspar,
est otro Melchior, ad achest Baltasar.
Rei, un rei es nacido que es senior de tirra,
que mandara el seclo en grant pace sines gera.   85

(HERODES)

Es asi por uertad ?

(CASPAR)

Si, rei, por caridad.

(HERODES)

I cumo lo sabedes?
ia prouado lo auedes?

(CASPAR)

90   Rei, uertad te dizremos,
que prouado lo auemos.

(MELCHIOR)

Esto es grand ma[ra]uila.
un strela es nacida.

(BALTASAR)

Sennal face que es nacido
95   i in carne humana uenido.

(HERODES)

Quanto i a que la uistes
i que la percibistis?

(CASPAR)

Tredze dias a,
i mais non auera,
100   que la auemos ueida
i bine percebida.

(HERODES)

Pus andad i buscad,
i a el adorad,
i por aqui tornad.
105   Io ala ire,
i adoralo e.

ESCENA IV

(HERODES, SOLO)

¿Quin uio numquas tal mal,
Sobre rei otro tal !
Aun non so io morto,
ni so la terra pusto !   110
rei otro sobre mi?
numquas atal non ui !
El seglo ua a caga,
ia non se que me faga ;
por uertad no lo creo   115
ata que io lo ueo.
Uenga mio maiordo[ma]
qui mios aueres toma. (*Sale el mayordomo*)
Idme por mios abades,
I por mis podestades,   120
i por mios scriuanos,
i por meos gramatgos,
i por mios streleros,
i por mios retoricos ;
dezir m' an la uertad, si iace in escripto,   125
o si lo saben elos, o si lo an sabido.

ESCENA V

(SALEN LOS SABIOS DE LA CORTE)

Rei, qque te plaze ? he nos uenidos.

(HERODES)

I traedes uostros escriptos ?

(Los Sabios)

Rei, si traemos,
130   los meiores que nos auemos.

(Herodes)

Pus catad,
dezid me la uertad,
si es aquel omne nacido
que esto tres rees m' an dicho.
135   Di, rabi, la uertad, si tu lo as sabido.

(El Rabí)

Po[r] ueras uo lo digo
que no lo [fallo] escripto.

(Otro Rabí al Primero)

Hamihala, cumo eres enartado!
por que eres rabi clamado?
140   Non entendes las profecias,
las que nos dixo Ieremias.
Par mi lei, nos somos erados!
por que non somos acordados?
por que non dezimos uertad?

(Rabí Primero)

145   Io non la se, par caridad.

(Rabí Segundo)

Por que no la auemos usada,
ni en nostras uocas es falada.

IV

LA GESTA DE MYO ÇID EL DE BIUAR

(From R. Menéndez Pidal, *Poema del Cid*, Madrid, 1898)

. . . .

Delos sos oios tan fuerte mientre lorando
Tornaua la cabeça *z* estaua los catando.
Vio puertas abiertas *z* vços sin cañados,
Alcandaras uazias sin pielles *z* sin mantos,
E sin falcones *z* sin adtores mudados.   5
Sospiro myo Çid, ca mucho auie grandes cuydados.
Fablo myo Çid bien *z* tan mesurado :
" Grado ati, señor padre, que estas en alto !
Esto me an buelto myos enemigos malos."
Alli pienssan de aguiiar, alli sueltan las Riendas.   10
Ala exida de Biuar ouieron la corneia diestra,
E entrando a Burgos ouieron la siniestra.
Meçio myo Çid los ombros *z* en grameo la tiesta :
"Albriçia, Albarffanez, ca echados somos de tierra ! "
Myo Çid Ruy Diaz por Burgos en traua,   15
En su conpaña .Lx. pendones leuaua ; exien lo uer mugieres
        z uarones.
Burgeses *z* burgesas por las finiestras son,
Plorando delos oios, tanto auyen el dolor.
Delas sus bocas todos dizian una Razon :
" Dios, que buen vassalo, si ouiesse buen Señor ! " . . .   20

Fablo myo Çid, el que en buen ora çinxo espada :   78
" Martin Antolinez, sodes ardida lança !
Si yo biuo, doblar uos he la soldada   80
Espeso e el oro *z* toda la plata,

Bien lo vedes que yo no trayo auer, z huebos me serie
Pora toda mi compana :
Fer lo he amidos, de grado non aurie nada.

85 Con uuestro consego bastir quiero dos archas ;
Yncamos las darena, ca bien seran pesadas,
Cubiertas de guadalmeçi e bien en claueadas.
Los guadameçis uermeios z los clauos bien dorados.
Por Rachel z Vidas uayades me priuado :

90 Quando en Burgos me vedaron conpra z el Rey me a ayrado,
Non puedo traer el auer, ca mucho es pesado,
En peñar gelo he por lo que fuere guisado ;
De noche lo lieuen, que non lo vean christianos.
Vealo el Criador con todos los sos santos,

95 Yo mas non puedo z amydos lo fago."
Martin Antolinez non lo de tarua,
Por Rachel z Vidas apriessa demandaua.
Passo por Burgos, al castiello entraua,
Por Rachel z Vidas apriessa demandaua.

100 Rachel z Vidas en vno estauan amos,
En cuenta de sus aueres, delos que auien ganados.
Lego Martin Antolinez aguisa demenbrado :
"O sodes, Rachel z Vidas, los myos amigos caros?
En poridad flablar querria con amos."

105 Non lo de tardan, todos tres se apartaron.
"Rachel z Vidas, amos me dat las manos,
Que non me descubrades a moros nin a christianos ;
Por siempre uos fare Ricos, que non seades menguados.
El Campeador por las parias fue entrado,

110 Grandes aueres priso z mucho sobeianos,
Retouo dellos quanto que fue algo ;
Por en vino aaquesto por que fue acusado.
Tiene dos arcas lennas de oro esmerado.
Ya lo vedes que el Rey lea ayrado.

Dexado ha heredades z casas z palaçios.   115
Aquelas non las puede leuar, sinon, ser yen ventadas ;
El Campeador dexar las ha en uuestra mano,
E prestalde de auer lo que sea guisado.
Prended las archas z meted las en uuestro saluo ;
Con gran iura meted y las fes amos,   120
Que non las catedes en todo aqueste año."
Rachel z Vidas seyen se conseiando :
" Nos huebos auemos en todo de ganar algo.
Bien lo sabemos que el algo gaño,
Quando atierra de moros entro, que grant auer saco ;   125
Non duerme sin sospecha qui auer trae monedado.
Estas archas prendamos las amas,
En logar las metamos que non sean ventadas.
Mas dezid nos del Çid, ¿de que sera pagado,
O que ganançia nos dara por todo aqueste año ? "   130
Respuso Martin Antolinez a guisa de menbrado :
" Myo Çid querra lo que ssea aguisado ;
Pedir uos a poco por dexar so auer en saluo.
Acogen sele omes de todas partes menguados,
A menester seys çientos marcos."   135
Dixo Rachel z Vidas : " dar gelos de grado."
" Ya vedes que entra la noch, el Çid es presurado,
Huebos auemos que nos dedes los marchos."
Dixo Rachel z Vidas : " non se faze assi el mercado,
Si non primero prendiendo z despues dando."   140
Dixo Martin Antolinez : " yo desso me pago.
Amos tred alCampeador con tado,
E nos uos aiudaremos, que assi es aguisado,
Por aduzir las archas z meter las en uuestro saluo,
Que non lo sepan moros nin christianos."   145
Dixo Rachel z Vidas : " nos desto nos pagamos.
Las archas aduchas, prended seyes çientos marcos."

Martin Antolinez caualgo priuado
Con Rachel z Vidas, de volutad z de grado.
150 Non viene ala pueent, ca por el agua apassado,
Que gelo non ventanssen de Burgos oṁe nado.
Afeuos los ala tienda del Campeador contado ;
Assi coṁo entraron, al Çid besaron le las manos.
Sonrrisos myo Çid, estaualos fablando :
155 "Ya don Rachel z Vidas, auedes me olbidado !
Ya me exco de tierra, ca del Rey so ayrado.
Alo quem semeia, de lo mio auredes algo ;
Mientra que vivades non seredes menguados."
Don Rachel z Vidas a myo Çid besaron le las manos.
160 Martin Antolinez el pleyto a parado,
Que sobre aquelas archas dar le yen .v.j. çientos marcos,
E bien gelas guardarien fasta cabo del año ;
Ca assil dieran la fe z gelo auien iurado,
Que si antes las catassen que fuessen periurados,
165 Non les diesse myo Çid dela ganançia un dinero malo.
Dixo Martin Antolinez : "cargen las archas priuado.
Leualdas, Rachel z Vidas, poned las en uuestro saluo ;
Yo yre con uuso, que adugamos los marcos,
Ca amouer a myo Çid ante que cante el gallo."
170 Alcargar delas archas veriedes gozo tanto :
Non las podien poner en somo mager eran esforçados.
Gradan se Rachel z Vidas con aueres monedados,
Ca mientra que visquiessen refechos eran amos.
Rachel amyo Çid la manol ba besar :
175 "Ya Canpeador, en buen ora çinxiestes espada !
De Castiella uos ydes pora las yentes estranas.
Assi es uuestra uentura, grandes son uuestras ganançias ;
Vna piel vermeia morisca z ondrada,
Çid, beso uuestra mano, endon que la yo aya."
180 "Plazme," dixo el Çid, "da qui sea mandada.

Siuos la aduxier dalla ; si non, contalda sobre las arcas."...
En medio del palaçio tendieron vn almofalla,
Sobrella vna sauana de rançal z muy blanca.
Atod el primer colpe .iij. marcos de plata echaron,
Notolos don Martino, sin peso los tomaua ;   185
Los otros .C.C.C. en oro gelos pagauan.
Çinco escuderos tiene don Martino, atodos los cargaua.
Quando esto ouo fecho, odredes lo que fablaua :
" Ya don Rrachel z Vidas, en uuestras manos son las arcas ;
Yo, que esto uos gane, bien mereçia calças."   190
Entre Rachel z Vidas aparte yxieron amos :
" Demos le buen don, ca el no lo ha buscado.
Martin Antolinez, un Burgales contado,
Vos lo mereçedes, daruos queremos buen dado,
De que fagades calças z Rica piel z buen manto.   195
Damos uos endon auos .XXX. marchos ;
Mereçer nolo hedes, ca esto es aguisado.
Atorgar nos hedes esto que auemos parado."
Gradeçiolo don Martino z Recibio los marchos ;
Grado exir dela posada z espidios de amos.   200
Exido es de Burgos z Arlançon a passado,
Vino pora la tienda del que en buen ora nasco ;
Reçibiolo el Çid abiertos amos los braços :
" Venides, Martin Antolinez, el mio fiel vassalo !
Aun vea el dia que demi ayades algo ! "   205
" Vengo, Campeador, con todo buen Recabdo :
Vos .vj. çientos yo xxx he ganados.
Mandad coger la tienda z vayamos priuado."...

Aquis conpieça la gesta de myo Çid el de Biuar.   1085
Tan Ricos son los sos que non saben que se an.
Poblado ha myo Çid el puerto de Alucant,
Dexado a Saragoça z alas tierras duca,

E dexado a Huesca *z* las tierras de Mont Aluan.
1090 Contra la mar salada conpeço de guerrear;
Aorient exe el sol, e tornos aessa part.
Myo Çid gãno aXerica *z* a Onda *z* Al menar,
Tierras de Borriana todas conquistas las ha.
Aiudol el Criador, el señor que es en çielo.
1095 El con todo esto priso a Muruiedro.
Ya vie myo Çid que Dios le yua valiendo.
Dentro en Valençia non es poco el miedo.
Pesa alos de Valençia, sabet, non les plaze;
Prisieron so con seio quel viniessen çercar.
1100 Tras nocharon de noch, al alua dela man
Açerca de Muruiedro tornan tiendas afincar.
Violo myo Çid, tomos amarauillar : " grado ati, padre spirital !
En sus tierras somos *z* femos les todomal,
Beuemos so vino *z* comemos el so pan;
1105 Si nos çercar vienen, conderecho lo fazen.
Amenos de lid nos partira aquesto;
Vayan los mandados por los que nos deuen aiudar,
Los vnos aXerica *z* los otros a Alucad,
Desi a Onda *z* los otros a Almenar,
1110 Los de Borriana luego vengan aca;
Conpeçaremos aquesta lid campal,
Yo fio por Dios que en nuestro pro enadran."
Alterçer dia todos iuntados son,
El que en buen ora nasco compeço de fablar :
1115 " Oyd, mesnadas, si el Criador uos salue !
Despues que nos partiemos dela linpia christiandad,
Non fue a nuestro grado ni nos non pudiemos mas,
Grado a Dios, lo nuestro fue a delant.
Los de Valençia çercados nos han;
1120 Si en estas tierras quisieremos durar,
Firme mientre son estos a escarmentar.

Passe la noche *z* venga la mañana,
Apareiados me sed a cauallos *z* armas ;
Hyremos ver aquela su almofalla,
Coño oñes exidos de tierra estraña,   1125
Ali pareçra el que mereçe la soldada."
Oyd que dixo Minaya Albarfanez :
" Campeador, fagamos lo que auos plaze.
A mi dedes .C. caualleros, que non uos pido mas,
Vos con los otros firades los delant.   1130
Bien los ferredes, que dubda non y aura,
Yo con los çiento entrare del otra part,
Coño fio por Dios, el campo nuestro sera."
Coño gelo a dicho, al Campeador mucho plaze.
Mañana era *z* pienssan se de armar,   1135
Quis cada vno dellos bien sabe lo que ha de far.
Con los aluores myo Çid ferir los va :
" Enel nombre del Criador *z* del apostol santi Yague,
Ferid los, caualleros, damor *z* de grado *z* de grand voluntad,
Ca yo so Ruydiaz, myo Çid el de Biuar ! "   1140
Tanta cuerda de tienda y veriedes quebrar,
Arancar se las estacas *z* acostar se atodas partes los tendales.
Moros son muchos, ya quieren Reconbrar.
Del otra part entroles Albarfanez ;
Mager les pesa, ouieron se adar *z* a arancar.   1145
Grand es el gozo que va por es logar.
Dos Reyes de moros mataron en es alcaz,
Fata Valençia duro el segudar.
Grandes son las ganançias que mio Çid fechas ha. . . .

Salio de Muruiedro vna noch en trasnochada,   1185
Amaneçio amyo Çid en tierras de Mon Real.
Por Aragon *z* por Nauarra pregon mando echar,
A tierras de Castiella en bio sus menssaies :

" Quien quiere perder cueta *z* venir a rritad,

1190 Viniesse a myo Çid que a sabor de caualgar ;

Çercar quiere a Valençia pora christianos la dar.

Quien quiere yr comigo çercar a Valençia,

Todos vengan de grado, ninguno non ha premia,

Tres dias le sperare en Canal de Çelfa."

1195 Esto dixo myo Çid el que en buen ora nasco.

Tornauas a Muruiedro, ca el se la a ganada.

Andidieron los pregones, sabet, atodas partes,

Al sabcr dela ganançia non lo quiere de tardar,

Grandes yentes se le acoien dela buena christiandad.

1200 Creçiendo ua en Riqueza myo Çid el de Biuar.

Quando vio myo Çid las gentes iuntadas, compeços de pagar.

Myo Çid don Rodrigo non lo quiso de tardar,

Adelino pora Valençia *z* sobrellas va echar,

Bien la çerca myo Çid, que non y auya hart ;

1205 Viedales exir *z* viedales entrar.

Sonando va[n] sus nueuas todas atodas partes ;

Mas le vienen a myo Cid, sabet, que nos le van.

Metiola en plazo, siles viniessen huuyar.

Nueue meses complidos, sabet, sobrella iaz,

1210 Quando vino el dezeno ouieron gela adar.

Grandes son los gozos que van por es logar,

Quando myo Çid gaño a Valençia *z* entro enla çibdad.

Los que fueron de pie caualleros se fazen ;

El oro *z* la plata qui en vos lo podrie contar?

1215 Todos eran Ricos quantos que alli ha.

Myo Çid don Rodrigo la quinta mando tomar,

Enel auer monedado XXX mill marcos le caen,

Elos otros aueres quien los podrie contar?

Alegre era el Campeador con todos los que ha,

1220 Quando su seña cabdal sedie en somo del alcaçar.

V

DISPUTA DEL ALMA Y EL CUERPO

(From the edition of R. Menéndez Pidal in the *Revista de Archivos, Bibliotecas y Museos*, Madrid, 1900)

[S]i quereedes oir lo que uos quiero dezir,
Dizre uos lo que ui, nol uos i quedo fallir.
Un sabad[o e]sient, dom[i]ngo amanezient,
Ui una grant uision en mio leio dormient :
Eram' asem[eian]t que so un lenzuelo nueuo   5
Jazia un cuerpo de uemne muerto ;
Ell alma era fuera [e] fuert mientre que plera,
Ell ama es ent esida, desnuda ca non uestida,
E guisa [d' u]n jfant fazie duelo tan grant.
Tan grant duelo fazie al cuerpo maldizie,   10
Fazi [ta]n grant de duelo e maldizie al cuerpo ;
Al cuerpo dixo ell alma : " de ti lieuo ma[la] fama !
Tot siempre t' maldizre, ca por ti penare,
Que nunca fecist cosa que semeias fer[mo]sa,
Ni de nog ni de dia de lo que io queria ;   15
Nunca fust a altar por j buena oferda dar
Ni diez[mo] ni primicia ni buena penitenci[a] ;
Ni fecist oracion nunca de corazo[n],
Cua[n]do iuas all el[gue]si[a] asentauaste a conseia,
I fazies tos conseios e todos tos(dos) treb[e]ios ;   20
Apostol ni martjr [nunca] quisist seruir,
Iure par la tu tiesta que no curaries fiesta,
Nunca de nigun santo no [cure]st so disanto
Mas not faran los santos aiuda mas que a una bestia muda ;
Mezquino, mal [fadado], ta' mal ora fuest nado !   25
Que tu fu[este] tan rico, agora eres mesquinu !

Dim, o son tos dineros que tu mi[sist en] estero?
O los tos morauedis azaris et melequis
Que solies manear et a menudo contar?
30   O son los pala[fres] que los quendes ie los res
Te solien dar por to loseniar?
Los cauallos corientes, las espuelas [pu]nentes,
Las mulas bien amblantes, asuueras trainantes,
Los frenos esorados, los [petr]ales dorados,
35   Las copas d' oro fino con que beuies to uino?
Do son tos bestimentos? ¿o los [tos] guarnimentos
Que tu solies festir e tanbien te . . ."

VI

GONZALO DE BERCEO

A

AQUI ESCOMJENÇA LA UIDA DEL GLORIOSO CON-
FESSOR SANCTO DOMJNGO DE SILOS

(From the edition of J. D. Fitz-Gerald, Paris, 1904, in the *Bibliothèque de l'École des hautes études*, fascicule 149)

En el nonbre del Padre, que fizo toda cosa,   1
E de don Jhesu Christo, Fijo dela Gloriosa,
Et del Spiritu Sancto, que egual dellos posa,
De un confessor sancto quiero fer vna prosa.

Quiero fer vna prosa en roman paladino   2
En qual suele el pueblo fablar con su uezino,
Ca non so tan letrado por fer otro latino :
Bien ualdra, como creo, un vaso de bon vino.

Quiero quelo sepades luego dela primera   3
Cuya es la ystoria, meter uos en carrera ;
Es de Sancto Domjngo, toda bien uerdadera,
El que dizen de Silos, que salua la frontera.

Enel nonbre de Dios, que nonbramos primero,   4
Suyo sea el preçio, yo sere su obrero,
Gualardon del lazerio yo en El lo espero,
Quj por poco serujcio da galardon larguero. . . .

Señor Sancto Domjngo, leal escapulado,   86
Andaua enla orden como buen ordenado,
Los oios apremjdos, el capiello baxado,
La color amariella, como omne lazrado.

87   Que qujera que mandaua el su padre Abbat,
O Prior o Prepuesto dela soçiedat,
Obedesçia el luego de buena uoluntat,
Tenjangelo los buenos abuena Christiandat. . . .

91   Sy los otros sus fradres lo quisiessen soffrir,
Elli dela iglesia nunca querria exir,
Las noches e los dias y los querria troçir,
Por saluar la su alma, al Criador seruir.

92   A el catauan todos como avn espeio,
Que yazia grant tesoro su el su buen peleio,
Por Padre lo catauan, essi sancto conçeio,
Fuera algunt maliello, que ualia poquilleio.

93   Ante vos lo dixiemos (sibien uos remenbrades),
Que serie luenga soga dezir las sus bondades,
Mouamos adelante, si nos lo conseiades,
Que aun mucho finca, mas delo que cuydades.

94   El Abbat dela casa fablo con su conujento,
Asmaron vna cosa, fizieron paramjento
De prouar este omne, qual era su taliento,
Si era tal por todo qual el demostramjento.

95   Dixieron : "ensaemoslo, ueremos que tenemos,
Quando lo entendieremos mas seguros seremos,
Ca diz la escriptura, e leer lo solemos,
Que oymos la lengua mas el cuer non sauemos.

96   Mandemos li que uaya a alguna degaña
Que sea bien tan pobre como pobre cabaña :
Sy fer non lo quisiere o demostrare saña,
Alli lo entendremos que trae mala maña."

97   Cerca era de Cannas, z es oy endia,
Vna casa por nonbre dicha Sancta Maria,
Essa era muy pobre, de todo bien uazia :
Mandaronli que fuesse prender essa baylia.

Consintio el buen omne, non desujo en nada,   98
Fizo el encljn luego, la bendiçion fue dada,
Oro al Cuerpo Sancto oraçion breujada,
Dixo palabras pocas, razon bien acordada.

"Señor, dixo, que eres de conplido poder,   99
Que alos que bien quieres non los dexas caer,
Señor, tu me enpara, cayate en plazer
Que lo que he lazrado non lo pueda perder.

Siempre cobdiçie esto, e avn lo cobdiçio,   100
Apartarme del mundo, de todo su bolliçio,
Beuir solo en regla, morar entu serujçio ;
Señor, merçed te clamo, que me seas propiçio.

Por ganar la tu gracia fizi obediençia,   101
Por beuir en tormento, morir en penjtençia ;
Señor, por el tu mjedo non quiero fer falençia,
Sy non, non ixiria de esta mantenençia.

Sennor, yo esto quiero, como lo querer deuo,   102
Sy non, de mj faria alos diablos çeuo,
Contra la aguijada coçear non me treuo :
Tu saues esti uaso que sin grado lo beuo.

Quiero algunt serujçio fazer ala Gloriosa,   103
Creo bien z entiendo que es honesta cosa,
Ca del Señor del mundo fue madre z esposa :
Plaze me yr ala casa enna qual ella posa."

Ixo del monesterio el señor a amidos,   104
Despidiosse de todos los sus frayres queridos,
Los que bien lo amauan fincauan doloridos,
Los que lo basteçieron ya eran repentidos.

Fue a Sancta Maria el baron benedicto,   105
Non fallo pan en ella, njn otro njgunt uicto,
Demandaua ljmosnas como romero fito,
Todos li dauan algo, qui media qui çatico.

106   Con Dios e la Gloriosa, e la creençia sana,
        Vinjali buena cosa de offrenda cutiana,
        De noche era pobre, rico ala mañana,
        Bien partia la ganançia con esa yent Christiana.

107   El baron de buen seso por la Ley bien conplir,
        Queriendo de lazerio de sus manos beuir,
        Començo alabrar por dexar el pedir,
        Ca era graue cosa parael de soffrir.

108   Meioro enlas casas, ensancho heredades,
        Conpuso la iglesia, esto bien lo creades,
        De libros e de ropas, e de muchas bondades;
        Suffrio eneste comedio muchas aduersidades.

109   Yo Gonçalo, que fago esto asu honor,
        Yo la ui, asy uea la faz del Criador,
        Vna buena cozina, assaz rica lauor;
        Retrahen quela fizo essi buen confessor.

110   Fue en pocos de annos la casa arreada,
        De lauor de ganados assaz bien aguisada,
        Ya trouauan en ella los mezquinos posada,
        Por el fue, Deo gracias, la iglesia sagrada.

111   Conuertio asu padre, fizolo fradrear,
        Ouo ennas sus manos en cabo afinar,
        Soter[r]olo el fijo en el mjsmo fossar,
        Pesa me que non somos çerteros del logar.

112   La madre, que non quiso la orden reçebir,
        Non la qujso el fijo a casa aduzir,
        Ouo ensu porfidia la uieia a morir:
        Dios aya la su alma, sy lo quiere oyr. . . .

289   Queremos uos un otro libriello començar
        E delos sus mjraglos algunos renunçar,
        Los que Dios en su ujda qujso por el mostrar:
        Cuyos ioglares somos, el nos deñe guyar. . . .

Eran en essi tiempo los Moros muy bezinos,   353
Non osauan los omnes andar por los camjnos,
Dauan los cosas malas salto alos matinos,
Leuauan cruamiente ensoga los mezquinos.

Dieron por auentura salto vna uegada,   354
Alliñaron aSoto essa gent renegada,
Pris(s)ieron vn mançebo en essa caualgada,
Domjngo auja nonbre, non fallezco en nada.

Metieron lo en fierros e en dura cadena,   355
De lazar e de fanbre dauan li fiera pena ;
Dauan li yantar mala e non buena la çena,
Conbria, si gelo diessen, de grado pan dauena.

Aquel es bien mezquino que caye ental mano,   356
En cosiment de canes quando iaz el Christiano,
En dicho y en fecho affontan lo cutiano,
Anda mal en ybierno, non meior en uerano.

Parientes del captiuo aujan muy grant pesar,   357
Ouieron por çien çientos sueldos apleytear,
Mas non aujan conseio que podiessen pagar,
Canon podian por nada los dineros ganar.

De toda la ganançia, con toda su mjssion,   358
Apenas allegaron la media redemption,
Estauan en desarro y en conmedicion,
Tenjan que afincar abria enla prision.

Asmaron vn conseio, deDios fue enbiado,   359
Que fuessen apedir al confessor onrrado,
Omne que li pidiesse nunca fue repoyado,
Sy el non lis ualiesse todo era librado.

Quales que fueron dellos, o primos o hermanos,   360
Fueron al Padre sancto por besar li las manos,
Dixieron : "Ay, Padre de enfermos e sanos,
Oy nuestra rencura, algunt conseio da nos.

361   Es vn nuestro pariente de Moros captiuado,
           Enna presion yaziendo es fierament lazrado,
           Auemos con los Moros el precio destaiado,
           Mas non cumple lo nuestro, ni lo que nos an dado.

362   Señor bueno, ayuda te uenjmos pedir,
           Ya por nuestra uentura non sauemos do yr,
           Tu saues en que caye captiuos redemjr,
           Dios como lo gradesçe al qui lo puede conplir."

363   El Padre piadoso començo de llorar:
           "Amjgos, diz, daria, sy toujesse que dar,
           Non podria en cosa meior lo enplear
           Lo que meter podiesse en captiuos sacar.

364   Non auemos dineros njn oro njn argent,
           Vn cauallo tenemos en casa sola ment,
           Nos essi uos daremos de grado al present,
           Cumpla lo que fallere el Rey Omnjpotent.

365   Leuat agora esso, lo que dar uos podemos,
           Mientre esso guyades por al uos cataremos,
           Lo que catar podieremos enujar uos lo emos,
           Como en Dios fiamos el preso cobraremos."

366   Fueron ellos su uja su cosa aguisar,
           Por uender el cauallo en auer lo tornar:
           El Padre cordoioso entro asu altar,
           Como era usado, al Criador rogar.

367   La noche escorrida, luego alos aluores,
           Canto la sancta mjssa elli conlos señores,
           Touieron por el preso oracion e clamores,
           Que Dios lo delibrasse de tales guardadores.

368   La oracion del Padre dela grant sanctidat
           Leuola alos çielos la sancta caridat,
           Plego alas oreias del Rey de Magestat,
           Escapo el captiuo dela captiujdat.

Abrieron se los fierros en que yazia trauado,   369
El corral nol retouo que era bien çerrado,
Torno asus parientes delos fierros cargado,
Faziase el mjsmo dello marabillado.

Lo que lis prometiera el Padre uerdadero   370
Tardar non gelo quiso por al dia terçero,
Desembargo al Moro que era carçelero
De gujsa que non ouo delli vn mal dinero.

Sopieron del captiuo qual hora escapo,   371
Vidieron que fue essa que la mjssa canto,
Entendien que el Padre sancto lo basteçio :
Esta fue la ayuda que lis el prometio. . . .

B

LIBRO DE ALEXANDRE

ASCRIBED TO BERCEO

(From a manuscript in the Bibliothèque Nationale at Paris. The transcript of the present passage is due to Professor A. Morel-Fatio of the
Collège de France and the École des Chartes, who is about to publish
a critical text of the poem.)

[1] Ordeno su fazienda por yr mas acordados,   1
Que sy les auiniese fuesen apareiados :
Mando que de tal guisa fuesen todos armados
Como sy de fazienda fuesen asegurados.

Leuauan por Reliquias vn fuego consagrado,   2
Sienpre estaua biuo, nunca fue amatado :
Asy yua delante en vn carro dorado,
Sobre altar de plata e bien encortinado.

[1] 804 in the edition of the *Bib. de aut. esp.*, vol. 51.

3
La estoria de Jupiter con otros çelestiales
Yua apres del fuego con muchos capellanes :
Andaua ex conuento en diez carros cabdales,
Que eran de fino oro z de piedras xristales.

4
Doze pueblos que eran de sendas rregiones,
De diuersos vestidos, de diuersos sermones,
Que serien a lo menos bien doze ligiones,
Estos dio que guardasen a esas rreligiones.

5
Bien auie diez mill carros de los sabios senneros,
Que eran por escripto de el rrey conseieros,
Los vnos eran clerigos, los otros caualleros :
Qui quier los conosçrie que eran conpanneros.

6
Iuan en pues aquellos diez mill escogidos,
Todos eran de Dario parientes conosçidos,
Todos vistien presetes muy nobles vestidos,
Semejauan que fueran en vn dia nasçidos.

7
En medio yua Dario, vn cuerpo tan preçioso,
Semeja pphan, tanto era de sabroso :
El carro en que yua tanto era de fermoso,
Que qui lo podie veyer tenies por venturoso.

8
Los rrayos eran de oro fechos a grant lauor,
Las rruedas eso mismo dauan grant rresplandor,
El axo de fina plata que cantase meior,
El ventril de çipres por dar buena olor.

9
El cabeçon del carro nol tengades por vil,
Era todo ondado de muy buen marfil,
Todo era listado de obra de grafil,
De piedras de grant presçio auie mas de mill.

10
Las puntas delos rrayos eran bien caleadas,
De bestiones bien fechos, de piedras preçiadas,
Eran tan sotil mente todas engastonadas,
Semejauan que eran en vno ajuntadas.

Digamos vos del yugo sy quiere de la lazada, 11
Obra era greçisca nueua mente fallada,
Toda vna serpiente la tenie enbraçada,
Pero cadena era de oro era muy delgada.

El escanno de Dario era de grant barata, 12
Los piedes de fino oro e los bancos de plata,
Mas valien los anillos en que ome los ata
Que non farie la rrenta de toda Damiata.

Uiene puestos los piedes sobre quatro leones, 13
Que semejauan biuos, tanto eran lydones,
Tenien enlas cabeças otros tantos grifones,
E tenien solas manos todos sendos bestiones.

Uenien sobre el rrey por tenprar la color 14
Vn aguilla bien fecha de preçiosa lauor,
Las alas espandidas por fer sonbra mayor,
Sienpre tenie al rrey de tenprada color.

Eran enla carreta todos los dioses pyntados, 15
Como son tres çielos e como son poblados,
El somero muy claro lleno de blanqueados,
Los otros mas de yuso de color mas delgados.

Iuan syn todo esto de cuesta e delante 16
Diez mill aguardadores çerca el enperante :
Todos auien astas de argente blanqueante,
E cuchillas brunnidas de oro flameante.

Leuaua mas de çerca dozientos lorigados, 17
Todos fillos de rreyes e a ley engendrados,
Todos eran mancebos, todos rrezien baruados,
De paresçer fermosos e de cuerpos granados.

Avn fizo al Dario por las huestes saluar, 18
Que las non pudiesen los griegos desbalçar,
Saco treynta mill otros varones de prestar,
Por gouernar la çaga e las huestes saluar.

19   Uynie çerca del rrey su muger, la rreyna,
       En preçiosa carreta, su preçiosa cortina,
       Vn fiio e dos fijas, mucha Rica vezina,
       Mas cabera la madre con muy grant cozina.

20   Auie y doze carros, todos bien adobados,
       De mugeres de rreyes todos vinien cargados,
       Por guardar estas donas auie y dos mill castrados,
       Quando eran chiquillos fueron todos cortados.

21   Los Reyes de oriente auien todos tal manna
       De yr en apellido con toda su conpanna,
       Bien de antiguedat tenien aquesta manna,
       Mas fue para Dario mas negra que la graja.

VII

POEMA DE FERNAN GONÇALEZ

(From the edition of C. C. Marden, Baltimore, 1904)

Quando fueron las armas des[f]echas e quemadas,   71
Fueron aquestas nuevas a Marruecos pas[s]adas ;
Las gentes afrycanas fueron luego juntadas,
Al puerto de la mar fueron luego [l]legadas.

Todos muy vyen guisados por a Spanna passar,   72
Quando fueron juntados pas[s]aron allend(e el) mar,
Arryvaron al puerto que dizen Gybraltar,
Non podrya ningun omne quantos eran asmar.

Todos estos paganos que [a] Afryca mandavan,   73
Contra los de Oropa despechosos estavan,

·   ·   ·   ·   ·   ·   ·   ·   ·

Entraron en la tierra do entrar non cuydavan.

Llegaron a Sevylla la gente rrenegada,   74
Es[s]a çibdat nin otras non se les fyzo nada ;
Era de mala guisa la rrueda trastornada,
La cavtyva dEspanna era mal quebrantada.

(Estonces) el vuen rrey don Rrodrygo a quien avia con-   75
      t(eç)ido,
Mando por tod(o) el rreyno dar luegol apellido :
" El que con el non fues[s]e ante del mes conplido,
El aver e el cuerpo tovies(e) lo por perdido."

Las gentes quando oyeron pregones aquexados,   76
Que daveres e (de) cuerpos eran mal (a)menazados,
Non era[n] y ninguno[s] pora fyncar osado[s],
Fueron ante del tienpo con el rrey ayuntados.

77   Quando ovo (el rrey) [don] Rrodrygo sus poderes juntados,
     Era poder syn guisa mas todos desarmados ;
     Lidiar fueron con (los) moros, levaron (los) sus pecados,
     Ca (les) fue de los profe(c)tas esto profetizado.

78   Tenia (el rrey) don Rrodrigo syenpre la delantera,
     Salio contra los moros, tovo les la carrera,
     Ayunto se en el canpo que dizen Sangonera,
     Çerca [es] de Guadiana en que a su rryvera.

79   Fueron damas las partes los golpes avyvados,
     Eran pora lidiar todos escalentados,
     (E) fueron de la primera los moros arrancados,
     (Rre)cojieron se con todo essora los cruzados.

80   Era la cosa puesta e de Dios otorgada
     Que seryan los dEspanna metidos a espada,
     A los duennos primeros [non] serya tornada ;
     Tornaron en el canpo ellos otra vegada.

81   Cuydavan los cristianos ser vien asegurados,
     Que avyan a los moros en el canpo rrancados;
     Fueran se los paganos es[s]as oras tornados,
     Sy non por quien non ayan perdon de sus pecados.

82   Otro dia mannana los pueblos descreydos
     Todos fueron en (el) canpo de sus armas guarnidos,
     Tanniendo annafyles e dando alarydos,
     (E) las tierras e los çielos semejavan movydos.

83   Volvieron es[s]as oras vn torneo pesado,
     Començaron los [moros] (a)do lo avyan dexado,
     Moryeron los cristianos todos   ¡ Ay, mal pecado !
     Del [buen] rrey es[s]as oras non sopieron mandado.

84   En Vyseo fallaron despues vna sepultura,
     El qual yazia en vn sepulcro escrito desta figura :
     "Aqui yaz(e) (el rrey) don Rrodrygo, vn rrey de grran[d] natura,
     [El] que perdio la tierra por su desaventura.". . .

El conde [de] Pyteos e (el) conde de Tolosa,   328
—Paryente(s) era(n) del rrey (don Sancho), esto es çierta cosa—
Tomo de sus condados conpanna muy fermosa,
Movyo pora Casty[e]lla en ora muy astrrosa.

El conde non vyo [por] a la lid llegar,   329
Pero quando lo sopo non quiso detardar ;
Al buen rrey de Navarra [bien] cuydo lo vengar,
Al puerto de Getarea ovo [de] arrybar.

Los navarros al conde todos a el (se) llegaron,   330
Commo fue la fazienda todo ge(l)lo contaron :
Quantos fueron los muertos, quantos los que fyncaron,
Commo a el en antes (de) dos dias le esperaron.

El conde de Tolosa dio les muy grrand esfuerço,   331
Coydo con es[s]e fecho con el salir a puerto,
. . . .
"Ca me han castellanos fecho [este] grran[d] tuerto."

El conde don Fernando avya lo ya oydo   332
Commo era aquel conde al puerto ya venido ;
El conde don Fernando, maguer [tan] mal fer(r)ydo,
Atal commo estava pora alla fue ydo.

Los vas[s]allos del conde tenien se por errados,   333
Eran contrra el conde fuerte m[i]ente yrados,
Eran de su sennor todos muy despagados,
Por que avyan por fuerça syenpre dandar armados.

Folgar non les dexa[va] nin estar (a)segurados,   334
Dizien : "Non es esta vyda sy non pora los pecados
Que andan (de) noche e (de) dia e nunca son cansados,
El semeja a Satan(as) e nos a (los) sus criados.

Por que lidiar queremos e tanto lo amamos,   335
Nunca folgura tenemos sy non quando almas saquamos,
A los del estantygua [a] aquellos semejamos,
Ca todas cosas cansan e nos nunca cansamos." . . .

338 Dyxo Nunno Layno : "Sennor, sy tu quisieres,
Sy a ty semejare o tu (lo) por bien tovyeres,
Que estes aqui quedo fasta que guaresçieres,
Que por mala codiçia en yerro non cayeres. . . .

342 Dexa folgar tus gentes, (e) a ty mesmo sanar,
Tyenes muy fuerte llaga, dexa la [tu] folgar,
Dexa venir tus gentes que avn son por llegar,
Muchos son por venir, deves los esperar.". . .

345 Quando ovo acabada don Nunno su rrazon,
Començo el buen conde, es[s]e fyrme varon ;
Avya grran[d] conplimiento del sen de Salamon,
Nunca fue Alexandrre mas grrand(e) de coraçon.

346 Dyxo : " Nunno Laynez, buena rrazon dixestes,
Las cosas commo son as[s]y las departyestes,
' Dalongar esta lid,' creo que assy dixestes,
[Quien] quier que vos lo dixo vos mal lo aprendiestes.

347 Non deue el que puede esta lid alongar,
Quien tyene buena ora otra quiere esperar,
Vn dia que perdemos non podrremos cobrar,
Jamas en aquel dia non podemos tornar. . . .

350 Todos los que grran[d] fecho quisieron acabar,
Por muy grrandes travajos ovyeron a pas[s]ar,
Non com[i]en quand(o) quisieron nin cena(n) nin (an) yantar,
Los vyçios de la carne ovyeron doluidar,

351 Non cuentan dAlexandre las noches nin los dias,
Cuentan sus buenos fechos e sus cavalleryas,
Cuentan del rrey Davyt que mato a Golias,
De Judas (el) Macabeo fyjo de Matatyas,

352 Carlos [e] Valdouinos, Rroldan e don Ojero,
Terryn e Gualdabuey, (e) Arnald e Oliuero,
Torpyn e don Rrynaldos e el gascon Angelero,
Estol e Salomon e el otrro (su) conpan[n]ero.

Estos e otrros muchos que [non] vos he nonbrado[s], 353
Por lo que ellos fyzieron seran syenpre ementados,
Sy tan buenos non fueran oy seryen oluidados,
Seran los buenos fechos fasta la fyn contados.

Por tanto ha me(ne)ster que los dias contemos, 354
Los dias e las noches en que los espendemos,
Quantos (dias) en valde pas[s]an nunca los cobrraremos,
Amigos, byen lo vedes que mal seso fazemos."

Cavalleros e peones ovo los de vençer, 355
A cosa quel dezia non sabyan rresponder,
Quanto el por byen tovo ovyeron lo (a) fazer,
Su rrazon acabada mando luego mover.

El conde don Fernando con toda su mesnada, 356
Llegaron a vn agua muy fuerte e muy yrada,
Ebrrol dixeron syenpre assy es oy llamada,
Vieron se (y) en grran[d] rrevate que fues(e) y su posada.

Tovyeron la rrybera tolosanos (byen) guardada, 357
Non dieron castellanos por es[s]o todo nada,
Dando e rresçebyendo mucha buena lançada,
Ovyeron much(o) ayna el agua traves[s]ada.

Ovyeron grran[d] rrevato en pas[s]ar aquel vado, 358
Ovo (y) de petavynos grran[d] pueblo derrybado,
Maguer [que] non querian venian (a) mal de su grrado,
Dellos se afogavan, dellos salian a nado.

Abrio por mediol agua el conde la carrera, 359
Ovyeron tolosanos a dexar la rrybera ;
Ordeno las sus azes en medio duna glera,
Fue los acometer dun estrranna manera.

Quando ovo el [buen] conde el rrio atraves[s]ado, 360
Fferio luego en ellos commo venia yrado ;
Al que el alcançaba much(o) era de malfado,
Del yva(n) a sus parientes ayna mal mandado.

361   El conde don Fernando, de coraçon loçano,
       Fyrie en pytavynos e fazie les grran[d] danno,
       Ronpya (les) las guarniçiones com(mo) sy fuessen vn
          panno,
       Non les valia esfuerço nin les valia engan[n]o.

362   Acorrian le luego [los] sus buenos varones,
       Ca tenia (a)y muchos [de] buenos infançones,
       Dun logar eran todos e dunos cor(r)açones,
       Lazravan tolosanos e lazraban (los) gascones.

363   Pero com(mo) eran muchos yvan los acoytando,
       (Ya) yva de fyera guisa la lid escalentando,
       Yva se domnes muertos [tod] el canpo poblando,
       Maltraye (a) los afyrmes el conde don Fernando.

364   Andava por [las] azes muy fyera mient(e) yrado,
       Por que non los podia vençer andava muy cuytado,
       Dixo : " Non puede ser maguer pes(e) al pecado,
       Nos pueden tolosanos fallar byen dest mercado."

365   Metyo se por las azes muy fuerte (mente) espoleando,
       La lança sobre mano, [el] su pendon alçando.
       "¿Donde estas, el buen conde?" assy yua llamando.
       "¡Sal, [sal] aca al canpo! (que) ¡cata aqui (a) don
          Fernando!"

366   Antes que ellos amos venies[s]en a (las) fer(r)idas,
       (Con las vozes de don Fernando las gentes eran desma-
          yados)
       Las gentes tolosanos todas fueron foydas ;
       Nunca ningunas gentes fueron tan mal fallidas,
       Ca fueron en grran[d] miedo e en mal preçio metidas.

367   Fueron todos foydos por vna grran[d] montanna,
       Fincol conde [en el canpo con] muy poca conpanna,
       Nunca fue el (conde) tolosano en quexa atamanna,
       Ca el cond(e) de Casty[e]lla le tenia fuerte sanna.

El conde de Tolosa mucho fue espantado,   368
Ca vyo (a) don Fernando venir mucho yrado,
Por non tener [la] gente que era des(m)anparado,
Con sus armas guarnido salio luego al canpo.

El conde don Fernando, omne syn crueldat,   369
Oluido con la yra mesura e vondat,
Fue feryr al [buen] conde dyra e (de) voluntat,
Non dudo de feryr lo syn nulla piedat.

El conde castellano, (vn) guerrero natural,   370
Feryo al (conde) tolosano de vn(a) golpe mortal,
Cuytado fue el gascon de la ferida muy mal,
Dixo a altas vozes : "¡ Santa Maria, (sennora e) val !"

El conde de Tolosa assy fue mal ferydo,   371
Fue luego del cavallo a tierra avatydo,
Dezir non pudo nada ca fue luego transido,
Luego que el fue muerto su pueblo fue vençido. . ₀ ₀

VIII

A

LA CRÓNICA GENERAL QUE MANDÓ COMPONER EL REY DON ALFONSO X

(*a*. From the extracts published by R. Menéndez Pidal in his *Leyenda de los Infantes de Lara*, Madrid, 1896, pp. 207 ff.)

[CHAPTER I.] DE CUEMO ROY BLASQUEZ DE ALFFOZ DE LARA FIRIO A SO SOBRINO GONÇALUO GONÇALUEZ, ET SO SOBRINO A ELL, ET DE CUEMO LOS FIZO EL CONDE GARÇI FERRANDEZ QUE SE PER- DONASSEN

Andados veynte et tres annos dell regnado del rey don Ramiro, et fue esto en la era de nueueçientos et nouaenta et siete annos, et andaua otrossi ell anno dela encarnaçion del Sennor en nueueçientos et çinquaenta et nueue et el dell
5 inperio de Otho, emperador de Roma, en veynte et seys, assi acaesçio en aquella sazon que un alto omne, natural de alffoz de Lara, que auie nonbre Roy Blasquez, que caso otrossi con una duenna de muy grand guisa et era natural de Burueua, et prima cormana del conde Garçi Ferrandez, et dezien le
10 donna Llambla ; et aquel Roy Blasquez era sennor de Biluestre, et avie una hermana muy buena duenna et complida de todos bienes et de todas buenas costumbres, et dizienle donna Sancha, et era casada con don Gonçaluo Gustioz, el bueno, que fue de Salas, et ouieron siete fijos alos que llamaron los siete inffantes de
15 Salas, et criolos a todos siete un muy buen cauallero que auie nonbre Munno Salido, et ensennoles todas buenas mannas, et guisolos por que fueron todos fechos caualleros en un dia, et armolos el cuende Garçi Ferrandez. Aquel Roy Blasquez de

quien dixiemos, quando caso con aquella donna Llanbla, fizo
sus bodas en la çibdad de Burgos, et enbio conuidar todos sos
amigos a muchas tierras : a Gallizia, a Leon, a Portogal, a
Estremadura, a Gasconna, a Aragon, a Nauarra, et conuido
otrossi todos los de Burueua, et a los otros de toda Castiella, et   5
fueron y llegadas muchas yentes ademas ; et fue en estas bodas
don Gonçaluo Gustioz con donna Sancha, su mugier, et con
aquellos sos siete fijos et con don Munno Salido, ell amo que
los criara. Estas bodas duraron çinco sedmanas, et fueron y
grandes alegrias ademas : de alançar a tablados et de boffordar   10
et de correr toros et de iogar tablas et açedexes et de muchos
ioglares, et dieron en estas bodas el conde Garçi Ferrandez et
todos los otros altos omnes grand auer ademas et muchos
dones. Mas una sedmana antes que las bodas se acabassen,
mando Roy Blasquez parar un tablado muy alto en la glera,   15
çercal rio, et fizo pregonar que qui quier quel crebantasse quel
darie ell un don muy bueno. Los caualleros que se preçiauan
por alançar fueron todos y allegados, mas pero nunqua tanto
se trabaiaron que pudiessen dar en somo delas tablas nin llegar a
ellas. Quando esto uio Aluar Sanchez, que era primo cormano   20
de donna Llanbla, caualgo en so cauallo, et fue alançar a aquel
tablado, e dio en las tablas tan grand colpe quel oyeron dentro
en la villa, segund dize la estoria. Donna Llanbla quando lo oyo,
e sopo que so cormano Aluar Sanchez fiziera aquel colpe, plogol
mucho, e con el grand plazer que ende ouo, dixo ante donna   25
Sancha, su cunnada, et ante todos siete sos fijos que seyen y
con ella : "agora veet, amigos, que cauallero tan esforçado es
Aluar Sanchez, ca de quantos alli son allegados non pudo ninguno ferir en somo del tablado sinon el solo tan sola mientre,
et mas valio el alli solo que todos los otros." Quando aquello   30
oyeron donna Sancha et sos fijos, tomaronse a riir ; mas los
caualleros, como estauan en grand sabor de un iuego que auien
començado, ningun dellos non paro mientes a aquello que

donna Llanbla dixiera, sinon Gonçaluo Gonçaluez, que era el
menor daquellos siete hermanos; et furtose de los hermanos,
et caualgo en so cauallo, et tomo un bofordo en su mano, et
fuesse solo, que non fue otro omne con ell sinon un so escudero
5 que le leuaua un açor. Et Gonçaluo Gonçaluez, luego que llego,
fue alançar al tablado, et dio un tan grand colpe en el, que
crebanto una de las tablas de medio. Quando esto vieron donna
Sancha et sos fijos, ouieron ende grand plazer, mas en verdad
peso mucho a donna Llanbla. Los fijos de donna Sancha caual-
10 garon estonçes et fueronse pora ell hermano, ca ouieron miedo
que se leuantase dend algun despecho, cuemo contescio luego
y, ca Aluar Sanchez començo luego de dezir sus palabras tan
grandes, por que ouo a responder Gonçaluo Gonçaluez et dixo:
"tan bien alançades uos, et tanto se pagan de uos las duennas,
15 que bien me semeia que non fablan de ótro cauallero tanto
como de uos." Aquella ora dixo Aluar Sanchez: "si las duennas de mi fablan, fazen derecho, ca entienden que valo mas
que todos los otros." Quando esto oyo Gonçaluo Gonçaluez,
pesol muy de coraçon et non lo pudo sofrir, e dexosse yr a ell
20 tan braua mientre, et diol una tan gran punnada en el rostro,
que los dientes et las quexadas le crebanto, de guisa que luego
cayo en tierra muerto a pies del cauallo. Donna Llanbla
quando lo oyo, començo a meter grandes bozes, llorando muy
fuerte e diziendo que nunqua duenna assi fuera desondrada en
25 sus bodas, cuemo ella fuera alli. Roy Blazquez quando aquello
sopo, caualgo a grand priessa, et tomo un astil en la mano, et
fuesse pora alla, do estauan; et quando llego a los siete inffantes, alço arriba el braço con aquell astil que leuaua, et dio con
ell un tan grand colpe en la cabeça a Gonçaluo Gonçaluez que
30 por çinco logares le fizo crebar la sangre. Gonçaluo Gonçaluez
quando se vio tan mal ferido, dixo: "par Dios, tio, nunqua
uos yo meresçi porque uos tan grand colpe me diessedes como
este; et ruego aqui a mios hermanos que si yo por uentura
ende muriero, que uos lo non demanden, mas pero tanto uos

ruego que me non firades otra uez, por quanto uos amades, ca
vos lo non podria soffrir." Roy Blasquez quando aquello oyo,
con la grand yra que ende ouo, alço otra uez aquella uara por
darle otro colpe, mas Gonçaluo Gonçaluez desuio la cabeça
del colpe, assi quel non alcanço sinon poco por ell onbro, et 5
pero tan grand ferida le dio que dos pieças fizo ell asta enel.
Gonçaluo Gonçaluez quando uio que non auie y otra mesura
nin meior que aquella, priso en la mano ell açor quel traye ell
escudero, et fue dar a Roy Blasquez con ell vna tan grand
ferida en la cara a bueltas con el punno, que todo gele crebanto 10
enel rostro daquel colpe, de guisa que luegol fizo crebar la sangre por las narizes. Roy Blasquez estonçes quando se uio assi
tan mal trecho, començo a meter bozes, et a dezir, " armas,
armas," muy apriessa, que luego fueron y ayuntados con ell
todos sos caualleros. Los inffantes quando aquello uieron, 15
apartaronse a un logar con su conpanna, et podrien seer por
todos dozientos caualleros, ca bien veyen que sse darie a grand
mal aquel fecho si Dios non lo desuiase. Mas el cuende Garçi
Ferrandez, que era sennor et era y en Burgos, et Gonçaluo
Gustioz, padre de los inffantes, luego que sopieron aquella 20
pelea, fueron pora alla, e metieronse entrellos e departieron
los, que non ouo y estonçes otro mal ninguno ; et tan bien
andido y el cuende Garçi Ferrandez que luego y los fizo perdonar. Sobresto dixo alli estonçes Gonçaluo Gustioz a Roy
Blasquez : "don Rodrigo, vos avedes mucho mester caualleros, 25
ca sodes del mayor prez darmas que otro que omne sepa, de
guisa que moros et christianos vos han por ende grand enuidia,
et uos temen mucho ; et por ende ternia yo por bien que uos
siruiessen mios fijos et uos aguardassen, si uos por bien lo
touiessedes et uos ploguiesse, et vos que les fuessedes bueno et 30
lo fiziessedes en manera que ellos valiessen mas por uos, ca
vuestros sobrinos son, et non han de fazer al sinon lo que uos
mandaredes et touieredes por bien." Et ell otorgol que assi
serie et le cumplirie.

(*b.* From the extracts published by C. C. Marden in his edition of the *Poema de Fernan Gonçalez*, Baltimore, 1904, pp. 118 ff.)

[CHAPTER V.] DE COMO EL CONDE FERNAND GONÇALUEZ LLAMO SUS UASSALLOS A CONSSEIO E DE LO QUE DIXO GONÇALUO DIAZ

Andados V annos del regnado daquel Rey don Ramiro, e fue esto en la era de DCCCC e XL e tres annos, e andaua otrossi estonces ell anno de la Encarnation del Sennor en DCCCC e V annos, e el dell imperio de Loys Emperador de
5 Roma en VII. En este anno aqui dicho, Almançor, que era el mas poderoso moro de aquend la mar so Abderrhamen Rey de Cordoua, quando oyo dezir como el Conde Fernand Gonçaluez auie preso el castiello que dizien Caraço, ouo ende muy grand pesar e touose por maltrecho. E enuio luego muchos
10 porteros con sus cartas por toda tierra de moros que fuessen luego con ell caualleros e peones. E cuenta la Estoria que tan grand fue el poder que ayunto de Reys e de caualleros e de otros omnes de armas, que ouo y mas de VII legiones. . . .
E el Conde Fernand Gonçalez, quando oyo dezir que Alman-
15 çor auie mouido con tan grand hueste e uinie menazando quel non fincarie tierra nin logar o nol fuesse buscar, enuio luego sus cartas por toda Castiella que uiniesen a el todos sos uassallos ca mucho era mester. E ellos, luego que uieron las car- tas, uinieron se por el muy de grado. E el ouo con ellos so
20 acuerdo e rogo les quel conseiassen qual serie lo meior, de yr a los moros o atender los. E estonces fablo Gonçalo Diaz, un cauallero muy sesudo, e dixo : " Sennor, non me semeia que tiempo tenemos nin sazon pora lidiar con los moros. Mas si alguna carrera pudiessemos fallar poro se desuiasse esta lid,
25 tenerlo ya yo por bien. E non nos deuemos recelar de pecho nin de otra cosa qualquier poro pudiessemos amanssar los moros e ganar dellos treguas, ca en muchas otras cosas se despiende ell auer.". . .

[Chapter VI.] De como el Conde Fernand Gonçalez esforço
  sos caualleros pora la batalla

El conde non se pago del conseio que Gonçalo Diaz daua e
fue muy sannudo por ende, pero que lo non mostro nin le
recudio brauamientre mas contradixol todo lo que dixiera, e
razono assi : "Quiero responder a don Gonçalo e contar quanto
el dixo, que las cosas que ell a aqui mostrado sol non son de   5
oyr nin de retraer. Dixo de la primera que escusemos el lidiar,
mas pero digo yo a esto que pues que omne non puede escusar
la muerte nin foyr della, deue morir lo mas onrradamientre que
pudiere. E en ganarnos treguas de los moros por pechar les
algo, de sennores que somos fazer nos emos sieruos ; e en uez de   10
sacar Castiella de la premia en que esta, doblar gela emos. . . .
Quando el Rey Rodrigo perdio la tierra, assi como sabedes, non
finco en toda Espanna tierra de cristianos si non Asturias e Castiella Uieia sennera. E es esta en que nos uiuimos agora e la
que nuestros auuelos deffendieron con muy grand lazeria, ca   15
fueron muy affrontados por que eran pocos e tenien muy poca
tierra e padescieron mucha lazeria de guerra e de fambre. E
con tod aquello, de lo ageno siempre ganaron e de lo suyo non
perdieron. E por miedo de muerte non quisieron fazer yerro
nin cosa que les mal estidiesse, e por esta carrera uencieron sos   20
enemigos. . . .

B

GENERAL ESTORIA

(From a fourteenth century MS., No. 816 of the Biblioteca Nacional
at Madrid, published in excerpts by R. Menéndez Pidal in his *Poema
de Yuçuf*, Madrid, 1902)

Libro 8°, Cap. 9. De como sonnaron en la carçel el copero
  et el çatiquero de Pharaon sus suennos, et gelos solto
  Josep que yazie y, et fueron uerdaderos

En la sazon que Josep yazie en la carcel, acaescio que dos
sergentes del rey fizieron por que cayeron en la su yra del rey.

. . . Et ell uno daquellos officiales que cayeron en la yra del
rey era copero del rey, et ell otro çatiquero. Et cuenta la
Estoria de Egipto que sopiera el rey Pharaon Nicrao la culpa
en que aquellos sus officiales cayeron contra el, et fuera desta
5 guisa : diz que yazie el rey durmiendo una noche, et uino ael
en suennos uno en semeiança de omne et dixol : el tu copero
et el tu çatiquero an conseiado como te maten, et guarda te
dellos. El rey esperto en cabo del suenno, como contesce a
todos los omnes las mas uezes, et asmo la razon et paro mientes
10 en el suenno et acordol bien, et grand mannana enuio por el
copero et por el çatiquero et dixoles lo que sonnara et deman-
doles quel dixiessen si era uerdad. El copero non quiso mentir
assu sennor el rey et dixol que assi era fablado. El rey estonçes, por sacar dellos mas la uerdad et saber mas del fecho, dixo
15 les esta razon : ¿como podiedes asmar atamana nemiga et
tamanna traycion como esta, ca yo nunca me apparto mucho
con tales como uos nin esto sennero, mas siempre muy acompannado, por que deuedes entender que non me podriedes uos
matar. Respuso el copero : sennor, la fabla fue tal que te diesse
20 yo poçon en el uino et el çatiquero enel pan, mas non quelo
yo otorgasse nin fuesse mi uoluntad delo fazer ; et assi como
te descubri la uerdad en lo al, assi telo digo en esto quem assi
contescio. En todo esto el çatiquero callosse que non dixo
nada. Et auie nombre Aracen et el copero Matis. Et el rey,
25 maguer que touo por bien al copero en que nol negara la uerdad, pero mando los prender de cabo a amos por saber aun
mas del fecho. Et echaron los en la carcel del rey o era Josep.

IX

CANTICUM CANTICORUM IN SPANISH

(From *Das Hohelied in castilianischer Sprache des XIII. Jahrhunderts nach der Handschrift des Escorial I. i. 6*, printed by J. Cornu in *Beiträge zur romanischen und englischen Philologie ; Festgabe für W. Foerster*, Halle, 1902)

II. 1. E yo so flor del campo e lilio de los valles. 2. Assi como el lilio entre las espinas : assi es la mi amiga entre las fijas. 3. Como el maçano entre los arboles de las selvas : assi es el mio amigo entre los fijos. Assenteme so la sombra daquel que amava. e el so fructo es dulçe al mio paladar. 4. Metio me el 5 rey en la bodega. ordeno caridat en mi. 5. Sostenet me con flores e cercat me de maçanas. ca damor so enferma. 6. La su siniestra so la mi cabeça. e la su diestra abraçar ma. 7. Coniuro vos fijas de Iherusalem por las corças e por los ciervos de los campos que no levantedes ni fagades despertar ala mi amiga. 10 fasta que ella quiera. 8. Voz del mio amigo. he que este viene saliendo los oteros. traspassando los collados. 9. Semeia el mio amigo ala corça. e el enodio de los ciervos. he que el esta tras nuestra paret. catando por las finiestras. oteando por las ventanas. 10. He el mio amigo que me fabla. Levantat e anda 15 amiga mia paloma mia. fermosa mia e ven. 11. Ca ya passo el yvierno e fuesse el agua. 12. Las flores parecieron en nuestra tierra. tiempo de cuedar vino. La voz de la tortola es oyda en nuestra tierra.

X

JUAN RUIZ, ARCIPRESTE DE HITA

LIBRO DE BUEN AMOR

(From the edition of J. Ducamin, Toulouse, 1901)

11   Dyos padre, dios fijo, dios spiritu santo :
El que nasçio de la virgen esfuerçe nos de tanto
Que sienpre lo loemos en prosa e en canto,
Sea de nuestras almas cobertura e manto.

12   El que fizo el çielo, la tierra e el mar,
El me done su graçia e me quiera alunbrar,
Que pueda de cantares vn librete Rimar
Que los que lo oyeren puedan solaz tomar.

13   Tu, señor, dios mjo, quel oñe crieste,
Enforma e ayuda amj, el tu acipreste,
Que pueda fazer vn libro de buen amor aqueste,
Quelos cuerpos alegre e alas almas preste.

14   Sy queredes, senores, oyr vn buen solaz,
Escuchad el rromanze, sosegad vos en paz,
Non vos dire mentira en quanto enel yaz,
Ca por todo el mundo se vsa e se faz.

15   E por que mejor de todos sea escuchado,
Fablar vos he por tobras e cuento rrimado ;
Es vn dezir fermoso e saber sin pecado,
Rrazon mas plazentera, ffablar mas apostado.

16   Non tengades que es libro neçio de devaneo,
Nin creades que es chufa algo que enel leo ;
Ca, segund buen djnero yaze en vil correo,
Ansi en feo libro esta saber non feo.

El axenuz de fuera mas negro es que caldera,   17
Es de dentro muy blanco, mas quela peña vera;
Blanca farina esta so negra cobertera,
Açucar negro e blanco esta en vil caña vera.

Sobre la espina esta la noble Rosa flor,   18
En fea letra esta saber de grand dotor;
Como so mala capa yaze buen beuedor,
Ansi so el mal tabardo esta buen amor. . . .

ENSSIENPLO DEL LEON E DEL CAUALLO

Vn cavallo muy gordo pasçia enla defesa;   298
Venje el leon de caça, pero conel non pesa;
El leon tan goloso al cavallo sopessa:
"Vassalo"—dixo—"mjo, la mano tu me besa."

Al leon gargantero rrespondjo el cavallo,   299
Dyz: "tu eres mj Señor e yo tu vasallo;
En te besar la mano yo en eso me fallo,
Mas yr aty non puedo, que tengo vn grand contrallo.

Ayer do me ferrava, vn ferrero mal dito   300
E[c]ho me en este pie vn clauo tan fito,
Enclauo me; ven, Señor, con tu djente bendito
Sacamelo e faz de m̃y como de tuyo quito."

Abaxose el leon por le dar algund confuerto,   301
El cavallo ferrado contra sy fizo tuerto,
Las coçes el cavallo lanço fuerte ençierto,
Diole entre los ojos, echole frio muerto. . . .

ENXIENPLO DE LA PROPIEDAT QUEL DJNERO HA

Mucho faz el djnero e mucho es de amar,   490
Al torpe faze bueno e om̃e de prestar,
Ffaze correr al coxo e al mudo fabrar,
El que non tiene manos dyneros quiere tomar.

491   Sea vn ome nesçio e Rudo labrador,
         Los dyneros le fazen fidalgo e sabydor,
         Quanto mas algo tiene, tanto es mas de valor,
         El que non ha djneros non es de sy Señor. . . .

497   El djnero quebranta las cadenas dañosas,
         Tyra çepos e grujllos e cadenas peligrosas;
         El que non tiene djneros echan le las posas;
         Por todo el mundo faze cosas maravillosas.

498   Yo vy fer maravillas do el mucho vsaua,
         Muchos meresçian muerte quela vida les daua,
         Otros eran syn culpa e luego los matava,
         Muchas almas perdja e muchas salvaua:

499   Fazer perder al pobre su casa e su vyña,
         Sus muebles e Rayzes todo lo des alyña,
         Por todo el mundo anda su sarna e sutyña,
         Do el djnero juega, ally el ojo gujña. . . .

509   El djnero es alcalde e juez mucho loado,
         Este es conssejero e sotil abogado,
         Alguaçil e meryno, byen ardyt, esforçado,
         De todos los ofiçios es muy apoderado.

510   En suma te lo digo, tomalo tu mejor:
         El djnero del mundo es grand rreboluedor,
         Señor faze del syeruo, de señor serujdor,
         Toda cosa del sygro se faze por su amor. . .

Del aue marja de santa marja

1661   Aue marja, gloriosa,
                   Virgen santa preçiosa,
                   Coṁo eres piadosa
                   Toda vja.

Graçia plena, syn manzjlla,   1662
Abogada,
Por la tu merçed, Señora,
Faz esta maraujlla,
Señalada,
Por la tu bondad agora
Guardame toda ora
De muerte vergoñosa,
Por que loe aty, fermosa,
Noche e dya.

Domjnus tecum,   1663
Estrella Resplandeçiente,
Melezina de coydados,
Catadura muy bella,
Reluziente,
Syn manzilla de pecados,
Por los tus gozos preciados
Te pido, virtuosa,
Que me guardes, lynpia rrosa,
De ffollya.

Benedita tu,   ·664
Onrrada syn egualança,
Syendo virgen conçebiste,
De los angeles loada
En alteza ;
Por el fijo que pariste,
Por la graçia que oviste,
O bendicha fror e Rosa,
Tu me guarda, piadosa,
E me guja.

XI

JUAN MANUEL

A

EL LIBRO DEL CAUALLERO ET DEL ESCUDERO

(From the edition of S. Gräfenberg in the *Romanische Forschungen*, VII. 443 ff.)

Asi commo ha muy grant plazer el que faze alguna buena obra, señalada mente si toma grant trabajo e[n] la faz[er], quando sabe que aquella su obra es muy loada et se pagan della mucho las gentes, bien asi ha muy grant pesar et grant
5 enojo, quando alguno a sabiendas o aun por yerro faze o dize alguna cosa por que aquella obra non sea tan preciada o ala-bada commo deuia ser. Et por probar aquesto, porne aqui vna cosa que acaeçio a un cauallero en Perpinnan en tiempo del primero Rey don Jaymes de Mallorcas. Asi acaeçio que
10 aquel cauallero era muy grant trobador et fazie muy buenas cantigas amarabilla et fizo una muy buena ademas, et avia muy buen son. Et atanto se pagauan las gentes de aquella cantiga, que des[d]e grant tiempo non querian cantar otra cantiga si non aquella. Et el cauallero que la fiziera auia ende muy
15 grant plazer. Et yendo por la calle un dia, oyo que vn çapa-tero estaua diziendo aquella cantiga, et dezia tan mal [et] errada mente, tan bien las palabras commo el son, que todo omne quela oyesse, si ante non la oyie, tenia que era muy mala cantiga et muy mal fecha. Quando el cauallero quela fiziera
20 oyo commo aquel çapatero confondia aquella tan buena obra commo [fiziera], ovo ende muy grant pesar et grant enojo et descendio de la bestia et asentose cerca del. Et el çapatero,

que non se guardaua de aquello, non dexo su cantar et quanto mas dezia mas confondia la cantiga que el cauallero fiziera. Et desque el cauallero vio su buena obra tan mal confondida por la torpedat de aquel çapatero, tomo muy passo vnas tiseras et tajo quantos çapatos el çapatero tenia fechos, et esto fecho, caualgo et fuesse. Et el çapatero paro mientes en sus çapatos, et desque los vido asi tajados, entendio que avia perdido todo su trabajo, ovo grant pesar et fue dando vozes en pos aquel cauallero que aquello le fiziera. Et el cauallero dixo le : amigo, el Rey nuestro señor es aqui, et uos sabedes que es muy buen Rey et muy justiçiero, et uayamos antel, et librelo commo fallare por derecho. Anbos se acordaron a esto, et desque legaron antel Rey, dixo el çapatero commo le tajara todos sus çapatos et le fiziera grant danno. El Rey fue desto sannudo et pregunto al cauallero si era aquello verdat, et el cauallero dixole que si, mas que quisiesse saber por que lo fi[zi]era. Et mando el Rey que dixiese, et el cauallero dixo que bien sabia el Rey que el fiziera tal cantiga que era muy buena et abia buen son, et que aquel çapatero gela avia confondida, et que gela mandasse dezir. Et el Rey mando gela dezir et vio que era asi. Estonçe dixo el cauallero que, pues el çapatero confondiera tan buena obra commo el fiziera et enque avia tomado grant dampno et afan, que asi confondiera el la obra del çapatero. El Rey et quantos lo oyeron tomaron desto grant plazer et Rieron ende mucho, et el Rey mando al çapatero que nunca dixiesse aquella cantiga nin confondiesse la buena obra del cauallero, et pecho el Rey el danno al çapatero et mando al cauallero que non fiziesse mas enojo al çapatero.

B

EL LIBRO DE LOS ENXIEMPLOS DEL CONDE LUCANOR ET DE PATRONIO

(From the edition of Knust and Birch-Hirschfeld, Leipzig, 1900, pp. 43 ff.)

EXEMPLO X

DE LO QUE CONTESCIO A UN OMNE QUE POR POBREZA ET MENGUA DE OTRA VIANDA COMIA ATRAMUZES

Otro dia fablava el conde Lucanor con Patronio [su conse-
jero], en esta manera : " Patronio, bien conosco a Dios que me
ha fecho muchas mercedes, mas quel' yo podria servir, et en
todas las otras cosas entiendo que esta la mi fazienda asaz con
5 bien et con onrra ; pero algunas vegadas me contesce de estar
tan afincado de pobreza que me paresce que quer[r]ia tanto la
muerte commo la vida. Et rruegovos que algun conorte me
dedes para esto."

"Sennor conde Lucanor," dixo Patronio, "para que vos
10 conortedes, quando tal cosa vos acaesciere, seria muy bien
que sopiesedes lo que acaescio a dos omnes que fueron muy
rricos."

E el conde le rrogo quel' dixiese commo fuera aquello.

"Sennor conde Lucanor," dixo Patronio, "de estos dos
15 omnes el uno dellos llego a tan grand pobreza quel' non finco
en el mundo cosa que pudiese comer. Et desque fizo mucho
por buscar alguna cosa que comiese, non pudo aver cosa del
mundo sinon una escudiella de atramizes. Et acordandose de
[quando] rrico solia ser e que agora con fambre era et con
20 mengua avia de comer los atramizes que son tan amargos et
de tan mal sabor, começo de llorar muy fiera mente, pero
con la grant fanbre começo de comer de los atramizes et en

comiendolos estava llorando et echava las cortezas de los atramizes en pos [de] si. Et el estando en este pesar et en esta
coyta sintio que estava otro omne en pos del et volvio la cabeza
et vio un omne cabo del, que estava comiendo las cortezas de
los atramizes que el echava en pos de si, et era aquel de que 5
vos fable desuso. Et quando aquello vio el que comia los atramizes, pregunto a aquel que comia las cortezas que porque fazia aquello. Et el dixo que sopiese que fuera muy mas rrico que
el et que agora avia llegado a tan grand pobreza et en tan grand
fanbre quel' plazia mucho quando fallava aquellas cortezas que 10
el dexava. Et quando esto vio el que comia [los] atramizes
conortose, pues entendio que otro avia mas pobre que el, et que
avia menos rrazon porque lo devie seer. Et con este conorte
esforçose, et ayudol' Dios, et cato manera en commo saliese
de aquella pobreza, et salio della et fue muy bien andante.'' 15

'' Et [vos], sennor conde Lucanor, devedes saber que el
mundo es tal et aun que nuestro sennor Dios lo tiene por bien
que ningun omne non aya conplida mente todas las cosas.
Mas pues en todo lo al vos faze Dios merced et estades con
bien et con onrra, si alguna vez vos menguare[n] dineros o 20
estudierdes en afincamiento, non desmayedes por ello et cred
por cierto que otros mas onrrados et mas rricos que vos estaran
afincados, que se ternian por pagados si pudiesen dar a sus
gentes et les diesen aun muy menos de quanto vos les dades a
las vuestras.'' 25

E al conde plogo mucho desto que Patronio [le] dixo, et
conortose et ayudose el, et ayudol' Dios, et salio muy bien de
aquella quexa en que estava.

Et entendiendo don Johan que este enxienplo era muy
bueno, fizolo poner en este libro et fizo estos viessos que 30
dizen asi :

> Por pobreza nunca desmayedes.
> Pues otros mas pobres que vos veedes.

XII

PERO LÓPEZ DE AYALA

RIMADO DE PALACIO

(From a MS. in the Biblioteca Nacional at Madrid — MSS. 4055. A paleographic edition of the whole poem will be published by Professor A. F. Kuersteiner of Indiana University, who has kindly furnished the present extract.)

Aquí comiença de los fechos del palaçio

422   Grant tienpo de mi vida pase mal despendiendo,
A señores terrenales con grant cura seruiendo ;
Agora ya lo veo e lo vo entendiendo,
Que quien y mas trabaja mas yra perdiendo.

423   Las cortes de los rreyes, ¿ quien las podria pensar ?
¡ Quanto mal *z* trabajo el oñe ha de pasar,
Perigros en el cuerpo *z* el alma condenar,
Los bienes *z* el algo sienpre lo aventurar !

424   Si mill años los siruo *z* vn dia fallesco,
Dizen que muchos males *z* penas les meresco ;
Si por ellos en cuytas *z* cuydados padesco,
Dizen que como nesçio por mi culpa peresco.

425   Si por yr a mi casa liçençia les demando,
Despues a la torrnada, nin se como nin quando,
Fallo mundo rrebuelto, trastorrnado mi vando,
z mas frio que nieue en su palaçio ando.

426   Fallo porteros nueuos, que nunca conosçi,
Que todo el palaçio quieren tener por sy :
Sy llego a la puerta, dizen : " Quien esta y ? "
" Señores," digo, " yo, que en mal dia nasçy.

Grant tienpo ha que cuydaua esta corte saber;   427
Agora me paresçe que non se que fazer;
Querria, sy pudiese, al rrey fablar z veer."
Dizen : " Estad alla, ca ya non puede ser.

Esta el rrey en consejo sobre fechos granados,   428
z non estan con el si non dos o tres priuados,
z a todos mando que non sean osados
De llegar a la puerta, avn que sean onrrados."

"Señor," le digo yo, "de ver al rrey non curo;   429
Mas acojed me alla, sy quiera en eso escuro,
z de mi vos prometo, z por mi fe vos juro,
De uos dar vn tabardo, desto vos aseguro."

Dize el portero : "Amigo, non podes entrar,   430
Ca el rrey mando agora a todos daqui echar;
Esperad alla vn poco, podredes despues tornar;
Alla estan otros muchos con quien podedes fablar."

"Señor," le digo yo, "alla estan mas de çiento :   431
Desde aqui oyo yo el su departimiento;
Pues non so yo agora de tan astroso tiento
Que alla non este tan quedo que non me sienta el viento."

"Tirad uos alla," dize el portero tal;   432
" Paresçe que auedes sabor de oyr mal :
Yo nunca vi tal ome z tan descomunal;
O vos tirare dende, sy Dios me val."

"Señor," le digo yo, " sy quier esta vegada   433
Me acojed alla z yd a mi posada,
z dar vos he vna hopa que tengo enpeñada."
Diz : " Entrad agora muy quedo z non fabledes nada."

Entro dentro apretado z asiento me muy quedo;   434
Que calle z non fable me faze con el dedo.
" ¿Quien sodes," diz otro, "que entrastes y tan çedo?"
"Señor," le digo yo, " vn ome que vengo de Toledo."

435   " Salid luego," diz, " fuera, aqui non estaredes."
     Trauo me luego del braço, yo apego me a las paredes :
     Viene luego el otro, dize : " Vos fincaredes,
     Mas lo que me mandastes luego cras lo daredes."

436   " Si señores," digo luego, " yo lo dare de grado,
     Todo lo que ouiere e mas de lo mandado."
     Con esta pleytesia finco asosegado,
     E esto entre los otros como oñe asonbrado.

437   Leuanta se el consejo z veo al rrey estar ;
     Vo luego espantado por le querer fablar ;
     El buelue las espaldas z manda luego llamar
     Que vengan rreposteros, que quiere yr çenar.

438   Yo esto en mi cŏmidiendo : " Mesquino, ¿que fare? "
     Muy grant verguença tengo, non se si lo fablare,
     O por ventura cras mejor ge lo dire :
     Desputando comigo nunca buen tiento he.

439   Pero allego a el, asy como a morir.
     " Señor," digo yo, " merçed, quered me agora oyr :
     Yo so vuestro vasallo z mandastes me venir
     Aqui a vuestra guerra, z agora mandastes me yr.

440   De sueldo de tres meses non puedo ser pagado,
     De la tierra de antaño dos terçios no he cobrado ;
     He perdido mis bestias, mis armas enpeñado ;
     A dos meses que yago doliente, muy lazrado."

441   Rresponde me vn priuado : " Los contadores an carga
     De librar los tales fechos, quel rrey nunca se enbarga."
     Desque veo mi fecho, que va asy a la larga,
     Leuanto me muy triste, con boca muy amarga.

442   Viene luego el portero, quexoso a mas andar,
     Dize : " Amigo, auedes librado, ca vos vi agora fablar
     Con el rrey ; por tanto vos vengo a acordar
     Que me dedes lo mandado, dar lo hedes en buen logar."

XIII

LA ESTORIA DEL RREY ANEMUR E DE IOSAPHAT E DE BARLAAM

(From the edition of F. Lauchert in the *Romanische Forschungen*, VII. 376 and 379)

A. Vn rrey non podia auer fijos maslos e estaua muy triste e teniase por esto por muy mal auentorado. E el qual commo estouiese en este cuydado, nasçio le vn fijo, e tomo muy gran gozo. E dexieron le los menges muy sabios que sy fasta X años viese sol o fuego, que seria de todo priuado de la lunbre ; 5 ca aquello synificauan los sus ojos. E es dicho, que commo el rey lo oyese, fizo tajar vna cueua en vna piedra e ençerrolo y con sus amas, por que non viese claridat de luz fasta los X años conplidos. E acabados los X años, sacaron el moço de la cueua non auiente conosçençia ninguna de las cosas mundanales por 10 los ojos. Entonçe ma[n]do el rrey que le diesen e le mostrasen todas las cosas, cada vna de su manera, e que le muestren en vn logar varones e en otro mogeres e aqui oro e plata e alli margaritas e piedras preçiosas e vestiduras muy fermosas e afeytamientos e carros anchos con cauallos rreales. E por que 15 fable breuemente, mostraron al moço todas las cosas por orden, e preguntando el commo fuese llamada cada vna de aquellas cosas, los ministros del rey mostraron le commo llamauan a cada vna cosa. E commo demandase que le dixiesen commo dezian a las mogeres, dezien que vn adelantado del rey que le 20 dixiera jugando que eran demonios los quales engañan a los omnes. Mas el coraçon del moço sospiraua mas por el deseo dellas que por las otras cosas. E despues que le mostraron todas las cosas tornaron lo. Entonçe preguntole el rey, qual cosa amaua mas de todas las que viera. E dixo el fijo : que, 25 padre, sy non aquellos demonios los quales engañan a los omnes. Ca ninguna de aquellas cosas que me son oy mostradas non ame tanto commo la amistad dellas. E marauillo se el rey de la palabra del moço e vey que cosa cruel es el amor de las 5 mogeres. . . .

B. Por muchas oras orando con lagrimas e fincando muchas vegadas los ynojos, pósose [Iosafat] en el suelo; e dormiendo vn poco vio a sy mismo arrebatado de vnos espantables e pasar por logares que nunca viera. E aduzido a vn prado grande 10 afeytado de flores bien olientes de fermusura, do via los arboles de todas maneras e afeytados de desuariadas flores estraños e marauillosos; e las fojas de los arboles dauan dulçe son meneadas de vn viento agradable e echauan olor non fartable; e estauan siellas puestas de oro muy linpio e fechas de piedras 15 preçiosas e dantes muy gran rresplandor, e lechos luzibles de colchas e de estrados, los quales por su fermusura sobran todo rrecontamiento; e pasan aguas muy linpias alegrantes los ojos. E aquellos espantables pasando lo por aquel canpo muy grande e marauilloso, metieron lo en vna çiubdat rresplandesçiente de 20 rresplandesçimiento non fablable; e los muros eran de oro puro e de piedras preçiosas, las quales nunca vio omne, e los muros eran muy altos. E quien puede rrecontar la fermusura e la claridat de aquella çiudat. E luz derramada de suso con rrayos alunbra todas las plaças della. E moran en ella vnas 25 conpañas çelestiales rresplandesçientes cantantes canto el qual nunca oyo oreja mortal. E oyo boz deziente: esta es la folgança de los justos e esta es la alegria de aquellos que plogieron a Dios. . . .

XIV

EL LIBRO DE EXENPLOS POR A.B.C. DE CLIMENTE SANCHEZ

(From the edition of A. Morel-Fatio in *Romania* VII. 481 ff.)

18

Amicus verus est qui, cum seculum defecit, tunc sucurrit

El amigo es de alabar
Que al tiempo de la priessa quiere ayudar.

Vn omne de Arabia, estando a la muerte, llamo a su fijo e
dixole : "¿Quantos amigos tienes?" E el fijo rrespondio e
dixo : "Segund creo, tengo çiento." E dixo el padre : "Cata   5
que el philosofo dixo : non alabes al amigo fasta que lo ayas
prouado. E yo primero nasci que tu e apenas pude ganar la
meytad de vn amigo, e pues assi es, ¿como tu ganaste çiento?
Ve agora e prueualos todos, porque conoscas sy alguno de todos
ellos te hes acabado amigo." E dixo el fijo : "¿Como me   10
consejas que lo faga?" Dixo el padre : "Toma vn bezerro e
matalo e fazelo pieças e metelo en vn saco en manera que de
fuera paresca sangre, e quando fueres a tu amigo, dile assy :
amigo muy amado, trago aqui vn omne que mate, rruegote que
lo entierres secretamente en tu casa, que ninguno non avera   15
sospecha de ty e assy me podras saluar." El fijo lo fizo commo
le mando el padre. El primero amigo a que fue dixole : "Lieua
tu muerto a cuestas, e como feziste el mal, parate a la pena.
En mi casa non entraras." E assy fue por todos los otros amigos e todos le dieron aquella misma rrespuesta. E tornosse   20
para su padre e dixole lo que feziera e dixo el padre : "A ti
acaescio segund dixo el philosofo : muchos son llamados amigos
e al tiempo de la nescesidat e de la priessa son pocos. E ve

agora al mi medio amigo e veras lo que te dira." E fue a el e
dixole : " Entra aca en mi casa, porque los vezinos non entien-
dan este secreto." E enbio luego a la mugier con toda su
conpaña fuera de casa e cauo vna sepultura. E quando el man-
5 çebo vio lo que avia fecho e la buena voluntad de aquel medio
amigo de su padre, descobriole el negoçio como era, dandole
muchas gracias. E dende tornosse a su padre e contole lo que
le feziera. E dixole el padre : " Por tal amigo dize el philosofo : aquel es verdadero amigo que te ayuda quando el mundo
10 te fallesçe."

69

Cogita quid accidere semper possit.

Sienpre deues pensar e ver
Las cosas que te pueden acaescer.

Dizen de vn principe que vna vegada le diera vn filosofo vna
cedula en que eran escriptas estas palabras : " En todas las
15 cosas que ouieres de fazer ssienpre pienssa lo que te puede
acaescer." Este principe mando que esta cedula que la
escreuiessen de letras de oro, e mandola poner en las puertas
de su palaçio. E dende a poco vnos de sus enemigos trataron
con su baruero que lo degollasse. E el baruero veniendole a
20 fazer la barua, vio la escriptura en la puerta e leyola e quando
vino ante el principe començo a temblar e mudarssele la color,
e mandolo prender, e por amenazas e tormentos conoscio la
verdat. El principe conoscio e perdonolo e mando degollar a
los que tratauan la maldat. Por lo qual paresce que es muy
25 grand prouecho en todas las cosas penssar el ffin.

XV

EL POEMA DE JOSÉ

(From the transcript made by M. Schmitz, *Romanische Forschungen*
XI. 357 ff., of the edition of the aljamiado text published by H. Morf,
Leipzig, 1883)

Zaliha, wife of Potiphar, complains of Joseph and he is cast into prison.

I cuando aquesto fue fecho, Zaliha fue rrepentida,   89
No le ab(i)ria quesido fazer en dias de su vida,
Dixendo : " ¡ O meçquina ! nunca sere guarida
D'este mal tan g(a)rande en que soy caida.

Que si yo supiera qu'esto abia de venir,   90
Que por ninguna via no se a podido cump(i)lir,
Que yo no e podido d'este mal guarir,
Por deseyo de Yuçuf abre yo de morir."

Alli jaze dieç annos, como si fuera cordero,   91
Daqui a que mando el rrey a un su portero
Echar en la p(e)resion dos omb(e)res yel terzero,
El uno su escançiano yel ot(o)ro un paniçero.

Porque abian pensado al rrey de fer t(a)raiçion,   92
Qu'en el vino yen el pan que le echasen pozon ;
P(o)robado fue al paniçero yal escançiano non,
Porque mejor supo catar yencubrir la t(a)raiçion.

Alli do'staban p(e)resos, muy bien los castigaba ;   93
I cualquiere qu'enfermaba, muy bien lo curaba ,
Todos lo guardaban por doquiere qu'el estaba,
Porqu'el lo mereçia, su fegura gele daba.

94 Sonno el escançiano un suenno tan pesado,
Contolo a Yuçuf, i sacoselo de g(a)rado ;
Disso : " Tu fues escançiano de tu sennor onrrado,
Mas aun seras a tu ofiçio torrnado.

95 Yabras perdon de tu sennor,
Ayudete el seso i guiete el k(i)riador,
Ya quien Allah da seso, dale g(a)rande onor,
Volveras a tu ofiçio con muy g(a)ran valor."

96 Disso el paniçero al su compannero :
" Yo dire a Yuçuf qu'e sonnado un suenno
De noche en tal dia, cuando salia el luzero,
I vere que me dira el su seso çertero."

97 Contole el paniçero el suenno que queria,
I sacosele Yuçuf i nada no le mentia ;
Disso : " Tu fues paniçero del rrey todavia,
Mas aqui jazeras porque fiziestes falsia.

98 Que al terçero dia seras tu luego suelto
I seras enforcado tu cabeça al tuerto,
I comeran tus miollos las aves del puerto,
Alli seras colgado fasta que sias muerto."

99 Disso el paniçero : " No sonne cosa zertera,
Que yo me lo dezia por ver la manera."
Disso Yuçuf : " Esta es cosa verdadera,
Que lo que tu dixestes, Allah lo envio por carrera."

100 Disso Yuçuf al escançiano aquesta rrazon :
" Rruegote que rrecuerdes al rrey de mi p(e)resion,
Que arto me a durado esta g(a)ran maldiçion."
Disso el escançiano : " P(a)lazeme de coraçon."

101 Que al terçero dia salieron de g(a)rado,
I fueron delante del rrey, su sennor onrrado,
I mando al paniçero seyer luego enforcado ;
Disso al escançiano : " A su ofiçio a torrnado."

Olvidosele al escançiano de dezir el su mandado,   102
I no le memb(o)ro por dos annos ni le fue acordado
Fasta que sonno un suenno el rrey apoderado;
Doze annos p(e)reso estuvo, yesto a mal de su g(a)rado.

Aqueste fue el suenno qu'el rrey obo sonnado: 103
De que salia del agua un rrio g(a)ranado:
Annir era su nomb(e)re, p(e)reçiado i g(a)ranado,
I vido qu'en salia[n] siete vacas de g(a)rado.

Eran bellas i gordas i de ley muy cargadas,   104
I vido otras siete magras, f(a)lacas i delgadas;
Comianse las magras a las gordas g(a)ranadas,
I no seles pareçia, ni enchian las illadas.

I vido siete espigas muy llenas de g(a)rano,   105
Verdes i fermosas como en tiempo de verano,
I vido otras siete secas, con eng(a)rano vano,
Todas secas i b(a)lancas, como cabello cano.

Comianse las secas a las verdes del dia,   106
I no seles pareçia ninguna mejoria,
Tornabanse todas secas, cadaguna vaçia,
Todas secas i b(a)lancas como de niebla f(i)ria.

El rrey se maravillo de como se comian las f(a)lacas a las gor- 107
     das g(a)ranadas,
I las siete espigas secas a las verdes mojadas,
Yentendio qu'en su suenno abia largas palabras,
I no podia pensar a que fuesen sacadas.

I llamo a sus sabidores yel suenno les fue a contar,   108
Que selo sacasen i no ye diesen vagar,
Yellos le dixeron: " No's querais aquexar,
Miraremos en los libros i no te daremos vagar."

XVI

DANÇA GENERAL

(From the edition of C. Appel in the *Beiträge zur romanischen und englischen Philologie dem X. deutschen Neuphilologentage überreicht*, etc., Breslau, 1902, pp. 12 ff.)

Prólogo en la trasladaçion

Aquí comjença la dança general, en la qual tracta commo la muerte dize abisa a todas las criaturas que pare mjentes en la breujedad de su vjda e que d' ella mayor cabdal non sea fecho que ella meresçe. E asy mesmo les dize e Requiere que vean e oyan bien lo que los sabios pedricadores les dizen e amonestan de cada dia, dando les bueno e sano consejo que pugn. . . en fazer buenas obras, por que ayan conplido perdon de sus pecados; e luego syguiente mostrando por espiriençia lo que dize, llama e Requiere a todos los estados del mundo que vengan de su buen grado o contra su voluntad.

Començando dize ansy:

Dise la muerte:

I

Io so la muerte çierta a todas criaturas
Que son y serán en el mundo durante.
Demando y digo: o, omne, por qué curas
De vida tan breue, en punto pasante,
Pues non ay tan fuerte njn Rezio gigante
Que d'este mj arco se puede anparar?
Conuiene que mueras quando lo tirar
Con esta mj frecha cruel traspasante.

II

Qué locura es esta tan magnifiesta
Que piensas tu, omne, que el otro morrá
E tu quedarás por ser bien conpuesta
La tu conplisyon ! e qué durara ?
Non eres çierto sy en punto verná
Sobre ty a dessora alguna corrupçion
De landre o carbonco, o tal ynplisyon
Por que el tu vil cuerpo se dessatará.

III

O piensas por ser mançebo valiente
O njnno de dias, que a luenne estaré
E fasta que liegues a viejo inpotente
La mj venjda me detardaré ?
Avisate bien, que yo llegaré
A ty a desora, que non he cuydado
Que tu seas mançebo o viejo cansado,
Que qual te fallare, tal te levaré. . . .

DISE EL PEDRICADOR :

V

Sennores honrrados, la santa escriptura
Demuestra e dize que todo onre nasçido
Gostará la muerte, maguer sea dura,
Ca traxo al mundo vn solo bocado ;
Ca papa o Rey o obispo sagrado,
Cardenal o duque e conde exçelente
E 'l enperador con toda su gente
Que son en el mundo, de morir han forçado. . . .

VII

Fazed lo que digo ! non vos detardedes,
Que ya la muerte encomjença a hordenar

Vna dança esquiua de que non podedes
Por cosa njguna que sea, escapar,
A la qual dize que quiere leuar
A todos nos otros, lançando sus Redes.
Abrid las orejas, que agora oyredes
De su charanbela vn triste cantar !

DISE LA MUERTE:

VIII

A la dança mortal venjt los nasçidos
Que en el mundo soes de qual quiera estado !
El que non quisiere, a fuerça e amjdos
Fazer le he venjr muy tost' e priado.
Pues que ya el frayre vos ha pedricado
Que todos vayaes a fazer penitençja,
El que non quisiere poner diligençia
. . . . . non puede ser mas esperado.

PRIMERA MENTE LLAMA A SU DANÇA A DOS DONZELLAS

IX

Esta mj dança traxe de presente
Estas dos donzellas, que vedes fermosas.
Ellas vinjeron de muy mala mente
Oyr mjs cançiones, que son dolorosas.
Mas non les valdrán flores e Rosas
Njn las conposturas que poner solian.
De mj, sy pudiesen, partir se querrian ;
Mas non puede ser, que son mjs esposas. . . .

DIZE EL RREY:

XVIII

Valia, valia, los mjs caualleros !
Yo non querria yr a tan baxa dança.

Llegad vos con los vallesteros !
Hanparad me todos por fuerça de lança !
Mas qué es aquesto? que veo en balança
Acortarse mj vida e perder los sentidos ;
El coraçon se me quexa con grandes gemjdos.
Adios, mjs vasallos ! que muerte me trança.

DIZE LA MUERTE:

XIX

Rey, fuerte tirano, que syenpre rrobastes
Todo vuestro rreyno e fenchistes el arca,
De fazer justiçia muy poco curastes,
Segunt es notorio por buestra comarca.
Venjt para mj, que yo so monarca
Que prenderé a vos e a otro mas alto.
Llegat a la dança cortés en vn salto ! —
En pos de vos venga luego el patriarca. . . .

DIZE EL ABOGADO:

XLII

Qué fué ora, mesquino, de quanto aprendy
De mj saber todo e mj libelar?
Quando estar pensé, estonçe cay.
Çegó me la muerte, non puedo estudiar.
Resçelo he grande de yr al lugar
Do non me valdrá libelo njn fuero,
Peores amjgos, que syn lengua muero.
Abarcó me la muerte ; non puedo favlar.

DIZE LA MUERTE:

XLIII

Don falso abogado, preualicador,
Que de amas las partes leuastes salario,

Venga se vos mjente commo syn temor
Boluistes la foja por otro contrario.
El Chino e el Bartolo e el Coletario
Non vos librarán de mj poder mero.
Aquí pagaredes commo buen Romero. —
E vos, canónigo, dexad el breujario ! . . .

DIZE EL MONJE :
LII

Loor e alabança sea para sienpre
Al alto sennor que con piadad
Me lieua a su santo Reyno, adonde contenple
Por syenpre jamas la su magestad.
De carçel escura vengo a claridad,
Donde abré alegria syn otra tristura.
Por poco trabajo avré grand folgura.
Muerte, non me espanto de tu fealdad !

DIZE LA MUERTE :
LIII

Sy la Regla santa del monje bendicto
Guardastes del todo syn otro deseo,
Syn dubda tened que soes escripto
En libro de bida, segunt que yo creo ;
Pero sy fezistes lo que fazer veo
A otros que handan fuera de la Regla,
Vida vos darán que sea mas negra. —
Dançad, vsurero ! dexad el correo ! . . .

LO QUE DIZE LA MUERTE A LOS QUE NON NONBRÓ :
LXXVIII

A todos los que aquí non he nonbrado,
De qual quier ley e estado o condyçion,

Les mando que vengan muy tost' e priado
A entrar en mj dança syn escusaçion.
Non Resçibiré jamas exebçion
Njn otro libelo njn declinatoria.
Los que bien fizieron avrán syenpre gloria,
Los que 'l contrario, avrán danpnaçion.

DIZEN LOS QUE HAN DE PASAR POR LA MUERTE:

LXXIX

Pues que asý es que a morir avemos
De nesçesidad, syn otro Remedio,
Con pura conçiençia todos trabajemos
En serujr a Dios, syn otro comedio;
Ca el es prinçipe, fyn e el medio,
Por do, sy le plaze, avremos folgura,
Avn que la muerte con dança muy dura
Nos meta en su corro en qual quier comedio.

CORRECTIONS FOR THE NOTES

P. 74, l. 30 : After *Domna* **2** 19 add " This is also C. L. form."

P. 77, l. 27 : Omit *kematu* 9.

P. 98, l. 23 : Instead of " early " read " middle of the."

P. 104, l. 8 : Add " Perhaps our MS. has only the sign for 'and' and not a real *i*."

" l. 10 : *dios* should be *Dios*. Add at the end of the line " Simply omit *Dios*."

" l. 30 : Omit **qui** . . . *que*.

P. 105, l. 2 : Omit *que*.

" l. 5 : Omit " Perhaps . . . l. 29."

P. 109, last line : Add " and 686."

P. 114, l. 25 : For " no " read " few, if any."

P. 115, l. 17 : After " and " add " some of them."

P. 124, l. 7 : Add " 137 *presurado* should be *pressurado*."

" l. 11 : *Misterio* should be *Auto*.

P. 133, l. 28 : After " **6** 14 " add " The MS. may have *z e*, i.e. 'and' written twice."

P. 142, l. 32 : Add " and Id. in Herrig's *Archiv* (1905)."

P. 143, l. 34 : " Sánchez " should be " González."

P. 144, bottom : Add " 368 *b* The *a* is needed in the verse."

P. 153, l. 26 : After " edition " add " (*Romania*, 1903)."

" l. 32 : *vierso* should be *vieso*.

P. 166, l. 33 : " J. F. Crane " should be " T. F. Crane."

P. 167, l. 24 : For " did so, too," read " had a like custom."

P. 173, l. 23 ; " Academia " should be " Accademia."

NOTES

I. DOCUMENTS OF THE CHURCH OF VALPUESTA FROM THE NINTH TO THE ELEVENTH CENTURY

L. Barrau-Dihigo, who has published the documents in question in the *Revue hispanique* VII. 273 ff., writes as follows regarding them: " Les chartes que nous publions ci-après sont extraites des deux cartulaires de Valpuesta [a town in the province of Burgos], conservés récemment encore à la Bibliothèque provinciale de Burgos, et classés aujourd'hui sous les numéros 1166 B et 1167 B à l'*Archivo histórico nacional* de Madrid. Elles vont de 804 à 1087, et limitées ainsi, forment un tout, car elles embrassent la période pendant laquelle Valpuesta a été le siège d'une église cathédrale." Of these two cartularies, 1167 B is a copy of 1166 B, made in 1236, and therefore useful chiefly for the help which it affords in deciphering the doubtful readings in 1166 B. This latter is not itself a homogeneous document: " c'est un recueil où l'on a réuni pêle-mêle, sans souci de l'ordre chronologique, des fragments divers, qui renferment une série de pièces dont les plus anciennes remontent à 804, et dont les plus récentes datent de la fin du XIe siècle." (Barrau-Dihigo says *XIIe siècle*, but this must be an error.) . . . " De plus, quoique l'on ait parfois désigné ce volume sous le nom de *becerro gótico* [i.e. an ecclesiastical register in Gothic script], il n'est pas entièrement écrit en *letra gótica*; la *letra francesa* [i.e. the French minuscule of the 11th and 12th centuries] y est fréquente; et si cette dernière semble due à des copistes du début du XIIIe siècle, la première offre des spécimens du Xe et du commencement du XIe siècle. Beaucoup de scribes ont pris part à la transcription des originaux visigothiques."

Having made clear that the documents are not all in a hand contemporary with the operations recorded in them, Barrau-Dihigo gauges the dates of the writing of those from which we give extracts, as follows: I, probably of the end of the 9th or of the early 10th century; XV, of the end of the 10th century; LII, of the end of the 10th or of the early 11th century; LXVI, of the second half of the 11th century.

Among the traits in the documents indicative of the Vulgar Latin stage or of the rise of the Spanish vernacular are these (some of which, of course, are found generally in Romance regions):

Acc. -*m* is gone: *eglesia* **1** 3; *collatu* **1** 7; *uilla alta* **1** 8; *uinea* **1** 12; etc.; *limite* **1** 12; etc.

h- is gone: *odie* **1** 15; *abeas* **1** 16; etc.

-*b*- intervocalic appears for -*v*- (-*u*-): *confirmabi* **1** 5; *nobi* **1** 11; *bobes* **1** 13; *temptaberi* **2** 3. This peculiarity, perhaps more common in documents written in Spain than elsewhere, may indicate that Lat. -*b*- and -*v*- (-*u*-) intervocalic had both become a bilabial spirant, as in mod. Spanish; the scribe, in view of the identity of sound, was puzzled as to what character to use; cf. *Gundesalbiz* **2** 6 with *Gundesaluo* **2** 8. See Cuervo in *Revue hispanique* II. 1 ff. for a discussion of *b* and *v*.

-*np*- is written for -*mp*-: *conparatione* **2** 9; *conparaui* **2** 9, 14; *inprimis* **2** 17; *Conposita* **1** 2. This is only a scribal convention: the *np* means *mp*, and does not necessarily denote a nasalization of the preceding vowel as has sometimes been said. Cf. *Romania* XXVII. 176 ff. It is frequent in manuscripts of Classic Latin texts, and is common in Spanish texts from the 12th century on, as is evidenced by the many cases contained in our extracts following.

Double consonants are simplified: *comorantes* **1** 6; *quatuor* **1** 13; *excomunicatus* **2** 28.

ae > *e*: *Sancte Marie* **1** 3; **2** 10, 21; *anime mee, anime nostre,* **2** 10, 20; etc. This, of course, is common in manuscripts of Classic Latin texts and also represents the Vulgar Latin pronunciation.

ŭ > *ǫ*: *pretio* **1** 13; 23; *plumazo* **1** 14; *iudicio* **2** 3; *atrio* **2** 10 (cf. *atrium* **2** 21); etc. This is Vulgar Latin.

uu > *u*: *perpetum* **2** 25.

The unaccented penult of proparoxytones is lost: *Domna* **2** 19.

-*ct*- after *ī* > *t*: *fita* **1** 3.

-*cl*- intervocalic > *gl*: *eglesia* (V. L. *eclesia) **1** 3, 5.

-*cy*- intervocalic > *z*, which may denote a voiced sound or a voiceless one, but, at all events, shows the assibilation: *plumazo* 'mattress,' 'pillow' (V. L. *plŭmacĕum), **1** 14.

-*ty*- intervocalic > *cy*, a learned treatment, showing, however, the assibilation of the sound: *uindicionis* (Lat. *venditio, venditionis*) **2** 4.

-*ty*- after a consonant > *ç* = voiceless *ts*, a popular change, showing the assibilation: *ifançones* 'nobles' (Lat. *infans, infantem,* V. L. *infantiones) **2** 16.

-ny- intervocalic $>$ *ñ*: *uinga* 'vineyard' (Lat. *vīnĕa*) **2** 13; cf. *uinea*
1 12, 16; etc. This confusion of *ng* and *nę*, which are equivalent
at all only in that both gave palatalized *n* under certain conditions,
shows that the palatalization had already taken place.

ge͡ ı́ $>$ ye: *iermanis, coniermanis,* **2** 27. Later this *i* = *y* from initial *g*
before unaccented *e* (Lat. *germanus*) disappeared entirely: cf. mod.
hermano, obs. *cormano = cohermano.* The *O. Sp. Glosses,* no. 198,
show the form *iermano.* Priebsch (*Ztschr. f. roman. Philol.* XIX. 29)
remarks thereon: "*coniermano* Urkunde vom Jahre 974 bei Escalona 418 a, *cojermano jermano* (*j* = *i*) *ib.,* *giermanis* Urkunde vom
Jahre 997 Escalona 473 a gegen *hermanos* aus dem IX. Jahrh. be-
legt bei Muñoz 153. S. Meyer-Lübke, *Gramm.* I, 329."

d before voiceless consonant $>$ *t*: *adque* = Lat. *atque,* **1** 11; *aput te* for
Lat. *apud te,* **1** 15. Of course *adque* is an erroneous spelling due to
the fact that original *d* $>$ *t* in such a position.

-d final disappeared as a sound: *quiquid* for Lat. *quiqui,* **2** 26; i.e. the
-d is written erroneously here because it still continued to be written
in cases in which it was not pronounced. Of course this may be
also the *quid* which regularly gave Span. *que.*

-nf- intervocalic $>$ *ff* or *f*: *ifançones* **2** 16. This *n,* lost in V. L., was restored later.

-xt- $>$ st: *iusta* (Lat. *juxta*) **1** 12; **2** 22, 23.

Lat. *-x-* intervocalic $>$ *ȷ̌*: *usor* **2** 19. It is likely that this *s* stands for
palatalized *s.*

Metathesis of *r* has not yet occurred: *Fredenando* **2** 6.

The breaking down of the Latin cases (for the development of Spanish the accusative took on, in general, the functions of the other Latin
cases) is clearly seen in the mistakes made by the writers of the documents. Thus, the acc. appears in an abl. construction:

    in caput **2** 12; used of rest in a place;

    cum meos gasalianes **1** 6;

    sapiente [for *sapientes*] *meos confratres* **2** 13;

    spontaneas nostras uoluntantes [for *uoluntates*] **2** 20.

Cf. also these examples:

        Domino Adefonso (as gen.) **1** 4;

        Didacus (dat.) **1** 10; (acc.) **2** 2;

        filiis meis (nom. pl.) **2** 1;

        iermanis, coniermanis, neptis, (nom. pl.) **2** 27;

        posteritas tua (acc.) **2** 2;

        sagone (nom.) **2** 16;

Ranemiri (abl.) **2** 6;

abbate (dat.) **2** 26.

The use of prepositional phrases to denote genitive and dative relations is seen in these instances:

de + noun = gen. of the noun:

de Pineto **1** 7; *de Munio* **1** 13; **2** 13; *de terris, de uineis,* **2** 9; *de monte* **2** 12; *de regula* **2** 22; etc.;

ad + noun = dat. of noun:

tibi et ad tuos gasalianes **1** 11;

ad episcopo **2** 11;

abeas ad me **2** 3;

excomunicatus ad fide **2** 29. (The last two cases are datives of deprivation.)

In *Sancti Emeteri* (Santander) **1** 9, we seem to have the genitive-locative with the preposition.

que (Lat. *quĕm*, unaccented, and *quĭd*; cf. Vocabulary) appears as a relative pronoun, sing. and pl., **1** 2; **2** 9, 22, 23: cf. *qui* (which remained for persons in O. Sp.) **2** 26.

latus appears seemingly as a prep. = *juxta*: *latus uinga* = *cerca de la viña,* **2** 12. Cf. Fr. prep. *lès*, Prov. *latz*.

sedere appears as the verb "to be": *sedeat ipsa terra . . . confirmata* **2** 25.

Among the more interesting of the remaining word forms are these. uindere (Lat. *vendere*) **1** 11 and uindicionis (Lat. *venditionis*) **2** 4. The *i* instead of *e* in the unaccented first syllable appears also in early western (Portuguese) texts. It indicates, doubtless, the accent on the infin. ending in *uindére* (Sp. *vendér*), as the accented Lat. *e* could not easily have become *i*. In the *çi* of *uindicionis* we see a common Late Lat. confusion of *ty* and *cy*. — For moiare **1** 8 there occurs the variant *molare* (Lat. *molaris* 'millstone,' but here 'boundary-mark'). If = Sp. *mojon* (Lat. *moles*, V. L. *moliōnem), 'boundary-mark,' *moiare* may mean *mojar(e)* from a V. L. *moliārem* based on *moles* 'pile,' 'heap' (of stones etc.), 'mark.' — In canape **1** 14 we appear to have the modern word: doubtless an early loan-word in the peninsula, it corresponds to a Late Lat. form of Gk. κωνωπεῖον (also κανωπεῖον). — The spelling nicil **1** 15 accords with a frequent *nichil* found in the Latin documents of the Middle Ages; if the *c* denotes a real pronunciation, it reflects the influence of *nec*; the *O. Sp. Glosses* show *mici* for *mihi* and therefore the *c* may be meaningless. —The patronymic -*az*, -*iz*, of unknown origin (Basque ?, Latin genitive -*acis* ?), appears in **Beilaz 2** 13 and **Gundesalbiz 2** 6. — In adtorralinia

1 14 we may have a formation on Lat. *toral* ' valance of a couch '; but ?
— **conllatione 2** 26 represents the learned *colación*. — Is **uocita 2** 22 for
vocitant ' people call ' ? — An interesting word is **gasalianes 1** 6, 12,
which harks back to Germanic *gasalho*, mod. Ger. *Geselle*, ' room-
mate ' etc. Diez (*Etym. Wörterbuch der roman. Sprachen*, p. 158) says
that *gasalianes* — citing our passage — must have been formed according to the Gothic plural *gasaljans*. The word remains in mod. Sp.
agasajar, *agasajo*, etc.

II. OLD SPANISH GLOSSES

According to Priebsch (cf. p. 5) there are about 400 words of the
Spanish vernacular contained in the MS. with which he deals. This
was known, in the 18th century, to the Benedictine monk Francisco de
Berganza, who utilized it in his *Antigüedades de España*, Madrid, 1719–
1721. (Cf. Menéndez Pidal in *Revista Crítica de Historia*, etc., Madrid,
1895, and see also *Romania* XXVI. 148.)

The glossator strove sometimes to give a Latin aspect to the endings
of his words : cf. his retention of intervocalic *t* in the participial ending
-atu, etc.; *fueret* for *fuere*, 8, 57, etc.; *fuerent* for *fueren*, 92 ; *ficieret* =
fiziere, mod. *hiciere*, 28 ; etc.; but he revealed his real pronunciation
when he wrote *fuere* 167 ; *son* < Lat. *sŭnt*, 233 ; *sierben* 46 ; *matan* 82 ;
etc. Of course he Latinizes, keeping the etymological vowels and
consonants, in many other cases ; as when he writes infinitives with
a final *e*.

The diphthongization of accented Lat. *ĕ* and *ŏ* is seen in *lieben* < *lĕvent*
(mod. Sp. *lleven*), 56 ; *mientre* 91, 116 ; *sierben* < *sĕrvent*, 46 ; *ierba* 61 ;
muerte 53 ; *mueran* 182 ; *luenge* 76 ; *cuerpos* 274 ; etc. The loss of the
labial element in Lat. *qu(e,i)* is clear in the use of *k* in *kematu* 9 ; *ke* 31,
42, 233 ; etc.; cf., however, *que* 182, and *quisieret* 96, beside *kisieret* 244.
For the voiceless velar stop, Lat. *c(a,o,u)*, we find *k* in *kadutu* 167, beside *cadutu* 86 (not included here). In *aplekan* 112, *aplekat* 208, the *k*
renders imperfectly the voiced velar stop *g*; while *g* itself, if not etymological, seems to appear in the Glosses with the value of *y*, cf. *siegat*
11, 27, 211, 240, etc. But the interpretation of the *g* in *siegat* is doubtful. Cf. also 74 *negant* = *necant*.

The equivalence of *b* and *v* (*u*) as a bilabial spirant may be inferred
from cases like *labatu* 11 ; *grabe* 91 ; *sierben* 46 ; *lieben* beside *leuatos* 56 ;
ueuetura 61 ; etc.

The prosthetic *e* is not indicated, *stando* 76.

The vocalization of *l* shows itself in *sotare* < *saltare*, 216; *sota* 222. This passed, of course, through the stage *au*, whose change to *o*, where the *au* was originally Lat., is seen also in *cosa* 31.

In -*ct*-, vocalization of the first element has occurred : *adduitos* < *adduc-tos*, 56; *aflitos* 25. In the latter case the resulting *i̯* has been absorbed by the preceding *i*, Lat. *ī*. 54 etc. *matare* seems to show assimilation of *c*.

The assibilation of *c*(*e,i*), *ti̯*, *ci̯*, is visible in *mortizino* < *mortĭcīnus* -*um* (mod. Sp. *mortecino*), 260 ; *anzes* < **anties*, 161 ; *brazaret* (based on *brac*(*ch*)*ium*) 122.

The assimilation of *p* to *t* is seen in *acetore* (mod. *azor*; cf. Vocab. s.v. *açor*) < *acceptorem*, 272.

For other changes phonological, morphological, and lexical cf. Priebsch l.c., and see also the notes below and the Vocabulary. The sense-difficulties in the Glosses are sometimes baffling because we have not the whole Latin text before us.

3 1–2 (5, 8) **aflaret** = O. Sp. *fallare* (fut. sbj. 3d sg.). — **aflatu** = O. Sp. *fallado* ; cf. Vocab. s.v. *fallar*. The writing of *u* for final unaccented *ŭ* in *aflatu* and other participles here — cf. 9 *kematu*, 11 *labatu*, 122 *con-strinitu*, 35 *incentitu*, 167 *kadutu*, 211 *osatu* — is a Latinism; the *o* is properly written in 57 *focato* : cf. 260 the adj. *mortizino*, and 44 the noun *periculo*. For intervocalic Lat. -*t*- the Glosses show regularly only *t*, although the voicing to -*d*- must have already occurred in Castilian. — The change of unaccented Lat. *ĭ* to *e* is shown in **fueret** < *fuerĭt*, cf. 57 etc., 92 *fuerent*, 96 *quisieret*, 244 *kisieret*, 167 *fuere*, 61 *ueuetura* < **bĭbĭtūra*, etc., just as that of the accented vowel appears in 81, 185 *estos* < *ĭstos*, 112 *aplekan* < *applĭcant*, 208 *aplekat* < *applĭcat*, 166 *uece* < *vĭcem*, etc. Early in Sp. the accent passed from *u* to the more sonorous *e* following.

The initial *f* of O. Sp. *fallar*, as in all other *f*- words treated popularly (unless before original *u̯* or *r*, as in *fuerent*, *frente*, etc.), became an aspirate *h* and then disappeared from pronunciation later on.

3 3–4 (9, 11) **kematu** : cf. Vocab. s.v. *quemar*. — Here we have two ex-amples of a Romance periphrastic construction taking the place of the Lat. passive voice. Neither of the glossed words passed into Romance. — In **siegat** (cf. also 27, 211, 240) we have a peculiar form. Lat. *sĕdĕat* > V. L. **sę̆yat* > *seya*, with a closing of the *e* due to the following palatal, > Castilian *sea*, with the usual Castilian absorption of *y* after *e*. The form *siega* is well attested in the Glosses, for Priebsch finds it there six times, along with *siegant* three times, *siegan* three times, and *siegam* twice (this last exhibiting a Portuguese-Galician feature in its -*m*). He is loath to regard the *g* of these forms as a device to prevent the hiatus (i.e., apparently as representing *y*, for in a few instances the Glosses seem to have a *g* meaning *y*), and finds the diphthong surprising in view of the usual development and the Aragonese *sia*, *sian*. Finally, he states his suspicion that the form is derived from a V. L. **sĕdat* and owes its *g* to the analogy of *diga* and *faga*. He cites the Catalan *sigui* (*estigui*), Valencian *siga*. Taking all in all, the form appears to indicate, unless it goes back to **sĕdat*, a non-Castilian origin for our glosses. In sense *siegat* is a pres. sbj. form of the substantive verb and copula "to be"; cf. Vocab. s.v. *seer* and *ser*. This weakening of the original sense of *sedēre* is seen also in 211 and 240, and in 65 *esse : sedere*.

3 5–9 (16, 26, 29, 119, 286) Everywhere in Romance territory, Lat. *ĭgnōrāre* seems to have been a learned word : for the people at large its place was supplied by V. L. *non *sapēre* : cf. Vocab. s.v. *saber*. The *p* of *sapet*, *sapiendo*, *sapiento* is probably a Latinism for the already developed *b*. *Sapiento* is a mistake for *sabiendo*, whether the glossator (or scribe) was thinking of *sapiens*, *sapientem*, or inadvertently wrote a *t = d* simply because he still represented the intervocalic *d* of the vernacular by *t*, cf. 8 *aflatu*, 9 *kematu*, etc. — The qui of Gloss 16 is the O. Sp. *qui*; cf. ante 2 26 note, and Vocab. s.v. *qui*. This *qui*, used only of persons, still lives on in *quizá*(*s*), O. Sp. *quiça*(*b*), probably from Lat. *qui te *sapet*, in which the *te* is an ethical dative, "who knows for thee," i.e. "who can tell thee," whence *quit sabe*, i.e. *quitsab*, *quiça*(*b*), since O. Sp. wrote *ç* for the *ts* sound.

3 10–12 (20, 91, 116) Cf. Vocab. s.v. *mientre*. The glossing words show the tendency to express adverbial ideas by phrases rather than by single words. The *za* of 116 is probably a scribal error.

3 13 (25) Neither of the glossing words, although both remain alive, is entirely popular in its development, as the *i* of *debiles* and the *fl* of *aflitos* show. Cf. Priebsch : "*aflito* from *afflīctum*, like Sp. *hito*, O. Sp., Ptg., and Aragonese *fito*, from *fīctum*." The Glosses also have 293 *anteditos* < Lat. *ante dictos*. In mod. Sp. the *c* has been restored in *aflicto*, which is therefore more learned still : it is less used than the regular participial form *afligido*. — As often in the Glosses, the glossing words ignore the case relation of the words glossed. — The *b* of **inbalidis** = *invalidis* shows that the scribe is so accustomed to the identity of *b* and *v* that he confuses them in the Latin word. Of course, in mod. Sp. even etymological *v* becomes the real labial stop *b* after a nasal (cf. *embestir* < V. L. *investīre*).

3 14 (27) Like all other Latin passive verbs, *fieri* disappeared in Romance, except for traces in Italian, Roumanian, etc.

3 15 (28) Apropos of **mentiru**, cf. Priebsch : " The MS. clearly shows *u* as opposed to the mod. Sp. and Ptg. fem. *mentira.*' Meyer-Lübke (*Grammatik der roman. Sprachen* I. 480) considers *mentira* as a case of forward (i.e. from the accented syll. toward the beginning of the word) dissimilation of *t–t* > *t–r*, i.e. the participial (*res, causa*, etc.) *mentita* > *mentida* > *mentira*. Diez (*Etym. Wörterbuch der roman. Sprachen*, p. 211) regards the Sp. word as an incomprehensible deformation of *mentida*, which appears properly in Catalan and Sardinian. Perhaps the *r* is rather due to analogy ; cf. the *r* of the correlative *verdadero -a, vero -a, de vero, veras*. One may think also of a possible influence of the abstract ending *-ura*. — In **ficieret** for the usual O. Sp. *fiziere* < Lat. fut. perf. indic. and perf. sbj. *fecerit* with the ending of the Lat. 4th conj. (*audīvĕrit* etc.), we see the retention of etymological intervocalic *c(e,i)*, as also in 166 *uece* and 224 *faces* ; cf., however 260 *mortizino* showing the voiced dental sibilant clearly.

3 16 (31) **periuratusset** = *perjuratus esset* (?) or *sit* (?). — The gloss shows in **se periuret** = mod. *se perjure* the Romance reflexive substitute for the Lat. passive. — **ke** = *que* ; cf. Vocab. s.v. *que*. The form appears here both as pron. and conjunction : cf. 42 (but 182 *que*), 233, 237, 79, 146, 234, 240. — Instead of **so** < Lat. *sŭŭm*, O. Sp. seems rather to have preferred *su* < Lat. *sua* before a fem. sg. noun : cf. Vocab. s.v. *so* and *su*. The Glosses also show 125 *sos* < *sŭŏs*, 187 *so caput*, and 250 (not given here) *so membra*. This last case is peculiar, since the poss. adj. stands before a glossing word derived from a Lat. ntr. pl. noun. Referring back to a plural antecedent, that is = 'their,' the Glosses show 224 *lures*. This is a pl. based on the Lat. gen. pl. of the pron. *ille*, [*il*]*lor*[*um*]. Cf. Priebsch : "*Lur, lures*, as opposed to general Sp. *so* (*su*) *sos* (*sus*) in *Gl.* 250 and 125, is confined to the east of the peninsula, Aragon and Catalonia, and is of Provençal stock." This last form is apparently, then, another non-Castilian trait in our Glosses. — For **sobre,** the regular Sp. derivative from Lat. *super*, cf. Vocab. s.v.

3 17 (42) The Latin construction with the future passive participle (gerundive) disappeared in Romance : instead of it we have here an infinitive phrase plus a *que* clause. — **por** : cf. Vocab. s.v. — **fere** is the O. Sp. *fer* ; cf. Vocab. — Instead of Lat. **faciat** (which gave Ptg. *faça*), it was a V. L. **facat* that gave the true O. Sp. form *faga*, mod. *haga.* — Priebsch rightly indicates that instead of **omiciero** we expect *omicio* here as an equivalent to the Lat. *homicidium* : *omiciero* is rather the agent noun 'homicide' = 'slayer.' As a term of the law, the Lat. *homicidium* and its derivatives passed to the people and produced a variety of forms more or less popular. For the simplex we have *omezo* beside [*h*]*omicio* etc.; for the agent noun in -*ero* < Lat. -*arius* we find *homiciero*, *omeciero*, etc.; for the diminutive (Lat. -*ĕllus*), *omicillo*, *ome-cillo*, etc. Cf. Priebsch: " *Omecillo* (which is the form occurring most frequently) denotes in the legal monuments not only the death-stroke and every crime of violence but also the fine imposed therefor, e.g. *pechará omecillo* in the *Fuero Juzgo* and the *Fuero Viejo de Castilla*" [i.e., in two of the oldest legal documents in Spanish]. Another early sense was that of ' hate,' ' deadly hate,' which still persists in the *Don Quijote*, Part I, Ch. XX, where Sancho uses it. Clemencín, in his ed. of the *Don Quijote*, points out that Juan Valdés, in his *Diálogo de la Lengua* (first half of the 16th century), marks it as a word passing into disuse in the sense of *enemistad*. Of course, locally it could maintain itself longer. A form with *z*, i.e. *omezillo* (cf. *omezo*), would seem more popular still.

3 18 (46) The Lat. *praebĕre*, as a verb = ' to offer,' ' serve,' disappeared in Romance. As a learned word, Sp. *ministrar* < Lat. *mĭnĭstrāre* remains. — Although glossing the same word, **ministrent** (sbj.) and **sierben** = mod. *sirven* < V.L. **sĕrvent* for Lat. *serviunt* do not agree in mood here.

3 19–4 1 (49, 54, 74, 82, 85) Among the words glossed here, **negare** for Lat. *necare* is interesting as showing that the scribe really pronounced as *g* in Sp. an originally intervocalic Lat. *c(a,o,u)*. He inadvertently wrote the *g* here, while, with a zealous endeavor to Latinize, he still wrote the *c* (*k*) in 112 *aplekan*, 208 *aplekat*, 244 *consico*, etc. Lat. *necare* still lives in Sp. *anegar* ' to drown,' which shows a specification of the method of " killing." Lat. *enecare*, which, according to Diez, *Etym. Wtb.*, p. 221, had already the sense of ' to drown ' in Gregory of Tours, may be back of *anegar*. An influence of the prefix *ad*- must be supposed however: one might argue for V.L. **adnecare*. **Interfĭcere** disappeared in Romance. **Ex(s)tinguere** did not survive in Spanish, although it is present in Italian, French, Portuguese, etc. — With regard to **occidunt**, Priebsch remarks that " *occidere*, supplanted in the Iberian peninsula by *mactare*, has been preserved there only in the old Catalan *aucire*." This, of course, is related to the Prov. *aucire*, which has been ascribed also to a V.L. **abcīdere* from *ab* and *caedere*. The noun *occisión* still survives in Sp. as a learned formation. — According to Diez (*Etym. Wtb.*) the Lat. **strages** remains in the Sp. verb *estragar*, ' to ravage,' ' destroy,' etc., and the noun *estrago*, ' havoc,' ' ruin,' etc. Priebsch, following Parodi (*Romania* XVII. 67), prefers as etymon a V.L. **extrahicare* from Lat.

trahere; but the case against *strages* is not settled. — For **matare** = mod. Sp. *matar*, cf. Vocab. s.v. — **matata**, scribal for *matada*, seems an abstract = mod. *matanza*. Priebsch cites also older Sp. *andada* = *andanza*.

4 2–4 (53, 92, 182) *Interitus* did not survive in Romance. *Pūnīre*, probably as a purely learned word, occurred in older Sp., but the popular term was *castigar* from Lat. *castigare*, in the ordinary sense of 'punish,' 'discipline.' Here the gloss shows a stronger sense. — **muertos** < Lat. *mŏrtŭos*, V. L. **mŏrtos*, has here the meaning 'killed,' 'put to death,' which it still preserves — only in the p.p., and even in the transitive use — in mod. Sp., when employed with reference to persons. — As to **fuerent** = O. Sp. *fueren*, cf. Vocab. s.v. *seer* and *ser*. — **infinem** = *in finem*, both of which remain in *en* and *fin*. — **usque** did not remain. It is represented here by the O. Sp. **ata que,** mod. *hasta que*. For the second element of this, cf. the Vocab. s.v. Apparently O. Sp. *ata* comes from the Arabic *ḥatta* 'up to,' 'until,' and appears also in the earlier form of *fata* (*f* = aspirate *h* as in Arabic). Sp. *hasta* (O. Sp. *fasta* with *f* = aspirate *h*) is troublesome. Diez, *Etym. Wtb.*, p. 458, although with misgivings, explained the word as Sp. *hácia* + *ata*. As to *hácia*, cf. Diez, ibid. p. 130, s.v. *faccia* : " Spanish knows the form *hácia* (*fácia*) used as a prep. instead of Lat. *versus* : *andaba hacia* (*á*) *la puente* really means ' he went with his face turned toward the bridge.' " *Hacia* + *ata* is impossible as the source of *hasta*. One might think of the O. Sp. *faz*, mod. *haz*, < Lat. *facies, facĭem*, + *ata*. But *fazata*, if with syncope it could become **fazta*, ought to result in **haza*, cf. Lat. *recitare* > Sp. *rezar*. The *s* may simply be intrusive in O. Sp. *fata*, for which the *ata* of the Glosses probably stands, and may be due to some analogy. Cf the Ptg. *te, ate*, O. Ptg. *atem*, whose history is also somewhat obscure.

4 5 (56) It would seem that already O. Sp. *levar* < Lat. *levare*, like mod. *llevar*, was used as an auxiliary with the past participle (i.e. here with both *adduitos* and *leuatos* treated as synonymous terms). The gloss does not exclude, however, the use of **lieben** in a literal sense. As to the relation of *levar* and the mod. *llevar*, cf. Vocab. s.v. *leuar*. — In **leuatos** = *levados*, the *u*, as so often in medieval documents, is scribal for *v* : the equivalence in O. Sp. of intervocalic *b* and *v* — both the bilabial spirant — may be seen in *lieben* beside *leuatos*. Cf. gl. 295 *leuare*. — **adduitos** < Lat. *addūctos* represents a prior stage to that of Sp. *aduchos*, m. pl. p.p. of O. Sp. *aduzir*, mod. *aducir*, < V. L. **addūcīre*, Lat. *addūcĕre*. The *ǐ* element infected the *t* of *adduitos* in Castilian, palatalizing it to *ť* > *ch*, and was itself absorbed. In dialects, the *ǐt* remained. Gl. 128 has *fruitu* < *frūctum*, which appears elsewhere in O. Sp., e.g.

in Berceo, as *frucho*, while mod. *fruto* is a Latinism. In mod. Sp. the
p.p. of *aducir* is of the regular type, *aducido*, and the word is used
rather in the figurative sense of 'to adduce,' 'quote,' 'cite,' than in
that of 'to bring.' Early in O. Sp. *dd > d*.

4 6 (57) The Lat. verb *vĕxāre* lives on in the mod. Sp. *vejar*, but the ~~vex, teach~~
latter has not the strong sense which the glossed word, *vexatus a
demonio*, 'injured (suffocated) by the devil,' seems to have in the text;
hence the gloss **focato** = mod. *ahogado*, O. Sp. *afogado*. Priebsch, however, thinks that the meaning here is that of *oprimir, acongojar*. *Afogar,
ahogar*, like the Lat. *suffocare*, points to Lat. *faux, faucem*, hence a V. L.
*affocare with the *f* of the main part of the word treated as initial.
"To kill by stopping the throat" was the original sense : by extension
the verb has come to signify 'suffocating' in other ways, as by
'drowning.'

4 7 (61) The glossed word, **poculum**, has here the meaning 'potion,'
'poison,' as the gloss 'herb-drink' shows. — Instead of **ueuetura**, we find
bebetura in glosses 51 and 280 not included here : the forms show again
the equivalence of *b* and *v*. The V. L. basis is *bĭbĭtūra from Lat. p.p.
bĭbĭtus. Cf. Priebsch : "*bebetura* [we might write it *bebedura* or *bevedura*]
and also *bebienda* [which likewise appears in early Sp.] stand for the
usual mod. *bebida* ; . . . *póculo = bebida* is limited to poetical diction." —
ierba < Lat. *hĕrba* ; cf. mod. *hierba* beside *yerba*, like *yedra* beside *hiedra*.

4 9–10 (233, 237) The glosses show the substitution in Spanish of
relative clauses for the convenient and pithy Lat. infinitive of the
accusative and infinitive construction. — Of course **esse** gave way in
Sp. to *sedēre* in so far as the infin. and certain other parts of the verb
are concerned : cf. Vocab. s.v. *ser, seer*. — **deesse**, having disappeared,
needed the explanation, "which is missing." — **iet** < Lat. *ĕst* is not
Castilian, for in that dialect the form received atonic treatment ;
hence *es*. Cf. Priebsch : "The diphthongization of Lat. *est*, already
appearing in almost regular fashion in the oldest Asturian texts, is
still a specific characteristic of that dialect : West-Asturian *yié yia*
(the *Fuero Juzgo* has *ia ya*, once each) ; Bable-Asturian *ye yes* ; and *yes*
in the dialect of Miranda, which has Asturian elements." He refers to
Munthe's *Anteckningar om folkmålet i en trakt af Vestra Asturien*,
Upsala, 1887, p. 51 ; Morel-Fatio's remarks in the *Romania* IV. 30, 35 ;
and E. Gessner's study of Old Leonese (1867), p. 27. E. Staaff, in his
Étude sur l'ancien dialecte léonais d'après des chartes du XIII siècle,
Uppsala and Leipzig, 1907, registers (p. 200) the forms *yes* and *ye*, and
he thinks that "there is no reason to doubt that we are face to face

2) Influence of *fazia* n *faza* . *fata* / contamination > *fasta
faza /

(= *fatsta*) simplified to *fasta*

E.g. *amicitate* > × *amiçtad* > *amistad* (occurs in Cid)
> *amicidad* ~ *amizdad*

with a case of real diphthongization. These forms could very well bear the accent, and there was doubtless a diphthongized form for the accented position and a form without the diphthong for the atonic position. Soon the two forms began to be employed the one for the other, and sometimes *ye* is the only form used. . . . If the verb is placed after the predicate, it takes on a certain accent, and then we have, doubtless, one of the cases in which the diphthongized form arose." On p. 310 he says: " *Yes* often becomes *ye* [and we may regard the *t* of our *iet = yet* as merely etymological] as a result of a tendency to bring this form into accord with the 2d person *yes*," i.e., the *s* was lost by dissimilation and in accord with the principle that 3d pers. sg. forms of the pres. indic. do not regularly end in *s*. Cf. Baist in Groeber's *Grundriss der roman. Philol.*, 2d ed., I, p. 914: " in the West and in Asturian *ye*, . . . in the Northeast, down to the *Glosses of Silos*, *yet*." — **ke** = mod. *que*: cf. Vocab. s.v. *que*. — **son** and **menos** are perfectly regular developments of *sŭnt* and *mĭnŭs*.

4 11 (76) The Lat. *absens*, *absentem*, remains in the non-popular mod. Sp. *ausente*. — In **luenge** = the obsolete *lueñe* < Lat. adv. *lŏnge* 'afar,' 'away,' we have doubtless the palatalized *n*, not yet sufficiently indicated any more than in 45 *punga* = obs. *puña* 'battle,' 224 *tingen* = *tiñen* 'dye,' 'color,' etc. It is better indicated in 77 *inpreinnaret*, 179 *preinnaret* (cf. mod. *preñado*, *empreñar*), from V. L. **praegnare*, **impraegnare*. Cf. Vocab. s.v. *luenne*. Priebsch records a variety of early forms of this word, finding *lueñe* (*luenne*) among the most usual. It is notable that the palatalized sound did not prevent the diphthongization of the preceding *ŏ*: in like fashion *somnium* may have given *sueño* ; of course one thinks of a possible influence of *luengo*. Cf. Baist in *Grundriss* I. 889. — In **stando** = *estando* the prosthetic *e* is not yet indicated, although undoubtedly a vowel sound was already developed before initial *s* + consonant. In the earliest O. Sp., however, as still in Italian, the prosthetic vowel may not have arisen in cases of close syntactical relation, if the preceding word ended in a vowel. We seem to have here a case of the use of *estar* to denote position : but O. Sp. did not differentiate consistently between *estar* and *seer*, *ser*, in this regard ; cf. Ford, " *Sedere*, **Essere* and *Stare* in the *Poema del Cid*," in *Modern Language Notes* XIV, No. 2.

4 12 (79) Cf. Vocab. s.v. *por* and *que*. — **quod** with the sense of 'because' did not survive in Spanish.

4 13–14 (81, 185) Except in certain combinations, as in **pero** < *per hoc*, **hogaño** 'this year' < *hoc anno*, **agora** 'now' < *hac hora*, the pure demonstrative adjective *hic, haec, hoc*, did not survive in Spanish. In ordinary usage its place was taken by one of the other Lat. demonstratives, as here by *iste, ĭstos > estos*.

4 15 (93) inici = *injici*, pres. infin. passive of *injicere*, which did not survive. — The frequentative **jactare** took the place of *jacĕre* and its derivatives, as here. So gl. 50 *relictis* : *iectatis*. Priebsch finds *iectar, ietar, getar*, in such early Sp. documents as the *Fuero de Aviles* (12th cent.) and the *Fuero Juzgo* (13th cent.), and calls attention to the mountaineer form *jitar*, the Aragonese *getar gitar*, the Portuguese *geitar*. Körting, s.v. *ejectare*, lists also the dialectal Sp. *jitar*. Cf. Vocab. s.v. *echar*. Diez (*Etym. Wtb.*, p. 161) felt that *jactare* explained sufficiently the Sp. *echar*, but, in view of the It. *gettare*, he set up the Lat. *ejectare* as the etymon. Cornu (*Romania* VII. 354) returns with good reason to *jactare* for the Sp. word. The *j* was lost before the unaccented syllable, as in the infin. and the p.p. (cf. *iectatis*) : *jactare jactatum >* *jaitar *jaitato > *jeitar *jeitado > *jechar *jechado, and, with the usual loss of initial *j* before unaccented *e*, > *echar echado*. Under the influence of the forms not accented on the first syll., those accenting the first syll. dropped the *j*. — The **por** here is apparently not part of the gloss equivalent.

4 16 (96) Although glossed here, the Lat. *nĕgāre* seems to have developed in Sp. as a popular word. — For O. Sp. **non** cf. Vocab. — In **quisieret** = *quisiere* < Lat. *quaesīvĕrĭt* we see the loss of *v* after *ī*, which frequently happened also in classic Latin, and already the closing effect of the *i* of the accented syll. upon a preceding unaccented *e* (Lat. *ae*, V.L. *e*). The *i* was caused by the usual V.L. shift of accent in *ie* to the more sonorous second element; cf. *mulíerem* > V. L. *muliérem.

4 17 (100) Of course *augŭrĭŭm* became masculine in Romance. In V.L. the first *u* of the combination *au–ŭ* disappeared, hence V.L. *agŭrĭŭm, mod. Sp. *agüero*. In the Sp. development, apparently the *i* closed the V. L. *o* (Lat. *ŭ*) to *u* and then, by epenthesis, joined it as *e*, which, as the more sonorous vowel, soon assumed the accent. This is, however, a doubtful phonetic process. — The practice of augury continued throughout the Middle Ages in Spain, in spite of the condemnation of it by the Church : the Penitential in question here arraigns it.

4 18 (111) According to the scribe's usual process of writing the Lat. voiceless for the Romance voiced consonants, *alquantre* = *alguandre*. Cf. Priebsch : "In the welcome *alquantre* we perceive clearly the rare *alguandre*, '*jamás*,' which is found twice in the *Cid* and once, reënforced by *nunquas*, in the *Reyes Magos* [cf. **7** 34 and Vocab. s.v. *alguandre*].

According to Cornu, *Romania* X. 75, this is Lat. *aliquando*. The difficulty which the *t* presents is resolved if we suppose a contamination
with *aliquantum*. [Or, rather, the *t* may be scribal and erroneous for
original *d*, written just as the scribe still wrote *t* for Lat. *t* which had
become *d*.] The word probably did not live after the 12th century; it
is lacking in documents of the archives." The *-re* Priebsch does not
seek to explain; cf. Vocab.

4 19–20 (112, 208) Both the Romance verb forms are inexact as to
mood, since the glossed words require the subjunctive; the sense is
that of " coming forward," or in general that of mod. Sp. *llegar*. In
O. Sp. *allegar* may have had occasionally the intransitive sense of
' arrive,' ' come forward '; cf. *Poema de Fernán González*, ed. Marden,
101 *d*. In mod. Sp. *allegar* is used only in the transitive sense, ' to
bring together,' yet Diez (*Etym. Wtb.*, p. 463) is of the opinion that
the intransitive sense began with the derivative *allegar*, Lat. *applĭcare*
(' to adapt to,' ' tend toward '), and passed thence to the simplex *llegar*.
The present glosses seem to bear him out. As their *k* probably represents the already developed *g*, they are forms of a verb *aplegar* <
applĭcāre, found in variants in Berceo, *Santo Domingo*, 518 and 667, in
the reflexive and passive use, and in the reflexive use in the *Libro de
Alexandre* (ed. Morel-Fatio, stz. 137), all with the sense of ' to reach,'
' arrive.' The transition to the intransitive sense is parallel to that of
pasear, transitive, which, through *pasearse*, has become *pasear*, intransitive. The simple verb *llegar* corresponds to Lat. *plĭcare*, and, independently of the influence of Lat. *applicare*, it should be remarked that the
change of sense from ' bend,' ' wend,' to ' go ' is illustrated also in the
history of the English verb " wend," " went," " he turned his way," " he
wended his way," therefore " he went." Among other examples of an
early date, Priebsch cites one from the *Fuero de Castrojeriz*: " *et plegamos
nos totos, et fuimus ad illos*." The same development may still hold true
of O. Sp. *troçir* as from V. L. **torcere*, **torcīre*, Lat. *torquĕre*, in spite of
Baist's assertion in the *Kritischer Jahresbericht ü. d. Fortschritte der
roman. Philol.* VIII. i. 214. The history of *llegar*, *allegar*, ought to be
considered by him, as well as the history of the English *wend*, *went*.
The writing of *pl* in *aplekan*, *aplekat*, *plegar*, etc. may be only conventional and etymological: the sound may have been already the palatalized
sound of *l*.

4 21 (122) In the Lat. **conplexu** observe *np* for *mp*. The gloss
seems to mean ' shall embrace constrained,' i.e. tightly. — **constrinitu**
= *constriñido* < V. L. **constrĭngītum*, p.p. of Lat. *constrĭngĕre*, instead

of Lat. *constrictum*. The mod. word is *constreñir constreñido*, but older Sp. shows also *co(n)stringir, co(n)strinir, co(n)striñir*, etc. — In the fut. sbj. **brazaret** = mod. *abrazare* we note the absence of the prefix — perhaps as a result of a scribal error — and the early use of *z* for the sibilant developed out of Lat. *cį*. In the later period, when conditions became fixed, *z* was reserved, in the intervocalic position, for the voiced dental sibilant, and *ç* denoted the corresponding voiceless sound of the present word, *abraçar < ad + brac(h)ium, *abbrac(h)ĭare*.

4 22 (124) *Femur* has left no traces in Romance. — The gloss **campas** has also passed from mod. Sp. Priebsch calls attention to the entry in the Cassel Glosses, so interesting for Old French, *campa : hamma*, in which the sense of 'ham' or 'upper leg' is clear. He says further: "This interesting gloss agrees with the *camba* of the *Alexander* [i.e. the *Libro de Alexandre*] and the *cama* of the *Cid*. The later Spanish and Catalan *gamba*, Portuguese *gambia*, with a voiced initial consonant ... are certainly not native, but probably came from Italy. In the first edition of the Dictionary of the Spanish Academy, it is said of *gamba*: '*Es voz italiana y de poco uso.*'" The word is general Romance: cf. Italian *gamba*, French *jambe*, and English *gammon, jamb*, etc. Diez supposed it to be of Celtic origin, and related to the stem *cam (camb-, camm-)* 'crooked,' 'bent,' found also, as general Indo-European, in Greek καμπή. So he says (*Etym. Wtb.* p. 155) : "The root is found in the Latin domain in *cam-urus, cam-erus*, 'crooked,' *cam-era* 'vault,' *camerare* 'to arch over,' French *cambrer*, in the simplex in the Celtic *cam* 'bent,' 'crooked' (Cymric *camineg*, 'felly of a wheel,' like the Portuguese *camba*)." Whatever the case may be with regard to a Celtic source (cf. Thurneysen, *Keltoromanisches*, s.v. *gamba*), the word has affinities with the English *ham*. In mod. Sp. *pierna* has supplanted *campa, camba, gamba*. See Körting, *Lat.-Roman. Wtb.*, 3d ed., s.v. *camba*. The development of the idea "crooked," "crooked limb," into that of "upper leg," "ham," is certainly not impossible. Descriptive features and pleasantry have much to do with the evolution of the Romance terms for the parts of the human frame. See also Gröber in *Archiv f. lat. Lexicographie* II. 432 and Rönsch in *Jahrbuch f. roman. u. engl. Sprache* XIV. 174.

4 23 (125) Of course **propris** stands for the dat. and abl. pl. *propriis. Proprius -a -um* has survived in Sp. as *propio -a* and is often used as an intensive with the possessive adjective. — For **sos**, cf. Vocab. s.v. *sǫ*; it is interesting to find *sŭōs > sos* in the 11th century. Cf. 187 *so < sŭŭm*.

4 24 (138) In Romance there is no trace of a popular development
of **quot.** — *Quantus -a -um*, with its flexional capabilities, had better
fortune : hence mod. Sp. *cuanto -a*.

4 25 (146) Of course the deponent *utor*, like all other deponent
verbs, disappeared in V.L. The p. p. *usus* and its derivatives have
had a better fate : cf. Sp. *uso, usar, usual* < Lat. *ūsūalis, usualem.* —
The **aiat** here, and in the next gloss 188 *habeat: aiat*, represents the
regular V.L. contraction of the pres. sbj. *habeat*, especially for the
Western part of the Romance territory and certainly for Sp. From
V.L. *(h)ayat* we obtain Sp. *(h)aya*, for which the gloss *aiat* stands.
The reduction of the Lat. word is due to proclitic and enclitic use in
verbal combinations, e.g. in perfect tenses, in which the accent in
V.L. was thrown on the accompanying and more important p.p. As
a result the auxiliary verb was slurred and soon was shortened in
pronunciation. In direct phonological development *-by-* did not become *y* in Spanish. — The word **lege** in Gloss 146 — whose correspondence with *uti* is not perfectly clear — is the Sp. *ley*, 'law' : *lex lēgem* >
lege > *lee* (since intervocalic *g* was lost before *e, i*, and in fact had already
become *y* in V.L.) and > *ley* (since the last *e*, being in hiatus, is really
a *y*) ; cf. Vocab. s.v. *ley*.

4 27–31 (153, 223, 274, 35, 88) All these glosses illustrate the early
Spanish use of the definite article. In 153, 223, 274, we have the full
forms of the article, corresponding directly to the Lat. demonstrative
adj. *ille* etc., with its first syllable retained. Priebsch deems these
forms, in so far as *elo, ela, elas* are concerned, common to the earliest
Old Spanish, and he states : " They have maintained themselves longest
(as late as the 13th cent.) in Leonese texts, as numerous examples from
the *Alexandre*, from the decrees of the Councils at Leon, and from the
archives of this province as published by Muñoz, Guerra y Orbe, and
Escalona prove." He calls attention to Gessner, *Das Altleonesische*,
Berlin, 1867, and Morel Fatio in *Romania* IV. 53. We have now the
well founded judgment of E. Staaff in his *Étude sur l'ancien dialecte
léonais d'après des chartes du XIIIe siècle*, Uppsala and Leipzig, 1907,
pp. 262 ff. He finds the forms *ela* (*ella*), *elas* (*ellas*), *elos* (*ellos*) instead
of *la, las, los*, i.e. the Latin forms preserved without apocopation
of the final syllable as regards the sing. *ela*, and, what is more interesting, without loss of the initial syllable for all of them. The forms
with a single *l* prevail, and he says, " The almost constant reduction
of *ll* to *l* is due doubtless to the influence of the masculine form " ; i.e.,
Lat. *ille* > *elle* > *elle* > *ell*, with loss of palatalization before a word

beginning with a consonant, *el*. But it should be observed that *aquella*, *aquellas*, *aquellos*, have maintained themselves in spite of *aquel*. Menéndez Pidal, *El Dialecto Leonés* (Madrid, 1906), p. 50, also registers *ela*, *elas*, *elos* for Old Leonese, but does not find the forms in the modern dialect. While there is a tendency in modern Asturian and in part of the Leonese territory to palatalized initial *l*, the shortened forms of the article, *la*, *las*, etc., do not show the palatalization (cf. ibid. pp. 31 and 50, and Staaff p. 265). In the original demonstrative use our Glosses show 62 and 168 *elos* and 178 *ela(s)*. In gloss 88 *lo* appears to be the masc. sg. of the article, and it may be the same form — if not the neuter — in 35. Like the other short forms, *la*, *los*, *las*, which at an early date became regular in Castilian, *lo* arose in the combination with a preceding preposition, e.g. *de ĭllŭ(m) > de ello > del(l)o*, and this, by redivision, *> de lo*. So also *de ĭlla(m) > del(l)a > de (l)la*, cf. *de la* of Gloss 61. In Gloss 214 we see *alas = á las*. While Castilian preferred the masc. form *el*, Leonese used *lo*, but generally only in combination with a preceding preposition, as in our Glosses; cf. Staaff, l.c., p. 265, note 2. Cf. the still more westerly form *o* of Portuguese, which appears to have arisen in such combinations as *a + lo*, *alo >*, with the usual Ptg. loss of intervocalic *l*, *ao*, and, by redivision, *a + o*. Some think that *ille* became *ile, *ila, etc. in V.L., but the history of the Sp. pron. *el*, *ella*, etc. must be borne in mind. Staaff, l.c., p. 253, says: "An important trait of the Leonese dialect consists in the tendency which this dialect has to assimilate the final consonant of certain words and the initial consonant of certain other words. This is the case above all with the final *n* of the prepositions *en* and *con* and the initial *l* of the article and the personal pronoun." He gives examples of *en + lo(s) > enno(s)*, *en + la(s) > enna(s)*, *en + los > enos*, *en + la(s) > ena(s)*; *con + lo(s) > conno(s)*, *con + la(s) > conna(s)*, *con + lo(s) > cono(s)*, *con + la(s) > cona(s)*. The forms with *nn* seem to be in the majority in the 13th-century charters examined by him. Perhaps the *n* of our *eno*, *ena*, *enas*, in Glosses 44, 200, 222, 105 (**4** 32–33; **5** 1–2) represents *nn*, but the matter is open to discussion. It is of importance in that it raises the question as to a Leonese or Western Spanish origin of our document. Gessner, in his article *Das Leonesische, Ein Beitrag zur Kenntniss des Altspanischen* (Berlin, 1867), had called attention to *enno*, *conno*. Staaff (p. 256) says that these forms "can go back only to the form *lo* of the article, a form which is that of Portuguese, and which . . . has also left traces in Leonese. This form represents the final syllable of *illum*, while the Sp. article goes back to the nominative *ęlli*, whose vowel has undergone the influence of *ellum*." Here he follows Baist, Gröber's *Grundriss* I, 2nd ed., 909. But there is no real need of asserting a V. L. *elli* as the basis. The occasional O. Sp. *elli* (masc. sg.), in view of which Baist supposes *elli*, may have its *-i* explained as a pronominal *i* due to the influence of Lat. *qui*, O. Sp. *qui*. Staaff (p. 257) discusses an Old Leonese *enne, ene*, in which, he says, " we must see a trace of the nominative [i.e. of *ille*] with a loss of the initial syllable: *en + elle > en le > enne* and likewise *tras elle > tras le*." It is much more likely that we start with *en le*, i.e., the first syllable of *elle* was probably lost first of all in combinations such as *de + elle > delle, dele*, whence, by redivision, *de (l)le*. Another significant statement of Staaff is this (p. 257) : " the assimilation of *n* and *l* gives either *nn* or *n*, spellings which are often found in the same document. The forms with single *n* increase toward the west. In the central and eastern region it is probable that *en* was first combined with the article when the latter was pronounced with palatalized *l*: *en + llo > enno (eño)*, after which *ñ* was frequently reduced to *n* under the influence of the preposition." The feminine article *el*, still used in mod. Sp. before a fem. noun beginning with accented *a* or *ha*, was much more used in early Sp., occurring both in Castilian (cf. Vocab. s.v. *el*) and in Leonese (cf. Staaff, p. 264) before fem. nouns and adjs. in general, provided they began with a vowel. It is to be noted that Cornu has endeavored — but hardly with success — to establish the fuller forms of the article, *elle* etc., for the *Poema del Cid*: cf. *Études romanes dédiées à G. Paris*; *Ztsch. f. rom. Philol.* XXI; etc.

As a learned adjective *predator -ora* of Gloss 153 lives on in mod. Sp. The noun is seen in the somewhat more popular *depredador*. O. Sp. had the verb *prear* < Lat. *praedare*, which was truly popular in form.

In 223 the unpronounced *h* of *habitum* has been omitted. — The gloss **similia** (Lat. ntr. pl. of *sĭmĭlis* treated as a V. L. fem. sg.) has given the Sp. *semeja*, 'likeness,' 'resemblance,' 'mark,' 'sign.' In the latter senses it is used rather in the pl. than the sing., but the word is not very common.

In 274 it is evident that **cuerpos** is really a pl. and not the representative of a sg. Lat. *cŏrpŭs*. Of course it is not impossible that a form *cuerpos* could do duty as both a sg. and a pl., but the chances are that a sg. *cuerpo* already existed. Cf. Menéndez Pidal, *Manual elemental de gramática histórica española* (Madrid, 1905), pp. 134–135. — The mod. Sp. *cadáver* is purely learned: in his writing of the Lat. word as **cadabera** the scribe shows again his inability to distinguish between *b* and *v* in the intervocalic position.

córpus > cuerpos + sg. cuerpo then derived from it

periculu > × peigulo > periglo > pelígro
os perigro
g must voice before loss of u

Lat. *incĕndĭum* remains in the learned development *incendio*. — The gl. **incentitu** owes its erroneous first *t* to the constant tendency of the scribe to write a *t* where the pronunciation was that of *d*. The word is the p.p. used with substantival force: mod. Sp. *encendido*, p.p. of *encender*, Lat. *incĕndĕre*, V. L. *incĕndēre*.

Lat. *hostīlis* maintains itself as Sp. *hostil*, but is hardly a word of common use. — **gentile** = mod. *gentil* 'Gentile' < Lat. *gentīlis*; here it may be used with the sense of *gente*. — **aduersario** = *adversario*, which remains as a learned form < *adversārĭus*.

collituras: this word, according to Priebsch, p. 22, "is mod. Sp. *cogedura* (cf. Ital. *coglitura*) 'the act of collecting something,' and goes with O. Sp. *coller*, Ptg. *colher*, more usually *colligir*, mod. Sp. *coger*." The *ll* (palatalized *l*, if it is really such) of *coller* and of our *collitura* may indicate Leonese origin: cf. the early examples of *ll < ly* given by Staaff (*coller* etc., already listed by Cuervo in *Rev. hisp.* II. 52 ff.) p. 227 ff. and by Menéndez Pidal in *Dialecto Leonés* p. 38 (*fillo* 'son,' *muller* 'wife,' etc.). In mod. Leonese the *ll > y*, which, indeed, appears relatively early also.

pullutione is represented in Castilian by the learned *polución* < Late Lat. *pollutio -onem*.—For **periculo**, mod. Cast. *peligro*, cf. Vocab. s.v. *perigro*.

With **sota** cf. 216 *saltare: sotare*. The sense is that of 'jumping' and 'hopping' in a dance, and the verb is the Lat. *saltare*, 'to dance,' 'hop.' Cf. Priebsch, p. 30: "For older *sotar* 'bailar, alegrarse' the mod. language has again *saltar*. . . . The substantive *sota* (mod. Sp. *saltación* and *salto*, which latter is also Portuguese, < *saltus*) is derived from the verb." If the forms *sotar*, *sota* are Castilian, one wonders why the reversion to *saltar*, *salto*, etc. took place. Cf. the noun *soto* 'grove' < Lat. *saltus -um*, which shows the same process of development as these old Sp. words (*saltum > *sauto > *souto > soto*) and has maintained itself. It should be indicated that *l* before a voiceless consonant has shown different treatments, now vocalizing to *u* (or to *i*, *y*, after *u*), and again persisting: cf. Baist in Gröber's *Grundriss* I, 2d ed., pp. 886 and 903, and Menéndez Pidal, *Gramática elemental*, 2d ed., p. 87.

5 3 (161) **prius: anzes.** Lat. *prius* did not remain in Sp. The glossing word *anzes* is a decidedly interesting form, with which Diez was not familiar when he wrote (*Etym. Wtb.* p. 21), s.v. Ital. *anzi*: "The derivation from *antea* is contradicted by the Sp. form [i.e. *antes*, the regular Sp. form]. . . . Ménage [in his *Dictionnaire étymologique*] argues for an undiscovered but easily admissible *antius*, as the comparative of *ante*, which is satisfactory for *anzi* as well as *ains* [the

O. S. Dialect. colli...
Cf colligere > Vl colligere > collir   Mod. coger
cf. malleare

corresponding Old French word], but throws *antes* out of court. And yet it must be a guiding principle of etymologizing, in so far as the letter does not stand in decided contradiction therewith, to hold to a common origin of words of the different sister languages which are alike in meaning and close in form." The *anzes* of our *Glosses* belongs to the same category as *anzi* and *ains*, and therefore Ménage's etymology deserves serious consideration. This it has received from Schuchardt in the *Ztschr. f. roman. Philol.* XV. 240, where he explains *anzi* as from *antie, an adverb framed on *antius -a -um. In O. Sp., *antie should give *anze ançe* (the spelling with *ç* for the voiceless sibilant being the better), and this might assume an adverbial *s*. Cf. Vocab. s.v. *antes*. Cf. Priebsch, p. 26: "*Anzes*, which must be referred to an *antie + *s* (cf. Ital. *anzi*), is, in the presence of Sp. and Ptg. *ante antes*, very strange. Perhaps from the present form [i.e. *anzes*], which unfortunately has not been found elsewhere, we may infer a derivative *anzano*, now also lost, which would correspond better to *antianum than the mod. *anciano* (*ancião* in Ptg.)." Of course, it must be said that *anciano* corresponds perfectly to *antianum, but as a learned development.

5 4 (166) Aside from certain Italian dialect forms, and possibly certain Provençal forms, **semel** seems to have left no trace in Romance, although the related *insimul* *insĕmul has given an O. Sp. *ensiemo* as well as other Romance forms. — In the gloss **uece** = *vece* is from Lat. *vĭcem*. Cf. Priebsch, p. 26: "*vice* is common Romance: Ptg. and Sp. *vez* (beside *vegada*, now obs., from *vĭcata), Provençal *vetz*, French *fois*. See the Reichenau Glosses 205: *semel : una vice*, and a marginal gloss of the MS. of the British Museum Add. 30,851, fol. 120 verso: *uicissim : aveces* (as in mod. Sp.)."

5 5 (167) Cf. Gloss 86, *lapsi sunt : cadutu fueret*. In both cases it is notable that *ser* is used as auxiliary with a verb of motion, as it often was used in O. Sp. — Priebsch, p. 21, registers also gloss 89 *cadieret* = mod. *cayere*, and *cadiot* (see below gl. 234) = *cayó*. He judges that this *cadudo* (for which *cadutu* and *kadutu* stand), which has not been discovered anywhere else, must early have given way to *ca(d)ido*, i.e. *caído* < *cadītum. He mentions as common in O. Sp. such past participles as *cognozudo*, *defendudo*, *venzudo*, etc. He says: " In a very old, richly illuminated Lat. MS. from Silos I find the gloss *casus* (subst.): *caditas*, and this latter word represents mod. *caída* 'fall.'" Priebsch also mentions the O. Sp. infin. *cader*, with preserved intervocalic *d*: cf. Menéndez Pidal, *Gramática elem.*, 2d ed., p. 200.

5 6 (187) The **so caput** corresponds to the *se ipsum*; the conj. *si* is not concerned here in the gloss. The sense is then that of the mod. *si mismo*, according, as Priebsch indicates, to the figure of the part for the whole, the head for the whole person. He has found in a document of 1233 the expression *ueuir en so cabo = vivir por sí*. We may add here the mod. Sp. *en su solo cabo = á sus solas*, the French *de son chef = de son propre mouvement*, and the Ital. *di suo capo = di proprio arbitrio*. Some doubt has been thrown on the derivation of *cabo* from the V.L. **capŭm*. Baist, *Grundriss*, 2d ed., I. 895, would derive it directly from Lat. *caput*; cf. Bernitt, *Lat. caput u. *capum*, etc. (Kiel, 1905). Of course final *t* would drop in *caput* and we should be reduced to **capu-* just as in **capu(m)*. But Sp. *cabeza* points to a **capiciam* based on **capum*.

5 7 (191) **noberce** represents the Lat. genitive *novercae* of *noverca*: the interchange of intervocalic *b* and *v* occurs as in other cases; the final *e* shows the V.L. change to *ę*. During the Middle Ages the scribes often used *e* for *ae* in transcribing classic texts. — Cf. Priebsch, p. 28, with regard to **matastra**: "for *matrastra* (with dissimilation, i.e. of the *r*), mod. Sp. *madrastra* beside *madrasta* (also Portuguese) from *matrasta* (in Isidore of Seville)." The ordinary dictionaries do not record a mod. *madrasta* for either Sp. or Ptg. As Priebsch indicates, Ducange (*Glossarium Infimae Latinitatis*) lists *matrasta*. The French *marâtre* is the same word and keeps both *r*'s. — Priebsch is doubtless right in regarding the obs. *noverca*, given in the Sp. dictionaries, as a term of legal usage and not a popular word.

5 8 (192) Perhaps the use of **cusina** here as a glossing word is due to a tendency to distinguish between the meaning of the Lat. *sobrina*, which became limited in Sp. to the sense 'niece,' and the more general meaning of Lat. *consobrina*, which appears to have given the Fr. *cousine*, Ital. *cugina*, etc., 'cousin.' In Lat. *sobrīnus -a*, standing as it did for *sororinus -a*, was properly used of cousins by the mother's side, while *consobrīnus -a* seems to have had its sense extended to that of 'cousin' and 'relative' in even a remote degree. It is not certain, however, that the glossator was refining in this way. For Priebsch, our *cusina* is a French loan-word [i.e. represents Fr. *cousine*, which some regard as a deformation in child's speech — where it occurred frequently, and often too in the proclitic use — of the Lat. *consobrina*]. As Fr. loan-words he regards also the Old Galician *cosino* and a 15th-century Aragonese *cosino*, and he has found the word in Portuguese courtly poetry of the 15th century, which underwent French influence.

In both Sp. and Ptg. the usual term for 'cousin' is *primo -a*, i.e. first in relationship after 'brother' and 'sister.'

5 9–11 (193, 194, 243) Lat. *matertera* 'aunt on the mother's side' did not survive in Sp. In **matertere** we have the genitive *materterae*. — **abunculi** stands for Lat. genitive *avunculi*. In Sp. there seems to be no trace of Lat. *avunculus* 'uncle on the mother's side.' It is, of course, the French *oncle*, whence the Eng. *uncle*. In Romance no attempt was made to distinguish by different words the uncle and aunt on the mother's side from those on the father's side. — Like Italian, Sp. and Ptg. have derived their words for 'uncle,' 'aunt,' from the Greek θεῖος, θεία, which included the uncles and aunts on both sides of the house. Thence came the V. L. *thīus, *thīa, Italian *zio, zia*, and our Sp. terms.

5 12 (211) In Romance the Lat. *audēre* gave way to a frequentative, V. L. *ausare*, whose pp. *ausatum* > our form **osatu** = *osado*, just as in gl. 230 its pres. sbj. *auset* > *oset* = *ose*. — Apropos of 211, Priebsch says: "*Sit ausus* for *audeat* is a constant expression in the old legal monuments and documents. In a document of 964 it is said, *nullus homo aus(e)us non sedeat per ibi entrare*; and in a document of 1277, *no sea ossado*."

5 13 (214) Lat. *nūptiae* (with influence of *novius*) has been potent in the other Romance languages; cf. French *noces*, Ital. *nozze*, etc.; but in Sp. it has been supplanted by the ntr. pl. *vōta* '(marriage) vows,' 'marriage,' 'wedding.' Hence O. Sp. *vodas* represented by our gloss. The O. Sp. tendency to use *b* even for etymological *v* in the initial position seems to have fixed the mod. spelling *bodas*. There is also exemplified here the tendency of a Lat. ntr. pl. in *-a* to be treated popularly as a fem. sg.; hence the new pl. in *-s*. In *nubtias* the scribe follows the reverse process and erroneously writes the voiced *b* for voiceless *p*, while he maintains voiceless *-p-* in *capo* for mod. *cabo*. In mod. Sp. a *b* before a voiceless consonant, if pronounced at all, becomes *p*: cf. *abstener*, pronounced either *apstener* or *astener*.

5 15 (224) The gloss, 'who stain their faces,' corresponds to the fuller expression in the Penitential *qui . . . monstruose fingunt*, 'who make themselves up strangely (unnaturally),' which it therefore interprets rather specifically. — On the O. Sp. rel. pron. **qui**, cf. Vocab. s.v. and the remarks to **3** 5 ff.; of course *quien* < *quĕm* appears regularly as the rel. and interrog. pron., used of persons, in mod. Sp. — As to the non-Castilian **lures** cf. the note on **3** 16. — **tingen** = *tiñen* corresponds to V. L. *tĭngent* for Lat. *tingunt*. It is difficult to say whether the *i* is the Latin vowel preserved or is the fully developed Sp. *i* of *teñir, tiño, tiñen,* etc. Palatalization under certain conditions explains the Sp. *i.* — According to Priebsch **faces** is not clear in the MS. It is, however, the form that we should expect from the pl. *facĭes* of the Lat. *facĭes facĭem,* as it is probable that the combination *-cĭe* was early reduced to *-ce*: cf. Ford in *Studies and Notes in Philology* etc. VII (Boston, 1900), p. 48, and Horning, *Lat. C im Romanischen* (Halle, 1883), p. 8. The resulting form in O. Sp. was *fazes,* for which our gloss stands.

5 16 (234) **Emersise** seems to be the active perf. infin. of *emergĕre* (*emersisse*): this part of the verb did not survive in Romance, and its place was taken most often by a subordinate clause, such as the *ke cadiot = que cayó* here. The Lat. text glossed is *si quis dicit diabolum . . . ex cahos emersise,* etc. — Apropos of the pret. indic. 3d sg. form **cadiot** cf. Priebsch, p. 18, where he deals with the pret. *tolliot* 'took away' of gl. 38: "*tollio tolló* from **tolluit* through *tolliut* like *cadiot* out of **caduit* through *cadiut*; later *cadió cayó* (*caió*)." In a note he says: "*absorbiut* is in a document of 969." Just what process Priebsch is thinking of is not clear, or what part **tolluit* and **caduit* play in the supposed development. In *ui* preterits the *u* generally passed beyond the consonant to join a preceding *a*; whence *au > ou > o* in O. Sp., cf. *habuit > ovo, sapuit > sopo,* etc. So from **caduit* we might expect **codo.* We are really dealing here with a weak preterit developed on the analogy of the pret. of the Lat. 4th conjugation, which became very important for Spanish and took over many verbs from other conjugations and certainly imposed itself for certain tenses. In Lat. we find already the development *audīvit > audĭit.* This form, continuing in V. L., could by analogy to the 1st conjugation, *amāvit > amáut,* become **audíut,* or perhaps we may say, without appealing at all to *audĭ.t,* that Lat. *audīvit* (whose *v* should regularly be lost in Span. after *ī*) was made over straightway to **audíut* through the analogy of *amáut.* The accent on the *i* could also be explained by the analogy of *audísti* for *audivísti, audímus* for *audivímus,* etc., which all tended to produce a uniform accent on the characteristic vowel *i* throughout the 1st, 2d, and 3d sg. and the 1st and 2d pl. See, for various statements as to the lines of development pursued by these preterit forms, Baist in the *Grundriss* I, 2d ed., 913; Meyer-Lübke, ibid. 479; Menéndez Pidal, *Gram. elem.,* 2d ed., 216 ff.; and in general A. Gassner, *Das altspanische Verbum* (Halle, 1897). If now we suppose a V. L. **cadíut,* its development would be *cadiot >,* with a shift of accent to the more sonorous vowel *o, ca(d)ió, cayó.* The shift of accent may have been helped by the analogy of the accented

-ó from *-aut* in the 1st conjugation, and also by the fact that in the 3d pl. ending *-īvērunt* > *-iĕrunt* > Sp. *-iéron*, the accent was regularly on the second element of a diphthong. It is not without interest that the Glosses contain, as 1st conjugation forms, 80 *duplicaot*, mod. Sp. *duplicó* < Lat. *duplicavit*, and 266 *betait* [mod. *vedó*] < Lat. *vetavit*. Here we seem to have indicated two different developments of *-avit*. Baist, *Grundriss* I. 913, says: "In the Glosses of Silos, *betait* vetavit beside *duplicaot*, *tolliot*, corresponds to mod. North Aragonese *costé* [i.e. *-áit* > *-é*] etc., as also to the Provençal." Accordingly, just as we find western (Leonese) traits in our Glosses, we seem to find eastern ones also. Baist, ibid. p. 895, finds the final *t* of *tolliot* etc. surprising, because he does not think that they were forms influenced easily by Latin considerations. But it must be obvious to all who go through the Glosses that the glossator or scribe usually added a *-t* to all 3d person forms and Latinized as much as possible.

5 17 (240) The Latin text runs here *mulier quamuis docta et sancta*, " a woman however much (= although) learned and holy." The gloss then means " although she be." — The word **macare** is both interesting and fraught with difficulty as to its source and development. It is certainly the same as the O. Sp. *maguer* (cf. Vocab. s.v. *mager*), which has often been written erroneously as *magüer* (cf. Cuervo in *Romania* XXXIII. 255). It seems also to be the Italian *magari*, *magara*, which Petrocchi (*Dizionario universale della lingua ital.*) terms an " exclamation which expresses an affirmation of probability or wish, desire "; i.e., the general sense is ' Yes, indeed ! ' ' I hope so ! ' He finds it combined with *Dio* in *Magari Dio*, *Magaraddio*, in uses quite like those of the Span. *¡ ojalá !* and, what is more in point still, he finds it in the sense of *quand' anche* ' although,' as in *Deve andar di là : magari ci andasse tutto il patrimonio*, i.e. ' even though all his patrimony were concerned.' Diez (*Etym. Wtb.*, p. 381) says, treating of the Italian forms : " *Macari*, *magari*, *magara* (popular), an interjection, ' utinam '; from the Greek μακάριος 'blessed,' ' happy ' (mod. Gk. μακάρι), vocative μακάριε. In the old poem of *Ciullo* [i.e. *C. d'Alcamo* or *Cielo dal Camo*] it has the sense of a concessive particle : *macara se dolesseti* ' even though thou didst grieve.' " He treats also of its appearance in Wallachian (Roumanian), Rhæto-Romance, and mod. Provençal, and continues: " Whether the O. Sp. concessive particle *maguar*, *maguer*, *maguera* (*mager de pie* ' even though on foot,' *Poema del Cid*) is from the same source, or, as Sánchez [*Poema del Cid*, note to v. 755, in his *Colección de Poesías Castellanas*, etc.] will have it, is a deformation of the French *malgré*, *maugré*, may be regarded as still a subject of consideration; a Ptg. *maguer* of the 12th cent. is given by Santa Rosa [in his *Elucidario*]." Baist (in Vollmöller's *Kritischer Jahresbericht*, VIII. i. 213) has very well called attention to a case in Juan Ruiz's *Libro de Buen Amor*, stz. 1034 (ed. J. Ducamin), of the exclamative use of *maguera* in Sp. Priebsch, pp. 33–34, has given examples of the forms of the concessive particle in the oldest Sp. texts, and thinks that its diffusion in Old Ptg. was not great. "It is strange," he says, "that neither the Sp. nor the Ptg. archives show a trace of the forms cited." In Bable-Asturian he finds *magar* and *de magar* in the temporal sense of *desde que, desde cuando*. He confesses himself unable to decide whether the Hispanic forms have any relation to the Italian interjections, and he rejects the possibility of a relation with the Fr. *maugré*.

As we have seen, Petrocchi notes a concessive as well as an exclamative use of the Italian word, and, on the whole, the Hispanic and the Ital. words would appear to hark back to the same source. Menéndez Pidal, *Gramática elem.*, p. 242, has accepted μακάριε for *maguer*. As to the appearance of the word with and without a final *a*, cf. such pairs in Sp. as *siquier* and *siquiera*, etc. Perhaps, when all is said and done, one may be pardoned for still wondering whether the Gk. etymon proposed is the correct one. The difficulties of semasiology are, perhaps, not insurmountable, but have they been met yet? Then, too, what are the historical conditions back of the adoption and preservation in Romance of such a Greek word? Körting (*Lat.-Roman. Wtb.*, s.v. μάκαρ) refers to the doubts cast by Miklosich on Diez's derivation of the Ital. word from the Oriental word, but he does not himself deal with the Hispanic and other forms mentioned above.

5 18 (244) As the scribe seems regularly to write the Lat. voiceless intervocalic stop for the Romance voiced form of it, **consico** probably means *consigo*. Therefore we see that in *sigo* the sense of the prep. was gone already and *cŭm* > *con* had to be added. Already, also, we see in *si* a prepositional form of the pers. pron., as opposed to *se* the conjunctive obj. form with the verb; cf. Vocab. s.v. *si*.

5 19 (260) Judging by the correspondence of *suffocato* and its Sp. Gloss **mortizino** (mod. *mortecino -a* < Lat. *mortĭcīnus -a*), the latter has here the strong sense of the Lat. word, 'dead' (of animals), 'carrion' (of flesh). This sense remains in Sp., which has, however, developed the further sense of 'dying away,' 'pining,' 'half-dead.' To the assibilation of Lat. *-c(e,i)*, as illustrated here, attention has already been called.

5 20 (272) V. L. *acceptor -em* (based on the p. p. of *accĭpĕre*) supplanted Lat. *accipiter* in V. L. *Acceptorem* > *açetór* (the *acetore* of our Gl.) > *açtor* > O. Sp. *açor* = mod. *azor* 'falcon,' 'hawk.' The transition from *açtor* to *açor* is due to a simplification of adjacent consonant sounds : *ç* = *ts* in O. Sp. therefore *açtor* = *atstor*, and the combination *tst*, by dissimilation of the second *t*, > *ts*, i.e. *ç*; hence *açor*: cf. *recĭtare* > *rezdar*, i.e. *redzdar*, > *redzar*, i.e. *rezar*, since O. Sp. *z* = *dz* in sound. See Ford in *Studies and Notes in Philol.*, Boston, 1900, VII. 37.

5 21 (295) **ferre** disappeared in Romance. — In Lat. *lĕvāre* had the senses 'to make light,' 'lift,' and 'take away.' For O. Sp. *levar*, mod. *llevar* (cf. Vocab. s.v. *leuar*, and the remarks to **4** 5), the senses 'to carry,' 'to take away' (this latter especially in the reflexive use in mod. Sp.), prevail. The mod. Sp. *levar* is used in the limited sense 'to lift (anchor),' 'to weigh (anchor).'

III. AUTO DE LOS REYES MAGOS

The best edition of this oldest monument of the Spanish drama, termed generally the *Misterio de los Reyes Magos*, is that published by R. Menéndez Pidal, — in the *Revista de Archivos, Bibliotecas y Museos* and in a reprint, Madrid, 1900, — who indicates earlier editions of importance and gives a description of the manuscript. The latter is now in the Biblioteca Nacional of Madrid (*Hh*–115). Along with several documents in handwriting of the 12th century, it contains, on folios 67 verso and 68 recto, our *Auto* in script of the early 12th century. In the ed. of 1900 Menéndez Pidal stated that the script was of the middle of the 13th century, but linguistic and scribal considerations have since led him to deem it of the 12th: cf. his *Gramática del Cid*, p. 144. Menéndez Pidal includes in his edition a slightly enlarged facsimile of it.

Among the early editions are the unscientific one of J. Amador de los Ríos in his *Historia Crítica de la Literatura Española* III. 655 ff. (Madrid, 1863), which gave rise to a study of the play and an attempt at an arrangement of the dialogue by the Italian littérateur Arturo Graf, in his *Studi drammatici*, Turin, 1878, pp. 251 ff.; that of E. Lidforss, in the *Jahrbuch für romanische und englische Litteratur* XII. (1871), pp. 44 ff., with a distribution of the parts not indicated in the MS., and accompanied by scholarly but improperly founded remarks regarding the date and the language of the piece; that of K. M. Hartmann, *Ueber das altspanische Dreikönigsspiel*, Bautzen, 1879, which textually marks no advance on the edition of Lidforss, but in its study of the language of the document and the question of its date brings up important matters which attracted the attention of A. Morel-Fatio and G. Paris in *Romania* IX. 464, and of G. Baist in the *Zeitschrift für romanische Philologie* IV. 443; and the paleographic edition of G. Baist, *Das altspanische Dreikönigsspiel*, Erlangen, 1887, which is surpassed only by Menéndez Pidal's edition. Reprints of the editions preceding Baist's and Menéndez Pidal's appear in A. Keller, *Altspanisches Lesebuch*, Leipzig, 1890; in E. Monaci, *Testi basso-latini e volgari della Spagna*, Rome, 1891; in E. Gorra, *Lingua e letteratura spagnuola delle origini*, Milan, 1898 (with a useful bibliographical note); and in E. de la Barra, *Literatura arcáica*, Valparaiso, 1898 (rather unscholarly). For various opinions regarding the nature and the versification of the *Misterio*, see also F. Wolf, *Jahrbuch für romanische und englische Litteratur* VI. 60 ff.; A. Mussafia, ibid. pp. 220 ff.; M. Milá y Fontanals, *De la poesía heroico-popular castellana*, Barcelona, 1874, pp. 450 ff.; K. Lange, *Die lateinischen Osterfeiern*, Munich, 1887; A. d'Ancona, *Origini del teatro italiano*, 2d ed., Turin, 1891; G. Baist, *Die spanische Litteratur* in Gröber's *Grundriss der romanischen Philologie* II. ii. 400 f.; J. Fitzmaurice-Kelly, *La Littérature espagnole*, Paris, 1904, pp. 42 ff. and 464 f.; R. Beer, *Spanische Literaturgeschichte*, Leipzig, 1903, I. 100 ff.; E. Mérimée, *Précis d'histoire de la littérature espagnole*, Paris, 1908, pp. 48 f. See further Von Schack, *Geschichte der dramatischen Literatur u. Kunst in Spanien*; Creizenach, *Geschichte des neueren Dramas*; Puymaigre, *Les Vieux Auteurs castillans*; and Morel-Fatio and Rouanet, *Le Théâtre espagnol*.

In the *Grundriss*, II. ii. 400, Baist has characterized the *Misterio* in succinct terms. " It could hardly fail to be the case that, along with the French ritual [which was adopted by the Church in Spain as a result of the large influx of French ecclesiastics in the 11th century], the dramatic ceremonies appertaining thereto should be taken over. . . . There is preserved, besides the isolated fragment of an Easter play [which Baist thinks Berceo introduced into his *Duelo de la Virgen*, stz. 178 ff.], only the first half of a Christmas mystery, the so-called *Misterio de los Reyes Magos*. An inexperienced hand of the first half of the 13th century has written it, in a rather defective way, on the last pages [it is on pp. 67 verso and 68 recto] of a MS. of the Chapter Library at Toledo. Its four scenes (the entrance of the Magi, their meeting one another, the Conversation with Herod, and the Council) show a rich metrical structure in lines of 8, 12, and 6 syllables, such as similar French and Latin pieces present; the prototype must, however, have been in Latin. The rime is somewhat imperfect, the conception and the language clerkly and simple; the place of the performance was in any event the Church. A rather advanced point of view is revealed in the way in which the elements of the liturgy are broken up and distributed; of a primitive character seem to be the lack of a pastoral prologue and the individual entrance of the Shepherds, while the dismissal of the Wise Men before the Consultation of the Jews is peculiar to the piece. . . . In view of the general development of the drama, the model of the piece must have belonged to the 12th century."

Hartmann, in his opuscule referred to above, discusses many matters of importance. He has been successful in disproving the arguments of Lidforss, who, basing himself on the fact that the diphthongs *ie* and *ue* are not written in the MS., maintained that the document belongs to the period when these latter were not yet fully developed and is therefore of the second half of the 11th century, if it is Castilian at all (and there are no traits in it, he thinks, belonging to the northeast or the northwest of the peninsula). Lidforss simply confused spelling and pronunciation. He was of the opinion that the diphthongization of Lat. $\breve{e}$ and $\breve{o}$ to *ie*, *ue* did not take place before the 12th century. Our 11th-century *Glosses* show it already, and other earlier documents display it. Moreover, an examination of our *Misterio* shows that the scribe writes now *e* (which may be the etymological spelling) and now *i* for an original Latin $\breve{e}$: *celo* < *caelum*, V. L. *cęlum; *seglo, seclo*, < *saeculum*, V. L. *sęculum; but *cilo*; *bine* < *bĕne*; *uinet* < *vĕnit*; *quin* < *quĕm*; *tine* < *tĕnet*; *quiro* < *quaero*, V. L. *quero; *tirra* < *tĕrra*. So also he writes now *o* (which may be etymological) and now *u* for an original Lat. $\breve{o}$: *morto* < *mŏrtŭum*; *bono*; *longa*; *uostros* < *vestros*, V. L. *vŏstros; but *pusto* < *pŏsĭtum*, V. L. *pŏstum; *pudet* < *potest*, V.L. *pŏtet; *cudo* < *cŏgĭtat* (or *cōgitat*). These forms show, as Hartmann declares, and as Morel-Fatio agrees (*Romania* IX. 468), that the Latin vowels in question had changed their sound in Spanish, and had really become sounds of which the first element was *i* and *u* respectively. Sometimes the scribe, bothered as to what he should do, held to the etymological vowel: again he wrote a character which rendered more exactly the first part of the diphthong developed out of it. The late Gaston Paris remarked (*Romania*, l.c.): "cette graphie [i.e. *i* < $\breve{e}$ and *u* < $\breve{o}$] est surtout intéressante en ce qu'elle paraît bien attester l'ancienne prononciation de *ie*, *uo* (plus tard *ue*) avec l'accent sur la première voyelle: *cilo* est pour *cielo*, *pudet* pour *puodet* ou *puedet*. *Celo* et *bono* peuvent s'interpréter ou comme graphies latines ou comme indices du déplacement de l'accent." There are good phonological reasons for supposing that the accent, in the development of a diphthong out of a simple vowel, rested originally on the first element of the new sound (cf. the history of the German diphthongs evolved from simple vowels), but it is open to discussion whether the accent, at the time when our *Misterio* was written down in the extant MS., still remained on that first element. For *ie* one is tempted to think so — although there is no absolute necessity — in view of the development of Lat. *ĕ* before *ll*: *castéllum* > *castiello* > *castillo*. (Were the intermediate stages *castíello* > *castíeĭlo*, i.e. *ĭl* = palatalized *l* from *ll*, > *castillo*, somewhat as *lectum* > *lieit* > *lit* in French? The process would be *ieĭ* > *ieĭ* > *iĭ* > finally *í*. But perhaps a stage -*iéi*-, with forward and back assimilating force of *i*, may suffice to explain the change.)

In so far as *uo* > *ue* is concerned, it should be said that Menéndez Pidal, in his *Cantar de Mio Cid, Texto, Gramática*, etc., Vol. I (Madrid, 1908), pp. 144 ff., argues for *uó*, with the accent on the second element, in both the *Misterio* and the *Poema del Cid*.

Lidforss stressed also the preservation of final *t*, in forms like *pudet* and *vinet*, as indications of the antiquity of our document. But the appearance of this *t* is due to a Latinizing tendency (Paris, l.c., p. 469, note, thinks it simply archaic and therefore indicative of a pronounced final *t* in such cases in O. Sp.), as it is in the *Glosses* : besides, other forms in the *Misterio* show that the -*t* is gone: cf. *fure* < *fuerit*, *trae* < *trahit*, V. L. **tragit*, *tine* < *tenet*, *salue* < *salvet*, etc.

Having disposed of Lidforss's phonological arguments, Hartmann seeks to fix somewhat exactly the date of the *Misterio* by studying the history of the Magi in the Latin dramatic literature of the Middle Ages. Spain does not possess, in so far as the discovered documents are concerned, any early Latin plays of a liturgical nature. France and Germany, however, have examples of the literary tradition concerned. The liturgy being the same in all these lands, and especially in France and Spain, there is every reason to believe that the liturgical dramas, which paraphrase the liturgy, had in Spain a composition not unlike that of French and German pieces. After studying the French liturgical plays or offices, — and the added play of Freisingen, — all of which belong to the 11th and 12th centuries, Hartmann finds that our *Auto* or *Misterio* is closest to the Latin liturgical play written at Orleans (12th century). He deems the Orleans document superior to the earlier pieces of Limoges, Rouen, Nevers, Compiègne, and Freisingen. This last alone has the prologue in which the shepherds figure. The Spanish piece, incomplete as preserved, since it breaks off at the point in which Herod is conferring with his rabbis and sages, shows a great advance over even the Orleans play: motivation, action, dialogue, and characterization are all much better. It is especially by a study of the history of the names given in the Spanish piece to the three kings — Caspar, Melchior, and Baltasar — that Hartmann seeks to arrive at a date for the document, and he thinks that there is reason to believe that these names were not definitively attached to the personages until after the mid-point of the 12th century. His view has been accepted by Morel-Fatio (*Romania* IX. 467), who says: "in order that a text as popular as ours should make an allusion to them, the names had to be universally known and accepted; that takes us perforce to the end of the 12th century." It is a little too much to say that our text is a "popular" one. Besides, Baist has thrown considerable doubt (cf. *Ztschr. f. roman. Philol.* IV. 455) on Hartmann's arguments as to the late acceptance of the names of the Magi. He believes — and he speaks from a knowledge of details — that at an early date, even so far back as 700, the names began to receive diffusion in Western Europe, and, with seeming good reason, he does not see why a twelfth-century writer in Spain should not be acquainted with them. Menéndez Pidal, *Cantar de Mio Cid*, Vol. I (Madrid, 1908), pp. 25 ff., also deems the names much older in the Occident and even quotes them in a document of the end of the 7th century, which, however, has them in a more archaic or distorted form. In fact, Hartmann's arguments are not conclusive against an assignment of the *Misterio* to at least the same period of the 12th century as that in which the *Poema del Cid* (or *Gesta de Myo Cid*) was written, and, as we have said above, Menéndez Pidal is of the opinion that on the basis of linguistic and scribal considerations the *Misterio* MS. is to be placed in the middle of the 12th century.

To the complicated nature of the riming scheme Baist has called attention, pointing out that Latin and other prototypes present the same features. Rime of the rich sort, and not simple assonance, is preferred in the document. Some of the faulty rimes appear due to the scribe.

6 1 We begin with verses of eight syllables. — Instead of **marauila** we need *maravella* (or *maraviella*), whose *e* answers better to the Lat. *ĭ* of *mirabĭlia*, for the rime with *strela* (= *strella*). Confusion with the diminutive ending *-iello(a)* or a contamination of *maravella* and *maravilla* will explain a *maraviella*. The *Loores* of Berceo, stz. 29, shows *maraviella* in rhyme with *estrella* and *ella*; in his *Milagros* we see, stz. 327, *maravella* rhyming with those same words, whereas in stz. 215 we find *marabilla* rhyming with *villa* etc. Of course these texts have not been edited in the most critical fashion in the *Biblioteca de autores españoles*, 57, yet these rimes may all be good and indicative of varying forms of our word. The Aragonese *José* (ed. M. Schmitz in *Roman. Forschungen* XI) has, stz. 31, *maravella* in rime with *ovecha* (i.e. *oveja*, *ovella*), *peleja* (Arag. *pelella*), etc.; in stz. 38 it rimes with *camella, ella*, etc.; in stz. 252, with *bella, aquella*, etc.

6 2 achesta: *ch = k, qu.* — **strela** = *strella*: *l* = palatalized *l* as in l. 34 *falada*, etc. The prosthetic *e* is not needed here after the vocalic ending of *achesta*: it was required at first only after a consonantal ending of the preceding word syntactically related to it; cf. ll. 19, 37, etc., and l. 36.

6 3 Without synalephe of **la e**, the line seems too long. In early Spanish, hiatus in verse was more likely than synalephe, and the latter occurred usually only when the final and initial vowels were the same, as in l. 4 *que es*.

6 6 la: scribal error for *las*: cf. l. 57.

6 7 uerdad: it is curious that, while we have some three cases of this form in the earlier part of the play, in the latter and greater part it is *uertad* that appears, as already in l. 10.

6 8 We may read, for the meter, *ual* and *un*. After *l*, in verbal forms as elsewhere, unaccented *e* could drop.

6 9 nocte: *noch*, used in the *Cid* and elsewhere (cf. Vocab.), will improve the meter; in O. Sp. palatal sounds of the sort are occasionally found in the final position. Of course *noche* had already developed and *nocte* is only etymological in spelling; cf. v. 27.

6 10 bine: *bien*, certainly the pronunciation of the scribe, makes the meter good. So in ll. 11, 38, 50, etc.

6 12 Assonance appears here.

6 13 seer: as in l. 25, so here *seer* seems a monosyllable = *ser*. Perhaps the poets used now the dissyllabic and now the contracted form according to verse exigencies.

6 14 i: it is curious that, while *e < et* is the more usual form of the conjunction " and " in O. Sp., the *Misterio* shows regularly *i = y*, whether the following word begin (or the preceding word end) with a vowel or not. Cf. Vocab. s.v. *et* and *i*. Menéndez Pidal, *Gram. elem.*, 2d ed., p. 241, (and before him Gessner, *Das Altleonesische*) regarded the Leonese *ie* and the occasional Old Castilian *ie* as representing a diphthongization of *ĕt* in a certain quasi-tonic position, as when adjacent to another atonic word (*los cuendes ye los res*, 'the counts and the kings'). He thinks, then, that this *ye* > *y* before a word beginning with *e*. It is very doubtful, however, that *ĕt* ever had a strong enough accent to lead to its diphthongization. Cf. Staaff, l.c., pp. 195 ff.: for him the Leonese form arose in syntactical and not purely phonological conditions: *e* was the original form < *et*; this before a vowel, and especially before the *e* of the article, became the semivowel *y*, e.g. *e ella* > *yella*; then, by erroneous redivision, *ye* (*l*)*la*, a division due to the tendency to generalize *la*, *lo*, etc., which had been developed in various combinations. ✗

6 15 The verse is bad: the omission of *por uer* suggests itself, but *dios* would then have to be a dissyllable, which is unlikely: cf. l. 18 etc. There is neither rime nor assonance in 15–16. *Simply omit Dios.*

6 16 Read *acheste*.

6 17 Menéndez Pidal notes that the MS. puts a mark of division of the verse after *Ala ire*. May we not then read (admitting a verse of 4–5 syllables):

> *Alla iré,*
> *O que fuer, aorallo e.*

For the sequence of three rimes, cf. ll. 102–104. — **aoralo e** = *aorallo* < *aorar* + *lo* (with assimilation of *r* to *l*, whence palatalized *l*) and *e* 'I have'; 'I have to adore him,' i.e. 'I shall (will) adore him.' In early Span. there was still consciousness of the compound nature of the indic. fut. and cond. (infin. of main verb + the pres. indic. and impf. indic., or the endings thereof, of the verb 'to have'), wherefore the parts are regarded as divisible and the object pronoun could appear between them.

7 22 Is **mos** a scribal error for *mios*? Cf. ll. 119, 121, etc. The latter is probably monosyllabic in our document. — **on**: a scribal error for *non*.

7 23 The rime shows that we must read *tiérra*.

7 24 **qui**: perhaps a Latinism for *que*. — For the meter read *paz*; cf. 85. — **guera** = *guerra*; *r* scribal for *rr* as *l* is for *ll*: *ala* for *allá*.

7 25 Synalephe of *a a* and contraction of *seer* > *ser* give a good verse. — **da**: seems Lat. *de* + *ad*; cf. Ital. *da*. It is more probably scribal for *de*.

7 26 For the meter omit *in*.

7 29 May we read *tod* for the first *todo*? Cf. Vocab. s.v. and cf. l. 40.

7 31 Cf. l. 58; both are good seven-syllabled lines. On the basis of 17, 51, and 105, and omitting the not really essential *lo* (cf., however, 17, 58, 59, 62), perhaps we may read in both cases

> *Al*[*l*]*a iré, aoraré.*

✗ *Perhaps our MS has only the sign for "and" and not a real 'i'*

7 33 There is no line to rime with this.

7 38–39 There is neither rime nor assonance here. — Perhaps *que uno* should be omitted: in O. Sp. *omne* had sometimes the value of an indefinite pronoun; cf. Fr. *on* and early Ital. use of *uomo*.

7 40 Perhaps we may read *tod*; cf. l. 29. — The rime with l. 41 is imperfect. Was there a popular *mondo* < Lat. *mŭndum*? As 41 is metrically imperfect, perhaps we may regard 40 and 41 as an interpolation, anticipating the statement as to *senior* in 42.

7 42 But for 49 and 57, we might be tempted to read *de toda gent* (cf. Vocab. s.v.); cf. the parallel singular in 43 *todo seglo*.

7 43 **iugara:** cf. Vocab. s.v. It is a question whether we must interpret this as *judgará*. It is true that the usual O.Sp. result of Lat. *judĭcāre* is *judgar*, but is the loss of the *d* impossible? Cf. *sosegar*, which has been referred to V. L. **subsedĭcāre*, and *trigo* from Lat. *trĭtĭcum*. The mod. *juzgar* probably owes its *z* to the influence of *juez*, O.Sp. *juizio* (*juicio*), etc.

7 44–45 **non** is Menéndez Pidal's resolution of the *ñ* of the MS., which seems to occur elsewhere in it too. — The relation of these two verses to the metrical and rime structure is not clear. Cf. 131–132. Certainly they correspond well enough with the emotions of the characters concerned at these particular stages of the drama.

8 52–53 **strelero:** we have Alexandrines here as in other parts of Scenes II and III. Baist (*Ztschr. f. roman. Philol.* IV. 450) thinks that he reads *estrelero* (= *estrellero*) here: the line calls for that. The facsimile published by Menéndez Pidal shows how bad the MS. is here. — The rime shows **quiro** = *quiéro*.

8 54–55 The MS. seems to show fairly well the two last syllables of *nacida*; may we not write it [*na*]*cida*? L. 54 is Menéndez Pidal's conjecture, and is not unreasonable. Of course the rime requires *marauiela* = *maraviella*. L. 55 is not a good six-syllabled line; *la strela* would make it one. Cf. the note of Menéndez Pidal: "By a cut made by the binder there were destroyed the words which I restore conjecturally. There can be seen only the top of a *d* under the *l* of the *strelero* of the preceding line; something like a small *s* a little more to the right; . . . *cida* under *uertad* is almost certain."

8 60–62 The MS. is in a poor condition as regards parts of these lines. — In 62 the order of *lo* is a common one for the O.Sp. conjunctive object pron.; it is often simply enclitic to the preceding word, as here to *auedes*. Cf. 63 *sil* = *si le*, 72 *quel* = *que le*, where the pron. is enclitic to a conjunction.

8 64 As Baist says (*Ztschr. f. roman. Philol.* IV. 450), we must read *la strela* here.

8 65 The order *prouar podremos* will give a good Alexandrine half-line, with the allowable unaccented syllable after the accented 6th syllable; cf. 89 and 91.

8 67 Read *bien* and *saberemos* for the meter. The latter has been proposed by Lidforss and Morel-Fatio, as well as *ofreceremos* in 68 and *querera* in 69. In the last case we might suggest *el oro él quera.* — In the first half-line of 68 perhaps the conjunction may be omitted between *mira* and *acenso* ; a comma suffices there.

9 70 Read *fur = fuer*; cf. Vocab. s.v. *fust.*

9 73 Perhaps the first half-line should be *Andemos tras la strela* ; cf. 64. — There is no rime for this line; cf. 33.

9 74 **te el** : one syllable ; so *que* and *es* in 78.

9 78 The MS. clearly shows *fallar* here as against the *falar* of 63, *falada* of 34, etc.

9 79–81 These three lines recalled to Hartmann certain verses in the Latin piece of Orleans :

> Quae rerum novitas aut quae vos causa subegit
> Ignotas tentare vias ? quo tenditis ergo ?
> Quod genus ? unde domo ? pacemne huc fertis an arma ?

These Latin verses are obviously from Vergil, *Æneid* VIII. 112–114. Hartmann supposed that the author of the Spanish piece and the author of the Orleans play simply used a common source ; Morel-Fatio (*Romania* IX. 467) deems that the Spaniard drew from the Frenchman. Without impugning Morel-Fatio's contention, we may point out that the verbal resemblances between the Spanish passage and the two Latin passages are not very great. From Cañete (ed. of *Farsas y églogas de Lucas Fernández*, Madrid, 1867) Morel-Fatio derives other testimony to the taking over into Castilian of the Latin plays of France, and especially to the translation from Latin into Castilian, at the end of the 13th century, of the *Office of the Shepherds* and the *Sibyl of Christmas Night*, which belonged to the ritual of the French Benedictines.

9 81 *Nom* would be better than *no m'* ; the *m(e)* is enclitic to *non* : *non + me > nom(e)*. — The second half-line has a syllable in excess.

9 82 Have we a combination of a six-syllabled line with Alexandrines, or is the first half-line of 82 lost ?

9 84–85 Cf. 24–25 for the rime. — *paz* is needed here as in 24.

10 89 Perhaps *ia = ya* may be omitted here and *que* in 91. Ll. 92, 93, 95, 98, 101, all present greater or less difficulty as regards converting them into six-syllabled lines (or rather seven-syllabled lines from the Spanish point of view, since where the ending is feminine the line has that number of syllables).

10 92–93 ma[ra]uila : the MS. has only *mauila* without any indication of a contraction ; hence Menéndez Pidal puts brackets on his emendation. We need *marauiela* to agree with the *strela* of 93, which must be rearranged to *es nacida una strela* (or *la strela*, which will correct the meter). — By omitting *grand*, we make 92 a line of seven (six) syllables.

10 94 Read *faz*. Synalephe is needed in *que es*.

10 95 A ready correction is not clear, unless we omit *carne*.

10 96 Perhaps the particle *i* < Lat. *hīc* 'here' may be omitted.

10 97 percibistis : a Latinism for *percibistes*.

10 98 Tredze is Menéndez Pidal's interpretation of the "XIII" of the MS. — 98 and 101 lack each a syllable ; in 101 *bine* is for *bien* ; in 100 there is synalephe in *la auemos*.

10 101 percebida : in O. Sp. the p. p. conjugated in the perfect tenses with *aver* (*haber*) might agree with the direct object. The agreement seems to have been optional ; in a sporadic way it continued down into the Golden Age, when it must have smacked of the archaic.

10 105 Read *i io ala ire*, and put a comma after *tornad* in 104.

11 109–110 Menéndez Pidal (*Cantar del Mio Cid, Gramática*, pp. 144–145) thinks that in the *Misterio* the stage *ue* of the diphthong from Lat. *ǒ* had not yet been reached, and would read here *muorto* and *puosto* instead of *muerto, puesto*. The theory has not much evidence back of it for the *Misterio*. He has developed it chiefly in connection with the *Cid* and its assonances. It is clear that we have only assonance in 109–110, as also in 121–122, 125–126, 127–128, 134, 136–137.

11 113 caga : scribal for *çaga*. The scribe does not use *ç* before *e* and *i*, as is so commonly done in many other O. Sp. documents, and has omitted the cedilla in the only case of *ça-* in the *Misterio*.

11 115 no lo : the MS. seems to have *nolo*, which is the better reading for this early period ; the redivision, which produced *no*, is perhaps somewhat later, and *non* is the regular O. Sp. form in the independent use. Cf. 137.

11 116 ueo: observe the indicative after *ata que* referring to the future.

11 117 mio : the scribe here uses *mio, mios* (both monosyllabic) before masc. nouns, and *mi, mis* (120, 142) before fem. nouns ; cf. Vocab. *Meos*, 122, is a Latinism for *mios*.

11 118   **qui**: does this represent *el que*, or is it a Latinism?

11 121–124   Read *escriuanos* and *estreleros*. There is a syllable lacking in 122, 124. In 123–124 we have neither rime nor assonance. Baist (*Ztschr. f. roman. Philol.* IV. 450) seems to think that 121–124 should be read as two Alexandrines; in which case, as he says, *gramatgos*, an " einfacher Schreibfehler," rimes with *retoricos*. For what does he deem *gramatgos* erroneously written here?

11 127   Read *Rei, que te plaz ?* etc. — **he**: here is one of the earliest examples of the use of the word still found in *hé aquí* etc., in which it appears with imperative or interjectional force. O. Sp. shows also the forms *afe* and *fe*, as well as *e, ahe, ae*. Dealing with *afe* and *fe* as existing in the *Cid*, I have proposed (in *Modern Philology* I. 49 ff., following clues given by Diez, Cuervo, Bello, etc.) that we see in these forms with *f* the primitive forms of the word, that we regard *afe(vos)* as a possible starting-point, and that it may be regarded as *habete + vos >* *avedvos >*, by assimilation of the *d, avevos >*, by dissimilation of the first *v*, under the possible influence of the interjectional *á fé* 'on my faith,' *afevos*. Under the influence of *á fé*, it was possible for the *afe* of *afevos* to be divided into *a + fe*, whence a new interjectional and demonstrative *fe*. In all this there is much assumption and mere suggestion, and Pietsch (*Modern Philology* II. 197 ff.) properly challenged many of my remarks, which were intended, however, only to raise the whole question. The semasiology of the case is clear enough : ' have ye here,' ' behold.' The assimilation of the *d* to the *v* following, Pietsch believes unlikely, as there are no similar cases of *dv > v* (I have referred to other possible cases of *dl > ll*, and there are also *septĭmāna > *setmana > O. Sp. sedmana >* mod. *semana*, and *advocatum > abogado*). It is true that the *dv* generally occurred only in combinations in which the *v* was first lost and then later the *d* : *amadvos > amados > amaos* (although the *v* may have gone first in other combinations, e.g., *dígovos, ámovos*), but the *vos* there was an atonic object pronoun. In *habete vos* it is the vocative (if not nominative or ethical dative). Could not the *v* of this latter maintain itself and could there not have occurred the more usual process of assimilation, that of the first consonant to the second ? Baist (in Vollmöller's *Kritischer Jahresbericht* VIII. i. 211) thinks the dissimilation of *v* to *f* in **avevos* " a strange one." Perhaps it is unparalleled, for *v–v* like *b–b*, where dissimilation has occurred, might be expected to result in the total loss of one of the *v*'s ; but the possible influence of the interjectional *á fé* must not be overlooked. However, all that I have said lacks absolute proof, as does also the derivation from the imperative of *vīdēre,* already suggested by Diez. Pietsch argues for the priority of our *he,* occurring here in the *Misterio* and listed by him for other early documents. This would represent an imperative sing. of *habere,* viz. *habe,* or rather V. L. **hae* (contracted even as *habes, habet,* were to **has, *hat*), whence *(h)e,* with meaningless *h,* which also was often not written in O. Sp. Ere long this assumed interjectional demonstrative use, and then, its true verbal origin being forgotten, its association with a plural *vos* was not impossible. O. Sp. *ahe, ae* he deems to have the same relation to *(h)e* that *ahí* has to O. Sp. *(h)i* (the *y* of *hay*). It remains for Pietsch to dispose of the *Cid* forms with *f.* Here, regarding the *fe* as the important form, he declares that all the *Cid* forms (between 20 and 30 cases) are dialectal, i.e. are Asturian. Asturian has retained original Lat. initial *f,* and occasionally seems to change, he says, forms having initial Lat. *h* to forms with *f.* Now, as Vulgar Latin *h* meant nothing, this seems to mean a change of nothing to *f.* This part of Pietsch's argument is not supported. Menéndez Pidal in his study of modern Leonese-Asturian seems to find no cases of *f-* for Lat. *h-* words; cf. *El Dialecto Leonés,* p. 29. In seeking to find Asturian dialect forms in the *Cid,* Pietsch is ranging himself on the side of Cornu, who has argued therefor on the basis of fuller article-forms and certain assonances found in the *Cid.* But Menéndez Pidal (*Gramática del Cid,* p. 36 et passim) controverts Cornu's arguments, and there seems to be no basis for the supposition that the *Cid* is Asturian. For the *Cid* I am still of the opinion that *afevos* is the original form, since it serves to correct verses into the *romance* type, as I believe with Cornu (*Études romanes dédiées à G. Paris; Romania* XXII. 153; *Ztschr. f. roman. Philol.* XXI. 461) that the *Cid* was originally composed in *romances* (8 or 7 syllables + 8 or 7 syllables, i.e. in two half-lines) : see per contra Menéndez Pidal, *Gramática del Cid* pp. 80 ff.

After all is said and done, the origin of *he, fe,* etc. remains in doubt. Menéndez Pidal, in a recension of the article in *Modern Philology* I, states his belief in an Arabic origin, but has not cited any Arabic form. As in line with this early appearance in the *Misterio* of *he* as a form in *h-* resulting from a form *fe* with *f-,* we may cite the *prohio* (*pro-* + a simplex having initial *h-*) of l. 12, the *hata* of l. 26 beside the *ata* of l. 116, all of which suppose an original initial *f-* which aspirated, or an Arabic initial strong aspiration which O. Sp. generally denoted by *f-.* Pietsch knows these forms, but is disposed to disregard them. Cf. further Menéndez Pidal. *Gramática del Cid,* pp. 173 ff. and 686

12 129–135 We seem to have lines of different lengths riming or assonating together.

12 134 Read *estos*. — **rees** : represents the proper development of Lat. *rēges*, whose *g* should drop ; cf. Vocab. s.v.

12 136 **uo** : This is for *uos = vos* ; cf. Vocab. s.v. *uo*.

12 137 Read *scripto* after the word ending in a vowel ; *fallo* is a conjecture of Menéndez Pidal ; the scribe ran *escripto* on after *nolo*.

12 138–147 G. Paris proposed (*Romania* IX. 469, note 2) the present distribution of these lines, which Lidforss had arranged otherwise.

12 138 **Hamihala** : this word, apparently interjectional in force, has not yet been explained satisfactorily. Morel-Fatio (*Romania* IX. 469) would connect it with the preceding speech as Lidforss did. He interprets then : " In truth I tell you, my Allah (God) has not written it," and then says : " It matters little that a rabbi is speaking, and the presence of the initial *h* is of no importance." Of course he has not Menéndez Pidal's conjectural *fallo*. But, as the latter points out, the MS. has the usual mark denoting the end of a verse after *escripto*. The enjambment is not likely. G. Paris, l.c., also objects to Morel-Fatio's interpretation : does not think that the combination *mi Ala* has ever been found, or that any one would ever think of having a rabbi invoke Allah. He agrees with Hartmann in finding the verse a mangled one. May we possibly read *Ha Mihala!* ' Ah, Michael! ' (or whatever *Mihala* represents), assuming that we have here the name of the rabbi addressed ?

12 146 Synalephe in *la auemos*.

12 147 The verse seems to have a syllable too many.

IV. LA GESTA DE MYO ÇID EL DE BIUAR

The title which we use is derived from l. 1085, which clearly marks the beginning of a new division of the poem. No less appropriate would be the term *Cantares de Myo Çid*, for the designation *Cantar* is used in l. 2276, which indicates the close of another division of it. The name most employed is *Poema del Cid*. For brevity's sake " the *Cid* " may suffice as a reference.

As for certain other O. Sp. documents, so for the *Cid* there is extant but a single MS., which is now in the possession of the family of the Marqués de Pidal. It is said to have been sent across the Atlantic at one time, in order that Ticknor, the historian of Spanish literature, might examine it. The MS. is in a handwriting of the 14th century. Near the end of it (ll. 3732–3733) it is stated : " *Per abbat le escriuio*

enel mes de mayo, En era de mill. ꝫ. CC. XL.V. años." Per Abbat is generally considered to have been the scribe to whom we owe the MS.;
the date 1245 of the era corresponds to 1207 of our calendar, but in
the vacant space between the second *C* and the *X* it is deemed probable that another *C* has been erased, and that the real date of the completion of the MS. is 1307. It belongs, therefore, to the early 14th
century. The first printed edition of it is that prepared by T. Sánchez
for his *Colección de poesías castellanas anteriores al siglo XV,* Vol. I
(Madrid, 1779). The most important reprint of this is that of Janer in
Vol. LVII of the *Biblioteca de Autores Españoles* (Madrid, 1864). Based
directly upon the MS. was the edition of K. Vollmöller (Halle, 1879).
This has given way to the best edition now accessible, that of R. Menéndez Pidal (Madrid, 1900). To this same scholar we owe, as a companion volume to his edition of the text, a very valuable *Gramática*
dealing with it (Madrid, 1908), in which will be found a wealth of information regarding all things appertaining to the poem. A *Vocabulario*
is to follow. A splendid *édition de luxe,* with an English translation
and much apparatus criticus, is that of A. M. Huntington (New York,
1897–1903). Resort to the MS. was apparently also had by Damas-
Hinard for his edition (Paris, 1858), accompanied by a juxtalinear
French translation and a large amount of annotation of a lexical and
geographical nature, etc. The South American savant A. Bello, who
died in 1865, prepared a text (modified to suit his views): this, with a
Glosario, notes, etc., appeared in Vol. II of his *Obras Completas* (Santiago de Chile, 1881). To the Swedish student of Spanish philology,
E. Lidforss, we are indebted for an edition with an introduction and
notes, including a discussion of the prosody of the document (Lund,
1895). Extracts from the poem have been given by Keller (in his *Altspanisches Lesebuch*), by E. Gorra (*Lingua e letteratura spagnuola delle
origini,* Milan, 1898, pp. 187 ff.; with a good bibliographical note), by
A. Restori (*Le Gesta del Cid,* Milan, 1890; contains extracts also from
other documents dealing with the story of the Cid), by A. Zauner (in
his *Altspanisches Elementarbuch,* Heidelberg, 1908, pp. 136 ff.; his text
follows that of Menéndez Pidal), etc.

Into the literature dealing *in extenso* or only partially with the *Cid*
we may not enter here. An excellent statement of the essentials is
given by G. Baist in his *Spanische Literaturgeschichte* (Gröber's *Grundriss* II. ii. 395 ff.); a full and clear exposition is that of Menéndez
Pidal in his precious *Gramática* of the Cid, already mentioned. For a
very useful bibliography, with entries coming down to a recent period,

cf. J. Fitzmaurice-Kelly's *Littérature espagnole* (Paris, 1904, pp. 452–453). There references are given to the publications of Wolf, Cornu, Dozy, Koerbs, Restori, Milá y Fontanals, Beer, Hinojosa, and others.

As preserved, the MS. is in a deplorable state, especially as regards the versification of the poem. There are also some lacunæ, for the first page of the MS. is missing and within it two other pages are wanting. The losses consist then of some verses preceding l. 1 of Menéndez Pidal's edition, and some more following l. 2337 and l. 3507. In extent they are not great, and the substance of them can be supplied from other documents, especially from the O. Sp. Chronicles that treat of the *Cid*. In the course of time various copyists have altered the original readings here and there in the MS., but by the use of reagents Menéndez Pidal has usually been able to decipher the words of the scribe Per Abbat.

In the opinion of Baist and Menéndez Pidal the MS. is not the first in which the poem was set down; it is clearly a copy, as certain errors (e.g. *lapsus calami*) show, of a preceding MS.; and the theory of Cornu (cf. his articles in *Études romanes dédiées à Gaston Paris*, Paris, 1891, and in *Symbolae Pragenses*) that the extant MS. represents something written down from memory is untenable. Several copies doubtless intervened between our MS. and the original composition of the poem. This is generally put at about 1140 — or half a century after the death of the hero — on the basis of general linguistic conditions, which seem to indicate the 12th century, and in consonance with certain fairly definite references in the body of the poem and in other works not much later than it.

To the fact that the versification of the *Cid* is in a sorry state we have already adverted. It is very obviously in assonance, as is the case with so many of the Old French epic poems; but the lines — and there are somewhat more than 3700 of them — vary greatly in length at times, some being very short and others very long. This has led some persons — and Menéndez Pidal is now of their number — to think that the poet was a rimester who had no idea of metrical regularity. In reply to this it may be said (cf. *Modern Language Notes* XXIV. 86) that the poet of the *Cid* — and there is a unity of composition in the work which implies a single poet for the form represented by our MS. — shows himself otherwise too good an artist to be so ignorant of metrical principles, and that there is no reason to suppose the work a primitive one in the evolution of the Spanish epic tradition or of Spanish poetry. Already, dealing with the *Misterio*, we have made reference to the theory, to which Cornu has given its greatest development (cf. *Études romanes dédiées à Gaston Paris*, Paris, 1891, pp. 491 ff.; *Romania* XXII. 531 ff.; *Ztschr. f. roman. Philol.* XXI. 461 ff.; *Symbolae Pragenses*, Vienna, 1893, pp. 17 ff.), that the meter of the *Cid* is the same as that of the ballads, the *romance* line, which in the ballads appears as a line of 8 syllables with the stress on the 7th (and with only 7 syllables if the line end with the accented syllable). Each ballad line is really only half of an original long line of 16 (14) syllables, and the long lines all assonated together, while the shorter ballad lines assonate only for the second, fourth, sixth, etc., i.e. only for the second half of the former long line. Now, we have preserved, in a 13th-century form, another long epic on the *Cid*, the *Rodrigo* or *Crónica rimada del Cid* (cf. Baist, *Grundriss* II. ii. 398 ff.), and we have discernible still in verse form some parts of an epic poem on the Infantes de Lara (cf. Menéndez Pidal, *Leyenda de los Infantes de Lara*, Madrid, 1896), in both of which the principle of the long line of 8 (7) + 8 (7) syllables prevails. It is this long line that Cornu would regard as the proper verse of the *Cid*. Upon examination he has found that many lines and half-lines are already true to this type: 8 (7) + 8 (7) or simply 8 (7). By means of corrections based on internal criticism he can restore many more of the same type. On the whole his theory has been regarded as acceptable by many scholars, while others, e.g. Restori (in *Propugnatore* XX), Lidforss, etc., think that the original meter was the Alexandrine. It is true that there are many good Alexandrines in the poem, but the difficulties of the situation are me. if we say that a redactor, taking a poem written originally in the long 8 (7) + 8 (7) lines, made it over in the 13th and 14th centuries — the time when the Alexandrine was used so largely in the didactic and religious verse of Castile and for epic purposes in the *Fernán González* — into Alexandrines as well as he could. He had but poor success. Some of the lines and half-lines he had to leave as they were; others he distorted without making Alexandrines out of them; in some other cases — and these are not the majority — he produced good Alexandrines. Baist (*Grundriss* l.c.) believes in Cornu's theory and thinks that the 8 (7) + 8 (7) type was evolved out of the French Alexandrine. Paris (*Journal des Savants*, 1898) believes it of antiquity in Spain: he says, "the verse of 14 (16) syllables, **which continues the trochaic tetrameter of popular Latin,** had doubtless maintained itself in Spain, and there was adapted to this national measure the French system of *laisses* made up of long verses having the same assonance"

It is an attractive theory that the measure of the popular Latin trochaic tetrameter, found in soldiers' songs during the classic period, was the basis of what even Menéndez Pidal (*Gramática del Cid*, p. 101) admits as probably a popular form in ancient Spain.

Not only have we these longish lines in the *Cid*, but we have them arranged in irregular stanzas, such as in the French epic (*chansons de geste*) are called *laisses* or *tirades*. The stanzas may embrace but a few lines, they may comprise a hundred or more. The lines of each stanza (*laisse, tirade*) are bound together by assonance, i.e. by vocalic rime, independently of consonantal agreement, as a glance at our extracts will show. The assonances are in a fairly good condition, wherefore Menéndez Pidal (l.c., p. 103) has argued that assonance was developed earlier in Spain than the metrical principle; for this, however, there is no proof. A study of the assonances and of the theories based on them has been made by several scholars; cf. those cited by Menéndez Pidal, and also by A. Coester (in *Revue hispanique* XV). Baist and Menéndez Pidal have opposed the theory based in part upon certain assonances in *o*, *ue*, that our poem was written in Asturian. Menéndez Pidal, following a theory already put forth by Fitzmaurice-Kelly (*Littérature espagnole*, p. 48), has tried to fix the region to which the poet belonged, and finds that he is acquainted at first hand — as his itineraries and descriptions of places show — only with the region between Medinaceli and San Esteban de Gormaz, i.e. in Castilian territory not far from Aragon. This region was under Aragonese dominion for part of the 12th century, yet our poem displays no Aragonisms; it is in Castilian. Cf. Coester, l.c., for a theory that the poem as preserved represents a reduced form of the original document. On the other hand, Menéndez Pidal (*Gramática del Cid*) thinks that the poem is substantially the original epic.

Paris, in the passage quoted above, says that to the national measure there was adapted the French system of *laisses*. This means that he regards the Spanish epic, as we know it, as one modeled on the French epic (*chansons de geste*). This may certainly hold true for the *Cid* and other Spanish epics, especially for that of Bernardo del Carpio, which, as Milá y Fontanals has made clear (in his *Poesía Heroico-popular Castellana*, Barcelona, 1896) is, in so far as the hero is concerned, a transformation of the *Chanson de Roland*, or rather of the latter's hero. There are elements of the *Cid* that recall others of the *Roland*; cf. especially the part played by the militant bishop Gerónimo in the *Cid* with that of Turpin in the *Roland*. The pilgrims from France who were constantly visiting Santiago de Compostella in the peninsula, and the knights who, from the 11th century on, came into Spain to aid the Spaniards in reconquering the land from the Arabs, brought with them their epic poems and their minstrels, and from them the Spaniards could gain an early knowledge of the French epic; cf. the *Légendes épiques* of J. Bédier (Paris, 1908 ff.) on the importance, for epic genesis, of these wanderings of pilgrims and soldiers. Of course this theory, holding good, as it doubtless does, for a good part of the extant Spanish epic matter, should not preclude the possibility of a purely native epic, exemplified possibly in the Fernán González story and even in that of Roderick the Goth. There is much uncertainty, however, in this regard. What is certain is, that any theory according to which the Spanish epic grew out of antecedent epico-lyric ballads (a theory exploited with debatable success for the Greek and the German epic traditions) is hardly true. The oldest epic ballads preserved in Spanish are later than the epic period, and seem to derive from the epics or from the Chronicles dealing with the epic heroes.

In so far as its contents go, our poem on the Cid deals with his banishment from Castile, where he was the most powerful baron, by his over-lord Alfonso VI, the King of Leon and Castile. He had offended that monarch and was therefore driven forth. He betook himself to the territory occupied by the Moors, and there, joined by many free lances who came from Castile to help him, he was able to take many Moorish strongholds, and finally to establish himself in Valencia as a virtually independent ruler. Then, after a reconciliation between himself and King Alfonso, there were arranged by the latter the marriages of the Cid's two daughters with the Aragonese Infantes de Carrión. These proved to be cruel husbands as well as poltroons, and, because of the gross insults which they inflicted upon his family honor, the Cid sought vengeance from the monarch. The Infantes were compelled to fight in the lists against the Cid's champions, and were ignominiously overcome. The poem closes with an announcement of the coming second marriages of the Cid's daughters, really historical marriages as opposed to the former fictitious ones, for now the poem deals with the union of the ladies in question with the heirs to the kingdoms of Navarre and Aragon. As a result of these second marriages, the royal house of Spain is of the Cid's kindred. So the poem states, l. 3724:

Oy los rreyes d'España sos parientes son.

With the element of history in the *Cid* — and it is no slight one —
there has been blended much that is pure poetic fiction. This is due
to the poet's tendency, as a good Castilian, to laud the virtues and
prowess of a great Castilian noble, who represented Castilian aspira-
tions and efforts at a time when Castile was still subject to the overlordship of the hated Leon, as was the case under Alfonso VI. On
the various documents treating of the historical Cid see Baist, *Grundriss* II. ii. 395 ff. First mentioned in 1064, he was a doughty warrior
under Sancho II of Castile and helped the latter to dispossess his
brother — later his successor — Alfonso, whence the latter's hatred of
the Cid, which was intensified when the Cid, at the head of a body of
nobles, compelled Alfonso to swear that he had no part in the murder
of Sancho before the walls of Zamora in 1072. Although married to
the king's cousin Ximena (the Chimène of Corneille's *Cid*), the Cid
was banished by Alfonso in 1081. Then he spent some time, with a
following of free lances, in serving this or that Moorish princeling
against an enemy, and even fought against a Christian antagonist in
the person of the Count of Barcelona, until finally in 1094 he took
Valencia from the Moors. He died in 1099. According to Baist
(*Grundriss*, l.c., p. 396), "the first half of the poem, from the banishment to the taking of Valencia, is rather a piece of biography carried
through in epic fashion; it became an epic through the addition of a
wholly fictitious tradition, the marriage of the Cid's daughters to the
Infantes of Carrion." In the opinion of Menéndez Pidal (l.c.) the
author of this poem was a mere minstrel with little knowledge of
the leading historical facts of the Cid's life, and interested chiefly in
keeping alive a certain local legend relating to his daughters. With this
view it is perhaps unwise to agree fully, yet the marriages are certainly
very important for the poet. For objections to the view cf. *Modern
Language Notes* XXIV. 83 ff. See also the interesting chapter *Le Poème
de mon Cid*, in Menéndez Pidal's *Epopée castillane*, Paris, 1910.

As has been stated above, the first page of the MS. is missing. It
described the preliminaries of the Cid's departure into exile from his
native place Bivar. In our opening line he is departing from Bivar and
looking back regretfully at it.

The first laisse extends from l. 1 to l. 9. Its assonance is *á–o*.

13 1 **Delos**: the modern division of words developed syntactically,
as for Lat. *de + íllos > de ellos > dellos > de (l)los*, is not regularly observed in the *Cid* or in O. Sp. generally. Moreover, the scribe often
divides words erroneously here, and again he erroneously runs them

together. — **sos** : the poss. adj. is here combined with the definite art., as often in O. Sp. — **oios** : the $i = j$. In O. Sp. script i stands for i, j, or y. — The second half-line, **tan . . . lorando**, is of the ballad type, 8 (7) syllables, and so is the second half of l. 2. According to Cornu's very reasonable theory, the second half-lines, containing as they do the assonating words, and therefore commending themselves to the memory of scribes and all others, are likely to preserve their integrity better than the first half-lines.

13 2 cabeça : cf. Vocab. s.v. In O. Sp. ç denoted a voiceless dental sibilant sound $= ts$, while z denoted properly in the intervocalic position a voiced dental sibilant $= dz$, as in *uazias*, l. 4. Before a consonant and at the end of a word $z = ç$ in value. Cf. Ford, *The Old Spanish Sibilants* (in *Studies and Notes in Philol.*, Boston, 1900). — **los** = the *palaçios* of the Cid, which he was leaving.

13 6 The Arabic title *Cid* = 'Lord' would seem to indicate the respect in which the Moors held the hero. — **mucho** : this is practically an instrumental use of the adverb. Cf. F. Hanssen, *De los adverbios mucho, mui i much* (in *Anales de la Universidad de Chile*, 1905, p. 30) : "The adverb which modifies the verb has invariably the form *mucho*. Everywhere there is said *mucho amaba*. . . . When the adverb is separated from the adjective, participle, or adverb which it modifies, *mucho* is used : *ca mucho auie grandes cuydados* (*Cid*). . . . This construction is much used in the *Poema del Cid*; in the other documents [i.e. of O. Sp.] examples are not lacking, but they are exceptional." Cf. the same scholar's *Dos problemas de sintaxis* (in the *Anales*, 1907). Of course Lat. *mŭltum* is here developed in an emphatic and not in an atonic proclitic position : hence it should have its full form *mucho* as distinguished from *mui* (*muy*), which properly can stand only before adjectives, passive participles, and adverbs.

13 9 buelto : on the use of b and v in O. Sp. cf. Cuervo (*Revue hispanique* II, and in the Notes to his edition of Bello's *Gramática*). The scribes often wrote b for either initial b or initial v of Latin origin; in the intervocalic position they preferred u ($= v$) or v for the Sp. results of both Lat. b and v; cf. *beuir, bevir*, < Lat. *vīvere*, V. L. **vīvīre*.

13 10 From here through l. 14 the assonance is in *ié–a*. This particular laisse has no *é–a*. — **pienssan** = *piensan*. After n and l (cf. *falssar*) the s is often written double in O. Sp. The reason thereof is not clear. Were the l and s pronounced far enough forward in the mouth, i.e. with so marked a dental quality, as to convert a following s into a sound almost that of ts (written ç in O. Sp.), and did the scribe

protest against such a change of the *s* by writing *ss* which meant a
clear voiceless *s*? — **aguiiar** = *aguijar*; cf. Vocab. The *i* after the *u*
has not been explained yet, any more than the diphthong *ui* of French
aiguille. Cf. Cornu in the *Grundriss*, I, 2d ed., p. 934, note 3. —
Riendas : the scribes often denoted the reënforced (double) *r* sound by
writing a capital in the initial position. Sometimes they wrote *rr* initially
as well as in the intervocalic position or after certain consonants.

13 11   Biuar : Bivar, the Cid's native place and fief, was not far from
Burgos. — **corneia** = *corneja*. The Cid seems to have lent much credence
to augury. His enemy, the Count of Barcelona, is said, in the *Crónica
General*, to have written a letter taxing him with this superstition.
References to augury occur in the poem also in ll. 859, 1523, 2366,
2369, 2615. Menéndez Pidal (*Leyenda de los Infantes de Lara*, p. 8,
note) gives information and references as to the widespread belief in
augury in Spain and southern France. See likewise Restori (*Gesta del
Cid*, p. 28).

13 12   la : this is the pers. pron. obj., enclitic to *ouieron*.

13 14   Albriçia : the Arabic etymon generally cited for this word
(cf. Vocab.) is not satisfactory. Baist (*Roman. Forschungen* IV. 408)
doubts it. Cf. Ford, *The Old Spanish Sibilants* (Boston, 1900), p. 64. —
Albarffanez : Álvar Fánez (or Fáñez ?) was a doughty warrior of the
Cid's time, and survived him by some fifteen years. In the poem, the
Cid calls him his " right arm " (l. 753 etc.), and he really figures as
the chief lieutenant of the hero. So also in a Latin poem on the taking
of the town of Almería from the Moors in 1147 — the Latin poem was
probably written shortly after the event — he is celebrated as only
second in importance as a fighter to the Cid. Historically it does not
seem certain that Álvar Fánez was closely associated with the Cid.

The Latin poem just mentioned is interesting in that, written about
the middle of the 12th century, it states that the deeds of the Cid were
already in song, and the presumption is that the *Poema del Cid* is meant.
It says (ll. 220 ff.) :

> Ipse Rodericus, Mio Cid saepe vocatus,
> De quo *cantatur* quod ab hostibus haud superatur,
> Qui domuit Mauros, domuit comites quoque nostros,
> Hunc [i.e. A.F.] extollebat, se laude minore ferebat.
> Sed fateor verum, quod tollet nulla dierum,
> Meo Cidi primus fuit, Alvarus atque secundus.

And this Roderick, often called " my Cid " (my lord), about whom it is *sung*
that by his enemies he was in no way overcome, who conquered the Moors, and

also conquered our Counts [it is an Aragonese poet who speaks, and he means the Count of Barcelona, twice defeated by the Cid, according to traditional accounts], extolled him [Álvar Fánez], and termed himself less praiseworthy. But I acknowledge the truth, which no course of time shall obliterate, Meo Cidi was first and Álvar second.

It was apropos of a descendant of Álvar Fánez, who played a part in the taking of Almería, that the Aragonese poet felt prompted to write the verses cited.

The doubling of *f* in *Albarffanez* may seem strange. Fánez must have been clearly the patronymic here, and therefore the *ff* is initial. Did the doubling of the *f* indicate a desire to retain the real *f* sound, as against the ordinary *popular* process of changing initial Latin *f* to *h-* (originally an aspiration and now nothing)? The doubling may have conveyed the sense of reënforcement. Ordinarily the *Cid* has *Albarfanez*. On Spanish names cf. J. Jungfer, *Über Personennamen in der Ortsnamen Spaniens*, etc., Berlin, 1902, and W. Meyer-Lübke, *Romanische Namenstudien*, Vienna, 1904 (in *Sitzungsberichte der Akademie der Wissenschaften*, Vol. CXLIX). For the patronymic ending *-ez, -az*, as a Latin genitive, see Jungfer, p. 15.

13 15 en traua : scribal for *entraua* = mod. *entraba.* — There seems to be no assonance for *en traua*, but l. 16 is really two lines written as one, and should end with *leuaua*. The rest forms a new line, which we may call 16 *a*. The laisse *á–a* is then limited to two lines only. The chances are that the original poem had other verses in this same *laisse* : a system of compression has eliminated them ; cf. Coester, l.c. Does the *uarones* of 16 *a* make a good assonance with *ó* of ll. 17–20? Menéndez Pidal (*Gramática del Cid*, p. 116) thinks that the poet assonated *ó–e* with *ó* and *á–e* with *á*. It is to be remarked that the sense, the meter, and the assonance of 16 *a* are satisfied with *la mugier e el uaron* instead of *mugieres z uarones*.

13 16 pendones : the streamers on the lances of the knights ; poetically the knights themselves.

13 17 son : *ser* and *estar* were not kept apart, with respect to the idea of place, in O. Sp. ; cf. Ford, *Sedere, *Essere and Stare in the Poema del Cid* (in *Modern Language Notes* XIV).

13 18 auyen = *avien* = *avían* = mod. *habían.* As in l. 6 *auie*, 16 *exien*, we see here, and in many cases in the poem, the impf. ending *-ía, -ían* changed to *-ie, -ien*. The weakening of the ending *-ia, -ian* seems to be a current O. Sp. phenomenon. Various articles and remarks have been written on it by Hanssen, *Sobre la formación del imperfecto*, etc. (Santiago de Chile, 1894), *Sobre la pronunciación del diptongo* ie, etc. (ibid., 1895), *Das Possessiv-Pronomen in den altspanischen Dialekten* (Valparaiso, 1897); by Gassner, *Das altspanische Verbum* (Halle, 1897); by Baist (in *Kritischer Jahresbericht der roman. Philol.* IV. i. 307); by Pietsch, *Preliminary Notes on Two Old Spanish Versions of the Disticha Catonis* (Chicago, 1902); by Zauner (in *Literaturblatt f. germ. u. rom. Philol.* XIX and XX); by Porębowicz, *Revision de la loi des voyelles finales en espagnol* (Paris, 1897); and by Fitz-Gerald, *Versification of the Cuaderna Via* (New York, 1905, pp. 68 ff.). Cf. also Menéndez Pidal, *Gram. elem.* (2d ed., pp. 212 ff.). Fitz-Gerald sums up the findings of all the investigators: cf. l.c., p. 84: "Hanssen, Gassner and Pietsch prove that there was an O. Sp. paradigm *-ía, -iés, -ié, -iémos, -iédes, -ién* [i.e. *a* weakened to *e* in all forms but the 1st sg., and the accent shifted to the *e* in those forms]. Zauner proves, in agreement with Baist, that there was an O. Sp. paradigm *-ía, -íes*, $\left\{ \begin{matrix} -ie \\ -ía \end{matrix} \right.$, *-íemos, -íedes, -íen* [i.e. with *e* in all but the 1st sg. and with the accent retained on the *i*, as in mod. Sp.]. Hanssen and Pietsch admit as a doublet to their 3d *-ié* a form *-ía*. Porębowicz calls attention to the fact that there is much evidence in favor of the forms *-ías, -íes, -íamos, -íemos, -ían, -íen*." Fitz-Gerald finds also an *-ie* for the 1st sg. In spite of all that has been written upon the matter, it cannot be said that all the evidence has been examined; and, besides, corrupt or badly edited texts have been given undue weight among the material used. The change of *-ía* to *-ie* in all the forms seems clear (although not so frequent for the 1st sg.), and the forms with *a* maintained themselves beside those with *e*. There seems to be evidence in favor of the shift of accent to the *e*, especially in the forms in which a consonant followed the *e* (cf. Fitz-Gerald, p. 87, *sabiémos* rhyming with *auémos*, and *podriédes*, a conditional with impf. ending, rhyming with *temédes*). That the consonant determined the *-ia > -ié* seems phonologically unlikely in the cases concerned, in spite of what Hanssen and Zauner say. Granting the endings *-iémos, -iédes*, etc., may we not rather opine that the analogy of other past tenses occasioned the change? The pret. indic. in O. Sp. showed in the 2d and 3d conjugations not only the regular *-imos, -istes* endings, but also *-iémos* (cf. *Cid*, 1116 *partiémos*, 1117 *pudiémos*) and *-iéstes* (*Cid*, 3260 *descubriéstes*, 3265 *firiéstes*): these latter endings reflect the analogy of the 3d pl. *-iéron* and also of the impf. subj. forms in *-iésse* etc. The combined influence of *-iémos, -iéstes, -iéron, -iésse* (and in the 1st and 3d sg. it seems that *-iésse* could become *-iés*, cf. *toviés* of Marden's *Fernán*

González, so that we have an impf. indic. form ending in *-iés* like the impf. indic. 2d sg.), etc., provides a possible factor in the change of the impf. indic. endings which we should not ignore. The phonological change of *a > e* in Castilian is not very likely unless a palatal follow the vowel. In dialectal mod. Sp. *-ie, -ies*, etc. may still be heard in certain localities and *-ié, -iés*, etc. in others, all as impf. indic. endings; cf. Menéndez Pidal, *Gram. elem.* (2d ed., p. 214). Through the analogy of *-ia, -ias*, etc. the O. Sp. *-ié, -iés*, etc. might become *-ie, -ies*.

13 19 **dizian**: the first *i* corresponds properly to the *ī* of Lat. *dīcere*, V. L. **dīcīre*. It is dissimilation from the accented *i* following that explains O. Sp. *dezían*, mod. *decían*, just as it does *dezir* and other forms.

13 20 **si . . . Señor**: an optative use: 'Oh, if he only had a good lord!' 'Would that he had,' etc.

13 78 ff. Here comes the trick played upon the Hebrew bankers of Burgos, while the Cid is encamped not far from that city. The incident is narrated with great zest, a zest which is easily understood when we remember the traditional Spanish hatred of the Jews, who really seem to have been allies of the Arabs in the subjugation of Spain. But the poet, it is to be observed, does not let our hero appear here as a barefaced swindler. The Cid says (cf. ll. 84 and 95) that he does the deed against his will and because just now he has no other way of raising the money needed to pay his men and obtain provisions. The 13th-century *Crónica general* of Alfonso X — which records both historical fact about the Cid and also the contents of the songs about him — makes him say (ed. Menéndez Pidal, p. 524): *sabe Dios que esto que lo fago yo amidos; mas si Dios me diere conseio, yo gelo emendare et gelo pechare todo* ('God knows that I do this in spite of myself; but if God gives me counsel — i.e. shows me how — I will make amends for it and pay it all back to them'). In the ballads (15th–16th centuries) the moral speculation and the safeguarding of the Cid's character are carried further. Later in the *Cid* (ll. 1431 ff.), where the hero sends back money to Castile for certain purposes by Álvar Fáñez, the Jews come to the latter and beg for payment, and he, apparently not having the wherewithal to pay them, promises to "see about it" when he returns to the Cid.

13 78–87 Assonance in *á–a*, broken in l. 82. But the first part of l. 82 (*Bien . . . auer*) is not necessary to the sense and may be an interpolation. Instead of the present ll. 82–83 perhaps we may read: *E huebos me serie pora toda mi compaña.*

13 79 **Martin Antolinez**: the chronicles appear to treat this trusty follower of the Cid as one of his kinsmen.

13 80 On the position of **uos** cf. the note to l. 17 of the *Misterio*.

13 81 Espeso e : in the 12th century the auxiliary could not begin its clause, the present order was the normal one. Cf. Hanssen, *Dos Problemas de Sintaxis*, p. 22.

14 88–95 Assonance in *á–o*.

14 89 Rachel ⱬ Vidas : the Hebrews formed a firm and are always mentioned together.

14 90 As the Cid was now an outlaw, the King had sent letters to Burgos and elsewhere forbidding loyal subjects to entertain him or sell him anything.

14 91 el auer : in ll. 109 ff. we see what this *aver* 'wealth' is supposed to be, viz. booty taken from the Moors.

14 92 gelo : cf. Vocab. Baist in the *Grundriss*, I, 2d ed., p. 910, thinks that *gelo* (pronounced *dželo*, i.e. with an initial sound like that of English *j*), through enclitic use after verb forms in *-r* and *-n*, changed its *dž* to *z* (as happened in a few cases in O. Sp.), and then the *ze* became assimilated in value to the reflexive *se*, whence the mod. *se* as a nonreflexive pronoun as well as a reflexive pronoun. But O. Sp. *z* did not change to *s*. Moreover, the regular development of O. Sp. *dž* (written as *g* before *e*, *i*, or as *j*) was > *ž* (i.e. it lost its dental stop element) and then > *š* (i.e. English *sh*). When the stage of *š* or palatal *s* was reached, then the confusion of the two pronouns occurred. In the late O. Sp. and down into the 16th century the spelling *xe* (= *še*) occurs instead of *ge*. Cf. Ford, *Old Spanish Sibilants* (Boston, 1900).

14 96–99 Assonance in *á–a*. — **de tarua** is a scribal error for *detardaua*. Cf. the frequent use here of the imperfect tense where the modern rule calls rather for the preterit. This use — a popular one — continued in the ballads of the Golden Age.

14 97 Probably an erroneous anticipation of l. 99 by the scribe. It has been pointed out that Martín Antolínez would hardly inquire for Rachel and Vidas before entering Burgos. He needed secrecy in his movements ; cf. ll. 106–107.

14 98 castiello : Damas-Hinard (cf. his ed. of the poem, p. 10, note) thought that 'castle' here meant the Jewish quarter. Bello (in his ed., p. 210) says: "There were many rich Jews in Burgos. In 1123 they played a leading part in the rising against the Aragonese, whom they dislodged from the castle of the city; perhaps on this account it was thought that the castle was guarded or inhabited by them."

14 100–173 Assonance in *á–o*, with several brief interruptions, which are perhaps due to scribal errors in the case of l. 116, which seems corrupt, and l. 124, which might be changed to *que el gaño algo* or *que el algo a gañado*.

14 101 **ganados**: the *Cid* seems to have both *ganar* (which remains the mod. Sp. verb) and *gañar*. Cf. Fr. *gagner* and It. *guadagnare* with palatalized *n*; mod. Sp. has also the noun *gañán* 'day laborer.' Cf. note to *Misterio*, l. 101.

14 109 **Campeador**: one of the current epithets applied to the Cid in the poem. From an early date in his career the Cid is said to have signalized himself in single combats. These we find recorded in the *Crónica General* of Alfonso X and elsewhere, e.g. in the *Rodrigo* (*Crónica Rimada*). For a brief statement of the supposedly historic facts of the Cid's life cf. Restori, *Gesta del Cid*, p. 257. It is a question whether *Campeador* may not have also the general sense of 'fighter,' 'campaigner.' — **parias**: the assumption here is — but, of course, Martín Antolínez is not necessarily stating facts — that the Cid made an incursion into Moorish territory to exact tribute from the Moors, that he made much booty and retained a good part of it. The king had the right to a certain part of all booty taken from the Moors, and the Cid was accused of not having delivered over this part, wherefore the king exiled him. But the *Crónica General* (ed. Menéndez Pidal, p. 523) gives a different account. It says that the Cid was accused of making an unwarranted attack upon Moorish territory (at *Sant Esteuan*) which was protected by a treaty between the Moors and King Alfonso, and that the king believed the accusation because he did not like the Cid " on account of the oath which he had exacted from him at Burgos, with regard to the death of King Sancho, . . . and straightway he sent his letters to the Cid to go forth from the realm." The *Crónica General*, in explaining the aversion of Alfonso to the Cid, is referring to another tradition, to the effect that the Cid, at the head of a body of nobles, had compelled Alfonso to swear solemnly that he had had no hand in the murder of King Sancho, his brother and predecessor. — **fue entrado**: as often in O. Sp., the perfect tense of a verb of motion is here made with the auxiliary *ser*.

15 116 **Aquelas**: i.e. the *arcas* of l. 113.

15 122 **seyen se conseiando**: 'were sitting, taking counsel with each other.'

15 124–125 Although we have proposed a possible amendment of 124, both of these lines may be corrupt as to their assonance. As they stand they form a couplet in *ó*, and some admit a couplet as a good laisse breaking a long laisse. In ll. 127–128 we appear again to have a couplet, now in *á–a*, breaking the same laisse. Ll. 124 and 127 are manifestly too short.

15 136 Dixo: the verb agrees with the nearer of its two subjects; cf. 139, 146, etc. Of course the two men form a single firm. With the present punctuation we must supply *hemos* after *gelos*. Some editors prefer to omit the colon after *Vidas* and treat the rest of the line as an accusative-and-infinitive construction.

15 142 tred: cf. Vocab. Menéndez Pidal, *Gramática del Cid*, p. 272, would derive *tred* directly from a V. L. imper. pl. *tragĭte* = Lat. *trahĭte*. But this etymon is not sure.

16 152 Afeuos: cf note to *Misterio*, l. 127.

16 154 estaualos: the conj. obj. pronoun, as an enclitic, is properly joined to the preceding word, as here. In his very capricious writing, the scribe often neglects to join it so. Instead of *los* we expect *les* here.

16 163 dieran: the collocation of *dieran* with *auien iurado* in the same construction must indicate that it is also a pluperfect indic. here. It is still occasionally used as an indic. pluperfect (its force in Latin) or preterit.

16 170 gozo: the origin of this word is not clear. Lat. *gaudium* should give Sp. *goyo*, and this form is found in Aragonese. Cf. Vocab. for other unsatisfactory etyma. May not the word be a loan-word from Provençal? As *gauz* (beside *gaug*, *jauz*) and the verb *gauzir* (*jauzir*) it occurs in the language of the troubadours as a stock term descriptive of one of the necessary courtly attributes. The wandering troubadours may have brought it to Spain.

16 174 This line does not assonate fully with the laisse in *á–a* following.

16 175–190 Assonance in *á–a*, broken in l. 184 by *echaron*. This, as Lidforss says, may be placed before *.iij.* or it may be changed to *echaban*. The line is bad anyway as to its length.

16 179 que la yo aya: this is an example of the interposition of another word, not an unstressed object pronoun, between the conjunctive object pronoun and its verb. Common in Portuguese-Galician, i.e. in the western part of the peninsula, it appeared not infrequently in older Castilian, yet it was not a feature of that language. The phenomenon is one of interpolation. It has been studied with much care by W. H. Chenery in his *Object-Pronouns in Dependent Clauses: a Study in O. Sp. Word-Order* (in *Publications of the Modern Language Association of America* XX. 1 ff.). He finds that (p. 1) "in O. Sp. this phenomenon is almost without exception confined to dependent clauses, i.e. clauses that begin with a subordinating conjunction, a relative pronoun, or a relative adverb with conjunctional force." It is a phenomenon (p. 6) " hardly appearing in Castilian texts before the latter part of the 13th century and then probably due to western [i.e. Ptg.-Galician] influence. . . . It is most prevalent in works of the courtly school of Alfonso X and his successors, and least frequent in works farthest removed from the influence of that school." It should be said here that that courtly school, although made up of Castilians like King Alfonso X and his nephew Juan Manuel, wrote love lyrics and other verse compositions in Portuguese-Galician. Chenery seeks to prove further (p. 7) " that in Castilian there is no enclisis of the pronoun in interpolation, and that the phenomenon is merely one of word-order, influenced by analogies of certain frequent collocations." In the *Cid* he finds (p. 38) only 8 cases of interpolation of this sort, and one anomalous case, while the cases of the normal order are in a great majority, wherefore he suspects " that the phenomenon is not a feature of the *Cid* in its original form, but is due to later scribes." He adds : " The proportion of interpolated subject pronouns is much greater than that of examples in other categories [4–9] and it is possible that some of these cases may be original." . . . " After the close of the 14th century," he says (p. 67), " interpolation becomes very rare in Castilian texts ; in works of the second half of the 15th century we can regard it only as an archaism inherited from older sources ; and in texts of the 16th century the phenomenon is nearly or quite absent." Chenery advances certain theories with respect to the origin of the phenomenon in O. Sp. and contends (p. 91) that " the problem of interpolation in O. Sp. resolves itself mainly into one of the relative order among words of weak stress." He argues that the O.Sp. object pronoun preceding the verb was proclitic to that verb and not enclitic to the word preceding. He does not allow the theory that one weak word may be enclitic to another word of weak stress. On this side, and in other particulars, the discussion should be carried further. For other interesting suggestions regarding the possible rise of the construction, cf. pp. 95–96. In our selections we meet other examples in **42** 32 and **54** 3. See E. Staaff, *Contribution à la syntaxe du pronom personnel dans le Poème du Cid*, in *Romania* XXIII.

16 180–181 **da qui** (= *de aquí*), etc.: the words seem to mean ' From here [i.e. this moment] let it be promised to you. If I bring it to you from yonder — the land of the Moors — [you shall have it] ; otherwise, you may count upon getting it out of the chests.' Cf. Lidforss (p. 109) for a discussion of the passage. He thinks that there is an anacoluthon in l. 181. Cornu would put a comma after *mandada*, in which case we translate 'from this moment be it promised to you, if I bring it to you from yonder.' The *Cid* seems to have other examples of the anacoluthon in a conditional statement.

17 182   The scribe has omitted a passage which described the return of the Jews and Martín Antolínez to the castle of Burgos to get the money; *palaçio = castiello* of l. 98; but cf. *posada* in l. 200. — **vn** = *un* = *una*. In O. Sp. *un* might stand before a fem. noun beginning with unaccented *a*.

17 185   Note the full form *Martino* used when it is not proclitic to the patronymic: cf. ll. 187, 199.

17 190   **calças** = mod. *calzas*. As Restori says, the price of a pair of hose or breeches is asked here as a commission or fee. The *Libro de Alexandre* (ed. Morel-Fatio, stz. 1065) has *non gano calças* 'he derived no advantage.'

17 191–208   Assonance in *á–o*.

17 192   **no lo** = *nos lo*. This may be a phonetical loss of *s* before *l* (cf. also 197, *nolo*), like that which occurs in Portuguese. If this be so, it is probably due to the scribe.

17 1085   Here begins a new division of the poem, which provides a possible name for the whole.

17 1085–1093   Assonance in *á*.

17 1086   This verse seems to have been misplaced by the scribe. It really belongs to a passage anterior to l. 1085, which describes the defeat and capture of the Count of Barcelona by the Cid and his men and dwells upon the great booty which they took from him.

17 1087   **Alucant**: cf. l. 1108, a variety of the same name. For the names mentioned in the lines following here, cf. in general Menéndez Pidal, *Gramática del Cid*, pp. 41 ff., where the itineraries mentioned in the poem are traced out as well as possible. Some of the places have disappeared. See also Restori, *Gesta del Cid*, p. 254, as to *Alucant*.

17 1088   **duca**: probably a scribal error for *daca = de acá* 'on this side.'

18 1092   **Al menar**: this is metrically equivalent to *a Almenar* with synalephe.

18 1094–1097   Assonance in *ié–o*.

18 1095   **Muruiedro** = *Murviedro*. Of the many places mentioned in the poem as captured by the Cid, this is the most important next to Valencia. The poet has inverted the historical order of their capture, for he really took Valencia first, in 1094, and Murviedro only later, in 1098.

18 1098–1121 Assonance in *á*. In l. 1098 we may read *plaz*; in l. 1106, *aquesto nos* (= *no se*) *partirá*. In l. 1105 *fazen*, and l. 1115 *salue*, we may have *á–e* in an *á* laisse : Menéndez Pidal admits this concomitance. L. 1113 is faulty beyond amendment. Cornu would change *fazen* of l. 1105 to O. Sp. *fan* (cf. *far* beside *fazer*), which is found elsewhere ; and Restori suggests simply the rearrangement of the line to *Con derecho lo fazen si nos vienen çercar.* In l. 1113 Lidforss would change *son* to *se han.*

18 1099 **viniessen çercar :** in O. Sp. the verb of motion often, as invariably now, takes a preposition (*á*) before the dependent infinitive, but again we find no preposition used. Before infinitives beginning with *a-* the preposition *á* is frequently suppressed.

18 1100 Perhaps the comma after *noch* should be omitted ; Lidforss prints without the comma.

18 1111 **conpeçaremos :** *compeçar* is related to O. Sp. *pieça* 'piece,' *empeçar* 'begin.' Cf. Vocab. and also Ford, *Old Spanish Sibilants*, p. 50.

18 1112 **enadran :** Lidforss derives this from Lat. *inaddere*, whence O. Sp. *eñadir*, mod. *añadir.* He does not explain the *ñ* of these latter. Cf. Vocab. He translates " ajouteront *à notre avantage.*" The syncope of *i* in the infin. stem is not rare in O. Sp. for regular verbs. The *Libro de Alexandre* (ed. Morel-Fatio, stz. 953) has *A los que fueren Ricos añadire en riqueza.*

18 1116 **partiemos** = *partimos*, 1117 *pudiemos* = *pudimos.* On these preterit forms, due to the analogy of *partieron, pudieron,* etc., cf. above, note to **13** 18.

18 1117 This line is parenthetical.

18 1121 **son a escarmentar :** a gerundival construction, ' are to be given a warning lesson.'

19 1122–1126 Assonance in *á–a.*

19 1125 *Oñe* and *ome*, both found in O. Sp. texts, must represent *omne*; De Lollis probably argues wrongly for *ome* as a good form (cf. *Studi di filologia romanza* VIII. 371).

19 1126 **pareçra :** as a result of syncopation *ç* coming before a consonant was sometimes allowed to stand in O. Sp. ; generally, however, the scribe wrote *z* = *ts.*

19 1127–1128 Couplet in *á–e.* This may be admitted as a good concomitance with the following laisse in *á* extending to l. 1149. Of course

l. 1128 and l. 1134 *plaze* may be changed to *plaz*; but ll. 1127, 1138, 1142, cannot be corrected away easily.

19 1132 **del otra part:** 'from the other side,' cf. 1144. Note *el, del*, standing even before a feminine adj. not beginning with *á*.

19 1146–1147 **es logar, es alcaz:** this *es* is Lat. *ípse* > *ese* > *es*. It is not necessary to assume (as Meyer-Lübke does, *Grammatik der roman. Sprachen* I. 522) that it is *íste* > *este* > *est* > *es*.

19 1185 This line, ending in *á–a*, does not adapt itself well to the *á* laisse following. It is preceded also by a series of lines in *á*. Although *á–e* may be admitted as a concomitance for *á*, there does not seem to be sufficient evidence to admit *á–a*; cf. Menéndez Pidal, *Gramática del Cid*, p. 114.

19 1186–1191 Assonance in *á*, with *á–e* in l. 1188.

19 1186 **amaneçio amyo** (= *á mio*) **Çid:** we expect *amaneçer* here in a direct personal construction, with *Çid* as the subject. Cornu and Lidforss dubiously suggest the suppression of the *á*. As the line stands, the construction is impersonal, 'it dawned for (dawn came to) my Cid,' etc.

20 1189 **cueta:** cf. Menéndez Pidal, *Gramática del Cid*, p. 146: "The word *cueta* [and he cites other instances of it in Berceo] is an Aragonesism, being a reduction of *cueyta* [this he finds in other early documents, including the *San Millán* of Berceo]; there are also found without the diphthong [*ue*] *coyta* [this he finds in Berceo's *Santo Domingo*; we have it here in Juan Manuel, **55** 3] and *cuyta* [in Berceo etc.], forms likewise dialectal in the treatment of the consonants." He finds *cueta < cueyta* an Aragonesism because a following *y* does not prevent diphthongization in the Aragonese dialect. On p. 76 he says that the *Cid* possesses few certain examples of Aragonesisms, and he does not include *cueta* among them. Diez (*Etym. Wtb.*, p. 103, s.v. *coitar, cochar*) takes as etymon the V. L. frequentative *cŏctāre from Lat. *coquĕre, cŏctum*, and points out that Lat. *coquĕre* had already the sense 'to vex,' 'harass,' etc., which is possessed by the O. Sp. *cochar, coitar*. The noun *coita* (*coyta*) he seems to regard as a derivative from the verb. Admitting an Aragonese development for the forms with *t*, we may say that the *oi* (*oy*) forms reflect the treatment in the unaccented syllable (as in *coitar, coytar*), while the *ue < uei* forms reflect the treatment in the accented syllable (e.g. **cŏctat > cueyta > cueta*). In *cuyta* = mod. *cuita* perhaps the *uy* (*ui*) is due to the influence of *cuydar* (*cuidar*) < Lat. *cō(g)ĭtare* (from which came O. Sp. *coydar*, with a diphthong never popular in Sp.). The closing force of the *y* may have produced *uy, ui*, in Castilian itself.

That *uey* ever gave *ui* in Castilian is not certain. Of course *cochar* is the proper development from *cŏctāre in Castilian. *Coyta*, if adopted early enough from Aragonese into Castilian, might also have closed of itself to *:uyta, cuita*. Restori would derive all the forms mentioned from *cog:tare*.

20 1192–1194   A brief laisse in *é–(i)a*.

20 1194   **sperare** : even though written *esperaré*, this would count the same after *le*.

20 1195   There is no assonance for this line, nor for l. 1196.

20 1197–1220   Assonance in *á* with the concomitance in *á–e* in ll. 1197, 1206, 1213, 1217.

20 1198   **quiere** : probably a scribal mistake for *quieren* ; cf. *yentes* in l. 1199.

20 1203   **sobrellas** = *sobre ella se*.

20 1208   **siles**, etc.: 'to see if they (any one) would come to succor them [the Valencians].'

20 1212   **çibdad** : what is the value of the *b* ? Corresponding to Lat. intervocalic *v*, it should have become the bilabial spirant *ƀ*, and this, before a consonant after the loss of the intervening vowel (*cīv(i)tātem*), should have vocalized as *u* (cf. *audīvit > audiut*). Our extracts show also **60** 19 *çiubdat* — whose *u* can only have been developed from the *ƀ* (*v*), and therefore *b* is erroneously written in it, perhaps through the influence of *çibdad* — and **60** 23 *çiudat*, which is the mod. *ciudad*. The writing of final *-t*, where Lat. had intervocalic *-t-*, shows the O. Sp. unvoicing of consonants at the end of a word. The mod. regular spelling — and the occasional O. Sp. spelling — with *-d* is due to the analogy of the properly written intervocalic *-d-* of the plural and derivatives. Are we to assume that in *çibdad* we have at so late a period as the 12th–14th centuries a bilabial *ƀ* before *d* ? It is not unlikely that in popular use *civitas* developed at a relatively late date in O. Sp.: *la(s) casa(s)* was a current term for 'town,' 'city' (cf. *Cid*, l. 62 *en Burgos la casa*, 'in the city or town of B.'; l. 1161 *Deyna la casa* ; l. 1550 *entrados son a Molina, buena e Rica casa* ; and again in l. 1232 *casa* 'city' in apposition with *Valençia*) ; *villa* was also a current term. Note the *b* also in the half-learned *dubda* (see Vocab.), where it vocalized and was absorbed by the preceding *u*.

20 1214   **qui en** = *quien* ; cf. l. 1218.

20 1216   **quinta** : the Cid, acting now like an independent ruler, takes to himself the fifth part of all booty, even as, under the old Spanish laws, the rulers of Castile and Leon did.

20 1218 **elos :** probably *e los*, 'and the,' as Lidforss believes, and not the full form of the article. Cf. note to **4** 27. Cornu (cf. his articles cited above) believes in restoring *elle*, *ella*, etc. as the forms of the article in the *Cid*, but this is a questionable policy to follow.

V. DISPUTA DEL ALMA Y EL CUERPO

This Spanish version of a debate between body and soul — a not un-common medieval form of the debate — is found written on the back of a document (now in the *Archivo Histórico-Nacional*) containing a deed of gift made by the Abbot of San Salvador de Oña in 1201. The docu-ment is cut on one side in such fashion that the initial letters of each of the 18 lines on it are missing, one letter in the earlier lines and several letters in the later lines. The debate is not complete : it ends in the middle of a phrase. According to Menéndez Pidal, in the Intro-duction to his edition reproduced here, the handwriting of the fragment is of the very beginning of the 13th century and contemporary with that of the deed of gift (1201) ; it might even belong to the 12th century. Baist (*Grundriss* II. ii. 401) ascribes the debate to the 13th century and believes that its 74 verses (as printed by Octavio de Toledo) belong to the western part of the Spanish speech domain. He thinks that it renders, although not in a perfect fashion, the six-syllable verses of a French original, and that the original Spanish form of our debate was metrically correct, although it ventured upon certain strong contrac-tions to achieve that correctness. The first edition of our fragment was that of the Marquis Pidal (Madrid, 1856; also in his works pub-lished in the *Colección de Escritores Castellanos*, Madrid, 1890). A reim-pression appeared in F. Wolf's *Studien zur Geschichte der span. u. port. Nationalliteratur* (Berlin, 1859, pp. 55 ff.), along with the corre-sponding verses of the supposed French original, whose likeness to our Spanish text is perfectly obvious. Directly from the MS. an edition was made by F. Monlau, in his *Escuela Superior de Diplomática* : *Colección de documentos*, etc. (Madrid, 1865), in which he improved upon Pidal's ed. and even gave better readings, in certain cases, than those appearing in the next edition, that of J. M. Octavio de Toledo in the *Ztschr. f. roman. Philol.*, II. 60. Besides a paleographical edition of the poem, Toledo gave a transcription in heptasyllabic verses or modifications thereof. Toledo also printed two later Spanish versions (the *Visión de Filiberto* and the *Revelaçión de un Hermitanno*) of this same debate form. Finding the versification rude, he admitted that many of the defects might be due to the negligence of the copyist. In regarding the composition as made up of short verses —and not of long verses as printed in our text — he follows Pidal and Wolf. The latter thinks that the Spanish rimer was striving to render the six-syllable verses of his Northern French original and generally succeeded, although occasional verbal difficulties in translation compelled him to lengthen or shorten the line.

Beyond a doubt, the Debate, like the *Misterio*, is a borrowing from France. It is a form, showing reductions and also additions, of the French (Anglo-Norman) original reprinted by Wolf from an edition of it given by T. Wright in his *Latin Poems Commonly Attributed to Walter Mapes* (London, 1841). Wright ascribes the French poem to the beginning of the 13th century; but as Menéndez Pidal finds that the MS. of the Spanish fragment is of the very beginning of the 13th century, if not of the 12th century, we should expect to date the French document back in the 12th century, and in fact there seem to be reasons for placing it at the mid-point of the 12th century : cf. Gröber in his *Grundriss*, II, i, 482, for the literature on the subject. The tradition of the *Debate between Body and Soul* is an old and widespread one in the Middle Ages. On the forms of it in Latin (the *Rixae animi et corporis*) cf. E. Du Méril, *Poésies populaires latines antérieures au 12ᵉ siècle* (Paris, 1843). Among the oldest forms is the Anglo-Saxon of the 10th century, which is in the Exeter Book. Cf. E. Mätzner, *Altenglische Sprachproben* I. 90 (Berlin, 1867) ; Kleinert, *Über den Streit zwischen Leib u. Seele* (Halle, 1880) ; *Romania* XX. 1 ff. and 513 ff. The general situation, in so far as our document is concerned, is that of a soul returning to chide its body for the evils that it did.

21 1 In the present state of the MS., sometimes we find perfect rime of the couplets, as here in *oir* and *dezir*, again we have assonance, as in *ui* and *fallir*, and again all form of rime is missing, as in l. 4 *uision* and *dormient*. Menéndez Pidal, like the previous editors, has filled in the lacunæ of the MS., according to his judgment, with the bracketed letters and words. His facsimile, printed with the text here given, shows that the ends of the lines (which are written as though they were prose) are sometimes impaired.

21 2 i: superfluous here, as *j* is in l. 16. — **quedo** = *cuedo*; cf. l. 30 *quendes* = *cuendes*.

21 3 esient = *exiente* with the force of *exiendo*; **amanezient** (*z* = *ts*, i.e. *ç*) = *amaneçiente* for *amaneçiendo*. Wolf (l.c., p. 58) puts the question whether the appearance of these present participial forms with the force of the usual Spanish gerund in -*ando*, -*iendo* is not due to French influence, i.e. are not the forms Gallicisms? The same question suggests itself with regard to **60** 17 *alegrantes* and 26 *deziente*, as well as the other forms in the present extract.

21 6 Western Spanish (Leonese) showed a tendency to diphthongize *ŏ* even more than Castilian did in certain cases : hence *uemne* here, if Baist is right in considering our document as western. Cf. Menéndez Pidal, *El Dialecto Leonés*, p. 18 ; Staaff, *Étude sur l'ancien dialecte léonais*, p. 206.

21 7 **ell** : note that *ell* and *all* appear here only before words beginning with a vowel. — **plera** : Lat. *plōrat* should have given only *plora*, mod. *llora*. Menéndez Pidal believes the rimes here to be *fuóra*, *plora*, i.e., the former word represents here an earlier stage of the development of Lat. *ŏ* (*fŏra*(*s*) > *fuora* > *fuera*). He says : " The scribe, copying these rimes, rejuvenated the first, putting down *fuera*, and, on reaching the second, went on regardless of facts and put down *plera*." Of course Menéndez Pidal believes that for the *Cid* the stage of *uo* was the regular one for original Lat. *ŏ*: this *uo* has been found also in Leonese and persists still in Asturian; cf. Menéndez Pidal, *El Dialecto Leonés*, p. 18, and Staaff, l.c., p. 205. If about 1201 a scribe was "rejuvenating" a form, our text would seem to antedate that period considerably.

21 8 **ama** : scribal error for *alma* : cf. *leio = leito* in l. 4.

21 9 **e** : Menéndez Pidal in his edition says : " I do not know whether *e* for *en* is a piece of forgetfulness on the scribe's part or corresponds to some phonetic law." No such law seems concerned here ; we need *en*.

21 10 **al** : Menéndez Pidal finds the *a* of this word not very clear, yet does not think that he can read *el* ; cf. *al* in l. 11.

21 11 **fazi** : the meter calls for this form, which represents *fazie* with loss of final unaccented *e*. — **grant de** : scribal error for *grande*.

21 16 **oferda** : perhaps a scribal error for *oferta* ; cf. mod. Sp. *oferta*, Ital. *offerta*, Fr. *offerte*. The scribe may have been thinking of *ofrenda*, and in any event his *d* is an emendation of an *a* which he wrote first. Cf. the *da* of *dar* following.

21 19 **elguesia** : cf. Menéndez Pidal : " The *a* of *el*[*gue*]*si*[*a*] was forgotten, like that of *penitencia* in l. 17 ; the cut on the margin compels us to supply three letters or four, and I find the form *elguesia* in a document of San Millán de la Cogolla of 1244, and *elglesia* in another of La Vid of 1212." The phenomenon would, then, seem to be one of the metathesis of *l*.   The western *igreja* (cf. Menéndez Pidal, *El Dialecto Leonés*, p. 40) would make a perfect rime here. — **asentauaste**: *sentáuast* (enclitic *t* = *te*) would make a good line: cf. *Dim*, l. 27.

21 20 Is it *I fazîes* (with dissyllabic *fazies*), or should *el* be omitted? Cf. l. 29 *solies*, seemingly *solîes*. — As to **tos(dos)** Menéndez Pidal says, " The copyist made a mistake, repeating the word *todos*, and then intercalated an *s* without striking out the superfluous *dos*."

21 22 **iure**: we expect here the 2d pers. sg. of the pret. indic. *iurest* (= mod. *juraste*).

21 24 This line is manifestly too long for a double verse of 7 (6) syllables.

21 25 **fadado**: this is simply a guess of all the editors. — For **ta' mal** the MS. has simply *tamal*.   The scribe forgot the *n*, or the nasal dash above the *a* which regularly denoted an *n* after a vowel.

21 26 **Que**: an early case of *que* = adverbial conjunction ' though.'

22 27 The letters *sist en* supplied here are conjectural only.   Menéndez Pidal says : " There are lacking four or five letters which I cannot restore in any better way ; I understand *estéro* = *estelo*."   What is this *estelo*?   The passage is obscure.   The O. Fr. text (Wolf, p. 57) has *Ou sont ore li denier ki tant estoient chier*.

22 28 **morauedis**, etc.: the MS. has *m̂azaris*. Cf. Menéndez Pidal : " All the editors read, without concerning themselves with the meter, *o los tos moazaris et melequis*.   I do not know the word *moazari*; it is true that I have not found *azari* either; but I suppose that it is an adjective like *melequi*, modifying the substantive *morauedi*; in a document of Sahagún, 1140, . . . we find *III morabitis melquis*."   Octavio de Toledo (l.c., p. 62) says : " *Moazaris et melequis*, Arabic coins."

22 30 **ie**: cf. note to **6** 14. — **res**: the true development of Lat. *reges*: cf. *Vocab*. s.v. *rees*.

22 33 **asueueras**: cf. Octavio de Toledo, l.c., p. 62 : " from *azvver* [sic], which means in Arabic the rope or strap joining the breast-leather to the crupper."   If the first *s* means ʃ (*sh*) here — cf. l. 3 *esient* = *exient*, etc. — this word may be related to the O. Sp. *axuar* ' outfit ' < Arabic *aʃ-ʃuar*, mod. *ajuar* ' bridal outfit,' used here perhaps in the general sense of ' trappings.'

22 36 **Do**: elsewhere, the document uses *o*.

22 37 **festir**: the scribe certainly means *vestir*; cf. *bestimentos* = *vestimentos* in l. 36.   One thinks here of the O. Sp. *femença* < Lat. *vehementia*.

VI. GONZALO DE BERCEO

A. VIDA DE SANTO DOMINGO DE SILOS

This critical edition of one of the several works of Gonzalo de Berceo has been based by Fitz-Gerald upon two 14th-century MSS., the one of them in the library of the Real Academia Española de la Lengua at Madrid and the other in the library of the Real Academia de la Historia at the same place, and upon the first printed edition of the poem made by the cleric Fray Sebastian de Vergara at Madrid in 1736. He gives to Vergara's edition the importance of a MS. because it is based on a lost MS. which seems to have been different from the extant MSS. There are some omissions in both of the latter: cf. the description by Fitz-Gerald (in the *Bibliothèque de l'École des hautes études*, fascicule 149, pp. xvi ff.). Cf. for a critique of Fitz-Gerald's edition F. Hanssen, *Notas á la Vida de Sto. Domingo de Silos*, etc. (Santiago de Chile, 1907).

The other printed editions — that of T. A. Sánchez in Vol. II of his *Colección de Poesías Castellanas* (Madrid, 1780), which reprints Vergara's without improving it and was itself reproduced by E. de Ochoa (Paris, 1842), and that of F. Janer in Vol. LVII of the *Biblioteca de Autores Españoles* (Madrid, 1864), which marks little critical advance over Sánchez's edition — are of little value for the reconstituting of the original text.

The source of Berceo's poem on the life and miracles of this St. Dominick was a Latin account, *Vita Beati Dominici Confessoris*, etc., written by a monk Grimaldus. It was published by Vergara in his edition already mentioned. Cf. Fitz-Gerald, l.c., pp. xii, xliii, lx.

For a general account of the labors of Berceo, cf. J. Fitzmaurice-Kelly, *Littérature espagnole*, pp. 55 and 447, with the literature cited by him; E. Mérimée, *Précis d'histoire de la littérature espagnole*, p. 36; Puymaigre, *Les Vieux Auteurs castillans* I. 267 ff.; and especially G. Baist in Gröber's *Grundriss* II. ii. 402.

Gonzalo de Berceo seems to be the oldest Spanish poet known to us by name, as a certain Lope de Moros (cf. Fitzmaurice-Kelly, l.c.), supposed to have preceded him, was probably only a scribe. He was also very fertile in his vein, having left us over 20,000 verses (if the *Libro de Alexandre* be included) in the *cuaderna vía*, i.e. in monorimed quatrains of Alexandrines, a metrical form much affected by the didactic and religious poets of the 13th and 14th centuries and used by them as something quite distinct from the measures of the minstrels who dealt with the epic matter. They termed these latter measures the *mester de joglaría* (meaning probably the double *romance* verses of the *Cid* etc.), while they styled their own the *mester de clerecía*. The Alexandrine was an importation from France.

Berceo's name is found in about a dozen documents ranging in date from 1220 to 1246. It is thought that he did not long survive this latter date. He became a priest, and as such (not as a monk) was attached to the monastery of San Millán de la Cogolla in the diocese of Calahorra in Old Castile. His compositions (exclusive of the *Alexandre*, to which we return later) embrace the *Vida de Sto. Domingo de Silos*, the *Estoria de S. Millan*, the *Vida de Sta. Oria* (his last work), the *Martyrio de S. Laurençio*, the *Milagros de Nuestra Señora*, the *Duelo que fizo la Virgen*, the *Signos del Juiçio*, all of which seem to follow written sources, and the *Loores de Nuestra Señora* and the *Sacrifiçio de la Misa*, which appear to show a more original treatment. Three hymns ascribed to him are of doubtful authenticity.

Berceo emphasizes in the course of these works his purpose of speaking in plain terms to his fellow-man. As Baist indicates, he eliminates the bombast and rhetoric of his sources, he allows his fancy little play and expresses the dry fact in a realistic and pious fashion, combining therewith, however, no little harmless humor.

For a study of the *cuaderna vía* cf. Fitz-Gerald, *Versification of the Cuaderna Vía as found in Berceo's Vida de Sto. Domingo de Silos* (N. Y., 1905), and F. Hanssen, *Metrische Studien zu Alfonso u. Berceo* (Valparaiso, 1903).

23 1 *c* **que egual :** note the hiatus, which is frequent here.

23 1 *d* **prosa :** used here in the general sense of " composition."

23 2 *b* We seem to need *En* [*el*] *qual* here. — It is doubtful that **su** had already became generalized in the masculine use at the time when Berceo was writing.

23 2 *d* Berceo speaks of himself whimsically as though he were a minstrel and entitled to a minstrel's reward. — **bon :** cf. 86 *b* **buen**, and many other cases in the document. The MS. of the *Academia de la Lengua* seems to have *un buen uaso de vino*, which is what we need here. But the poem seems to require the rime *bonas* in 233 *c* : still ?

23 3 *d* **Silos :** on the road to Burgos from Madrid ; it is not far from Burgos and therefore is in Old Castile.

24 91 *a* **fradres :** Cf. 104 *b* **frayres**. One wonders whether Berceo could have used these two forms interchangeably. Yet there are strange phenomena here. Compare *el* in 87 *c* with *elli* in 91 *b*. Our

MS. and other information is not sufficient for a critical edition unless that edition be based on a general study of the linguistic conditions of Berceo's time and locality.

24 92 *d* **algunt :** O. Sp. shows *algund* and *algunt* beside *algun* and the full form *alguno* ; cf. Vocab. The *d* and *t* are inorganic. They are due to the analogy of *grande, grand, grant, segund, segunt, segun, quando, quand,* and other words having an etymological -*nd*-.

24 96 *d* **entendremos :** an example of the tendency in O. Sp. to abridge the infinitive basis in the future and conditional even for regular verbs.

24 97 *a* Not only have we hiatus in *e es,* but *oy* has to be read as a dissyllable here, if the half-line is correct.

25 103 *d* *Plaz,* a true O. Sp. form, would make the line good. Apparently the editor does not care to admit apocopated forms in such cases as this. Cf. *iaz* in 356 *b,* and his own correction of *plaze* to *plaz* in the present line, on p. xxxii. — **enna :** on this dialect form cf. Baist, *Grundriss* I, 2d ed., p. 905. Like other forms found here, e.g. *fizi, elli, essi,* it probably belongs to the dialect of the scribe. Instead of *enna* for this line, the MS. of the Academia de la Lengua has *enla,* the Castilian form ; and again where 361 *b* shows here *enna,* that same MS. shows *enla.* Into his text Fitz-Gerald has also admitted 108 *a enlas,* 358 *d enla,* and 367 *b conlos* (instead of *connos*). The complete text shows many more examples of the same sort.

26 108 *d* **este :** the verse requires *est* ; cf. Fitz-Gerald, p. xxxii.

26 109 *a* **Gonçalo :** cf. **40** 13 *Gonçaluo = Gonçalvo* and **44** 7 *Gonçaluez = Gonçalvez* ; cf. also **2** 8 and 13 *Gundesaluo = Gundesalvo* and **2** 6 *Gundesalbiz. Gundesalbus* is a frequent Latinized form of this originally Germanic name.

26 110 *c* **mezquinos :** the MS. of the Academia de la Historia has *mesquinos,* the earlier and better form, here and in 353 *d,* 356 *a.*

26 111 *b* **ouo afinar,** and 112 *c* **ouo a morir :** these are periphrases equivalent to the pret. indic. *finó* and *murió. Aver* + *á* or *de* + an infin. = pret. indic. of the main verb occurs frequently in the 15th and 16th century ballads.

26 289 *a* Note *un otro* contrary to the modern usage.

27 353 *c* **los cosas malas :** Fitz-Gerald treats *los* as agreeing logically with the masc. obj. to which *cosas malas* applies, i.e. the *Moros* of 353 *a,* In 480 *a* the fem. art. is used with *cosas* under similar circumstances to the present. The *Libro de Alexandre* (ed. Morel-Fatio), stz. 689 *d,* has *el otro cosa mala* (but possibly the construction is different there), while in 2337 *a* it has *la cosa mala.* Cf. Cornu, *Romania* XIII. 313, for other cases of *cosa* used of persons and seemingly always treated as feminine.

27 354 *d* **fallezco**: for this substitute *fallesco*, the good early form, which is given by the MS. of the Academia de la Historia and by Vergara's MS. : the *z* supplanted the *s* only later in the inceptive verb. On the analogy of *falleçes* (*ç* = *ts*), *falleçe*, etc., *fallesco* was made over into *fallezco* (with *z* originally = *ts* when before a consonant).

27 356 *c* **affontan** : O. Sp. *fonta*, in the *Cid*, is a loan-word through the French *honte* (with aspirated *h*) from the Germanic. Lat. *f* initial had in popular treatment before a vowel given O. Sp. aspirated *h*, but the *f* long continued to be the only character used for the new sound; hence it was used also for the aspirate sound at the beginning of the borrowed word.

28 361 *b* **presion**: the Academia de la Historia MS. and Vergara's have *prision*, the reading already accepted by Fitz-Gerald for 358 *d*.

28 362 *d* **al qui**, etc.: this half-line has a syllable in excess. Omit *al*, and *qui* remains = 'if one,' 'if any one'; cf. O. Fr. *qui* and also Ital. *chi* = *se alcuno*.

B. Libro de Alexandre

Since the present extract was published, M. Morel-Fatio's critical edition of the Paris MS., whence it was taken, has appeared (*El Libro de Alexandre, Manuscrit esp. 488 de la Bibliothèque nationale de Paris*, published in the series of the Gesellschaft für romanische Literatur, Vol. X, Dresden, 1906). What changes M. Morel-Fatio has found it advisable to make since he did me the favor of letting me use his transcript of several years ago, will be indicated in the notes.

In the *Romania*, IV. 7 ff. (1871), M. Morel-Fatio presented his dissertation entitled *Recherches sur le texte et les sources du Libro de Alexandre*. This useful study is in certain respects modified by the Introduction to his edition of the text. Therein he indicates the great importance of the *Alexandre*, as being "the sole example of the ancient [i.e. the Greco-Roman] epopee in Spanish literature of the 13th century." He continues: "The principal source of the *Libro* is the poem of Gautier de Chatillon, the *Alexandreis*, which dates from the end of the 12th century [cf. the note thereon by Gröber in his *Grundriss* II. i. 408, and see the edition prepared by Müldener, 1863, of this Latin poem by a Frenchman]. . . . But, in addition, the Castilian rimer has derived inspiration from several Latin writings, notably from the *Liber de praeliis* [an epitome of the Pseudo-Callisthenes.

This Greek document, really a novel on Alexander, was made around 200 A.D. The epitome, called *Liber* or *Historia de praeliis*, was made by the Neapolitan priest Leo in the second half of the 10th century]. Then, he derived inspiration from French poems, or, at least, from the best-known of them, the *Roman d'Alexandre* of Lambert le Tort and Alexandre de Paris."

The first edition of the *Alexandre* was that of Sánchez in 1782, in Vol. III of his *Colección de Poesías Castellanas*. This edition, based on a MS. which for a while was in the private collection known as the Osuna Library — whence it is referred to as O. — but is now at Madrid in the Biblioteca Nacional, was repeated by F. Janer in 1864, in Vol. LVII of the *Biblioteca de Autores Españoles*. In his *Recherches* of 1871, Morel-Fatio noted that an Augustinian community at Lyons had still in the 17th century a MS. of the poem. This MS., after having been long lost from view, came to light again in 1888, and is now at Paris — therefore known as P. — in the Bibliothèque Nationale (*Fonds espagnol*, 488). "The importance of P.," says Morel-Fatio, "results first of all from the fact that it contains about a hundred more strophes than O., and fills in an important lacuna in this latter MS." In fact, in O. there are missing 111 strophes between stz. 1183 and stz. 1184 of the Sánchez-Janer edition, and these appear as strophes 1213–1323 of Morel-Fatio's edition. P. is in a handwriting of the middle of the 15th century, and may be due to several scribes, and like O. it seems to show much garbling by scribes. Yet, bad as they are, P. and O. often mutually correct each other; nevertheless, it must be borne in mind that they have, in all probability, greatly impaired an original MS., from which they are somewhat distant, and which had greater merits than they exhibit on its behalf. On brief remnants of two other MSS. — or, possibly, of a single MS. — cf. Morel-Fatio, Introduction, p. ix ff.; they concern only some 18 to 19 strophes of our poem, which extends to 2639 strophes in P.

A reference in O., the MS. published by Sánchez-Janer, led to the idea that a certain *Johan Lorenzo* was the author of the poem. Nothing is known of him, and he may merely have been the scribe of that MS. Now the last strophe of P. attributes the authorship to *Gonçalo de Berceo, natural de Madrid* (a little town near the monastery of San Millán de la Cogolla), *en sant Myljan criado*. Baist (*Roman. Forschungen* VI. 292) thinks that the Berceo of our *Sto. Domingo* is meant. But Morel-Fatio thinks that a falsification is possible here: cf. Introduction, p. xxi, " En somme, rien ne s'oppose à ce que la strophe ait été fabriquée par quelqu'un qui avait lu les *explicit* de Berceo, savait certaines circonstances de sa vie et qui, pour une raison à lui seul connue, voulut faire passer le *Libro de Alexandre* pour une œuvre de ce versificateur."

In his edition, Morel-Fatio does not concern himself at all about O., published in a faulty way by Sánchez and Janer. He simply hopes that a critical edition of it may appear soon. " It is easy to see," he states, " that the language of P. is neither central Castilian nor the Leonese which characterizes MS. O. Beyond a doubt we find in it in great number forms purely Castilian, but, beside them, others peculiar to the Aragonese dialect and more particularly to that part of the Aragonese domain which borders on the region of the Catalan language." He is not ready to say yet whether the Leonesisms in O. belong to the scribe or to the poet. Menéndez Pidal argues (in *El Dialecto Leonés*, Madrid, 1906, p. 7) that if they belong to the poet, he must have been some one other than Berceo. Of course, in discussing the question of authorship, it must be borne in mind that the undoubted works of Berceo are religious in nature ; could he have written this long secular poem on Alexander? In all probability, the composition of the work belongs to the mid-point of the 13th century ; certainly its use by the *Fernan Gonçalez* would make this appear to be the case. For a list of other sources of it, cf. Baist, *Grundriss* II. ii. 403, and see E. Mérimée, *Précis d'histoire de la littérature espagnole*, p. 40, and M. Menéndez y Pelayo, *Orígenes de la Novela* (in *Nueva Biblioteca de Autores Españoles*, Madrid, 1905), I. lxix. Much interesting matter regarding the nature of the medieval literature on Alexander will be found in P. Meyer's *Alexandre le Grand dans la littérature française du moyen âge* (Paris, 1886). Our passage (whose metrical conditions are not perfect) describes a procession of Darius's household etc. The Spanish author got his information rather from Quintus Curtius's *Historia Alexandri Magni*, III. iii, than from the abridged account in Gautier de Chatillon.

29 1 This is stanza 831 of Morel-Fatio's edition.

29 1*a* **fazienda :** Morel-Fatio writes *fasienda* here and *fazienda* in d. In the Introduction, p. xxiii, he says : " I cannot always answer for having distinguished well between *z* and *s*, which are easily confused in cursive script : our scribe seems to have employed them indifferently, and it even happens to him to write *z* at the end of words with the value of a final *s*." Cf. Ford, *Old Spanish Sibilants*, p. 100. O. Sp. *z* never became *s*. Many printed O.Sp. texts showing, apparently, *s* for *z* (i.e. in cases where the phonetic development calls for *z*), are uncritical; their editors confused cursive *s* and *z* of the MS. But 15th-century scribes must also have been guilty of some confusion, as Morel-Fatio's text shows. We have printed *z* here according to the best O. Sp. usage in *diez*, *lazada*, *dozientos*, etc., where Morel-Fatio gives the real or seeming *s* of his MS. The peculiar scribal diacritics of his edition have not been employed here, as they are for the most part, if not wholly, without phonological importance: cf. the description of them in his Introduction, pp. xxiii ff.

29 1 *b* **fuesen**: the O. Sp. voiceless *ss* of the intervocalic position seems already simplified in the modern way: cf. *asy*, *esas*, *eso*, *guardasen*, etc. Of course these are scribal spellings, not those of the 13th-century author.

30 5 *a* **mill carros**: cf. 6 *a* *mill escogidos*. Before the vowel of the next word *mill* had the palatalized *ll*; although written before a word beginning with a consonant the *ll* meant in Castilian the simple *l* sound.

30 5 *b* **de el rrey**: perhaps *el rrey* formed a compound title — cf. *el rey* still so used in Portuguese — and therefore the contraction *del* did not occur.

30 5 *d* **conosçrie**: as a result of syncope of the vowel of the infinitive basis in the fut. and cond. indic. *ç* came sometimes before a consonant.

30 6 *c* In this passage *muy* seems always dissyllabic.

30 7 *b* **pphan**: in the edition Morel-Fatio now reads *prophan*, which is obscure. May the abbreviation stand for *Prest Johan = Preste Juan*, i.e. Prester John, who for the Spaniards is a paragon of magnificence?

30 7 *d* The *que* is superfluous both for the meter and for the syntax.

30 8 *d* **olor**: in O. Sp. and down into the Golden Age, the abstracts in -*or* were treated as feminine; *labor* still remains so.

31 11 *d* Morel-Fatio's edition puts a comma after *oro*. But should we not rather omit one of the *era's* ?

31 13 *a* Morel-Fatio now prints *Viene[n]*, supplying an *n* to make the verb pl. In this case, the *piedes* of this same line is its subject.

31 13 *b* **lydones**: obscure. Some such sense as 'rampant' seems required here.

31 13 *d* **solas**: Morel-Fatio now reads *so las*, 'under the.'

31 14 *a* **Uenien**: Morel-Fatio now reads *Venje = venía*, for which *aguilla* (= *águila*, with erroneous scribal *ll*) appears to be the subject. — **color**: should not this, or the *color* of *d*, be changed to *calor*?

31 15 *b* A *los* before *tres* would correct the verse.

31 16 *b* Morel-Fatio now reads *enperant*, but the final *e* is needed.

31 16 *c* Morel-Fatio now has *argent*.

31 18 *b* **las non**, etc. : observe the interpolation already noted above in other documents.

VII. POEMA DE FERNÁN GONÇALEZ

Our extract is taken from Professor C. C. Marden's critical edition of the incomplete and sole MS. of the epic on the historical Fernán González (died 970 A.D.), a lusty warrior who fought against the Moors and at the same time, as the chief noble of Castile, protested against the suzerainty exercised over that region by the king of Leon. Hence the appeal to the patriotic feelings of the Castilians and the epic importance given to his story. The MS., now in the Escurial Library (*Escurialense* B–iv–21), is not earlier than the 15th century. It shows the writing of two scribes, who modernized earlier readings of the text, and is very defective in that it often omits whole lines and lacks the conclusion of the poem. We are fortunate, however, in having other documents that deal with Fernán González's career and give us the complete account. The most important of these is the *Crónica General* of Alfonso X (second half of the 13th century), which gives exactly the same account as the *Poema* in so far as the latter extends, and, therefore, may be deemed to contain the narrative of the missing final part of it. The *Crónica* dwells, in particular, upon a supposed redemption of Castile from the overlordship of Leon through the sale by Fernán González to the king of Leon of a certain horse and a hawk, whose price, if not paid on a fixed day, was to double on every succeeding day. As the king allowed the day of payment to pass by, his treasurer found that not all the gold in the world could pay the large sum entailed (as a simple computation in geometrical progression shows) ; and to redeem his royal word the king had to accede to the request of Fernán González that Castile be declared independent of Leon. As a matter of fact, the battlesome Fernán González, as Count of Castile, was virtually, although not nominally, ruler of that region. Other early documents recounting events of Fernán González's career are — in the 13th century — Berceo's *Vida de San Millán* and the *Crónica Rimada del Cid*.

In all probability the *Poema* was composed by a monk of the monastery of San Pedro de Arlanza, and, as certain references in it indicate, it was put together about 1250; cf. Marden in *Revue hispanique* VII. 22. The author drew from Berceo's religious verse and also from the *Alexandre*, therefore his work is subsequent to them. It is likely that he was acquainted with other epic songs (*cantares de gesta*) and especially with the *Poema del Cid*.

Baist (*Grundriss* II. ii. 393) has analyzed the whole poetic tradition of Fernán González, and believes that only that part of it which deals with his marriage to an Infanta of Navarre and his double captivity in Leon and Navarre may be deemed to have been originally treated in a popular epic ; the rest is of the category of the school epic. From the fact that the monk to whom we owe the present form of the epic repeatedly mentions his source of information as an *escriptura*, a *lehenda*, etc., Baist infers that he used Latin material. Perhaps so, but in any event he was certainly working over an antecedent popular poem which dealt already in epic fashion with either part — as Baist says — or a good deal of the heroic career of Fernán González. The monk uses the learned form of the *cuaderna vía*, the quatrain of monorimed Alexandrines, but a considerable number of his verses show only assonance ; and in the imperfect half-Alexandrines of the work, which are clearly good *romance* verses or epic hemistichs containing irreducible epic formulæ, we are tempted to see remnants of an earlier *cantar de gesta* which furnished the monastic writer with his basis.

Utilizing all the documents that have treated poetically or historically of Fernán González, and governed by his own knowledge of O. Sp. phonology, morphology, and syntax, Professor Marden has endeavored to establish a critical and restored text of the monk's poem. Cf. his discussion of all the apparatus criticus in the Introduction to his edition ; Baist, *Grundriss* II. ii. 393 ; Milá y Fontanals, *De la Poesía Heroico-popular Castellana* (Barcelona, 1896, p. 173) ; *Modern Language Notes*, February, 1905 ; Puymaigre, *Les Vieux Auteurs castillans*, II. 153 ff. ; Gorra, *Lingua e letteratura spagnuola*, p. 265 ; Janer's earlier edition of the poem in the *Biblioteca de Autores Españoles* LVII ; Menéndez Pidal, *Notas para el Romancero del Conde Fernán González* in the volume *Homenaje á Menéndez y Pelayo*, I. 429 (Madrid, 1899).

33 71 In the opening stanzas of the poem there is given a compendium of the early history of Spain. The present passage deals with the legend of Count Julian and Roderick the Goth. According to the chronicles, as well as the poetical accounts, Roderick seduced the daughter (Cava) or wife of one of his nobles, Julian, who was in command of a fortress on the sea-coast. In revenge, Julian went over to Africa and urged the Moors to invade Spain. Then he treacherously induced his master, King Roderick, to convert all his weapons of war into plowshares and other instruments of peace, and when the land was devoid of means of defense he admitted the Moors, who rapidly overran Spain after defeating Roderick in 711. As to whether there ever was an epic on the story of Roderick the Goth much doubt has been expressed: cf. Baist, *Grundriss* II. ii. 395, Milá y Fontanals, *De la Poesía Heroico-popular Castellana* p. 107, J. Menéndez Pidal, *Leyendas del Último Rey Godo* (Madrid, 1906). While Milá and Baist deny the existence of *cantares de gesta* on the subject and consider it as a matter which passed from early fictitious Arabic accounts in chronicle form to the O. Sp. chronicles, J. Menéndez Pidal, like Menéndez y Pelayo (*Antología de Poetas Líricos Castellanos* XI. 156), believes that there were epics on the loss of Spain in 711.

33 71 *a* In Marden's text the brackets indicate the letters and words which he restores, the parentheses mark the letters and words which he expunges.

33 72 *a* **Spanna**: this form, by redivision of preposition and noun, could easily arise from *dEspanna* 74 *d*, 80 *b*, etc.

33 73 *b* **de Oropa**: cf. Vocab., and see Baist, *Grundriss* I, 2d ed., p. 890, where he gives other instances of *eu > o*: *Santoveña < Sancta Eufemia*, *Santolalla < Sancta Eulalia*.

34 78 *b* **tovo**, etc.: i.e., he intercepted them on their way.

34 78 *c* **Sangonera**: a river and the neighboring territory in the province of Murcia. According to Milá y Fontanals (cf. Marden, p. 168) the poet has confused his geography here.

34 81 *d* **sy**, etc.: 'If it were not for him (Julian?) on account of whom may they have no pardon for their sins.'

34 83 *d* and 84 Accounts vary as to the fate of Roderick. Cf. J. Menéndez Pidal, l.c., pp. 141 ff. He perished in the battle according to some; he survived it, and, being captured, was tortured to death, according to others; while still others speak of his repentance in a hermitage.

34 84 *b* This line is corrupt. The general sense is that an inscription stone was found on a grave.

35 328 Fernán Sánchez had laid low King Sancho of Navarre, and to obtain revenge for the deed the latter's kinsman, a southern French noble, invaded Castile. By a study of this passage Marden (*Revue hispanique* VII. 22) has obtained a certain basis for the dating of the poem. The scribe, botching the passage, made it speak of two invading counts; but a critical examination of it clearly shows that but one person was meant and he was Count of both Poitou and Toulouse. In

1250, Alphonsus, Count of Poitou, became also Count of Toulouse; the two titles ceased to be united in 1271. We therefore have 1250 as a *terminus a quo* for the dating of this passage. Other evidence of an internal nature places the date of the poem at a period not long after 1250.

35 329 *a* **vyo**: this would be better written *uvyó* = pret. indic. 3d sg. of *uviar* < Lat. *obviare* 'to go to meet,' 'travel,' etc. Cf. Berceo's *Santo Domingo* (ed. Fitz-Gerald), stz. 506 *huujados* (= *uviados*) and 507 *huujar* (= *uviar*), which in the *Biblioteca de Autores Españoles*, Vol. LVII, stzs. 506 and 507, are printed improperly as *viados* and *uyar*.

35 329 *d* **Getarea**: a place in French Navarre.

35 330 *b* There is no satisfactory phonological explanation of **commo** with double *m*.

35 335 *c* **estantygua**: this term denoted a body of demons which were supposed to roam about in the twilight or at night; cf. C. M. de Vasconcellos in *Revue hispanique* for 1900. In *Don Quijote*, I, chap. xxxi, Cervantes seems to allude to the belief in the *estantigua* when he makes Don Quixote speak of *una legión de demonios, que es gente que camina y hace caminar sin cansarse todo aquello que se les antoja*. As the *estadea* the same superstition is found in Portugal: it is mentioned by G. Borrow in his *Bible in Spain*.

36 338 *a* **Layno**: we expect the patronymic here as in 346 *a*.

36 342 *a* **mesmo**: A. M. Espinosa, *Studies in New Mexican Spanish*, finds that *mismo* is the current form in O. Sp. and argues for the etymon **metīpsimus > meísmo > mismo*.

36 345 *d* **Alexandrre**: cf. 351 *Alexandre*. The scribe has many cases of this doubling of the *r* where the usual O. Sp. graphic conditions do not admit it.

36 347 *b* **quien**, etc.: should not this line be regarded as a question?

36 350 *b* and *d* Note the equivalence of *aver a* and *aver de* with a dependent infinitive.

36 351 This stanza was copied from the *Libro de Alexandre* (ed. Morel-Fatio), stz. 2266.

37 355 *c* **ovyeron**, etc.: the omission of the *a* is questionable.

37 356 *c* A comma is needed after *syenpre*.

37 356 *d* The sense seems to be: They saw themselves in great distress as to having any camp there.

38 367 *b* **fincol**: note the article treated here as enclitic to the word preceding it. Is it really assured for this document?

39 368 *c* Marden interprets: *A fin de que la gente no le tuviese por desamparado*.

VIII. LA CRÓNICA GENERAL AND LA GENERAL ESTORIA

To the personal interest of King Alfonso X (Alfonso el Sabio, who was born in 1230, came to the throne in 1252, and died in 1284) we have to attribute the first large use of Spanish prose. As a result of his personal endeavor and of the incentive which he gave to the many scholars whom he gathered about him at his court, Spanish became a supple medium of scientific and literary expression. The many works which have in the past been ascribed to him cannot all have been his individual compositions. For the more extensive among them he doubtless suggested the plan and superintended the working of it; in all probability he also corrected the style of certain of them.

He had a great liking for astronomy and caused compilations to be made which are valuable to those studying the Ptolemaic system; these are the *Libro de Saber de Astronomía* and the *Tablas Alfonsíes* (cf. ed., Madrid, 1863–1867). He showed the usual medieval fondness for games, by preparing, or commissioning others to prepare, manuals dealing with chess, draughts, etc.; and for lapidaries, or studies of gems and their relations to human fortunes, by having translated from Arabic a *Libro de las Piedras*. Other minor works have been attributed to him on no very certain evidence.

Beyond a doubt he was closely concerned with some four important works: the *Crónica General* (which more properly might be called the *Crónica de España*), the *General Estoria*, the *Siete Partidas*, and the *Cantigas de Santa María*. The last-named work we may dismiss at once, interesting and attractive as it is, because it is in Portuguese-Galician; for, following the custom of his time in Castile, Alfonso wrote love lyrics and religious verse in the language of the west of the peninsula. The *Siete Partidas* (edited by the Real Academia, 1807) is a codification of the laws of Spain arranged under seven headings, whence the title. The document gains in importance from a literary point of view in that it is more than a mere statement of the laws; it adds thereto moral and philosophical speculation, and is written in an engaging style. That part alone in which Alfonso discusses — or approves the method of discussing — the duties of monarchs to their subjects is a remarkable counterpart to Machiavelli's *Principe*, and is especially noteworthy for the way in which it stresses morality and religion, which Machiavelli excludes.

The *Crónica General* is the first great history of Spain. For its in-formation — and it goes back as far as the history of humanity outside of Spain allows — it draws upon the Bible and certain ancient historians, upon contemporary historians dealing in Latin with the progress of affairs in Spain (Bishop Roderick of Toledo and Bishop Lucas of Tuy), and upon the knowledge which Alfonso himself and his coadjutors had of recent events. To us far more important than the information de-rived from these sources is that which he appropriated from the epic poems, the *cantares de gesta*. Dealing with national heroes, legendary or historical, such as Bernardo del Carpio, the Cid, Fernán González, the Infantes de Lara, etc., Alfonso and his cohistorians inform us also of the terms in which the minstrels sang of those personages. Doing this, they often cast into prose form the contents of lost poems; again they kept snatches of the lost poems, and it has been possible for Menéndez Pidal in the case of the Infantes de Lara to reconstruct in verse form portions of the lost epic or epics on them; for, apart from the chronicle accounts and the ensuing ballads, we have no important literary record of them. As the ostensibly poetic accounts of the Cid and Fernán González given by the *Crónica General* run parallel with the preserved poems, we may infer that its similar accounts of the Infantes de Lara, of Bernardo del Carpio, etc., likewise represent the contents of lost poems.

As regards its text the *Crónica General* is in a state well nigh dis-maying to the scholar. In 1541, Florián Docampo (De Ocampo) pub-lished at Zamora a text which long passed as the *Crónica General*. But the studies of various scholars, and especially of Menéndez Pidal, have shown that Ocampo's edition represents a later and modified form of Alfonso's Chronicle. As a result of Menéndez Pidal's investigations (cf. his *Leyenda de los Infantes de Lara*, Madrid, 1896, pp. 49 ff., his *Catálogo de Crónicas Generales de España manuscritas*, Madrid, 1898, and his forth-coming study which will form Vol. II of his edition of the *Crónica*), it proves to be the case that, at the best, Ocampo's edition represents a form of a third edition of the text.

For some time it has been Menéndez Pidal's chief purpose to arrive at a pristine text of the *Crónica*. The difficulties in the way are enor-mous. As he says (in the Introduction *Al Lector* of his edition in the *Nueva Biblioteca de Autores Españoles*, Madrid, 1906) : "What dis-heartens him who studies the *Crónica* is the great divergency which he discovers when he compares several MSS. out of the many in which this so long text is preserved." He thinks that in his text he has arrived at the "*Primera Crónica General*, free from large interpolation and rearrangements of any sort," and he states the following with respect to former versions: "The MSS. previously confounded with one another under the common title of *Crónica General del Rey Sabio* are the result of almost two centuries of historiographical activity, beginning with the *Primera Crónica General*, which Alfonso X had made, and continuing with the *Crónica General de 1344*, that of *Veinte Reyes*, the *Tercera* and the *Cuarta Crónica General*, that of *1404*, and others of less importance."

From the text of our extract, published originally in the *Leyenda de los Infantes de Lara*, the editor has departed somewhat in the edition of the whole Chronicle: the important divergencies will be noted in the remarks following. In the passage chosen we have a bit of the epic tradition of the Infantes de Lara, so excellently studied by Menéndez Pidal in his *Leyenda*. It is the very opening of their tragic story that is presented here. The treacherous plot devised by Ruy Velásquez at the instigation of Doña Lambra, the betrayal of the Infantes into the power of a Moorish army which slays them, the carrying of their heads to Cordova, the Moorish stronghold in which their father had already been confined by the knavery of Ruy Velásquez, the father's recognition of the heads of his seven sons, all these traits, as well as the later vengeance wrought upon Ruy Velásquez and Doña Lambra by the Moorish half-brother of the Infantes, Mudarra, passed into the ballads of the 15th and 16th centuries and into the 19th-century Romantic production of the Duke of Rivas, the *Moro Expósito*.

The various details of the story have been worked out, not only by Menéndez Pidal, but also by G. Paris in his article *La Légende des Infants de Lara* in the *Journal des savants*, Paris, 1898.

The *General Estoria* (or *Grande e General Historia*) remains still unedited as a whole. Apparently Alfonso intended it to be a compendium of universal history, especially of ancient history, and perhaps to form an introduction to the *Crónica General*, which preceded it in date of composition. Much use is made in it of the Biblical narratives and of classical and Oriental works. As to the particular way in which the *General Estoria* utilized the Bible, cf. S. Berger, *Les Bibles castillanes*, p. 361 etc. in *Romania* XVIII. In the later aljamiado poem (cf. p. 63) we have the story of Joseph again told. The source of Alfonso's account of Joseph was an Arabic work, the *Book of Roads and Realms* of Abū Obaid, King of Niebla, according to Menéndez Pidal, *Poema de Yuçuf*, p. 72. Cf. Menéndez y Pelayo, *Orígenes de la Novela*, I. xlv.

On Alfonso el Sabio and his various works, cf. Baist in the *Grundriss* II. ii. 408 ff.; Fitzmaurice-Kelly, *Littérature espagnole*, pp. 60 ff.; Mérimée, *Précis d'histoire de la littérature espagnole*, pp. 58 ff.; Puymaigre, *Les Vieux Auteurs castillans* II. 3 ff. On the tradition of the Infantes cf., besides the works already cited, Milá y Fontanals, *De la Poesía Heroico-popular Castellana*, p. 202.

40 2 era: the era was 38 years ahead of our normal reckoning, whence the date 959 A.D. given in l. 4.

40 7 alffoz: as *f* here represents an Arabic aspirate, the doubling may indicate the force of the aspiration. However, the doubling of *f* is also often inorganic in O. Sp. — **caso**: note *casar* used already in O. Sp. with the force of *casarse*.

40 9 Ferrandez: in the complete edition Menéndez Pidal writes Fernández, the more usual form. He also uses *como*, *conde*, etc. instead of the diphthongized forms. It is somewhat a matter of doubt whether his use of *su* instead of our *so*, before masculine nouns, is an improvement upon his present text. Garci-Fernández is but one of several really historical figures in the Infantes legend: he ruled Castile from 970 to 995.

40 10 Llambla: the later documents, ballads, etc. call her Lambra. It seems to be the Lat. *Flammula*; cf. Boccaccio's *Fiammetta*.

40 14 inffantes: this term does not necessarily imply that the young men in question were of royal origin. Menéndez Pidal (*Leyenda*, p. 443) calls attention to the fact that in the O. Fr. epic *enfant* meant the youth who had not yet received the dubbing to knighthood (cf. Gautier, *La Chevalerie*, p. 193). He adds: "In Spain it seems that the name *infante* was given to noble youths, even though they were already knights (perhaps until such time as they inherited from their fathers), as happened to the Infantes de Lara."

40 15 Salas: Salas, the domain of Gonzalo Gustioz and his sons, was situated in the district of Lara. Hence, by extension, the later and more general use of the term *Infantes de Lara*.

41 11 iogar tablas: cf. the mod. *jugar á tablas*. Suppression of prepositions was more common in O. Sp. than now, if we may trust MS. readings; cf. l. 21 etc. *fue alançar.* — **açedexes**: Menéndez Pidal now reads *açedrexes*. This represents the mod. Sp. *ajedrez* 'chess,' which looks back to O.Sp. *axedrez*. The word may have some connection with the Persian *shah* 'king'; cf. the importance of the king in chess, and the terms "checkmate" etc. The Fr. *échec* and Ital. *scacchi* suggest *shah*. Cf. Diez, *Wtb.*, p. 428: "from the Arab. *ash-sha'treng*

' chess-board,' and this from the Persian, and the latter is of Indian origin and means ' having a hundred, i.e. different, colors,' " etc.

41 30 Menéndez Pidal now reads *alli el solo*.

42 11 Menéndez Pidal now prints the better O. Sp. *leuantasse*. So also in **43** 18 he now has *desuiasse*.

42 32 **uos yo meresçi**: for the interpolation cf. also l. 34 and **43** 2 and 5.

42 34 **muriero**: instead of this interesting form, Menéndez Pidal now prints *murier*. Cf. his *Gram. elem.*, 2d ed., p. 219: " In the fut. subj. the 1st person with etymological final *-o* was used in the 12th–14th centuries: *fallaro, tomaro, pudiero, sopiero*, beside the forms in *-r* or *-re* which later prevailed entirely."

43 6 **enel**: Menéndez Pidal now has *en ell*.

43 9 **ell**: observe the *ll* of the pronoun retained even in the final position. It is ordinarily so in the article before a word beginning with a vowel.

43 11 **enel rostro**: Menéndez Pidal now omits this from his text, but mentions it as a variant.

43 25 Menéndez Pidal now reads *muy mester*.

43 26 **del mayor prez**: this use of the article with the true comparative is found as late as the *Don Quijote*, where (with archaic effect) it appears in Part I, Chap. IX: *Esta Dulcinea . . . tuvo la mejor mano para salar puercos, que otra mujer de toda la Mancha.*

43 34 Menéndez Pidal now has *complirie*, which is the better O. Sp. form. The *u* appeared first in the unaccented position before a following accented diphthong *ie* or *io*.

44 1 The extracts dealing with Fernán González were taken by Marden from the MS. of the *Crónica General* numbered X–i–4 in the Escurial Library. The text printed by Menéndez Pidal (p. 392) is substantially the same. The incident in Fernán González's career treated here is dealt with briefly in the 37th *Exemplo* of Juan Manuel's *Conde Lucanor* (Knust-Birch-Hirschfeld ed., p. 165).

44 10 **fuessen . . . con ell**: ' should . . . go to him '; cf. mod. *ir con*, ' to go to.'

44 17 **uiniesen**: Menéndez Pidal has *uiniessen*.

44 21 **atender los**: in such cases Menéndez Pidal writes the pronoun as enclitic, *atenderlos*.

44 24 **poro**: here and in l. 26, Menéndez Pidal has *por o*.

45 2 **lo non mostro**: another instance of interpolation: cf. **45** 20.

45 3 **mas**: here the modern language would prefer *sino*.

45 4 **contar** : Menéndez Pidal has *cotar* and gives *contar* as a variant. *Cotar*, = mod. *acotar*, is based on the Lat. *quot, quotus -a -um*, and here has the meaning of ' comment upon,' ' interpret.'

45 9 **ganarnos** : Menéndez Pidal prints *ganar nos*, apparently regarding *nos* as the subject pronoun. — **pechar les** : read *pecharles*, and in l. 10 *fazernos emos*, and in l. 11 *doblargela emos*.

46 3 **sopiera** : here an indicative pluperfect or preterit.

46 15 **atamana** = *atamaña*. Cf. *tamanna* l. 16.

IX. CANTICUM CANTICORUM

The manuscript I–j–6 of the Escurial library, in which this Old Spanish translation of the *Canticle of Canticles* (*Song of Solomon*) occurs, is described by S. Berger in *Romania* XVIII. 380 ff., 391 ff., 560 ff. According to him the portions of the Old Testament and the Four Gospels comprised in the manuscript constitute " la plus ancienne traduction textuelle de la Bible " in Spanish. Cornu, who intends to publish the Four Gospels also, attributes the language of the manuscript to the 13th century (cf. *Festgabe f. Foerster*, p. 121, note); Berger (l.c., p. 560) states that the manuscript itself seems to be of the first half of the 14th century. Moreover, he finds that this manuscript is not the only one to transmit to us all or part of the Old Spanish translation in question. " Nous en retrouvons," he says (l.c., p. 391), " le Nouveau Testament dans un manuscrit interpolé de l'*Historia general* [i.e. the *Grande y General Historia* of Alfonso X, a thirteenth-century document still unedited, except for some passages of it] . . . et peut-être les Prophètes, en tout ou en partie, dans un autre manuscrit interpolé." These manuscripts are also in the Escurial library (I–j–2 and Y–j–8). In his interesting general account of the Bible in Spain, the land which in the age of the Renaissance presented us with the first polyglot edition of the Bible, Berger remarks (l.c., p. 361) : " Avec Alphonse X l'amour de la Bible se manifeste, uni à une conception historique très remarquable, dans l'*Historia general*. . . . Vers le même temps on commence à traduire la Bible elle-même en castillan et ces traductions textuelles rentrent peu à peu dans l'*Historia general* pour la compléter, pour se fondre avec elle et pour en faire une Bible autant qu'un livre d'histoire."

Cornu publishes the whole *Canticle*. Six of the twelve verses given here are printed by Berger, whose transcript differs slightly from

Cornu's. Sometimes the translator quite mistook the meaning of his original — the Vulgate — but in general he is rather faithful to it.

47 10 **levantedes :** observe *levantar* in the transitive use : cf. l. 15, where *levantat* seems to be *levántate*.

47 18 **tiempo,** etc. : the Vulgate has *tempus putationis advenit* 'the time of pruning has come.' Ordinarily the Sp. verb *cuedar* has only the sense of 'to think': here it seems that the other sense of Latin *putare*, 'to prune,' is passed over to it. The translator is not too clear as to the meaning of the word, as the correlation with *vino* shows.

X. JUAN RUIZ : LIBRO DE BUEN AMOR

In the preface to his paleographical ed., Ducamin has described fully the 3 MSS. of Ruiz's work. One of them, *S*, is in script of the end of the 14th or the early 15th century and is posterior to the other two. It was originally at Salamanca (whence the *S*), but is now at Madrid in the Library of the Royal Palace. Ducamin has made it the basis of his text, taking variants from the other MSS. The second MS., *G*, once belonged to the archivist Gayoso ; it is now in the Library of the Real Academia de la Lengua at Madrid. It is in script of the 14th century, having been completed in 1389, and, like *S*, is the work of a single scribe : it lacks the first ten quatrains of the work as well as a passage in prose which follows them. The third MS., *T*, belonged once to the Cathedral at Toledo : it is now in the Biblioteca Nacional at Madrid. It is also due to a single scribe and is of the same time as *G*. A fragment, *F*, containing a few verses, is in a manuscript of the private library of the King ; it is valueless : cf. Ducamin, p. xxx.

The first edition of the work was that of Sánchez, who published it as *Poesías del Arcipreste de Hita* in Vol. IV of his *Colección de Poesías Castellanas*, etc., in 1790. It is neither critical nor paleographical, and suppresses certain stanzas deemed immoral. It was reprinted by Ochoa (Paris, 1842). Amador de los Ríos, in Vol. IV of his *Historia Crítica de la Literatura Española* (1863), printed some of the suppressed verses, but his text is very faulty. In 1864 Janer reprinted Sánchez's text in Vol. LVII of the *Biblioteca de Autores Españoles*, pretending, however, to include all the passages omitted by Sánchez. But he did not do this with completeness, and his text is also uncritical. Hence the necessity for a complete text. Ducamin aimed at giving the paleographic conditions and has not sought to amend the text.

Juan Ruiz, Archpriest of Hita, is the first true poet in the history of Spanish literature. Not inaptly he may be termed the Villon of Spain, for, like Villon, he was both a reprobate and a real singer. We have not the dates of his birth and death; but as he was imprisoned by his ecclesiastical superior, Gil de Albornoz, Archbishop of Toledo from 1337 to 1367, and remained in prison for thirteen years, and as another cleric is mentioned as Archpriest of Hita in 1351, it is generally assumed that his activity belonged to the first half of the 14th century. His incarceration was probably occasioned by the irregularities of his life. As it seems, he improved the opportunities presented by his enforced leisure to develop his poetic genius, but just how much of his preserved verse was written in jail is a matter of conjecture. As we have it, his work must represent a selection out of a larger mass of compositions : it really forms a kind of versified diary of his amorous experiences, interspersed with many other poetical elements, erotic, didactic, religious, etc., in their nature. He appears to have intended to give the title *Libro de Buen Amor* to his book — it is not actually so styled in the MSS. — in order to indicate to us that we should all strive to love divine things and not the things of this world. This is humoristic on his part and quite in keeping with the general humorism of the book, for the moralizing purpose is entirely subordinated to the amorous and playful impulses of the author, who unblushingly narrates the vicissitudes of his culpable love affairs, in the conduct of which he is aided by a go-between, the old woman Trota-Conventos. She is one of the chief characters in the work, and is interesting for the later history of Spanish literature as being the prototype of the Celestina of the similarly-named dramatic novel. Trota-Conventos is herself a descendant from the go-between in the Pseudo-Ovid or *Pamphilus de Amore* (cf. Gröber, *Grundriss* II. i. 427), a medieval document of amorous import. Of course the great authority on scabrous love affairs was known to Juan Ruiz, for the impress of the *Ars Amatoria* of Ovid is clear. Fables drawn from Old French *Isopets* and possibly other collections, smutty stories derived from Old French fabliaux and revealing their origin by even retaining Old French words, a version of the contest between Lent and the Carnival season, based on an Old French *Debat de Quaresme et de Charnage*, — all these evince the author's acquaintance with foreign literature. Not the least charming elements in the book are the religious lyrics (like the one addressed to the Virgin Mary), undoubtedly sincere in tone, — for in characters like Ruiz extremes touch, and they easily pass from the immoral to the devout.

—and the little pastoral poems in which he tells humorously of his encounters with mountain girls (*serranas*) and dairymaids, thus anticipating the similar poems of the Marquis of Santillana (15th century).

The meters used by Ruiz are of the most varied kind. In the more purely narrative and descriptive parts of the book he uses Alexandrines in the *Cuaderna vía* arrangement. In the more lyrical passages he employs verses of 4, 5, 6, and 7 syllables. The exact metrical constitution of the whole work cannot be determined independently of a critical study of the text, and this has not yet been made; see, however, F. Hanssen, *Los Metros de los Cantares de Juan Ruiz* (*Anales de la Universidad*), Santiago de Chile, 1902.

Cf. Baist in the *Grundriss* II. ii. 405 ff.; Fitzmaurice-Kelly, *Littérature espagnole*, pp. 71 ff.; E. Mérimée, *Précis d'histoire de la littérature espagnole*, pp. 76 ff.; M. Menéndez y Pelayo, *Antología*, III. liii ff., *Revue hispanique* VIII. 553; Puymaigre, *Vieux Auteurs castillans* II. 257 ff.

48 11 *a* **crieste**: The MSS. seem to show *s* and *z* confused: we have here interpreted the sibilant signs in accordance with the correct O. Sp. usage of the 14th century. Ducamin tried to render the conditions of the MSS., but of course, as Morel-Fatio states for the *Alexandre*, it is not always easy to distinguish the scribes' cursive *s* and *z* from each other, and, besides, the scribes ignorantly interchanged them. By writing *espiritu* in l. *a*, and suppressing the *El* of l. *b*, we obtain a perfect stanza in *cuaderna vía*. In like fashion many of the irregularities in the text might be remedied. The text shows Leonesisms, as Menéndez Pidal indicates in his review of Ducamin's edition.

48 13 *a* **crieste**: under the influence of the ending *-é* of the first pers. sg. pret. indic. of the 1st conj., that of the second pers. was often changed from *-aste* to *-este*.

48 13 *b* **acipreste**: why the loss of *r*? Did it disappear in popular speech before the dental sibilant *ts* (*ç*) as before the sibilant *s* (*coso* < *cursum*; O. Sp. *vierso* < *vĕrsum*)?

48 13 *c* This line gives the true title of the book. For *fazer* we should substitute *far* or *fer* to correct the line; cf. stz. 498 *a*. No attempt is made here to correct all the faulty lines.

49 298 *a* As a story of the wolf, the fox, and the mule, this little apologue appears in the Italian *Novellino* (ed. Gualterazzi, No. XCIV). A form of it occurs also in the Old French *Roman de Renard*. On its history in general cf. A. d'Ancona, *Del Novellino e delle sue fonti* (in *Studj di critica e storia letteraria*, Bologna, 1880, p. 339).

49 298 *b*   **conel . . . pesa**: is the idea this: *la caça non pesa con el*, i.e. 'he is not overburdened with prey'?

49 299 *c*   **en eso**, etc.: i.e. 'I find myself resting under that obligation.'

49 300 *d*   **faz . . . quito**: does this mean 'deal with me as with the one whom thou hast freed'? Probably not, although *quito* = 'set free,' 'left free,' occurs in O. Sp.; cf. *Cid* 1370 *De mi sean quitos* 'Let them be left free by me' and 1539 *quito seua Minaya* 'Minaya goes off free (of expense),' and Berceo, *Loores*, stz. 147, *Era todo cativo quito de la presion* 'Every captive was set free from prison.' The more exact sense here is 'deal with me as with one left free to thy treatment,' i.e. with whom thou mayst deal freely. Cf. Berceo, *Milagros*, stz. 86, where the demons are claiming a certain soul and striving to drive the angels away from it:

> Fizieron los diablos luego muy grant querella,
> Que suya era quita, que se partiessen della.

> 'The Devils then made very great complaint,
> For it [the soul] was freely theirs, so that they [the angels] should depart from it.'

49 490 *a*   The theme of this passage reappears in the 17th century in Francisco de Quevedo's poem

> *Poderoso caballero*
> *Es don Dinero.*

50 491 *a*   This *ome*, like the *ome* of 490 *b*, should be interpreted as *omne*. De Lollis in his *Noterelle spagnole* (in *Studj romanzi* for 1900) expressed belief in a form *ome*, but Baist (in *Ztschr. f. roman. Philol.* IV. 451) had already termed *omme* very doubtful. There is no evidence of the survival of *homo* in Spanish; besides, it could only give *uemo* or *omo*; *hŏm(ĭ)nem* has the secondary combination *mn*, which dissimilated one of its nasals to *r*, after persisting for a while (*omne* > *omre* > *hombre*; *nomĭnare* > *nomnar* > *nomrar* > *nombrar*, etc.). Original *mn* assimilated the *m* to the *n* (*damnare* > *dannar* > *dañar*).

50 509 *c*   **alguaçil**: this should be *alguazil*, as its Arabic etymon has a voiced sibilant *z*.

50 1661 *a*   The verses of this song are intended to be eight-syllabled lines with the stress on the seventh syllable, and four-syllabled lines with the stress on the third.

51 1662 *d*   It would be better to put no mark after *maraujlla* and a period at the end of the next line.

XI. JUAN MANUEL

Like his uncle Alfonso X, Juan Manuel (1282–1348) gave himself up with great zeal to the cultivation of the vernacular prose. His life was a very busy one, spent in good part on the battle-field or in the council-chamber. Still a youth, he was in Murcia fighting against the Moors. When Fernando IV died (1312) he became regent during the minority of his kinsman, Alfonso XI. Later, when the latter had assumed the reins of power, some unpleasantness arose between them and active hostilities resulted. They were reconciled, however, and in 1340 Juan Manuel helped the King to win his great victory over the Moors of Andalusia on the battle-field of Salado. Two years later he seems to have been present at the siege and capture of Algeciras by Alfonso XI.

In spite of this great activity, Juan Manuel found opportunity for a large amount of composition in Spanish prose, impelled thereto — as passages in his work, e.g. in the Prologue of his *Libro de la Caça*, expressly state — by the example of his uncle, Alfonso X, for whom he evinces the greatest admiration. He has left us two lists of his works: the one appears at the beginning of his *Conde Lucanor* (or *Patronio*); the other is in the Prologue to a MS. collection of all his works, which he thus brought together in corrected form and gave to the Monastery of Peñafiel. Unfortunately that MS. collection in its original form is not now discoverable. In the 15th-century copy of it (cf. Gräfenberg, 446, note 2), MS. S–34 of the Biblioteca Nacional at Madrid, several of the twelve works that should be there are missing, and some contained in it are defective, as e.g. the *Libro del Cauallero et del Escudero*, out of whose 51 chapters at least 13 are lacking.

It is at the beginning of the Prologue of this imperfectly preserved collection of his works that Juan Manuel narrates the little story given on pp. 52–53 of our Extracts. This has no direct relation to the *Libro del Cauallero et del Escudero*, although, following the example of Gräfenberg, we print it under that heading.

On the basis of the two lists mentioned, and in accordance with other references to his works made here and there by Juan Manuel as well as with the circumstances of his life, Baist (in his edition of the *Libro de la Caça*, Halle, 1880, p. 154) has drawn up a chronological list of the various compositions. It is this:

Crónica Abreviada ⎫
Libro de la Caballería ⎬ 1320–1324
Libro de la Caza 1325-1326

The second, third, and fourth Parts of the *Patronio* (or *Conde Lu-canor*) probably belong between 1329 and 1334. It is thus seen that this great literary activity belonged to the years 1320 to 1335. Of the works indicated, the *Libro de la Caballería* is not to be found. Also missing are the *Libro de los Sabios*, the *Libro de los Engeños*, and the *Libro de los Cantares*, which Baist assigns to the period between 1320 and 1328, and the *Reglas como se debe trobar*, which he places between 1328 and 1335.

The *Crónica Abreviada* is a compendium of his uncle's *Crónica General*. The *Libro de la Caballería* may have been of the same nature as the preserved *Libro del Caballero y del Escudero*. This latter has a novelesque framework borrowed from the Catalan Ramon Lull's *Libre del Orde de Cavalleria*, and through the medium of conversations between an old knight, now a hermit, and a young squire, who soon becomes a knight, conveys much information of an encyclopedic nature. For this information J. M. drew upon other books, notably his uncle's *Siete Partidas*, but he also reflects his own experience of men and things. The idea of the *Libro de la Caza*, a treatise on falconry, came to J. M., as he tells us in the Prologue of the book, from one which Alfonso X had caused to be made; it ranks well among the books of its kind. The *Libro del Infante* is an earlier and still discernible form of the *Libro de los Estados*. In the earlier form it was J. M.'s Apology for his warlike attitude with regard to the sovereign, Alfonso XI; in the extended form it becomes a general consideration of the various stations and callings in life and of their relative value for human happiness and worth. The *Libro Infinido* ('Unfinished Book') is addressed to his eldest son and deals with the duties of rulers. The *Libro de las Armas* is a history of his own family, its emblazonments, etc. The *Prólogo General*, prepared, as has been said, for the MS. containing his collected

works, must come late. Also one of his latest documents is that addressed to the Dominican monk Masquefa : it treats of the Assumption
of the Blessed Virgin Mary. As to the nature of the lost works we can
only speculate. The *Libro de los Sabios* was doubtless didactic ; the
Libro de los Engeños must have treated of engines of war, and may have
been based directly or indirectly on Vegetius, *De re militari*, which
J. M. cites elsewhere. According to most opinions, the *Libro de los
Cantares* contained compositions in Galician-Portuguese, in which J. M.
could probably indite verse, even as his uncle had done ; and it is generally assumed that the *Reglas como se debe trobar* simply stated rules
for such conventional verse compositions of the Provençalizing sort as
those of the Catalonian and Portuguese-Galician schools. Baist is of
the opinion (cf. *Grundriss* II. ii. 419 and 426) that the *Reglas* was a redaction of one of the several early Catalan treatises of the class. In
Castilian, of course, we have some specimens of J. M.'s power of versi-
fying in the rimed moralizations to the tales in the *Conde Lucanor*.

This last is the Golden Book of the Old Spanish period, in so far as
Part I is concerned. Parts II–IV (in the Knust ed., Parts I–III) consist merely of sententious sayings derived chiefly from the older *Boca-
dos de Oro* (cf. Baist, *Grundriss* II. ii. 411) ; Part V (in the Knust ed.,
Part IV) is concerned with spiritual and religious matters. The *Libro
de los Enxienplos del Conde Lucanor et de Patronio*, as J. M. himself
calls it in the opening of the book, is a framework of tales antedating
the *Decameron* of Boccaccio and the *Canterbury Tales* of Chaucer.
The framework is this : a ruling count, Lucanor, when in doubt as to
the course to pursue in some matter of statecraft or with regard to
affairs in general, seeks advice of Patronius, formerly his tutor and
now his counselor. The latter does not respond directly to him, but
answers with a tale involving a similar situation and the solution that
was there found possible for the difficulty. Basing himself thereon, the
count proceeds to act in a suitable fashion in his own case. The moral
of the tale is reënforced, for not only does Patronius state it in prose,
but J. M. repeats it at the end in verse form, employing meters of several
sorts (cf. F. Hanssen, *Notas á la Versificación de Juan Manuel*, in *Anales
de la Universidad*, Santiago de Chile, 1902, p. 26).

Baist, who knows so well the whole work of J. M., has given a succinct account of the sources of the *Conde Lucanor* (*Grundriss*, II. ii.
419) : " The contents of the 51 tales, from which everything obscene
is excluded, are of the most varied : historical matter or half-historical
matter dealing with Spain, the author's own experiences, some Arabic

traditions, Phædrus, the *Calila and Dimna*, the *Barlaam*, along with the whole European stock of anecdotes. Some of all this is told in incomparable fashion, all of it from memory; the diction is lively, the manner original." Above all, Baist (p. 414) stresses the author's indebtedness to the general European fund of anecdotes. Rhetorical flourish is lacking in J. M.'s style; he coördinates his clauses and avoids turgidness, the besetting sin of later Spanish prose and verse.

With the exception of the *Crónicas* and the *Libro de la Caça*, Gayangos published J. M.'s works, in a very incorrect form, in Vol. LI of the *Biblioteca de Autores Españoles*; of some of the works he made improper divisions. The *Libro de la Caça* was edited by Baist, Halle, 1880, and by Gutiérrez de la Vega in *Biblioteca Venatoria*, Vol. III, Madrid, 1877; the *Crónica Complida* by Baist, in *Roman. Forschungen* VII. 551 ff., the volume which has also Gräfenberg's good edition of the *Libro del Cauallero et del Escudero*, with a study of the text. As the *Libro del Cauallero et del Escudero*, in the collective MS. S–34, is preceded only by the General Prologue, Gräfenberg has included the latter in his edition. It is preserved only in the one MS., at the head of which it stands, being followed immediately by the *Libro del Cauallero et del Escudero*.

Besides S–34 there are four other MSS. of the *Conde Lucanor* (some of which omit Parts II–V): viz. (1) one in the Biblioteca Nacional, M–100; (2) one in the Library of the Academia de la Historia at Madrid, Est. 27. gr. 3 a; (3) one which belonged to the Conde Puñonrostro and was purchased by E. Krapf; all of these are of the 15th century; and (4) one which was owned by Gayangos and belongs to the 16th century. The first printed edition was that of Argote de Molina, Seville, 1575. Practically reprints of this are the edition of Madrid, 1642, that of A. Keller, Stuttgart, 1839, and that of Barcelona, 1853. Better than these is that of the *Biblioteca de Autores Españoles*, LI, but, like the other documents printed in that volume, it is philologically unsatisfactory, being neither paleographic nor critical. Two different editions by E. Krapf, Vigo, 1898, and Vigo, 1900 (this latter giving the Puñonrostro MS.), are likewise unsatisfactory. The best available edition is that of H. Knust, prepared for the press, after his death, by Professor Birch-Hirschfeld, Leipzig, 1900. It is based upon MS. S–34 and aims to give variants from the other four MSS. and from the edition of Argote de Molina and that of Gayangos. It is not a definitive edition, however, as it leaves no little to be desired.

Cf. Baist, *Grundriss* II. ii. 418 ff.; Fitzmaurice-Kelly, *Littérature espagnole*, pp. 76 ff., and the bibliography on p. 462; Mérimée, *Précis d'histoire de la littérature espagnole,* pp. 64 ff.; Puymaigre, *Les Vieux Auteurs castillans* II. 177 ff.; the Introduction to Gräfenberg's edition of the *Cauallero et Escudero,* and the introduction to the Knust edition of the *Conde Lucanor.* There is a French translation of the *Conde Lucanor* by A. de Puibusque, Paris, 1854; and an English translation by J. York, London, 1868, based perhaps upon the French. An older version is the German by Von Eichendorff, Berlin, 1840. For congeners to Juan Manuel's tales see Liebrecht's edition of Dunlop's *Prose Fiction,* Berlin, 1851, pp. 501 ff., and Puymaigre, l.c., as well as the notes appended to Knust's edition. Much remains to be done in the way of comparative literature studies on the *Conde Lucanor.*

52 1 To explain why he took the trouble to prepare a corrected collection of his works, J. M. narrates this tale in his General Prologue. He localizes it at Perpignan in a time not long before his own birth, but the story is an old and widespread one. It is told in Greek by Diogenes Laertius (2d or 3d century A.D.) in his *Lives and Teachings of the Famous Philosophers of Antiquity,* apropos of the Greek poet Philoxenus (4th century B.C.) and some brickmakers. The Italian taleteller F. Sacchetti (1335–1410) has a similar tale about Dante and a blacksmith (Tale CXIV; cf. also CXV, and see Papanti, *Dante secondo la tradizione e i novellatori,* Leghorn, 1873, p. 61, note 4), and Dunlop, *History of Prose Fiction,* London, 1896, II. 152, indicates it as told of Ariosto and still other poets (cf. the London *Athenæum,* June 17, 1854). See further Menéndez y Pelayo, *Orígenes* I. xcv, and Landau, *Beiträge zur Geschichte der ital. Novelle,* p. 20. — **Asi:** in the original document it was *assi.* According to the editors, S–34 seems to have simplified intervocalic *ss.*

52 2 e[n] la faz[er]: the MS. has *e la faz.* Baist, Gräfenberg, and others propose the change. The other changes indicated here in [ ] are necessitated by scribal omissions.

52 9 primero: even in the *Don Quijote* we find traces of the full form before a noun. — **don Jaymes:** Jaime I of Mallorca, 1248–1311.

53 23 afan: there is no satisfactory etymology for this word. Fitz-Gerald, *Sto. Domingo,* p. 137, proposes an unexplained *ad* + **fannum.* There seems to have been an older Sp. *afaño,* still used in Aragon; *afan* may be a Provençal loan-word, as Fitz-Gerald suggests.

54 1 This story was utilized by Calderón in *La Vida es Sueño* I. ii. 253 ff. Cf. Liebrecht's edition of Dunlop's *Prose Fiction,* p. 544, and Knust's note, pp. 323–324, where an Oriental variation is given.

54 5 contesce de estar: observe the linking preposition which is not used now.

54 18 **atramizes**: the *i* appears regularly in our text; we expect *a* as in the heading. Apparently only S. 34 has the *i*; the other MSS. have *u* (*atramuces, atarmuces*, etc.). The Arabic source is *attormoç* or *attormuç*.

55 21 **cred**: just as *seer > ser, seed > sed*, so other verbs, as *creed*, show occasionally the same contraction.

XII. PERO LÓPEZ DE AYALA: RIMADO DE PALACIO

There are two long MSS. of this work, the one at Madrid and the other in the Escurial. They will be described by Professor Kuersteiner in the paleographic edition which he is preparing for the *Bibliotheca Hispanica*. Previous to the appearance of the edition of Janer in Vol. LVII of the *Biblioteca de Autores Españoles*, only portions of the work had been printed; cf. F. Wolf, *Studien zur Geschichte der span. u. portug. Nationallitteratur*, pp. 138 ff. Janer's edition is unsatisfactory for philological purposes, as it shows modernizations and arbitrary editorial changes.

A leading noble of Castile, López de Ayala was born in 1332 and lived until 1407. He was active in both politics and warfare, and served in succession four sovereigns, Pedro I, Enrique II, Juan I, and Enrique III, apparently modifying his political views to suit the changing administrative conditions, and becoming Grand Chancellor of Castile in 1398. He suffered two periods of captivity, being captured first by the English at the battle of Nájera in 1367, and again by the Portuguese at Aljubarrota in 1385. Legend has it that upon the occasion of his first capture he was carried off to England by the Black Prince, and, a prisoner there, wrote his *Rimado de Palacio* under conditions similar to those under which James I of Scotland and Charles d'Orléans wrote their works. But substantial proof of his having ever been in England has not yet been given. Fitzmaurice-Kelly, *Littérature espagnole*, p. 83, says: "We can determine approximately the different periods in which the *Rimado de Palacio* was composed. In the first part of the poem an allusion to the schism which declared itself under the pontificate of Urban VI must date from 1378 or the following years; a reference to the death of Hernán Pérez de Ayala, father of the author, takes us to 1385 or shortly thereafter, and the mention that the schism had lasted twenty-five years fixes the date of composition at 1403."

López de Ayala's literary output is no slight one. He shows himself an early man of the Renaissance in his translations from Livy (the

Decades), Boethius (*De Consolatione Philosophiae*), and Isidore of Seville (*De Summo Bono*), and he added to these versions his renderings of the *Historia Trojana* of Guido delle Colonne and the *De Casibus Virorum Illustrium* of Boccaccio. Like Juan Manuel, he also produced his treatise on falconry, the *Libro de Cetrería* (ed. in the *Bibliófilos Españoles*, Vol. V; cf. also *Biblioteca Venatoria* of Gutiérrez de la Vega, Madrid, 1879, Vol. III).

As an historian Ayala has his merits. "With this contemporary of the Frenchman Froissart and the Italian Villani [Villani died when Ayala was sixteen years old], history loses the impersonal character which it had usually had up to that time; the author, the man, shows himself at last, and communicates to the narrative an accent of individuality. Ayala also makes of it — or, at least, strives to make of it — an artistic work, according to the ancient models with which he was familiar, and which at times he strives to reproduce, especially Titus Livius" (E. Mérimée, *Précis d'histoire de la littérature espagnole*, p. 84). These capabilities as a historian he shows in his continuation of the official chronicles of the realm (*Crónicas de los Reyes de Castilla* : ed. in *Biblioteca de Autores Españoles*, Vol. LXVI, and by Llaguno y Amírola in *Crónicas Españolas*, Madrid, 1779), which embraces the periods of the four monarchs whom he served.

But the most important of the works of Ayala is his *Rimado de Palacio*, which, like the *Libro de Buen Amor* of Ruiz, is, at least partly, autobiographical in its nature. It differs from Ruiz's work in being eminently serious of tone in the satirical arraignment of the society of the time, which forms a large part of the whole. All classes are passed in review, from the lowest to the highest, and the Court especially is pilloried. Our extract deals with the tribulations of the soldier who vainly seeks in a venal court for any requital of his service of his king and country.

The autobiographical and satirical parts of the work are in *cuaderna vía*, and this is one of the last important examples of the use of this form. In some interspersed hymns and songs, most of which are addressed to the Virgin Mary, Ayala employs lyric measures common in the Provençal-Galician school, using especially the short line of 8 (7) and 7 (6) syllables with interwoven rimes. In conclusion, it may be said that the *Rimado* has much value as a picture of manners of the time. The title *Rimado de Palacio* is not due to the author; Baist says (*Grundriss* II. ii. 421, note 3) : " its meaning is not quite clear, for ' rime ' in Spanish [i.e. the term *rime*] is doubtful at this early time."

But see above, **48** 15 *b*, where Ruiz says : *Fablar vos he por tobras e cuento rrimado.*

Cf. M. Menéndez y Pelayo, *Antología de Poetas Líricos Castellanos*, Vol. IV, pp. ix ff.; R. Floranes Robles, *Vida Literaria de Pero López de Ayala*, in *Colección de Documentos Inéditos*, Vols. XIX–XX ; Baist in *Grundriss* II. ii. 421 ff. and 434 f.; Fitzmaurice-Kelly, *Littérature espagnole*, pp. 83 ff., and p. 463 (*Notes bibliographiques*); Mérimée, *Précis*, pp. 82 ff.

56 422 It is apparently from this part of the whole book that the title was taken : it means, perhaps, *Libro Rimado de Palacio*. Cf. *Biblioteca de Autores Españoles*, Vol. LVII, stz. 422.

In certain cases the imperfect Alexandrines may be amended easily ; e.g. by omitting *A* in line b and inserting *y* before the second *mas* in line d. In other cases the emendation is not easy. We shall not try to correct the whole passage.

56 423 *d* Note *algo* as a noun; it was often such in O. Sp.

57 427 *c* veer = *ver* for the verse; cf. 429 *a.*

57 430 *a* podes = *podedes.*

58 438 *a* The reading *comidiendo* is good.

58 439 *a* allego : note the intransitive use. Cf. note to **4** 19–20.

XIII. LA ESTORIA DEL RREY ANEMUR E DE IOSAPHAT E DE BARLAAM

Lauchert prints this document from a 15th-century MS. of the Library of Strassburg University, which has also another O. Sp. text, *Estoria de los Quatro Dotores de la Santa Eglesia* (ed. by Lauchert, Halle, 1897). Our *Estoria del Rrey Anemur* etc. is simply a translation of an abridged redaction of the *Barlaam and Josaphat* story given by Vincent of Beauvais in his Latin *Speculum Historiale* of the 13th century. The translation was probably made in the 15th century : cf. Baist, *Grundriss* II. ii. 445 ; *Romania* X. 300 ; and F. de Haan in *Modern Language Notes*, 1895, pp. 11 ff.

The general framework of the originally Oriental mystical novel of *Barlaam and Josaphat* is well known; with the *Sindibad* (*Seven Sages*) and *Calila and Dimna*, it is one of the most widespread of Oriental fictions in the West. In its origin it seems to have been an Indian story of the Buddha, which narrated his seclusion from the world in his veriest childhood, his education, from which was carefully excluded all knowledge of the objects of the outer world, especially of its diseases and miseries and the things that caused them, and then, in spite of these precautions, his gradual learning, through fortuitous circumstances, just the things against which he had been guarded. Many more factors entered into the make-up of the *Barlaam and Josaphat*, but not the least interesting are the tales and visions, such as those illustrated from our Spanish translation of Vincent of Beauvais's version of the Christian adaptation of the Buddhistic story.

The Christian form of the story has been summed up by J. Dunlop in his *History of Prose Fiction*, London, 1896, I. 66 ff. In early Christian times, Abenner, a king of India, signalized himself by persecuting the Christians. After years of fruitless expectancy, a son, Josaphat, was born to him. Of the astrologers summoned to cast his horoscope one announces that Josaphat is destined to become a Christian. To guard against this, Abenner secludes the child in a splendid palace, where, with suitable teachers and attendants, he is to be brought up in ignorance of the miseries and evils of this life. But, through various accidents, the young prince eventually comes into contact with examples of all such things. Finally, to frustrate completely the king's plans, he becomes a Christian, when a noted hermit named Barlaam gains access to his palace and acquaints him with the doctrines of Christianity. His father is angry upon learning of this event, and seeks, by various wiles, to win the lad back. It is all in vain, and finally the father becomes a Christian himself. He is succeeded by his son Josaphat, who ere long renounces the throne to go forth into the desert as a hermit.

This Occidental form of the legend seems to be represented earliest by a Greek version (first published by Boissonade, *Anecdota Graeca*, Vol. IV, 1832), which was long attributed to St. John of Damascus. But it is now ascribed to another John, of a monastery near Jerusalem (cf. Zotenberg, in *Notices et extraits des MSS. de la Bibliothèque nationale*, Vol. XXVIII, Part I, 1886), who preceded St. John of Damascus by more than a century. Before the 13th century the Greek version appeared in a Latin form wrongly ascribed to George of Trebizond, as it is earlier than his time (cf. Menéndez y Pelayo, *Orígenes de la Novela* I. xxviii). In the 13th century appears Vincent of Beauvais's epitome, which forms the basis of the Spanish version.

Cf. Menéndez y Pelayo, *Orígenes de la Novela* (in *Nueva Biblioteca de Autores Españoles*), Madrid, 1905, p. xxvi, for a good bibliography of the legend.

59 1 This story is important, not only for Spanish literature, but for comparative literature in general (cf. Dunlop, *History of Prose Fiction*

I. 76, note). It appears in the early Italian collection of tales, the *Novellino* (cf. A. d'Ancona, in *Studj di critica e storia letteraria*, Bologna, 1880, pp. 279 ff., and p. 307, note) ; in Odo of Cherrington's *Narrationes* written in England in the 12th century; in Boccaccio's *Decameron*, where it forms an addition to the hundred tales, since it is found in the Introduction to the Fourth Day. In Spanish it appears in the *Libro de Enxemplos* of Clemente Sánchez (cf. below, p. 61, and see *Biblioteca de Autores Españoles*, Vol. LI, 504, *Enxemplo* CCXXXI). The general influence of the Barlaam legend (and the related Sindibad or Seven Sages legend) is seen in Lope de Vega's play *Barlam y Josafá* (1611), whose first act operated powerfully upon the construction of Calderón's famous play *La Vida es Sueño*. For other instances of the literary influence of the story, cf. Menéndez y Pelayo, l.c., p. xxxvii. See also Mérimée, *Précis*, p. 72.

59 4 dexieron: the *e* may be due to the influence of *dezir*; cf. 19 *dixiesen*, etc.

59 6 commo . . . oyese : this construction of *como* with the impf. sbj. is quite old.

59 9 moço : on this word of unknown origin cf. Ford, *Old Spanish Sibilants*, pp. 73 ff.

59 10 auiente = *aviente* < Lat. *habiens, habientem*. Throughout, this document shows the Lat. pres. part. in -*ans* -*antem*, -*ens* -*entem*, retained with sufficient verbal force to take a direct object. Regularly, in Spanish, it was the gerund of Latin that assumed such a function; whence the Sp. -*ando*, -*iendo* forms. The use of the pres. participial forms here is probably a Latinism, due to a close imitation of the Latin text of Vincent of Beauvais.

59 11 diesen: this, and many other forms, show the reduction of intervocalic -*ss*- to -*s*-.

59 20 dezien : we expect *dizen* 'people say,' 'it is said.'

60 6 With the hope of shaking Josaphat's Christian convictions and his expressed celibate purpose, his father has him exposed to carnal temptation. When he is about to succumb thereto, a vision comes to him, in which he sees the glories of Paradise. This vision has certain relations to the general medieval literature dealing with journeys to, or visions of, Paradise and the Earthly Paradise. Cf. A. d'Ancona, *I precursorsi di Dante* (Florence, 1874); A. Maury, *Essai sur les légendes pieuses du moyen âge* (Paris, 1843); D'Ancona e Bacci, *Manuale della letteratura italiana*, 2d ed. (Florence, 1904), pp. 437 ff.

XIV. EL LIBRO DE EXENPLOS POR A.B.C. DE CLIMENTE SÁNCHEZ

In 1860, Gayangos published in the *Biblioteca de Autores Españoles*, Vol. LI, the *Libro de los Enxemplos*, from an incomplete MS. of the Biblioteca Nacional, which gives no indication as to the author. Later there came to light the MS. (now in the Bibliothèque Nationale of Paris, *Fonds espagnol*, no. 432) utilized by Morel-Fatio in *Romania* VII, whence we publish our extracts. The Paris MS. has a short prologue, in which the author announces himself with the words *Yo Climente Sanchez, arcediano de Valderas en la iglesia de Leon*, and says that it had been for some time his intention to *copilar vn libro de exenplos por a. b. c. e despues rreduzirle en romançe.* Further he stresses the didactic purpose by saying : *ectiam exenplis utimur in docendo et predicando ut facilius intelligatur quod dicitur.* Of this Clemente Sánchez, Archdeacon of Valderas, we have some knowledge. Nicolás Antonio, in his *Bibliotheca Hispana Vetus* (Rome, 1696) II. 138, speaks of a MS. of the Escurial Library containing the *Suma de exemplos del arcediano de Valderas*, i.e. our document. This MS. is not discoverable now. It is known also that Sánchez wrote a *Sacramental* or liturgical manual (printed several times from 1475 on), and that he finished this at Leon in 1423. Morel-Fatio argues (*Romania* VII. 482 f.) that he was born about 1370 and composed his collection of examples between 1400 and 1421.

Combining the Paris MS. with that of Madrid, we seem able to obtain the complete text of Sánchez's work. " The 71 examples that we are going to read [i.e. those published by him]," says M.-F., " represent the part of the text contained in the first sheets, now lost, of the Madrid MS. In this latter there was also omitted the example published at the end of this first series and numbered CCXVI *a* [so that M.-F. really prints 72 additions to the Madrid MS.] : it is, moreover, the only example that the Paris MS. has in excess ; on the other hand, it lacks a certain number, above all at the end of the text. The scribe, it seems, was in a hurry to finish it. As one might expect, the language of the collection in the Bibliothèque Nationale, which was copied in the last years of the 15th century, presents a less archaic character than the text of Madrid." This last, like all the documents in the *Biblioteca* series, is not printed in such a fashion as to make it available for philological purposes. M.-F. thinks that the Madrid MS. dates from the beginning of the 15th century.

As regards the actual date of compilation, Menéndez y Pelayo (*Orígenes de la Novela*, I. cii) agrees with M.-F., although he thinks it possible that the work was done in the last years of the 14th century.

The Madrid MS. has 395 examples or tales and the Paris MS. 72 additional ones, so that the complete collection consists of 467.

Because of a lack of local and national color in the tales, M.-F. thinks that Clemente Sánchez de Vercial (his full name given in the prologue to his *Sacramental*) did not go directly to the various sources which he mentions for them. He deems it more likely that he simply translated (in spite of his use of the word *copilar*) one of the *Alphabeta Exemplorum* or *Narrationum*, often put together in the 13th century for the use of preachers. He is not able, however, to identify Sánchez's work with any of the known *Alphabeta*. Menéndez y Pelayo believes in more real activity on Sánchez's part. Cf. *Orígenes de la Novela* I. ciii: " The narratives of the Archdeacon of Valderas belong to the common fund, and he himself indicates the sources of many of them; but did he himself consult these sources ? In some cases we think that he did. The *Disciplina Clericalis* of Petrus Alphonsus is integrally and faithfully translated in the *Libro de Exemplos*. We have not made a similar comparison with the *Dialogues* of St. Gregory, which he cites at every moment, with the *Lives of the Holy Fathers*, with the *Memorable Deeds and Sayings* of Valerius Maximus, with the *City of God* of St. Augustine, etc. . . . but we believe it certain that all these works, so commonly read in the Middle Ages, were familiar to him, and he exploited them directly. Other citations may be at second hand." Baist (*Grundriss* II. ii. 414) seems to agree with M.-F.; he says: " Perhaps a smaller Latin *Alphabetarium* has been combined here with another Latin collection." On the *Alphabeta* cf. P. Toldo in *Archiv f. das Studium d. neueren Sprachwissenschaften u. Literaturen* for 1907.

The proper comparative literature studies have not yet been made of the various *exemplos* of the collection. See, however, Puymaigre, *Les Vieux Auteurs castillans* II. 107 ff., *Jahrbuch f. roman. Literatur* VI. 128, and J. F. Crane, *The Exempla*, etc., London, 1890 (Vol. XXVI of the Folk-Lore Society publications).

Each of the examples is preceded by a Latin maxim, translated at once into two imperfect (at least in the MSS.) Spanish verses. In these the moral to be conveyed is stated beforehand, just as in the *Conde Lucanor* it is stated at the end of the tale. The Latin maxims are arranged in alphabetical sequence : hence the title of the collection *por A. B. C.* This arrangement would seem to suggest a Latin *alphabetum* as source.

A scholarly edition of the whole text of the *Libro de Exemplos* is a desideratum: we may expect it from Professor M. A. Buchanan of Toronto University, who has already done some work on the Paris MS.

The text of our extracts seems Castilian. G. T. Northup, *El Libro de los Gatos* (*Modern Philology* V, Chicago, 1908), points out (p. 489) that " Valderas is almost exactly on the border-line between Leon and Castile. We should expect a MS. written there to show traces of the eastern Leonese dialect. These peculiarities abound in the Madrid MS. of the *Exenplos*."

61 1 This often used tale is in the *Disciplina Clericalis*, in the *Castigos* of Don Sancho (*Biblioteca de Autores Españoles* LI. 156), in the *Conde Lucanor* (No. 2), in the *Espejo de los Legos* derived from John of Hoveden's *Speculum Laicorum* (a 13th-century work), etc. A transcript of the Paris MS. made by Professor Buchanan shows slight variations from Morel-Fatio's text: l. 8 *como* is *coõmo*, l. 15 *secretamente* and **62** 4 *sepultura* have initial *ss*, etc.

62 13 Cf. Puymaigre, l.c., p. 112, note, for other applications of the advice contained in the inscription.

62 25 Observe *penssar* taking a direct object.

XV. EL POEMA DE JOSÉ

There are still extant a number of literary documents written in Spanish by Spanish Moors. In obedience to a hieratical custom, or for some other reason, these Moors used Arabic characters when writing their Romance text. The Spanish Jews did so, too, in the older period, and Yiddish is still written and printed in Hebrew characters. The Spanish documents thus written in Arabic characters are *aljamiados*, or texts in *aljamía*, from the Arabic word meaning 'barbarian,' applied by the Spanish Moslem to the Mozarabes, i.e. the Arabs who were not of pure blood or Christians whose blood was mingled with that of Arabs. In their turn (cf. M. Schmitz, l.c., p. 323) the Spaniards applied the term *aljamía* to the somewhat degenerate Spanish, intermingled with Arabic elements, which was spoken by the Mozarabes and the Moriscos. Here, we use the term in the general sense of works in Spanish written in Arabic characters. Of these the best is the *Poema de José*, or, to use the aljamiado form of the name, *Poema de Yuçuf*.

There is no complete MS. of the *José* that has yet come to light, but the larger part of its contents is known to us from two MSS. Of these the older, once possessed by the scholar Gayangos and now at Madrid in the Library of the Academia de la Historia (T–12), is the one published by R. Menéndez Pidal in his *Poema de Yuçuf* (in the *Revista de Archivos, Bibliotecas y Museos*, Madrid, 1902), along with a transliteration of it and a study of the text and its literary relations. There has been some variety of opinion as to the date of this MS. That part of it containing the *José* was by Gayangos placed first in the 16th century and then in the 15th. H. Morf (*El Poema de José*, Leipzig, 1883, p. x) does not believe that it belongs farther back than the end of the 15th century nor that it is more than three quarters of a century older than the other MS. (Gg–101). On the other hand, Menéndez Pidal, following the statement of E. Saavedra (in *Discursos leídos ante la Real Academia Española*, Madrid, 1878, p. 162), believes that the *José* part of this MS. — obviously the oldest part of it, much older than other parts, which are clearly of the 16th century — is of the 14th century, and thinks that the language of the document is a good argument to this effect. " The absence," he says (*Yuçuf*, p. 2), " of the strong Castilian influence which is observed in Aragonese writings of the 15th century, is an indication, and another is the retention of the dental in the paroxytonic ending of the 2d pers. pl. forms of verbs." This MS. has 95 stanzas of *cuaderna vía* (like Ayala's *Rimado* it still uses that form), extending from the beginning of Joseph's story down to the affair with Zalifa or Zaliha (Potiphar's wife). The account given has many things in it not found in the Biblical account in Genesis. The document (and this is true of the other MS. also, for they give the same account in their corresponding parts) follows rather the 12th sura or chapter of the Koran, with its variations from the Biblical story, and also adds elements due neither to the Bible nor to the Koran, but to the fantastication of such Oriental writers as the Hebrew Cab of Yemen, who became a Mohammedan under the caliphate of Omar. Throughout the whole poem, as exhibited by the combined MSS., there is little evidence of originality on the poet's part. On the lacunae and other defects in its text, cf. Menéndez Pidal, l.c., p. 2.

The other MS. (Gg–101) is preserved in the Biblioteca Nacional at Madrid. It was published by H. Morf in his *Gratulationsschrift der Universität Bern an die Universität Zürich*, etc., *El Poema de José*, Leipzig, 1883, with a description of the MS. Of the text thus published a transliteration was printed by M. Schmitz in *Roman. Forschungen* XI. 315. Schmitz repeats Morf's description of the MS. and enters into a discussion of the linguistic and literary nature of the document. This, in its turn, has been discussed by Menéndez Pidal in the article mentioned. This MS. Gg–101 appears to be of the 16th century. It lacks the beginning of the poem, some nine strophes, and also the end of it. The beginning is supplied by the other MS., but for the end we have no such help. Morf thinks that about 50 strophes are lacking, i.e. about eight folios of the MS., as he deems that in that space the poet would have covered fully the remainder of the account given in the 12th chapter of the Koran. Other defects in Gg–101 are described by Morf and Schmitz.

Schmitz believed that he found Orientalisms in the syntax of the *José*, but Menéndez Pidal (p. 52) regards his arguments as untenable.

Another very fragmentary MS., containing but four strophes, is described by Morf, p. x, and by Schmitz, p. 319. It belonged to the great collection of MSS. of *aljamía* made by Gayangos.

The language of the *José* is clearly the Aragonese dialect. This is even more markedly the case in the older MS. (T–12). Cf. Menéndez Pidal, p. 40 : " Both *A* [i.e. T–12] and *B* [i.e. Gg–101] present Aragonese traits, but with this difference : *B* is very modern, of the second half of the 16th century, and its Aragonese is much Castilianized, although not completely so ; *A*, being much older, presents the dialect with greater purity. Both represent a language more popular than that generally used by the Aragonese littérateurs at the respective dates." A detailed study of the Aragonese elements in the language of both MSS. is given by Menéndez Pidal, pp. 40–56. For another account of Aragonese traits cf. Saroïhandy in *Annuaire de l'École des hautes études*, 1898 and 1901.

As to the date of composition of the original poem, Menéndez Pidal naturally places it at not later than the 14th century ; cf. also Menéndez y Pelayo, *Orígenes*, etc., I. lxv. Morf assigns it to the second half of the 15th century.

Schmitz, pp. 325–356, gives full directions for a system of transliteration of the Arabic script. For another description of a method of transliteration cf. Ford, *Old Spanish Sibilants*, pp. 159–160. The transliteration made by Gayangos of Gg–101 for Vol. LVII of the *Biblioteca de Autores Españoles* is quite incorrect, as was the earlier form which he provided for Ticknor's *History of Spanish Literature*. This is no longer included in the American edition, but appears in the German and Spanish translations.

On a later Moorish treatment of Joseph's story, the *Leyenda de José*, cf. *Leyendas Moriscas*, etc., published by F. Guillén Robles (Madrid,

1885–1886). Compare our *José* passage with that from the *Estoria General* given on p. 45; this latter was taken by Alfonso or his collaborator from an Arabic source also, the *Book of Roads and Realms* of the Moorish King of Niebla (near Seville). See Puymaigre II. 169 ff.

63 89 *a*   It will be quite obvious that many of the verses are metrically imperfect, and that the rimes are sometimes supplanted by assonance.

63 89 *b*   **abiria** : in Arabic two consonants cannot stand together in the same syllable. So, if two consonants come together in a syllable in Spanish, the *José* inserts between them a duplicate of the vowel following the second of them : therefore *abria* becomes *abiria*, *ombres* becomes *omberes*, etc. For such cases as *abria*, however, the Moorish scribe sometimes does not do this, regarding the *b* and *r* as in different syllables ; cf. 90 *d abre*, 95 *a Yabras*. — **quesido** : in this dialect form the consonant of the pret. indic. etc. has been carried over to the past part.

63 89 *c*   **dixendo** : this seems a dialect form and not simply a scribal error : the pret. stem has entered even into the present participle. 90 *d deseyo*, 91 *c jaze*, 93 *d fegura*, 97 *c fues*, and other forms here show sufficiently the dialectal nature of the language; cf., however, Menéndez Pidal's remark as to the large Castilianizing that this MS. Gg–101 has undergone.

63 91 *a*   **dieç** : here the text has, at the end of the word, the letter *sīn* which answers to the early Spanish *ts* sound. This O. Sp. wrote regularly as *ç* at the beginning of a word and between vowels, and as *z* before a consonant and also at the end of a word. This use of *z* was only scribal and conventional ; it was not phonological, since O. Sp. *z* properly denoted the *ds* sound. Now, only in this one case does the *José* in our MS. write final *sīn* = *ç* (i.e. *ts*) for what in Roman script is regularly final O. Sp. *z* = *ts*. In 1 *b* and 16 *b* it writes *diez* with Arabic *zāy* ; but *zāy* was never *ts* in value in Arabic. Again in 91 *a annos*, 94 *a suenno*, etc., the Arabic text indicates a double *nūn*, which accords with the O. Sp. spelling *nn*, but not with the pronunciation, which was palatalized *n*. Could not the Arabic scribe have approximated more to the sound, writing *ny* or something of the sort? I have already pointed out (*Old Spanish Sibilants*, p. 158) that 105 *b* has *tiepo* (so in Morf's text and not *tiempo*) for *tienpo* and 103 *d salia* for *salian*, and ventured to suggest that the Arabic scribe was "rendering literally the words of a MS. in Roman characters, in which the nasal dash was sometimes lacking [i.e. the dash over a vowel indicating that a nasal consonant belongs after it], a common enough occurrence in other O.Sp. documents." Menéndez Pidal denies the copying from a MS. in Roman characters, and thinks that here, and in other cases cited by him (p. 57), we are in the presence of a phonetic phenomenon, the disappearance of the nasal consonant through a nasalization of the preceding vowel. Have we evidence enough of that? However the case may be, Schmitz (p. 355), in view of the care with which the Arabic scribe regularly differentiates *r* and *rr*, *l* and *ll*, *n* and *nn*, *s* and *ç* and *z*, infers that "the scribe of the *José* was adequately informed regarding both the pronunciation and the orthography of Spanish." Herein we see that the phonetic value of aljamiado texts must not be overrated : they give us certain corroborative information regarding O. Sp. sounds which have changed in the modern language, since the equivalence of the Arabic characters adopted impels us to suppose (as other testimony indicates) O. Sp. $z = dz$, $ç = ts$, j and $g(e,i) = d\check{z}$, etc. ; but, on the other hand, they adopt also conventionalities of the Roman-script writing of Spanish; cf. Ford, l.c., p. 158.

63 91 *c* **terzero** : here, and in 99 *a zertera*, the scribe confused sibilants, erroneously writing *zāy* (*z*) for *sīn* (*ç*).

63 93 *a* *Yuçuf*, understood, is subject to *castigaba* and *curaba*.

63 93 *b* Schmitz must be wrong in taking *el rrey*, understood, as subject to *enfermaba* ; *cualquiere qu(e)* is the subject.

63 93 *d* **gele** : observe *le* here and in 89 *b* ; elsewhere *lo* is used; cf. 94 *b*, 99 *b*, etc.

64 94 *c* **disso** : the MS. has *šīn*, which in aljamía stands for both O.Sp. *s* and *x* (i.e. *š*, *sh*). The *tešdīd* or sign of doubling stands over the *šīn*. This is probably an error of the scribe, who meant only *dixo*. At all events *dixxo* would be as correct as *disso*. Cf. 99 *c*. — **fues** = here and in 97 *c fueste*. So in 31 *b fues* stands for subj. *fueses*. With this loss of the final syllable Schmitz compares *ley = leite* in 104 *a*.

64 95 *c* **ya** = *y a*.

64 96 *c* If *luzero* means the morning star, we have an allusion to the belief that the dreams just before dawn come true. To this Dante refers several times.

64 97 *b* **sacosele** : cf. also 94 *b sacoselo*. Note the equivalence of *sele*, *selo*, with *gele* of 93 *d*. This writing of *se = ge* shows the lateness of the MS. So also does the regular appearance here of *s* for intervocalic double *s*.

64 97 *d* **fiziestes** : apparently here, and in 99 *d dixestes*, the 2d pl. form is mingled with the 2d sg. in addressing the same person.

65 103 *b* **de que** : i.e. a dream to the effect that, etc.

65 103 *d* The MS. has *salia*. Here, and in one other case, Schmitz needlessly saw an Arabicism of syntax, in the appearance of a singular verb *before* a plural subject. The scribe simply forgot his nasal sign; cf. note to 91 *a*.

65 106 *c* **vaçia**: again the scribe has confused his sibilants, writing voiceless *sīn* (*ç*) for voiced *zđy* (*z*).

65 108 *b* **ye**: Schmitz takes this as = *le*. It thus occurs side by side in this passage with *ge* and *se*.

XVI. DANÇA GENERAL

This anonymous document is preserved in but a single MS. It is in the Escurial Library (IV–b–21) and contains the *Fernán González* and several other important documents. According to Appel, the script of the part containing the *Dança* is not earlier than the 15th century.

The *Dança* appeared in print (and in a very imperfect form) first in Ticknor's *History of Spanish Literature* III. 459 ff. (cf. last ed., p. 531). Janer then printed it at Paris in 1856, and in 1864 reprinted it at Madrid in Vol. LVII of the *Biblioteca de Autores Españoles*. Janer's text is also bad, and therefore Appel prepared his edition, from which our extracts come. There is also now the edition of Barcelona, 1907, which agrees with that of Appel, yet shows the correct form *dize* in the three or four cases near the beginning of the poem in which Appel seems clearly to find *dise* (cf. p. 5, note 1, of Appel's ed.).

In point of composition the *Dança* is probably of the 15th century and not later than the middle of it (cf. Baist, *Grundriss* II. ii. 428); some put it in the first half of the century. A later elaboration of it, first printed in 1520, has been reprinted by A. de los Ríos in his *Historia Crítica de la Literatura Española* VII. 507 ff: this Appel deems of some value in suggestion of corrections to be made in the text of the *Dança*, which is, metrically and otherwise, sometimes at fault.

The Dance of Death is a subject which has figured in both the literary and the pictorial art of several countries, and there is reason to suppose that, at least originally, the literary forms interpreted the paintings. W. Seelmann, in his *Totentänze des Mittelalters* (Leipzig, 1893), has studied the literary category concerned, and has pointed out a certain resemblance between the Spanish poem and a Lübeck *Totentanz* of 1463. But the *Dança* also has affinities with a French *Danse Macabré* of the 15th century (published by V. Dufour in *Recherches sur la Danse macabre*, Paris 1873; cf. id., *La Danse macabre des SS. Innocents de Paris*, 1874). For a comparison of the three documents, cf. Appel, pp. 2 ff. The Spanish piece is far superior to the others in literary merit, excelling them in liveliness of spirit, in characterization, and in the keenness of its satire. Still, the origin of the Spanish work is probably to be sought in some earlier French poem. Cf. Fitzmaurice-Kelly, *Littérature espagnole*, p. 93 : " This Dance of Death (*Danse Macabré*) is thought (as well as the German *Totentanz*) to be imitated from a French original as yet unknown ; it is at present the oldest version of the legend that has come down to us. Although its form is superficially dramatic, the *Danza* is not a real drama. Death summons mortals to his sinister festival, forcing them to take part in his dance. The thirty-three victims — a pope, an emperor, a cardinal, a king, and so on (a cleric and a layman always alternate in it) — respond to the invitation in a series of octaves which will soon be surpassed by the sonorous music of Mena [Juan de Mena, the poet, 1411–1456], but mark an advance over the *versos de arte mayor* which some think they see in the *Libro de Buen Amor* of Ruiz (cf. F. Wolf, *Studien*, 413 ; Morel-Fatio, *L'Arte mayor et l'hendécasyllabe*, in *Romania* XXXIII ; Foulché-Delbosc, *Étude sur le Laberinto de Juan de Mena*, in *Revue hispanique* IX). The poet of the *Danza de la Muerte* was an expert in morbid allegory."

In addition to the articles on the *arte mayor* cited by Fitzmaurice-Kelly, cf. F. Hanssen, *Zur spanischen u. portug. Metrik* (Valparaiso, 1900) ; id., *El Arte Mayor de J. de Mena* (in *Anales de la Universidad de Chile*, Santiago de Chile, 1906) ; and J. Schmitt, *Sul verso de arte mayor* (in the proceedings of the Reale Academia dei Lincei, Rome, 1905) ; as well as the older statement of A. Bello in his *Ortología y Métrica* (cf. his *Obras Completas*, Santiago de Chile, 1884, Vol. V). Appel (pp. 9 ff.) discusses the metrical condition of our poem. It has one of the usual stanzaic arrangements of the *arte mayor*, viz. that of the octave with its lines rhyming *a b a b b c c b*. What the original and perfect type of the individual line of *arte mayor* was, has been the subject of some debate. " The peculiarity of this verse," says Appel, " as compared with French, Provençal, and Italian verses, is, as is well known, that the number of its syllables seems to be no definitely fixed one. If, as usually happens, we regard as the basic form the decasyllable, which by a cæsura after the fifth syllable is divided into two equal parts, then the number of syllables should vary between 10 and, with feminine cæsura and feminine verse-ending, 12. (Even two unaccented syllables may stand at the cæsura.) But, now, the first syllable of every hemistich may also be omitted, so that we have in the half-verse 4 syllables instead of 5 (or, with feminine ending, 5 instead of 6) ; and just as the regular number of syllables may be diminished by one, so also one may be added, so that we may count 6 (or 7) of them in the half-verse."

When all is said and done, it is the accent that furnishes the fixed principle of the line of *arte mayor*. One wonders whether the initial principle was not that of two accents in each half-line. Perhaps the unaccented syllables were arranged symmetrically around those accented, and the perfect type was that represented by stz. I, l. *h* :

Con ésta | mj frécha || cruél tras|pasánte.

This, under a rhythmic stress scheme, corresponds to an amphibrachic arrangement under a quantitative scheme. Cf. Ford, *An Old Spanish Anthology* (N.Y., 1901), pp. xxxvi ff. To avoid monotony and sing-song effect various modifications may then have been made. Secondary accents might occur in the second and eighth syllables ; and, even more than that, the accent might fail entirely in those syllables. But, of course, it is not certain whether the seemingly perfect type is fundamental or an elaboration.

Taking for the half-line a scheme such as we propose, viz.

$$\cup \; \prime \; \cup \; | \; \cup \; \prime \; (\cup)$$

with an optional suppression of the final unaccented syllable, Appel finds that 693 out of the 1264 half-verses of the *Dança* correspond to it. To these we may add 33 more, if we count the cases in which the first accent yields to a secondary accent, viz.

$$\cup \; \diagdown \; \cup \; | \; \cup \; \prime \; (\cup)$$

The next most frequent type appears in but 106 half-verses. On the other probable varieties represented in the document, cf. Appel, l.c.

66 1 trasladaçion : Appel (l.c., *Anmerkungen*, pp. 32 ff.) thinks that this indicates a literary taking-over, a translation or free rendering of, say, a French original, rather than a mere scribal copying.

66 2 tracta : this seems to have no subject. Appel thinks that it may stand for *tractan* (i.e. the nasal dash, = *n*, was forgotten over the last *a*) with indefinite subject. The indefinite 3d pl. occurs elsewhere in the poem. Of course the *en* might be suppressed.

66 3 abisa : was this originally the imper. sg. of the verb *avisar*, 'look out!' — **pare** = *paren*. The scribe forgot the nasal dash over *e*.

66 7 pugn : the MS. has *pugnīi* : but *pugnen* must be meant ; l. 482 has *pugnastes*.

66 I *a* The 1520 ed. has the metrically better line

Yo la muerte encerco á las criaturas.

This may represent the original reading of this verse, or it may be an elaboration.

66 I *g* This is an interesting early use of *cuando* as a preposition. See Bello-Cuervo, *Gramática Castellana*, 1183, 1240. Cf. Eng. 'we did it *when* children' for a possible transition stage.

67 II *g* **landre** : the reference is to the bubonic plague or pest. — **ynplisyon** : Appel would derive this from Lat. *implēre* and translate 'filling out,' 'swelling.'

67 II *h* **el tu** : the article occurs frequently here with the poss. adj.

67 III *d* **me** : this is an ethical dative. The 1520 print has *Que en mi venida me detardaré*.

67 V *b* **nasçido** : the rime requires *nado*.

67 V *d* **traxo** : there is a correction in the MS. here and Appel is not entirely certain whether *traxo* or *truxo* was the first reading. The 1907 ed. says that *truxo* was the original reading. At all events the correction is in the same hand as the original word. The sense is not quite clear here. The 1520 print has *que traxo al mundo un solo bocado*, i.e. '(death) which a single mouthful (i.e. of the apple of Paradise) brought into the world.' In v. 165 f. our poet speaks of mother Eve as having gained death for us by tasting forbidden fruit.

67 V *h* **forçado** : an adverb = *forzadamente, forzosamente*.

68 VII *f* **nos otros** : the modern form of the pronoun in prepositional use seems clear here.

68 VIII *b* **soes** : the *d* intervocalic is now gone. In later script a corrector of the MS. changed this to *soys*, i.e. our *sois*. Cf. *f, vayaes*.

68 VIII *h* Appel cannot make out what stood originally at the beginning of this line. In later script there is *Per mj*, not *Por mi* as Janer has it.

68 IX *a* We need *A esta mj dança* etc., as the 1520 print reads. The 1907 ed. has [*A*] *Esta*.

68 XVIII *a* Observe the article even in the vocative use of the poss. adj. In O. Sp. the article is found even directly before nouns in the vocative. Technically the nouns are in apposition with a pronoun " ye " understood.

69 XVIII *c* The first half-verse is too short. The 1520 print has *agora* after *vos*.

69 XVIII *e f* Appel says : " The MS. reading can hardly be kept unmodified. The 1520 print reads *que veo en balança Estar mi vida, perder mis sentidos*."

69 XVIII *g* The first half-line is improved by reading, as the print does, *cor* for *coraçon*.

69 XLII *g* **peores amjgos :** 'the worst of friends,' viz. *libelo* and *fuero*. The 1520 print has *Lo peor es, amigos*.

70 XLIII *c* Appel proposes nothing here, but one wonders whether there should not be an *en* before *mjente*. If not, the latter seems to mean 'memory.'

70 XLIII *e* Cf. Appel: " Cino (da Pistoja, died 1337) and Bartholo (died 1357) are the well-known teachers of law. But who is meant by *el Cole(c)tario* (a real proper name is certainly not before us here), I have not been able to determine even with the help of jurists among my friends. Nor have I been able to discover a particular work called *Collectarium*."

70 XLIII *h* **E vos :** the print has *Venid vos*.

70 LII *a* **sea :** the print has *será*.

70 LII *c* The print omits **santo** ; it should be stricken out here. — In **contenple** we have a poor rime. Did the poet say *contempre*? — Does the attitude of the monk here suggest that the poet was himself a monk ? Of course our *Dança* is anonymous.

71 LXXIX *e* **prínçipe :** Appel asks whether we should not read *principio*. The print has *comienzo*.

71 LXXIX *h* **comedio :** here apparently ' place,' ' site,' ' scene,' and in *d* ' course,' ' behavior.' But ?

CORRECTIONS FOR THE ETYMOLOGICAL
VOCABULARY

P. 180 : s.v. **aguiiar**. " L. *acūlea* " should be " V. L. **acūlea* "

P. 182 : After **amanezient** insert " **amanssar** (*ad* + V. L. **mansare* from
V. L. *mansus* ' tame ' = L. *mansuetus* and *mansues*) to tame,
pacify, **44** 26."

" s.v. **amariello**, l. 7. Before **23** insert " yellow, livid,"

P. 187 : s.v. **ata**, l. 2. Add " (cf. **fata**)."

P. 193 : s.v. **buelto**, l. 3. Add " (V. L. **vŏltus* = C. L. *volūtus*)."

P. 203 : s.v. **corteza**, l. 1. *cortĭcĕa* should be **cortĭcĕa*

P. 205 : s.v. **cuedar**, l. 4. *cŏgito* should be **cŏgito*

P. 213 : s.v. **dizeremos**. Read " **dizeremos, dizremos** (fuller forms " etc.
after " **9** 75 " add " **10** 90."

P. 234 : After **fure** insert " **furtarse** (refl., V. L. **fŭrtare* from C. L.
fŭrtum ' theft ') to steal away, **42** 2."

P. 242 : s.v. **lea**. For " **14** 104 " read " **14** 114."

P. 247 : s.v. **mannana**, l. 2. For *gran* read *grand*

P. 252 : s.v. **mi**, l. 3. For **míęa* read **miea*

P. 263 : After **palaçio** insert " **paladar** (V. L. **palatalis*, **palatalem*, from
C. L. *palātum*) palate, **47** 5 (the *r* is due to dissimilation)."

P. 265 : Before **pedir** insert " **pecho** (C. L. *pactum* ' pact, agreement ')
tax, tribute, **44** 25."

P. 278 : s.v. **Rayzes**, l. 2. After " roots," insert " real estate,"

" After **Razon** insert " **razonar** (V. L. **rationare* from C. L. *ratio*)
to speak, **45** 4."

" After **reçebir** insert " **recelar** (based on *çelo*, ' zeal,' ' fear,' from
C. L. *zēlus*) to fear, **44** 25."

" After **Reconbrar** insert " **recudio** (pret. indic. 3 sg. of O. Sp.
recodir, from C. L. *recŭtĕre*, V. L. **recŭtīre*, ' to strike back ')
retorted, **45** 3."

P. 283 : s.v. **salir**, l. 5. Add " go up, **47** 12."

P. 289 : s.v. **si**, l. 4. " *nos* " should be " *uos* "

" l. 5. After " you " add " ; still, this may be *si* ' if ' "

P. 292 : Between **sol** and **solaz** insert " **sol** (for *solo*, advb., C. L. *sōlum*)
only, even, **45** 5."

1766

P. 295: column 2, l. 1. "close" should be "reduce"

" column 2, l. 3. After *alma*. add "So, also, msc. *so amo> sǫ amo > sụ amo*, etc."

" Between **suso** and **suyo** insert "**sutyña** = su **tyña**."

P. 298: s.v. **tirar**, l. 4. After "**66** I 7" add in parentheses "(infin. noun)"

P. 299: s.v. **tomar**, l. 2. "**10**" should be "**20**"

P. 300: s.v. **tost'**. Change *toste* to *tosto* and add "(C. L. *tostum*, p.p. of *torrēre*, 'to roast') quickly,"

P. 303: s.v. **tuerto**, l. 5. Before "inscription" insert "cross-piece;"

P. 305: s.v. **uo**, l. 1. Omit "before *lo* and"

P. 306: s.v. **vaçia**. After *vazio -a* add "< C. L. *vacīvus*"

P. 308: s.v. **vey**, l. 3. Add "It may be imper. *ve* + advb. *y* there.'"

ETYMOLOGICAL VOCABULARY

Note. Wherever possible, Vulgar Latin etyma have been given for words not found in Latin. Of course, the V. L. forms did not necessarily ever exist in many of the cases. Analogy (especially in the verb system), working at an early date in the already developed vernacular, can explain many phenomena without recourse to V. L. bases.

A

a prep. (L. *ad*) to, at, with, for, sign of the accusative.

a = *ha* (V. L. **hat* for L. *habet*) has, there is (are), ago, **6** 4 etc.; **14** 90 etc.; **34** 78 *d*; **58** 440 *d*; **63** 90 *b* etc.

aaquesto = *á aquesto*, **14** 112.

abades (cf. *Abbat*) abbots, clerics, **11** 119.

abarcar (V. L. **abbrachicare* from *ad* + *brachium* with metathesis of *r*) to embrace, grasp; *abarcó* **69** XLII 8.

abaxose (pret. indic. 3d sg. of *abaxar* + *se*; cf. V. L. **bassius > baxo*) stooped, bent over, **49** 301 *a*.

Abbat (L. *abbas, abbātem*) abbot, **24** 87 *a*, 94 *a*.

Abderrhamen (pr. n.) **44** 6.

abia (impf. 3; cf. *auer, aver*) had, **53** 18; there were, **65** 107 *c*; *abia de* had to, was to, **63** 90 *a*.

abian had, **63** 92 *a*.

abierto, -a, (L. *apertus*) cf. *abrir*.

abisa counsel, advice, **66** 3; cf. mod. *aviso* (L. **advīsum*).

abogado, -a, (L. *advocatus, -a*) advocate, **50** 509 *b*; **51** 1662 *b*.

abraçar (cf. L. *bra(c)chium*, whence V. L. **abbrachiare*) to embrace, **47** 8 (cf. mod. *abrazar*).

abras (fut. 2; cf. *auer, aver*) thou shalt have (indep.), **64** 95 *a*.

abre (fut. 1; cf. *auer, aver*) I shall have, **63** 90 *d*; **70** LII 6.

abria (cond. 3; cf. *auer, aver*) **27** 358 *d*; **63** 89 *b*.

abrir (L. *aperire*) to open, **37** 359 *a*; **29** 369 *a*; **13** 3; **17** 203; *abrid* **68** VII 7.

a bueltas = *avueltas*.

abuena = *á buena*, **24** 87 *d*.

aca (L. *eccum*, under influence of *ac, atque*, + *hac*) hither, here, **18** 1110; **38** 365 *d*; **62** 2.

acabado, -a, (cf. *acabar*) entire, perfect, **61** 10.

acabar (V. L. **accapare*) to achieve, end, fulfill, **36** 345 *a*, 350 *a*; **37** 355 *d*; **41** 14; **59** 9.

acaeçer (V. L. **accadescēre*) to happen; *acaecio* **52** 8, 9.

acaesçer (cf. *acaeçer*) to happen, **40** 6; **45** 22; **54** 10, 11; **61** 22; **62** 12, 16.

açedexes (possibly a form of the Arabic *ash-sha'treng*, chessboard)
chess, **41** 11.

acenso (cf. *encenso*) incense, **8**
68.

açerca de (L. *ad + cǐrca* and *de*)
near, **18** 1101.

achest (L. *eccum*, under influence
of *ac,* + *iste*), -a, this, **6** 2, 16;
achesto, pron., **6** 14.

acipreste (L. *archi-*, Gk. ἀρχι-, +
presbyter) archpriest, **48** 13 *b*.

acoger (V. L. *accollǐgēre*) to join;
acogerse to join, gather about,
rally around, **15** 134.

acoien (cf. *acoger*) **20** 1199.

acojed (cf. *acoger*) receive, take in,
57 429 *b*, 433 *b*.

acometer (L. *ad + commǐttere*) to
attack, **37** 359 *d*.

acompannado (p.p. of *acompannar*,
related to early Sp. *compannón*,
companno, from V.L.*companio*,
based on *cum-* + *panis*) accompanied, **46** 17.

açor (L. *acceptor, acceptōrem*, for *accipiter*) hawk, **42** 5; **43** 8.

acordada (p.p. of *acordar*) suitable,
fit, prudent, **25** 98 *d*.

acordar (V. L. *accordare* from *ad
+ cor, cǒrdis*, with perhaps some
influence of *chǒrda*) to remind,
58 442 *c*; *acordado* recalled, **65**
102 *b*; *acordados* agreed, in har-
mony, **12** 143, systematic, arranged, **29** 1 *a*; *acordandose de*
remembering; *se acordaron* they
agreed, **53** 12; *acordol* he remem-
bered it, **46** 10.

acordol = *acordó + le*, **46** 10.

acorrer (L. *ad + cǔrrere*) to run to,
hasten to, succor; *acorrian* **38**
362 *a*.

acortar (L. *ad + cǔrtare*) to cut
short, **69** XVIII 6.

acostar (V. L. *accostare* from *cǒsta*)
to lay down, throw down; *acostar
se* to fall flat, **19** 1142.

acoytar (V. L. *accǒctare* from *ad +
cǒctus*, p.p. of *cǒquere*) to distress,
annoy; *acoytando* **38** 363 *a*; cf.
mod. *cuita, acuitar*.

açucar (Arab. *al + çuccar*) sugar,
49 17 *d*; cf. mod. *azúcar*.

acuerdo (cf. *acordar*) agreement,
44 20.

acusado (L. *accusatus*) accused, **14**
112.

ad (= *a*, L. *ad*) sign of the accusative, **9** 83.

adar = *á + dar*, **19** 1145; **20** 1210.

adelante (L. *ad + de + ǐn + ante*,
with dissimilation of *n*) forward,
24 93 *c*.

adelantrado (cf. *adelante*; the intrusive *r* is not found in the mod.
adelantado) governor, high officer, **59** 20.

adelino (*n* = *ñ*; V.L. *addelineare*)
he moved forward, advanced,
20 1203 (forms with *ñ* or *nn*
occur in *Cid* 467, 1984, 2237).

ademas (L. *ad + de + magis*) besides, exceedingly, in the ex-
treme, **41** 6, 10, 13; **52** 11.

-ades (L. *-atǐs*) mod. Sp. *-áis*, ending
of pres. indic. 2d pl.

adios (*á + Dios*) good-by, **69** XVIII 8.

ado (L. *ad + de + ǔbi*) whither,
where, **34** 83 *b*.

adobados (p.p. of *adobar*, based on Germanic *dubb-*, cf. Eng. *dub*) fitted up, furnished, **32** 20 *a*.

adonde (L. *ad* + *de* + *ŭnde*) whither, where, **70** LII 3.

adoralo = *adorarlo* ; *adoralo e* = *lo adoraré*, **10** 106.

adorar (L. *adōrare*) to adore. **9** 77 ; *adorad* **10** 103.

adtores (perhaps an imperfect spelling for *aztores*, an intermediate between L. *acceptores* and O. Sp. *açores*) hawks, **13** 5.

aduchas (p.p. of *aduzir* ; L. *ad* + *dūctas*) brought, **15** 147.

aduersidades (L. *adversitātes*) adversities, **26** 108 *d*.

adugamos (L. *addūcamŭs* ; cf. *aduzir*) **16** 168.

aduxier (L. *addūxĕrim* ; cf. *aduzir*) **17** 181.

aduzir (L. *addūcĕre*, V.L.*addūcīre*) to bring, lead, **15** 144 ; **26** 112 *b* ; *aduzido* **60** 9.

ael = *á él*, **46** 5.

aessa = *á essa*, **18** 1091.

afan (? ; cf. Körting³ § 206) anxiety, trouble, **53** 23.

afeuos = *afe* + *vos* (*afe* = (1) L. *habe*, or (2) L. *habete*, or (3) it is *a* + *fe*, confused with *fe* = L. *vĭde*. But?) behold you, see you, **16** 152. (See the discussion in the Notes.)

afeytamientos (cf. *afeytar*) adornments, **59** 15.

afeytar (V.L.*affactare* from *facere*, *factus*) to adorn ; *afeytado* **60** 10, 11.

affontan cf. *afontar*.

affrontados cf. *afrontar*.

afinar = *á finar*.

afincamiento (cf. *afincar*) distress, **55** 21.

afincar = *á fincar*, **18** 1101 ; **27** 358 *d*.

afincar (V. L.*affīgicare*, from *ad* + *fīgere*, with intrusive *n*) to distress, bring to dire straits ; *afincado* **54** 6; **55** 23; cf. mod. *ahinco*.

afogar (V.L.*affōcare*, cf. L.*affocare*, *suffocare*, based on *faux*, *faucem*) to stifle, drown; *se afogavan* **37** 358 *d* ; cf. mod. *ahogar*.

afontar (based on French *honte*, Germanic *hauniþa*) to shame, vilify, insult ; *affontan* **27** 356 *c*.

afrontar (L. *affrŏntare*, from *ad* + *frŏns*, *frŏntem*) to insult, affront, injure; *affrontados* **45** 16; cf. mod. *afrentar* from *frente*.

Afryca (l.w.; L. *Africa*) **33** 73 *a*.

afrycanas (cf. *Afryca*) African, **33** 71 *c*.

afyrmes (adv. based on L. *firmus*, with *ī* instead of *ĭ* as required for most Romance forms. It may be a loan-word. The *-s* is adverbial) firmly, stoutly, **38** 363 *d*.

ageno (L. *alienus*) of another; *lo ageno* another's goods, **45** 18.

agora (L. *hac hōra*) now, **6** 3; **21** 26; **28** 365 *a* etc.

agradable (L. *ad* + *grat · us* + *-abilis*) agreeable, **60** 13.

agua (L. *aqua*) water, rain, body of water, stream, **16** 150; **37** 356 *b* ; **47** 17 ; **65** 103 *b*.

aguardadores (cf. *aguardar*) guards, **31** 16 *b*.

aguardar (*a* + Germanic *ward-*; cf. Old Saxon *wardon*, O. H. G. *warten*, Eng. *ward*) to wait, attend, guard, watch; *aguardassen* **43** 29.

aguiiar = *aguijar* (a formation on V. L. **acúcula* or L. *acúlea*; cf. mod. *aguja*, a regular development thereof) to spur on, **13** 10.

aguijada (cf. *aguiiar*) goad, spur, pricks, **25** 102 *c*.

aguilla = *aguila* (L. *aquĭla*, but of semi-learned or irregular development) eagle, **31** 14 *b*.

aguisa = *á guisa*, **14** 102.

aguisado (cf. *aguisar*) proper, **15** 132, 143; **17** 197.

aguisar (*a-* + *guisar*, from Germanic *wīsa*, Eng. *wise*) to arrange, provide, **26** 110 *b*.

aguisar = *á guisar*, **28** 266 *a*.

aiuda = *ayuda* aid, **21** 24.

aiudar = *ayudar* to aid, **18** 1107; *aiudaremos* **15** 143; *aiudol* = *ayudóle*, **18** 1094.

ajuntadas = *ayuntadas* (*j* = *i* = *y*; cf. *ayuntado*) joined, united, **30** 10 *d*.

al (*á* + *el*) to the, etc., **25** 98 *c* etc.; (*á* + *él*) to him, etc., **28** 362 *d* etc.

al (L. *alĭd*, ancient for *aliud*) else, something else, anything else, **6** 14; **9** 75; **28** 365 *b*; **31** 18 *a*; **43** 32; *lo al* other things, **55** 19.

ala = *á la*, **13** 11; **16** 150 etc.

ala = *alla*, thither, there, **6** 17; **7** 51; **10** 105.

ala (L. *ala*) wing, **31** 14 *c*.

alabança (abstract noun of the L. *-antia* class, formed on stem of *alabar*) praise, **70** LII 1.

alabar (L. *allaudare*, or V. L. **alapare*, cf. Körting³ § 397. The source is uncertain, yet *allaudare* seems to impose itself) to praise, **61** 1; *alabada* **52** 6; *alabes* **61** 6.

alabrar = *á labrar*.

alançar (L. *ad* + V. L. *lanceare* formed on L. *lancea*) to throw lances, **41** 10, 18, 21; **42** 6; *alançades* = mod. *alanzáis*, **40** 14.

alarydos = *alaridos* (Arab. *al-arîr* 'din, uproar,' or V. L. **ululitus* for L. *ululatus*. The source is not clear; cf. Körting³ § 401) shouts, cries of alarm, war-cries, **34** 82 *c*.

alas = *á las*, **17** 1088; **28** 368 *c*; **48** 13 *d*.

Albarfanez (pr. n.) Alvar Fánez **19** 1127, 1144; *Albarffanez* **13** 14.

albriçia (related to Arab. *al-bashârah* 'good news'; cf. Ptg. *alviçaras*) reward for good news, hurrah! be merry! **13** 14.

alcaçar (Arab. *al-qaçar* 'castle') castle, citadel, **20** 1220; mod. *alcázar*.

alcalde (Arab. *al-qâḍī* 'judge') mayor, magistrate, **50** 509 *a*.

alcançar (possibly Arab. *al-qanaç* 'spoils of the chase,' influenced by O. Sp. *encalçar* from V. L. **incalceare*, and by O. Sp. *acalçar* from V. L. **accalceare*) to obtain, reach, strike; *alcançaba* **37** 360 *c*; *alcanço* **43** 5; cf. mod. *alcanzar*.

alcandara (Arab. *al-kandarah*) perch **13** 4; cf. mod. *alcándara*.

alçar (V. L. **altiare* from L. *altus*) to raise, lift; *alçando* **38** 365 *b*;

alço (pret. 3) **42** 28 ; **43** 3 ; cf. mod. *alzar*.

alcargar = *al cargar*, **16** 170.

alcaz (a derivative from *alcançar*; the loss of the *n*, if not scribal, may be due to the influence of *caça*, mod. *caza*, which is similar in meaning) pursuit, **19** 1147.

alegrantes (cf. *alegre*) delighting, **60** 17 ; cf. *alegrar*.

alegrar (cf. *alegre*) to rejoice, delight; *alegre* (pres. sbj. 3) **48** 13*d*.

alegre (L. *ălăcer* became V. L. *alę̄cer*, *alę̄crem*, possibly under the influence of L. *laetus*, V. L. *lę̄tus*. But this source is not certain ; cf. Körting³ § 391. On V. L. *alicer*, *alįcrem* > *alęcrem*, whose close *e* better explains the Spanish form, cf. Grandgent, *Vulgar Latin*, § 195) merry, **20** 1219.

alegría (formation on *alegre*) joy, **41** 10 ; **60** 27 ; **70** LII 6.

Alexandre (L. *Alexander, Alexandrum*, to which the mod. *Alejandro* corresponds better) Alexander, **36** 351*a* ; *Alexandrre* **36** 345*d*.

alfoz (Arab. *al-ḥawz*) district, region ; *alffoz de Lara* **40** title, 7.

algo (L. *aliquod*) something, somewhat, anything, **7** 30 ; **15** 123, 124 ; **16** 157 ; **17** 205 ; **25** 105*d* ; **45** 10 ; **48** 16*b* ; of account, valuable, **14** 111 ; (as a noun) property, means, wealth, money, **50** 491*c* ; **56** 423*d*.

alguaçil (Arab. *al-vazîr*) bailiff, policeman, **50** 509*c*. (The correct early Spanish form is *alguazil*.)

alguandre (L. *aliquando*, with analogical adverbial -*re*, cf. -*mientre*) at any time, **7** 34. ✓

algun (apocopated form of *alguno*) **42** 11 ; **54** 7.

algund (apocopated form of *alguno*) **49** 301*a*.

alguno, -a, -os, -as, (V. L. *alicūnus* etc., from L. *aliqu[is] unus* etc.; cf. L. *alicubi, alicunde*) some, any, some one, any one, **24** 96*a* ; **26** 289*b* ; **52** 1 etc.

algunt (apocopated form of *alguno*) **24** 92*d* ; **25** 103*a* ; **27** 306*d*.

ali = *allí*, **19** 1126.

all (before a feminine word beginning with a vowel) = *al* ; *á la* to the ; *all el[gue]si[a]* **21** 19.

alla (L. *ĭllắc*, with its first syllable modified under the influence of *á* or of the L. particle *ac* found in *aquel* etc.) thither, there (of motion and rest, both), **42** 27 ; **57** 427*d*, 430*c d*, 431*a d*, 432*a* ; mod. *allá*. ✓

Allah (Arab. *Allâh*) Allah, **64** 95*c* ; mod. *Alá*.

allegar (L. *applĭcare*) to bring together, collect, gather ; *allegados* **41** 18, 28 ; *allegaron* **27** 358*b* ; to come, approach, *allego* **58** 439*a*.

allende (*allí* + *ende* from L. *ĭnde*) beyond, **33** 72*b*.

alli (L. *ad* + L. *illĭc*, whose accent is due to *hīc* ; or L. *atque*[?] + *illĭc* ; or L. *eccum*, influenced by L. *ac*, + *illĭc*) there, thereby, then, **13** 10 ; **20** 1215 ; **24** 96*d* ; etc.

alliñaron = *aliñaron* (*aliñar*, L. *ad* + L. *lineare*) they advanced, **27** 354*b*.

ally = *allí*, **50** 499 *d.*

alma (L. *anĭma*, with dissimilation of *n*) soul, **21** 7, 12, etc.

Almançor (Arab. pr. n.) **44** 5, 14.

Almenar (Arab. pr. n.) **18** 1092.

almofalla (Arab. *al-maḥallah*) army, camp, **19** 1124; (perhaps Arab. *al-moḥallā*[?]) carpet, rug, **17** 182.

alo = *á lo*, **16** 157.

alongar (L. *ad* + formation on *longus*, V. L. *allongare*) to defer, **36** 346 *c*, 347 *a*.

alos = *á los*, **18** 1098 etc.

altar (L. *altāre*) altar, **21** 16 etc.

alterçer = *al terçer*, **18** 1113.

alteza (L. *altĭtia* from *altus*) height; *en alteza* on high, **51** 1664 *e.*

alto, -a, -os, -as, (L. *altus* etc.) high, lofty, noble, mighty, loud, **39** 370 *d*; **40** 6; **41** 13, 15; etc.; *en alto* on high, **13** 8.

alua = *alba* (L. *albus*, *alba*, 'white') dawn, **18** 1100.

Aluan = *Albano* (from L. *albus*, V. L. *albanus*); *Mont Aluan* **18** 1089.

Aluar = *Álvaro* (pr. n.), **41** 20.

Alucad (cf. *Alucant*) **18** 1108.

Alucant (pr. n.) **17** 1087.

✓ **alunbrar** = *alumbrar* (V. L. *allūmĭnare* from *ad* + *lumen*) to illumine, **48** 12 *b*; *alunbra* **60** 24.

aluores (pl. of *albor*, V. L. *albor*, *alborem*, from *albus*) dawn, **19** 1137; **28** 367 *a*.

alyña cf. *desaliñar* to derange, disturb, destroy; *des alyña* **50** 499 *b*.

ama (V. L. *amma*, cf. Körting³ § 604) nurse; *amas* **59** 8.

ama = *alma*, **21** 8.

amades (L. *amatĭs*) **43** 1; cf. *amar.*

amaneçer (inchoative formation on L. *mănĕ*; *ad* + *mane* + *-escere* > **-escēre*) to dawn; *amaneçio* it dawned, morning came, **19** 1186.

amanezient = *amaneçiendo*, **21** 3; cf. *amaneçer.* ✱ *See correction p 176 a*

amar (L. *amāre*) to love, **49** 490 *a*; *amamos* **35** 335 *a*; *amades* **43** 1; *ame* (pret. 1) **60** 3; *amaua* = *amaba*, **59** 25; *amauan* **25** 104 *c*; *amava* **47** 5; *amado* **61** 14.

amarabilla = *á maravilla* marvelously, **52** 11.

amarauillar = *á maravillar*, **18** 1102.

amargo, -a, (V. L. **amaricus*, *-a*, based on L. *amarus*, *-a*) bitter, **54** 20; **58** 441 *d.*

amariello, -a, (V. L. **ambarĕllus*, *-a*, formed on Arab. *'ambar* 'amber,' •r V. L. **amarĕllus*, *-a*, formed on L. *amarus*, *-a*, 'bitter,' with an unexplained change of sense. Ety. doubtful. Cf. Körting § 579) **23** 86 *d.* *yellow, livid*

amas both, **69** XLIII 2; cf. *amos.*

amatar (*a-* + *matar* 'to kill,' from *māt* found in such expressions as Persian *shāh māt* 'the king is dead,' whence Eng. "checkmate" and Sp. *jaque mate.* Phonologically this ety. is better than L. *mactare*, which should have given in Sp. **mechar.* But the source is still thought doubtful by some: cf. Körting³ §§ 5783, 5996) to deaden, extinguish; *amatado* **29** 2 *b.*

amaua = *amaba*, **59** 25; cf. *amar.*

amauan = *amaban*, **25** 104 *c*; cf. *amar.*

amava = *amaba*, **47** 5; cf. *amar*.

amblantes (L. *ambŭlāre, ambulantes*) ambling, **22** 33.

amenaza (cf. L. pl. *mĭnaciae* 'threats,' *mĭnax*, *mĭnacem*) threat; *amenazas* **62** 22.

amenazar (cf. *amenaza*; the verb indicates V. L. **amminaciare*; thence, perhaps, the noun) to threaten; *amenazados* **33** 76 *b*.

amenos = *á menos*, **18** 1106.

amidos (L. *ĭnvītŭs*, perhaps influenced by *á miedo*; the *-s* is adverbial) in spite of one's self; in spite of myself, **14** 84; *a amidos* against his will, **25** 104 *a*; cf. *amjdos* **68** VIII 3; *amydos* **14** 95. (The correlation with *a fuerça* in **68** VIII 3 could also explain the *a*).

amigo, -a, (L. *amīcŭs*, *-a*) beloved, friend, **41** 3; **47** 1, 2; **61** 1.

amistad (V. L. **amīcĭtas*, **amīcĭtatem*, based on *amīcus*. This gave regularly O. Sp. *amizad*, whence, by the analogy of abstracts in *-stad*, L. *honestatem* > *honestad*, etc., the more usual and modern *amistad*) friendship, **60** 3.

amj = *á mí*, **48** 13 *b*.

amjdos = *amidos* in spite of himself (*a fuerça e amidos*) **68** VIII 3.

amjgos = *amigos*, **28** 363 *b*; **69** XLII 7; cf. *amigo*.

amo (masc. formed on *ama*) tutor, **41** 8.

amonestar (V. L. **admonestare*, based on **monestus*, a p.p. derived from *mŏnēre, monitus*; cf. Körting³ § 243) to admonish; *amonestan* **66** 6.

amor (L. *amor, amōrem*) love, **19** 1139; **47** 7 etc.

amos, -as, (L. *ambo, -os, -as*) both, **14** 100, 104, 106; **15** 120, 127, 142; **16** 173; **17** 191, 200, 203; **38** 366 *a*; **34** 79 *a*; **46** 26.

amouer = *á mover*, **16** 169.

amydos = *amidos* against my will, **14** 95.

amyo = *a myo*, *á mío*, **16** 174; **19** 1186.

an (V. L. **hant* for L. *habent*) they have, (as aux.) **11** 126; **12** 134; **13** 9; **17** 1086; **28** 361 *d*; **46** 7; (as indep. verb) **58** 441 *a*.

anbos = *amos*, both, **53** 12.

ancho, -a, (L. *amplŭs, -a*) broad, **59** 15.

andante (cf. *andar*) progressing; *bien andante* prosperous, **55** 15.

andar (L. *ambulare*; or V. L. **ambitare* from *ambīre, ambitus*; or L. *adnare*; or V. L. **amb-*, from *ambire, + dare*. For the sense and sound development **ambitare* is most engaging, but none of the etyma proposed can be deemed certain. Cf. Körting³ § 588) to go, walk, proceed, pass, act, be, **8** 60; **9** 80; **27** 353 *b*; **35** 333 *d*; *ando* **56** 425 *d*; *anda* **27** 356 *d*; **50** 499 *c*; *andan* **35** 334 *c*; *andaua* = *andaba*, **23** 86 *b* etc.; *andava* = *andaba*, **38** 364 *a* etc.; *andido* (analogy of *estido* = L. *stetit*) **43** 23; *andidieron* **20** 1197; *andemos* **8** 64; **9** 73; *anda* (imper.) **47** 15; *andad* **10** 102; *andados* (p.p.) past, elapsed, **40** 1; **44** 1.

andar (n.) gait, rate; *a mas andar* at full speed, with all one's might, **58** 442 *a*.

andaua (impf. 3 of *andar*) **23** 86 *b*; **30** 3 *c*; **40** 3; **44** 2.

andava cf. *andaua*, **38** 364 *a*; *andava muy cuytado* he was greatly distressed, **38** 364 *b*.

andidieron (pret. 3 pl. of *andar*, on the analogy of *estidieron* = L. *steterunt*) **20** 1197.

andido (pret. 3 of *andar*, on the analogy of *estido* = L. *stetit*) **43** 23.

Anemur (pr. n.) **59** *title*.

angel (L. *angĕlus*) angel, **51** 1664 *d*.

Angelero (pr. n.) Engelier, **36** 352 *c*. (One of Charlemagne's peers.)

anillo (L. *anĕllus* from *anus*) ring, **31** 12 *c*.

annafyl = *añafil* (Persian and Arab. *an-nafīr*), Moorish pipe or trumpet, **34** 82 *c*.

Annir (pr. n.) **65** 103 *c*.

anparar = *amparar* (L. *in* + *parare*; for the *a* cf. obs. *mamparar* from L. *manu parare*) to protect, **66** I 6. (Cf. *enparar*.)

ansi (L. *ac* + *sīc*, with intrusive *n*) so, thus, **48** 16 *d*; **49** 18 *d*; cf. *assi* and *asi*.

ansy = *ansi*, **66** 12.

antaño (*ante* + *año*) last year, previously, **58** 440 *b*.

ante prep. (L. *ante*) before, into the presence of, **41** 25, 26; **53** 11; **62** 21; etc.; (adv.) before, previously, **24** 93 *a*; **52** 18; *ante de* (prep.) before, **33** 75 *c*; *ante que* (conj.) before, **16** 169.

antel = *ante el*, **53** 11, 13.

antes adv. (*ante* + adverbial -*s* found in *después*, *menos*, *fueras*; cf. Menéndez Pidal, *Gramática elemental*, 2d ed., p. 240) previously, earlier, **16** 164; *en antes* previously, **35** 330 *d*; *antes que* before, **38** 366 *a*; **41** 14.

antiguedat (L. *antīquĭtas*, *antīquĭtatem*) antiquity, **32** 21 *c*; cf. mod. *antigüedad*.

Antolinez (pr. n.) **13** 79 etc.

aoralo = *aorallo* < *aorarlo*, **6** 17.

aorar (L. *adorare*); [*aor*]*ar* **8** 62; *aorare* (fut. 1) **7** 31; **8** 58; *aoralo e* (fut. 1) **6** 17; cf. *adorar* in the same document, **9** 77; **10** 103, 106.

aorient = *á orient*[*e*], **18** 1091.

apareiados (V. L. **apparĭcŭlatos* from *pariculus*, a diminutive of *par*) prepared, ready, **19** 1123; **29** 1 *b*; cf. mod. *aparejar*.

apartar (V. L. **appartare* from *ad* + *pars*, *partem*); *apartarme* to depart, **25** 100 *b*; *se apartaron* went apart, **14** 105, and *apartaronse* **43** 16.

aparte (L. *ad* + *partem*) apart, to one side, **17** 191.

apassado = *a passado*, *ha pasado*, **16** 1 50.

apedir = *á pedir*, **27** 359 *b*.

apegar (V. L. **appĭcare*); *apego me* I cling, shrink close, **58** 435 *b*.

apellido (V. L. **appellītus*, -*um*, connected with *appellare*) call, muster, levy, **32** 21 *b*; *dar el apellido* to give the call to arms, order a levy, **33** 75 *b*.

apenas (L. *ad* + *poenam* with adverbial -*s*, or *ad* + *poenas*) hardly, **27** 358 *b*; **61** 7.

apleytear = *á pleytear*, *á pleitear*, **27** 357 *b*.

apoderado (*a-* + participial formation on *poder* from V. L. *potēre for L. *posse*) empowered, mighty, **65** 102 *c*; *apoderado de* charged with, given power over, **50** 509 *d*.

apostado (V. L. *appositatum from L. *ad* + *posĭtus*) appropriate, elegant, **48** 15 *d*.

apostol (learned word from L. *apŏstŏlus, -um*) apostle, **19** 1138; **21** 21.

appartar (cf. *apartar*); *me apparto* I go apart, am alone, **46** 16.

apremjdos = *apremidos* (p.p. of obs. *apremir*, L. *apprĭmere* with change of conjugation) pressed together, closed, **23** 86 *c*.

aprendiestes (pret. 2 pl. of *aprender*, L. *apprehendere*) learned, understood.

aprendy (pret. 1 of *aprender*) cf. *aprendiestes*.

apres (loan-word, cf. Prov. *apres*, Fr. *après*, L. *apprimere*, *appressum*); *apres de* after, **30** 3 *b*.

apretado (V. L. *appectorare [?], *appectoratum [?], from *ad* and *pectus*, *pectoris*) constrained, hurried, in haste, **57** 434 *a*.

apriessa (*á* + *priessa* from L. p.p. *prĕssus, prĕssa*, etc.) quickly, **14** 97, 99; **43** 14; cf. mod. *apriesa*, *aprisa*.

aquel adj. (L. *eccum*, under influence of *ac*, + *ĭlle*) that, **9** 77; **12** 133 etc.; (dem. pron.) the one, he, him, **7** 24; **27** 356 *a*; etc.

aquela = *aquella* adj. and pron. (L. *eccum*, under influence of *ac*, + *ĭllam*) that, the one, she, her, **19** 1124; pl. *aquelas* = *aquellas*, **15** 116; **16** 161.

aquell (before a vowel) **42** 28; cf. *aquel*.

aquella (adj. and pron.) that, the one, she, her; cf. *aquela* **52** 3, 20; **61** 20; **52** 14.

aquello dem. pron. ntr. (L. *eccum* or V. L. *accum + *ĭllŭd*) that, **53** 1; **53** 9.

aquellos pl. of *aquel* (L. *eccum* or V. L. *accum + *ĭllōs*) those, **30** 6 *a*; **60** 27.

aquend = *aquende* prep. (L. *eccum* or V. L. *accum + *ĭnde*) on this side of, **44** 6.

aquesta adj. and pron. fem. (L. *eccum* or V. L. *accum + *ĭstam*) this, this one, **18** 1111; **32** 21 *c*; **64** 100 *a*; pl., **33** 71 *b*.

aqueste adj. and pron. masc. (L. *eccum* or V. L. *accum + *ĭste*) this, this one, **15** 121, 130; **48** 13 *c*; **65** 103 *a*.

aquesto dem. pron. ntr. (L. *eccum* or V. L. *accum + *ĭstud*) **14** 112; **18** 1106; **52** 7; **63** 89 *a*; **69** XVIII 5.

aquexados (p.p. of *aquexar*) distressing, **33** 76 *a*.

aquexar (*a-* + *quexar* from V. L. *questiare based on L. *questus*, rather than from L. *coaxare*) refl. to complain, **65** 108 *c*.

aqui (L. *eccum* or V. L. *accum + *hĭc*) here, **10** 104 etc.; *por aqui* hither, this way, **10** 104.

aquis = *aqui se*, **17** 1085.

Arabia Arabia, **61** 3.

Aracen pr. n., **46** 24.

Aragon Aragon, **19** 1187; **41** 4.

arancar = *arrancar* (Germanic **ranc* 'twisted'?) to pull out, pull up, **19** 1142; refl. to break ranks?, go in rout?, **19** 1145.

arbol (L. *arbor*, *arbŏrem*) tree, **47** 3; **60** 10.

arca (L. *arca*) chest, box, **14** 113; **17** 181 etc.; cf. *archa* **14** 85 etc.

archa = *arca*, **14** 85; **15** 119, 127, etc.

arco (L. *arcus*, *arcum*) bow, **66** I 6.

ardida (p.p. of *arder*, L. *ardēre*, or a by-form of O. Sp. *fardido*, *fardida*, from O. Fr. *hardi*, Germanic verb *hartjan* 'to make hardy') hardy, bold, **13** 79.

ardyt = *ardido* (cf. *ardida* ante) bold, daring, hardy, **50** 509 *c*.

arena (L. *arena*) sand, **14** 86.

argent (L. *argĕntum*; possibly a Fr. loan-word) **28** 364 *a*; **31** 16 *c*.

Arlançon (pr. n.) Arlanzon, **17** 20.

arma (L. ntr. pl. *arma*) arm, weapon; pl. arms, armor, **19** 1123; **34** 82 *b*; etc.; *armas*, *armas*, to arms! **43** 13.

armar (L. *armare*) to arm, **19** 1135; *armados* **29** 1 *c*; **35** 333 *d*; to dub, *armo* pret. 3, **40** 18.

Arnald pr. n., **36** 352 *b*.

arrancados (cf. *arancar*) routed, **34** 79 *c*.

arreada (p.p. of *arrear*, V.L. **arredare*, **redare* from Germanic or Celtic; cf. Gothic *rêdan* 'to arrange, prepare,' and Celtic *rēd*-, **reidho*-, 'to make ready') prepared, fitted out, **26** 110 *a*.

arrebatado (p.p. of *arrebatar*. The etymon is uncertain, but there seems to be a sense-connection with L. *arripio*, *arreptus*) carried off, **60** 8.

arriba (L. *ad* + *rīpam*) up, on high, **42** 28.

arrybar = *arribar* (V.L. **arripare*; cf. *arriba* above) to arrive, **35** 329 *d*.

arryvaron (cf. *arrybar*) landed, **33** 72 *c*.

arto = *harto* (L. *fartus*, p.p. of *farcire*) too much, too long, **64** 100 *c*.

as = *has* (V.L. **has* for L. *habes*; cf. *aver*) thou hast, **12** 135.

asaz = *assaz* sufficiently, quite, **54** 4.

asegurar, **assegurar** (V.L. **assecūrare* from *secūrus*): *asegurados* assured, certain, in security, **29** 1 *d*; **34** 81 *a*; **35** 334 *a*; *aseguro* I assure, **57** 429 *d*.

asemeiant (pres. part. of *assemejar*, *asemejar*, V.L. **assimiliare* from *sĭmĭlis*) seeming, apparent, **21** 5.

asentar, **assentar** (V.L. **assĕdĕntare* from L. *sedens*, *sedentem*): *asentose* (refl. pret. 3) seated himself, **52** 22; *assenteme* seated myself, **47** 4; *asiento me* I sit down, **57** 434 *a*.

asentauaste = *asentabas* + *te* (cf. *asentar*) thou didst seat thyself, **21** 19.

asi (L. *eccum*, under influence of *ac.* + *sīc*; or simply *ac sīc*) so, thus, as, **7** 41 ; **9** 73 ; **52** 1 ; etc. The older form was *assi*.

asmar (L. *aestimare*, with its first syllable modified by *ad*, *a*-) to estimate, judge, decide on, conceive, think of, consider, **33** 72 *d*; **46** 15; *asmaron* **24** 94 *b*; **27** 359 *a*; *asmo* pret. 3, **46** 9.

asonbrado = *asombrado* (p.p. of *assombrar*, *asombrar*, formed on *sombra* from L. *sub* > Sp. *so* and L. *ŭmbra*) bewildered, **58** 436 *d*.

asosegado (p.p. of *assossegar*, *asosegar*, from V. L. *ad-sŭbsĕdĭcare based on *sĕd-ere*) at ease, satisfied, **58** 436 *c*.

aSoto = *á Soto*, **27** 354 *b*.

assaz (L. *ad* + *satis*) enough, much, **26** 109 *c*; **26** 110 *b*; cf. *asaz*.

assenteme (cf. *asentar*) I seated myself, **47** 4.

assi (older form of *asi*) **15** 139, 143; **16** 153, 163; etc.; cf. also *ansi*, *assy*.

assil = *asi* + *le*, **16** 163.

assu = *á su*, **46** 13.

assy = *assi*, *asi*, **36** 346 *b*, *c*, 356 *c*; **61** 13, 16, 19 ; cf. also *asy*.

asta (L. *hasta*) staff, lance, **31** 16 *c*.

astil (L. *hastīle*) handle, shaft, **42** 26, 28.

astroso (V. L. *astrōsus* from L. *aster*, *astrum*) disastrous, unfortunate, wretched, evil, fateful, **57** 431 *c*.

astrrosa (cf. *astroso*) disastrous, **35** 328 *d*.

Asturias pr. n., **45** 13.

asu = *á su* (cf. *assu*), **26** 109 *a*, 111 *a*; etc.

asuueras (ety. ?) harness strap running from the breast-leather to the crupper, **22** 33.

asy = *assi*, *asi*, so, thus, as, just, **26** 109 *b*; **29** 2 *c*; etc.; cf. *assy*; *asý* **71** LXXIX 1.

ata prep. (Arab. *ḥatta*) until; *ata que* until, **11** 116.

atal adj. and pron. (L. *ac* = *eccum* + *talis*) such, such a, such a thing, as, just, **7** 22, 33; **11** 112; **35** 332 *d*.

atamana = *atamanna* (L. *ac* = *eccum* + *tam* + *magnus* -*a*) so great, **46** 15; cf. *tamanna* **46** 16 and modern *tamaño*.

atanto adv. (L. *ac* = *eccum* + *tantŭm*) so much, **52** 12.

atar (L. *aptare*) to fasten ; *ata* pres. 3, **31** 12 *c*.

atender (L. *attĕndĕre*, which joined the 2d conj.) to await, **44** 21.

ati = *á ti*, **13** 8 ; **18** 1102.

atierra = *á tierra*, **15** 125.

atod = *á todo*, **17** 184.

atodas = *á todas*, **19** 1142 ; **20** 1197.

atodos = *á todos*, **17** 187.

atorgar (V. L. *auctorĭcare > *actoricare, from L. *auctor*; cf. L. *auctorare* and *auctoritas*) to grant; *atorgar nos hedes* you shall grant us, **17** 198.

atramizes (ety. Arabic) lupines, **54** 18, 20, 22, etc. (The proper form would be *atramuçes*; cf. notes.)

atramuzes (cf. *atramizes*) lupines, **54** title.

atravessado (p.p. of *atravessar*, *atravesar*, V. L. *attraversare formed on L. *tra*[*ns*]*vĕrsus*) crossed, **37** 360 *a*.

aty = *á ti*, **49** 299 *d*.

aue = L. *ave*, hail, **50** 1661 *a*.

auedes = *avedes* (cf. *aver*), **8** 62 ; **10** 89 ; **16** 155; etc.

auemos = *avemos* (cf. *aver*), **10** 91, 100 ; **12** 146; etc.

auentorado = *aventurado* (p.p. of *aventurar*, formed on *aventura*) fortunate; *mal auentorado* unfortunate, **59** 2.

auentura = *aventura* (V. L. **adventūra* from L. *advenio*) chance, fortune, **27** 354 *a*.

auer = *aver* to have, **59** 1 ; (n.) property, means, money, wealth, possessions, **11** 118; **14** 82; **15** 118, 125; etc.; *auer monedado* money, **20** 1217.

auera = *avera*, *avra* (cf. *aver*) there will be, **10** 99.

auia = *avia* (cf. *aver*), **52** 14.

auie = *avia* (impf. 3 of *aver*) had, there was (were), **13** 6; **40** 7, 15; **43** 7; **44** 8, 15; **46** 24; **30** 5 *a*, 9 *d*; *auie y* **32** 20 *a*, *c*.

auien = *avian* (impf. 3 pl. of *aver*), **14** 101; **16** 163; **31** 16 *c*; **32** 21 *a*; **41** 32.

auiente (part. adj. from *aver*) having, **59** 10.

auiniese = *aviniese* (from *avenir*) should occur, be necessary, **29** 1 *b*.

auja = *avia*, **27** 354 *d*.

aujan = *avian* (from *aver*), **27** 357 *a*, *c*.

aun (L. *ad + hūc*, whence, with intrusive *n*, **adhūnc*; cf. *tunc*, *hinc*; or L. *ad + ūnum*) yet, even, **11** 109; **17** 205; **24** 93 *d*; etc.

auos = *á vos*, **17** 196; **19** 1128.

aura = *avrá* (from *aver*) : *y aura* there will be, **19** 1131.

auredes = *avredes* (fut. 2 pl. of *aver*), **16** 157.

aurie = *avria* (cond. 1 of *aver*), **14** 84.

auuelo = *avuelo*, *abuelo* (V. L. **aviŏlus -um*, dimin. of L. *avus*) ancestor, **45** 15.

auya = *avia* (impf. 3 of *aver*) there was, **20** 1204.

auyen = *avian* (impf. 3 pl. of *aver*), **13** 18.

avatydo (p.p. of *avatir*, *abatir*, L. *batuere*, *battere*) beaten down, **39** 371 *b*.

ave (L. *avis*, *avem*) bird, **64** 98 *c*.

avedes (pres. 2 pl. of *aver*) **43** 25.

avemos (pres. 1 pl. of *aver*) : *a morir avemos* we shall die, **71** LXXIX 1.

avena (L. *avēna*) oats, **27** 355 *d*.

aventurar (from *aventura*, V. L. **adventūra* from L. *advenio*, *adventum*) to venture, risk, **56** 423 *d*.

aver (L. *habēre*) to have, get, **54** 17 ; cf. *auer* **59** 1 etc.; part. adj. *auiente* (with gerund force) **59** 10.

Indic. pres.

Sg. 1 *he* **17** 207 etc.; *e* **6** 3.

2 *as* **12** 135.

3 *a* **6** 4 etc. ; *ha* **15** 115 etc.

Pl. 1 *avemos* **71** LXXIX 1 ; *auemos* **10** 91 etc.

2 *avedes* **43** 25; *auedes* **8** 62.

3 *an* **11** 126; *han* **18** 1119 etc.

Indic. impf.

Sg. 1

    2

    3 *avia* **33** 75 *a* etc.; *auia* **52**
      14; *auja* **27** 354 *d*; *avya*
      35 332 *a*; *auie* **13** 6 etc.;
      avie **40** 11 etc.; *abia* **53**
      18 etc.

Pl. 1

    2

    3 *aujan* **27** 357 *a*; *avyan* **34**
      81 *b*; *auien* **14** 101 etc.;
      abian **63** 92 *a*.

Indic. fut.

Sg. 1 *avre* **70** LII 7; *abre* **63** 90 *d*
      etc.

    2 *abras* **64** 95 *a*.

    3 *auera* **10** 99; *avera* **61** 15.

Pl. 1 *avremos* **71** LXXIX 6.

    2

    3 *avrán* **71** LXXVIII 7 etc.

Indic. cond.

Sg. 1

    2

    3 *abria* **27** 358 *d* etc.

Sbj. pres.

Sg. 1 *aya* **16** 179.

    2 *ayas* **61** 6.

    3 *aya* **55** 18.

Pl. 1

    2 *ayades* **17** 205.

    3 *ayan* **34** 81 *d*.

For pret. tenses cf. *ouo, ovo, obo,*
ouieron, oviste, etc.; for past
and fut. sbj. forms cf. *ouiesse,*
ouiere, ouieres, etc.

aver n. (cf. *aver* ante) property,
goods, **33** 75 *d*; cf. *auer* **11** 118
etc.

avera (fut. 3 of *aver*), **61** 15.

avia (impf. 3 of *aver*) had, there
was (were), **33** 75 *a*; **52** 11; **53**
7; etc.; *avia de* had to, **54** 20.

avie = *avia*, **40** 11.

avisar (V. L. *advisare, from *ad* +
visum, p.p. of L. *videre*) to
advise, put on guard.

avisate (cf. *avisar*) be on thy
guard, **67** III 5.

avn = *á un*, **24** 92 *a*.

avn = *aun* still, yet, even, **25**
100 *a*; **31** 18 *a*; **36** 342 *c*: *avn*
que even though, although, **57**
428 *d*; **71** LXXIX 7.

avrán (fut. 3 pl. of *aver*), **71**
LXXVIII 7.

avré (fut. 1 of *aver*), **70** LII 7.

avremos (fut. 1 pl. of *aver*), **71**
LXXIX 6.

avya = *avia*, **35** 332 *a*; **36** 345 *c*.

avyan = *avian* (impf. 3 pl. of *aver*),
34 81 *b*, 83 *b*; **35** 333 *d*.

avyvado (p.p. of *avivar* from V. L.
*avvivare, i.e. L. *ad* + *vivare
from *vivus*) lively, strong, **34** 79 *a*.

axenuz (Arab. *ash-shenuz*) fennel,
49 17 *a*; cf. mod. *ajenuz*.

aXerica = *á Xerica*, **18** 1092.

axo (a by-form of *exe*, mod. *eje*,
from L. *axis, axem*) axle, **30**
8 *c*; cf. Ptg. *eixo*.

ay (L. *ai*) alas! **27** 360 *c*; **34** 83 *c*.

ay = *ahí* (L. *ad* + *híc*) there, **38**
362 *b*.

ay (V. L. *hat = L. *habet* + *híc*, i.e.
Sp. *a* 'has' + *y* 'there') there
is, **66** I 5.

aya (V.L. *haya, *hayat, L. *habeam*,
habeat; pres. sbj. 1 and 3 of *aver*)
16 179; **26** 112 *d*; **55** 18.

ayades (V. L. *hayatĭs*, L. *habeatis*; pres. sbj. 2 pl. of *aver*) **17** 205.

ayan (V. L. *hayant*, L. *habeant*; pres. sbj. 3 pl. of *aver*) **34** 81 *d*; **66** 8.

ayas (V. L. *hayas*, L. *habeas*; pres. sbj. 2 of *aver*) **61** 6.

ayer (L. *ad + hĕrī*) yesterday, **49** 300 *a*.

ayna = *aína* (V. L. *agīna* from *agere*; cf. *ruina* from *ruere*) quickly, **37** 357 *d*, 360 *d*.

ayrado (L. *ad + īratus*, *īratum*, from *īrascor*) held in anger, inimical, **14** 90, 114; **16** 156; cf. *en yra . . . yo sere metido*, *P. del Cid*, v. 74.

ayuda (abstract from *ayudar*) aid, **28** 362 *a*; cf. *aiuda*.

ayudar (L. *adjŭtare*) to aid, **61** 2; **62** 9; **48** 13 *b*; **55** 14; **64** 95 *b*; *ayudose* he got along, prospered, **55** 27.

ayudol' = *ayudó* + *le* (cf. *ayudar*), **55** 14, 27.

ayuntado (p.p. of *ayuntar*, V. L. *adjunctare* from L. *adjunctus*) assembled, arrived, **33** 76 *d*; **43** 14.

ayuntar (cf. *ayuntado*): *ayunto* assembled, mustered, **44** 12; *ayunto se* the meeting took place, they clashed, **34** 78 *c*.

azaris (? See notes) **22** 28.

azes (L. pl. *acies*) lines of battle, ranks, **37** 359 *c*, 364 *a*, 365 *a*.

ba = *va* (pres. 3 of *ir*; L. *vadit* under the influence of *dat*, *stat*, etc.) goes, **16** 174.

balança (V. L. *bĭlancia* from L. *bĭlanx*, *bĭlancem*; possibly a loan-word from French *balance*) balance, scales, **69** XVIII 5; cf. mod. *balanza*.

Baltasar (pr. n.) Balthasar, **9** 83.

banco (Germanic *bank*) bench, seat, **31** 12 *b*.

barata (abstract from a verb *baratar* based on the Gk. πράττειν 'to do,' 'deal,' or on the Celtic word for 'treachery,' 'trickery,' Irish *brath*, Welsh *brad*) bargain, price, value, **31** 12 *a*.

Barlaam pr. n., **59**.

baron (of uncertain source, but seemingly connected with the L. *baro*, *barōnem* 'simpleton,' 'stupid person,' therefore 'a servant,' 'one doing service,' 'a vassal,' and with O. Fr. *baron*, acc. of *ber* = Germanic *bero* 'bearer') man, **25** 105 *a*; cf. mod. *varón* 'man,' 'male.'

Bartolo pr. n., **70** XLIII 5.

barua (L. *barba*) beard; *fazer la barua* to shave, **62** 20; cf. mod. *barba*.

baruados (cf. *barua*) bearded, **31** 17 *c*; cf. mod. *barbados*.

baruero (V. L. *barbarius*) barber, **62** 19; cf. mod. *barbero*.

basteçer (inceptive formed on V. L. *bast-*; cf. *bastir*): *basteçio* provided, secured, **29** 371 *c*; *basteçieron* contrived, devised; cf. mod. *abastecer*. (The sense of 'building,' 'contriving' is the basic one.)

bastir (V. L. stem *bast-*) to build, make, **14** 85.

baxado (p.p. of *baxar*, V.L. **bassiare* based on V. L. **bassius* from *bassus* 'thick,' 'thick set,' 'low,' which latter is found in Classic Latin as a personal name, indicative, doubtless, of a bodily characteristic) bowed, bent, **23** 86 *c*.

baxo -a (V. L. **bassius -a*; cf. *baxado*) low, base, **68** XVIII 2.

baylia = *bailía* (a formation on L. *bajŭlus* 'bearer,' 'one having a charge or burden'; cf. Eng. 'bailiff') charge, jurisdiction, office, **24** 97 *d*.

bello -a (L. *bellus -a*, a contraction of *benulus -a*; cf. L. *bonus* and *bene*) handsome, fair, **65** 104 *a*.

bendicho -a (L. *benedĭctum*. The Sp. *i* is due to the analogy of *digo*, *dixe*, and other forms in which the *i* is phonologically and historically correct; cf. L. *dīco*, *dīxi*) blessed, **51** 1664 *h*.

bendiçion (learned word, L. *benedictio*, *benedictionem*) blessing, **25** 98 *b*.

bendicto (L. *benedĭctum*) blessed, **70** LIII 1; cf. *bendicho*.

bendito (cf. *bendicto*) blessed, **49** 300 *c*.

benedicto=*bendicto*,*bendito*,blessed, **25** 105 *a*.

benedita = *bendito -a* blessed, **51** 1664 *a*.

besar (L. *basiare* from *basium*) to kiss, **16** 174; **27** 360 *b*; etc.

bestia (learned word, L. *bēstĭa*) beast, **21** 24; **52** 22; **58** 440 *c*.

bestimento = *vestimento* (learned word, L. *vĕstīmĕntum*) vestment, garment, **22** 36.

bestion (augmentative of *bestia*) big beast, **30** 10 *b*; **31** 13 *d*.

beuedor = *bebedor* (V. L. **bĭbĭtor*, **bĭbĭtōrem*, from L. *bĭbo*) drinker, tippler, toper, **49** 18 *c*.

beuer = *beber* (L. *bĭbĕre*, V. L. **bĭbēre*) to drink; *beuo = bebo*, **25** 102 *d*; *beuemos = bebemos*, **18** 1103; *beuies = bebías*, **22** 35.

beuies = *bebias* (impf. 2 of *beuer* = *beber*) **22** 35.

beuir = *vevir*, *vivir* (L. *vīvĕre*, V. L. **vīvīre*, with dissimilation in the first syll. in Sp.) to live, **25** 100 *c*, 101 *b*; **26** 107 *b*; *biuo* I live, **13** 80.

bezerro (ety. uncertain; hardly the Basque *beia* + *cecorra*) calf, **61** 11; cf. mod. *becerro*.

bezino = *vezino*, mod. *vecino* (L. *vīcīnus*, *vīcīnum*, with dissimilation in the first syll. in Sp.) near, neighboring, **27** 353 *a*.

bida = *vida* (L. *vīta*) life, **70** LIII 4.

bien (L. *bĕne*) well, very, certainly, **13** 7; **14** 86 etc.; (n.) welfare, **54** 5; goods, property, **24** 97 *c*; **56** 43 *d*; good qualities, **40** 12.

Biluestre = *Vilvestre*, pr. n., **40** 10.

bine = *bien*, **6** 10, 11; etc.

bio (cf. *en bio* = mod. *envió* he sent) **19** 1188.

Biuar = *Vivar*, pr. n., **13** 11; **17** 1085; etc.

biuo = *vivo* (pres. 1 of *beuir*) I live, **13** 80.

biuo -a = *vivo -a* (L. *vīvus -a*) alive, active, **29** 2 *b*; **31** 13 *b*.

blanco -a (Germanic *blank-*) white, **17** 183 etc.

blanqueado (n. from p.p. of *blanquear*, derived from Germanic *blank-* + V. L. verbal ending *-ĭdĭare*) white spot, **31** 15 *c*.

blanqueante (pres. part. of *blanquear*; cf. *blanqueado*) gleaming white, **31** 16 *c*.

Blasquez = *Velasquez*, pr. n., **40** 7 etc.

boca (L. *bŭcca* 'cheek') mouth, **13** 19 etc.

bocado (*boca* + *-ado* from Lat. *-atus*, *-atum*, a suffix signifying 'full') mouthful, morsel, **67** v 4.

boda (L. *vōta*, pl. of *vōtum* 'vow'): pl. *bodas* wedding, **41** 2, 6, etc.

bodega (L. *apothēca*, which lost its initial *a-* in syntactical combination, as with the preceding article *illa*, Sp. *la*) store-room, wine-cellar, **47** 6.

boffordar (cf. *bofordo*) to cast *bofordos*, i.e. lances or stakes, wands, and the like, at a scaffold erected as a target, **41** 10.

bofordo (the word may consist of two parts, of which the first, *bo-*, is of obscure origin, while the second, *fordo*, with *f* denoting the aspirate *h* sound, may be a Germanic *hurd-*, found e.g. in Eng. 'hurdle,' and denoting a 'wand,' 'reed,' 'staff,' etc. The Sp. words *bofordo* and *bofordar* are probably derived directly from the O. Fr. *bohorder*) a wand, stake, or similar object cast, as a knightly exercise, against a

tablado or scaffolding, **42** 3; cf. mod. *bohordo*.

bollicio (perhaps from L. *bŭlla* 'bubble'; *bŭllire*, *bŭllare*, 'to bubble,' 'seethe,' and therefore probably 'to make a noise'; cf. Sp. *bulla* 'noise,' 'clatter') tumult, **25** 100 *b*; cf. mod. *bullicio*.

boluistes = *volvistes*, mod. *volvisteis*, pret. 2 pl. of *bolver*, mod. *volver* (L. *volvĕre*, V. L. **volvēre*) to turn, turn over, **70** XLIII 4.

bon = *buen, bueno*, **23** 2 *d*.

bondad (L. *bonĭtas, bonĭtātem*) goodness, **51** 1662 *f*; pl. good qualities, good things, **24** 93 *b*; **26** 108 *c*.

bono = *bueno*, **7** 37.

Borriana (pr. n.) Burriana, **18** 1093; **18** 1110.

boz = *voz* (L. *vox, vōcem*) voice, **60** 26; pl. shouts, **42** 23; **43** 13.

braço (L. *brachĭum*) arm, **17** 203; **42** 28; etc.; cf. mod. *brazo*.

brauo -a = *bravo -a* (L. *barbarus -a* > **barbus -a* > V. L. **brabus -a*. But the source is not absolutely certain) wild, fierce, brave; *braua mientre* fiercely, wildly, **42** 20.

breue = *breve* (L. *brĕvis -em*) brief, short.

breuemente = *brevemente* (L. *brĕvis, breve* + *mens, mĕnte*) briefly, **59** 16.

breujado -a = *breviado -a* (formed on *breve*; cf. *abreviar*) brief, **25** 98 *c*.

breujario (learned word, L. *breviarium* 'epitome') breviary, **70** XLIII 8.

breujedad (by-form of *brevedad* from L. *brevitas, brevitatem*) brevity, **66** 4.

brunnidas (fem. pl. p.p. of *brunnir* from Germanic *brun*, whence V. L. **brunio, *brunire*) burnished, **31** 16 *d*.

bueltas in *a bueltas = abueltas, avueltas* (seemingly an indef. fem. pl. p.p. of *aboluer, avolver* from L. *advolvĕre*, V. L. **advolvēre*). It occurs with a following *con*, with which it formed a compound preposition, *a bueltas con* along with, **43** 10. The *P. del Cid* (ed. Menéndez Pidal) has 589 *abuelta con*, 1761 *en buelta con*, 716 *abueltas de*, 3616 *abueltas con*, which all seem to mean 'along with.' Possibly it is a combination of the noun *vuelta, vueltas* with prepositions.

buelto (p.p. of *boluer, volver*; cf. *boluistes*) turned, brought upon, **13** 9. ᵛ Lˣ vᴏ... ≈ C L . vᴏ...

buelue = *vuelve* (cf. *boluistes*) turns, **58** 437 *c*.

buen = *bueno* (L. *bŏnum*), **17**, 192 etc.; = *buena* (proclitic to word beginning with a vowel in *en buen ora*), **13** 78; **16** 175.

buestro -a = *vuestro -a* (*vŏster, vŏstrum, vŏstram*, which in V. L. supplanted L. *vester*), your, **69** XIX 4.

Burgales (pr. n.) native or citizen of Burgos, **17** 193.

burges (Germanic *burg* + L. *-ensis*) burgher, citizen; *burgeses, burgesas* **13** 17. (The *Apolonio* 80 and 202 seems to have *burges*,

with change of *dž* to *dz* after *r*. The mod. *burgués* shows the stop *g* and not the spirant sound or its development. Baist, in the *Grundriss* I, 2d ed., p. 889, states a *Burgensis* = 'native of Burgos.' The fem. is based on the masc.)

Burgos (pr. n.) Burgos, **13** 12 etc.

Burueua = *Burbueba, Bureba*, **40** 8; **41** 5. (Cf. Menéndez Pidal, *Leyenda*, p. 4.)

buscar (of obscure origin. Perhaps from a stem *busc-* found in Romance words for 'bush,' 'wood,' 'forest,' as in Ital. *bosco*, Fr. *bois*, Sp. *bosque*, and related to Eng. *bush*, German *Busch*. According to Diez, *Etym. Wtb.*, the original sense of the verb may have been "to go through the bushes (cf. *montar* to go up the mountain), and, therefore, to hunt, to seek ") to seek, seek out, get, **9** 79; **44** 16; **54** 17; **10** 12; **17** 192.

byen = *bien* well, well off, **37** 354 *c*; **38** 364 *d*.

C. = *ciento*, **19** 1129; *C.C.C.*, **17** 186.

ca (L. *qua* as found in *quare = qua re*; the suppression of *y* may be due to unaccented use) for, because, but, **13** 6, 14; **14** 86; etc.

cabaña (V. L. *capanna*, related to L. *capere*, or V. L. *cabanna* with possible Celtic origin. But?) cabin, **24** 96 *b*. (Isidore of Seville says this: "tugurium parva casa est; hoc rustici capanna vocant." In the 8th century the Reichenau glosses have *cabanna.* Cf. Murray's *English Dict.* s.v. *cabin.*)

cabdal n. (L. *capitalis, capitalem*) capital, account, **66** 4; (adj.) of a chief or leader, **20** 1220; princely, excellent, **30** 3 *c*.

cabeça (V. L *capĭcia,* based on V. L. *capum* for *caput*) head, **13** 2; **31** 13 *c*; etc.; cf. mod. *cabeza.*

cabeçon (V. L. *capicionem,* i.e. an augmentative of *cabeça*) large head, headpiece, dasher, **30** 9 *a*.

cabello (L. *capĭllus, capĭllum*) hair, **65** 105 *d*.

cabera (Sp. *cabo* 'end,' + -*ero -era* from L. -*arius -a*) near the end, last, **32** 19 *d*.

cabeza (bad reading for *cabeça*) **55** 3.

cabo (L. *capŭt,* or rather, V. L. *capŭm*) end, **16** 162; *cabo de* beside, near, **55** 4; *de cabo,* anew, again, **46** 26; *en cabo* finally, at last, **26** 111 *b*; *en cabo de* at the end of, **46** 8.

caça (abstract from *caçar* 'to chase,' 'hunt,' based on V. L. *captiare* from L. *capere, captum*) hunt; *de caça* a-hunting, **49** 298 *b*; cf. mod. *caza.*

cada (V. L. *cata* from Gk. κατά as used distributively) each, **66** 7; *cada vna* (adj.) each, **59** 19; (and pron.) each one, **59** 12, 17; *quis cada vno* each one, **19** 1136.

cadaguna (= *cada una,* under influence of *alguna, ninguna* with *g*; cf. *cada*) each one, **65** 106 *c*.

cadena (L. *catēna*) chain, **27** 355 *a* etc.

caer (V. L. *cadēre* for L. *cadĕre*) to fall, **25** 99 *b*; to fall to the lot of, **20** 1217; *caida* p.p. **63** 89 *d*.

caga = *çaga*; *a caga* backward, **11** 113.

çaga (Arab. *sâqah* 'rear-guard,' with initial *sīn,* which gave O. Sp. *ç*) rear, rear-guard, **31** 18 *d*; cf. mod. *zaga.*

calças pl. (V. L. *calcĕas*; cf. L. *calceus* 'boot,' from *calx*), hose, trousers, **17** 190, 195; cf. mod. *calzas.*

caldera (L. *caldaria,* from *caldus* for *calidus*) caldron, boiler, **49** 17 *a*.

caleadas (perhaps a by-form of *caladas* p.p. of *calar*) fitted in, **30** 10 *a*; cf. *callar.*

callar (L. *calare* from Gk. χαλᾶν 'to slacken,' 'cease.' But the Sp. palatalized *ll* could not come from L. or Gk. single *l*.) to be silent; *calle* pres. sbj. 1, **57** 434 *b*.

calle (L. *callis, callem*) street, **52** 15.

callosse = *calló + se* (cf. *callar*) he was silent, **46** 23.

camjno = *camino* (V. L. *camminus* from Celtic *cammin-*) road, way, **27** 353 *b*.

campal (V. L. *campalis, *campalem* from L. *campus*) in the field; *lid campal* pitched battle, **18** 1111.

Campeador (agent formation on p.p. of *campear* from L. *campus, camp-* + V. L. -*ideare,* therefore, 'to be in the field,' 'carry on a campaign.' Possibly the Germanic *kampa* 'battle,' cf. the O. H. G. *kampfjan* 'to fight,' influenced the formation) Champion, Campaigner, Fighter, **14** 109; **15** 117; etc.

campo (L. *campus, campum*) field, battle, **19** 1133; **47** 10.

can (L. *canis, canem*) dog, **27** 356 *b*.

caña vera = *cañavera* (*caña* < L. *canna* + *vera* 'true cane'; the sense seems that of 'sugar cane'; *vera* may be the L. adj. *varia*), **49** 17 *d*.

cañado (L. *catenātum* from *catēna*) padlock, lock, bolt, **13** 3; cf. mod. *candado*.

canal (L. *canal, canālem*) canal; *Canal de Çelfa* pr. n., **20** 1194.

cançion (learned word from L. *cantĭo, cantĭōnem*) song, **68** IX 4.

Cannas pr. n., **24** 97 *a*. (A place name.)

cano -a (L. *canus -a*) hoary, white, **65** 105 *d*.

canon = *ca non*, **27** 357 *d*.

canónigo (half-learned word, L. *canŏnĭcus -um*) canon, **70** XLIII 8.

Canpeador = *Campeador*, **16** 175.

canpo = *campo*, **34** 78 *c*, 80 *d*; etc.

cansar ((1) L. *campsare* 'to bend,' 'avoid,' related to Gk. κάμπτειν, 'to bend,' 'bow,' or (2) L. *quassare* 'to shatter,' 'break,' with intrusive *n*. Semasiologically both sources are open to objection) to tire, weary, wear out; *cansado* **35** 334 *c*; **67** III 7; to grow weary, **35** 335 *d*.

cantantes (participial adj.; cf. *cantar*) singing, **60** 25.

cantar (L. *cantare*) to sing, **28** 367 *b*; to crow, **16** 169; to creak, **30** 8 *c*.

cantar (infin. noun; cf. *cantar* ante) singing, music, song, **48** 12 *c*; **52** 13; **53** 1; etc.

cantiga (formation in L. *cant-* from *cantare* or *cantus*; cf. L. *cantĭcum*) song, **52** 11, 12; etc.

canto (L. *cantus, cantum*) song, singing, **60** 25; **48** 11 *c*.

capa (L. *cappa*) cape, cloak, **49** 18 *c*.

çapatero (agent noun in *-ero*, L. *-arius*, based on *çapato*; cf. L. *argentum* and *argentarius*. Cf. *çapato*) shoemaker, cobbler, **52** 15, 20 etc.; cf. mod. *zapatero*.

çapato (origin obscure. Arabic and Basque etyma have been suggested. These and the Germanic *stap* are all doubtful. Apparently related are the Fr. *savate*, Ital. *ciabatta*, etc.) shoe, **53** 5, 6; etc.; cf. mod. *zapato*.

capellan (L. L. *cappellanus*, guardian of the *cappella* or bit of St. Martin's cloak, and of the place, also called *cappella* 'chapel,' where it was kept) chaplain, priest, **30** 3 *b*.

capiello (L. L. *cappellus -um*, a dimin. of L. *cappa*) hood, cowl, **23** 86 *c*.

captiuado = *captivado* (learned word; p.p. of *captivar*, V.L. **captīvare*) captured, **28** 361 *a*; cf. mod. *cautivado*.

captiujdat = *captividad* (learned word; L. *captīvĭtas, captīvĭtatem*) captivity, **28** 368 *d*; cf. mod. *cautividad*.

captiuo = *captivo* (learned word; L. *captīvus*) captive, **27** 357 *a* etc.; cf. mod. *cautivo*.

cara (V. L. **cara*; cf. Gk. χάρα 'head') face, **43** 10.

Caraço pr. n., **44** 8.

carbonco (back formation from L. *carbŭnculus*, based on *carbo*, Sp. *carbúnculo*) carbuncle, **67** II 7.

carçel (L. *carcer, carcerem*, with dissimilation of *r* to *l*) prison, jail, cell, **45** 22 etc.

carçelero (L. *carcerarĭus -um*) jailer, **29** 370 *c*.

cardenal (L. L. *cardĭnalis, cardĭnalem* from L. *cardo, cardinis*) cardinal, **67** v 6.

carga (abstract from *cargar*) charge, task, **58** 441 *a*.

cargar (V. L. **carricare* from L. *carrus* 'cart') to load, fill, take up, **16** 170; *cargaua* impf. **17** 187; *cargen* pres. sbj. **16** 166; *cargado* **29** 369 *c*; **32** 20 *b*; **65** 104 *a*.

cargaua = *cargava* (imp. 3 of *cargar*), **17** 187.

cargen = *carguen* (pres. sbj. 3 pl. of *cargar*) pick up, **16** 166.

caridad (half-learned word; L. *carĭtas, carĭtatem*) charity, **7** 51; **9** 87; etc.; *par* or *por caridad* for the love of God, of a verity, forsooth, **7** 51; **9** 87; etc.

caridat = *caridad* (the *t* represents properly the unvoicing of final *-d*) charity, **28** 368 *b*; **47** 6.

Carlos (L. L. *Carŏlus*) Charles, **36** 352 *a*.

carne (L. *caro, carnem*) flesh, **7** 39; **10** 95; etc.

caro -a (L. *carus -a*) dear, beloved, **14** 103.

carrera (V. L. **carraria* from L. *carrus* 'cart') way, path, course, road, **23** 3 *b*; **34** 78 *b*; *por carrera* on its way, **64** 99 *d*.

carreta (dimin. in *-ĭtta* of L. *carrus*, Sp. *carro*) car, chariot, **31** 15 *a*; **32** 19 *b*.

carro (L. *carrus -um*) cart, chariot, **29** 2 *c*; **30** 3 *c*; etc.

carta (L. *charta*) letter, **44** 17.

casa (L. *casa* 'cottage') house, home, **15** 115; **24** 94 *a*; etc.

casar (V.L. **casare* 'to set up house,' from L. *casa*) to marry, take in marriage, **40** 7, 13; **41** 1.

Caspar pr. n., **9** 82.

castellano -a (V. L. *castellanus -a -um* appertaining to a castle. Castile took its name from its many castles) Castilian, **39** 370 *a*; **35** 331 *d*.

Castiella (fem. sg. from ntr. pl. of L. *castĕllum, castĕlla*) Castile, **16** 176; **19** 1188; etc.; cf. mod. *Castilla*.

castiello (L. *castĕllum*) castle, **14** 98; **44** 8; cf. mod. *castillo*.

castigar (L. *castīgare*) to instruct, lecture, **63** 93 *a*.

castrado (p.p. of *castrar*, L. *castrare*) eunuch, **32** 20 *c*.

Castyella = *Castiella*, **35** 328 *d*; **38** 367 *d*.

catadura (noun formation in *-ura*, L. *-ūra*, on *catado*, p.p. of *catar*, 'to look at,' from L. *captare* 'to

take in,' that is, with the eye)
aspect, face, **51** 1663 *d.*

catar (L. *captare*) to get, manage,
seek, behold, look, look at, look
for, consider, **6** 9 ; **12** 131 ; **13** 2 ;
15 121 ; **28** 365 *b* ; etc.

catassen = *catasen* (cf. *catar*), **16**
164.

catauan = *catavan* (impf. of *catar*)
looked at, **29** 92 *a* ; regarded, respected, **24** 92 *c.*

çatico (dimin. of *çato*, from Basque
zatoa ; but ?) bit of bread, **25**
105 *d* ; cf. mod. *zatico.*

çatiquero (agent formation in *-ero*,
L. *-arius*, on *çatico*) pantler,
baker, **46** 2 etc.

caualgada = *cavalgada*, mod. *cabal-
gada* (n. from p.p. of *caualgar*)
cavalcade, raid, foray, **27** 354 *c.*

caualgar = *cavalgar*, mod. *cabalgar*
(V. L. *caballĭcare* from L. *caballus*) to mount, ride, ride on, make
forays, **20** 1190; **16** 148; **41** 21; etc.

cauallero = *cavallero*, mod. *caballero*
(V. L. *caballarius* from L. *caballus*) horseman, trooper, knight,
19 1129 ; **19** 1139 ; etc.

cauallo = *cavallo*, mod. *caballo* (L.
caballus -um) horse, mount, **19**
1123 ; **22** 32 ; etc.

cauar = *cavar* (L. *cavare*) to dig,
62 4.

cavalleros cf. *cauallero*, **37** 355 *a.*

cavalleryas (formation on *cavallero*)
chivalrous deeds, **36** 351 *b.*

cavallo cf. *cauallo*, **39** 371 *b* ; **49**
298 *a* ; etc.

cavtyva = *cautiva* (cf. *captiuo -a*)
wretched, poor, **33** 74 *d.*

cay = *caí* (cf. *caer*), **69** XLII 3.

caye = *cae* (cf. *caer*) falls, is in-
cumbent, **27** 356 *a* ; **28** 362 *c.*

çedo (L. *cĭto*) quickly, **57** 434 *c.*

cedula (learned word, L. *schĕdŭla*)
slip of paper, scroll, **62** 14, 16.

çegar (L. *caecare*) to blind.

celar (L. *cēlāre*) to conceal, hide,
9 8.

çelestial (learned word, V. L. **cae-
lestialis -em* from L. *caelestis*)
celestial, celestial being, **30** 3 *a* ;
60 25.

celestrial (cf. *çelestial* ; V. L. **caele-
strialis -em* under influence of L.
terrestris, which has the combination *-str-*) **8** 66 ; **9** 71.

Çelfa, Canal de pr. n., **20** 1194.

celo = *cielo*, **7** 36.

çena (L. *cēna, coena*) supper, **27**
355 *c* etc.

çenar (L. *cēnare*) to sup, take supper, **58** 437 *d* etc.

çepo (L. *cĭppus -um*) stock (for
punishment) **50** 497 *b.*

çerca prep. (L. *cĭrca*) about, around,
beside, near, **31** 16 *b* ; **41** 16 ;
çerca de re̦ar, **24** 97 *a* etc. ; *de
çerca* near, at hand, **31** 17 *a.*

çercal = *çerca + el*, **41** 16.

çercar (V. L. *cĭrcare* from *cĭrca*) to
surround, besiege, **18** 1099 ; **18**
1105 ; etc.

çercat = *cercad* (cf. *çercar*), **47** 7.

çerrar (V. L. **sĕrrare*, L. *sĕrare* from
L. *sĕra* 'bolt,' 'bar.' The *ç* may be
due to the influence of *çercar* 'to
surround,' 'shut up,' which has
certain sense affinities, rather
than to the desire to distinguish

it from *serrar* 'to saw,' as Diez says) to close, enclose, **29** 369 *b* ; cf. *ençerrar*.

certas = *ciertas* (formation in adverbial -*s* on *cierto* -*a*, or the fem. pl. adj. *ciertas* used adverbially; cf. Eng. 'certes') certainly, **7** 23.

çertero -a (V. L. *certarius -*a* from L. *cĕrtus* -*a*) certain, sure, trusty, **26** 111 *d* ; **64** 96 *d*.

çeuo = *cevo*, mod. *cebo* (L. *cĭbus* -*um*) food, **25** 102 *b*.

charanbela (etym. ? Sp. shows also *charamela, churumbela*. Is there a connection with Fr. *chalumeau* < L. *calamellus* ?) oboe, **68** VII 8.

Chino (pr. n.) Cino, **70** XLIII 5.

chiquillo -a (dimin. in -*iello*, -*illo*, L. -*ĕllus* -*a* -*um*, of Sp. *chico* -*a*, which is of obscure etym., as the derivation from L. *cīccum* is phonologically unlikely) little, young, **32** 20 *d*.

christiandad (half-learned; L. *Christianĭtas, Christianĭtatem*) Christianity, Christendom, **18** 1116 ; **20** 1199.

Christiandat = *christiandad*, **24** 87 *d*.

Christiano -a (learned ; L. *Chrīstĭanus* -*a* -*um*) Christian, **14** 93 ; **20** 1191 ; etc.

chufa (possibly connected with L. *sibilare*, as an onomatopoetic or other variation of it. But ?) mockery, jest, **48** 16 *b*.

çibdad (L. *cīvĭtas, cīvĭtatem*) city, **20** 1212 ; **41** 2 ; cf. *çiubdat, çiudat*, and mod. *ciudad*.

çibdat = *çibdad*, **33** 74 *b*.

Çid (Arab. *seid* 'lord' with initial *sīn*, which gave O.Sp. *ç*) Cid, lord, chief, **13** 6 etc.

çielo (L. *caelum*) heaven, sky, **18** 1094 ; **28** 368 *b* ; etc.

çien = *çiento* (first apocopated to O. Sp. *çient*, and then, before a cons. to *çien*, which was next generalized in the proclitic position), **27** 357 *b*.

çiento (L. *cĕntum*) hundred, one hundred, **15** 135 etc.

çierto -a (L. *cĕrtus* -*a* -*um*) certain, a certain, **35** 328 *b* ; **55** 22 ; etc.

ciervo (L. *cĕrvus* -*um*) deer, stag, **47** 8, 13.

cilo = *çielo*, **7** 41.

çinco (L. *quīnque*, V.L. *cīnque*. The -*o* is due to analogy ; cf. *ocho*) five, **41** 9.

çinquaenta (L. *quīnquagĭnta*, V. L. *cīnqŭagĭnta*) fifty, **40** 4 ; cf. mod. *cincuenta*.

çinxiestes (pret. 2 pl. of *ceñir*. L. *cinxistis* gave Sp. *cinxistes* ; the diphthong is due to the analogy of the endings -*ieron*, -*iese*, etc.) girded on, **16** 175 ; cf. mod. *ceñisteis*.

çinxo (pret. 3 of *ceñir* ; L. *cinxit*. The -*o* is analogical.) girded on, **13** 78 ; cf. mod. *ciño*.

çipres (probably a loan-word ; cf. O. Fr. *ciprès*. L. *cypressus*, rather than *cupressus*, from Gk. κυπά-ρισσος) cypress, **30** 8 *d*.

çiubdat = *çibdad*, **60** 19.

çiudat = *çibdad*, **60** 23.

clamar = *llamar* (L. *clamare*) to call, name, entreat, **12** 139 ; **25** 100 *d*.

clamor (L. *clamor*, *clamōrem*)
clamor, entreaty, **28** 367 *c.*

claridad (half-learned; L. *clarĭtas*,
clarĭtatem) light, **70** LII 5.

claridat = *claridad* brightness, effulgence, **59** 8; **60** 23.

claro (L. *clarus -um*) clear, bright,
31 15 *c.*

claueadas cf. *enclaueadas*, **14** 87.

clauo = *clavo* (L. *clavus -um*) nail,
14 88; **49** 300 *b.*

clerigo (half-learned; L. *clerĭcus
-um*) cleric, **30** 5 *c.*

cobdiçiar (half-learned; V.L. **cŭ-
pĭdĭtĭare*, based on V.L. **cŭpĭ-
dĭtĭa* from L. *cupĭdus*) to covet;
cobdiçio pres. 1; *cobdiçie* pret. 1,
25 100 *a*; cf. *codiçia*.

cobertera (formation in *-era*, L.
-aria, on *cŏ-ŏpĕrt-us*, p.p. of L.
cŏ-ŏpĕrīre 'to cover') cover, cov-
ering, **49** 17 *c.*

cobertura (formed like *cobertera*,
but with the suffix *-ura*) cover,
shelter, **48** 11 *d.*

cobrar (back formation from *recobrar*, L. *rĕcŭpĕrāre* 'to recover')
to recover, collect, get, re-
ceive, **28** 365 *d*; **36** 347 *c*; **58**
440 *b.*

cobrraremos = *cobraremos* (cf. *cobrar*) **37** 354 *c.*

cocear (formation in *-ear*, V.L.
-ĭdĭare on *coz* 'kick,' from L.
calx, *calcem*) to kick, **25** 102 *c.*

coçes (pl. of *coz*; cf. *cocear*) kicks,
49 301 *c.*

codiçia (half-learned; V.L. **cŭpĭ-
dĭtĭa* from L. *cupĭdus*) covetous-
ness, cupidity, **36** 338 *d.*

coger (V.L. *cŏllĭgĕre for L. *collĭ-
gĕre*) to take, take in; *coger la
tienda* to strike tent, **17** 208.

colcha (apparently L. *cŭlcĭta*. But
should *c't* give *ch* after a cóns. ?)
quilt, coverlet, **60** 16.

Coletario pr. n. ?, **70** XLIII 5.

colgar (L. *collŏcare*) to hang, **64** 98 *d.*

collado (V.L. *collatum from L.
collis) hill, ridge, **47** 12.

color (L. *color*, *colōrem*) color, **23**
86 *d* etc.

colpe (V.L. *colpus, for L. *cŏlăphus*
from Gk. κόλαφος; perhaps a
loan-word in Spanish; cf. *Grundriss* I, 889) blow, **17** 184; **41** 22;
etc.; *a tod el primer colpe* at the
outset, at once, **17** 184; cf. mod.
golpe (**34** 79 *a*).

comarca (L. *cŭm* + Germanic *marka*
'mark,' 'boundary,' 'border-
land') region, **69** XIX 4.

comedio (L. *cŭm* + *mĕdium*) middle,
mean, mean course, **26** 108 *d*;
71 LXXIX 4, 8; *en este comedio*
in the meantime.

començar (L. *cŭm* + *ĭnĭtiare*) to
commence, begin, **26** 107 *c*,
289 *a*; etc.; with *de* before an
infin. **28** 363 *a* etc.; with *a* before an infin. **42** 23 etc.; cf.
mod. *comenzar.*

comer (L. *cŏmĕdĕre*, V.L. *comedēre)
to eat, **18** 1104; **54** 16; etc.; *comianse* ate up, **65** 104 *c.*

comidiendo pres. part. of *comedir*
(L. *cŭm* + *mētīri*, V.L. *mētīre),
meditating, **54** 438 *a.*

comien = *comian* (impf. 3 pl. of
comer), **36** 350 *c.*

comiença (pres. 3 of *començar*, with *ie* analogical to that of O. Sp. *compieça, empieça*) begins, **56** title.

comigo = *conmigo*, **20** 1192; **58** 438 *d*.

comjença = *comiença*, **66** 2.

commo (V. L. **quōmǫ* for L. *quōmŏdo*; the form *como* seems the more natural development) how, as, like, that, **35** 330 *b, d*, 332 *b, d*; etc.; *en commo* whereby, **55** 14. (Cf. Vising in *Tobler Festschrift*, Halle, 1895.)

como (cf. *commo*) as, how, like, that, **23** 2 *d*, 86 *b*; **24** 92 *a*; etc.; *como si* as though, **63** 91 *a*.

coño = *commo*, **16** 153; **19** 1125, 1133; etc.; *coño sy* as though, **29** 1 *d*.

compana = *compaña* (V. L. **compania*, an abstract formation from L. *cŭm* and *panis* 'sharing bread') company, troop, **14** 83.

compannero (formation in *-ero*, L. *-arius*, on L. *cŭm + panis, panem*) companion, **64** 96 *a*; cf. mod. *compañero*.

compeçar (probably O. Sp. *empeçar* — which is in the *Cid*, v. 3308, 3542 — with a change of prefix due to the influence of *començar*. The basis is uncertain. It may be a stem **pec-* or **pecc-*, whence V. L. **pecia* or **peccia*, O. Sp. *pieça*, and V. L. **impeciare* or **impecciare*, O. Sp. *empeçar*) to begin (with *de* before an infin.), **18** 1114.

complido -a (p.p. of O. Sp. *complir* from L. *complēre*, V. L. **complīre*) complete, full, perfect, accomplished, **20** 1209; **40** 11.

con (L. *cŭm*) with, to, **14** 85; **23** 2 *b*; etc.; *con todo esto* in the meantime, **18** 1095.

conbria (cond. 3 of *comer*, with shortened infin. stem *com'r* and phonetically developed *b*) **27** 355 *d*.

conçebiste (pret. 2 of O. Sp. *concebir* from L. *concĭpĕre*, V. L. **concĭpīre*) didst conceive, **51** 1664 *c*.

conçeio = *concejo* (L. *concĭlĭum*) council, assembly, **24** 92 *c*.

conciencia (learned word, L. *conscĭentĭa*) conscience, **71** LXXIX 3.

condado (*comĭtātus, comĭtātŭm*) county, earldom, **35** 328 *c*.

conde (L. *cŏmes, cŏmĭtem*. The *o* was kept in proclitic development; cf. the independent form, O. Sp. *cuende*. *Conde* was generalized in the later O. Sp. period) count, earl, **35**, 328 *a*, 329 *a*; etc.

condenar (learned word, L. *condĕmnāre*) to condemn, damn, **56** 423 *c*.

conderecho = *con derecho*, **18** 1105.

condyçion = *condición* (learned word, L. *condĭtĭo, condĭtĭōnem*) condition, **70** LXXVIII 2.

conel = *con él*, **49** 298 *b*.

confessor (agent formation in *-or* *-ōrem* on *confessus*, p.p. of L. *confiteor*) confessor, **26** 109 *d* etc.

confondiesse = *confundiese* (see *confondir*), **53** 26.

confondir (L. *confŭndĕre*, V. L. *confŭndīre*) to confound, confuse, spoil, **52** 20; **53** 2; etc. (The mod. *confundir* owes its *u* to forms like *confundió, confundieron, confundiese, confundiera*, in which it was developed out of unaccented *o* by the *į* of the following accented syllable. The earlier O. Sp. period often still shows *o* everywhere; cf. *confondiesse* **53** 26; *confondiera* **53** 21, 23.)

confuerto (abstract from *confortar, confuerto, confuertas*, etc., derived from L. *confortāre*, based on *fŏrtis*) comfort, **49** 301 *a*; cf. mod. *conforte*.

coniuro = *conjuro* (L. *conjūro*) I conjure, entreat, **47** 8.

conlos = *con los*, **28** 367 *b*.

conmedicion (learned word; abstract in *-icion*, L. *-ītio -ītionem*, based on *conmedir* from L. *cŭm* + *metiri*, V. L. **metīre** ' to measure,' ' estimate,' ' think ') meditation, thought, **27** 358 *c*; cf. *comedir, comedición*.

conmigo (L. *cŭm* + *mīhī* > *mī* + *cŭm*; *mī* supplanted *mē* in *mēcŭm*, and, the identity of the second syllable of *migo* < *mīcŭm* being forgotten, *cŭm* > *con* was prefixed) with me, **8** 61 ; cf. *comigo*.

conortar (V. L. **conhŏrtāre** from L. *hortari*, with influence of the sense of L. *confortare*) to counsel, comfort, **54** 10; **55** 11, 26.

conorte (abstract from *conortar*) advice, comfort, **54** 7 ; **55** 3.

conortedes (pres. sbj. 2 pl. of *conortar*) **54** 10.

conoscas = mod. *conozcas* (see *conoscer*), **61** 9.

conoscencia (learned word; abstract in *-encia*, L. *entia*, from *conosc-er*) knowledge, **59** 10.

conosçer (L. *cognōscĕre*, V. L. **conoscēre**, based on L. *nosco* instead of *gnosco*) to know, **30** 5 *d*, 6 *b*; **54** 2 ; **56** 426 *a* ; etc.; cf. mod. *conocer*.

conosco = mod. *conozco* (see *conosçer*), **54** 2.

conosçrie = mod. *conocería* (see *conosçer*), **30** 5 *d*.

conpaña (cf. *compana, compaña*) company, troop, companionship, following, household, **13** 16; **60** 25; **62** 4.

conpanna (cf. *conpaña*) **32** 21 ; **35** 328 *c*; **38** 367 *b* ; **43** 16.

conpannero (cf. *compannero*) **30** 5 *d* ; **36** 352 *d*.

conpeçar (cf. *compeçar*) **17** 1085; **18** 1090, 1111.

conplido p.p. of *conplir*, completed, fulfilled, full, perfect, **25** 99 *a* ; **33** 75 *c*; **59** 9; *conplida mente* fully, entirely, **55** 18.

conplimiento = *complimiento* (mod. *cumplimiento*; L. *complēmĕntum*, V. L. **complīmĕntum**) perfection, **36** 345 *c*.

conplir = *complir* (mod. *cumplir*; L. *complēre* ; V. L. **complīre**) to fulfill, accomplish, **26** 107 *a* ; **28** 362 *d*.

conplisyon = *complision* (semi-learned word; L. *complexio*, *complexiōnem*) physique, constitution, **67** II 4 ; cf. mod. *complexión*.

conpostura = *compostura* (L. *compositūra*) finery, cosmetic, **68** IX 6.

conpra = *compra* (abstract from *conprar*, *comprar*, L. *comparare*, V. L. *compĕrāre*) purchase, purchasing, **14** 90.

conpuesto -a = *compuesto* -a (p.p. of *componer*, L. *componere*, *compŏsĭtus*) composed, constituted, **67** II 3.

conpuso = *compuso* (pret. 3 of *componer*; see *conpuesto*) furnished, provided, **26** 108 *b*.

conquisto -a (p.p. ; L. *conquīsītus* -a -um, V. L. *conquīsītus* -a -um) conquered, **18** 1093.

consagrado (L. *consecratus* -a -um, V. L. *consacratus* -a -um, reconstructed on L. *sacer*) consecrated, sacred, **29** 2 *a*.

consego (scribal error for *consejo*) counsel, advice, **14** 85.

conseia ⪪ *conseja* (L. ntr. pl. *consĭlĭa*, or an abstract from *consejar*) fable, story-telling, **21** 19.

conseiades (pres. sbj. 2 pl. of *conseiar*) **24** 93 *c*.

conseiar = *consejar* to counsel, advise, plan, **15** 122 ; **46** 7 ; etc.

conseiassen (impf. sbj. 3 pl. of *conseiar*) **44** 20.

conseiero = *consejero* (L. *consĭlĭarĭus* -um) counselor, **30** 5 *b*.

conseio = *consejo*, **18** 1099 ; **21** 20 ; etc.

consejar (L. *consiliari*, V. L. *consĭlĭāre*) to counsel, advise, **61** 11.

consejo (L. *consĭlĭum*) counsel, advice, plan, **66** 7 ; council, **57** 428 *a* ; **58** 437 *a*.

consintio (pret. 3 of *consentir*; L. *consĕntīre*) **25** 98 *a*.

consseio = *consejo*, **44** title.

conssejero = *consejero*, *conseiero*, **50** 509 *b*.

contado -a (p.p. of *contar*) famous, noted, **15** 142 ; **16** 152.

contador (V. L. *computator*, *compŭtatōrem* from *computare*) accountant, steward, **58** 441 *a*.

contalda = *contadla* (see *contar*), **17** 181.

contar (L. *cŏmpŭtāre*) to count, reckon, estimate, tell, relate, **17** 181 ; **20** 1214 ; etc. ; *cuenta* **44** 11 etc.

contecer (V. L. *contĭgescĕre* for L. *contingere*) to happen, **33** 75 *a*.

contenple = *contemple* (pres. sbj. 1 of *contemplar*; L. *contĕmplare*) contemplate, **70** LII 3.

contesçer (older form of *contecer*) to happen, **42** 11 ; **46** 8, 23 ; etc.

contido (p.p. of *contir* V. L.*contigīre*, L. *contingĕre*) happened, **33** 75 *a*.

contra (L. *cŏntra* ; proclitic use prevented the diphthongization of *ŏ*) toward, in the direction of, against, **18** 1090 ; **25** 102 *c* ; etc.

contrallo (L. *contrarius* -um, Sp. *contrario*, whence by dissimilation *contralio*, and, with a palatalization of *l* by the *i*, *contrallo*) impediment, check, **49** 299 *d*.

contrario (learned word, L. *contrarius* -um) opponent, opposite, **70** XLIII 4 ; **71** LXXVIII 8.

contrra = *contra*, **35** 333 *b*.

conuento = *convento* (L. *conventus -um*) convent, gathering, agreement, **30** 3 *c*. (Here the Latin word.)

conuertio = *convertió* (pret. 3 of *convertir*, L. *convertĕre*, V.L. **convĕrtīre*) converted, **26** 111 *a*.

conuidar = *convidar* (L. *invitare*, whence V.L. *convītāre*, under the influence of *convivium*) to invite, **41** 2, 4.

conuiene = *conviene* (pres. 3 of *convenir*, L. *convĕnīre*) it is necessary, **66** I 7.

conujento = *conviento* (L. *convĕntum*) convent, monastery, community,**24** 94*a*; cf.mod.*convento*.

copa (L. *cŭppa*, by-form of *cūpa*) cup, glass, **22** 35.

copero (formation in *-ero*, L. *-arĭus*, on *copa* or V.L. **cupparius -um*) cup-bearer,**45** *B* title ; **46** 2 ; etc.

coraçon(L.*cor*+ *-acium* + *-o -ōnem*, V. L. **coracio*, **coracĭōnem*) heart, **36** 345*d* ; **38** 361*a* ; **59** 22 ; **69** XVIII 7 ; *de coraçon* heartily, **42** 19 ; **64** 100*d* ; cf. mod. *corazón*.

corazon = *coraçon*, **21** 18.

corça (ety. obscure ; L. *caprea* is impossible) roe, hind, **47** 8, 13 ; cf. mod. *corza*.

cordero (V.L. **chordarius -a -um* from L. [*agnus*] *chordus* ' new-born lamb ') lamb, **63** 91 *a*.

cordoioso = *cordojoso* (V.L. **cordolĭōsus -a -um* from L. *cordolium*) distressed at heart, grieved, **28** 366 *c*.

Cordoua = *Córdoba* (L. *Cordŭba*) (pr. n.) Cordova, **44** 7.

corientes = *corrientes* (verbal adj. from*correr*) running, swift, **22** 32.

cormano (L. *con-*, *co-* + *germanus -a -um* ; cf. also obs. *cohermano -a*) first cousin, **41** 24 ; *primo -a*, *cormano -a*, **40** 9 ; **41** 20.

corneia = *corneja* (V. L. **cornĭcŭla*, dimin. of L. *cornix*, *cornĭcem*) raven, **13** 11.

corraçones (cf. *coraçon*) **38** 362 *c*.

corral (possibly a V.L. **cŭrrālis*, **cŭrrālem*, based on the stem of L. *cŭrrĕre*, ' a place to run in,' ' yard.' But ?) courtyard, **29** 369 *b*.

correo (perhaps a masc. form of *correa*, L. *corrĭgĭa*) leather strap, leather bag, moneybag, **48** 16*c* ; **70** LIII 8.

correr (L. *cŭrrĕre*, V. L. **cŭrrēre*) to run, **49** 490 *c* ; *correr toros* to course bulls, **41** 11.

corro (perhaps a formation from the stem of *correr*, ' a running together,' ' assembly ') circle, round dance, **71** LXXIX 8.

corrupçion (learned word ; L. *corruptio*, *corrŭptĭōnem*) corruption, disease, **67** II 6.

cortado (p.p. of *cortar*, L. *cŭrtare*) cut, castrated, **32** 20 *d*.

corte (L. *cŏhŏrs*, whence V. L. *cŏrs*, *cōrtem*) court, **56** 423 *a*.

cortés (V.L.**cortensis*,**corte*[*n*]*sem*, from *cors*, *cortem*) courteous, courtly, **69** XIX 7.

corteza (V.L.*cortĭcĕa* from L. *cortex*, *cŏrtĭcem*) bark, husk, pod, **55** 1, 4 ; etc.

cortina (V. L. *cortīna*, which is in the Vulgate, Exodus xxvi, 1 ff. Its relation to L. *cortina* 'round vessel,' 'circle,' 'arch,' is not clear.) curtain, **32** 19 *b*.

cosa (L. *causa*) thing, matter, anything, **21** 14; **24** 94 *b*; etc.; *buena cosa* a good amount, **26** 106 *b*.

cosiment (perhaps a formation in *-ment[e, o]* on the Germanic *kausian* 'to choose') will, control, power, **27** 356 *b*. (Du Cange has *causimentum = judicium, arbitrium*.)

costumbre (V. L. **consuetūmen*, **co[n]s[ue]tuminem* for L. *consuetudo*) custom, way, **40** 12.

coxo (V. L. **coxus -a -um*, related to L. *coxo, coxonem*) lame, crippled, **49** 490 *c*; cf. mod. *cojo*.

coydado (L. *cōgĭtatum*, p.p. of *cōgitare*) care, **51** 1663 *c*; cf. *coydo, cuydado, cuidado, cuydar, cuedar*, etc.

coydo (pret. 3 of *coydar, coidar*, L. *cōgitare*) expected, believed, **35** 331 *b*; cf. *coydado* and mod. *cuidar*.

coyta (abstract from *coytar, coitar*, V. L. **cŏctare*, a frequentative of L. *coquere, coctum*. The form is dialectal or a loan-word: O. Sp. *cochar* is the normal development.) distress, care, **55** 3; cf. *cuyta, cuytado, cueta*, mod. *cuita*.

cozina (L. *cocīna*, based on L. *coquere, cocere*) kitchen, **26** 109 *c*; **32** 19 *d*; mod. *cocina*.

cras (L. *cras*) to-morrow, **58** 435 *d*, 438 *c*.

creades = *creáis* (pres. sbj. 2 pl. of *creer*), **26** 108 *b*.

crebantar (V. L. **crepantare* from L. *crepare, crepans, crepant-em*) to break, **41** 16; **42** 7, 21; **43** 14; cf. *quebrantar* with metathesis of *r*.

crebantasse = *crebantase* (cf. *crebantar*), **41** 16.

crebar (L. *crĕpāre*) to break, break out, burst, burst forth, **42** 30; **43** 11; cf. *quebrar* with metathesis of *r*.

creçiendo (pres. part. of *creçer*, L. *crēscĕre*, V. L. **crēscēre*) growing, **20** 1200.

cred = *creed* (V. L. **crēdēte*; cf. *sed* for O. Sp. *seed*), see *creer*, **55** 21.

creençia (learned word; V. L. **crēdĕntĭa* from L. *crēdĕre, credens, credentem*) belief, faith.

creer (L. *crēdĕre* V. L. **crēdēre*) to believe, think, **11** 115; **23** 2 *d*; etc.

criado (L. *creatus -um* 'one brought up,' 'one trained,' p.p. of *creare*) servant, **35** 334 *d*.

Criador (L. *Creator, Creatōrem*) Creator, **6** 1, 5; etc.

criar (L. *creare*) to create, **48** 13 *a*; to breed, bring up, train (cf. *criado*), **40** 15; **41** 9.

criatura (L. *creatūra*) creature, **66** 3.

crieste = *criaste* (pret. 2 of *criar*) thou didst create, **48** 13 *a*.

cristiano (learned word, L. *Chrīstĭanus -um*) Christian, **34** 81 *a* etc.

cruamientre (L. adj. *crūda + mĕnte*, abl. of L. *mens*, with intrusive *r*) cruelly, **27** 353 *d*.

cruel (L. *crudelis, crūdēlem*) cruel, terrible, **60** 4; **66** I 8.

crueldat = *crueldad* (L. *crudelitas*, *crūdēlĭtatem*) cruelty, **39** 369 *a*.

cruzado (Sp. *cruz* [from L. *crux*, *crŭcem* — and not wholly popular in its development] + *-ado* from L. p.p. ending *-atus -atum*) crusader, Christian soldier, **34** 79 *d*. (But the sense here is rather "those who had crossed the sea" = the Moors. In which case it is the p.p. of *cruzar*.)

cualquiere (*cual* from L. *qualis*, *qualem* + *quiere* from *querer*) whoever, **63** 93 *b*.

cuando (L. *quando*) when.

cubierto -a (p.p. of *cubrir*, L. p.p. *coopĕrtum* > *cobierto* > *cubierto*) covered, **14** 87.

cuchilla (derived from *cuchillo* 'knife,' L. *cultellus -um*, dimin. of L. *culter*) sword, **31** 16 *d*.

cudo = *cuedo* (cf. *cuedar*) I believe, **7** 45.

cuedar (L. *cōgĭtare* or V.L.*cŏgitare*) to believe, think. (The form *cueido* has been found and seems to point to *cŏgito*.)

cuemo (L. *quomodo*, V.L. **quomo*: this is the development of the accented form) how, as, **40** title; **42** 11, 25.

cuende (L. *comes*, *cŏmĭtem*, developed originally as an accented form and not as a proclitic) **40** 18; **43** 18, 23.

cuenta (abstract from the verb *contar*, *cuento*, *cuentas*, etc., 'to count') count; *en cuenta de* counting up, **14** 101.

cuenta, cuentan (cf. *contar*) **44** 11; **46** 2; **36** 351 *a*; etc.

cuento (abstract from *contar,cuento*, etc.) tale, **48** 15 *b*.

cuer (L. *cor*, *cŏrdis*, V. L. *cor*, **cŏrem*) heart, **24** 95*d*.

cuerda (L. *chŏrda*) cord, rope, **19** 1141.

cuerpo (L. *cŏrpus*, V.L. **cŏrpum*) body, person, frame, **21** 6, 7; **30** 7 *a*; etc.; *Cuerpo Sancto* Host, **25** 98 *c*.

cuesta (L. *cŏsta*) rib, side; *de cuesta* on the side, on the flank, **31** 16 *a*; *a cuestas* on the back, **61** 18.

cueta (cf. *coyta*, like which it seems either dialectal or a loan-word) distress, care, **20** 1189.

cueua = *cueva* (L. *cavus -a -um*; V. L. **cŏvus -a -um*) cave, **59** 7, 9.

culpa (learned word, L. *cŭlpa*) fault, crime, **46** 3; **50** 498*c*; **56** 424 *d*.

cumo = *cuemo*, how, as, **7** 41; **8** 65, 67; **10** 88; **12** 138.

cumplir (cf. *conplir*; the *u* was developed first in the unaccented position, under the influence of the palatal *y* of the next syllable, as in *complió* > *cumplió*, *complieron* > *cumplieron*) to fulfill, complete, suffice; *cumple* **28** 361 *d*; *cumpla* **28** 364*d*; *cumplir* **63** 90*b*; *cumplirie* **43** 34.

cumplirie = *cumpliria*, **43** 34; cf. *cumplir*.

cunnada = *cuñada* (L. *cŏgnata*: the *o* seems to have been closed to *u* by the palatal following) sister-in-law, **41** 26.

cura (L. *cūra*) care, **56** 422 *b*.

curar (L. *cūrāre*) to care, attend, strive, keep, **21** 22, 23; **57** 429 *a*; **63** 93 *b*; **66** I 3; **69** XIX 3.

curaries = *curarías*, **21** 22; cf. *curar*.

curastes = *curasteis*, **69** XIX 3; cf. *curar*.

curest = *curaste*, **21** 23; cf. *curar*.

curie (pres. sbj. 3 of *curiar*, V. L. *curiare based on V. L. *curia; cf. L. *incuria*) save, guard, **9** 74, 76.

cutiano -a (L. *quŏttĭdĭanus -a -um* > *cotiano -a > *cutiano -a*) daily, **26** 106 *b* ; (adv.) **27** 356 *c*.

cuydades = *cuidáis* (cf. *cuydar*), **93** 4.

cuydado = *cuidado* (L. *cōgĭtatum*, p.p. of *cogitare*; see *coydado*, of which it is a later form) care, trouble, affliction, distress, concern, tribulation, **13** 6; **56** 424 *c*; **59** 3; **67** III 6.

cuydar = *cuidar* (a later development of *coydar*) to believe, expect, think, mean, **33** 73 *d*; **34** 81 *a*; **35** 329 *c*; **57** 427 *a*.

cuydaua = *cuidaba* (see *cuydar*), **57** 427 *a*.

cuyo -a (L. *cujus -a -um*) whose, **23** 3 *b*; **26** 289 *d*.

cuyta (a later form of *coyta*, with *o* closed to *u* by the palatal following, or perhaps reflecting the influence of *cuidar*, *cuydar* 'to have thought or care') distress, trouble, **56** 424 *c*.

cuytado -a (a later development of *coytado -a*; see *coyta* and *cuyta*) distressed, afflicted, pained, **38** 364 *b*; **39** 370 *c*.

d' = *de* (prep.) of, **22** 35; **63** 89 *d*.

da = *de a* from in, **7** 25; cf. Ital. *da*. (It may be erroneous for *de*.)

da qui = *de aquí*, **16** 180.

dades (L. *datĭs*, mod. *dais*) you give, **55** 24 ; cf. *dar*.

dado (L. *dătum*) gift, **17** 194.

dalla = *d'alla, de allá*, from yonder, **17** 181.

dalongar = *d'alongar*, *de alongar*, as to prolonging, **36** 346 *c*; cf. *alongar*.

damas = *d'amas, de amas* (L. *ambo*, *ambos -as*), on both, **34** 79 *a*.

Damiata (pr. n.) Damiata, **30** 12 *d*.

damor = *d'amor, de amor*, **19** 1139 etc.

dampno (learned form; L. *damnŭm*, *dampnum*; cf. *danno*, mod. *daño*) damage, **53** 22.

dança (from Fr. *danse*, which may be of Germanic origin; cf. O.H.G. *dansōn* 'to draw forth'; after *n* the *s* may have become O.Sp. *ç* = *ts* ?) dance, **66** title; cf. mod. Sp. and Ital. *danza*.

dançar (cf. *dança*): *dançad* dance ye, **70** LIII 8.

dandar = *d'andar, de andar*, **35** 333 *d*.

danno = mod. *daño* (popular form of L. *damnum*; cf. *dampno*) harm, danger, **38** 361 *b*; **53** 14, 27.

dañoso -a (L. *damnōsus -a -um*) harmful, **50** 497 *a*.

danpnaçion (learned word, L. *damnatio, dampnatio, dampnatiōnem*) damnation, **71** LXXVIII 8.

dantes (L. pres. part pl. *dantes* from *dare*) giving out, **60** 15. (A Latinism ?)

daquel = *d'aquel, de aquel*, **43** 11 etc.

daqui = *d'aqui, de aquí*, **57** 430 *b*; **63** 91 *b*.

dar (L. *dare*) to give, strike, **15** 130; **9** 76; etc.; *dar le yen = le darían* they would give him, **16** 161; *diera* (L. *dĕdĕrat*, plpf. become a pret.) he gave, **62** 13; *dieran* (L. *dĕdĕrant* plpf. remaining as such in Sp.) had given, **16** 163 (cf. the correlation with *auien iurado*, **16** 163); *non dieron nada* they did not give a rap, they did not care at all, **37** 357 *b*; *darse* to surrender; *ouieron se adar* they had to surrender, **19** 1145.

daredes (L. *dar(e)* + *(hab)ētis*; mod. *daréis*) **58** 435 *d*; cf. *dar*.

darena = *d'arena, de arena*, **14** 186.

darie = *daría* (cond. 3 of *dar*), **41** 17; **43** 17.

Dario (pr. n.) (L. *Darīus* and L.L. *Darĭus*) Darius, **30** 6 *b*, 7 *a*.

darmas = *d'armas, de armas*, **43** 26.

dat = mod. *dad* (L. *dăte*, imper. pl. of *dar*), **14** 106.

daua = *dava, daba* (cf. *dar*), **50** 498 *b*.

dauan = *davan, daban* (cf. *dar*), **25** 105 *d*; **27** 353 *c*; etc.

davena = *d'avena, de avena*, **27** 355 *d*.

daveres = *d'averes, de averes*, **33** 76 *b*.

Davyt = mod. *David* pr. n., **36** 351 *c*.

de (L. *dē*) of, from, with, by, in, to (with infin.), than, **6** 6, 15; etc.

december (Latinism for *diciembre*, L. *december, decĕmbrem*) December, **6** 16.

decid imper. pl. and *decides* (= mod. *decís*) pres. 2 pl. of O. Sp. *dezir*, mod. *decir* (L. *dīcĕre*, V. L. **dīcīre*), **9** 81. (The *c* is etymological.)

declinatoria (learned word formed in *-oria*, L. *-oria* on L. *declinare, declinatum*) plea denying a judge's competency, demurrer to jurisdiction, **71** LXXVIII 6.

dedes (mod. *deis*, L. *dētĭs*) sbj. pres. 2 pl. of *dar*, **15** 138; **19** 1129; etc.

dedo (L. *dĭgĭtŭs -ŭm*) finger, **57** 434 *b*.

defesa (L. p.p. *dēfēnsa*, V.L. **dēfēsa*, as in *terra *defesa*, i.e. ' defended land,' ' land fenced in ') pasture, **49** 298 *a*.

deffendieron = *defendieron* (pret. 3 pl. of *defender*; L. *defendĕre*, V. L. *defĕndĕre*) defended, **45** 15.

degaña (L. *dĕcānĭa*) hermitage, farm attached to a hermitage, **24** 96 *a*; cf. obs. Sp. *decania*.

degollar (L. *dēcŏllāre*) to behead, **62** 23.

degollasse = *degollase* (cf. *degollar*), **62** 19.

del (Sp. *de* + *el*) of the, from the, **23** 1 *a* ; **25** 100 *b* ; etc. ; (before fem. noun or adj. beginning with any vowel, accented or not) **19** 1132, 1144 ; **35** 335 *c*.

del (Sp. *de* + pron. *él*) of him, from him, **37** 360 *d* etc.

dela, delas = mod. *de la, de las*, of the, from the, **16** 165, 170 ; etc.

delant (apocopated form of *delante*) in front, **19** 1130 ; *a delant* forward, ahead, **18** 1118.

delante (L. *dē* + *ĭn* + *ante*, whence *denante* and by dissimilation, *delante*) in front, forward, onward, **29** 2 *c* ; **31** 16 *a* ; *delante de* before, into the presence of, **64** 102 *b* ; cf. *adelante*.

delantera (formation in *-era*, L. *-aria*, on Sp. *delante*) van, vanguard, **34** 78 *a*.

delgado -a (L. *dēlĭcātus -a -um*) delicate, thin, faint, fine, **31** 11 *d*, 15 *d* ; **65** 104 *b*.

delibrasse = mod. *delibrase* (impf. sbj. 3 of *delibrar*, L. *de* + *lībĕrāre*), should deliver, should free, **28** 367 *d*.

dell (L. *de* + *ĭllum*, as developed before a word beginning with a vowel) of the, from the, **40** 5 ; **44** 4 ; (sporadically before a consonant) **40** 1. (Before a word beginning with a consonant the *ll* soon became *l*, as neither gemination nor palatalization of *l* could continue there.)

della, dellas = *de ella, de ellas*, **52** 4 ; **59** 23 ; etc.

delli = *de* + *elli*, from him, **29** 370 *d*.

dello = *de ello*, **29** 369 *d*.

dellos = *de ellos*, of them, from them, **19** 1136 ; etc. ; (partitive use) some of them, **37** 358 *d*.

delo = *de lo*, **24** 93 *d*.

delos = *de los*, **13** 1 ; **14** 101 ; etc.

demandar (L. *dēmăndāre*, ' to intrust,' ' commend '; the Romance words show a sense development made already in V.L.) to ask, ask an account, **42** 3 *d* ; **46** 11 ; etc.

demandaua = *demandava, demandaba* (cf. *demandar*), **14** 97 etc.

demenbrado = *de menbrado*, **14** 102.

demi = *de mí*, **17** 205.

demonio (learned word, L. *daemon*, L. L. *daemonium*, based on Gk. δαιμόνιον from δαίμων, δαιμον-) demon, **59** 21 etc.

demostramjento = *demostramiento* (O. Sp. abstract in *-miento*, L. *-mĕntum*, from *demostrar*) appearance, **24** 94 *d*.

demostrar (L. *demonstrare*, V. L. **demōstrāre*) to show, **24** 96 *c* ; **67** v 2.

demuestra (cf. *demostrar*) : the *ue* is due to the analogy of L. or V. L. *ŏ* verbs.

dend (apocopated form of *dende*) whence, **42** 11.

dende (L. *dē* + *ĭnde*) thence, hence, **57** 432 *d* ; etc.; *dende a poco* shortly after, **62** 18.

deñar (L. *dĭgnāre*) to deign, **26** 289 *d*.

dentro (L. *de* + *ĭntro*) within, **18** 1097 etc. ; *de dentro* inwardly, within, **49** 17 *b*.

Deo (L. dative) to God, **26** 110 *d*.

departimiento (V. L. **departīmĕntum* based on V. L. **departire*) argument, debate, talk, conversation, **57** 431 *b*.

departir (V.L. **departīre*) to part, separate, argue, debate, **43** 21.

departyestes = mod. *departisteis* (cf. *departir*) you argued.

derecho (L. *directum*, from p.p. of *dirigere*) right, reason, law, **18** 1105; **53** 12; *fazen derecho* they act rightly, **42** 17.

derramar (V. L. **de-ex-ramare*, or **dis-ramare*, or simply **de-ramare* ' to break branches,' ' disrupt,' ' spread about ') to shed, **60** 23.

derrybado = mod. *derribado* (V.L. **de-ex-rīpare*, or **dis-rīpare*, or simply **de-rīpare* ' to throw down from the bank,' ' to ruin,' ' to destroy ') overthrown, routed, **37** 358 *b*.

des- a prefix from L. *dĭs-*, or *dē +* *ex*.

desanparado -a = mod. *desamparado -a* (*des-*, L. *dē + ex* or L. *dĭs-*, *+ anparado -a*; cf. *anparar*. The original text has *desmanparado*, p.p. of O. Sp. *desmamparar* from *des-* and *mamparar*, L. *manuparare*) forsaken, **39** 368 *c*.

desarmado -a (L. *dis-*, or *de + ex*, whence Sp. *des-* + p.p. of *armar*, L. *armāre*) unarmed, **34** 77 *b*.

desarro (according to Janer, ed. in *Bib. de Aut. Esp.* 57, from O. Fr. *desarroi* ' disarray,' ' unreadiness,' therefore ' perplexity.' This is from L. *dĭs-*, or *dē ex*, +

ad + Germanic *rēd-*, akin to English ' ready ' and German *Rath*) perplexity, bewilderment, **27** 358 *c*.

desaventura (*des- + aventura*, cf. *aventurar*) misfortune, **34** 84 *d*.

desbalçar (Ety.? Cf. Ital. *balzare* ' to jump,' ' leap.' See Körting, s.v. *balteus*) to rout, dislodge, **31** 18 *b*.

descender (L. *dēscĕndĕre*, V. L. **dēscĕndēre*) to descend, alight, **52** 22.

descobrio (pret. 3 of O. Sp. *descobrir*; L. *dĭscŏŏperīre*) revealed, **62** 6. (The modern *descubrió* is due to the closing influence of the palatal *i* or *y* upon the *o*. Analogy extended the *u* to all forms.)

descomunal (*des-*, from L. *de + ex*, and V.L. **communalis -em* from L. *commūnis*) uncommon, extraordinary, **57** 432 *c*.

descreydo -a = *descreído -a* (p.p. of *descreer*, L. *dĭs- + crēdĕre*, V.L. **discrēdēre*) unbelieving, infidel, **34** 82 *a*.

descrubades = mod. *descubráis* (cf. *descobrio*) reveal, **14** 107.

descubri (cf. *descobrio*) revealed, **46** 22.

desde (L. *dē + ex + dē*) from, since, for, **52** 13; **57** 431 *b*.

desembargar (*des-*, from L. *dĭs-* or *de ex*, *+ embargar* from V.L. **imbarrĭcāre* based on a stem *barr-* of uncertain, possibly Celtic, origin and akin to English *bar*) to relieve, **29** 370 *c*.

deseo (possibly from L. *dĭssĭdĭŭm* 'separation,' 'lack,' 'want,' therefore, 'wish,' 'desire.' In view of difficulties presented by other Romance forms, some propose V.L. **dēsīdĕiŭm* for L. *dēsīdĕrĭum*. Perhaps it is a case of a contamination of *dĭssĭdĭŭm* and *dēsīdĕrĭum*) desire, **59** 22 etc.

deseyo (Aragonese form of *deseo*) desire, **63** 90 *d*.

desfecho -a (*des*, L. *dĭs*- or *de ex*, + *fecho -a*, L. *factum -am*) destroyed, **33** 71 *a*; mod. *deshecho -a*.

desi (L. *dĕ ex hīc*, or rather, since this should give O. Sp. **dexi* with a palatal sibilant, it is O. Sp. *des*, from L. *de + ex*, regularly developed in *desde*, O. Sp. *desque*, etc., plus the O. Sp. adverb *i*, *y*, from *hīc*, still preserved in *hay*. Before a cons. the *x* might become *s*) thence, **18** 1109.

desmanparado -a (*des-* + *mamparado -a*, p.p. of O. Sp. *mamparar* 'to protect,' from L. *manu + parare*) unprotected, forsaken, **39** 368 *c*; cf. *anparar* and mod. *desamparado*.

desmayar (V. L. **desmagare*, i.e. *des* + a Germanic stem *mag-*, still found in German *mag*, *mögen*, *Macht*, Eng. *may*. The evolution of *y* from *g* is not entirely clear. Cf. earlier Ital. *smagare* and O. Fr. *esmaiier*; this latter may have influenced the Sp. form) to become dismayed, lose heart, **38** 366 *b*; **55** 21; **55** 32.

desmayedes = mod. *desmayéis* (cf. *desmayar*), **55** 21, 32.

desnudo -a (*des-*, as intensive prefix, + L. *nūdus -a -um*) naked, **21** 8.

desondrado -a (*des-* + L. *hŏnōrātum -am*, with regular loss of *o* and the popular development of *d* between *n* and *r*; cf. *tendré*, *vendré*) dishonored, **42** 24; cf. mod. *deshonrado*.

desora (*des-*, from L. *de + ex*, and L. *hōra*; cf. *desi*): *a desora* unexpectedly, **67** III 6. (Cf. *dessora*, with a better indication of the voiceless *s*, and mod. *deshora*.)

despagado -a (*des-* + p.p. of *pagar*, L. *pacare*) displeased, **35** 333 *c*.

dEspanna = *d'España* or *de Spana*, **34** 80 *b*.

despecho (L. *dēspĕctus -um*) contempt, anger, strife, **42** 11.

despechoso -a (adj. in *-oso -osa*, L. *-osus -a -um*, from *despecho*) angry, rancorous, **33** 73 *b*.

despender (L. *dĭspendĕre*, V. L. **dĭspendēre*) to spend; *mal despendiendo* wasting, **56** 422 *a*.

despertar (V. L. **dē-ĕxpĕrgĭtāre*, i.e. *de* + a frequentative from L. *expergitus*, p.p. of *expergere*) to awaken, **47** 10.

despidiosse = mod. *se despidió*, pret. 3 of *despedir* + *se* (V. L. **de-expĕtīre*, based on L. *pĕtĕre*), he took leave, **25** 104 *b*.

despues (L. *dē + ex + pŏst*) afterwards, later, **15** 140 etc.; *despues que* after, since, **18** 1116 etc.

desputando by-form of *disputando*, p.p. of *disputar* (learned word, L. *dĭspŭtāre*), arguing, **58** 438 *d*.

desque (L. *de* + *ex* + *quĭd*) since, as soon as, after, **53** 3, 7, 12 ; etc.

dessatará fut. 3 of O. Sp. *dessatar*, mod. *desatar* (*des-*, intervocalic *dess-*, + *atar* from L. *aptare*), he will unbind, **67** II 8.

desso = *d'esso, de esso*, **15** 141.

dessora (cf. *desora*) : *a dessora* of a sudden, unexpectedly, **67** II 6.

dest = *d'est, de este*, **38** 364 *d*.

desta = *d'esta, de esta*, **34** 84 *b* etc.

destaiado = *destajado*, p.p. of *destajar* (*des-* + *tajar* from L. *talĭare* 'to cut '), neatly cut, stipulated, agreed, **28** 361 *c*.

d'este = *de este*, **66** I 6.

desto = *d'esto, de esto* of this, **7** 37 etc.

desuariado -a = *desvariado -a* (learned word ; *des-* + p.p. of *variar*, L. *varĭare*) variegated, **60** 11.

desuiar = *desviar* (V. L. **dē-ex-vĭāre*) to deviate, avert, **43** 18 ; (refl.) turn aside, **43** 4.

desujo = *desvió* (cf. *desuiar*) deviated, objected, **25** 98 *a*.

desuso = *de suso* (V. L. *sūsum*, L. *sursum*) further back, **55** 6.

detardar (L. *dē* + *tardāre*) to delay, defer, **14** 105 ; **20** 1198 ; etc.

detardedes = mod. *detardéis ; non vos detardedes* do not delay, **67** VII 1 ; cf. *detardar*.

detarua scribal error for *detardaua*, mod. *detardaba* (cf. *detardar*), **14** 96.

deuedes = mod. *debéis* (cf. *deuer*), **46** 18.

deuer = *dever*, mod. *deber* (L. *debēre*), to be obliged, have duty, owe, **18** 1107 etc.; *deuo* I should, ought, **25** 102 *a* etc.

devaneo (abstract from *devanear* ' to rave,' ' talk nonsense,' V. L. **devanĭdĭare*, based on L. *vanus -a -um*, Sp. *vano -a*) nonsense, **48** 16 *a*.

devedes = mod. *debéis* (cf. *deuer*), **55** 16.

deves = mod. *debes* (cf. *deuer*), **36** 342 *d*.

devie = mod. *debía* (cf. *deuer*), **55** 13.

dexar (L. *laxāre*, with its first syll. made over under the influence of the prep. and prefix *dē*, which has a privative force) to leave, leave aside, abandon, leave off, cease, let, **9** 71 ; **15** 115, 117 ; etc.; cf. mod. *dejar*.

dexieron = *dixieron*, mod. *dijeron*, **59** 4.

dexosse = *dexose, se dexó* (cf. *dexar*), **42** 19.

dezeno -a (V. L. **decēnus -a -um*, based on L. *decem* as L. distributive *septeni* is on *septem*. In Sp. the function is that of the ordinal) tenth, **20** 1210.

dezien = mod. *decían*, said, called, named, **40** 9 etc.

deziente (pres. part., with verbal force, of *dezir* ; L. *dīcens, dīcĕntem*, with the vowel of *dezir* in the initial syll.) saying, **60** 26.

dezir (L. *dīcĕre*, V. L. **dīcīre* with dissimilation in the initial syll.)

to say, tell, **8** 53; **12** 132; etc.;
dezir m'an they will tell me, **11**
125; (n.) discourse, speech, **48**
15 *c*; cf. mod. *decir*.

di (imper. of *dezir*, L. *dīc*) say, **61**
13 etc.

dia (L. *dĭēs*, *dĭem*; V. L. **dia*; the
Sp. *i* may be due to the hiatus,
cf. Sp. *via*, L. *vĭa*, or, as the Fr.
lundi, etc., Ital. *lunedi*, etc., suggest, to a V. L. *ī*) day, **17** 205;
21 15; etc.; *de dia* by day, **35**
334 *c*; (pl.) life, **7** 22 etc.

diablo (half-learned; L. *dĭabŏlus*)
devil, **25** 102 *b*.

Diaz pr. n., **13** 14 etc. (L. documents have *Didaci*, indicating a
genitive *-aci* as equivalent to the
patronymic *-az*.)

dicho -a (p.p. of *dezir*; L. *dictum*;
the *i* is due to a V. L. **dīctum*
or to the L. *ī* of the pres. and
pret. stems; cf. Sp. *endecha*, L.
ĭndĭcta, Ital. *detto*, etc.) said,
told, called, mentioned, **12** 134;
19 1134; etc.; (n.) word, **27**
356 *c*.

dieç (Aragonese writing of *diez*)
ten, **63** 91 *a*.

diente (L. *dens*, *dĕntem*) tooth, **42**
21.

diesse (impf. sbj. 1 and 3 of *dar*;
stem *d-* of Sp. *di*, *dió*, etc., +
ending *-iesse*, L. *-ĭvĭssem*, *-ĭvĭsset*
of the 4th conj.) should give, **46**
19; **16** 165; cf. mod. *diese*.

diessedes (impf. sbj. 2 pl. of *dar*;
stem *d-* of the pret. + ending
from L. 4th conj. *-ĭvĭssētĭs*, with
accent like that of the sg. and

3 pl.) should say, **42** 32; cf.
mod. *dieseis*.

diessen (impf. sbj. 3 pl. of *dar*;
stem *d-* + *-iessen* from L. 4th
conj. *-ĭvĭssent*; cf. *diesse*) should
give, **27** 355 *d*; cf. mod. *diesen*.

diestra (L. *dĕxtĕram* [*manum*])
right hand, **47** 8; (adv.) on the
right, **13** 11.

diez (L. *dĕcem*) ten, **30** 5 *a* etc.

diezmo (L. *dĕcĭmus -um*) tenth part,
tithe, **21** 17.

digamos (pres. sbj. 1 pl. of *dezir*;
L. *dīcamŭs*) **31** 11 *a*.

digo (pres. 1 of *dezir*; L. *dīco*) I
say, **6** 7 etc.

diligençia (learned word; L. *dīlĭ-
gĕntĭa*) diligence, effort, **68** VIII 7.

dim = *di* + *me* tell me **22** 27.

dinero (L. *dēnārĭus -um* which
should have given **denero*; is
the *i* due to dissimilation?)
penny, **16** 165; (pl.) money, **22**
27 etc.

diol = *dio*, *dió* + *le*.

Dios (L. *Dĕŭs*, very common as a
vocative; whence **Dieos*, *Díos*,
Diós) God, **6** 1 etc.; pl. *Dioses*
(newly made on *Dios*) **31** 15 *a*.

dira, dire (fut. 3 and 1 of *dezir*,
based on a contracted infin.
stem, L. *dīcĕre* > **dicre* > **dire*
+ O. Sp. *a*, *e*, mod. *ha*, *he*) **48**
14 *c*; **62** 1; etc.

disanto (*dia*, apocopated to *di-*,
[cf. *María* apocopated to *Mari-*
in *Mari-Sánchez*, etc.] + *santo*)
holy day, religious feast, **21** 23.

dise = *dize*, mod. *dice* (L. *dīcĭt*)
says, **66, 67, 68** titles.

disso (Aragonese transliteration = O. Castilian *dixo*, mod. *dijo*) said, **64** 94 *c* etc.

dito (V. L. **dĭctum*, cf. L. *dīco*, *dīxi*, and L. *dĭctum*): *mal dito* accursed, **49** 300 *a*. (*Dĭctum* is due to the influence of the preterite.)

diuerso -a (mod. *diverso -a* ; learned word, L. *dīvĕrsus -a -um*) diverse, different, various, **30** 4 *b*.

dixendo (Aragonese pres. part. of *dezir*, basɜd on pret. stem *dix-*) saying, **63** 89 *c*.

dixeron = *dixieron* (with *i̯* absorbed by preceding palatal *š*) said, called, **37** 356 *c* ; **65** 108 *c* ; cf. mod. *dijeron*.

dixestes (pret. 2 pl. of *dezir*; for an earlier *dixiestes*, whose *i* was absorbed by the preceding palatal *š*; L. stem *dix-* + 4th conj. ending *-ĭvĭstĭs*, or simply the analogy of the 3 pl. *dixieron*) said, **36** 346 *a*, *c* ; **64** 99 *d*.

dixiemos (pret. 1 pl. of *dezir*; it is O. Sp. *diximos* remade on the analogy of *dixieron*) we said, **24** 93 *a* ; **41** 1 ; mod. *dijimos*.

dixiera = mod. *dijera* (a pret. or plpf. in force), **59** 21.

dixieron (pret. 3 pl. of *dezir*; L. pret. stem *dix-* + pret. ending 4th conj. *-ĭvērunt*) they said, **24** 95 *a* ; **27** 360 *c* ; cf. mod. *dijeron*.

dixiese, dixiesen (cf. *dixiesse*) **53** 7 ; **54** 13 ; **59** 19.

dixiesse, dixiessen (impf. sbj. 3 sg. and pl. of *dezir*; L. pret. stem *dix-* + endings of plpf. sbj. 4th

conj. *-ĭvĭsset -ĭvĭssent*) said, uttered, told, **53** 25 ; **46** 12 ; cf. mod. *dijese, dijesen*.

dixo (pret. 3 of *dezir*; L. *dix-* + Sp. strong ending *-o* from L. *-ĭvĭt > -iut > io* or L. and V. L. *-ŭit*) said, **12** 141 ; **15** 136 ; etc. ; cf. mod. *dijo*.

dixol = *dixo* + *le*, **46** 6.

diz (apocopated form of *dize*) **24** 95 *c* ; **28** 363 *b* ; etc.

dize (pres. 3 of *dezir*; L. *dīcĭt*) says, **41** 23 ; **58** 435 *c* ; etc. ; cf. mod. *dice*.

dizen (pres. 3 pl. of *dezir*; L. *dicunt*, V. L. **dīcent*) they say, call, tell, **9** 82 ; **23** 3 *d* ; etc. ; cf. mod. *dicen*.

dizeremos (fuller form of fut. *diremos* ; cf. *dezir* and *dizre*) **9** 75.

dizian (imper. 3 pl. of *dezir*; V. L. **dīcēant*, with ending like that of L. *habebant > *habeant*, by dissimilation) were saying, **13** 19 ; cf. mod. *decían* (whose *e* is due to dissimilation).

dizien = *dizian* called, **35** 334 *b* ; **40** 12 ; **44** 8.

diziendo (pres. part. of *dezir*; L. *dīcĕndum*) **42** 24 ; **52** 16 ; cf. mod. *diciendo*.

dizre = mod. *diré* (fut. 1 of O. Sp. *dizir, dezir*), **21** 2.

dizremos = mod. *diremos* (cf. *dizeremos, dizre*), **10** 90.

djente = *diente*, **49** 300 *c*.

djnero = *dinero*, **48** 16 *c* ; **49** 490 *a*.

do (L. *de* + *ŭbi*) where, whither, when, **22** 36 ; **28** 362 *b* ; **33** 73 *d* ; etc.; *por do* whereby, **71** LXXIX 6.

(Now found only in *doquiera*; cf. *donde*. It is in combinations like *de ub(i) quierat*, in which the spirant *b* before a cons. became *u*, that the form *do* arose.)

doblar (L. *dŭplāre*) to double, 45 11; *doblar uos he* I shall double for you, 13 80.

doliente (L. *dolens, dolĕntem*) suffering, grieving, 58 440 *d*.

dolor (L. *dolor, dolōrem*) grief, 13 18.

dolorido -a (Sp. *dolor* + part. and adj. ending *-ido*, L. *-ītus*) grieved, grieving 25 104 *c*.

doloroso -a (L. *dolorōsus -a -um*) dolorous, sorrowful, 68 IX 4.

doluidar = *de oluidar*, 36 350 *d*.

domingo (L. [*diem*] *domĭnĭcum*; the *i* shows either a half-learned treatment or the influence of *día*) Sunday, 21 3.

Domjngo = *domingo*, 23 3 *c*; 27 354 *d*.

Domjnus = *Dominus* (L.), 51 1663 *a*.

domnes = *de omnes*, 38 363 *c*.

don (L. *dōnum* should have given **dono*; *don* may be a loan-word from Fr. or Prov., or an abstract from *donar*) gift, reward, 16 179; 17 192; etc.

don (L. vocative *dŏmĭne*; the retention of *o* and the shortening of the form are due to unaccented proclitic use; cf. accented *dueño*) lord, Mr., sir, 16 155, 159; 17 185; etc.

dona (L. *dŏmĭna*, or rather a fem. formed on Sp. *don*) woman, 32 20 *c*; cf. proclitic *doña* and ac-

cented *dueña*, both of which show a regular treatment.

dond (apocopated form of *donde*) whence, 6 19.

donde (L. *de* + *ŭnde*) where, 38 365 *c*; 70 LII 6. (The original sense "whence" is found in 6 19.)

donna = *doña* (L. *dŏmĭna*, in proclitic and unaccented use), lady, Mrs., Miss, 40 10, 12; etc.

donzella (V. L. **domĭnĭcĕlla*, dimin. of L. *domina*; we should expect **donzilla*. Perhaps the Prov. *donzella* explains the *e*) damsel, maiden, 68 IX 2; cf. mod. *doncella*.

doquiere = *do* + *quiere* (L. *quaerit*): *por doquiere* wheresoever, 63 93 *c*.

dorado -a (L. *de* + *auratus -a -um*) gilded, golden, 14 88; 22 34; etc.

dormiendo (L. gerund *dormiĕndum*) sleeping, 60 7. (The form *durmiendo* shows the closing effect of the *j*.)

dormient (L. pres. part. *dormiens, dormientem*) sleeping, 21 4; cf. mod. adj. *durmiente*.

dormir (L. *dŏrmīre*) to sleep, 15 126 (L. *dŏrmĭt* > *duerme*); 46 5.

dos (L. *duo*, V. L. **dŭōs*) two, 9 71 etc.

dotor (learned word; L. *dŏctor, dŏctōrem*) doctor, scholar, 49 18 *b*.

doze (L. *duodecim*, V. L. **dōdĕcĭm*) twelve, 30 4 *a*; 32 20 *a*; etc.; cf. mod. *doce*.

dozientos (based on L. *duo* and *cĕntum*) two hundred, 31 17 *a*;

43 17. (The *z* is properly developed from intervocalic L. *c(e,i)*; the mod. *doscientos* is a reconstructed form.)

dubda (half-learned word; abstract from *dubdar*, L. *dŭbĭtāre*) doubt, hesitation, fear, **19** 1131; **70** LIII 3; cf. mod. *duda*.

duca = mistake for *daca? = de acá* on this side, **17** 1088.

dudar (cf. *dubda*) to hesitate, **39** 369 *d*.

duelo (abstract from *doler*, *duelo*, *dueles*, etc., L. *dŏlēre*) grief, lament, **21** 9, 10; etc.

duenna = *dueña* (L. *dŏmĭna*) woman, lady, **40** 8, 11; **42** 16; etc. (Used here in the general and not in the modern restricted sense.) Cf. *donna*.

duenno = *dueño* (L. *dŏmĭnus -um*) master, owner, **34** 80 *c*; cf. *don*.

dulçe (learned word; L. *dŭlcis -em*) sweet, **47** 5; **60** 12.

dun = *d'un, de un*, **37** 359 *d*.

duna = *d'una, de una*, **37** 359 *c*.

duque (learned formation on L. *dux*, *dŭcem*) duke, **67** v 6.

durante (cf. *durar*) lasting, **66** I 2.

durar (L. *dūrāre*) to last, continue, **18** 1120; **19** 1148; etc.

duro -a (L. *dūrus -a -um*) hard, harsh, **27** 355 *a*; **67** v 3.

dya = *día* (V. L. *dia* for L. *dies*) day, **51** 1662 *j*.

Dyos = *Dios*, **48** 11 *a*.

dyra = *d'yra* = *de ira* (L. *īra*) with anger, **39** 369 *c*.

dyxo = *dixo*, **36** 338 *a*, 346 *a*.

dyz = *diz*, **49** 299 *b*.

e (cf. *he*) I have; (in perf. tenses) **6** 3; **7** 30; etc.; (separable element of fut. indic.) **6** 17; **7** 46; etc.

e (L. *et*) and, **13** 5, 12; etc.; **21** 7, 11; etc.; **26** 106 *a* etc.; cf. *et, z, i, y*.

-ear verbal ending (V. L. *-ĭdĭare*).

Ebrro (pr. n.) Ebro, **37** 356 *c*.

Ebrrol = *Ebrro* + *le*, **37** 356 *c*.

echar (L. *jactare* > **jeitar* > *echar*) to throw, cast, throw down, expel, pour out, dispatch, put, put on, **13** 14; **17** 184; **19** 1187; **20** 1203; **46** 27; etc.

echauan = *echavan*, *echaban* (cf. *echar*), sent forth, **60** 13.

Egipto (L. *Ægyptus -um*) Egypt, **46** 3.

egual (L. *aequalis -em*) equal, **23** 1 *c*. (Cf. mod. *igual*, whose *i* may be due to the closing force of the following *ʒ*.)

egualança (*egual* + *-ança* from L. abstract suffix *-antia*) equality, equal, peer, **51** 1664 *b*. (Cf. obs. *igualanza*, mod. *igualdad*.)

el def. art., masc. sg. (L. *ĭlle* > *ell* and, before a masc. word beginning with a cons., *el*, which was then generalized before all masc. nouns), the, **7** 40 etc.; **23** 1 *a* etc.; (before a noun in the vocative, which may be regarded, however, as in apposition to the subject of a verb) **38** 365 *c*; fem. art. sg. (L. *ĭlla*, *ĭllam* > *ella* and before a fem. word beginning with *a-, ha-,* > *ell*. This became *el*, whether

through the analogy of the
masc. art. *el*, or through a loss
for both, in an apparently final
position, of the palatalization of
the *l*. The analogy of the demonstrative and personal pronouns *ell* > *el* doubtless had
influence he.e. In O. Sp. it became possible to use the fem.
art. *el* before fem. *nouns and
adjectives* beginning with any
vowel, accented or not. In mod.
Sp. the form is restricted to use
before fem. *nouns* beginning
with accented *a- ha-*), **16** 150;
47 17; **56** 423 *c*; cf. *ell*.

el masc. dem. adj. and pers. pron.
(L. *ĭlle* > *ell*, which in proclitic
use or in the absolute *Auslaut*
lost its palatalization and > *el*),
he, him, it, that, the one, **13** 78;
17 1085; etc.; **8** 68; **15** 124; etc.

el[gue]sia = *eglesia, iglesia*, **21** 19.

ell (cf. *el*; def. art. masc. sg. before
word beginning with a vowel
sound) the, **40** 3; **41** 8; **42** 10;
43 5, 8, 9; **44** 3; **46** 1, 2; (fem.
sg. before word beginning with
a vowel sound) **21** 7, 8, 12; **43** 6.

ell (cf. *el*; pers. pron. masc. sg.) he,
him, it, **40**; **41** 17; **42** 4, 19, 29;
43 9, 14, 33; **44** 11.

ella (L. *illa, illam*) she, her, it, **25**
103 *d*, 105 *b*; etc.

elli pers. pron. masc. sg.(L. *ĭlle* > *elle*
and, under influence of the pro-
nominal *qui*, which remained in
O. Sp., > *elli*; the form is perhaps
dialectal in Berceo), he, him, it,
24 91 *b*; **28** 367 *b*; **29** 370 *d*.

ello pers. pron. ntr. sg. (L. *ĭllŭd* or
V. L. **illŭm*), it, **29** 369 *d*.

ellos pers. pron. masc. pl. (L. *ĭlle*,
ĭllōs), they, them, **27** 360 *a*; **28**
366 *a*; etc.

elos = *ellos*, **11** 126. (The *l* means
palatalized *l*.)

elos = *e* 'and ' + *los* 'the,' or (but?)
the masc. pl. art. in fuller form,
20 1218.

ementar (perhaps for O. Sp. *en-
mentar*, which may represent
mentar, V. L. *mentare* under the
influence of *en mente*) to remember, **37** 353 *b*. (*Mentar* remains
the mod. word.)

emos = *hemos* (L. *habēmŭs* or rather
a new pl. based on Sp. *he*; cf. *so,
somos*), **28** 365 *c*; **45** 10, 11. (In
all these cases it forms the separable and second element of the
fut. indic., and obj. prons. intervene between the infin. basis and
emos.)

emperador (L. *imperator, ĭmpera-
tōrem*) emperor, **40** 5; **44** 4.

en (L. *ĭn*) in, into, on, upon, with
respect to, as, during, **6** 12; **7**
22; etc.; *en todo esto* during all
this, **46** 23; *en todo* wholly, **6** 12
etc.

en = *ende* > *end* and *ent* > *en* (cf.
grande > *grand* and *grant* >
gran), thence, **65** 103 *d*; *por en*
thereby, therefore, **14** 112.

enadran (fut. 3 pl. of *enadir* = mod.
añadir, L. *in* + *addere*, V. L.
*addīre) they will add, **18** 1112.

enartado (p.p. of O. Sp. *enartar*, L.
ĭn + *arctare, artare* 'to press,'

'to hem in,' therefore 'to hem in with wiles,' 'to beguile') beguiled, deceived, **12** 138.

enbargar = *embargar* (V. L. **imbarrĭcare* based on a stem *barr-* of uncertain origin but widespread in Romance) to bother, impede, embarrass, **58** 441 *b*.

enbiar = mod. *enviar* (L. *ĭn* and *vĭa*, whence V. L. **invĭāre*) to send, **27** 359 *a*; **41** 2; **62** 3. (The *nb* doubtless meant what is meant by the mod. *nv*, viz. the sound *mb*; cf. *enviar* and *enuiar*.)

enbraçar = mod. *embrazar* (V. L. **ĭmbrac(ch)iare* from L. *ĭn* and *bracchium*) to embrace, take hold of, **31** 11 *c*; cf. *abraçar*.

encarnaçion (learned word; L. L. *incarnatio, incarnationem*; cf. L. L. *incarnari* based on L. *in* and *caro, carnem*) incarnation, **40** 3.

Encarnation = *encarnaçion*, **44** 3.

encenso (n. from *ĭncēnsum*, p.p. of L. *incendere*) incense, **9** 72. (The mod. *encienso* either shows an *ĕ* in *incensum* or owes its diphthong to analogy. The form *acenso* is due to a confusion of prefixes; cf. old *acender* = *encender*.)

ençerrar (V. L. **inserrare*, L. *ĭn* + *serare*. The doubling of *r* is peculiar. The change of *s-* to *ç-*, originally = *ts*, is also strange; perhaps after the *n* the *s* organically developed to *ts*. A combination with the L. adv. *ĭntus* > **ents* could produce the *ç*,

but it seems unlikely. The simplex *çerrar* also has *ç*; cf. this latter and the possible relation with *çercar*) to inclose, **65** 104 *d*.

enchir (L. *ĭmplēre*, V. L. **ĭmplīre*) to fill, swell out, **65** 104 *d*. (In mod. Sp. *henchir*, whose *h-* would seem to be inorganic yet is apparently represented by *f-* in an early Sp. *fenchir*. Cf. L. *inflare*, mod. Sp. *hinchar*, early Sp. *finchar*. For this latter we might suspect a mistaken V. L. **finflare*, and *finchar* might have superinduced *fenchir*.)

ençierto = *en çierto* surely, really, **49** 301 *c*; cf. mod. *por cierto*.

enclauar = *enclavar* (V. L. **inclavare*, based on *clavus*) to prick a horse when driving nails into his shoe, **49** 300 *c*.

enclaueadas = *enclaveadas* (fem. p.p. of O. Sp. *enclavear*, L. *ĭn* + a formation in *-ear*, V. L. *-idiare*, on L. *clavus -um*) to nail, stud with nails, **14** 87.

encljn = *enclin* (loan-word? cf. learned word *inclinar*, L. *ĭnclīnare*, and the Fr. adj. *enclin*) bow, **25** 98 *b*. (It is now obsolete.)

encomjença = *encomiença* (pres. 3 of *encomençar*, L. *ĭn* + *cŭm* + *ĭnĭtĭare*) to begin, commence, **67** VII 2. (The diphthongization is due to the influence of *empiezo* and other verbs; cf. mod. *comenzar*.)

encortinado -a (p.p. of *encortinar*, based on *cortina*) curtained, draped, **29** 2 *d*.

encubrir (*en-*, L. *in*, + *cubrir*, L. *coopĕrīre*. O. Sp. had *cobrir*, whose *o > u* through closing in *cobriendo* and similar forms) to conceal, **63** 92 *d*.

ende (L. *ĭnde*) thence, therefrom, thereat, thereof, over it, **41** 25; **42** 34; **43** 3; **44** 8; **52** 14; etc.; *por ende* on that account, **43** 27, 28.

endia = *en día*, **24** 97 *a*.

endon = *en don* as a gift, **16** 179; **17** 196.

enel = *en el*, **19** 1138; **20** 1217; **23** 4 *a*; etc.

enemigo (L. *ĭnĭmīcŭs -ŭm*) enemy, **45** 21; **62** 18.

eneste = *en este*.

enfermar (L. *ĭnfĭrmāre*) to fall sick, **63** 93 *b*.

enfermo -a (L. *ĭnfĭrmus -a -um*) sick, infirm, **27** 360 *c*; **47** 7.

enforcar (V. L. *ĭnfŭrcare*, based on L. *fŭrca*) to gibbet, hang, **64** 98 *b*, 101 *c*; cf. mod. *ahorcar*

enformar (L. *ĭnfōrmare*) to inform, inspire, **48** 13 *b*. (In mod. Sp. it is the learned *informar*.)

engañar (Ety.? Said to be Germanic stem *ganja-*, Eng. 'yawn,' etc.) to deceive, beguile, **59** 21; **60** 1.

enganno = *engaño* (abstract from *engañar*) wile, stratagem, **38** 361 *d*.

engastonar (L. *ĭn*, Sp. *en-* + a verb based on augmentative in *-on* of Germanic *Kast-*; cf. Germanic *Kasten* 'chest,' 'receptacle') to fit in, enchase, set, **30** 10 *c*.

(Cf. mod. *engastar*; the *g* may be due to a weaker utterance of the Germanic voiceless *k*.)

engendrar (L. *ĭngĕnĕrare > *engen-'rar*, and, with a dental stop developed between *n* and *r*, *engendrar*) to engender, beget, **31** 17 *b*.

engrameo (Ety.? Said to be connected with Germanic *Gram* 'sorrow,' etc. But?) shook, **13** 13. (Cf. Bello, *Obras* II. 373, for other instances of *engramear*, 'to shake.')

engrano (L. *in* + *granum*) the fullness of grains on an ear of corn, **65** 105 *c*.

enla = *en la*, **20** 1212 etc.

enlas = *en las*, **26** 108 *a*; **31** 13 *c*.

enna (Western Sp. for *en la*, with assimilation of *l*) **25** 103 *d*; **28** 361 *b*.

enodio (L. L. *enodĭus -um*, L. *enodis* 'free from knots,' 'clear.' But?) fawn, **47** 13.

enojo (L. *ĭn* + *ŏdĭum*; this should have given *enoyo*, and the *j* has been ascribed to Catalan influence, since there *-dy- > j* and *tj*) annoyance, anger, **52** 5, 21; etc. (The influence of *ojo*, 'eye,' has also been suspected, for the eye expresses anger and ill will.)

enparar (L. *ĭn* + *parare*) to protect, **25** 99 *c*; cf. *anparar*.

enpeñar (V. L. *ĭmpĭgnāre*, based on L. *pignus*) to pledge, pawn, **14** 92; **57** 433 *c*; **58** 440 *c*.

enperador = *emperador*, **67** v 7.

enperante = *emperante* (L. pres. part. *împĕrans*, *împĕrantem*) ruler, emperor, **31** 16 *b*.

enplear = *emplear* (perhaps a loan-word; cf. O. Fr. *empleier*, mod. Fr. *employer*, L. *împlĭcare*) to employ, **28** 363 *c*.

ensaemos = *ensayemos*, pres. sbj. 1 pl. of *ensayar* (V. L. *exagiare*, based on *exagĭum*, with influence of the prefix *en*, L. *in*), let us test, **24** 95 *a*.

ensanchar (verb formed, with a contamination of prefixes *ex-* and *in-*, on V. L. *amplare* or L. *ampliare*, from L. *amplus -a -um*) to extend, increase, **26** 108 *a*.

ensenno = *enseñó*, pret. 3 of *enseñar* (V. L. *însĭgnāre* from L. *sĭgnum*), taught, showed, **40** 16.

ensoga = *en soga*, **27** 353 *d*.

enssienplo (by-form of *enxienplo*) example, story, **49** title.

ensu = *en su*, **26** 112 *c*.

ent = *ende* (cf. *en*) thence, **21** 8.

ental = *en tal*, **27** 356 *a*.

entender (L. *întĕndĕre*, V. L. *întĕndēre*) to understand, perceive, learn, **24** 95 *b*; **25** 103 *b*; **42** 17; etc.

entendes = *entiendes* (cf. *entender*) understandest, **12** 140.

entendien = *entendían*, **29** 371 *c*.

entendremos = *entenderemos*, fut. 1 pl. of *entender* (in O. Sp., verbs not strictly of the irregular class might have a contract infin. stem in the fut. and cond. of the indic.), **24** 96 *d*.

enterrar (V. L. *întĕrrāre*, based on L. *tĕrra*) to inter, bury, **61** 15.

entonçe (L. *în + tŭncce*) then, **59** 11, 24. (Cf. mod. *entonces*, which has a final, so-called adverbial, *-s*, due to *después* and similar forms.)

entrar (L. *întrāre*) to enter, go in, come in, **13** 12; **14** 109; **15** 125; etc. (Sometimes it completes its construction with *d*; cf. **13** 12; **15** 125.)

entrastes = *entrasteis* (cf. *entrar*), **57** 434 *c*. (The O. Sp. form represents properly the L. *amastîs* for *amavistis*; the *i* of the mod. form is due to analogy.)

entraua = *entrava*, *entraba* (cf. *entrar*), **14** 98.

entre (L. *înter*, V. L. *între*; cf. L. *intra*) among, **47** 2 etc.; *entre* . . . *e* both . . . and, **17** 191.

entrellos = *entre ellos*, **43** 21.

entu = *en tu*, **25** 100 *c*.

enuidia = *envidia* (partly learned word; L. *învĭdĭa*) envy, **43** 27.

enuio = *envió* (cf. *enbiar*), **44** 9, 16 etc.

enujar = *enviar* (cf. *enbiar*), **28** 365 *c*.

envio pret. 3 of *enviar* (cf. *enbiar*), **64** 99 *d*.

enxiemplo (L. *exĕmplŭm*; the apparent prefix *ex-* has suffered contamination with L. prefix *în-*) exemplar, instructive story, **54** title. (Cf. *exenplo* and mod. *ejemplo*.)

enxienplo = *enxiemplo*, **49** title; **55** 29.

era (L. L. *aera*, a sg. noun from ntr. pl. of L. *aes*. In L. *aera* meant

'counters used in calculating')
era, **44** 2.

era (L. *ĕram*, *ĕrat* in atonic and
proclitic use, wherefore the *ĕ*
did not diphthongize; cf. *ser*) **19**
1135 etc.; (auxiliary of verb of
motion, *era venido* = mod. *había
venido*) **35** 332 *b*. (In O. Sp. *era*
could be used where only *estaba*
is now allowed.)

erados = *errados* astray, in error,
12 142.

eram' = *era* + *me*, **21** 5.

eran (L. *ĕrant* in atonic use, wherefore the *ĕ* did not diphthongize;
cf. *ser*) **16** 171 etc. (In O. Sp.
eran could be used where only
estaban is now allowed.)

eres (L. fut. *ĕrĭs* in atonic use and
therefore without diphthongization; cf. *ser*. As L. *ĕs* would
have produced a Sp. form not
distinguishable from that derived from L. *ĕst*, a new pres. 2
was created by borrowing the
fut. 2, which already had the
function of a present of probability) **12** 138; **21** 26; etc. (In
O. Sp. *eres* could be used where
only *estás* is now allowed.)

-ero -era (L. *-arĭus -arĭa*) suffix denoting agent, 'full of,' etc.

errado -a (L. p.p. *erratus -a -um*) in
error, astray, mistaken, **35** 333 *a*;
(adv.) *errada mente* erroneously,
52 17.

es (L. *ĕst*, developed in an atonic
position and therefore without
diphthongization; cf. *ser*) **6** 2
etc.; (as auxiliary with verbs of

motion, *exido es* = mod. *ha
salido*) **17** 201; **21** 8; *es de amar*
is to be loved, **49** 490 *a*; *es de
alabar* is to be praised, **61** 1;
es = mod. *está*, **7** 36; **15** 137;
etc.

es = *ese* (L. *ĭpse*; the loss of the
final unaccented *e* is frequent
here in O. Sp.), **19** 1146, 1147;
20 1211. (The theory that this
is *este* > *est* and, before a consonant, > *es* does not appear correct.)

esa (L. *ĭpsa*, *ĭpsam*; fem. of *ese*,
O. Sp. *esse*, *essa*) **26** 106 *d*; **30**
4 *d*.

escalentar (V. L. **excalentare*, based
on L. *calēre*, *calens*, *calentem*) to
warm, excite, **34** 79 *b*; **38** 363 *b*.

escançiano (Germanic *skankjo*,
mod. German *schenk*, + *-ano*,
L. *-anus -a -um*) cup-bearer, **63**
92 *c* etc.; cf. mod. *escanciador*.

escanno = *escaño* (L. *scamnum*)
stool, chair, **31** 12 *a*.

escapar (V. L. **excappare*, based on
L. *ex* and *cappa* 'to come from
under the cape,' 'to get free')
to escape, **28** 368 *d*; **29** 371 *a*;
etc.

escapulado -a (p. p. based on L.
scapula 'shoulder') wearing a
scapular, having a monastic
habit, **23** 86 *a*.

escarmentar (of uncertain origin.
It has been referred to L. *car-
pĕre* 'to carp at,' whence a V. L.
*excarpĭmĕntare, and to L. *car-
men*. From this latter we might
conceive of a derivative V. L.

*excarmĭnĭtare, but its formation, like that of *excarpimentare, is open to grave doubt. A relation to the Ital. scarnamento, L. ex and caro, carne, is also hard to justify) to punish, make a warning example of, **18** 1121.

escarno = escarnio? (apparently of Germanic origin. Cf. O.H.G. skërnon 'to flout,' O. Sp. escarnir. The a may be due to the following consonants or to some exterior analogy) mockery, jeering; sines escarno beyond a cavil, **7** 38.

escogido -a (p.p. of escoger, V. L. *excollĭgĕre; cf. coger) chosen person, **30** 6 a.

escomjença = encomjença (with L. prefix ex- instead of ĭn-), begins, **23** title.

escorrido -a (p.p. of escorrir, V. L. *excŭrrīre based on L. cŭrrĕre) passed, elapsed, **28** 367 a. (The forms escurrir, escurrido, etc., which survive, show the closing influence of the following palatal in escorriendo > escurriendo, and similar forms.)

escreuiessen = escreviessen = mod. escribiesen (impf. sbj. 3 pl. of escribir, L. scrībĕre, V. L. *scrībīre. The e of the second syll. may be due to dissimilation in the infin., i.e. escribir > escrebir, or it may be a scribal mistake) should write, **62** 17.

escripto -a (partly learned spelling of escrito -a) written, **12** 137; **70** LIII 3; (n.) writing, decree, scripture, **11** 125, 128; **30** 5 b.

escriptura (partly learned spelling of escritura, L. scrīptūra) writing, inscription, scripture, **7** 35; **24** 95 c; **62** 20; **67** v 1.

escrito -a (L. p.p. scrīptus -a -um; cf. escreuiessen) written, **34** 84 b; cf. escripto.

escuchar (L. auscŭltāre, V. L. *ascŏltāre, whence O. Sp. ascuchar and, by confusion of as- with the prefix ex-, Sp. es-, escuchar. The u is due to the closing of V. L. o by the palatal developed in the change of -lt- to tš, i.e. ch) to hear, listen to, **48** 14 b, 15 a.

escudero (L. scŭtarĭus -um) shield-bearer, esquire, squire, **17** 187; **42** 4; etc.

escudiella (L. scŭtĕlla, dimin. of scŭtum 'tray,' 'dish') porringer, dish, **54** 18. (Mod. escudilla shows change of -iella > illa through the palatalizing force of ll.)

escuro -a (L. obscūrus -a -um, whence Sp. obscuro -a, oscuro -a, and also, in O. Sp., escuro -a, which shows the influence of the prefix ex-, Sp. es-) dark, **70** LII 5; **57** 429 b; en eso escuro in some dark place.

escusaçion (learned word; L. excūsatĭo -ōnem) excuse, evasion, **71** LXXVIII 4.

escusar (L. excūsāre) to avoid, **45** 6, 7.

esforçado-a (p.p. of esforçar) strong, sinewy, mighty, **16** 171; **41** 27; etc.; cf. mod. esforzado.

esforçar (V. L. *exfŏrtĭare, based on L. fortis -e) to strengthen, **16**

171 ; **48** 11 *b* : etc. ; (refl.) to be strengthened, pluck up courage, **55** 14 ; cf. mod. *esforzar*.

esfuerço = mod. *esfuerzo* (abstract from *esforçar*, *yo esfuerço*, etc.) might, strength, **38** 361 *d* ; reënforcement, help, **35** 331 *a*.

esida = *exida* (fem. p.p. sg. of *exir*) gone forth, **21** 8. (As elsewhere in the *Disputa*, the *s* = *š*, i.e. *x*.)

esient = *exiente* (participial adj. connected with *exir*. By a Latinism it is used in the absolute construction, as a verbal, instead of *exiendo*) departing, **21** 3 ; cf. *esida*.

esmerado -a (p.p. of *esmerar*, V. L. *exmĕrāre*, based on L. *merus* -a -um) refined, pure, **14** 113.

eso dem. adj., ntr. sg. (L. *ĭpsŭd* or *ipsŭm*, if in V. L. the latter became the ntr. form), this, that, **49** 299 *c* etc. ; *eso mismo* likewise, **30** 8 *b*.

esorado -a = *exorado* -a (V. L. *exauratus* -a -um, based on L. *aurum*) gilded, golden, **22** 34. (As elsewhere in the *Disputa*, the *s* = *š*, i.e. *x*.)

espada (L. *spatha*) sword, **13** 78 ; **16** 175 ; etc.

espalda (L. *spatŭla* > *espadla* and, by metathesis, > *espalda*, for metathesis of *dl* to *ld* was frequent in O. Sp.) shoulder ; (pl.) back, **58** 437 *c*.

espandir (V. L. *expandīre*, L. *expandĕre*) to spread out, extend, **31** 14 *c*. (It is obs.)

Espanna = *España* (L. *Hĭspanĭa*) Spain, **33** 74 *d* ; **45** 13.

espantable (formation on the stem of *espantar*) frightful being, **60** 8, 18. Cf. Fr. *épouvantable*.

espantar (seemingly from a contraction of V. L. *expavĕntare* based on L. *expavēre*, *expavens* -entem) to frighten, bewilder, **39** 368 *a* ; **58** 437 *b* ; (refl.) to be afraid, **70** LII 8.

espeio = *espejo* (L. *spĕculum* ; the palatal sound following closed the *ĕ* and prevented diphthongization) mirror, **24** 92 *a*.

espender (L. *expĕndĕre*, V. L. *expendĕre*) to spend, pass, **37** 354 *b* ; **13** 81. (Also spelled *expender*.)

esperar (L. *spērāre*) to hope, hope for, expect, await, **23** 4 *c* ; **35** 330 *d* ; etc.

espertar (V. L. *expĕrgĭtāre*, a frequentative from L. *expergĕre*, *expergĭtus*) to awake, awaken, **46** 8. (The mod. verb is *despertar* = O. Sp. *espertar* + prefix *de*-.)

espeso -a p.p. of *espender* (L. p.p. *expēnsus* -a -um), expended, spent, **13** 81.

espidios = *espidió* + *se* (refl. form of pret. 3 of *espedir*, V. L. *expĕtīre*, ' to ask from [some one] leave to go,' etc. ; based on L. *pĕtĕre*. The mod. verb *despedir* shows the addition of the prefix *de*-), took leave, **17** 200.

espiga (L. *spīca*) ear of corn, **65** 105 *a*.

espina (L. *spīna*) thorn, **19** 18 *a* ; **47** 2.

espiriençia (a more popular but still partly learned form of *experiencia*, L. *expĕriĕntĭa*) experience, experiment, trial, test, **6** 9. (The *i* of the second syll. is due to the closing influence of the *i̥* following.)

espolear (formation on noun *espuela*, with the original *o* of the Germanic *sporo* and the verbal ending *-ear*, V.L. *-ĭdĭare*) to spur, spur on, **38** 365 *a*.

esposa (L. *sponsa*, V.L. **spōsa*) spouse, bride, **25** 103 *c*; **68** IX 8; gyves, fetters, **50** 497 *c*.

espuela (Germanic *sporo*; cf. Eng. *spur.* Thence in O. Sp. *esporon* and, without the augm. suffix *-on*, *espuera*. Thence, by confusion with the dimin. suffix *-uela* [cf. also O. Sp. *espolon* beside *esporon*], *espuela*) spur, **22** 32.

esquivo -a (related to *esquivar* 'to shun,' Germanic *skiuhan*, **skiuan.* Cf. Eng. *shy*, German *scheu*) disagreeable, antipathetic, **68** VII 3.

essa (L. *ĭpsa*; fem. of O. Sp. *es*, mod. *ese*) this, that, **18** 1091 etc.; (pron.) this, that, it, that one, **24** 97 *c* etc.

essi masc. adj. sg. (L. *ĭpse*, whence *esse* and, under influence of O. Sp. *qui*, *essi.* The form is western), this, that, **24** 92 *c*; **27** 353 *a*; **26** 109 *d*; (pron.) **28** 364 *c*. Cf. *es*, mod. *ese*.

esso dem. pron. ntr. (L. *ĭpsŭd* or V. L. *ĭpsŭm*), that, this, it, **15** 141, etc. Cf. mod. *eso*.

essora (O. Sp. *essa*, apocopated in compound word, + *ora*) at once, straightway, **34** 79 *d*.

est (apocopation of *este*) : *est otro* this other, **9** 83.

esta, estas (L. *ĭsta*, *ĭstam*, *ĭstas*; fem. of *este*, *est*) this, that, these, those, **6** 19 etc. ; (pron.) **29** 371 *d*.

estaca (Germanic **staka*; cf. A.S. *staca*, Eng. *stake*) stake, peg, **19** 1142.

estades = mod. *estáis* (L. *statĭs*, pres. 2 of *stare* ; cf. *estar*).

estado (L. *status*, *statum*) estate, calling, rank, **66** 10; **68** VIII 2.

estantygua = (*h*)*ueste antigua* (L. *hŏstis antīqua*, *hŏstem antīquam* 'ancient host,' i.e. of roving demons ; for the change of *ue* > *e* some explanation is needed) demon army, **35** 335 *c*.

estar (L. *stāre*, for variation of sense cf. *seer*) to be, be standing, stand, be firm, remain, **35** 333 *a*; **69** XLII 3; **54** 5; **58** 437 1; etc.: pres. 1 *esto* **46** 17; **58** 436 *d*; etc.; 2 *estas* **38** 365 *c*; 3 *esta* **45** 11 etc.; 2 pl. *estades con bien* you are well off, **55** 19; 3 pl. *estan* **57** 428 *b* etc.: impf. 3 *estaua* **13** 2; **16** 154; **29** 2; etc.; *estava* **35** 332 *d*; **55** 3; etc.; *estaba* **63** 93 *c*; 3 pl. *estauan* **27** 358 *c*; **14** 100; etc.; *estavan* **33** 73 *b*: pret. 3 *estuvo* **65** 102 *d*: fut. 1 *estaré* **67** III 2; 2 pl. *estaredes* **58** 435 *a*; 3 pl. *estaran* **55** 22: imper. 2 pl. *estad* **57** 427 *d*: pres. sbj. 1 *este* **57** 431 *d*; 2 *estes* **36** 338 *c*: impf. sbj. 3 *estidiesse* **45** 20;

estouiese **59** 3 : fut. sbj. 2 pl.
estudierdes **55** 21 : aux. in progressive tenses, **13** 2 ; **16** 154 ; etc.

estaredes = mod. *estaréis* (*estar* + -*edes*, L. (*hab*)*ētĭs* ; the intervocalic *d* disappeared, whence **estarées* and the second *e* was in the hiatus position, therefore = *y*, whence *estareys*, i.e. *estaréis* ; cf. *estar*), **58** 435 *a*.

estaua, estauan = *estava*, *estavan* = *estaba*, *estaban* (L. *stabat*, *stabant*) ; cf. *estar*.

estava, estavan cf. *estaua*.

este dem. adj. and pron. masc. sg. (L. *ĭste*), this, that, that one, he, him, **24** 94 *c* ; **47** 11 ; etc.

estero (?) **22** 27.

esti dem. adj. masc. sg. (L. *ĭste*, under influence of pronominal *i* of O. Sp. *qui* ; the form seems to be Western Sp.), this, that, **25** 102 *d* ; cf. *este*.

estidiesse (impf. sbj. 3 of *estar* ; L. perfect stem *stet-* from *stare*, + ending of plpf. sbj. of 4th conj. -*īvĭsset*, O. Sp. -*iesse*. The attraction of -*ŭi* perfects produced O. Sp. *estudiesse*, and entire assimilation to O. Sp. *oviesse*, *toviesse* gave *estoviesse*, whence, through the influence of the *į*, mod. *estuviese* ; cf. *estar* and *estouiese*) **45** 20.

esto dem. pron. ntr. (L. *ĭstŭd* or V. L. *ĭstŭm*), this, that, it, **6** 8 ; **10** 92 ; etc. ; *por esto* on this account, **59** 2 ; *con todo esto* in the meantime, withal, **18** 1095 ;

(scribal mistake for *estos*) **12** 134.

esto (L. *stō* ; the *y* of mod. *estoy*, like that of *soy*, *voy*, is unexplained ; it may be due to the production of a glide vowel when the subject pron. was postfixed, *esto yo* > *estoy yo*. Perhaps the process started with O. Sp. *so* < *sŭm*, which appears in Western Sp. as *soe*, regarded by some as the source of mod. *soy* ; cf. *estar*) **46** 17 etc.

Estol pr. n. (perhaps for O. Fr. *Estolt*, L. *Stŭltus -um*, whence also O. Fr. *Estout*, and, with modifications, Ital. *Astolfo*), **36** 352 *d*.

estonçe (= O. Sp. *entonçe*, with change of prefix due to influence of L. *ex-*, O. Sp. *es-*) then, **53** 21 ; **69** XLII 3 ; cf. *estonçes*.

estonçes (= O. Sp. *estonçe*, with an adverbial -*s* taken from *pues*, etc.) then, **33** 75 *a* ; **42** 10 ; **43** 12, 22 ; etc. ; cf. mod. *entonces*.

estoria (partly popular development of L. *hĭstŏrĭa* or L.L. *storia*) history, story, title, **30** 3 *a* ; **41** 23 ; **44** 11 ; **46** 3 ; **59**. Cf. the mod. learned form *historia*.

estos adj. and pron. (masc. pl. of *este* ; L. *ĭstōs*), these, those, **9** 71 ; **18** 1121.

estouiese = early O. Sp. *estoviesse*, mod. *estuviese*, **59** 3. Cf. *estidiesse* and *estar*.

estrado (L. *strātum*) canopy, dais, **60** 16.

estranas = *estrañas*, **16** 176.

estraño -a (V. L. **extranĕus -a -um*, based on L. *extra*) strange, foreign, exotic, **19** 1125; **60** 11.

estrela = *estrella* (the *Misterio* writes *l* for palatalized *l*), **7** 36. (Cf. also *strela* in the *Misterio*.)

estrella (L. *stēlla* influenced by L. *astrum*) star, **51** 1663 *b*.

Estremadura pr. n., **41** 4.

estrranna (cf. *estraño -a*) strange, terrible, **37** 359 *d*.

estudiar (learned word; V. L. **stŭdĭāre* from L. *stŭdĭum*) to study, **69** XLII 4.

estudierdes syncopated form of *estudieredes* (L. pret. stem *stet-*, from *stāre*; by analogy of *-ui* perfects, e.g. *pude*, the stem *estud-* was created. The ending is that of the L. perfect sbj. 4th conj. *-īvĕrītis > -ĭĕrītis > -ieredes >* mod. *-iereis*. The analogy of *ovieredes*, mod. *hubiereis*, *tovieredes*, mod. *tuvieireis*, produced mod. *estuviereis*. Cf. *estar*, *estidiesse*), **55** 21.

et (L. *ĕt*, which, being an unaccented word, should not diphthongize. The spelling with *t* is a Latinism; it may appear, in the same document, side by side with *e* which represents the true sound. In mod. Sp. *é* remains before words beginning with *i-* and *hi-*, where its greater sonority has preserved it; in enclitic or proclitic use with words ending in a vowel or beginning with any vowel except *i-* (*hi-*), the *e*, as an hiatus vowel, became *y*, whose

use was then extended to the position before consonants) and, **22** 28, 29; **40**; **46** 1; **52** 3; etc. Cf. *i* (= *y*), *y*.

ex = L. *ex*, **30** 3 *c*.

exçelente (learned word; L. *excellens*, *excellentem*) excellent, **67** v 6.

exco (L. *exĕo* under influence of inceptive ending *-sco*): *me exco* I am going forth, **16** 156; cf. *exir*.

exebçion (mistaken spelling of *ex-[c]epcion*, learned word, L. *exceptio*, *exceptionem*) exception, demurrer, **71** LXXVIII 5.

exenplo = *exemplo* (L. *exĕmplŭm*; this could give *exiemplo*, cf. *enxiemplo*, and the palatal *x* could absorb the *i*. The retention of *-mpl-* may indicate a learned treatment; cf. *amplum > ancho*) exemplar, exemplary tale, **61** title. (Mod. *ejemplo* comes from *exemplo*.)

exida (noun from fem. p.p. of O.Sp. *exir*, L. *exīre*, *exĭtus -a -um*, V.L. **exītus -a -um* by attraction to the 4th conj.) exit, departure, **13** 11.

exien = *exían*, **13** 16; cf. *exir*.

exir (L. *exīre*) to go forth, come forth, issue, **17** 200; **20** 1205; **24** 91 *b*; *exe* (L. *ĕxĭt*) comes forth, **18** 1091; *exido -a* (p.p., L. *exĭtus -a -um*, V.L. **exītus -a -um*) gone forth, **19** 1125; *exido es* he has gone forth, **17** 20.

fabla (L. *fabŭla*) speech, agreement, plan, **46** 19; mod. *habla*.

fablable (formation in -able, L. -abĭlis -abĭlem, on the stem of fablar) describable, **60** 20.

fablar (L. fabŭlāre and fabŭlāri based on fari) to speak, **13** 7, 78; **18** 1114; etc.; fut. 1 fablar vos he **48** 15 b; era fablado it had been spoken of, conceived, **46** 13; mod. hablar.

fablaua = fablava, **17** 188.

fablava = mod. hablaba, **54**.

fabledes = mod. habléis, **57** 433 d; cf. fablar.

fabrar = dialect form of fablar, **49** 490 c.

✓ **face** (Latinism for faze, faz) it makes, **10** 94.

✓ **facinda** (scribal spelling of facienda or rather fazienda from L. facĭenda or, perhaps, V. L. *facĕn-da, fut. pass. part. of facĕre. The ntr. pl. became a fem. sg.) matter, affair, thing, **7** 33.

fadado -a (V. L. p.p. *fatatus -a -um from *fatare, based on L. fatum and Fata) fated, **21** 25; cf. mod. hadado -a.

✓ **faga** (V. L. *facam, L. facĭam, pres. sbj. 1 of facere, V. L. *facĕre, O. Sp. fazer) do, **11** 114; **61** 11; mod. haga.

✓ **fagades** (V. L. *facātĭs, L. facĭātis, pres. sbj. 2 pl. of facĕre; cf. faga) do, make, **17** 195; **47** 10; mod. hagáis.

✓ **fagamos** (V. L. *facāmŭs, L. facĭā-mus, pres. sbj. 1 pl. of facĕre, V. L. *facĕre, O. Sp. fazer) let us do, **9** 73; **19** 1128; mod. haga-mos.

fago (V. L. *faco, L. facĭo) I do, **14** 95; **26** 109 a; etc.

falar = fallar, **7** 34; **8** 63; **12** 147. (In the Misterio l sometimes = palatalized l.)

falcon (L. L. falco, falcōnem, perhaps connected with L. falx, falcem, and named from the curved shape of the bird's claws) falcon, **13** 5; mod. halcón.

falençia (learned word; L. fallĕre, fallens, fallentem; it is an abstract formation on this latter) mistake, **25** 101 c; cf. fallir.

✗ **fallar** (L. afflāre 'to breathe upon,' 'to scent,' therefore 'to find,' as a Romance development of sense. A metathesis of *faflare is said to explain the Sp. word. But the ety. is not too certain. If it be accepted, perhaps we had better assume as the intermediate form *fafflare, whose initial sound is due to anticipation of that ending the first syllable and beginning the second, or is due to onomatopœia, i.e. represents the puffing of a dog on the scent) to find, **9** 78; **25** 105 b; **34** 84 a; **38** 364 d; etc. Cf. Glosses, 5 and 8.

fallesçer (V. L. *fallescĕre from L. fallĕre) to fail, **56** 424 a; **62** 10; cf. mod. fallecer.

fallezco (= fallesco, the correct O. Sp. pres. 1 from V. L. *fallesco. On the analogy of the ç = ts in falleçes, falleçe, etc. a z, which in O. Sp. = ts before a cons., took the place of the s) I fail, err, **27** 354 d.

fallir (V. L. *fallīre*, L. *fallĕre*) to fail, be lacking, deceive, **21** 2; **28** 364 *d*; **38** 366 *d*. (This verb persists in mod. Sp. only in the p.p.)

falsia (noun formed on *falso -a* by the addition of the learned abstract ending *-ia*, L. *-ia*) falsehood, treachery, treason, **64** 97 *d*.

falso -a (L. *falsus -a -um*) false, **69** XLIII 1.

fama (L. *fama*) fame, repute, **21** 12.

fambre (L. *fames, famem, famis*; on basis of the two latter forms a V. L. nom. **famis* may be supposed and thence an acc. **famĭnem* by the attraction of such words as L. *sanguis, sanguĭnem*; cf. also the L. *-o, -inem* class, e.g. *homo, homĭnem, hirundo, hirundinem*, and the ntr. class, e.g. *nomen, nominis*, V. L. **nominem*, Sp. *sangre, hombre*, [*golondrina*], *nombre*) famine, hunger, **45** 17, **54** 19; mod. *hambre*.

fanbre = *fambre*, **27** 355 *b*; **55** 10.

far (L. *facĕre* > **facre* > *far*. The form *fer* shows the proper reaction of the palatal *c* > *g* > *y*, which should close the *a* to *e* and then be absorbed by it; **fagre* > **fayre* > **feyre* > *fer*. Doubtless the analogy of *dar, estar*, etc. explains *far*. This form occurs as basis of the fut. and cond., or in periphrastic constructions equivalent to them): *ha de far* has to do, will do,

19 1136; *fare* I will make, I shall do, **14** 108; **58** 438 *a*; *faran aiuda* they will give aid, **21** 24; *faria* I should make, **25** 102 *b*; *farie = faria* cond. 3, would do (as a substitute for another verb), **31** 12 *d*; (cf. mod. *haré, haría*, etc.; *he de hacer*, etc.); cf. *fazer* and *fer*.

faran = mod. *harán*; cf. *far*.

fare = mod. *haré*; cf. *far*.

faria = mod. *haría*; cf. *far*.

farie = *faria*.

farina (L. *farīna*) flour, **49** 17 *c*; mod. *harina*.

fartable (adj. in *-able*, L. *-abĭlis -abĭlem*, based on stem of O. Sp. *fartar*, 'to sate,' V. L. **fartare*, a frequentative formed on *farctus, fartus*, the p.p. of L. *farcīre*) satiating, **60** 13.

fasta (apparently connected with O. Sp. *fata, ata* 'up to,' 'until,' from Arabic *ḥatta*; the *s* is unexplained, but cf. the *s* of the correlative *desde*) up to, until, **16** 162; **37** 353 *d*; **59** 4; etc.; *fasta que* until, **36** 338 *c*; **47** 11; etc.

fata (Arabic *ḥatta*; L. initial *f*, in popular treatment, became aspirate *h* in O. Sp. as to sound, but the sign *f* was retained long after the change; so the Arabic aspirate could be rendered by the same sign. So also in O. Sp. the O. Fr. aspirate *h-* was rendered by *f-* in *fonta* = O. Fr. *honte, fardido* = O. Fr. *hardi*, etc.) up to, as far as, until, **19** 1148.

favlar = *fablar*, **69** XLII 8.

faz (L. *facĭes -em*) face, **26** 109 *b*.

faz = apocopated form of *faze*, pres. 3 of *fazer*, and also of the imper. sg. of that verb, **48** 14 *d*; **49** 490 *a*, 300 *d*; **51** 1662 *d*; cf. mod. *hace* and *haz*.

fazer (V. L. *facēre for L. *facĕre*, which is represented by *far* and *fer* somewhat more closely) to do, make, commit, cause, have, **25** 103 *a*; **37** 355 *c*; **43** 22; **45** 10, 19; **46** 21; etc.: pres. 1 *fago* **14** 95 etc.; 3 *face* **10** 94; *faze* **49** 490 *b* etc.; *faz* **48** 14 *d* etc.; *ffaze* **49** 490 *c*; 1 pl. *fazemos* **37** 354 *d*; beside *femos* **18** 1103; 3 pl. *fazen* **18** 1105: impf. 2 *fazies* **21** 20; 3 *fazia* **29** 369 *d* etc.; *fazie* **38** 361 *b* etc.; *fazi* **21** 11: pret. 1 *fizi* **25** 101 *a*; 2 *fecist* **21** 14; *feziste* **61** 18; 3 *fizo* **23** 1 *a* etc.; 2 pl. *fezistes* **70** LIII 5; *fiziestes* **64** 97 *d*; 3 pl. *fizieron* **24** 94 *b*: fut. 1 *fare* **14** 108 etc.; *fazer . . . he* **68** VIII 4; *fer . . . he* **14** 84; 1 pl. *fazer . . . emos* **45** 10; 3 pl. *faran* **21** 24: cond. 1 *faria* **25** 102 *b*; 3 *farie* **31** 12 *d*: sbj. pres. 1 *faga* **11** 114 etc.; 1 pl. *fagamos* **9** 73 etc.; 2 pl. *fagades* **17** 195 etc.: sbj. impf. 3 *fiziesse* **53** 28; 2 pl. *fiziessedes* **43** 31: plpf. 3 *feziera* had made, had done, **61** 21; *fiziera* **52** 14 etc.: imper. 2 *faz* **49** 300 *d*; 2 pl. *fazed* **67** VII 1: p. p. *fecho* **17** 188 etc. Cf. mod. *hacer, hago, haces*, etc., *hacía, hice, haré, haría, haga, hiciese, hiciera, haz, haced, hecho*, etc.

fazi = apocopated form of *fazie*, **21** 11.

fazie = *fazia* with *-a* weakened to *-e* (impf. 3 of *fazer*), **21** 9, 10; **38** 361 *b*; **52** 10.

fazienda (L. *facĕnda*, or V. L. *facĕnda, fem. sg. or ntr. pl. of fut. pass. part. of *facere*, 'thing(s) to be done') business matter, affairs, **29** 1 *a*, 1 *d*; etc.; cf. mod. *hacienda*.

fazies = *fazias* with *-a-* weakened to *-e-* (impf. 2 of *fazer*), **21** 20.

fe (L. *fĭdes, fĭdem* > O. Sp. *fee* > O. Sp. *fe*) faith, pledge, promise, **57** 429 *c*; (pl. L. *fĭdes* > *fees* > *fes*) **15** 120. (Cf. popular *he*; the *f* is due to learned influence.)

fealdad (formation on *feo -a*, analogical to Sp. *lealtad, liberalitad*, O. Sp. *mortaldad*, mod. *mortalidad, mortandad*, all constructed with the L. double suffix *-alĭtas, -alitatem*) ugliness, **70** LII 8.

fecho -a p.p. of *fazer* (L. *factus -a -um*), made, done, caused, **17** 188; **19** 1148; **30** 8 *a*; etc.; n. (L. *factum*) fact, deed, matter, event, affair, **27** 356 *c*; **35** 331 *b*; etc.; cf. mod. *hecho*.

fecist pret. 2 of *fazer* (cf. the more popular form *feziste*), didst, didst do, **21** 14, 18.

fegura (L. *fĭgūra*; the mod. word is the learned *figura*) aspect, appearance, **63** 93 *d*. (In the *José* it is dialectal.)

fembra (L. *fēmĭna* > *femna > by dissimilation *femra, and, with a *b* developed organically in the transition from *m* to *r* > *fembra*) female, woman, **6** 15; cf. mod. *hembra*.

femos pres. 1 pl. of *fer* (L. *facĭmus* > **facmus* > **faimos* > **feymos* > *femos*), we do, **18** 1103; cf. also *fazer*.

fenchistes pret. 2 pl. of *fenchir* (cf. *enchir*), filled, **69** XIX 2.

fĕo -a (L. *foedus -a -um*) nasty, ugly, **48** 16 *d*; **49** 18 *b*.

fer (L. *facĕre* > **facre* > **fagre* > **fayre* > **feyre* > *fer*. The form may have been reconstructed on the analogy of *femos* < *facĭmus* and O. Sp. *feches* < *facĭtĭs*, but the *fere* of the *Glosses* makes this seem unlikely) to do, make, **14** 84; **23** 2 *a, c*, 1 *d*; **24** 96 *c*; **25** 101 *c*; **31** 14 *c*; **50** 498 *a*; **63** 92 *a*. (The form is not restricted, like *far*, at least in great part, to use in the periphrasis forming a future tense or a conditional. Cf. *fazer*.)

ferida (noun from L. fem. p.p. *ferīta* of *ferīre* ' to strike ') blow, wound, **39** 370 *c*; **43** 10. Cf. mod. *herida*.

ferir (L. *ferīre*) to strike, wound, **19** 1130, 1137, 1139; **37** 360 *b*; **38** 351 *b*; **41** 29; **42** 31; **43** 1; **19** 1131. Cf. mod. *herir*.

fermoso -a (L. *formōsus -a -um*, with dissimilation of the initial *o* from the accented *o*, a process helped by the obscuring force of *r*) beautiful, fine, **21** 14; **30** 7 *a*; **35** 328 *c*; etc. Cf. mod. *hermoso -a*.

fermusura = O. Sp. *fermosura*, with assimilation of *o* to the accented *u* (it is a formation, with the abstract ending *-ura*, on the stem of *fermoso -a*), beauty, **60** 10, 16. Cf. mod. *hermosura*.

Fernand = *Fernando*, **44** 7, 14.

Fernando (pr. n.) Ferdinand, **35** 332 *a* etc.

Ferrandez = *Fernández*, pr. n. (with assimilation of *n* to *r*), **40** 9 etc. Cf. mod. *Hernández*.

ferrar (L. *ferrāre*) to shoe, **49** 300 *a*, 301 *b*. Cf. mod. *herrar*.

ferrava = *ferraba* (cf. *ferrar*), **49** 300 *a*.

ferredes = mod. *heriréis* (fut. 2 pl. of *ferir*, L. *fer(i)r(e)* *(hab)ētĭs* ; syncopation of the infin. basis of the fut. and cond. occurred more often in O. Sp. than in mod. Sp.) you shall strike, **19** 1131.

ferrero (L. *ferrarĭus -a -um* ' of iron ' ; *faber ferrarĭus* ' smith ') smith, **49** 300 *d*. Cf. mod. *herrero*.

ferrida = *ferida*, **38** 366 *a*.

feryr = *ferir*, **39** 369 *c, d*, 370 *b* ; 371 *a*.

festir = *vestir* < L. *vestīre*, **22** 37.

feziera (L. plpf. indic. *fēc-ĕrat* with the ending of the 4th conj. *-ĭvĕrat*. In O. Sp. the form is usually still indic. plpf. or pret., as in the cases here ; in mod. Sp. the *-ra* forms are more often sbj. impf.) had made, had done, **61** 21 ; **62** 8. Cf. *fiziera*.

feziste (L. *fēc-* + *-isti*, ending of 4th conj. ; the *i* of mod. *hiciste*, *hicisteis*, etc. is due to the analogy of *hice* and *hicieron*, in which it was phonetically developed) pret. 2 of *fazer*, **61** 18.

fezistes (cf. *feziste*; L. *fēc-* + *-ístís*. In mod. *hicisteis*, the last *i* is analogical to that of *hacéis* and like forms) pret. 2 pl. of *fazer*, **70** LIII 5.

ffablar = *fablar* speech, converse, **48** 15 *d*.

ffaze = *faze* (cf. *fazer*), **49** 490 *c*.

fferio = *ferió* (cf. *ferir*), **37** 360 *b*.

ffin = *fin* (L. *finis -em*) end, **62** 25.

ffollya = *folia* (L. *follis*, *fŏllem*, whence O. Sp. *fol* + abstract *-ia*; the form is learned) folly, **51** 1663 *j*.

fiar (V. L. **fīdāre* from *fīdus*, instead of L. *fīdĕre*) to trust, **18** 1112; **19** 1133; **28** 365 *d*.

fidalgo (O. Sp. *fijo*; shortened to *fi-* in composition, + *de* + *algo*. The last was a noun meaning 'property,' 'means,' as well as a pron. in O. Sp.) noble, **50** 491 *b*. Cf. mod. *hidalgo*.

fiel (*fĭdēlis -em*) faithful, **17** 204.

fierament, fiera mente (cf. *fiero* and *mente*; the latter shows learned treatment) fiercely, terribly, bitterly, **28** 361 *b*; **54** 21.

fiero -a (L. *fĕrus -a -um*) fierce, terrible, **27** 355 *b*.

fierro (L. *fĕrrum*) iron; pl. fetters, **27** 355 *a*; **29** 369 *a*; etc. Cf. mod. *hierro*.

fiesta (L. ntr. pl. *fĕsta* from *fĕstum*; or the adj. *festus -a -um*, as in *dies festa*) feast, holy day, **21** 22.

figo (L. *fīcus -um*) fig, **6** 8.

figura (learned word; L. *fĭgūra*) figure, manner, way, **34** 84 *b*. Cf. *fegura*.

fiio = *fijo*, **32** 19 *c*.

fija (L. *fīlĭa*) daughter, maiden, **32** 19 *c*; **47** 2; mod. *hija*.

fijo (L. *fīlĭum*) son, boy; pl. sons, children, **26** 111 *c*, 112 *b*; etc.; mod. *hijo*.

fillo (western dialect form = *fijo*) **31** 17 *b*.

filosofo (learned word; L. *phĭlŏsŏphus*) philosopher, **62** 13.

finar (V. L. **fīnāre* based on L. *finis -em*) to die, **26** 111 *b*.

fincar (V. L. **fĭgĭcāre* based on L. *fīgĕre*. For Sp. we must suppose rather a V. L. **fingicare*, with that same *n* infix which occurs in L. in *fingere*, *pingere*, etc.) to fix, pitch (tents), **18** 1101; *fincando los ynojos* bending the knees, **60** 6; to remain, be left, **27** 358 *d*; **24** 93 *d*; **38** 367 *b*; etc. Cf. mod. *hincar*, used only in the transitive sense.

fincaredes = mod. *hincaréis* (fut. 2 pl. of *fincar*) you shall remain, **58** 435 *c*.

fincarie = *fincaria* (cond. 3 of *fincar*) would remain, **44** 16.

fincauan = *fincavan*, mod. *hincaban* (impf. 3 pl. of *fincar*), **25** 104 *c*.

fincol = *fincó*, from *fincar*, + the art. *el*, **38** 367 *b*.

finiestra (L. *fĕnĕstra* > *feniestra*, and, under the closing influence of the *i̯* > *finiestra*) window,

13 17; **47** 14. (It is now obs.; the mod. word is *ventana*.)

fino -a (V. L. **fīnus -a -um*; perhaps connected with L. *fīnītus -a -um*, 'finished,' 'polished,' 'fine,' especially of phraseology) fine, pure, **22** 35; **30** 3 *d*, 8 *c*; etc.

firades = mod. *hiráis* (L. *fĕrĭatĭs*; the initial *i* is due to the closing force of the *ị*), pres. sbj. 2 pl. of *ferir*, **19** 1130; **43** 1.

firio = mod. *hirió* (cf. *ferir*), **40**.

firme (perhaps learned word; cf. L. *firmus -a -um*, Fr. *ferme*, etc.) : *firme mientre* firmly, thoroughly, **18** 1121.

fito (L. *fīctus -um*, p.p. of *fingere* and related to *fīgĕre*) fixed, fixedly, regular, thorough, firm, firmly, **25** 105 *c*; **49** 300 *b*.

fizi (L. *fēcī*; the final *ī* closed the accented *ē*, whence *fizi*, which, except for its appearance in dialects, became *fize*, when final unaccented *i* opened regularly to *e*) pret. 1 of *fazer*, **25** 101 *a*.

fiziera plpf. 3 of *fazer* (cf. *feziera*, whose initial *e* > *i* under the influence of the following *ị*), had made, made, had done, done, **41** 24; **52** 14, 19; **53** 2; etc.; cf. mod. *hiciera*.

fizieron pret. 3 pl. of *fazer*, **24** 94 *b*; **45** 23; etc.; cf. mod. *hicieron*.

fiziesse impf. sbj. 3 of *fazer*, **53** 28; cf. mod. *hiciese*.

fiziessedes impf. sbj. 2 pl. of *fazer*, **43** 31 ; cf. mod. *hicieseis*.

fiziestes (L. pret. stem *fēc*- + ending of 4th conj. -*īstĭs* for -*ivistis* should have given *fezistes*. The initial *i* is due to the analogy of 1 *fize*, 3 pl. *fizieron*, etc.; the diphthong -*ie*- shows the influence of the accented syll. of *fizieron*, etc.) pret. 2 pl. of *fazer*, **64** 97 *d*; cf. mod. *hicisteis*.

fizo pret. 3 of *fazer* (L. *fēcĭt*, the *i* shows the analogy of 1 *fize*, etc.; the -*o*, common to all strong pret. 3 may have arisen in the 4th conj. -*īvit* > -*iut* > *io* or in such forms as V. L. **venŭit*, whence O. Sp. *veno*), **23** 1 *a*; **25** 98 *b*; etc.

flablar = *fablar* (with anticipation of the *l*), **14** 104.

flaco -a (L. *flaccus -a -um*; perhaps not wholly popular; cf. *flamma* > Sp. *llama*) thin, lean, spare, **65** 104 *b*.

flameante (pres. part. adj. from *flamear*, based on L. *flamma* and verbal ending -*ear*, V. L. -*ĭdĭare*) flaming, **31** 16 *d*. (The more popular form is *llameante*.)

flor (L. *flos*, *flōrem*) flower, **47** 1, 7 ; etc. (The retention of initial *fl*- here makes one doubt that the combination regularly became *ll*- in popular treatment; cf. *flaco* and *flameante*.)

foja (L. *fŏlĭa*, ntr. pl. of *fŏlĭum*; this ntr. pl. became a fem. sg. as of the first declension; the palatal sound following closed the *ŏ* and prevented its diphthongization) leaf, page, **60** 12 ; **70** XLIII 4.

folgança (formation in *-ança*, V. L. *-antĭa*, on the stem of *folgar*) recreation, delight, **60** 27 ; cf. mod. *holganza*.

folgar (said to be a formation on L. *fŏllis* 'bellows,' whence the sense of 'fool,' 'merry fellow,' because the fool or clown puffs out his cheeks like a bellows. So L. L. *fŏllĭcare* was framed, 'to play the fool,' 'have recreation,' 'rest,' and thence *folgar*, mod. *holgar*, with the latter two senses) to rest, have recreation, **35** 334 *a* ; **36** 342 *a, b*.

folgura (formation in *-ūra* on the stem of *folgar*) rest, recreation, ease, delight, **35** 335 *b* ; **70** LII 7 ; **71** LXXIX 6 ; cf. *folgança* and mod. *holgura*.

forçado p.p. of *forçar* (V.L. *fŏrtĭare*, based on L. *fortis*) used with adverbial force (= mod. *forzoso -a*, *forzosamente*), perforce, of necessity, **67** v 8.

fossar (formation on L. *fossa*, mod. Sp. *huesa* ; cf. also O. Sp. *fossal*, of which *fossar* may be a variant) graveyard, cemetery, **26** 111 *c*.

foyr = *foir* (L. *fŭgĕre*, V. L. *fŭgīre* ; the *u* of mod. *huir* is due to the analogy of *fugiámus* > *fuyamus*, *huyamus* and similar forms which spread the *u* throughout the verb) to flee, **45** 8 ; p.p. *foydos -as* (with *fueron* as aux.), **38** 366 *c*, 367 *a*.

fradre (L. *frater, fratrem*) brother (in ecclesiastical sense), friar, **24** 91 *a*.

fradrear (*fradre* + verbal ending *-ear*) to become a friar, **26** 111 *a*.

frayre = *fraire* (perhaps a loan-word from Provençal *fraire* ; thence, by dissimilation the form *fraile* ; or the form may be dialectal) friar, brother, **25** 104 *b* ; **68** VIII 5 ; cf. *fradre*.

frecha (Dutch *flits* ? or Irish *flesc* ? The ety. is unknown) arrow, shaft, **66** I 8 ; cf. mod. *flecha*.

freno (L. *frēnum*) bit, **22** 34.

frío -a (L. *frīgĭdus -a -um*) cold, **49** 301 *d* etc.

frontera (formation in *-arĭa* on L. *frons, frontem*) frontier, **23** 3 *d*.

fror = *flor* (with attraction of *l* to the final *r* ; the form is Western Sp.) flower, **51** 1664 *h*.

fructo (learned spelling of *fruto*, L. *frŭctus -um*) fruit, **47** 5.

fu = *fue* (with an O. Sp. apocopation of final-*e*, which was possible while the accent was still on the *u* ; L. *fŭĭt*), **7** 34.

fue pret. 3 of *ser* (L. *fŭĭt*), was, **14** 111, 112 ; **18** 1117 ; etc. ; aux. of verb of motion, *fue entrado*, **14** 109 ; *fue ydo*, **35** 332 *d* ; with the force of *estuvo*, pret. of *estar*, **38** 367 *c* ; **39** 368 *a* ; **53** 14 ; etc. ; pret. of *ir* 'to go,' **18** 1118 ; **25** 105 *a* ; **37** 359 *d* ; **39** 369 *c* ; etc. ; *fuesse* and *fuese* = *fue* + *se*, went off, **42** 27, 4 ; **47** 17 ; **53** 6. (The mod. *fué* shows a shift of accent, which had not been accomplished in the earliest O. Sp., as *fu* and similar forms show.)

ruego (L. *fŏcus -um*) fire, **29** 2 *a*; **59** 5.

fuera (L. *fŏras*. This seems to have given an O. Sp. *fueras*, of which *fuera* may be a back formation) (adv.) out, outside, **21** 7; **58** 435 *a*; (prep.) except, **24** 92 *d*; *fuera de* away from, out of, outside of, beyond, **62** 4; **70** LIII 6; *de fuera* outside, outwardly, **49** 17 *a*; **61** 12, 13.

fuera (L. *fŭĕrat*, plpf. 3 of *esse*; in O. Sp. the sense may be plpf. or pret. indic. or impf. sbj.) had been, was, **42** 24, 25; **46** 4; **54** 10; **55** 8; (after *si*) **63** 91 *a*; cf. *ser* and *fue*.

fueran (L. *fŭĕrant*; cf. *fuera*; the O. Sp. sense is that of the plpf. or pret. indic. and perhaps impf. sbj. of *ser*) had been, were, **30** 6 *d*; (as aux. of verb of motion) *fueran se tornados*, **34** 81 *c*; (after *sy*, *si*) **37** 353 *c*; cf. *fue*.

fuerça (L. *fŏrtĭa* from *fŏrtis*) force, dint, **35** 333 *d*; **68** VIII 3; **69** XVIII 4.

fuere (L. *fŭĕrĭt*, fut. perf. indic. and perf. sbj. 3 of *esse*, become in Sp. a fut. sbj.) **14** 92; cf. *fue*.

fueres (L. *fŭĕrĭs*, fut. perf. indic. and perf. sbj. of *esse*, become in Sp. a fut. sbj.) thou go, **61** 13; cf. *fue*.

fuero (L. *fŏrŭm* 'place of justice,' therefore, by transferal of sense, 'law') law, privilege, **69** XLII 6.

fueron (L. *fŭĕrŭnt*, perf. 3 pl. of *esse*) were, **27** 360 *a*; **32** 20 *d*; etc.; (aux. of verb of motion) **33** 71 *b* and *d*; **38** 366 *c*, 367 *a*;

(pret. indic. of *ir* 'to go') **27** 360 *b*; **28** 366 *a*; **34** 77 *c*; etc.; *fueronse* went off, **42** 10.

fuert cf. *fuerte* **21** 7.

fuerte (L. *fŏrtis -em*) strong, violent, **37** 356 *b*; **66** I 5; *fuert mientre*, *fuerte mientre* strongly, violently, bitterly, **13** 1; **21** 7; (adv.) violently, **42** 24; **49** 301 *c*.

fues (L. *fŭĭste* > *fuĕste* > *fuĕste* > *fuest* > *fues*; pret. 2 of *ser*) thou wast, **64** 94 *c*, 97 *c*. (The form occurs in an Eastern Sp. document.)

fues (apocopation of *fuesse*, *fuese*) **37** 356 *d*.

fuese = O. Sp. impf. sbj. *fuesse*, **37** 356 *d*; **59** 17.

fuese = *fue* + *se*, went off, **42** 27.

fuesen = earlier O. Sp. *fuessen*, **29** 1 *b*, *c*; **65** 107 *d*; etc.

fuesse (= *fue* + *se*; the *s* was doubled to indicate the retention intervocally of the originally initial voiceless *s* of *se*) went off, **42** 4; **47** 17; **53** 6; cf. *fuese* and *fue*.

fuesse (L. *fŭĭsset*; impf. sbj. 3 of *ser* and *ir*) should be, should go, **24** 97 *d*; **33** 75 *c*; **44** 16; **46** 21; cf. mod. *fuese*.

fuessedes (L. *fŭĭssētĭs*, which has a recessive accent by analogy of sg. forms and 3 pl. Thence > **fuéssees* > *fuéseis* in mod. Sp.) impf. sbj. of *ser* and *ir*, **43** 30.

fuessen (L. *fŭĭssent*) impf. sbj. 3 pl. of *ser* and *ir*, should be, should go, **16** 164; **38** 361 *c*; **44** 10; **27** 359 *b*; cf. *fuesen* and *fue*.

fuest (cf. *fues*) thou wast, **21** 25.

fure (scribal for *fuere*) **6** 17; **8** 69; **9** 70.

fust (by-form of *fuest*, which occurs in the same document) thou didst go, **21** 16. (Cf. *fu*, *fo*, etc.; the form is analogical to them as to its accent.)

fyera = *fiera* (cf. *fiero -a*) fierce, terrible, **38** 363 *b*.

fyjo = *fijo*, **36** 351 *d*.

fyn=*fin* end, **37** 353 *d*; **71** LXXIX 5.

fyncaron = *fincaron* (cf. *fincar*) were left, remained, **35** 330 *c*.

fyrie = *fería*, impf. 3 of *ferir*, **38** 361 *b*. (The *y*, i.e. *i*, is due to the analogy of *firió*, etc.)

fyrme = *firme* firm, resolute, **36** 345 *b*.

fyzieron = *fizieron*, **37** 353 *b*.

fyzo = *fizo*, **33** 74 *b*.

[O.Sp. *g* before *e* and *i* was pronounced like English *g* in *gem*.]

galardon (cf. *gualardon*) guerdon, reward, **23** 4 *d*.

Gallizia pr. n. (L. *Galicia*), Galicia, **41** 3.

gallo (L. *gallus -um*) cock, **16** 169.

ganado (a noun from p.p. of *ganar*) flock, herd, **26** 110 *b*. (The sense may have developed in the days of cattle-lifting and foraging, when the *gains* were often cattle. It may have arisen in business exchange; cf. L. *pecus* and *pecunia*.)

ganançia (learned word; formation in *-ancia*, L. *-antia*, on stem of verb *ganar*) gain, profit, yield,

results, **15** 130; **16** 165; **26** 106 *d*; **27** 358 *a*; etc.

ganar (Ety. ? Cf. Murray's Eng. Dict. s.v. *gain*. Argues for a Common Romance *guadaniare*, whence Fr. *gagner*, Ital. *guadagnare*, Sp. *guadañar* 'to mow.' This Com. Rom. he equates with an O.H.G. *weidinjan* [recorded as *weidenen*] used for (1) 'to graze,' 'pasture,' (2) 'to forage,' 'hunt,' etc.) to gain, **14** 101; **15** 123; **17** 190; etc.; cf. *gañar*.

gañar (cf. *ganar*. The *Cid* uses *ganar* and *gañar* side by side. The *ñ* is the form expected; cf. Fr. *gagner*, Ital. *guadagnare*) to gain, **15** 124; **18** 1092; **20** 1212.

Garçi pr. n. (= *Garcia* shortened in combination with a following patronymic), **40** 9.

gargantero -a (formation in *-ero -era*, L. *-arius -a -um*, on Sp. *garganta* from the onomatopoetic *garg*; cf. English 'gargle') gluttonous, greedy, **49** 299 *a*.

gascon (pr. n.) Gascon, **36** 352 *c* etc.

Gasconna = mod. *Gascuña* (pr. n.) Gascony, **41** 4.

ge (regularly prefixed to another pronoun, *gela*, *gelo*, *gele*, *gelos*, *gelas*; L. dative *illi* + acc. *illum*, *illam*, *illos*, *illas*; [*il*]*li illŭm* > *lyelo* (like Ital. *glielo*) whence *telo*, *yelo* and then *gelo*) to him, to her, to it, to them, **14** 92; **15** 136; **16** 151; **20** 1210; **19** 1134; **27** 355 *d*; etc.; cf. mod. *selo*, *sela*, etc. See *sele*.

* *furtarse* — see Corrections p. 176a

gemjdo =*gemido* (half-learned word, L. *gemĭtus -um*, V. L. **gemūtus -um* with the ending of p.p. of 4th conj.; cf. *gemir* ' to groan ') groan, moan, **69** XVIII 7.

general (learned word ; L. *generalis -em*) general, **66**.

gent (apocopation of *gente*) **27** 354 *b*.

✓ **gente** (L. *gens*, *gĕntem*, which should have given **yiente*, whence popular O. Sp. and popular mod. *yente*; learned influence has restored the *g*) race, people, household, men, **33** 71 *c*, 74 *a* ; **36** 342 *a* ; etc. ; (pl.) Gentiles, nations, **6** 6 ; **7** 42 ; etc.

gera = *guerra*, **9** 85.

gesta (learned word ; L. ntr. pl. *gesta*, which became a fem. sg.) deeds, exploits, song, epic (cf. Fr. *geste*), **17** 1085.

Getarea pr. n., **35** 329 *d*.

gigante (learned word ; L. *gĭgas*, *gigantem*) giant, **66** I 5.

✓ **glera** (L. *glarĕa* ; the more popular treatment of initial *gl-* seems to have produced *l-*, cf. *landre* and Ptg. *leira*) gravel, gravel-covered place, strand, **37** 359 *c* ; **41** 15.

gloria (learned word ; L. *glōrĭa*) bliss, glory, **71** LXXVIII 7.

glorioso -a (learned word ; L. *gloriosus -a -um*) glorious, blessed, **50** 1661 *a* ; *la Gloriosa* the Glorious One, the Virgin, **25** 103 *a*.

Golias (pr. n.) Goliath, **38** 351 *c*.

goloso -a (L. *gŭlōsus -a -um*) gluttonous, **49** 298 *c*.

golpe (by-form of *colpe* ; a weak utterance of the voiceless guttural may have produced the form with *g*. Baist deems it an imperfectly heard form of Fr. and Prov. *colp*) blow, **34** 79 *a* ; **39** 370 *b*. (The more usual O. Sp. form keeps the *c*.)

Gonçalez pr. n., **33** title ; **44** 14 ; cf. *Gonçaluez*, **44** 7.

Gonçalo pr. n., **26** 109 *a* ; **44** 21 ; cf. *Gonçaluo*, **40** 13 etc.

Gonçaluez = *Gonçalvez*, **44** 7 ; cf. *Gonçalez*.

Gonçaluo = *Gonçalvo*, **40** 13 etc. ; cf. *Gonçalo*.

gordo -a (L. *gŭrdus -a -um*) fat, sleek, **49** 298 *a* ; **65** 104 *a*.

gostar (L. *gŭstare*, which gave usual Sp. *gustar*; the present form requires V. L. *gŭstare* ; cf. Ital. *gustare* and Fr. *goûter*) to taste, **67** V 3.

gouernar = *governar*, mod. *gobernar* (L. *gŭbernare*), to care for, attend to, **31** 18 *d*.

gozo (L. *gaudĭum* ? L. *[ne]gŏtium* for *otium* ? V. L. *gŭstus -um* ? ? The etymon is uncertain) joy, **16** 170 ; **19** 1146 ; **20** 1211 ; etc.

graçia (learned word ; L. *gratĭa*) grace, **25** 101 *a* ; **48** 12 *b* ; etc. ; (pl.) thanks, **26** 110 *d* etc.

gradar (V. L. **gratare* from L. *gratus -a -um*) : *gradarse con* to delight in, **16** 172 ; *grado* he was glad, **17** 200. (In the expressions *Grado a Dios*, *grado a ti*, **18** 1102, 1118 ; **13** 8, we may have the verb ' to thank,' or the noun *grado*.)

gradeçer (V. L. *gratescēre* based on L. *gratus -a -um*) to thank, **17** 199.

gradesçer = *gradeçer* (the *s* was absorbed by the following ç = *ts*) to thank, reward, **28** 362 *d*.

grado (noun derived from L. adj. *gratus -a -um*) liking, pleasure, **25** 102 *d*; *a nuestro grado*, **18** 1117; *de grado* gladly, willingly, **15** 136; **16** 149; **27** 355 *d*; **58** 436 *a*; etc.; *de su buen grado* very willingly on their part, **66** 11; *de grado* at my will, **14** 84.

grafil (formation in *-il*, L. *-ilis -ilem*, on L. *graphĭum*, Gk. γρα-φίον 'writing stylus') engraving tool, **30** 9 *c*.

graja (L. *gracŭla*) jay, jackdaw, **32** 21 *d*.

✓ **gramatgos** (half-learned word; L. *grammatĭcus -os*) grammarians, **11** 122.

grameo cf. *engrameo*, **13** 13.

gran (apocopation of *grande*. This lost its *e*; then *grand* assimilated its *d*, in close syntactical connection, to the initial consonant of the following word. Later *gran* was extended to use before a word beginning with a vowel) grand, great, **15** 120; **42** 20; **59** 3; **60** 15; **64** 95 *d*, 100 *c*.

granado -a (perhaps a formation in *-ado*, L. p.p. ending *-atus -a- um*, on *grano*, i.e. 'grained,' 'full of grain,' 'perfect') full of grain, excellent, **65** 107 *a*; splendid, fine, large, important, **31** 17 *d*; **57** 428 *a*; **65** 103 *b* and *c*; **65** 104 *c*.

grand (apocopation of *grande* in close syntactical relation to an immediately following word of which it is an attribute; later it became *gran*) **10** 92; **19** 1139; **40** 8; **41** 13, 22; etc.; (in the predicate, before the copula *es*) **19** 1146. Cf. **grande**. ✓

grande (L. *grandis -em*; generally after a noun or in the predicate position in O. Sp.) grand, great, **60** 9, 18; **63** 89 *d*; **64** 95 *c*. ✓

grandes pl. of *grande*, *grand*, *grant*, *gran*, **13** 6 etc.

grano (L. *granum*) grain, corn, **65** 105 *a*.

grant (form assumed by *grand* before a word beginning with a voiceless consonant, or in the absolute *Auslaut*, where the *d* unvoiced to *t*. The scribes sometimes used the form in other than these original conditions and sometimes used *grand* for *grant*) **9** 85; **15** 125; **21** 4; **24** 92; **27** 357 *a*; **52** 2; **54** 22; etc.

graue = *grave* (L. *gravis -em*) heavy, burdensome, **26** 107 *d*.

greçisco -a (V. L. *Graecĭscus -a -um*, based on L. *Graecus* + ending *-iscus*) Greek, **31** 11 *b*. (Cf. mod. *Gregüescos* and *greguisco -a*, which follow *griego -a*.)

griego -a (L. *Graecus -a -um*) Greek, **31** 18 *b*.

grifon (augmentative in *-on*, L. *-onem*, of L. *grȳphus -um*) large griffin, **31** 13 *c*.

grrado = *grado*, **37** 358 *c*.

grran = *gran*, **36** 345 *c* etc.

grrand = *grand*, **34** 84 *c* ; **35** 331 *a* ; etc.

grrande = *grande*, **36** 345 *d*.

grujllo = *grillo* (L. *grȳllus -um* 'cricket'; thieves' slang or some onomatopoetic suggestion may explain the change of sense. Or the word may be connected with Fr. *grille* from L. *craticula*, in which case the resemblance in shape of the instruments may explain the term) gyves, fetters, **50** 497 *b*.

guadalmeçi (cf. *guadameçi*) **14** 87.

guadameçi (Arab. *wadameçi*? ; the term is supposed to be related to the name of the town *Gadames* in Tripoli, where this leather was prepared. But?) a kind of leather, **14** 88.

Guadiana pr. n., **34** 78 *d*.

gualardon (Germanic *wiðarlōn* 'counter, i.e. equal, reward.' The second part of the compound, *lōn*, mod. German *Lohn*, has been replaced by *don*, L. *donum*, of the same sense ; for the first element we may suspect, as Alfonso X seems to do in the *Siete Partidas*, that O. Sp. *egual*, mod. *igual*, has influenced its form) guerdon, reward, **23** 43. (Cf. *galardon*, which is the usual mod. form.)

Gualdabuey pr. n. **36** 352 *b*. (Cf. Marden : " Gandebaldus, King of Frisia, in the Chronicle of Turpin.")

guardador (an agent formation in *-or*, L. *-or -orem*, on *guardar*,

guardado) guardian, jailer, **28** 367 *d*.

guardar (Germanic stem **ward-* ; cf. O.H.G. *warta* 'guard') to guard, keep, **30** 4 *d* ; **32** 20 *c* ; etc. ; *guardaban* respected, **63** 93 *c*.

guardarien = *guardarian*, **16** 162.

guardastes = *guardasteis*, **70** LIII 2.

guardaua = *guardava*, *guardaba*, **53** 1.

guaresçer = mod. *guarecer* (an inceptive formation on Germanic *warjan* 'to defend,' hence 'to ward off [an illness] ') to be cured, get well, **36** 338 *c*.

guarir (Germanic *warjan* adapted to the 4th conj. ; cf. *guaresçer*. It is obsolete) to be cured, recover, **63** 89 *c*, 90 *c*.

guarniçion (learned formation in *-icion*, L. *-itio -itionem*, on the verb *guarnir*) accouterment, armor, **38** 361 *c*.

guarnimento (formation in *-mento*, L. *-mĕntum*, on *guarnir*) adornment, raiment, **22** 36.

guarnir (Germanic **warnjan* 'to equip,' adapted to the 4th conj.) to supply, array, accouter, **34** 82 *b* ; **39** 368 *d* ; cf. mod. *guarnecer*.

guera = *guerra*, **7** 24.

guerra (Germanic *werra* 'war') war, **45** 17 etc.

guerrear (formation in *-ear*, V. L. *-idiare*, on *guerra*) to make war, **18** 1090.

guerrero (formation in *-ero*, L. *-arius -um*, on *guerra*) warrior, **39** 370 *a*.

guiar (Germanic *wîtan* 'to see, observe') to guide, **64** 95 *b*.

guisa (Germanic *wîsa* 'way,' 'wise') way, wise, manner, **14** 102; **15** 131; **21** 9; etc.; *a guisa de* after the fashion of, **14** 102 etc.; *de guisa que* so that, **42** 21 etc.; *guisa* (adv.) in the manner, **21** 9; *syn guisa* extraordinary, **34** 77 *b*.

guisado -a (p.p. of *guisar*) prepared, adapted, appropriate, proper, **14** 92; **15** 118; etc.

guisar (based on *guisa*) to direct, arrange, prepare, **28** 366*a*; **33** 72*a*; **40** 17.

guja = *guia* (imper. sg. of *guiar*), **51** 1665 *j*.

gujña = *guiña* (pres. 3 of *guiñar*, Germanic *winkjan*, Eng. *wink*), winks, **50** 499 *d*.

gujsa = *guisa*, **29** 370 *d*.

guyades = mod. *guiáis* (cf. *guiar*) you attend to, look after, **28** 365 *b*.

guyar = *guiar*, **26** 289 *d*.

Gybraltar = *Gibraltar* (Arab. *Ǵibel Tarik* 'Tarik's Hill'), pr. n., **33** 72 *c*.

ha (V. L. **hat* for L. *habet*, shortened in proclitic use; cf. *a*) has (aux. in perf. tense), **15** 115; **17** 192; etc.; has (in independent use with a direct object = mod. *tiene*), **20** 1193; **50** 491 *d*; **52** 1; etc.; ago (in impersonal use), **57** 427 *a*; (a separable element of the fut. indic.) *dexar las ha* he will leave them, **15** 117; *ha de*

+ an infin., has to + an infin., **19** 1136; **56** 423 *b*; cf. *aver*.

Hamihala ? **12** 138.

han (V. L. **hant* for L. *habent*, shortened in proclitic use) have (aux. in perf. tense), **18** 1119; **35** 331 *d*; have (in independent use = *tienen*), **43** 27; *han de* + infin., have to (should) + infin., **43** 32; *de morir han forçado* must die, **67** v 8; cf. *aver*.

handan = *andan* (cf. *andar*), **70** LIII 6.

hanparad = *amparad* (cf. *anparar*) protect, **69** XVIII 4.

hart = *arte* (L. *ars*, *artem*) stratagem, artifice, **20** 1204.

hata (Arab. *ḥatta*) up to, as far as, **7** 26.

he = *hé* (L. imper. *habe* 'have thou,' shortened in proclitic use to **hae*; or L. *habete*; or L. imper. *vĭde* 'see thou.' The ety. is not clear) behold, **11** 127; **47** 11, 13, 15. Cf. Notes.

he (L. *habeo*; shortened to V. L. *hae[o]*, *hay[o]*, in proclitic use; > **hey* > *he*; cf. *e*) I have (aux. in perf. tense), **17** 207; **37** 353 *a*; etc.; I have (independent use = *tengo*), **58** 438 *d*; **69** XLII 5; (separable element of the fut. indic.) **13** 80; **14** 84, 92; **48** 15 *b*; etc.; cf. *e*.

hedes = *-éis* (L. [*hab*]-*ētĭs*, used as a separable element of the fut. 2 pl.): *merecer nolo hedes* = *nos lo mereceréis*, **17** 197; *dar lo hedes* = *lo daréis*, **58** 442 *d*. (The form may be deemed analogical to *hemos*.)

heredades (L. *hērēdĭtas*, pl. *hērēdĭtates*) estates, fields, **15** 115; **26** 108 *a*.

hermana (L. *gĕrmāna*) sister, **40** 11.

hermano (L. *gĕrmānus -um*) brother, **27** 36ᴄ *a*; **42** 2.

hes = *es*, **61** 10.

homne = *hombre* (L. *hŏmo, hŏmĭnem*, treated as a proclitic) man, **8** 65; cf. *omne*.

honesto -a (a learned word; L. *hŏnĕstus -a -um*) honorable, **25** 103 *b*.

honor (L. *hŏnor, hŏnōrem*) honor, **26** 109 *a*.

honrrado = *honrado* (L. *hŏn[ō]rātus -um*) honorable, **67** v 1.

hopa (ety. unknown, possibly Germanic; cf. Fr. *houppelande*) cassock, gown, **57** 433 *c*.

hora (L. *hōra*) hour, **29** 371 *a*.

hordenar = *ordenar* (L. *ōrdĭnāre*) to order, put in order, draw up, **67** vii 2.

huebos (L. *ŏpŭs*, with *h* prefixed to the initial diphthong) need; *huebos me serie* it would be needful for me, **14** 82; *huebos auemos* we have need, **15** 123, 128.

Huesca pr. n., **18** 1089.

hueste (L. *hŏstis, hŏstem*) host, enemy, army, **31** 18 *a* and *d*; **44** 15.

humano -a (L. *hūmānus -a -um*) human, **10** 95.

huuyar = *uviar* (mod. *obviar*; L. *ŏbvĭāre*; in the unaccented position, *o* > *u* under the influence of the following *i̯* or *y*, as in *ŏbvĭāre* > **ovi̯ár* > *uviar*) to go to meet, succor, relieve, **20** 1208.

hyremos = *iremos* (cf. *ir*), **19** 1124.

[In O. Sp. script *i* may stand not only for the vowel *i*, but also for *y* and *j*.]

i = *y* (L. *hīc*) there, **10** 96; **21** 2, 20.

i = mod. *y* (L. *et* in proclisis and enclisis) and, **6** 14; **7** 24; etc. (It appears regularly in the *Misterio* and frequently in the transliterated *José*.) Cf. *et*.

ia = *ya* (L. *jam*) already, now, **10** 88; **11** 114.

iace = *yace* (L. *jacet*) lies, is, **11** 125.

iaz (apocopation of *iace*, more properly O. Sp. *yaze*) **20** 1209; **27** 356 *b*.

ides (L. *ītĭs*) pres. 2 pl. of *ir*, **9** 79; cf. mod. *vais*.

ie (a mistake for *e* or rather an early Western form) and, **22** 30.

Ieremias pr. n., **12** 141.

iglesia (half-learned; L. *eclēsĭa* for *ecclesia*) church, **24** 91 *b*.

Iherusalem (pr. n.) Jerusalem, **47** 8.

illada (Aragonese form; Castilian *ijada*, L. *īlĭa*, ntr. pl. treated as fem. sg., whence V. L. *īlĭāta*) flank, **65** 104 *d*.

imos (L. *īmŭs*) pres. 1 pl. of *ir*, **8** 63; **9** 77; cf. mod. *vamos*.

imperio (learned word; L. *ĭmpĕrĭŭm*) rule, imperial sway, **44** 4.

in (L. *ĭn*, Castilian *en*; it is a Latinism in the *Misterio*, which has also *en*) in **6** 16; **7** 26, 36; etc.

infançon (L. *infans*, V. L. **infantio, *infantionem*; cf. L. *infantia*) noble, **38** 362 *b*.

inffante (mod. *infante*; L. *infans*, *infantem*) young noble, **40** 14; **42** 27; **43** 1 5, 20.

inpotente = *impotente* (learned word; L. *impotens*, *impotĕntem*) impotent, **67** III 3.

io = *yo* (L. *ĕgo*, V. L. **eo*), **6** 11; **7** 37; etc.; **21** 1 5; **66** I 1.

iogar (L. *jŏcari*, V. L. **jŏcāre*) to play, **41** 11; cf. mod. *jugar*.

ioglar (L. *jŏcŭlāris*, *jŏcŭlārem* 'facetious') minstrel, juggler, **26** 289 *d*; **41** 12; cf. mod. *juglar*.

Iosafat (pr. n.) Josaphat, **60** 7.

Iosaphat (pr. n.) Josaphat, **59**.

ir (L. *īre*) to go, **8** 61; **6** 17; etc.; *ides*, pres. 2 pl. (L. *ītis*), **9** 79; *imos*, pres. 1 pl. (L. *īmŭs*), **8** 63; **9** 77. Except for the sporadic *imos*, *ides*, *īre* did not keep its own pres. indic. or pres. sbj. in Sp.; it borrowed the forms from L. *vadĕre*. It also lost its pret. tenses and supplied these from *esse*. Cf. *vo*, *vas*, *vamos*, *fue*, *fuesse*, etc.

iuan = *ivan*, mod. *iban* (L. *ībant*), impf. 3 pl. of *ir*, **30** 6 *a*; **31** 16 *a*.

iuas = *ivas*, mod. *ibas* (L. *ības*), impf. 2 of *ir*, **21** 19.

iuego = *juego* (L. *jŏcus*, *jŏcum*) game, **41** 32.

iugara = *jugara* (regular O. Sp. *judgara*, mod. *juzgará*, fut. 3 of *judgar*, *juzgar*, L. *jūdĭcāre*) will judge, **7** 43.

iuntado = *juntado*, p.p. of *juntar* (L. *jŭnctare*, with *u* closed by adjoining palatals), assembled, **18** 1113.

iura = *jura* (abstract from *jurar*, L. *jūrāre*) oath, **15** 120.

iurado = *jurado* (p.p. of *jurar*; cf. *iura*) sworn, **16** 163.

iure ? **21** 22.

ixiria (cond. 1 of O. Sp. *exir*, L. *exīre*) I should go forth, **25** 101 *d*. (The initial *i* is due to *ixieron* and such forms.)

ixo (pret. 3 of O. Sp. *exir*; cf. *ixiria*) he went forth, **25** 104 *a*.

[In O. Sp. *j* was pronounced like the English *j*.]

j = *i* (L. *hīc*) there, **21** 16.

jamas (L. *jam* + *magis*) ever, **70** LII 4; (with negative) never, **71** LXXVIII 5; **36** 347 *d*.

Jaymes (pr. n.) Jaime, **52** 9.

jazer (see *yazer*, the more popular form) to lie, **21** 6; **63** 91 *a*; **64** 97 *d*.

jfant = *ifant*, *iffante*, mod. *infante* (L. *ĭnfans*, *ĭnfantem*, V. L. **īfantem*) child, **21** 9.

Johan (L. *Johannes*, *Johannem*) John, **55** 29; cf. mod. *Juan*.

José (apocopated form of *Josep* from L. *Josēp[h]us -um*) Joseph, **63** title.

Josep = *José*, **45** 22; **46** 27.

Judas (pr. n.) Judas, **36** 351 *d*.

juega pres. 3 of *jugar* (L. *jŏcatur*, V. L. **jŏcat*), plays, **50** 499 *d*.

juez (L. *jūdex*, *jūdĭcem* > *júez* > *juéz*) judge, **50** 509 *a*.

jugar (L. *jŏcāri*, V. L. **jŏcāre*. The *u* is unexplained, unless it be due to the closing force of the initial palatal; but cf. the regular

development of the vowel in
*jŏcat > juega) to play, sport;
yugando, **59** 21.

juntado -a (p.p. of juntar, L. jŭnctare; the u is due to the adjacent
palatals) joined, assembled, **33**
71 c, 72 b; **34** 77 a.

Jupiter (pr. n.) Jupiter.

justiçia (learned word; L. justĭtĭa)
justice, **69** XIX 3.

justiçiero -a (learned word; V. L.
justĭtĭarius -a -um) fond of
justice, impartial judge, **53** 11.

justo -a (learned word; L. justus
-a -um) just. **60** 27.

kriador ⸗ criador Creator, **64** 95 b.

[ll-words will be found here after lj-words.]

'l = el the (after e, 'and'), **67** V 7.

-l = le him, to him, to her (added
as enclitic to some other word,
e.g. si, as in sil, **8** 63; que, as in
quel, **9** 72; non, no, as in nol, **9**
78; a noun, as in manol, **16** 174;
a verb form, as in aiudol, **18**
1094; plogol, **41** 24 etc.).

la, las fem. def. art. (L. ĭlla[m], pl.
ĭllas, shortened in proclitic and
enclitic use, or the result of a
redivision of della, dellas, and
similar compositions in the case
of the article), the, **7** 49; **8** 53;
13 13; etc.; (fem. dem. pron.)she,
her, the one, that, **45** 14; (pers.
pron.) her, it, **6** 3, 20; **10** 96; etc.

labrador (V. L. *laborator, *labōra-
tōrem, an agent noun formed on
p.p. laboratus) tiller, worker of
the soil, plowman, **50** 491 a.

labrar (L. labōrāre) to work the
soil, till, labor, **26** 107 c.

lagrima (half-learned word; L.
lacrĭma) tear, **60** 6.

lança (L. lancĕa) lance, lancer,
fighter, **13** 179; **38** 365 b; cf.
mod. lanza.

lançada (lança + -ada from L. p.p.
-atus -a -um, a suffix denoting a
'blow from,' etc.) thrust of a
lance, **37** 357 c; cf. mod. lanzada.

lançar (L. lancĕāre) to launch, cast,
let go, **49** 301 c; **68** VII 6; cf.
mod. lanzar.

landre (L. glans, glandem, V. L.
*glandĭnem, with a change of
initial palatalized l to simple l)
glanders, **67** II 7.

Lara pr. n., **40** title and 7.

largo -a (L. largus -a -um, 'abundant,' 'large,' 'much') great,
long, momentous, **65** 107 c; a lc
larga slowly, **58** 441 c.

larguero -a (formation in -ero -a
on larg-o) bounteous, **23** 4 d.

las pl. of la: art., **22** 32 etc.; dem.
pron., **12** 141; pers. pron., **14**
86; **15** 117; etc.

latino (learned word; L. latīnus
-um) Latin, **23** 2 c.

lauor = labor (L. labor, labōrem;
the u may denote the bilabial
spirant value of the mod. b)
work, workmanship, cultivation,
farming, **26** 109 c, 110 b; **30** 8 a;
31 14 b.

Laynez = Lainez, pr. n., **36** 346 a.

Layno pr. n., **36** 338 a.

lazada (L. laqueus -um, V.L. *lacĕus
-um 'bond,'whence V.L.*lacĕāre,

lacĕātus -a -um. On the p.p. the Sp. noun is based. This seems to be used as coequal in sense with *yugo* ' yoke,' ' harness connecting two or more horses,'etc.) **31** 11 *a.*

lazar (L. *Lazarus,* the suffering beggar of the Bible, with perhaps influence of L. *lacĕrare*) suffering, disease, **27** 355 *b* ; cf. mod. *lazaro.*

lazeria (cf. *lazar.* It is a formation in *-ia* on the same basis) hardship, suffering, **45** 15, 17.

lazerio (by-form of *lazeria*) toil, labor, tribulation, **23** 4 *c* ; **26** 107 *b.*

lazrar (L. *lacĕrāre,* with influence of *Lazarus,* the diseased beggar of the Bible) to afflict, cut to pieces, suffer, **38** 362 *b* ; **23** 86 *d* ; **25** 99 *d* ; **28** 361 *b* ; **58** 440 *d.*

lazravan impf. 3 pl. of *lazrar.*

le (L. dative sg. [*il*]*lī > li* and, through use as enclitic, i.e. in the final unaccented syll., *> le*) him, to him, to her, **16** 153, 159 etc. ; **20** 1194 etc. (In O. Sp. it is enclitic and proclitic.)

lea = *le a, le ha,* **14** 104.

leal (L. *legalis -em,* whence the learned form *legal.* On the basis of Sp. *ley* was formed O. Sp. *leyal,* and thence regularly in Castilian *leal* ; cf. *sedeam > seya > sea*) loyal, faithful, **23** 86 *a.*

lecho (L. *lĕctŭm > leyĭo > lecho* ; the palatal following closed the L. *ĕ,* V. L. *ę̆,* and prevented diphthongization) bed, **60** 15.

leer (L. *lĕgĕre,* V. L. **legĕre.* The *e* of the unaccented first syll. passed to the forms stressing that syll., e.g. *leo, lees,* etc.) to read, **24** 95 *c* ; **48** 16 *b* ; **62** 20.

legaron = *llegaron* (in O. Sp. palatalized *l* is oftennot distinguished in writing from the simple *l* ; cf. *llegar*), **53** 12.

legion (learned word ; L. *lĕgĭo, lĕgĭōnem*) legion, **44** 13.

lego = *llegó* (cf. *legaron*), **14** 102.

lei = *ley* faith **12** 142.

leio (perhaps a scribal error for *leito,* a dialect Sp. form of *lecho,* showing arrested development) bed, **21** 4.

lengua (L. *lĭngŭa*) tongue, speech, **24** 95 *d* ; **69** XLII 7.

lennas (perhaps scribal for *llenas*) **14** 113.

lenzuelo (perhaps scribal for *lençuelo,* i.e. with *z* denoting a voiceless sound. L. *lĭntĕŏlum*) sheet, shroud, **21** 5.

Leon pr. n., **41** 3.

leon (L. *lĕo, lĕōnem*) lion, **31** 13 *a* etc.

les (L. dative pl. [*il*]*līs* ; cf. *le*) to them, of them, **16** 165 ; **18** 1098, 1103 ; **19** 1144 ; etc. (Although chiefly used as an enclitic in O. Sp. it was probably proclitic also.)

letra (L. *lītera* and *littera,* V. L. **lĭttera*) letter, handwriting, **49** 18 *b* ; **62** 17. (A V. L. **lettera* might be supposed as due to the influence of *legere, lectum.*)

letrado -a (participial adj. formed on *letra*) literate, trained, **23** 2 *c.*

leualdas = *levadlas* (with a frequent O. Sp. metathesis of *dl*; cf. *leuar*), **16** 167.

leuantar = *levantar* (V. L. **levantare* based on pres. part. *levans*, *levant-em* of L. *levare*) to raise; (refl.) to arise, rise, adjourn, **42** 11; **58** 437 *a*, 441 *d*.

leuar = *levar* (L. *lĕvāre*. In O. Sp. the *l* is not palatalized; the mod. *llevar*, *llevando*, etc. are due to the forms that stressed the first syll., whose *ĕ* > *ie*, *lievo*, *lieva*, *lieve*, etc. In these latter the *į* ere long palatalized the *l*, whence *llevo*, *lleva*, etc., and by analogy *llevar*, etc.) to take, take away, take along, carry, raise, bear up, **15** 116; **68** VII 5; **16** 167; **28** 368 *b*; etc. (Mod. Sp. has *levar* in the restricted sense 'to weigh anchor.')

leuastes = mod. *llevasteis* (with analogical *i*; cf. *lleváis*, *llevaseis*, etc.; L. *levavĭstĭs*, *levastĭs*), pret. 2 pl. of *leuar*, **69** XLIII 2.

leuat = *levad* (imper. pl. of *leuar*), **28** 365 *a*.

leuaua, **leuauan** = mod. *llevaba*, *llevaban* (cf. *leuar*), **13** 16; **31** 17 *a*; **42** 5; **27** 353 *d*; etc.

levantat = *levantad* (the *t* denotes the voiceless value in O. Sp. of final *d*), imper. pl. of *leuantar*, **47** 15.

levantedes (V. L. **levantētĭs* > *levantedes* > *levantees* > mod. *levantéis*) pres. sbj. 2 pl. of *leuantar*, **47** 10.

levaré (cf. *leuar*) **67** III 8.

levaron (cf. *leuar*) **34** 47 *c*.

ley (L. *lex*, *lēgem* > *lee*, whence, as the unaccented *e* is in post-hiatus, *ley*) law, faith, religious faith, **26** 107 *a*; **70** LXXVIII 2; *a ley* lawfully, legitimately, **31** 17 *b*.

ley (apparently an Aragonese form = Castilian *leche*. One would expect *leite*; L. *lac*, *lacte* > **laįte* > *leite*) milk, **65** 104 *a*.

li (earlier O. Sp. and also dialectal Sp. form of *le*) to him, of him, **24** 96 *a*, 97 *d*; **25** 105 *d*; etc. (It occurs here only in the extract from Berceo.)

libelar (learned word; L. L. **lĭbĕllāre*, from L. *libellus*) to present petitions, to bring an action, **69** XLII 2.

libelo (learned word; L. *lĭbĕllus* -*um*) memorial, petition, case, action, lawsuit, **69** XLII 6.

librar (L. *lībĕrāre*) to set free, dispatch, settle, decide, finish one's business, **27** 359 *d*; **53** 11; **58** 441 *b*, 442 *b*; **70** XLIII 6.

libriello (*libr-o* + the O. Sp. dimin. ending -*iello*, L. -*ĕllum*) little book, **26** 289 *a*; cf. O. Sp. and mod. *librete*.

librete (dimin. in -*ete* of *libro*) little book, **48** 12 *c*.

libro (half-learned word; L. *lĭber*, *lĭbrum*) book, **26** 108 *c*; **48** 13 *c*; etc.

liçençia (learned word; L. *lĭcĕntĭa*) license, leave, **56** 425 *a*.

lid (L. *lis*, *lītem*) contest, battle, **18** 1106, 1111; **35** 329 *a*; etc.

lidiar (L. *lītĭgāre*, whose *g* may have disappeared first in forms in which it was followed by *e*, *litigem*, etc. It is doubtful that *g* before *a* disappeared naturally after *e*, *i*) to fight, **34** 77 *c*, 79 *b*; **35** 335 *a*; (n.) **45** 6.

liegues pres. sbj. 2 of *llegar* (the spelling is probably scribal for *llegues*; cf. *lieuen*, etc.), **67** III 3.

lieua (L. *lĕvat*; cf. *leuar*) **70** LII 3; (L. imper. *lĕva*) **61** 17.

lieuen (L. *lĕvent*; cf. *leuar*) **14** 93.

lieuo (L. *lĕvo*; cf. *leuar*) **21** 12.

ligion (half-learned word. Cf.*legion*, whose *e* is here closed by following *į*) legion, **30** 4 *c*.

lilio (learned word; L. *līlĭum*) lily, **47** 1, 2. (The mod. *lirio* shows dissimilation.)

linpio -a = *limpio -a* (L. *līmpĭdus -a -um*) clear, pure, bright, **18** 1116; **60** 14, 17.

lis (L. [*il*]*līs*; earlier O. Sp. and Western Sp.; cf. *li*, *le*) to them, **27** 359 *d*; **29** 370 *a*, 371 *d*.

listado (participial adj. in *-ado -a* on *lista*, L. *līsta*) striped, streaked, **30** 9 *c*.

ljmosna = *limosna* (half-learned word; L. *ĕlĕēmŏsўna*; cf. Ital. *limosina*) alms, **25** 105 *c*.

llaga (L. *plaga*) wound, **36** 342 *b*.

llamar (L.*clamare*) to call, summon, name, ring, **37** 356 *c*; **38** 365 *c*; etc.

llamauan = *llamavan*, *llamaban* (cf. *llamar*), **59** 18.

Llambla (L. *Flammŭla*) pr. n., **40** 10.

Llanbla = *Llambla*, **41** 1, 21, 23; **42** 22.

llegar (L. *plĭcāre*, 'to bend,' therefore 'to bend, or wend, one's way toward,' etc.) to arrive, come, gather, reach, **33** 71 *d*, 74 *a*; **35** 329 *a*; etc.

llegat = *llegad* (*d* unvoiced to *t* in the final position in O. Sp.; cf. *llegar*), **69** XIX 7.

lleno -a (L. *plēnus -a -um*) full, **65** 105 *a*.

llorar (L. *plōrāre*) to weep, **28** 363 *a*; **42** 23; etc.

lo ntr. art., dem. and pers. pron. (L. [*il*]*lŭd* or V. L. *[il]lum* as ntr. and masc.), the, that, it, **28** 361 *d*; **44** 20; **45** 8; etc.; **21** 1; **30** 7 *d*; etc.; **6** 9; **24** 91 *a*, 95 *b*; etc.

lo pers. pron. masc., direct obj. (L. [*il*]*lŭm*), him, it, **6** 17; **7** 31; etc. (In O. Sp. *lo* is both enclitic and proclitic.)

loar (L. *laudare*) to praise, **48** 11 *c*; **50** 509; etc.

loçano -a (source uncertain. Perhaps Germanic *lust*, German adj. *lustig*, Eng. *lusty*. A V. L. *lŭstĭānus -a -um* might yield the form; cf. V. L. *ŭstĭum* > O. Sp. *uço*. A connection with Gothic *laus*, O.H.G. *lôs*, is hardly likely) lusty, sturdy, valiant, **38** 361 *a*; cf. mod. *lozano*.

locura (formation in abstract *-ura* on *loco -a*. This adj. is of uncertain origin. L. *alŭccus -um* 'owl' has been proposed. Also L. *glaucus -a -um*, Gk. γλαυκός 'bluish green or gray,' 'gleaming,' connected with γλαύξ ' owl.'

The wild, glaring stare of the owl might have suggested the sense of 'mad,' 'insane.' The derivation from Homeric *Glaucus*, the foolish warrior so called, is hardly likely. For *gl-* > *l-*, cf. *landre*) madness, **67** II 1.

logar (L. *lŏcalĭs -em*, from *lŏcus -um*, > *logal* and by dissimilation *logar*. The *u* of mod. *lugar* is unexplained; an influence of *luego* < L. *lŏcum*, *lŏco*, is not likely and not satisfactory as an explanation) place, **8** 64; **15** 128; **19** 1146; **20** 1211; **26** 111 *d*; **38** 362 *c*; etc.

longa (scribal Latinism in the *Misterio* for *luengo -a* < L. *lŏngus -a -um*) long, **9** 76.

loor (formation in *-or*, L. *-or -ōrem* on stem of *lo-ar*) praise, **70** LII 1.

lorando = *llorando* (*l* often for palatalized *l* in O. Sp.; cf. *llorar*), **13** 1.

lorigado (formation in *-ado*, L. p.p. ending *-atus -a -um*, on *loriga* 'cuirass,' L. *lorīca*) cuirassier, **31** 17 *a*.

los art., dem. adj. and pers. pron., direct obj., masc. pl. (L. [*il*]*lōs* from *ille*), the, those, them, **13** 2; **14** 88; **18** 1107; etc. (It is both enclitic and proclitic in O. Sp. Cf. *la*, *las* for the explanation of the rise of the form.)

loseniar = *losenjar* (probably from O. Fr. *losenger* 'flattering') flattering, flattery, **22** 31; cf. mod. *lisonjero -a*.

Loys (pr. n.) Louis, Lewis, **44** 4; cf. mod. *Luis*.

Lucanor pr. n., **54** 1 etc.

luego (L. *locŭs -um*, ablative sg. *lŏco*) then, at once, straightway, now, soon, **18** 1110; **23** 3 *a*; **24** 87 *c*; etc.; *luego syguiente* immediately afterwards, **66** 9; *luego que* as soon as, **39** 371 *d* etc.

luegol = *luego* + *el*, art., **33** 75 *b*; = *luego* + *le*, pron., **43** 11. (These are cases of the enclitic use of art. and pers. pron.)

luengo -a (L. *lŏngus -a -um*) long, **24** 93 *b*.

luenne = *lueñe* (L. adv. *lŏnge*) : a *luenne* afar, off, in the distance, **67** III 2.

lugar (cf. *logar*) **69** XLII 5.

lunbre = *lumbre* (L. *lūmen*, *lūmĭne* > *lumne*, by dissimilation *lumre* >, with development of labial stop between labial nasal and *r*, *lumbre*. In O. Sp. the scribes often wrote *n* for what was really pronounced > *m*, before a following labial) light, **59** 5.

luz (L. *lux*, *lūcem*) light, **59** 8; **60** 23.

luzero (L. *Lucifer*, *Lūcĭfĕrum* > *Luzevro* > *Luzero* ; or a formation in *-ero*, L. *-arĭus*, on *luz* or O. Sp. *luzir* 'to shine') morning star, Lucifer, **64** 96 *c*. Cf. *Luzbel* < *Lucĭfer*.

luzible (half-learned; V. L. *lūcĭbĭlis -em*) shining, resplendent, **60** 15.

lydones (ety. and sense ?) **31** 13 *b*.

Lyno = *Lino*, pr. n., **36** 338 *a*.

lynpio -a (cf. *linpio -a*) **51** 1663 *i*.

m' = *me* in proclitic use, **9** 81; **11** 125; **12** 134.

-m = *me* in enclitic use.

ma = *m'a* (cf. *m'*) = *me ha*, **47** 8.

Macabeo (pr. n.) Macabæus, **36** 351 *d*.

maçana (L. [*malŭm*] *Matĭānum*, a kind of apple. This should have given O. Sp. *mazana*, cf. Ptg. *mazãa*; the *ç* is due to a *Mattiana or the O.Sp. *mançana*, mod. *manzana*, probably from a V. L. *mantianum with an *n* due to the spreading of the initial nasal sound) apple, **47** 7.

maçano (cf. *maçana*) apple tree, **47** 3.

madre (L. *mater*, *matrem*) mother, **25** 103 *c*; **26** 112 *a*; etc.

mager = *maguer*, although, **16** 171; **19** 1145. Cf. note to **5** 17.

magestad (half-learned word; L. *majĕstas*, *majĕstātem*) majesty, **70** LII 4.

Magestat = *magestad* (-*d* normally unvoiced to -*t* in the final position), **28** 368 *c*.

magnifiesta (misspelling of *manifiesta*, half-learned word, L. *manĭfĕstus* -*a* -*um*. The *g* is due to its appearance in *dignus* -*a* -*um*, popular Sp. *dino* -*a*, often written *digno* -*a*, and similar forms in which the etymological *g* had no pronounceable force) manifest, **67** II 1.

magro -a (L. *macer* -*a* -*um*, *macrŭm* -*am*) thin, **65** 105 *b*.

maguer (cf. *mager*; the spelling with *u* is the correct one) although, **35** 332 *c*; **37** 358 *c*; **38**

364 *c*; **67** V 3; *maguer que* although, **46** 25.

maior = *mayor*, greatest, master, **7** 49.

maiordoma (learned word. We should expect *mayordomo*, as the form in -*a* is properly feminine. L. *major*, *majōrem* and *domus*, *domum*) majordomo, **11** 117.

mais (if not a mistake for *mas*, this = L. *magis* > **mag's* or **mac's* > *mais*; that is, it shows a different treatment from that of proclitic *magis*; cf. Ptg. *mais*) more, **10** 99. Cf. *mas*.

mal (L. adv. *malĕ* become a substantive) evil, harm, **9** 74, 76; **11** 107; **18** 1103; etc.; (adv.) ill, evil, badly, **21** 25; **27** 356 *d*; **39** 370 *c*; etc.; *a mal de su grado* in spite of himself, **65** 102 *d*.

mal (adj. = *malo*, *mala* in proclitic apocopated use) bad, sorry, **29** 370 *d*; *mal ora* inauspiciously, **21** 25.

maldat = *maldad* (V. L. *malĭtas, *malĭtātem* from *malus* -*a* -*um*, or a formation from *mal*, *mal.o*, on the analogy of *bondad*, etc. from L. *bonĭtas*, *bonĭtātem*, etc.) evil deed, iniquity, **62** 24.

maldiçion (learned word; L. *maledictio*, *maledīctĭonem*) curse, **64** 100 *c*.

maldizie = *maldezia*, mod. *maldecía* (with the original *i* of *dīcebat* and a weakening of the impf. ending -*a* to -*e*; L. *malĕdīcēbat*, V. L. *maledīcēat, from L. *malĕdī-cĕre*, V. L. *malĕdīcīre*), impf. 3 of

O. Sp. *maldezir*, was cursing, **21**
10, 11.

maldizre (fut. 1 of O. Sp. *maldezir*
(cf. *maldizie*) with a retention
of the *i* of L. *malědīcere*, V. L.
*malědīcīre, and a syncope of the
i of the infin. basis) I shall
curse, **21** 13.

malfado (L. *mal*[*um*] + *fatum*) ill
fate, misfortune, **37** 360 *c*. Cf.
O. Sp. adj. *malfadado*, mod. *mal-
hadado*.

maliello (*mal·o* + dimin. ending
-iello, L. *-ěllus -um*) evil person,
malicious person, **24** 92 *d*.

Mallorcas (pr. n.) Majorca Islands,
52 9.

malo -a (L. *malus -a -um*) evil,
bad, poor, sorry, **16** 165; **21** 12;
etc.

maltraye = *maltraía* impf. 3 of
maltraer (L. *mal*[*e*] + *trahěre*,
V. L. *trahēre) to treat ill, treat
harshly, **38** 363 *d*.

maltrecho -a (L. *mal*[*e*] + *tractus -a
-um*, p.p. of *trahere*) ill-treated,
44 9.

man (L. *mane*, both n. and adv.)
morning, **18** 1100.

maña (L. *machǐna* > *macna > *maña*) way, device, trick, skill,
ability, **24** 96 *d*.

mañana (formation in *-ana*, L. *-ana*,
on L. *mane*, *maněana, **manǐ-
ana*) morning, to-morrow, **19**
1122, 1135; etc.

mançebo (L. *mancǐpium* 'slave,'
'boy,' or V. L. *mancǐpum; cf.
L. *mancǐpare*) youth, **27** 354 *c*;
31 17 *c*; etc.

mandado (L. *mandatum*, ntr. p.p.
of *mandāre*) mandate, news,
message, **18** 1107; **34** 83 *d*; **37**
360 *d*; cf. *mandar*.

mandar (L. *mandare*) to command,
order, rule, govern, cause, have,
promise, **9** 85; **16** 180; **17** 208;
19 1187; **20** 1216; etc; *lo mandado* the thing promised, **58**
442 *d*.

mandaredes = mod. *mandaréis* (cf.
mandar), **43** 33.

mandasse = mod. *mandase* (cf.
mandar), **53** 19.

mandastes = mod. *mandasteis* (cf.
mandar), **58** 435 *d* etc.

mandaua = *mandava, mandaba* (cf.
mandar), **24** 87 *a*.

manear (V. L. *manǐdǐare, i.e. L.
manus -um + verb ending *-ǐdǐ-
are*) to handle, **22** 29.

manera (L. *manuarǐus -a -um*, adj.
based on *manus*; thence a fem.
noun) manner, way, port, **37**
359 *d*; **64** 99 *b*; etc.; *en manera
que* in such a way that, **43** 31.

manna = *maña*, **32** 21 *a* and *c*; **40**
16.

mannana = *mañana*, **34** 82 *a*; *de
gran mannana* very early in the
morning, **46** 10.

mano (L. *manus -um*) hand, **14**
106; **16** 153; etc.; *sobre mano*
held aloft, **38** 365 *b*; (pl.) the
two forefeet, **31** 13 *d*.

manol = *mano* + enclitic *le*, **16** 174.

mantenençia (learned word; formed
of L. *manu* and *tenentia from
pres. part. of L. *tenēre*) observ-
ance, rule, **25** 101 *d*.

manto (L. *mantum*; cf. *mantellum*) mantle, cloak, robe, **13** 4; **17** 195; **48** 11 *d*.

manzylla = *manzilla*, mod. *mancilla* (L. *macŭla*, with a substitution of suffix *-ĕlla* for the seeming suffix *-ŭla*, whence V. L. **macella*, O. Sp. *maziella*. The *n* is probably due to the influence of L. *mancus -a -um* 'defective,' which presents affinities of sense) stain, spot, blemish, **51** 1662 *a*, 1663 *f*.

mar (L. *mare*; ntr. in L., the word is masc. or fem. in Sp.) sea, **18** 1090; **33** 71 *d*, 72 *b*; **48** 12 *a*.

marabillado -a (p.p. of *marabillarse*, O. Sp. *marauillarse*) marveling, full of wonder, **29** 369 *d*.

marauila = *marauilla*, mod. *maravilla* (half-learned word; L. *mirabilis*, ntr. pl. *mīrābĭlĭa*, treated as a fem. sg. of the first declension. The first *a* is perhaps due to the influence of the *a* of the second syll.) marvel, wonder, **6** 1; **8** 54; **10** 92. (The *Misterio* writes *l* for *ll*.)

marauillar = *maravillar* (verb based on *marauilla*, *maravilla*; V. L. **mīrābĭlĭare*): *marauillo se* he marveled, **60** 3.

marauilloso -a = *maravilloso -a* (*marauilla* + *-oso -a*) marvelous, **60** 12, 19.

maraujlla = *marauilla*, *maravilla*, **51** 1662 *d*; cf. *marauila*.

maravilla (cf. *marauila*) **50** 498 *a*.

maravillar (cf. *marauillar*): *se maravillo* wondered, **65** 107 *a*.

maravilloso -a (cf. *marauilloso -a*) **50** 497 *d*.

marcho = *marco* (in the *Cid* the scribe sometimes uses *ch* for *c* = *k*), **15** 138; **17** 196, 199.

marco (Germanic *mark*) mark, coin, **15** 135, 147; etc.

marfil (probably of Arabic origin; *nâb-al-fil* and *adm-al-fil* have been proposed) ivory, **30** 9 *b*.

margarita (learned word; L. *margarīta*) pearl, **59** 14.

Maria (pr. n.) Mary, **24** 97 *b* etc.

Marja = *Maria*, **50** 1661 *a*.

Marruecos (pr. n.) Morocco, **33** 71 *b*.

Martin (apocopated form of *Martino*; it arose first in proclitic use before family names) pr. n., **13** 179 etc.

Martino (pr. n.) Martin, **17** 185.

martjr = *martir* (learned word; L. *martyr*, *martȳrem*) martyr, **21** 21.

mas (L. *magĭs* > **mags*, i.e. *max*. It was developed in unaccented proclitic use and lost the palatalization of its final sound before a word beginning with a cons. Hence *mas*, which then was generalized; cf. *mais*) (adv.) more, further, most, **7** 28; **10** 99; **14** 95; **19** 1129; **24** 93 *d*; *non pudiemos mas* we could not help it, **18** 1117; *non ... mas* no longer, **68** VIII 8 : (conj.) but, **15** 129; **21** 24; **28** 361 *d*; etc.; *mas pero* but, however, nevertheless, **41** 18; **42** 34; **45** 7 : (adj.) more, further, most, **46** 9; **53** 28.

maslo (half-learned; L. *mascŭlus -um* > *masclo* > *maslo*; the mod. *viacho* seems to show the popular treatment) male, **59** 1.

matar (in sense this agrees with the L. *mactare*. But the latter in true Sp. development should have given **mechar*. One thinks of the Persian *mât* in *shâh mât* 'the Shah is dead,' which early entered the Occident; cf. Eng. 'checkmate.' But for the change of *ct* to *t* in a word of popular use, cf. also L. *tractare* > Sp. *tratar*) to slay, kill, **19** 1147; **36** 351 *c*; **46** 7; etc.

Matatyas = *Matatias* (pr. n.) Mathathias, **36** 351 *d*.

matinos m. pl. (L. *matūtīnus -a -um*, acc. pl. *mat[ū]tīnos*), matins, morning prayers, the morning, **27** 353 *c*.

Matis pr. n., **46** 24.

mayor (L. *major, majōrem*) greater, **31** 14 *c* etc.

me pers. pron., direct and indirect obj. (L. *mē*, accusative sg., and *mihi* > *mī*, dative sg. In the enclitic unaccented final position *mī* would become *me* in O. Sp.), me, to me, for me, myself, to myself, etc., **7** 27; **13** 9; **14** 82; etc. (It is both enclitic and proclitic in O. Sp.)

meçer (L. *mĭscēre* 'to mix,' 'stir up,' 'move,' 'excite'): *meçio los ombros* he shrugged his shoulders, **13** 13.

meçquino -a (Arab. *meçkīn*, with a *sīn* which in Arab. words passing

into Sp. regularly gave O. Sp. *ç* = *ts*. Ordinarily in O. Sp. this *ts* was rendered by voiceless *z* before a following syllable beginning with a cons., as in Castilian *ç* could stand only before a vowel) wretch, woe 's me! **63** 89 *c*; cf. *mezquino* and *mesquino*.

medio -a (learned word; L. *mĕdĭus -a -um*) half, **27** 358 *b*; **62** 1; etc.; (n.) *media* half a hundredweight, **25** 105 *d*.

medio (learned word; L. *mĕdĭum*) middle, means, **17** 182; **30** 7 *a*; **71** LXXIX 5; *de medio* in the middle, **42** 7; *por medio* through the middle of, **37** 359 *a*.

mediol = *medio* + *el* art., **37** 359 *a*. (This shows the enclitic use of the article.)

meior = *mejor*, **12** 130; **27** 356 *d*; etc.

meiorar = *mejorar* (L. *melĭorare*; perhaps this gave **meldrar* > mod. *medrar*, and *mejorar* is analogical to *melĭoro* > *mejoro*, etc.) to make improvements, **26** 108 *a*.

mejor adj. and adv. (L. *melior, melĭorem*), better, best, **48** 15 *a*; **50** 510 *a*; **63** 92 *d*.

mejoria (formation in *-ia* on *mejor*) improvement, **65** 106 *b*.

Melchior pr. n., **9** 83.

melequis (?) **22** 28.

melezina (L. *medĭcīna*, with a possible influence of *mel*, Sp. *miel*, as honey and sirups are used in preparing medicines. Yet Columella seems to have already

a rustic *melicus* for *medicus*) med-
icine, relief, **51** 1663 *c*.

melo = *me* + *lo*, **49** 300 *d*.

membrar (L. *memŏrāre*) : *no le mem-
bro* he did not remember, **65**
102 *b*.

menar (cf. *Almenar*) **18** 1092.

menazar (a formation from L.
mĭnatus, p.p. of *mĭnor*, *mĭnāri*,
i.e. V. L. *mĭnātĭāre*, cf. L. *mĭ-
natĭo* 'threat,' if not a development from L. *minax, minacem*)
to threaten, **33** 76 *b* ; **44** 15.

menbrado -a = *membrado -a* (L.
mĕmŏrātus -a -um, p.p. of *me-
morare*) cunning, wily, **14** 102 ;
15 131.

menear (L. *minari*, V. L. *mĭnāre*
'to threaten,' 'drive,' 'move' ;
thence O. Sp. *menar*, and, with
a substitution of verbal suffix
-ear, V. L. *-ĭdĭare*, *menear*) to
move, stir, **60** 13.

menester (L. *mĭnĭsterĭum* 'office,'
'help,' 'need' ; genitive *mĭnĭ-
stĕrii habēre* 'to have as a need,'
'to need,' 'to want') : *a menester*
he has of need, he wants, **15**
135 ; *ha menester* it is needful,
37 354 *a*.

menge (perhaps a loan-word; cf.
O. Fr. *metges*, *meges*, Catalan
metge, from L. *mĕdĭcus* ; the *n*
might be due to a spreading of
the initial nasal) physician, **59** 4.

mengua (noun abstract from *menguar*) want, lack, **54** 20.

menguado -a (p.p. of *menguar*) im-
poverished, needy, **14** 108 ; **15**
134 ; **16** 158.

menguar (L. *minŭĕre* ; V. L. **mĭ-
nŭāre* from L. *mĭnus*. The Sp.
verb shows rather an intrans.
than a trans. use) to be lacking,
55 20.

menor (L. *minor*, *mĭnōrem*)
younger, youngest, **42** 2.

menos adv. (L. *mĭnŭs*), less, least, **55**
13, 24 ; *a menos de* without, **18**
1106 ; *a lo menos* at least, **30** 4 *c*.

menssaie = mod. *mensaje* (loan-
word from Fr. *message*, V. L.
*missatĭcum from L. *mĭttĕre*,
mĭssus. The *n* may be due to a
spreading of the initial nasal
sound) message, messenger, **19**
1188.

ment = *mente*, **28** 364 *b*.

mente (learned form of *miente*, L.
mens, *mĕntem*) spirit, mind, **68**
IX 3 : (element of adverb) **35**
333 *b* ; **52** 2, 17. (The mod. language prefers *mente*, and uses
miente only in certain phrases,
e.g. *parar mientes en*, 'to give
attention to.')

mentir (L. *mĕntīre*) to lie, **46** 12 etc.

mentira (formation on *mentir*) lie,
48 14 *c*. (Cf. Note to **3** 15.)

menudo (L. *mĭnūtus -a -um*, p.p. of
minuĕre) diminished, little ; *a
menudo* often, **22** 29.

meo (Latinism for *mio*) **11** 122.

mercado (L. *mercātus -um*) affair,
business, bargain, **15** 139 ; **38**
364 *d*.

merçed (L. *merces*, *mercēdem*) mercy,
favor, **25** 100 *d* ; **51** 1662 *c* ; etc.

mereçedes = mod. *merecéis* (cf.
mereçer), **17** 194.

mereçer (V. L. *merescēre*, an inceptive from L. *merēre*) to merit, deserve, 17 190, 197 ; etc.

meresçer = earlier form of *mereçer* (the *s* was later absorbed by the following *ç* = *ts*), 42 32 ; 50 498 *b* ; etc.

meresco = mod. *merezco* (pres. 1 of *meresçer, mereçer*), 56 424 *b*. (The *z*, originally = *ts* before a cons., in O. Sp. is due to the analogy of *mereçes, mereçe*, etc., which had the *ts* sound.)

mero -a (learned word ; L. *mĕrus -a -um*, 'pure,' 'real') : *poder mero* power (given to a sovereign or a high official) to inflict the death punishment, 70 XLIII 6 ; cf. *mero imperio*.

meryno = *merino* (V.L. **majorīnus -um*, from L. *major*) royal judge, district judge, 50 509 *c*.

mes (L. *mensis -em*, V. L. **mēsem*) month, 6 16 ; 20 1209 ; etc.

mesmo (V. L. **metĭpsĭmus -a -um*, from L. *met* + *ĭpse*) self, same ; *ty mesmo*, 36 342 *a* ; *asy mesmo*, 66 5. (The form remained in literary Sp. through the Golden Age, but the usual Castilian form is *mismo* ; cf. *mismo*.)

mesnada (V. L. **mansĭonata* based on L. *mansĭo, mansĭōnem* ; *mansĭōnata* > **maįsnata* > **meisnada* > *mesnada*) household, following, troop, retainers, 18 1115 ; 37 356 *a*.

mesquino -a (cf. *meçquino*) 58 438 *a* ; 69 XLII 1. (The *s* does not properly render the Arab.

sĭn of the etymon ; it may be due to scribal error or misreading of MS.)

mesquinu (perhaps an error for *mesquino* ; cf. *mezquino* in line preceding, 21 25) 21 26.

mester (a more popular development of *menester*, from L. genitive *mĭnĭstĕrĭi* > *menester* > **men'ster* > *mester*) : *ha mester* it is necessary, 37 354 *a* ; *avedes mucho mester caualleros* you have great need of knights, literally, you have knights [as a thing] of great need, 43 25 ; *mucho era mester* it was very necessary, 44 18. (*Menester* alone survives.)

mesura (L. *mensūra*) measure, moderation, 39 369 *b* ; 43 7.

mesurado -a (p. p. of *mesurar*, L. *mensurāre*) measured, moderate, with moderation, 13 7.

meter (L. *mĭttĕre*, V. L. **mĭttĕre* 'to send.' The sense development is this : 'to send' > 'to transfer' > 'to put,' i.e. somewhere else) to put, place, 15 119, 120 ; 20 1208 ; etc. ; *meter bozes* to emit shouts, 42 23.

metyo = *metió* (cf. *meter*), 38 365 *a*.

meytad (L. *medietas, medĭetātem* > **meyetatem* > *meçtad* > *meytad* ; whence mod. *mitad* ; the sense 'middle,' 'midpoint' developed that of 'half ') half, 61 8.

mezquino -a (cf. *meçquino*) unlucky, wretched, 21 25 ; 26 110 *c* ; 27 356 *a*.

mi pers. pron., obj. of prep. (L. *mihi*, *mī*), me, myself, **9** 82; **17** 205; **19** 1129; etc.

mi (as a poss. adj. this appears to have been at first only fem.; L. *mĕa* > **mīẹa* > *mía* and, in proclitic use before a word beginning with a vowel, especially with *a*, e.g. *mīaalma*, *mialma*, *mi alma*, > *mi*. It is possible that the V. L. had *mẹa*, whence directly *mía*; cf. Zauner, *Romanische Sprachwissenschaft*, 2d ed., I 69. Of the 19 cases in these extracts, only 3 are masc., and they are not in the earlier texts. As the form later became generalized for masc. and fem. use, they may mark the beginning of the change. It is doubtful that it is necessary to pass from *mía* to *mi* through a weakened fem. *míe*. Cf. Menéndez Pidal, *El Dialecto Leonés*, p. 49. On *mi* was constructed the pl. *mis*) my, **11** 120; **12** 142; **14** 83; **46** 21; **56** 422*a*, 424*d*, 425*a*; masc. **56** 425*c*; **57** 429*c*, 433*b*; **58** 440*c*; masc. **56** 441*c*; **61** 19; **62** 2; with prefixed art. as in Ital., *la mi*, **47** 2, 8, 10; **54** 4; masc. *al mi*, **62** 1. (Cf. the retention of this usage in the Lord's Prayer, *Vengạ el tu reino*. These extracts do not show *mía* as adj. before a noun. The masc. form as poss. adj. was regularly *mio*.) Cf. *mj*.

mia (fem. poss. adj. after its noun) my, **47** 16; cf. *mi*.

miedo (L. *mĕtus -um*) fear, **18** 1097; **38** 366*e*; etc.

miente (L. *mens*, *mĕntem*): *parar mientes* to mind, pay attention, **46** 9; **53** 6. (Only in this expression and similar ones *mientes* persists; cf. *mente*.)

miente (cf. preceding word and *mente*) element of adv.: *fyera miente* fiercely, **38** 364*a*.

mientra (ety. not clear. Perhaps L. *dum* + *ĭnterim*, whence **domentre*, and through some analogy, e.g. that of the adverbial *miente*, >*domientre*. Thence, by decomposition, *mientre*. Under the influence of advs. in *-a* (*fuera*, etc.), *mientra* may have been formed. But?): *mientra que* while, as long as, **16** 158, 173.

mientre element of adv. (= *miente* with intrusive *r* sometimes found in O. Sp. after cons. + *t* combinations): *fuerte mientre* violently, **13** 1; **21** 7; **41** 29; **42** 20; cf. *alguandre*.

mientre (cf. *mientra*) while, **28** 365*b*.

mill (L. *mīlle*. This maintained itself for some time in proclitic use before a vowel; before a cons. it soon became *mil*, i.e. lost its palatalization, and this form was then generalized) thousand, **20** 1217; **30** 5*a*, 6*a*, 9*d*; **31** 16*b*, 18*c*; **32** 20*c*; **56** 424*a*.

Minaya pr. n., **19** 1127.

ministro (learned word; L. *minister*, *mĭnĭstrum*) minister, servant, officer, **59** 18.

mio, mios poss. adj. masc. sg. in proclitic use (L. *mĕŭs -ŭm*, accusative pl. *mĕōs > míęo, míęos > mío, míos*), my, **11** 117, 118, 119, 121, 123, 124 ; **19** 1148 ; **21** 4 ; **42** 33 ; **43** 29 ; with the art. as in Ital., *el mio*, **17** 204 ; **47** 4, 5, 11, 12, 15. (There seems to be some evidence, e.g. that of assonance, in O. Sp., to the effect that *mio* was at least sometimes accented *mió*. To this the analogy of *to* and *so* might have led ; but the question is an open one. For mod. proclitic *mi* cf. *mi*.) Cf. *mjo* and *myo*.

mio poss. pron. ntr. sg. (L. *mĕŭm*) : *lo mio* mine, what's mine, **16** 157.

miollo (L. *mĕdŭlla*, with change of ending and gender) marrow, **64** 98 *c*.

mira (L. *myrrha*) myrrh, **8** 68 ; **9** 70.

mirar (L. *mīrāri* and *mīrāre* 'to look at with wonder.' In Sp. with neutral sense) to look, **65** 108 *d*.

misist (?) didst put (?), **22** 1.

mismo -a (cf. *mesmo*. Apparently *mismo* is equally early with *mesmo*, if not earlier, and has beside it also an O. Sp. *meísmo*, for which there may be supposed a V. L.**metípsimus -a -um*, with *í*. The word presents many difficulties, of which the entire disappearance in early O. Sp. of intervocalic L. *-t-* is not the least. On the supposition that *mesmo* was the earlier form, *mismo* has been ascribed to assimilating

influence in the combinations *mi mesmo, ti mesmo,* etc. > *mi mismo,* etc.) same, self, **60** 8 ; **61** 20 ; *esso mismo* likewise, **30** 8 *b*.

mj = *mi* poss. adj. proclitic, my, **49** 299 *b* ; **66** I 6 ; **68** IX 1 ; **69** XVIII 8 ; **70** XLIII 6 ; with art., *la mj*, **67** III 4 ; *los mjs*, **68** XVIII 1. (Cf. *mi* ; only two of the cases of *mj* are fem., but they are all relatively late.)

mj = *mi* pers. pron., **102** 25 *b*.

mjedo = *miedo*, **25** 101 *c*.

mjente = *miente*, **70** XLIII 3 ; **66** 3.

mjo = *mio* poss. adj. masc. (after its noun), my, **48** 13 *a* ; **49** 298 *d*.

mjraglo = *miraglo* (half-learned word ; L. *miracŭlum*) miracle, **26** 289 *b*.

mjsmo = *mismo*, **26** 111 *c* ; **29** 369 *d*.

mjssa = *missa*, mod. *misa* (learned word ; L. *mĭssa*, fem. p.p. of *mittĕre*, used in the dismissal by the priest at the end of the Mass, *Ite, missa est,* i.e. *ecclesia*, or *concio*, or *congregatio*, etc., *missa est*) Mass, **28** 367 *b* ; **29** 371 *b*.

mjssion = *mission*, mod. *misión* (learned word ; L. *mĭssĭo, mĭssĭonem*) mission, effort, **27** 358 *a*.

moço (origin unknown. Cf. Ford, *Old Spanish Sibilants,* p. 76) boy, youth, **59** 9, 16, 22 ; **60** 4.

moger = *muger* (a dialect form ; ordinarily the following palatal sound developed in L. *mŭlier, muliérem* closed the V. L. *ǫ* to *u*) woman, **59** 13, 20 ; **60** 5 ; cf. *mugier*.

mojado -a p.p. of *mojar* (V. L. *mŏl-lǐare* from L. *mŏllis*. The sense transition is from 'softening' to that of 'saturating' in order to soften), wet, moist, **65** 107 *b*.

Mon Real (*Mons Regalis, Montem Regalem* ; or rather Sp. *monte*, shortened in proclitic use, + Sp. *real*, from *rey + al, reyal > real* ; cf. *leal*) pr. n., **19** 1186.

monarca (L. L. *monarcha* from Gk. μονάρχης) monarch, **69** xix 5.

monedado -a p.p. of *monedar* (V. L. *monetāre* from L. *mŏnēta*), coined, in money, **15** 126 ; **16** 172 ; **20** 1217.

monesterio (learned word ; L. L. *mŏnĕstĕrĭum* by-form of L. L. *monasterĭum*, perhaps produced by the influence of *ministerium*) monastery, **25** 104 *a*. (The mod. word is *monasterio*.)

monje (perhaps a loan-word ; cf. Prov. *monge*. The L. L. *mŏnă-chus -um* could not give the Sp. word ; neither could a possible by-form *monichus*) monk, **70** liii *a*.

Mont Aluan (pr. n.) Montalvan, **18** 1089. (Cf. *Mon Real* ; before a vowel proclitic *monte* at first kept its *t*.)

montaina = *montaña* (V. L. *montanĕa* from L. *mons, montem*) mountain, **38** 367 *a*.

morar (V. L. *mŏrāre*, L. *mŏrāri*) to dwell, abide, **25** 100 *c* ; **60** 24. (The pres. tense forms with *o* instead of *ue*, e.g. *moran*, show either the analogy of the forms

not accenting the first syll., or a learned treatment.)

morauedi = *moravedí* (Arab. *morábiṭí*) a coin, **22** 28. (Cf. mod. *maravedí*, which perhaps shows the assimilating force of the *a* of the second syll.)

morir (L. *mŏri, mŏrīri*, V.L. *mŏrīre*) to die, **25** 101 *b* ; **26** 112 *c* ; etc. ; *muero* (V. L. *mŏro* for L. *morior*) **69** xlii 7 ; *mueras* (V. L. *mŏras* for L. *moriaris*) **66** I 7 ; *morrá* fut. 3, **67** II 2 ; *muriero* fut. sbj. 1., **42** 34 ; *muerto, -a*, p.p., **21** 6 etc.

morisco -a (L. L. *Maurĭscus -a -um, Morĭscus -a -um*) Moorish, **16** 178

moro (L. *Maurus -a -um*) Moor, **15** 125, 145 ; etc.

morrá fut. 3 of *morir* (with syncopated infin. basis), will die, **67** II 2.

mortal (L. *mortalis -em*) mortal, deadly, **8** 65 ; **9** 70 ; **39** 370 *b* ; etc.

morto (Latinism for *muerto*) **11** 109.

moryeron = *morieron* (older form of pret. 3 pl. of *morir* ; the *i* later closed the *o* to *u*, whence mod. *murieron*), **34** 83 *c*.

mos (scribal error for *mios*) my, **7** 22.

mostrar (L. *monstrāre*, V. L. *mŏstrāre*) to show, exhibit, **26** 289 *c* ; **59** 11 ; etc. (The pres. tense forms showing the diphthong are due to the analogy of *o, ue* verbs from L. etyma with *ŏ*.)

mouer = *mover*, **16** 169 ; **24** 93 *c* ; etc.

mover (L. *mŏvēre*) to move, start, **37** 355 *d*. (The pres. indic. *muevo*, pres. sbj. *mueva*, etc., are due to V. L. *mŏvo, *movam, etc., for L. *mŏvĕo*, *mŏvĕam*, etc.)

movydo = *movido* p.p. of *mover* (V. L. *movītus for L. *motus*), stirred, moved, **34** 82 *d*.

movyo = *movió* pret. 3 of *mover*, **35** 328 *d*.

much apocopated form of *mucho* (adv.).

mucho -a (L. *mŭltus -a -um*; the palatal developed after the *ŭ*, V. L. *ǫ*, closed it to *u*; *mŭltum* > *molto* > *moyto > *muyto > *mucho*) (adj.) much, many a, **32** 19 *c*; **37** 357 *c*; (pl.) many, **26** 108 *c* etc.; (pron.) much, **24** 93 *d*; (pl.) many, **61** 22.

mucho (L. *mŭltum*, ablative and instrumental *mŭlto* 'by much,' i.e. 'a great deal') a great deal, much, **53** 25; **54** 16; modifying a finite form of a verb, as in mod. Sp. **19** 1134; **41** 25; **43** 28; **52** 4; **55** 10; modifying an adj. or a part.: here (1) sometimes the verb intervenes between *mucho* and the adj. or part., and its instrumental use is clear, again (2) *mucho* stands immediately before the adj. or part. where the mod. Sp. uses only *muy*; (1) *mucho avie grandes cuydados* he had very great care, **13** 6; *mucho es pesado* it is very heavy, **14** 91; *mucho era de malfado* he was very unfortunate, **37** 360 *c*; *mucho fue espantado* he was greatly terrified,

39 368 *a*; *mucho era mester* it was of great need, **44** 18; (2) *mucho sobejanos* very abundant, **14** 110; *mucho ayna* very quickly, **37** 357 *d*; *mucho yrado* very angry, **39** 368 *b*; *mucho loado* greatly praised, **50** 509 *a*.

mudar (L. *mūtāre*) to change, molt, **13** 5; **62** 21.

mudarssele = *mudar* + *se* + *le*, **62** 21.

mudo -a (L. *mūtus -a -um*) mute, dumb, **21** 24; **49** 490 *c*.

mueble (L. *mōbĭlis -em*, V. L. *mŏbĭlis -em with *ŏ* due to *mŏvēre*) (pl.) movable objects, furniture, **50** 499 *b*.

muerte (L. *mors*, *mŏrtem*) death, **45** 8; **50** 498 *b*; etc.

muerto -a p.p. of *morir* (L. *mŏrtŭŭs*, V.L.*mortus -a -um), died, dead; (n.) dead man, etc., **21** 6; **35** 330 *c*; etc.

muger (cf. *mugier*) **32** 19 *a*, 20 *b*.

mugier (L. *mulier*, *mŭlĭĕrem*, V. L. *mŭlĭĕrem; the *lĭ* > *g* i.e. *dž*, which closed the preceding *ŭ*, V. L. *ǫ*, to *u*; the accented *ĕ* > *ie*; later the *g*, i.e. *dž*, absorbed the *ị* of *ie*, whence *muger*, mod. *mujer*) woman, wife, **13** 16; **41** 7; **62** 3; cf. *moger*.

mula (L. *mūla*) mule, she-mule, **22** 33.

mundanal (formation in *-al*, L. *-alis -alem*, on L. *mŭndānus -a -um*) mundane, worldly, secular, **59** 10.

mundo (learned word; L. *mŭndus -um*) world, **7** 40; **25** 100 *b*; etc.

Munno = *Muño*, pr. n., **40** 16.

muriero fut. sbj. 1 of *morir* (V. L. fut. perf. 1 **morivero*, **moriero*. The form is interesting as tending to show that the fut. perf. indic. as well as the perf. sbj. entered into the make-up of the Sp. fut. sbj.), I shall die, **42** 34.

muro (L. *mūrus -um*) wall, **60** 20, 22.

Murviedro pr. n., **18** 1095.

muy (L. *mŭltum*, ablative *mŭlto*, developed in proclitic position and therefore shortened before an adj., an adjectival p.p., or an adv.; e.g. *mŭltum*, or *mŭlto*, *bŏnum* > *moyto buono* > *muyt* [i.e. with a loss of palatalization in *t* before the following cons. after loss of *o*] *bueno* > *muy bueno*, with assimilation of *t* to *b*. The palatalizing effect of *lt*>*yi* closed the *ŭ*, V. L. *ọ*, to *u*. The form *mucho much* could develop as an adv. before a word beginning with a vowel, e.g. *much amado*, but the form *muy* became generalized) very, **17** 183; **24** 97 *c*; **27** 353 *c*; etc. Cf. *muy mas rico*, **55** 8, and *muy menos*, **55** 24, cases in which the mod. Sp. uses only the instrumental *mucho*; cf. *mucho*.

m̃y = *mi* me, **49** 300 *d*. (The tilde is a scribal error.)

myo = *mio* : *myo Çid*, **13** 6, 7 ; etc. ; *los myos amigos*, **14** 103.

naçido -a (p.p. of *naçer*, earlier *nascer*, p.p. *nasçido -a*, V. L. **nascītus -a -um*, which was developed beside L. *natus -a -um*, giving the p.p. for perfect tenses, while the latter gave the adjectival *nado -a*. The *s* was absorbed by the *ç* = *ts*) born, **6** 4, 5; etc.

nada (L. p.p. fem. *nata*, from *nascor*, used in such an expression as *res nata*, *rem natam* 'thing born,' 'thing existing,' 'anything.' In V. L. the noun was dispensed with. Originally the word was only positive in force; later by constant association with a negative *non*, *no*, it gained a negative force as well, and, when no verb was used with it, it could have this force. In these extracts it generally stands after a verb and *non* precedes the verb, as in mod. Sp., so that in and for itself it has only the positive sense) something, anything, **7** 47; (*non* + verb + *nada*) nothing, **14** 84; **25** 98 *a*; **27** 354 *d*, 357 *d*; **33** 74 *b*; **46** 24; **57** 433 *d*; (in one case it is *nada* + *non* + verb) nothing, not at all, **64** 97 *b*.

nado (perhaps an abstract from *nadar* 'to swim,' L. *natare*, rather than a direct derivative from the p p. *natus -a -um* of L. *no*, *nare* to swim.' Apparently it exists in O. Sp., as in mod. Sp., only in the phrase *á nado* = *nadando*): *salian a nado* they got out by swimming, **37** 358 *d*.

nado -a adjectival p.p. of *nacer* (L. *natus -a -um*), born, **21** 25; *om̃e nado* = *omne nado*, any one born, any living soul, any one,

16 151 ; cf. *naçido*. (O. Sp. uses *nado*, *nadi* [which owes its *i* — simply a pronominal ending and not necessarily a pl. one — to the influence of O. Sp. relative pron. *qui*], and *nadie*, which survives, all as pronominal forms. The *ie* of *nadie* has not been explained ; it may be due to the analogy of *alguien*, or to a contam'nation of O. Sp. *nadi* and a **nade* made up on the analogy of relative *que*, but this latter process has not been demonstrated.)

nariz (V. L. **narix*, **narīcem*, L. *naris*) nostril, nose : *narizes* (mod. *narices*) nostrils, **43** 12.

nasçer (L. *nasci*, V. L. **nascēre*) to be born ; pret. 1 *nasçi* **61** 7 ; *nasçy* **56** 426 *d* ; pret. 3 *nasçió* **48** 11 *b* ; **59** 3 (cf. the strong form *násco*) ; p.p. *nasçido -a* **30** 6 *d* ; **67** v 2 ; **68** VIII 1. (Later the *ç* = *ts* absorbed the preceding *s*, whence mod. *nacer*.)

nasçido = *naçido* ; cf. also *nasçer* and *nado*.

nasco strong pret. 3 of *nasçer* (V. L. pret. 3 **nascŭit*), was born, **17** 202 ; **20** 1195 ; **18** 1114. Cf. the weak pret. *nasçio*, mod. *nació* ; it is used side by side with this weak form in O. Sp.

nasçy = *nasçi* (cf. *nasçer*), **56** 426 *d*.

natura (learned word ; L. *natūra*) nature, race, kind, **34** 84 *c*.

natural (learned word ; L. *naturālis -em*) natural, native, born, **39** 370 *a* ; **40** 6, 8.

Nauarra = *Navarra* (pr. n.) Navarre, **19** 1187 ; **41** 4 ; etc.

Navarra (cf. *Nauarra*) **35** 329 *c*.

Navarro (pr. n.) Navarrese, **35** 330 *a*.

neçio -a (learned word ; L. *nĕscĭus -a -um* 'ignorant') ignorant, silly, **48** 16 *a* ; cf. *nesçio*.

negar (L. *nĕgāre*) to deny : *negara* (plpf. 3) had denied, **46** 25.

negoçio (learned word ; L. *negōtĭum*) business, affair, **62** 6.

negro -a (L. *nĭger*, *nĭgra*, *nĭgrum -am* ; the retention of *gr* may indicate that this is a learned word) black, dire, awful, disastrous, **32** 21 *d* ; **49** 17 *a* ; etc.

nemiga (*enemigo, enemiga*, with loss of its first syll.) diabolical deed, **46** 15. (Cf. *inimicus* used in the Bible for the devil.)

nescesidad (cf. *nesçesidad*) **61** 23.

nesçesidad (L. *necessĭtas*, *necessĭtā-tem* ; the *s* before the *ç* is due to scribal error. In the later O. Sp. period, L. *sc* before *e*, *i*, had become *ç*, but the *s* was still often written ; by transferal this meaningless *s* was written in cases in which it was not etymological) necessity, **71** LXXIX 2.

nesçio cf. *neçio* (the *ç* absorbed the etymological *s*), ignorant, silly, stupid, **50** 491 *a* ; **56** 424 *d*.

ni (L. *nĕc* > **ne* and this in unaccented proclitic use before a word beginning with a vowel > *ny*, *ni*, which was then generalized) neither, nor, **11** 110 ; **12** 147 ; **21** 15, 17 ; etc.

Nicrao pr. n., **46** 3.

niebla (L. *nĕbŭla*) cloud, mist, **65** 106 *d*.

nieue = *nieve* (this can hardly have come from L. *nix*, *nĭvem*, which should have given *neve. It is perhaps a derivative from the verb *nevar*, *nieva* [an analogical form], etc., 'to snow,' V. L. *nĕvare based on *nix*, *nĭvem*. It should be stated that L. has a p.p. *nĭvātus -a -um* 'cooled with snow') snow, **56** 425 *d*.

nigun (apocopated form of *niguno -a*; L. *nĕc* + *ūnus -a -um*, with influence on the first element of the already developed Sp. *ni*) no, not any, **21** 23; cf. *njguna*, *njgunt*.

nin (*ni* with an *n* due to the influence of O. Sp. *non*) neither, nor, **14** 107; **15** 145; **33** 74 *b*; **35** 334 *a*; **36** 350 *c*; etc.; cf. *njn*.

ningun (apocopated form of *ninguno -a*) **33** 72 *d*; **41** 33; **55** 18.

ninguno -a (*niguno -a* with an *n* due to O. Sp. *nin* and *non*) no, not any, none, **20** 1193; **33** 76 *c*; **38** 366 *c*; **41** 28; **43** 22; etc.

njguna = *niguna* (cf. *nigun*), **68** VII 4.

njgunt = *nigun* (with inorganic *t* due to the analogy of forms like L. *secundum* > O. Sp. *segund* > O. Sp. *segunt* > *según*), **25** 105 *b*.

njn = *nin*, **25** 105 *b*; **68** IX 6; **69** XLII 6; **71** LXXVIII 6.

njnno = *niño* (origin obscure; said to be connected with Ital. *ninna* 'cradle,' 'girl baby,' and to be derived from a lullaby formula such as *ninna-nanna*. But?) child, **67** III 2.

no = *nos*; possibly a scribal error, but as it occurs before *l*, *no lo ha buscado*, **17** 192; *mereçer nolo hedes*, **17** 197, it may be a Western dialectal suppression of *s* before *l*, as in Portuguese.

no (L. *nōn*, whence O. Sp. *non*, which in proclitic use, or in combination with a following pronoun, lost its final *n*, as in *nol*, *nolo*, *nola*, *nos*, for *non le*, etc. Hence, by redivision, *no*, which was then generalized) not, no, **6** 2; **9** 81; **11** 115; **12** 137, 146; **14** 82; **21** 22; **47** 10; etc.

no's = *no os*, **65** 108 *c*.

noble (L. *nōbĭlis -em*) noble, **30** 6 *c* etc.

noch = *noche* (whether it was dialectal or really Castilian or due to sentence phonetics, O. Sp. seems to have permitted palatalized sounds to remain in the final position), **15** 137; **18** 1100; **19** 1185.

nocharon (cf. *trasnochar*) **18** 1110.

noche (L. *nox*, *nŏctem*; the palatal sound following the *ŏ*, V. L. *ǫ*, closed it and prevented diphthongization) night, **6** 9; **7** 27; **19** 1122; etc.; *de noche* by night, **14** 93; etc.; cf. *noch*, *nog*.

nog (dialect form of *noch*; in Eastern Sp. *g* = *dž* unvoiced at the

end of a word and thus obtained
the value of Castilian *ch*; its
use here is unetymological. If
the *Disputa* is western, the *-g*
= *ch* is a little strange) **21** 15.

nol = *non* + *le*, **9** 78; **21** 2; **29**
369 *b*; **30** 9 *a*; **44** 16; **46** 25; cf.
no.

nolo = *nos lo* (cf. *no* = *nos*), **17** 197.

nombre (L. *nomen, nomine* > O. Sp.
nomne, and by dissimilation
nomre, whence, with a *b* developed in the transition from *m* to
r, *nombre*) name, **9** 81 ; **19** 1138;
46 24 ; etc.

non (L. *nōn*. This in great measure maintained itself in O. Sp.,
but in certain syntactical combinations it lost its final *n*,
whence *no*, which was then
generalized and remains as the
modern form) not, **6** 7, 13, etc. ;
9 75; **11** 109; etc.; cf. *no*.

nonbrar = *nombrar* (L. *nomĭnāre*)
to name, mention, **23** 4 *a*; **37**
353 *a*; **70** LXXVIII 1.

nonbre = *nombre*, **23** 1 *a*, 4 *a*; **27**
354 *d*; etc.

nos = *non se*, **18** 1106; **20** 1207 ;
38 364 *d*.

nos pers. pron., subj. and direct and
indirect obj. (L. *nōs*), we, us, **8**
63; **11** 127; **12** 130; **15** 123;
etc. (In O. Sp. this is the current
form for the 1 pers. nominative
pl. ; *nosotros -as* is late; cf. *nos
otros* **68** VII 6.)

nostras (Latinism for *nuestras*) **12**
147.

not = *no te*, **21** 24.

notar (learned word; L. *nŏtāre*) to
note, count, **17** 185.

notorio -a (learned word; L. *notō-
rĭus -a -um*) notorious, **69** XIX 4.

nouaenta = *novaenta* (L. *nonagĭnta*,
V. L. *novagĭnta on the analogy
of *nŏvem*) ninety, **40** 2. Cf. mod.
noventa.

nuestro -a poss. adj. (L. *nŏster* ;
nŏstrum -am) our, **18** 1117; **47**
17; etc.; (pron.) ours, **19** 1133;
lo nuestro our affair, **18** 1118.

nueua = *nueva* ; cf. *nueuo*.

nueuas (fem. pl. of *nueuo -a*, used
as a noun) fame, deeds, **20** 1206;
cf. *nuevas*.

nueue = *nueve* (L. *nŏvem*) nine,
20 1209 ; **40** 4.

nueueçientos = *nuevecientos* nine
hundred, **40** 2, 4. (Cf. mod.
novecientos ; in popular usage
nuevecientos still occurs.)

nueuo -a = *nuevo -a* (L. *nŏvus -a
-um*) new, **21** 5; **56** 426 *a* ; *nueuo
mente* newly, recently, **31** 11 *b*.

nuevas (cf. *nueuas*) news, **33** 71 *b*.

nulla (perhaps learned word; L.
nūllus -a -um) any (after *sin*),
39 369 *d*.

numquas (L. *nŭmquam* > *numqua*,
of which the accented *u* may
show learned treatment or the
closing influence of following
ỵ. Thence *nunqua*, with the
usual change of *m* > *n* before *k*.
The *s* is the so-called adverbial
-s derived from *pues*, etc.) never,
ever, **11** 107, 112 ; cf. *nunca*.

nunca (cf. *numquas* ; the change
of L. *-qua* to *-ca* is peculiar;

perhaps the position in an un-accented syll. explains it; cf. *ca*) never, ever, 21 14; 24 91 *b*; 27 359 *c*; 29 2 *b*; 35 334 *c*. (This is already the usual form in O. Sp.)

Nunno = *Nuño*, pr. n., 36 338 *a*, 345 *a*; etc.

nunqua (cf. *numquas* and *nunca*) never, 41 18; 42 24, 31.

nunquas (cf. *numquas*) never, 7 34.

O interj. (L. *o, oh*) oh! 51 1664 *h* etc.

o (L. *aut*) or, 6 20; 7 35; etc.; *o . . . o* either . . . or, whether . . . or, 27 360 *a*.

o interrog. and rel. (L. *ŭbī > *ove > *oue > *oe > o*. But?), whether, where, in which, 8 60; 9 79; 14 103; 22 27; etc.; *o que* wherever, 6 17.

obedesçia = *obedecia* (impf. 3 of *obedesçer*, mod. *obedecer*, L. *obēdīre*, V. L. *obēdēscēre) obeyed, 24 87 *c*.

obediençia (learned word; L. *obēdĭentĭa*) obedience, 25 101 *a*.

obispo (half-learned word; L. *ĕpĭscŏpus -um > *ebiscpo > obispo*; the initial *o* may be due to the labializing force of the *b*. But?) bishop, 67 v 5.

obo = *ouo, ovo* = mod. *hubo*, 65 103 *a*.

obra (L. *ŏpĕra* gave *huebra*, with a special and restricted sense; *obra* may be an abstract from *obrar*, in which the *o* of forms not accented on the first syllable was generalized; cf. also *obrero*) work, deed, 30 9 *c*; 31 11 *b*; etc.

obrero (L. *ŏpĕrārĭus -um*) workman, laborer, 23 4 *b*.

occidente (learned word; L. *ŏccĭdens, ŏccĭdĕntem*) west, 7 26.

odredes (L. *aud[ī]r[e]* + *[hab]ĕtĭs > *audrĕtĭs*) fut. 2 pl. of *oir*, 17 188.

oferda = *oferta* (learned word; L. L. *offĕrta for L. *oblata*, p.p. of L. *offerre*) offering, 21 16; cf. *offrenda* and *oferta*.

official = *oficial* (learned word; L. *officialis -em*) official, officer, servant, 46 1, 4.

offrenda = *ofrenda* (learned word; L. *offĕrĕnda* from *offerre*) offering, 26 106 *b*.

ofiçio (learned word; L. *offĭcĭum*) office, post, 50 509 *d*; 64 94 *d*; etc.

ofrecremos = *ofreçremos* = *ofreceremos* fut. 1 pl. of *ofrecer* (V. L. *offĕrĕscēre from L. *offerre*), we shall offer, 8 68.

oio = *ojo*, 13 1 etc.

oir (L. *audīre*) to hear, 21 1; 41 31; etc.

Ojero (pr. n.) Ogier, 36 352 *a*.

ojo (L. *ŏc[ŭ]lus -um*) eye, 49 301 *d* etc.

olbidado p.p. (cf. *olvidar*), forgotten, 16 155.

oliente (participial adj.; L. *oliens, oliĕntem* from *olēre*) odorous, fragrant, 60 10.

Oliuero = *Oliverio* (pr. n.) Oliver, 36 352 *b*.

olor (V. L. *olor, olōrem* for L. *odor, odōrem*; cf. *olēre*) odor, fragrance, 30 8 *d*; 60 13.

oluidar = *olvidar* to forget, **36** 350 *d*; **37** 353 *c*; **39** 369 *b*.

olvidar (V. L. **oblitare*, a frequentative from L. *oblitus*, p.p. of *obliviscor*; the *l* has undergone metathesis) **65** 102 *a*.

ombre = *hombre*; cf. *omne* and *uemne* (L. *homo*, *hŏmĭnem* > O. Sp. *omne*, which, arising perhaps in unaccented proclitic use as an indefinite pronoun, like the Fr. *on*, prevailed over the diphthongized *uemne*; by dissimilation *omne* > *omre*, whence, by the natural production of a transitional labial stop, *ombre* and with an etymological restoration of *h*, *hombre*) man, **63** 91 *c*.

ombro = *hombro* (L. *hŭmĕrus -um* > **omro*, whence, with transitional labial stop, *ombro*. In mod. Sp. the *h* has been restored in writing) shoulder, **13** 13.

ome (with nasal dash forgotten) = *oñe* = *omne* (cf. *ombre*), **50** 491 *a*.

oñe = *omne* (cf. *ombre*), **15** 134; **16** 151; **19** 1125; etc.

omne = *hombre* (cf. *ombre*; this is the regular O. Sp. form from L. *homo*, *hŏmĭnem*; [*h*]*ombre* is a later development) man, **9** 70; **12** 133; **23** 86 *d*; **24** 94 *c*; etc.; (in unaccented proclitic use as an indefinite pronoun) one, **45** 7. (The form developed in the unaccented position was extended to accented use.) Cf. *uemne*.

Omnjpotent = *Omnipotente* (learned word; L. *ŏmnĭpŏtens*, *ŏmnĭpŏtĕntem*) Omnipotent, **28** 364 *d*.

on = *non*? **7** 22; cf. *non* **11** 112.

onbro = *ombro*, **43** 5.

Onda pr. n., **18** 1092, 1109.

ondado -a (L. *ŭndātus -a -um*) undulated, streaked, provided with bands, **30** 9 *b*.

ondrado -a (L. *hŏnōrātus -a -um* > *onrado -a*, whence, with the development of a transitional dental stop, *ondrado*) honorable, **16** 178; cf. mod. *honrado -a*.

onre = *omre*, *ombre*, **67** V 2.

onrra (with *r* reënforced after *n*, while the more popular O. Sp. form developed a *d* between the *n* and the *r*) = mod. *honra* (an abstract from O. Sp. *onrrar*, mod. *honrar*) honor, **54** 5; **55** 20.

onrrado -a p.p. of *onrrar*, mod. *honrar* (L. *hŏnōrāre*, *hŏnōrātus -a -um*), honored, honorable, venerable, of high rank, virtuous, **27** 359 *b*; **51** 1664 *b*; **55** 22; **57** 428 *d*; **64** 94 *c*, 101 *b*; cf. *onrra* and the more popular O. Sp. *ondrado*.

ora n. (L. *hōra*) hour, **35** 328 *d*; **36** 347 *b*; etc.; *aquella ora* then, **42** 16; *en buen ora* auspiciously, **13** 78; **16** 175; etc.; *mal ora* inauspiciously, **21** 25; *toda ora* at all times, **51** 1662 *g*; *essas oras* now, **34** 81 *c*, 83 *a* and *d*; *ora* (adv.) now, **69** XLII 1.

oracion (learned word; L. *ōrātio*, *oratĭōnem*) prayer, **21** 18; **25** 98 *c*.

orar (L. *ōrāre*) to pray, **25** 98 *c* ; **60** 6.

orden (L. *ōrdo, ōrdĭnem*) order, series, community, holy orders, **23** 86 *b* ; **26** 112 *a* ; **59** 16.

ordenar (L. *ōrdĭnāre*) to ordain, regulate, order, arrange, draw up, **23** 86 *b* ; **29** 1 *a* ; **37** 359 *c* ; etc.

oreia = *oreja*, **28** 368 *c*.

oreja (L. *aurĭcŭla*) ear, **60** 26.

orient = *oriente*, **18** 1091.

oriente (L. *oriens, ŏrĭĕntem*) orient, east, **7** 25 ; **32** 21 *a*.

oro (L. *aurum*) gold, **8** 68 etc.

Oropa pr. n. (L. *Eurōpa* ; cf. *Eulalia* > O. Sp. *Olalla* ; in syntactical combinations the *e* of the unaccented diphthong may have been lost, as in *de Europa* > *de* *Uropa > *de Oropa*. But?), Europe, **33** 73 *b*.

osado -a (p.p. of *osar*) bold, venturesome, **33** 76 *c* ; **57** 428 *c*.

osar (V. L. *ausare, a frequentative from L. p.p. *ausus*) to dare, venture, **27** 353 *b*.

osauan = *osavan* = *osaban* (cf. *osar*), **27** 353 *b*.

otear (L. *optare* ‘to choose’ with a suffix change of *-are* > *-ar* for V. L. *-ĭdĭare* > *-ear*. But?) to examine, glance, peep, **47** 14.

otero (L. *altarĭum* from *altus*) height, **47** 12.

Otho (pr. n.) Otho, **40** 5.

otorgar (V. L. *auctōrĭcare from L. *auctor*) to authorize, agree to, grant, **34** 80 ; **43** 33 ; **46** 21.

otorgasse = *otorgase* (cf. *ōtorgar*), **46** 21.

otorgol = *otorgó* + *le* (cf. *otorgar*), **43** 33.

otro -a adj. and pron. (L. *alter, altĕrum, altĕram*), other, another, the next, the following, **6** 9 ; **9** 83 ; **11** 108 ; **26** 289 *a* ; etc. ; *el otro* the other man, your neighbor, **67** II 2 ; *un otro*, **26** 289 *a* ; *nos otros*, **68** VII 6.

otrosi (L. *altĕrum + sīc*) likewise, also, **8** 59, 63.

otrossi = *otrosi*, **40** 3, 7 ; **41** 5 ; etc.

otrro = *otro*, **36** 352 *d* ; **37** 353 *a*.

ouiere = *oviere*, mod. *hubiere*, fut. sbj. 1 of *aver* (L. *habuĕrĭm*), I shall have, **58** 436 *b*.

ouieres = *ovieres*, mod. *hubieres* (L. *habuĕrĭs*), thou mayest have, **62** 15.

ouieron = *ovieron*, mod. *hubieron* (L. *habuĕrŭnt*, but with 4th conj. ending), they had, **13** 11 etc.

ouiesse = *oviesse*, mod. *hubiese* (L. *habuĭsset*) : *si ouiesse* would that he had, **13** 20.

ouo = *ovo*, mod. *hubo* (L. *habŭĭt*), had, **17** 188 ; **26** 111 *b* ; etc. ; there was (were), **43** 22 etc.

oviste = mod. *hubiste* (L. *habuisti*) thou didst have, **51** 1664 *g*.

ovo (cf. *ouo*) had, there was (were), **34** 77 *a* etc.

ovyeron (cf. *ouieron*) **36** 350 *b* ; (with *a* or *de* before an infin.) **36** 350 *b* and *d* ; **37** 359 *b* ; etc. (This last construction is sometimes equal to a simple preterite of the main verb.)

oy = mod. *oye*, imper. sg. of *oir*, **27** 360 *d*.

oy = mod. *hoy* (L. *hodĭe*) to-day, **37**
353 *c*, 356 *c* ; **60** 2 ; *oy endia* now-
adays, **24** 97 *a*.

oyan = mod. *oyan* (popular), *oigan*
(L. *audĭant*), sbj. pres. 3 pl. of
oir, **66**.

oyd imper. pl. of *oyr*, **19** 1127.

oydo = mod. *oíd* (cf. *oir*), **35** 332 *a*.

oyesse = mod. *oyese* (L. *audīvissĕt*),
sbj. impf. 3 of *oir*, **52** 18.

oyie = mod *oía*, impf. 3 of *oir*, **52**
18.

oymos = *oímos* (cf. *oir*), **24** 95 *d*.

oyo = mod. *oyo* (popular), *oigo*
(L. *audĭo*), pres. 1 of *oir*, **57** 431 *b*.

oyr = *oir*, **26** 112 *d* etc.

oyredes = mod. *oiréis*, fut. 2 pl. of
oir, **68** VII 7.

pace (Latinism for *paz*, which is
required by the meter in both
cases) peace, **7** 24 ; **9** 85.

padesçer (V. L. **patescĕre*, an inceptive corresponding to L.
pati) to suffer, **45** 17 ; *padesco*
(mod. *padezco*) I suffer, **56** 424 *c*.
(Cf. mod. *padecer*, in which the
usual absorption of *s* in the
combination *sç* is shown.)

padre (L. *pater*, *patrem*) father, **13**
8 ; **23** 1 *a* ; etc.

pagado -a (p.p. of *pagar*) pleased,
happy, paid, **15** 129 etc.

pagano (L. *pagānus -um*) pagan,
33 73 *a*.

pagar (L. *pacāre* 'to pacify,' 'to
please,' 'to satisfy,' and hence
'to pay') to pay. **17** 186 ; **15** 129 ;
etc. ; (refl.) to be pleased, be satisfied, **15** 146 ; **42** 14 ; **52** 3 ; etc.

pagaredes = mod. *pagaréis* (fut. 2
pl. of *pagar*) you shall pay, **70**
XLIII 7.

pagauan = *pagavan*, mod. *pagaban*
(cf. *pagar*), **17** 186 ; **52** 12.

palabra (L. *parabŏla* > **parab'la*,
and, by metathesis of *r* and *l*,
palabra) word, remark, speech,
meaning, **25** 98 *d* ; **42** 12 ; **52** 17 ;
etc.

palaçio (learned word ; L. *pala-
tĭum*) palace, **15** 15 ; **17** 182 ;
etc.

< paladar[*]

paladino -a (L. *palatīnus -a -um*
'appertaining to a palace,' i.e. to
a public building, 'public,'
'manifest') clear, manifest, **23**
2 *a*.

palafre (an Eastern Sp. form, cf.
Catalan *palafre* ; L. *paravĕrēdus*.
The usual Castilian word is
palafrén, which seems to show
the working of popular etymologizing, i.e. the influence of *frēnum*, Sp. *freno* 'bridle') palfrey,
22 30.

paloma (L. *palŭmba* ; for popular
change of *mb* > *m*, cf. *lomo* from
lumbus -um) dove, **47** 16.

pan (L. *panis -em*) bread, loaf, **18**
1104 etc.

paniçero (V. L. **panīcĭarĭus -um*, a
formation on L. *panis*) baker,
pantler, **63** 91 *d* etc. ; cf. mod.
panadero.

panno = *paño* (L. *pannus -um*)
cloth, piece of cloth, **38** 361 *c*.

papa (L. *pappa*, from Gk. πάππας
'papa,' 'father,' 'bishop,' 'pope')
pope, **67** v 5.

[*] See Correction p. 176a

par (perhaps Fr. *par* as used in adjurations; by confusion with Sp. *para*, the latter appeared later in the same use) by; *par caridad* for pity's sake! **7** 51; **12** 145; *par mi lei* by my faith! **12** 142; *par la tu tiesta* by thy head (life)! **21** 22; *par Dios* by God! (cf. mod. *pardiez*) **42** 31.

para (from *pora*. In proclitic use, when the accent of the first vowel was weak, the *o* may have been assimilated to the *a*) for, to, in order to, toward, **32** 21 *d*; **54** 8; etc.; *para que* in order that, **54** 19.

parael = *para el*, **26** 107 *d*.

paramjento = *paramiento* (V. L. **paraměntum* from L. *parare*) determination, contrivance, device, **24** 94 *b*.

parar (L. *parare*, from *par* 'equal,' wherefore the original sense was 'to make something equal to another,' hence 'to oppose one thing to another,' 'to check a thing by another') to stop, fix, set up, settle, arrange, prepare, **16** 160; **17** 198; **41** 15, 33; etc.

pareçer (later and mod. form of *paresçer*; the *ç* = *ts* absorbed the *s*) to appear, seem, be apparent, **19** 1126; **47** 17; **65** 104 *d*; etc.

pareçra = syncopated fut. of *pareçer*, i.e. *pareçera*, **19** 1126.

pared (L. *paries*, *parětem*, V. L. **parětem* > **parětem*; the pl. *parētes* occurs in inscriptions) wall, **58** 435 *b*.

paresca = mod. *parezca*, pres. sbj. 3 of *paresçer*, **61** 13.

paresçer (V. L. **parescēre*, L. *parēre*) to appear, seem, **54** 6; **57** 427 *b*; etc.; (n.) appearance, aspect, **31** 17 *d*; cf. *pareçer*.

paret = *pared* (at the end of a word, O. Sp. *d* unvoiced to *t*) wall, **47** 14.

paria (learned word; L. *par* ' equal,' ntr. pl. *parǐa*, treated as a fem. sg. of the first decl. The sense development is ' things equal to a demand,' and hence a ' tribute '): *parias* tribute, **14** 109. (The word exists only in the pl. in Sp.)

pariente (L. *parens*, *parěntem*, pres. part. of *parěre* 'to beget.' Already in L. the original sense of ' parent ' had been developed beyond that of ' progenitor,' ' ancestor,' to that of ' relative ' in general) relative, **27** 357 *a*; **29** 369 *c*; **30** 6 *b*.

parir (L. *parěre*, V. L. **parīre*) to bear, bring forth, **51** 1664 *f*.

part (truncated form of *parte*) **18** 1091; **19** 1132.

parte (L. *pars*, *partem*) part, side, party, **15** 134; **19** 1142; **34** 79 *a*; etc.

partiemos = *partimos* (pret. 1 pl. of *partir*, analogous to 3 pl. *partieron*) we departed, **18** 1116.

partir (L. *partīre* ' to part,' whence the sense ' to part one's self from,' ' to depart ') to part, settle, decide, share, depart, **18** 1106, 1116; **26** 106 *d*; (refl.) to depart, **68** IX 7.

paryente = *pariente*, **35** 328 *b*.

pasante = older Sp. *passante* (adjectival pres. part. of *pasar*, *passar*) passing, **66** I 4.

pasar = *passar* (in later times intervocalic *-ss-* was simplified to *-s-*) to pass, go through, endure, **56** 422 *a*, 423 *b* ; etc.

pasçer (L. *pascĕre*, V. L. *pascēre*, 'to graze ') to feed, graze, **49** 298 *a*. (Mod. *pacer* shows the ʋsual O. Sp. absorption of *s* by *ç = ts*.)

passar (V. L. *passāre*, from L. *passus*, p.p. of *pandĕre* ' to extend,' i.e. the feet) to pass, pass over, **14** 198 ; **16** 150 ; **17** 201 ; etc.

passo = mod. *paso*, adv. from the noun *passo*, mod. *paso* (L. *passus -um* ' step.' The sense development seems to be ' with [stealthy] step,' ' stealthily,' ' quietly,' and 'quickly'), quietly, quickly, softly, **53** 4.

patriarca (learned word ; L. L. *patrĭarcha*, Gk. πατρίάρχης) patriarch (as a religious dignitary), **69** XIX 8.

Patronio (pr. n.) Patronius, **54** 1 etc.

paz (L. *pax*, *pacem*) peace, **48** 14 *b*.

pecado (L. *peccātum*) sin, **34** 77 *c* ; **35** 81 *d* ; **48** 15 *c* ; etc. ; *mal pecado !* what a pity ! **34** 83 *c* ; devil, **35** 334 *b* ; **38** 364 *c*. (The personification of " sin " as the " Devil " continues in popular Sp.)

pechar (V. L. *pactare* based on L. *pactum* ' bargain,' ' business affair ' ; cf. L. *pangere* and *paciscor*)

to pay, give as tribute, **45** 9 ; **53** 26.

< pecho *

pedir (L. *petĕre*, V. L. *petīre*) to ask, entreat, ask of, **15** 133 ; **19** 1129 ; etc. ; (n.) begging, **26** 107 *c*.

pedricador (half-learned word ; metathesized form of *predicador*, L. *praedĭcator*, *praedĭcatōrem*) preacher, **66** 6.

pedricar (learned word ; metathesized form of *predicar*, L. *praedĭcāre*) to preach, **68** VIII 5.

pelea (perhaps an abstract from *pelear* ' to fight.' This latter is of uncertain origin. The Gk. παλαίειν ' to struggle,' ' wrestle,' has been proposed. Not unlikely is a formation on *pelo*, L. *pĭlus -um* ' hair,' in *-ear*, V. L. *-ĭdĭare*, i.e. ' to clutch by the hair,' ' pull the hair out of,' ' fight ') struggle, fight, **43** 21.

peleio scribal for *pellejo* (masc. form corresponding to *pelleja*, L. *pellĭcŭla*, dimin. of *pellis*) skin, **24** 92 *b*.

peligroso -a (metathesis of L. *perĭcŭlōsus -a -um*) perilous, dangerous, **50** 491 *b*.

pena (L. *poena*, V. L. *pēna*) pain, penalty, punishment, **27** 355 *b* ; **61** 18 ; etc.

penar (V. L. *pēnare* ; cf. *pena*) to suffer pain, **21** 13.

pendon (apparently from L. *pĭnna* ' feather.' It may be a loan-word from O. Fr. *pennon*, an augmentative of L. *pĭnna* ; cf. Ital. *pennone*. The banner or pennon

* See Correction p. 176a

appears to have been originally a plume or bunch of feathers. The *d* may be due to the influence of *pender* 'to hang'; cf. the interworkings of Eng. *pennant* and *pendant*. In O. Sp., loan-words in *-nn-* were sometimes rendered with *-nd-*, i.e. the second dental nasal lost its nasality and remained as a dental stop) pennant, number of men going with a pennant, i.e. a knight and followers, **13** 16; **38** 365 *b*.

penitencia (learned word; L. *poenĭtĕntĭa*) penitence, penance, **21** 17; *penitençja* **68** VIII 6.

pensar (learned development, as the retention of *n* before *s* shows; cf. *pesar*, the popular development; L. *pensāre* 'to weigh,' 'consider.' The Romance form with *n* has the figurative sense only) to consider, imagine, think, intend, **56** 423 *a*; **62** 11; etc.; *pensarse de* to bethink one's self of, **19** 1135 etc.

penssar = *pensar*, **62** 25. (Frequently in O. Sp. *s* is written double after *n*; cf. *Alfonsso*, etc. This may have been done to stress the importance of pronouncing carefully the combination of *n* and *s*, which was not a popular one, since L. *ns* properly became *s* in V. L.; cf. the doubling also of *f* after *n*, *inffante*, for a similar reason, since L. *nf* tended to become *ff*, *f* in V. L.)

penytençia = *penitençia*, **25** 101 *b*.

peña vera (L. *pĭnna varĭa* 'variegated plumage'; cf. O. Fr. *panne* and *vair*) a skin or fur of variegated color, **49** 17 *b*. (L. *varia* may be itself an adaptation of some other word.)

peñar (cf. *enpeñar*) **14** 92.

peon (V. L. **pĕdo*, *pĕdōnem*, from *pes*) footman; (pl.) infantry, **37** 355 *a*; **44** 11.

peor (L. *pejor*, *pejōrem*) worse, worst, **69** XLII 7.

percebir (L. *percĭpĕre*, V. L. **percĭpīre*) to perceive; *percebida* (p.p. fem. sg. in pres. pf. tense and agreeing with the direct obj., as sometimes occurred in O. Sp.) **10** 101. (The form *percibir*, which remains in mod. Sp., owes its first *i* to forms like *percibiendo*, *percibieron*, etc., in which the following *i* closed the *e* to *i*.)

percibistis = *percibistes* (which the rhyme requires), **10** 97; cf. *percebir*. (It is the mod. *percibisteis*.)

perder (L. *perdĕre*, V. L. **perdēre*) to lose, destroy, **20** 1189; **25** 99 *d*; etc.

perdja = *perdía* (cf. *perder*), **50** 498 *d*.

perdon (abstract from *perdonar*) pardon, **34** 81 *d* etc.

perdonar (V. L. **perdōnāre*) to pardon, **43** 24 etc.

perdonassen = mod. *perdonasen* (cf. *perdonar*), **40** title.

peresco = mod. *perezco* (pres. 1 of O. Sp. *peresçer*, mod. *perecer*;

V. L. *perescēre, L. perīre) to perish, **56** 424 d.

perigro (L. perīcŭlum > periglo and, by assimilation, perigro ; the usual Castilian form is peligro, which shows interchange of l and r) peril, **56** 423 c.

periurar = perjurar (L. perjūrāre) to swear emphatically, commit perjury ; periurados perjured, perjurers, **16** 164.

pero (L. pĕr + hŏc ; without diphthongization because used syntactically as an unaccented proclitic combination) but, yet, however, nevertheless, **31** 11 d ; **41** 8 ; etc.

Perpinnan = Perpiñán (pr. n.) Perpignan, **52** 8. (This shows nn = Fr. palatalized gn.)

pertenecer (V. L. *pertenescēre, L. pertĭnēre) to appertain, belong, **9** 72.

pesado -a (p.p. of pesar) heavy, weighty, troubled, distressing, grievous, **14** 86, 91 ; **34** 83 ; **64** 94 a.

pesar (L. pensāre, V. L. *pēsar) to weigh, weigh upon, grieve, vex, displease, **18** 1098 ; **19** 1145 ; **26** 111 d ; **38** 364 c ; etc. ; (n.) grief, vexation, trouble, **27** 357 a ; **44** 9 ; etc. ; cf. pensar.

peso (L. pensum, V. L. *pēsum) weight, act of weighing (in this sense it may be an abstract from pesar), **17** 185.

pesol = pesó + le (cf. pesar), **42** 19.

petavynos = Petavinos pr. n. (L. Pĭctavīnus -a -um, accusative pl.

-os ; Fr. Poitevins), men of Poitou, **37** 358 b.

petral (L. pĕctŏrālis -e, [corium] pectŏrāle) breast leather of a horse, **22** 34. (Mod. Sp. pretal shows metathesis of the r ; it may be the real form in the text.)

Pharaon (L. L. Pharao, Pharaōnem) (pr. n.) Pharaoh, **45** title.

philosofo = mod. filósofo (learned word ; L. phĭlŏsŏphus -um) philosopher, **61** 6, 22 ; etc.

piadad (cf. piedat ; L. pĭĕtas, pĭĕtatem ; not wholly popular in its treatment ; the first a of piadad may be due to the influence of the second and accented a. The mod. form of the noun is piedad, but the a still stands in piadoso -a, apiadarse, etc.) pity, compassion, **70** LII 2.

piadoso -a (V. L. *pĭĕtōsus -a -um ; cf. piadad) pious, compassionate, **28** 363 a ; **50** 166 c ; etc.

pidiesse = mod. pidiese (impf. sbj. 3 of pedir), **27** 359 c.

pie (L. pes, pĕdem > piede > pie[e]) foot, **42** 22 ; **49** 300 b ; de pie on foot, **20** 1213.

pieça (V. L. *pĕcĭa from the stem pic-, picc-, whence comes also pequeño, Ital. piccolo, etc. A V.L. *pettia has also been proposed. The etymon is not clear) piece, **43** 6 ; **61** 12 ; cf. mod. pieza.

piedat = piedad (with the usual O. Sp. unvoicing of final d to t) pity, **39** 369 d ; cf. piadad.

piedes (cf. pie) feet, **31** 12 b, 13 a.

piedra (L. *pĕtra*) stone, gem, **30** 3 *d* ; **59** 7 ; etc.

piel (L. *pĕllis -em* > *pielle* > *piell*, and, with loss of palatalization in the final position, > *piel* ; the pl. *pielles* shows the retention of the palatalized *l* in the intervocalic position ; the form *pieles* is remade on *piel*. The *ll* did not palatalize early enough to prevent the diphthongization) skin, fur, **16** 178 ; **17** 195.

pielles pl. of *piel*, **13** 4.

pienssa, pienssan (cf. *penssar*) **62** 15 ; **13** 10 ; **19** 135.

plaça (V. L. **plattĕa* for L. *platĕa* ; the treatment of initial *pl-* is not wholly popular as *pl-* > *ll-*) place, square, **60** 24 ; cf. mod. *plaza*.

plata (noun from V. L. **plattus -a -um* ; cf. Gk. πλατύς ' flat,' ' flat surface,' ' plate,' ' plate or flat strip of metal,' ' silver [plate] ') silver, **13** 81 ; **17** 184 ; etc. ; cf. *plaça*.

plazentero -a (formation in *-ero -a* on L. *placens, placĕntem*, pres. part. of *placēre*) pleasing, **48** 15 *d* ; cf. mod. *placentero -a*.

plazer (L. *placēre* ; the *pl-* did not receive the more popular treatment > *ll-*) to please, **11** 127 ; **18** 1098 ; **19** 1128 ; etc. (cf. pret. indic. *plogo, plogieron* ; impf. sbj. *ploguiesse*) ; (n.) pleasure, **41** 25 ; **42** 8 ; etc. ; cf. mod. *placer*.

plazme = *plaze* + *me* (cf. *plazer*), **16** 180.

plazo (L. *placĭtum* from *placĭtus -a -um* > **plazedo* > **plazdo*, and, by absorption of *d* into *z* = *dz*, > *plazo*. The sense development is perhaps [*tempus*] *placitum* ' pleasing or suitable time,' ' time agreeable to both parties,' ' stipulated time ') appointed time ; *metiola en plazo* he set a time for it, **20** 1208 ; cf. *pleyto*.

plego = mod. *llegó* (cf. *llegar* ; this is either a Latinism for *llegó*, or a dialect form showing the retention of *pl-*) arrived, reached, **28** 368 *c*.

plena fem. adj. (L. word), full, **51** 1662 *a*.

plera (scribal for *pluera*, required by the rhyme ; but it is L. *plōrat* ; cf. *llorar*) weeps, **21** 7. (Cf. Notes.)

pleytear (verb formed on *pleyto* + *-ear*, V. L. *-ĭdĭare*) to plead, bargain, **27** 357 *b*.

pleytesia (learned formation on *pleyto* + *es*, L. *-ensis -em*, > *pleytes* ' skilled in pleas ' + *-ia* > *pleytesia*) agreement, covenant, **58** 436 *c*.

pleyto (L. *placitum* ' something pleasing,' ' a plea,' ' an affair,' > **plactum* > **playto* > *pleyto* = mod. *pleito*. The development is not wholly popular as regards Castilian; it should be **plecho* or **llecho*) affair, matter, business, compact, **16** 160. (Cf. the different treatment represented by *plazo*.)

plogieron = mod. *pluguieron*, pret. 3 pl. of *plazer* (with the usual closing force of * į* ; L. *placuērunt*, with a substitution in the ending of the 4th conj. *-iĕrunt*, > *plo-g[u]ieron*. The voicing of the *c* > *g* is peculiar, as epenthetic *ụ* seems to have prevented voicing; cf. *sapuit* > *sopo*. Of course the *pl* does not show the really popular treatment), pleased, **60** 28.

plogo = mod. *plugo* (analogous to *pluguieron*, etc.; L. *placŭit* > **plaugo*, with analogical *-o* [cf. **venŭit*, O. Sp. *veno*, etc.], > **plougo* > *plogo* ; for the *g* cf. *plogieron*), pret. 3 of *plazer*, **41** 24; **55** 26; etc.

plogol = *plogo* + *le*, **41** 24.

ploguiesse = mod. *pluguiese* (impf. sbj. of *plazer*), **43** 30.

plorando cf. *llorar* (the *pl-* is probably only etymological; cf. *lo-rando*, **13** 1), weeping, **13** 18.

poblar (V. L. **pŏpŭlāre*, based on L. *pŏpŭlus*) to people, settle, occupy, fill, **17** 1087; **31** 15 *b*; **38** 363 *c*.

pobre (L. *pauper*, *paupĕrem* ; in view of the voicing of *p* > *b* perhaps we must start from V. L. **poper*, **popĕrem* ; cf. *paucum* > *poco* and Ptg. *pobre* instead of **poubre*, Ptg. *pouco* and Ital. *poco* beside *povero*) poor, poor man, **24** 96 *b* ; **50** 499 *a*.

pobreza (*pobre* + abstract ending *-eza*, L. *-ĭtĭa*) poverty, **54** title, and 6; **55** 9; etc.

poco -a (L. *paucus -a -um* ; the *ụ*, partly consonantal in nature, seems to have prevented the *c*

from receiving the intervocalic voicing; cf. Ptg. *pouco*, Ital. *poco*) little, short, but little, **6** 4; **15** 133; etc.; (pl.) few, but few, **25** 98 *d*; (adv. and pron.) a little, **43** 5; *dende a poco* shortly after, **62** 18; (pl.) few, **45** 16 etc.; *po-cos de annos* a few years, **26** 110 *a*.

poçon (cf. *pozon*, which represents exactly L. *potio*, *potĭonem* 'po-tion,' 'poison.' The *ç* may be due to a form with intrusive *n* ; cf. *ponzoña* and *emponzoñar*; this shows the influence of *pŭnctus*, V. L. **punctĭare* > *punçar*, mod. *punzar* 'to sting,' i.e. 'give a poisonous bite') poison, **46** 20.

podedes = mod. *podéis* (V. L. **po-tētĭs* for L. *potestis* > *podedes* > **podeẹs* > *podéis*; as **podés* might be expected, the *i* may be ana-logical to the *i* of the first conj. *amáis*, etc. But cf. *rey*) pres. 2 pl. of *poder*, **57** 430 *d*; **68** VII 3.

poder (V. L. **pŏtēre* for L. *possum*, *posse* = *pot*[*is*] *sum*, *pot*[*is*] *esse* 'I am able,' 'to be able'; cf. L. *pot.es*, *pot.est*, etc.) to be able, **8** 63; **9** 78; etc. (already in O. Sp. the pret. shows *u* instead of *o* ; *potŭi* > *pude*, **61** 7 ; *potŭĭt* > *pudo*, **39** 371 *c*; etc.; yet, cf. *podieremos*, **28** 365 *c*; *podiesse*, **28** 363 *d* etc.) ; (n.) power, force, **25** 99 *a* ; **34** 77 *b*.

poderoso -a (formation in *-oso -a* on n. *poder*) powerful, **44** 6.

podes = mistake for *podedes*, **57** 430 *a*.

podestad (L. *potestas, potestātem*) power, authority, magistrate, **11** 120.

podie = weakened form of *podía* (cf. *poder*), **30** 7 *d*.

podiedes = weakened form of *podiades* > *podíais* (cf. *poder*), **46** 15.

podien = weakened form of *podían*, **16** 171.

podieremos = mod. *pudiéremos* (cf. *poder*), **28** 365 *c*.

podiesse, podiessen = mod. *pudiese*, *pudiesen* (cf. *poder*), **28** 363 *d*; **27** 357 *c*.

podredes = mod. *podréis* (cf. *poder*), **57** 430 *c*.

podrie = weakened form of *podría* (cf. *poder*), **20** 1214, 1218.

podriedes = weakened form of *podriades*, mod. *podríais*, **46** 18.

podrien = weakened form of *podrían* (cf. *poder*), **43** 16.

podrremos scribal for *podremos* (cf. *poder*), **36** 347 *b*.

podrya = *podría* (cf. *poder*), **33** 72 *d*.

poema (L. *pŏēma*; learned word) poem, **63** title.

poner (L. *pōnĕre*, V. L. **pōnēre*) to put, place, put on, wear, employ, **16** 167, 171; **62** 17; **68** VIII 7; etc.; cf. *porne*, *puesto*.

poquilleio = *poquillejo*, adv. (*poco* + *-illo* from L. *-ĕllum*, + *-ejo* from L. *-ĭcŭlum*), very little, **24** 92 *d*.

por prep. (L. *prō*, V. L. **por*; this may be due to the influence of *per* on *pro*, but L. shows *por* in the prefix of *porrigere*, *portendere*, etc., so that it may be an old popular L. form. Cf. Eng. *for*, *fore*, German *vor*, *für*, etc.; Fr. *pour*), for, by, through, to, in order to, trying to, as, during, with, **6** 15, 18; **7** 27; **11** 119; etc.; *por aqui* hither, this way, **10** 104; *por caridad* in charity, forsooth (cf. *par c.*), **9** 87; *por uer* in truth, **6** 15; *por uertad* in truth, **9** 86; **11** 15; *por todos* in all, **43** 16; *por siempre* (cf. mod. *para s.*) forever, **14** 108; *por al* = *pora 'l*, i.e. *pora el* until, **29** 370 *b*; *por que* (conj.) why, wherefore, in order to, so that, **12** 139; **14** 112; **40** 17; **42** 13; **46** 18; etc.; *son por llegar* are to come, have yet to come, **36** 342 *c*.

pora = *por* (V. L. **por* + *a*, L. *ad*) for, to, toward, in order to, **14** 83; **16** 176; **17** 202; **20** 1203; **33** 76 *c*; etc.; *pora alla* thither, **35** 332 *d*; **42** 27; etc.; *pora* = *pora* + *á*, **20** 1191. Cf. *para*, which has survived.

porfidia (learned word; L. *perfĭdĭa*, with influence on the first syll. of the prep. and prefix *por*. If the mod. *porfiar*, *porfía*, etc., are derived from this same source, they show an influence on the second syll. of the *ī* of L. *fīdus* *-a -um*. They may represent a V. L. **porfīdare* based directly on *fīdus*) obstinacy, **26** 112 *c*; cf. *prohio*.

poridad (L. *puritas, pūrĭtātem*; the *o* is peculiar; the mod. word is *puridad*) secrecy, **14** 104. (The retention of the *ĭ* is not popular.)

porne = mod. *pondré* (*poner* + [*h*]*e*, > *ponere*, with syncope > *ponre*, and with metathesis > *porne* ; so also in O. Sp. *verne* = *vendré*. It was, however, the tendency to keep intact the verb stem that prevailed. Hence the *pon-* of the stage *ponre* simply developed a transitional *d* after it before the *r*) I shall put, **52** 7 ; cf. *poner*.

porqu' = *porque*, **63** 93 *d*.

porque = *por* + *que*, wherefore, why, (as rel.) in order that, **6** 21 ; **42** 32 ; **55** 13. (Also written *por que* **12** 139 etc.)

portero 1 (L. *portārĭus -a -um* from *pŏrta* 'door') doorkeeper, **56** 426 *a* ; **57** 430 *a*.

portero 2 (perhaps a formation in *-ero* on the stem of O. Sp. *portar*, L. *portare*, 'to bear,' 'carry' ; cf. Fr. *porteur* < L. *portator*, *porta-tōrem*. Yet as janitors also have functions as messengers, this may be the same as *portero* 1) messenger, ambassador, officer, **44** 10 ; **63** 91 *b*.

Portogal (pr. n.) Portugal, **41** 3.

pos (L. *pŏst*, developed in proclitic unaccented use, hence without diphthongization ; cf. *pues*, the accented form) : *en pos*, *en pos de* (prep.) after, **53** 8 ; **55** 2, 3, 5 ; **69** XIX 8.

posada (noun from p.p. fem. of *posar*) abode, lodging, rest, quarters, inn, halt, **17** 200 ; **26** 110 *c* ; **37** 356 *d* ; **57** 433 *b*.

posar (L. *pausāre*) to rest, remain, be, **23** 1 *c* ; **25** 103 *d*.

posas (perhaps scribal error for *esposas*, which suits the meter better. This from L. *spōnsa*, V. L. *spōsa, is used as a term of thieves' jargon; 'bride,' 'spouse,' ' something bound to one,' there-fore ' fetters ') **50** 497 *c*.

posose = *póso*, mod. *puso*, from *poner* + *se*, **60** 7.

pozon (L. *potio*, *potĭōnem*) poison, **63** 92 *b*. Cf. mod. *ponzoña* and O. Sp. *poçon*.

pphan (perhaps scribal for *Preste Johan* or rather *Prest Johan*, which suits the meter better) Prester John, **30** 7 *b*.

prado (L. *pratum*) meadow, **60** 9.

preçiado -a (p.p. of *preçiar*) prized, esteemed, valuable, famed, **30** 10 *b* ; **51** 1663 *g* ; **52** 6 ; **65** 103 *c*.

preçiar (learned word ; V. L. *prĕ-tĭāre from L. *prĕtĭum*) to prize, esteem, vaunt, **41** 17 ; cf. *presçiar*.

preçiauan = *preciavan*, *preciaban* (cf. *preçiar*) : *se preçiauan por* vaunted of, **41** 17.

preçio (learned word ; L. *prĕtĭum*) price, prize, reward, **23** 4 *b* ; **28** 361 *c* ; *mal preçio* contempt, dis-grace, **38** 366 *e*.

preçioso -a (learned word ; L. *pre-tĭōsus -a -um*) precious, fine, **30** 7 *a* ; **31** 14 *b* ; etc.

pregar (L. *prĕcāri* and *prĕcāre*) to pray, **7** 32. ✓

pregon (L. *praeco*, *praecōnem* ' crier,' ' herald ' ; thence, by transferal, ' proclamation ') herald, procla-mation, **19** 1187 ; **20** 1197 ; **33** 76 *a*.

pregonar (L. *praecōnāre*) to proclaim, **41** 16.

preguntar (V. L. **percunctāre*, L. *percontari* and *percontare* for *percunctari* etc. There is a metathesis of *r* in the first syll.) to ask, **53** 14; **55** 7; **59** 17, 24.

premia (perhaps an abstract from O. Sp. *premiar* 'to press,' 'oppress,' formed on stem of L. *prĕmĕre*) force, compulsion, **20** 1193; **45** 11.

prender (V. L. **prendēre*, L. *prĕhĕndĕre*) to take, arrest, imprison, **15** 119, 127, 140, 147; **24** 97 *d*; **46** 26; etc.; cf. *priso*, *preso*.

prepuesto -a (L. *praepŏsĭtus -a -um* > V. L. **prepŏstus*, etc.) Superior, **24** 87 *b*.

presçio = *preçio* (the inorganic *s* is due to the analogy of *nesçio* > *neçio*, etc.) price, value, **30** 9 *d*.

present = *presente*: *al present* just now, for the present, **28** 364 *c*.

presente (learned word; L. pres. part. adj. *presens*, *presĕntem*) : *de presente* just now, **68** IX 1.

presetes (perhaps with metathesis of *r*, from Provençal *perset* 'dark,' 'dark red,' i.e. a cloth of this color) purple cloth garments(?), **30** 6 *c*.

presion (L. *prehensio -onem*, > **prensio -onem*, V. L. **presio*, *presĭōnem* > *presion*, whence, also, through the closing effect of *ĭ* > *prision*) prison, imprisonment, **28** 361 *b*; **63** 91 *c*; **64** 100 *b*.

preso -a (p.p. of *prender* and also adj.; L. *prehensus -a -um* >

*prensus > V. L. **prēsus -a -um*) taken, captured, imprisoned, **44** 8; **63** 93 *a*; **65** 102 *d*; (n.) captive, prisoner, **28** 365 *d*, 367 *c*.

prestalde = *prestad* + *le* (with a common O. Sp. metathesis of *dl* > *ld*; cf. *prestar*), **15** 118.

prestar (L. *praestare* 'to furnish,' 'offer,' 'present,' whence, in Romance, 'to lend') to lend, **15** 118; to be useful, **48** 13 *d*; (n.) (L. *praestare* 'to be of excellence') excellence, **31** 18 *c*; **49** 490 *b*.

presurado -a (formation in *-ado -a* on *presura*, L. *pressūra*) hasty, hurried, in haste, **15** 137. (Cf. mod. *apresurado* and *presuroso -a*.)

preualicador = *prevalicador* (and this, with dissimilation of second *r* from first, < *prevaricador*; half-learned word; L. *praevarĭcātor -ōrem*) prevaricator, **69** XLIII 1.

prez (perhaps a loan-word from Prov. *pretz* < L. *prĕtĭum*, which gave otherwise the learned Sp. *precio*) repute, fame, **43** 26.

priado = *privado* (with popular loss of *v* after L. *ĭ*; *prīvatus -um* become adverbial in use. The sense change is 'privately,' 'stealthily,' 'quickly.' There seems to be no need of appealing to Celtic *briga*. It is possible that in V. L. the sense was influenced by that of *prius*) quickly, **68** VIII 4; **71** LXXVIII 3; cf. *priuado*.

priessa = mod. *priesa* and *prisa* (fem. noun from L. p.p. *prĕssus*

-a -um) haste, **42** 26; distress, need, **61** 2, 23 (in the latter senses the word is now archaic).

primas adv. (from L. *prīmus -a -um* ; the -*s* is due to *pues* and other advs. having it etymologically; cf. *antes*, etc.), for the first time, **6** 3.

primero -a adj. (L. *prīmārĭus -a -um*), first, former, **23** 4 *a* ; **34** 80 *c* ; etc.; *de la primera, luego de la primera*, at the outset, **23** 3 *a* ; **34** 79 *c* ; **45** 6; adv. *primero* first, **15** 140; conj. *primero que* before, **61** 7.

primicia (learned word; L. *prīmĭtĭae*) first fruits, **21** 17.

primo -a (L. *prīmŭs -a -um* ' first,' i.e. ' one related in the first degree,' ' cousin ') cousin, **27** 360 *a* ; *primo-a cormano-a* cousin german, first cousin, **40** 9; **41** 20.

prínçipe (learned word; L. *princeps, prīncĭpem*) first, beginning, **71** LXXIX 5; prince, **62** 13, 16; etc.

Prior (L. *prior, prĭōrem*) Prior, **24** 87 *b*.

prisieron strong pret. 3 pl. of *prender* (L. *prehenderunt*, V. L. *presiérunt; the *ĭ* changed the first *e* to *i*), took, **18** 1099. (This, like other forms, shows that *prender* in O. Sp. had often the force of mod. *tomar*.)

prision (cf. *presion*) **27** 358 *d*. (This remains the mod. form.)

priso strong pret. 3 of *prender* (L. *prehendi*, V. L. *presī > O. Sp. *prise*; the *i* passed by analogy to the 3 sg. *priso*, which, coming

from L. *prehendit*, V. L. *presĭt, should have had *e* ; cf. also the *i* of *prisieron*), took, captured, **14** 110; **18** 1095; **43** 8.

prissieron scribal mistake for *prisieron*, **27** 354 *c*.

priuado = *privado* (L. *prīvātus -um*) one privy to a prince's counsels, favorite, courtier, **58** 441 *a* ; (p.p. of *privar*, L. *prīvāre*) deprived, **59** 5; (adv.; cf. *priado*) stealthily, quickly, **14** 89; **16** 148, 166; **17** 208.

pro n. (L. *prō*, existing as a prep. ' for,' ' for the advantage of,' ' in favor of,' and as a prefix, e.g. in *prosum, prodesse*, ' to be of advantage '), advantage, **18** 1112. (The word is masc. here; it is of common gender in mod. Sp.)

probar (L. *prŏbāre*) to prove, **52** 7 ; **63** 92 *c* ; cf. *prouar*.

profecia (learned word; L. L. *prophetia*; cf. Gk. προφητεία) prophecy, **12** 140.

profecta (learned word; L. *prophēta* ; the *c* is inorganic and unpronounced; it is due to its appearance in many -*ct*- Latin words) prophet, **34** 77 *d*.

profetizar (L. L. *prophetizare* ; cf. Biblical Gk. προφητίζειν) prophesy, **34** 77 *d*.

prohio pres. 1 of O. Sp. *prohiar* (apparently V. L. *prōfīdare, based on L. *fīdus -a -um*. But cf. *porfidia* and mod. *porfía, porfiar*): *lo prohio* I insist upon it, I maintain, **6** 12. (If the *f* of *prōfīdare were treated as initial, in popular Sp. it would become *h*.)

prólogo (learned word; L. *prŏlŏgus -um*) prologue, **66** 1.

prometer (L. *promĭttĕre*, V. L. *promĭttēre*) to promise, **29** 370 *a*, 371 *d*; **57** 429 *c*.

propiçio -a (learned word; L. *propĭtĭus -a -um*) propitious, **25** 100 *d*.

propiedat = mod. *propiedad* (L. *proprietas, proprĭĕtātem*, with dissimilation of *r* and usual O. Sp. unvoicing of final *d* > *t*) property, quality, **49** 490 *a*.

prosa (L. *prōsa*) prose, discourse, account, **23** 1 *d*, 2 *a*; **48** 11 *c*.

✓ **prouar** = *provar* (cf. *probar*) to test, prove, **8** 65; **10** 89, 91; **24** 94 *c*; etc.

prouecho = mod. *provecho* (L. *prōfĕctus -um*, with voicing of intervocalic *-f-* and the closing of *ĕ*, V. L. *ę*, by the following palatal. It is unnecessary to appeal to L. *provectus*) profit, advantage, **62** 25.

prueua = *prueva*, mod. *prueba*, imper. sg. of *prouar*.

pudet scribal for *puede* (cf. *poder*), **6** 13.

pudiemos = mod. *pudimos* (cf. *poder*; the *ie* is due to influence of *pudieron*, etc.): *non pudiemos mas* we could not help it, **18** 1117.

pudiessen = mod. *pudiesen* (cf. *poder*), **41** 19.

pueblo (L. *pŏpŭlus -um*) people, nation, men, **23** 2 *b*; **30** 4 *a*; **34** 82 *a*; etc.

pueent scribal error for *puent*, *puente* (L. *pons, pŏntem*), bridge, **16** 150.

puerta (L. *pŏrta*) door, gate, **13** 3; **56** 426 *c*; etc.

puerto (L. *pŏrtus -um*) port, pass, defile, **17** 1087; **33** 71 *d*, 72 *c*; etc.; *salir a puerto* to escape, succeed, **35** 331 *b*.

pues (L. *pŏst* developed in accented adverbial use; cf. unaccented *pos*) since, for, **53** 21; **55** 12, 19; etc.; *pues que* since, **45** 7; prep. *en pues* (cf. *pos*) behind, **30** 6 *a*.

puesto -a (p.p. of *poner*; L. *pŏsĭtus*, V. L. **pŏstus -a -um*) put, set up, settled, determined, **31** 13 *a*; **34** 80 *a*; **60** 18. ✓

pugn (perhaps for *pugnen* from *pugnar*, L. *pŭgnāre*. O. Sp. had also the popular form *puñar*, whose palatalized *ñ* closed the *ŭ*, V. L. *o*, to *u*) strive, **66** 7.

punentes (L. pres. part. pl. *pŭngentes* from *pŭngĕre*; the *n* may mean *ñ*) poignant, sharp, pricking, **22** 32.

punnada = *puñada* (a formation in *-ada*, L. *-ata*, on *punno*, *puño*) punch, blow of the fist, **42** 20.

punno = *puño* (L. *pŭgnus -um*; the palatalized *ñ* closed *ŭ*, V. L. *ǫ*, to *u*) fist, **43** 10. (This, like *punnada*, shows already the palatalization of O. Sp. *nn*; otherwise the *nn* could not appear here.)

punta (fem. n., corresponding to *punto*, L. *pŭnctum*; the *ŭ*, V. L. *ǫ*, was closed by the palatal following) point, sharp point, end, **30** 10 *a*.

punto (cf. *punta*) point of time, moment, **66** I 4; *en punto* in a moment, in a trice, **67** II 5.

puro -a (L. *pūrus -a -um*) pure, **60** 21 ; **71** LXXIX 3.

✓ **pus** scribal for *pues*, **10** 102; **12** 131.

✓ **pusto** scribal for *puesto*, **11** 110.

pyntado -a = *pintado -a* (p.p. of *pintar*, V. L. **pĭnctare*, from L. *pingere*, *pinctum* ; the palatal closed the *ĭ*, V. L. *ę*, to *i*) painted, **31** 15 a.

pytavynos = *petavynos*, **38** 361 b.

Pyteos (pr. n.) Poitou, **35** 328 a.

qque scribal error for *que*, what, **11** 127.

qu' = *que*, **63** 90 a, 93 b.

qual interrog. and rel. pron. and adj. (L. *qualis -em*), what, which, as, such as, **8** 60 ; **9** 80 ; **23** 2 b ; **24** 94 c ; **29** 371 a ; **44** 20 ; **59** 24 ; **67** III 8 ; rel. pron. *el qual, la qual*, etc., who, whom, **59** 2 ; **66** 2 ; **68** VII 5 ; etc. ; *quales que* whichever, whoever, **27** 360 a ; *qual quier, qual quiera* whatever, **68** VIII 2 ; etc.; (excl.) *¡qual!* what! what a! **6** 1 etc ; cf. mod. *cual*.

quand apocopated form of **quando**, **36** 350 c.

quando (L. *quando*) when, whenever, as soon as, since, if, **14** 90 ; **17** 188 ; **24** 95 b ; **52** 3 ; etc. ; (prep.) at the time of, **66** I 7 ; cf. mod. *cuando*.

quanto -a adj. and pron. (L. *quantus -a -um*), how much, all the, all that ; (pl.) how many, all the, those who, etc., **37** 354 c ; **41** 28 ; **48** 14 c ; **53** 5 ; etc. ; *quanto i a que* how long since, **10** 96; *quanto que* whatever, **14** 111 ; *quanto que* all who, **20** 1215; *quanto tanto* the...the, **50** 491 c; *quanto mas . . . mas* the more . . . the more, **53** 1 ; *¡quanto!* how much! **56** 423 b ; cf. mod. *cuanto -a*.

Quatro (L. *quattŭor* > V. L. **quattor*, and with influence of *unus -um*, > Sp. *uno*, of. L. *octo*, etc., *quáttoro* > *qua[t]tro*) four, **31** 13 a.

que 1, interrog. pron. and adj. (L. *quĭd*), what, which, **9** 79 ; **11** 114 ; **15** 129 ; (as indirect interrog. = *lo que*) **6** 7 ; **19** 1127 ; etc. ; *a que* for what, why, **65** 107 d ; *por que* why, **12** 139 etc.; *tener que dar* to have something to give, **28** 363 b ; *que qujera que* whatever, **24** 87 a ; (excl.) *qué* what! what a! **13** 20 ; **41** 27 ; **60** 4 ; etc.

que 2, interrog. and rel. pron. (L. *quī, quae, quĕm, quid*, developed in unaccented and proclitic or enclitic position, and therefore without diphthongization for *quae* and *quĕm* > V. L. *que* and *quem*, which latter could lose its *m*), who, whom, which, that, **6** 6 ; **7** 40 ; **13** 8 ; **18** 1094 ; **20** 1190 ; **21** 14 ; **23** 1 a ; etc.; cf. *qui* and *quien*.

que 3, conj. (L. *quĭd* with influence of *quod*), that, **6** 4 ; **21** 5 ; **24** 93 b ; etc. ; so that, **14** 93 ; **29** 1 b ; **30** 8 c ; etc. ; *a que* until, **63** 91 b ;

(pleonastic) *que si* yes, **53** 16;
(pleonastic after *preguntar*) **55**
7 ; (with sense of L. *quam* and
quod) than, **20** 1207 ; **21** 24 ; **41**
30 ; etc. ; (with sense of L. *quod*,
quia, etc.) for, because, **15** 143 ;
19 1129 ; **24** 92 *b* ; etc. ; though,
21 26.

quebrantar (metathesized form of
crebantar) to break, break down,
shatter, **50** 497 *a* ; **33** 74 *d*. (This
is the mod. form.)

quebrar (metathesized form of *crebar*) to break, **19** 1141. (This
form has survived as the mod.
form.)

quedar (V. L. **quētāre* from V. L.
*quētus -a -um for L. *quiētus* ;
the sense development is 'to be
quiet,' 'to remain behind in a
state of quiescence,' 'to remain') to be left, **67** II 3.

quedo 1, scribal for *cuedo* (cf. *cuedar*), I mean, I intend, **21** 2.
(The scribe improperly uses *qu*
= *kw* before *e* as he properly
used it before *a*.)

quedo -a 2 (V. L. **quētus -a -um* for
L. *quiētus*) quiet, at rest, **36**
338 *c* ; **57** 431 *d*, 433 *d* ; (adv.)
quietly, **57** 434 *a*.

quel' = *que + le*, **54** 3, 13, 15 ; etc.

quel = *que le*, **9** 72 ; **18** 1099 ; **41**
16 ; etc. (Like *quel'*, this shows
the enclitic nature of *le*.)

quel = *que + el* (art. and pron.), **37**
355 *b* ; **58** 441 *b* ; **48** 13 *a*. (This
shows the enclitic nature of *el*, *él*.)

quela = *que + la*, **26** 109 *d* ; **49** 17 *b* ;
50 498 *b* ; etc.

quelo = *que + lo*, **23** 3 *a* , **46** 20.

quelos = *que + los*, **48** 13 *d*.

quem = *que + me*, **16** 157 ; **46** 22.
(This shows the enclitic nature
of the pers. pron. *me*.)

quemar (L. *crĕmāre* with loss of
the first *r*, apparently due to
dissimilation in the infin., the
fut. indic., etc. ; of course *qu*
stands for *c = k* before *e*) to
burn, **33** 71 *a* ; cf. *Kemar* in the
Glosses.

quende scribal for *cuende* (cf.
quedo 1), count, **22** 30.

quera scribal for *querrá* (cf. *querer*),
8 69.

querades (L. *quaerātĭs*) = mod. *que-
ráis* (cf. *querer*), **9** 8.

queredes (V. L. **quaerētĭs*) = mod.
queréis (cf. *querer*), **8** 60, 61, 67 ;
9 80 ; **48** 14 *a*.

quereedes scribal error for *queredes*,
21 1.

querer (L. *quaerĕre*, V. L. **quĕrēre*)
to will, wish, desire, like, love,
25 102 *a* etc. ; pres. part. *que-
riendo*, **26** 107 *b* ; p.p. *querido -a*,
25 104 *b* ; pres. *quiero*, **14** 85
etc. ; *quieres*, **25** 99 *b* ; *quiere*, **20**
1189 etc. ; *queremos*, **9** 75 etc. ;
queredes, **8** 61 ; *quieren*, **19** 1143
etc. ; impf. 1 *queria*, **21** 15 ; 3,
64 97 *a* ; 3 pl. *querian*, **37** 358 *c*
etc. ; pret. 2 *quisist*, **21** 21 ; 3
quiso, **20** 1202 ; 3 pl. *quisieron*,
36 350 *a* etc. ; fut. 3 *querra*, **15**
132 ; cond. 1 *querria*, **57** 427 *c*
etc. ; 3, **24** 91 *b* ; 3 pl. *querrian*,
68 IX 7 ; sbj. pres. 3 *quiera*, **47**
11 etc. ; 2 pl. *querades*, **9** 81 ;

querais, **65** 108 *c* ; sbj. fut. 2 *qui-sieres*, **36** 338 *a* ; 3 *quisiere*, **68** VIII 3 etc. ; 1 pl. *quisieremos*, **18** 1120 ; *sy quiere* at least, at any rate, even, **31** 11 *a* ; *sy quiera* at least, **57** 429 *b*.

ꝗuesido (dialectal, i.e. Eastern Sp., p.p. of *querer*, with the distinctive cons. of the pret. *quise*, etc.) wished, desired, **63** 89 *b*.

quexa (abstract from *quexar*) complaint, tribulation, distress, lamentable state, **38** 367 *c* ; **55** 28 ; cf. mod. *queja*.

✓ quexada (ety. ? L. *capsus* cannot give the form) jaw, **42** 21 ; cf. mod. *quijada*.

quexar (V. L. *quĕstĭare* from L. *questus*) to complain, **69** XVIII 7 ; cf. mod. *quejar*.

quexoso -a (formation in *-oso a*, L. *-osus -a -um*, on *quexa*) querulous, scolding, **58** 442 *a* ; cf. *quejoso -a*.

✓ qui (L. *quī*) rel. pron. in accented use (cf. *que*, 2), who, he who, she who, etc., **11** 118 ; **15** 126 ; **30** 7 *d* ; (perhaps a Latinism for *que*) *aquel qui*, **7** 24 ; (perhaps a dialectal Sp. form ?) *al qui*, **28** 362 *d* ; *qui . . . qui* one . . . another, **25** 105 *d* ; *qui quier*, *qui quier que* whoever, anyone, **30** 5 *d* ; **41** 16.

ꝗui, da qui = *daqui* from here, right now, **16** 180.

qui en = *quien*, **20** 1214.

✓ quien (L. *quĕm*, acc. of *quis* and *qui*) interrog. and rel. pron. (subj. and obj. of prep.), who, whom, he who, etc., **20** 1189, 1192, 1218 ;

33 75 *a* ; **36** 347 *b* ; **41** 1 ; **56** 422 *d* ; etc. ; (obj. of prep. and pl. ; cf. mod. *quienes* now more common than *quien* as pl.) whom, **57** 430 *d* ; (indirect obj. without prep.) to whom, **64** 95 *c* ; *quien quier* whoever, **36** 346 *d*.

quier apocopated form of *quiere* (cf. *querer*) : *qui quier que* whoever, **41** 16 ; *quien quier* whoever, **36** 346 *d*.

quiera pres. sbj. 3 of *querer*: *sy quiera* at least, **57** 429 *b*.

quiere pres. 3 of *querer*: *sy quiere* at any rate, even, **31** 11 *a*.

quin scribal for *quien*, **6** 20 ; **9** 79 ; **11** 107.

quinta (L. [*pars*] *quīnta* 'fifth part') fifth part, **20** 1216.

quiro scribal for *quiero* (cf. *querer*), **8** 53.

quis (perhaps L. *quĭs[que]*] : *quis cada vno* each one, **19** 1136. (In mod. Sp. *cada uno* has simply supplanted L. *quisque*.)

quisiesse = mod. *quisiese* (cf. *querer*), **53** 16.

quisiessen = mod. *quisiesen* (cf. *querer*), **24** 91 *a*.

quisist = mod. *quisiste* (cf. *querer*), **21** 21.

quito -a (abstract from *quitar*, based on a V. L. form of L. *quietus -a -um*) something left free or at one's disposal, **49** 300 *d*.

quj = *qui* he who, **23** 4 *d*.

qujera = *quiera* (cf. *querer*) whatever, **24** 87 *a*.

qujso = *quiso* (cf. *querer*), **26** 289 *c*.

[Initial capital *R* usually denotes the rein-
forced *r*, which is also, in the initial position, often written *rr*, and again only
r as in modern Spanish.]

rabi (Gk. ῥαββί, Hebrew *rabī*) rabbi, **12** 135, 139.

Rachel pr. n., **14** 89 etc.

Ramiro pr. n., **40** 2.

rançal (Persian *ransan ?*) a fine
stuff, silken cloth, **17** 183.

Rayzes = mod. *raíces* (L. *radix*, pl.
radīces) roots, **50** 499 *b*.

Razon, razon (L. *ratio*, *ratiōnem*)
reason, remark, word, speech,
13 19 ; **28** 98 *d* ; etc.

Recabdo (abstract from verb *recab-
dar*, mod. *recaudar* ' to achieve,'
' order,' ' secure,' V.L. *recapĭ-
tare* from L. *caput*, *capit-*) prudence, caution, completeness,
message, **17** 206 ; cf. mod. *re-
caudo* and *recado*, with different
senses.

reçebir (L. *recĭpĕre*, V.L. *recĭpīre*)
to receive, accept, **26** 112 *a* ; *Reçibio, reçibio*, pret. 3, **17** 203, 199.
(In mod. *recibir*, the *e* of the
stem has been replaced by the
i which developed from it in
forms like *recibió, recibieron*,
etc.)

Reconbrar (L. *recŭpĕrare*, whence
the usual Sp. *recobrar*. The *n* is
perhaps due to the influence of
Sp. *con*, L. *cum*) recover, re-
form, rally, **19** 1143.

redemjr = *redemir* (L. *redĭmĕre*, V.
L. *redĭmīre*) to redeem, **28**
362 *c*. (Mod. *redimir*, with *i* instead of *e*, shows the analogical

influence of *redimió* and similar
forms.)

redemption (learned word ; L. *red-
emptio, redemptionem*) ransom,
27 358 *b*. (*Redención* is half popular.)

Redes pl. of *red* (L. *rēte* become
fem.) net, **68** VII 6.

redondo (L. *rotŭndus-a-um*, whence
*rodondo and by dissimilation
redondo) round, **7** 41.

rees (L. pl. *rēges*. By contraction
there resulted the pl. *res* ; by a
reduction of the *e* in hiatus to *į*,
y, there resulted *reys*. The pl.
reyes is remade on the Sp. sing.
rey) kings, **12** 134.

refecho (L. *refectum*, or V.L. **re-
factum* from the reconstituted
*refacere for *reficere*) remade, re-
imbursed, established, **16** 173.

Regla, regla (learned word ; L. *rē-
gŭla*. The popular derivative is
reja, with a different sense) rule,
reign, monastic life, **25** 100 *c* ; **70**
LIII 1.

regnado (half-learned ; L. p.p. *reg-
natum*) rule, reign, **40** 1 ; **44** 1.
(The popular form should be
*reñado ; the mod. *reinado* shows
the influence of *rei, rey*.)

rei (L. *rex, rēgem*) king, **8** 66, 69 ;
9 71 ; etc. ; cf. *rey, rees, res, reis,
reyes*.

Reliquias (learned word ; L. pl.
relĭquĭae, relĭquĭas) relics, **29**
2 *a*.

Reluziente (L. pres. part. *relūcens,
relūcĕntem*) shining, bright, **51**
1663 *e* ; mod. *reluciente*.

Remedio (learned word; L. *remĕdĭum*) remedy, help, escape, **71** LXXIX 2.

remenbrades (L. *rememŏrātĭs*, pres. 2 pl. of *rememorare*) you remember, **24** 93 *a*; cf. mod. *rememorar* and *recordar, acordarse*, which have taken the place of the obsolete *remembrar*.

rencura (a formation with the L. abstract ending *-ura* on L. *rancor, rancōrem*. The *e* is due to the influence of the prefix *re-*, indicative of the reflex nature of the sentiment) rancor, grief, complaint, **27** 360 *d*; cf. mod. *rencor*.

renegado -a (L. p.p. *renegātum -am*) renegade, infidel, **27** 354 *b*.

renunçar (half-popular; L. *renŭntĭare*) to announce, make known, **26** 289 *b*; cf. mod. *renunciar*.

repentido -a (V. L. p.p. *repoenĭtītŭm -am* of V. L. *repoenĭtēre*; cf. L. *poenĭtēre*) repentant, **25** 104 *d*.

repoyado (V. L. p.p. *re-pŏdĭātum* of V. L. *re-pŏdĭāre* based on L. *pŏdĭum*; cf. Sp. *apoyar* from V. L. *appodiare*) repulsed, **27** 359 *c*.

Requiere pres. 3 of *requerir* (V. L. *requĕrīre* from L. *re* and *quaerere*), requests, summons, **66** 5.

res (pl.) kings, **22** 30; cf. *rees*.

resçelo (abstract, with inorganic *s*, from O. Sp. *reçelar* 'to dread,' from V. L. *re-zēlāre*, based on L. *zēlus*, Gk. ζῆλος) dread, **69** XLII 5.

Resçibiré fut. 1, with inorganic *s*, of *recibir* (cf. *reçebir*), **71** LXXVIII 5.

Resplandeçiente (V. L. *resplendescens, resplendescĕntem*; cf. L. *resplendēre*; the *a* is due to some exterior influence, possibly that of Fr. *resplendir* or that of O. Sp. *espandir*) resplendent, **51** 1663 *b*.

responder (L. *respŏndēre*) to respond, **40** 13; cf. *respuso*.

respuso, Respuso (V. L. *respŏnsŭit* for L. *respŏndī*) responded, replied, **15** 31; **46** 19. (As pret. 3 of *responder* it is supplanted by the regular *respondió*. *Repuso*, still used in the sense of 'responded,' is probably only *respuso* influenced by the pret. of *reponer*.)

retorico (learned word; L. *rhetŏrĭcus -um*) rhetorician, orator, **11** 124. ✓

retouo, Retouo = *retuvo* (pret. 3 of *retener*, L. *retinēre*, V. L. *retĕnēre*. The form is due to the analogy of *ovo*, from L. *habŭit*, and is not derived from V. L. *retenui*. The mod. *u* of *retuvo* arose in *retuvieron* and similar forms) retained, detained, **14** 111; **29** 369 *b*.

Retrahen = *retraen* (pres. 3 pl. of *retraer*, L. *retrahĕre*, V. L. *retrahēre*) they bring back (a story, etc.), relate, **26** 109 *d*.

rey, Rey (cf. *rei*) king, **14** 90, 114; **16** 156; etc.; cf. also *rrey*.

Reyes (cf. *rees*) kings, **19** 1147.

Reyno = *reino* (half-learned; L. *rĕgnum* should have given **reño*; influence of *rei*, *rey*, explains *reino*) realm, **70** LII 3.

Reys (cf. *rees*) kings, **44** 12.

Rezio (*rĭgĭdus -um* ?) stout, sturdy, **66** I 5.

Rico -a, rico -a (Germanic *rîkja*; cf. Goth. *reiks*, O. H. G. *rîhhi*) rich, **14** 108; **17** 195; etc. (The original German sense of 'powerful' is partially preserved in *ricohombre*.)

Rienda (V. L. *rĕtĭna* > **redna* > by metathesis **renda* > *rienda*. The V. L. word is connected with L. *retinēre*; cf. L. *retinaculum* 'halter') rein, **13** 10.

Rieron pret. 3 pl. of *reir* (O. Sp. *riir*), laughed, **53** 24.

riir (L. *rīdēre*, V. L. **ridire*; the Sp. *reir* shows dissimilation of *i* to *e* in the protonic syllable, as in L. *dīcĕre*, V. L. **dīcīre* > *dizir* > *dezir*, *decir*, while Ptg. *rir* shows simple contraction) to laugh, **41** 31.

Rimado = *Libro Rimado* (cf. *Rimar*), **56** title.

Rimar (from the Germanic; cf. O. H. G. noun *rîm*, **rima* 'row,' 'series,' 'number') to rhyme, **48** 12 c.

Riqueza (abstract in *-eza*, L. *-ĭtia*, from adj. *rico -a*) wealth, riches, **20** 1200; cf. *rritad*.

Rodrigo pr. n. (of Germanic origin; cf. L. L. *Rodericus*), Roderick, **20** 1202 etc.

rogar (L. *rŏgāre*) to ask, entreat, pray, **7** 32; **8** 59; etc.

Roma pr. n. (L. *Rōma*), Rome, **40** 5 etc.

roman (a reduction in O. Sp. of *romance*, which also appears as *romanz*, from L. adv. *romanĭce*, as used in *loqui romanice*. Perhaps the analogy of *latín* caused the reduction. But ?) Romance, i.e. Spanish, **23** 2 a; cf. mod. *romance*.

romeria (abstract in *-ia* on the basis of *romero -a* 'pilgrim to Rome,' from V. L. *Romarius -a -um*) pilgrimage (originally to Rome, and then in general), **9** 77.

romero, Romero (cf. *romeria*) pilgrim, **25** 105 c; **70** XLIII 7.

Ronpya = *rompía*, impf. 3 of *romper* (L. *rŭmpĕre*, V. L. **rŭmpēre*), broke, **38** 361 c.

ropa (connected with Germanic **raubha*, O.H.G. *rouba* 'spoils,' 'garments'; the *p* may have originated in a form in which the German *b* became final, **raub-*, and therefore voiceless. But ?) robe, vestment, drapery, **26** 108 c.

Rosa (learned word; L. *rŏsa*) rose, **49** 18 a; **51** 1664 h; etc.

rostro (L. *rŏstrum* 'beak') face, **42** 20; **43** 11.

Roy pr. n. (shortened form of *Rodrigo*, L. L. *Rodericus*), **40** 7 etc.; cf. *Ruy*.

rrancado (p.p.) routed, **34** 81 b; cf. *arancar*.

rrayo (L. *radĭum*) ray, beam, spoke, **60** 24; **30** 8 a; **30** 10 a.

rrazon reason, argument, speech, remark, subject, talk, 36 345*a*, 346*a*; 37 355*d*; 48 15*d*; 55 13; 64 100*a*; cf. *Razon*.

rreal (L. *regalis, regālem*) royal, regal, 59 15.

rreboluedor = *revolvedor* (agent noun in *-dor*, L. *-tor -tōrem*, connected with *revolver*, L. *revŏlvĕre*, V. L. **revolvĕre*) disturber, 50 510*b*.

rrebuelto = *revuelto* (p.p. of *revolver*; L. p.p. *revolūtus*, V. L. **revolvitum*, **revŏltum*) upturned, topsy turvy, 56 425*c*.

rrecojieron = *recogieron*, pret. 3 pl. of *recoger* (L. *recollĭgĕre*, V.L. **recollĭgĕre*, **recolgĕre*), gathered, 34 79*d*.

rrecontamiento (abstract in *-miento*, L. *-mĕntum*, from *recontar*, L. *re* + *cŏmpūtare*) recounting, relation, description, 60 17.

rrecontar (cf. *rrecontamiento*) to tell, describe, 60 22.

rrecuerdes pres. sbj. 2 of *recordar* (L. *recŏrdāre*), remind, 64 100*b*.

rregion (learned word; L. *regio*, *regĭōnem*) region, 30 4*a*.

rreligion (learned word; L. *religio*, *relĭgĭōnem*) religion; (pl.) religious objects, 30 4*d*.

rrenegado -a (L. p.p. *renĕgātŭs -a*) renegade, infidel, 33 74*a*.

rrenta (V. L. ntr. pl. p.p. *rĕndĭta* of V. L. *rendĕre* for L. *reddĕre*, under the influence of L. *prehĕndĕre*, V. L. **prĕndĕre*) income, 30 12*d*.

rrepentido -a p.p. of *repentir* (V. L. **repĕnĭtīre* based on L. *poenĭtēre*), repentant, 63 89*a*.

rrepostero (V. L. **repostŏrĭum* or **repostārĭum*; cf. L. *repŏsĭtŏrĭum* 'tray,' 'waiter') butler, 58 437*d*.

rresçebyendo (cf. *reçebir*; the intrusive *s* is due to the analogy of inceptive verbs, *meresçer*, etc. Mod. *recibiendo* shows the change of *e* to *i* under the closing influence of the *y* or *i̯* of the next syllable) receiving, 37 357*c*.

rresplandesçiente (cf. *resplandeçiente*) 60 19, 25.

rresplandesçimiento (a noun formation in *-miento*, L. *-mĕntum*, from the verb *resplande[s]çer*; cf. *resplandeçiente*) splendor.

rresplandor (related to *resplandeçer*; cf. *resplandeçiente* and L. *splĕndor*, *splĕndōrem*) splendor, effulgence, 30 8*b*; 60 15.

rresponder (cf. *responder*) 37 355*b*; 58 441*a*; 61 4; 49 299*a*.

rrespondjo = *respondió*, 49 299*a*.

rrespuesta (noun from V. L. p.p. **respŏsĭtus -a -um*, **respŏstus -a -um*, corresponding to the V. L. pret. **resposui* of L. *respondere*) answer, 61 20; cf. Ital. *risposta*, O. Sp. *respuso*.

rrevate (ety.?) distress (?), 37 356*d*.

rrevato (ety.?) combat, 37 358*a*.

rrey (cf. *rei*, *rey*) 30 5*b*; 31 14*a*; etc.

rreyna = *reina* (L. *rēgīna* > O. Sp. *reína* and, under the influence of *rey*, *reino*, *reyno*, etc., *réina*) queen, 32 19*a*.

rreyno (cf. *Reyno*) realm, **33** 75 *b*; **69** XIX 2.

rrezien = mod. *recién* (L. *recens*, *recĕntem*, whence the O. Sp. adj. *reziente* and in proclitic use, as adv., *rezient*, *rezien*) recently, newly, **31** 17 *c*.

rrico (cf. *Rico*) rich, **54** 12 etc.

rrimado (cf. *Rimar*) rhymed, **48** 15 *b*.

rrio (L. *rivus -um*) river, **37** 360 *a*; **65** 103 *b*.

rritad (also O. Sp. *rictad*; abstract in *-tad*, L. *-tas -tatem*, from adj. *rico -a*; the *c* disappeared as in L. *fĭctŭm* > O. Sp. *fito*, mod. *hito*) riches, wealth, **20** 1189; cf. *Riqueza*.

rrobastes = mod. *robasteis*, pret. 2 pl. of *robar* (from Germanic *raub-*, O. H. G. *roubôn*), robbed, **69** XIX 1; cf. *ropa*.

Rrodrigo, Rrodrygo (cf. *Rodrigo*) **34** 78 *a*; **33** 75 *a*; etc.

rrogo pret. 3 of *rogar*, **54** 13.

Rroldan (Franco-Latin *Hruotolandus*, O. Fr. *Roland*) Roland, **36** 352 *a*.

rromanze (= *romançe*, *romanz*, O. Sp. forms of L. adv. *romanice*, as used in *loqui romanice* 'to speak Romance') a composition in Spanish, **48** 14 *b*.

rrosa (cf. *rosa*) **51** 1663 *i*.

rrueda (L. *rŏta*) wheel (of Fortune), **30** 8 *b*; **33** 74 *c*.

rruego (L. *rŏgo*; cf. *rogar*) I ask, **54** 7; **61** 14; **64** 100 *b*.

rrybera = mod. *ribera* (V. L. **rĭpăria*, i.e. *terra *riparia*, from L. *rĭpa*) bank, **37** 357 *a*, 359 *b*.

Rrynaldos = *Reinaldos* (L. L. *Regĭnaldŭs*, O. Fr. *Renaut*, Ital. *Rinaldo*) Reginald, Rinaldo, **36** 352 *c*.

rryvera (cf. *rrybera*) bank, shore, **34** 78 *d*.

Rudo -a (L. *rŭdis*, *rŭdem*, under influence of V. L. *rŭgĭdus -a -um* 'wrinkled,' 'rough,' 'rude'; cf. Ital. *ruvido -a* and Fr. *rude*) rude, **50** 491 *a*.

ruego (L. *rŏgo*; cf. *rogar*) I ask, **42** 33; **43** 1.

Ruy (cf. *Roy*) **13** 15; *Ruydiaz* = *Ruy Diaz*, **19** 1140. (Both *Roy* and *Ruy* were developed in proclitic use; cf. Menéndez Pidal, *Gram. del Cid*, p. 170.)

's = *os*, enclitic to *no*, **65** 108 *c*.

-s = *se*, enclitic to a verb form, **16** 154; **18** 1091, 1102; etc.; enclitic to a pron., *sobrellas* = *sobre* + *ella* + *se*, **20** 1203; enclitic to an adv. of place, *aquis* = *aquí* + *se*, **17** 1085; enclitic to *non*, *nos* = *non* + *se*, **18** 1106; **20** 1207. (In the last case we have the regular popular loss of *n* before *s*.)

sabad (L. *sabbătum*, usually in pl. *sabbata*, from Gk. σάββατον from Hebrew *shabbāth*) Saturday, **21** 3.

sabedes = mod. *sabéis* (cf. *saber*), **10** 88; **45** 12; **53** 10.

sabelo (*l* scribal for *ll*) = *sabello* = *saber* + *lo*, with assimilation of *r*, **8** 53.

saber (L. *sapĕre*, V. L. **sapēre*) to know, know how, understand, be able, learn, **8** 67 ; **46** 14, 26 ; etc. : pres. 1 *se* (L. *sapio*, V. L. **saio* [cf. **haio* for *habeo*] > **seio* > **seo* >, in proclitic aux. use, e.g. **se*[*o*] *leerlo*, > *se* ; cf. *he*), **6** 2, 7 ; etc. ; 2 *saues*, **28** 362 *c* etc. ; 3 *sabe*, **19** 1136 etc. ; 1 pl. *sabemos*, **15** 124 ; 2 pl. *sabedes*, **10** 88 etc. ; 3 pl. *saben*, **11** 126 etc. : impf. 3 *sabia*, **53** 17 ; 3 pl. *sabyan*, **37** 355 *b* : pret. 3 *sopo*, **35** 329 *b* etc. ; *supo* (V. L. **sapuit* > **saup.o* > **soup.o* > *sopo*, and this >, through analogy of *sopieron* > *supieron*, etc., > *supo*), **63** 92 *d* ; 3 pl. *sopieron*, **29** 371 *a* : fut. 1 *sabre*, **6** 10 etc. ; 1 pl. *sabremos*, **8** 67 : pres. sbj. 3 *sepa* (L. *sapiat* > **saipa* > **seipa* > *sepa* ; the *i* preserved the *p* as not intervocalic), **43** 26 ; 2 pl. *sepades*, **23** 3 *a* ; 3 pl. *sepan*, **15** 145 : impf. sbj. or plpf. indic. 1 *supiera*, **63** 90 *a* ; 3 *sopiera*, **46** 3 : impf. sbj. 3 *sopiese*, **55** 8 ; 2 pl. *sopiesedes*, **54** 11 : imper. *sabet* = *sabed*, **18** 1098 etc. : p.p. *sabido* (V. L. **sapitus* *-a -um*) known, learned, **11** 26 etc.

saber (n.) wisdom, knowledge, learning, **48** 15 *c* ; **49** 18 *b* ; etc.

sabet = *sabed* (cf. *saber*) you must know, **18** 1098 ; **20** 1197, 1207, 1209.

sabidor (formation in *-or*, L. *-or* *-ōrem*, on *sabido*, p.p. of *saber*) knower, sage, seer, **65** 108 *a*.

sabiendas (adverbial formation in *-s* on the pres. part. or gerund *sabiendo* of *saber*) : *á sabiendas* knowingly, **52** 5.

sabio (L. *sapidus* *-a -um*) sage, wise man, **30** 5 *a* ; **59** 4 ; **66** 6.

sabor (L. *sapor -ōrem*) liking, desire, taste, pleasure, delight, **20** 1190, 1198 ; **41** 32 ; **54** 21 ; etc.

sabroso -a (V. L. **saporōsus -a -um* ; or simply *sabor* + *-oso -osa* > *sab*[*o*]*roso -a*) pleasant, attractive, **30** 7 *b*.

sabyan = *sabian* (cf. *saber*), **37** 355 *b*.

sabydor = *sabidor*, **50** 491 *b*.

sacar (L. *saccāre* 'to strain or pass through a sack,' therefore, in the Romance of Spain, 'to take out of a sack,' whence 'to take out' in general) to take out, get out, derive, get, free, learn, interpret, **15** 125 ; **28** 363 *d* ; **46** 14 ; **64** 94 *b* ; etc. (The ety. is not satisfactory ; cf. Gk. σάκα.)

saco (L. *saccus -um*) sack, **61** 12.

sagrado -a (L. p.p. *sacratus -a -um*) consecrated, **67** v 5 ; **26** 110 *d*.

salado -a (V. L. p.p. as adj. *salātus -a -um* ; from L. *sal*) salty, salt, **18** 1090.

Salamon (pr. n.) Solomon, **36** 345 *c*.

salario (learned word ; L. *salārium* 'salt-money,' i.e. money given to soldiers for salt, thence 'pay' in general) salary, pay, **69** XLIII 2.

Salas pr. n., **40** 14 etc.

Salido pr. n., **40** 16.

salir (L. *salīre* 'to jump' ; thence, in Sp., 'to jump out,' 'come forth') to come out, go out, issue, rise, **19** 1185 ; **34** 78 *b* ; **35** 331 *b* ; etc. 80 w*p* 47,12 -

Salomon = *Salamon*, **36** 352 *d*.

salto (L. *saltus -um*) jump, bound, assault, **27** 353 *c*; *en un salto* in a moment, at once, **69** XIX 7.

saluar = *salvar* (L. *salvāre*) to save, safeguard, free, clear (a space), cross, **8** 52; **9** 74; **18** 1115; **23** 3 *d*; **24** 91 *d*; **31** 18 *a*; etc.

saluo = *salvo* (L. *salvus -a -um*): as noun ([*lugar*] *salvo*), safe place, security, safe, **15** 119, 133, 144; etc.

saña (V.L. **sanĭa* for L. *sanies* 'corrupted blood,' 'poisonous slaver of a serpent'; thence, because of the relation between physical and mental phenomena in the angry, 'anger.' This etymology is not certain. One thinks also of L. [*in*]*sanĭa* 'madness') anger, **24** 96 *c*; cf. *sanna*.

sanar (L. *sanāre*) to heal, cure, treat, **36** 342 *a*.

Sanchez pr. n., **41** 20.

Sancho (possibly V.L. **Sanctŭlus -um*, a diminutive of L. *Sanctus*) pr. n., **35** 328 *b*.

Sanctidat = mod. *Santidad* (half-learned word; L. *Sanctitas, sanctĭtātem*) sanctity, **28** 368 *a*.

sancto -a (learned spelling of *santo -a*, L. *sanctus -a -um*) holy, saintly, Saint, **23** 1 *c* etc.

Sangonera pr. n., **34** 78 *c*.

sangre (L. *sanguis, sanguĭnem* > **sangne* >, by dissimilation, *sangre*) blood, **42** 30 etc.

sanna = *saña*, **38** 367 *d*.

sannudo -a = *sañudo* (participial adj. in *-udo -a*, L. *-utus -a -um*, on *sanna, saña*) angry, **53** 14.

sano -a (L. *sanus -a -um*) sound, well, **26** 106 *a*; **27** 360 *c*; etc.

santi in *santi Yague* (L. vocative *Sancte Jacŏpe*, used as a war cry; the *e* of *sancte*, being in hiatus, = *y*, written also *i*) **19** 1138.

santo -a (cf. *sancto*) saint, **14** 94 etc.

saquamos (scribal error for *sacamos*; cf. *sacar*; *qu = k* before *e, i*, is here wrongly used before *a*) pluck out, **35** 335 *b*.

Saragoça (L. [*civitas Cae*]*sara*[*u*]*gŭstĭa*; the mod. *Zaragoza* for *Çaragoça*, shows the assimilation of *s* to *ç*) Saragossa, **17** 1088. (Possibly Arabic pronunciation of the name explains the *ç* and we may abide by a form [*Cae*]*sara*[*u*]*gusta*.)

sarna (seemingly an Iberian word, used as such by Isidore of Seville) itch, **50** 499 *c*.

Satanas (L.L. *Satanas*, Gk. Σατανᾶς) Satan, **35** 334 *d*.

sauana = mod. *sábana* (V.L. **sabăna*; cf. Gk. σάβανον 'linen cloth') sheet, **17** 183.

sauemos = *savemos, sabemos* (cf. *saber*), **28** 362 *b*; **24** 95 *d*.

saues = *saves, sabes* (cf. *saber*), **28** 362 *c*; **25** 102 *d*.

sazon (L. *satĭo, satĭōnem* 'sowing,' hence in Romance 'sowing season,' whence 'season' in general. Cf. Diez, *Etymologisches Wörterbuch*: 'For the sowing or planting of each crop there is a particular and favorable time in the year's course, a *satio verna, aestiva, autumnalis* — and this last term is in Columella; it was easy to denote the period of the year, for which Latin provided no simple term, by the sowing time.' The derivation from L. *statio -ōnem*, a 'standing still,' i.e. of the year's course, whence Ital. *stagione*, has been rejected by Diez, in view of the difficulty presented by the initial *st*. Still, one wonders whether a dissimilation of the first *t* — and its entire disappearance — was impossible) season, time, period, **40** 6; **45** 22. (In mod. Sp. the term is most common in *á la sazón*, in which it has the neutral sense of 'time,' 'period.')

√ **scriuano** = *scrivano* (the meter requires *escrivano*, mod. *escribano*; V.L. **scribānus -um* from L. *scrība*) scribe, **11** 120.

se (L. *sē* and perhaps also *sĭbi*, V.L. **sī* on the analogy of *mī* for *mihi*. In enclitic unaccented position *si* could become *se*. In O. Sp. the pron. is enclitic and proclitic) pers. pron. refl. 3 sg. and pl., himself, herself, itself, to himself, etc.; to themselves, themselves, etc., **17** 1086; **19** 1142, 1145; **20** 1199; **29** 369 *d*; **38** 365 *a*; etc. (On the whole, the pron. was more often enclitic than proclitic; hence the larger possibilities for *sī > se*; cf. *-s*.)

seades (L. *sedĕātĭs > *seyades > seades*, whence **seaẹs>*mod.*seáis*) pres. sbj. 2 pl. of *seer*, **14** 108.

seclo (learned word; L. *saecŭlum*) √ world, **9** 85; cf. *seglo*.

seco -a (L. *sĭccus -a -um*) dry, dried, withered, **65** 105 *c* and *d*.

secretamente (cf. *secreto* and *mente*) secretly, **61** 15.

secreto -a (learned word; L. *sēcrētus -a -um*) secret, **62** 3.

sedie = weakened form of *sedia* (L. *sedēbat*, impf. 3 of *sedēre*, V. L. **sedēat > sedía*), sat, stood, was, **20** 1220; cf. *seer*, *ser*.

sedmana (L.*septĭmāna>*settĭmana*, as in Ital., > **setmana* >, with assimilation of voiceless *t* to voiced *m*, *sedmana*, whence, with complete assimilation of *d*, mod. *semana*) week, **41** 9, 14.

seer (L. *sĕdēre* 'to sit.' The sense of 'to sit,' 'to be in a place,' weakened to 'to be.' So also *stare* 'to stand,' 'to stand in a place,' 'to be in a place,' 'to be.' O. Sp. still shows traces of the retention of the older sense 'to sit,' which in mod. Sp. is rendered by the derivative *sentar*, etc., from the pres. part. *sedens*, *sedentem*, **sedentare*. Later *seer* contracted to *ser*, which remains as the mod. form and in O. Sp. is already frequent as the basis of the fut. and cond. of the indic. In O. Sp. *seer* and *ser* are used often in the same construction and with the same sense as *estar*, as both had originally signification of place. While certain forms of *seer*, *ser* come from L. *sedere*, others, e.g. the

pres., the impf., and the pret.
indic. and related forms, come
from L. *esse*. Cf. the forms
listed under *ser* and *era*, *eres*,
etc., *fue, fuesse, fuera, fuere*, etc.)
to be, **6** 13; **7** 25; **43** 16; **55** 13.
See also *sedie*, *seades*, *ser*, *seyer*.

seglo (half-learned form; L. *saecŭlum*; it is intended in the *Misterio* for the current O. Sp. *sieglo*,
whence mod. *siglo*; the development of sense was, ' period of
years ' or ' century,' ' time during
which one is in this world,' ' this
world ') the world, secular things,
7 43; **11** 113; cf. *seclo*.

segudar (V. L. *secūtāre, frequentative from L. *sequor*, *secūtus*) to
follow, pursue; (n.) following,
pursuit, **19** 1148.

segund (L. *secŭndus -um* — the *ŭ*
does not show the popular treatment; thence *segundo*, which in
proclitic use lost its *o*, whence
segund, which, before a voiceless cons., became *segunt*. By
entire assimilation of the final
cons. to the cons. beginning the
following word both *segund* and
segunt became the mod. *según*)
as, just as, **41** 23; **48** 16 *c*; **61**
5, 22.

segunt (cf. *segund*) as, **69** XIX 4;
70 LIII 4.

segurado -a (V. L. p.p. of *secūrāre
from *secūrus -a -um*) secured,
sure, certain, in security, **35** 334 *a*.
Cf. mod. *asegurar*, *asegurado*.

seguro -a (L. *secūrus -a -um*) sure,
certain, **24** 95 *b*.

seio (cf. *conseio*) **18** 1099.

sele, seles, selo = *se + le*, *se + les*,
se + lo (in early O. Sp. the *se*
was always the reflexive pron.
in this construction; in late
O. Sp., e.g. in the *José*, we find
already the non-refl. *se* < O. Sp.
ge before another pron. beginning with *l*. The development
of the *se* from *ge* is this: it was
originally the L. dative *illi* before an accusative *illum*, *illam*,
etc.; hence *illi illum* ' it to him '
> [*il*]*lį el*[*l*]*o* > *lyelo* > *ŧelo*, = the
stage of Ital. *glielo*, > with total
absorption of the *l* element by
the palatal *y* [cf. Fr. *fille* > *fi.y*]
yelo >, as the *y* was very palatal,
i.e. produced with a very narrow
passageway between the tongue
and the palate, and therefore
with much friction, *gelo*, i.e.
dželo; cf. dialectal and American Sp. *jo* = *džo* for *yo*. The
dental element in *ge* = *dž* disappeared ere long, hence *ž*,
and in the late O. Sp. period all
voiced sibilants unvoiced, hence
š = Eng. *sh*. The spelling *ge*
still continued largely, but the
spelling *xe* is found beside it,
and O. Sp. *x* = *š*, i.e. *sh*. At the
stage *xe*, i.e. *še*, confusion with
the refl. *se* seems to have set
in, partly because the Sp. *s* was
then so cacuminal as almost to
be palatal, i.e. it approximated
greatly to *xe*, *she*, and partly because an aversion to the use of
initial *x*, or *g* meaning *x*, showed

itself, and *s*, as the sign nearest in value, recommended itself. So it is that the confusion of *se*, reflexive, and *ge*, *xe*, not reflexive, but simply dative, became absolute, and in mod. Sp. *se* does duty for both words), (as refl.) himself, themselves, etc. + to him, to her, to them, **15** 134; **65** 104 *d*; etc.; (as dative pron. not refl.) **64** 94 *b*, 97 *b*.

selva (L. *sĭlva*) forest, **47** 3.

semeiança = *semejança* (formation in -*ança*, L. -*antĭa*, on the stem of *semejar*) likeness, **46** 6; cf. mod. *semejanza*.

semeiar = *semejar*, **16** 157; **42** 15; **44** 22; etc.

semeias = apocopated form of *semeiasse* = *semejasse*, impf. sbj. of *semejar*, **21** 14.

semejar (V. L. *sĭmĭlĭare* formed on L. *sĭmĭlis*) to seem, resemble, seem fit, **30** 6 *d*, 7 *b*, 10 *d*; **31** 13 *b*; **34** 82 *d*; etc.

sen (Germanic *sin*; it is perhaps apocopated *seno*; cf. Ital. *senno*) sense, wisdom, **36** 345 *c*.

seña (L. *sĭgnum*, pl. *sĭgna* ' signs,' ' ensign ') standard, banner, **20** 1220.

señalada mente (cf. p.p. of *señalar*) signally, especially, **52** 2.

señalar (V. L. *sĭgnalāre* from V. L. *sĭgnālis*, from L. *sĭgnum*) to mark; p.p. *señalado* -*a*, signal, **51** 1662 *e*.

sendos -**as** (L. pl. *sĭngŭlos* -*as* > O. Sp. *seños* -*as* in a regular way. Then, because of sense relations

— since the word was always used with reference to each individual of *two* persons or things, etc. — a contamination with *dos* occurred; hence *sendos* -*as*) single, individual, as many, **30** 4 *a*; **31** 13 *d*.

senior scribal Latin spelling of *sennor*, *señor*, **6** 6 etc.

sennal = *señal* (V. L. **signalis*, ntr. **sĭgnāle* based on L. *sĭgnum* and used as a noun) sign, **6** 13, 21; etc.; cf. *señalar*.

sennero -**a** = *señero* -*a* (V. L. *sĭngŭlārĭus* -*a* -*um*, based on L. *singularis*) single, alone; (pl.) individual, **30** 5 *a*; **45** 14; **46** 17.

Sennor, sennor = *señor* (L. *Senĭor*, *senĭōrem*) Lord, lord, master, gentleman, sir, **25** 102 *a*; **35** 333 *c*; etc.; **13** 8; **18** 1094; etc.; *sennora* = *señora* (fem. formed on *señor*) lady, **39** 370 *d*.

sentido (noun use of the p.p. of *sentir*, L. *sentīre*) sense, consciousness, **69** XVIII 6.

sentir (L. *sentīre*) to feel, perceive, **55** 3.

sepades (L. *sapĭātĭs* > **saipades* > **seipades* > *sepades* > **sepaęs* > mod. *sepáis*; cf. *saber*) **23** 3 *a*.

sepulcro (learned word; L. *sepŭlcrum*) sepulcher, **34** 84 *b*.

sepultura (learned word; L. *sepŭltūra* ' burial ') burial place, grave, tomb, **34** 84 *a*; **62** 4.

ser (contraction of *seer* < L. *sedēre*; see *seer*) to be, **34** 81 *a*; **38** 364 *c*; etc.; *seryen* = *seryen*, weakened cond. 3 pl., **15** 116: indic. pres.

(all forms from L. *esse* or V. L.
variations thereof) 1 *so*, **7** 37 etc.;
soy, **63** 89 *d*, cf. *so*; 2 *eres*, cf.
eres; 3 *es*, cf. *es*; 1 pl. *somos* (<
L. *sŭmŭs*), **12** 142 etc.; 2 pl.
sodes, **8** 52 etc.; *soes*, **68** VIII 2
etc. (from V. L. **sŭtŭs*), cf. *soes*;
3 pl. *son* (< L. *sŭnt*), **13** 17 etc.:
impf. 3 *sedie* (weakened form of
sedía < L. *sedēbat*, V. L. **sedéa*),
20 1220; 3 pl. *seyen*, **15** 122 etc.;
all other forms occurring in the
extracts are from the impf. of
L. *esse*, cf. *era*, *eran*: pret.; all
forms used in the extracts are
from *esse*; cf. *fu*, *fue*, *fues*, *fuest*,
fust, *fueron*. But O. Sp. also possessed real pret. forms of *ser* <
sedere, such as *sovo*, *sovieron*,
which, of course, showed the
analogy of *ovo*, *ovieron*, pret. of
aver, *haber*: fut. 2 *seras*, **64** 94 *d*
etc.; 3 *sera*, **7** 42 etc.; 1 pl. *seremos*, **24** 95 *b*; 2 pl. *seredes*, **16**
158; 3 pl. *seran*, **14** 86 etc.:
cond. 3 *seria*, **54** 10; **59** 5; *serie*,
14 82; etc.; *serya*, **34** 80 *c*; 3 pl.
seryan, **34** 80 *b*; *seryen*, **37** 353 *c*;
serien, **30** 4 *c*; *ser yen*, **15** 116:
sbj. pres. 2 *seas* (from *sĕdĕas*),
25 100 *d* etc.; cf. *sias*; 3 *sea* (from
L. *sĕdĕat* > V. L. **sęyat*, as the
palatal closed the accented
vowel, > *seya* > *sea*), **15** 118 etc.;
2 pl. *seades*, cf. *seades*; 3 pl. *sean*
(from *sĕdĕant*), **15** 128 etc.: sbj.
impf.; all forms occurring here
are from *esse*; cf. *fues*, *fuese*,
fuesse, *fuessedes*, *fuessen*, *fuera*,
fueran; the forms in *-ra* still

usually retain indic. force; *se*
< *sedere* also had real impf.
forms, such as *soviesse*, *soviessen*,
analogical to *oviesse*, etc.: sbj.
fut.; all forms occurring here
are from *esse*; cf. *fuere*, *fure*,
fueres: imper.; no forms occur
here; but O. Sp. had *se* < *sĕde*,
developed in atonic use, and
sed from *sĕdēte* > *seed* > *sed*: pres.
part. *syendo* = *siendo*, **51** 1664 *c*;
but O. Sp. had also *seyendo* <
sedĕndum; the form *siendo* has
been remade on *s-er* + the regular ending for *-er* verbs: p.p.
does not occur here; but O. Sp.
had *seído* < V. L. **sedĭtus*; the
form *sido* has been remade on
s-er.

seredes (L. *sedēre* + [*hab*]*ētĭs*) fut.
2 pl. of *ser*, *seer* (*seredes* > **sereęs*
> *seréis*), **16** 158.

sergente (loan-word from Fr. *ser-
gent*, from L. pres. part. *serviens*,
servientem) servant, **45** 23.

serie, serien weakened form of
seria, *serian*, cond. 3 of *ser*, *seer*,
14 82; **24** 93 *b*; etc.; **30** 4 *c*.

sermon (L. *sermo*, *sermōnem*)
speech, language, idiom, **30**
4 *b*.

serpiente (L. *serpens*, *serpĕntem*)
serpent, **31** 11 *c*.

seruiçio = *servicio* (learned word;
L. *servĭtĭum*) service, **25** 103 *a*.

seruir = *servir*, **21** 21; **24** 91 *d*;
pres. part. *seruiendo*, **56** 422 *b*.
(The mod. *sirviendo* shows the
closing force of the *i̧*.)

serujcio = *seruicio*, **23** 4 *d*; **25** 100 *c*.

serujdor=*seruidor*, *servidor* (L. *servī-tor*, *servītōrem*) servant, **50** 510 c.

serujr = *seruir*, **71** LXXIX 4.

servir (L. *sĕrvīre*) to serve, deserve, **54** 3; cf. *seruir*, *serujr*.

serya = *sería* (cf. *serie*), **34** 80 c.

seryan, seryen = *serían* (cf. *serie*), **34** 80 b; **37** 353 c.

seso (L. *sensus -um*, V.L. **sēsus -um*) sense, judgment, **26** 107 a; **64** 95 b; etc.; *mal seso* senseless thing, **37** 354 d.

sesudo -a (participial adj. formed on *seso*) sensible, **44** 22.

Sevylla = *Sevilla* (pr. n.) Seville, **33** 74 a.

seýen impf. 3 pl. of *ser*, *seer* (L. *sedēbant*, V.L. **sedéant* > *sedian*, which weakened its ending > *sedien*, cf. *sedie*, > with loss of intervocalic *d*, *seíen*, here written *seyen*), were sitting, were, **15** 122; **41** 26.

seyer (perhaps an Eastern Sp. form of *seer*) **64** 101 c.

seyes scribal error for *seys*, **15** 147. (The occurrence of *reyes* beside *reys* might have led a scribe to write *seyes* for *seys*.)

seys = *seis* (L. *sĕx*, i.e. *sĕks*, developed in proclitic and atonic use. We might expect **ses*.)

si (L. *sīc* 'so,' which developed also the sense in Romance of affirmation) so (in an adjuration; *si el Criador nos salue* 'so may the Creator save you'), **18** 1115; yes, **9** 87 etc.

si (L. *sĭbi*; the Sp. form is not derived directly from this, but is analogical to *mi* < L. *mihi*, *mī*) himself, herself, **55** 2.

si (L. *sī*) if, whether, **6** 10; **7** 3c; etc.; *si non* but, except, **15** 140; **45** 13; etc.

sias = Castilian *seas* (cf. *ser*), **64** 98 d. (The form occurs in an Aragonese text.)

sibien = *si bien*, **24** 93 a.

siella (L. *sĕlla* > *siella* > **sieilla*, i.e. a palatal effect from the *ll*, once they palatalized, was exerted on the *ie*, whence mod. *silla*; cf. O. Fr. *iei* > *i*) chair, seat, **60** 14.

siempre (L. *sĕmper*, V.L. **sĕmpĕre*, **sĕmpre*, with final adverbial *e*; cf. *tarde*, *mane*, etc.) always, ever, **21** 13; **25** 100 a; etc.

sienpre = *siempre*, **29** 2 b; **31** 14 d; etc.

sieruo = *siervo* (L. *sĕrvus -um*) serf, servant, **45** 10.

siete (L. *sĕptem*) seven, **65** 103 d.

sil = *si* if, whether, + *le* (obj. pron.), **8** 63.

siles = *si* + *les*, **20** 1208.

Silos pr. n., **23** 3, 4 etc.

sin prep. (L. *sĭne*; this should have given **sen*. The *i* may be due to the influence of *sinon*, mod. *sino*, which, like *sin*, is privative in force), without, **13** 3; **17** 185; **25** 102 d; etc.

sines prep. (apparently an amplified form of *sin*; but the ending -*es* is rather adverbial than prepositional; is the form due to a combination of *sine* and *ex*? It is to be noted that O. Provençal has *senes*; is the Sp. form a loan-word?), without, **7** 38; **9** 85.

siniestro -a (L. *sĭnĭster, sĭnĭstrŭm -am*; this should have given **senestro -a*; the influence of the correlative *diestro -a* < L. *dĕxtĕrum -am*, produced a diphthong here, and the *į* closed the initial *e* > *i*) left: *siniestra* left hand, **47** 8; on the left, **13** 12.

sinon = *si* if + *non*, if not, otherwise, except, **15** 116; **41** 29; **42** 1; etc. Cf. mod. *sino* and *si no.*

siruiessen = *sirviessen*, mod. *sirviesen*, impf. sbj. 3 pl. of *servir*, **43** 29.

siruo = *sirvo* (L. *servĭo*), pres. 1 of *servir*, **56** 424 a.

siuos = *si* + *uos, vos*, mod. *si os*, **17** 181.

so (L. *sŭm*, pres. 1 of *esse*. This should have given **son*; but as this form would be identical with the 3 pl. L. *sŭnt* > Sp. *son*, and as most Sp. verbs [and especially the common monosyllabic forms, L. *do, sto*, etc. > O. Sp. *do, esto*] end in *-o*, the *n* was omitted) I am, **7** 37; **11** 109; **16** 156; **19** 1140; etc. (In late O. Sp. [cf. **63** 89 *d*] the mod. form *soy* begins to appear. The *y* is difficult of explanation. Some refer it to an intermediate O. Sp. *soe*, i.e. *sọẹ*, found in Leonese, whose *e* is likewise not easily explained; cf. Staaff, *L'ancien dialecte léonais*, p. 309. He registers *so, soy*, and *soey* and says:

" The ordinary form of the *Poema de Alexandre soe* [therefore Leonese] is not represented in our charters [thirteenth-century documents studied by him]. As in general usage *seyo* < *sedeo* ran parallel to *so*, it is not impossible that *soy* represents a contamination of these two forms. *Soey* might represent the primitive stage of this contamination, *soe* and *soy* might be different reductions of this form." Possibly the form arose in the cases of inversion, i.e. when the order was *so yo* > *soyo* and with backward and forward action of the palatal > *soy yo*. But? The *y* appears in mod. Sp. also in *voy* and *doy*.) Cf. *ser.*

so (L. *sŭb*; the disappearance of the *b* may be due to complete assimilation in proclitic use with a word beginning with a cons.) under, **11** 110; **21** 5; **44** 6; **47** 4, 8; **49** 17 *c*; etc. (In mod. Sp. *so* has given way to *bajo, debajo de*, except in certain set phrases, e.g. *so capa de, so color de, so pena de*.)

so, sos (L. *suus, sŭŭm, sŭŏs* > **soo*, **soos* > *so, sos*) his, her, their, its (before a masc. noun), **15** 133; **18** 1099, 1104; **21** 23; **40** title; **41** 2, 8, 21, 24, 26, 31; **42** 3, 4, 8; etc. (in mod. Sp. *so* has given way to *su*, which, apparently, in early O. Sp. was only fem. and was later generalized. Still, early texts show already much confusion of *so*, *su*; cf. the O. Sp. *Glosses*. It is to be borne in mind that in hiatus, as between different words, especially before *o-* and *a-*, *so* might also become *su*, *so ojo* > *su ojo* [cf. *ú* for *ó* 'or'], and a new masc. pl. *sus* could then be formed. Another possibility, *so ojo* > *s' ojo*, does not seem to have recommended itself); *el so*, *los sos* (as poss. adj. before masc. n.; cf. *la mi*, *el mio*, etc.; cf. mod. Ital. use) his, her, their, **13** 1; **14** 94; **18** 1104; **47** 5; *los sos* (as pron.) his men, **17** 1086; cf. *su*.

sobeiano -a = *sobejano -a* (said to be derived from V. L. **supĕrcŭlānus -a -um*, based on V. L. **supercŭlus*, cf. Ital. *soverchio*, from L. *sŭper*. But the etymon should give **soberchano*. The formation may rather be directly on L. *sub*: **subĭcŭlus*, **subĭcŭlanus*, which presents no phonetical difficulty. For sense development cf. *subir*) excessive, superior, excellent, **14** 110. (The term is obsolete; cf. mod. *sobrado -a*.)

sobrar (L. *supĕrāre*) to exceed, be in excess, **60** 16.

√ **sobre** (L. *sŭper*; it is a question whether the *-e* is one of support, or whether we must suppose a V. L. **sŭpĕre* > **sŭpre*, cf. L. *ante* and *supra*) on, upon, over, about, **11** 108; **16** 161; **20** 1203; **31** 13 *a*, 14 *a*; etc.

sobrella = *sobre ella*, **17** 183.

sobrellas = *sobre* + *ella* + *se* (enclitic), **20** 1203; *sobre ellas* **20** 1209.

sobresto = *sobre esto* upon that, thereupon, **43** 24.

sobrino (L. *sōbrīnus -um*, used at first of the children of sisters, and then for 'cousin' on the mother's side; in Sp. the sense was extended to that of 'nephew') nephew, **43** 32.

soçiedat = *sociedad* (half-learned word; L. *socĭetas*, *socĭĕtātem*) society, community, **24** 87 *b*.

sodes (V. L. *sŭtis*, which, framed on the analogy of *sŭmus* and *sŭnt*, displaced L. *estis*. From *sodes*, by natural loss of intervocalic *-d-*, came *soes*, i.e. *soęs*, whence mod. *sois*) you are (used sometimes as sg. of address), **8** 52; **13** 79; **14** 103; **43** 26; **57** 434 *c*; cf. *ser*.

soes (cf. *sodes*) you are, **68** VIII *b*; **70** LIII *c*.

sofrir (L. *sŭffĕrre*, V. L. *sŭffĕrīre* > *soffrir* > *sofrir*. Mod. *sufrir* arose in forms having *į*, *sofriendo* > *sufriendo*, etc.) to suffer, endure, stand, permit, **24** 91 *a*; **26** 107 *d*; **42** 19; **43** 2; cf. *suffrió*.

soga (of uncertain source; said to be connected with Basque *soca*, which may, however, be derived from the Sp. word. A Celtic **sōca* has also been proposed; cf. Irish *sūgān* 'hay rope,' 'straw rope.' As the Sp. word seems originally to mean only a grass rope, the Celtic etymology is not unlikely) rope, fetter, **27** 353 *d*; *luenga soga* a never-ending tale, **24** 93 *b*.

sol (L. *sol*, *sōlem*) sun, **18** 1091 ; **59** 5.

solaz (L. *solācĭum*. But this should have given **solaço* ; perhaps it is a loan-word from Provençal *solatz* ; the word is common in the troubadour poetry, which was early brought to Spain) solace, delight, **48** 12 *d*, 14 *a*.

soldada (formation on L. *sŏlĭdus -a -um* 'whole,' 'entire,' occurring in expressions such as *stipendium solidum* 'the entire pay' given to a soldier, and also as a n. denoting a coin. Hence V. L. **solĭdātus -a -um* 'one paid,' 'soldier,' Sp. *soldado*, and **solĭdāta* 'money paid,' 'pay') pay, **13** 80 ; **19** 1126.

soler (L. *sŏlēre*) to be wont, **24** 25 *c* ; **54** 19 ; **68** IX 6 ; etc.

solien = *solían*, weakened impf. 3 pl. of *soler*, **22** 31.

solies = *solías*, weakened impf. 2 of *soler*, **22** 29, 37.

solo -a (L. *sōlus -a -um*) sole, alone, single, only, **25** 100 *c* ; **41** 29 ; **67** V 4 ; *sola ment* only, alone, **28** 364 *b* ; *tan sola mientre* only, **41** 29.

soltar (V. L. **sŏltāre*, a frequentative from p.p. *solūtus*, V. L. **solūtus*, **soltus*, of L. *solvĕre*) to loosen, solve, interpret, **13** 10 ; **45** title.

sombra (apparently connected with L. *ŭmbra* ; but the *s* is difficult

of explanation. The noun is regarded as an abstract from the verb *sombrar*, mod. *asombrar* 'to throw a shadow upon,' 'to astound,' etc. The verb *sombrar* has been explained as L. *sŭb + ŭmbrāre*, *sŭbŭmbrāre*, whence by dissimilation of first *b* or by a vocalization of it, *so.ombrar*, *sombrar*. O. Sp. has also *solombra*, a form which shows the infl. of *sol* 'sun.' It is doubtful that the *s-* can be attributed, in *sombra*, to this form alone) shade, shadow, **47** 4.

somero (V. L. **sŭmmārĭus -um* from L. *sŭmmus -a -um*) upper, highest, **31** 15 *c*.

somo (L. *sŭmmum*) highest point, top : *en somo* on top, **16** 171 ; **20** 1220 ; **41** 19 ; etc.

son (L. *sŏnus -um* ; but this gave properly O. Sp. *sueno* ; *son* is either an abstract from *sonar*, or, more likely, since this had *ue* in stem-accented forms, it is a loan-word from Provençal *son.s*, Fr. *son* ; it was, of course, a troubadour word) tune, air, melody, **52** 17 ; **53** 18 ; **60** 12. (In the general sense of "sound," *sonido* prevails in mod. Sp.)

sonar (L. *sŏnāre*) to sound, resound, **20** 1206.

sonbra = *sombra*, **31** 14 *c*.

sonnar = *soñar* (L. *sŏmnĭāre* ; the *ue* forms, mod. *sueño*, *sueñas*, etc., may be due to the analogy of other *o-ue* verbs, in case the *ĭ* of *sŏmnĭo*, *sŏmnĭas*, etc., could

✳ See Corrections p. 176a

close the *o* and prevent diphthongization; cf. *suenno*) to
dream, **45** title; **46** 11; **64** 94 *a*,
96 *b*, 99 *a*; etc.

sonrrisos = *sonrisó* + *se*, pret. 3 of
the refl. verb, now obs., *sonri-
sarse* (L. *sŭb-* + V.L. **rīsāre*, a
frequentative from L. *rīdēre*, *rī-
sus*. We should expect **sobri-
sar*, or, if the V.L. form were
*sŭrrīsāre, a **sorrisar*. The Sp.
prefix *son-* for L. *sub-* occurs in
other words: *sonreir*, *sonrodar*,
sonrojar, *sonsacar*, etc. As *som-*
it stands before labials (or did
so originally) in *someter* < L.
submittere, *sompesar* < L. *sub* +
pensare. Its rise seems clear in
someter < **sŭb.mĭttēre* > **som.me-
ter* > *someter*. L. had already
summittere beside *submittere*. If
a consciousness of this *som-* as
a prefix = L. *sŭb-* persisted, we
could understand its substitution for the phonetic development of *sŭb-* in *sonrisar* and the
other forms above. Before den-
tals and linguals *son-* would be
the form. One thinks also of
an accumulation of prefixes:
sŭb, Sp. *so*, + *ĭn*, Sp. *en*, whence
so[e]n; but this seems unlikely.
The prefix *sŭb-* seems to have
undergone other deformations,
e.g. *sa-*, *za-*, *cha-*. The doubling
of *r* after *n* in *sonrisar* was
probably a scribal device to indicate the reënforced nature of
r in that position, as still in
mod. Sp. In thoroughly popular

treatment *nr* > *rr*), he smiled, **16**
154.

sopessa scribal for *sopesa* (pres. 3
of *sopesar*, more usually *sompesar*, cf. *sonrrisos*; L. *sŭb* +
pensāre, V.L. **pēsāre*), weighs,
takes the weight or measure of,
gauges, judges, **49** 298 *c*.

sopiera (plpf. 3 of *saber*) had learned,
46 3. (Hence, through the operation of *į̃*, *supiera*.)

sopieron (pret. 3 pl. of *saber*) learned,
29 371 *a*; **34** 83 *d*; **43** 20. (Hence,
through the operation of *į̃*, *supieron*.)

sopiese (impf. sbj. 3 of *saber*) **55** 8.
(Hence, through the operation
of *į̃*, *supiese*.)

sopiesedes (impf. sbj. 2 pl. of *saber*)
54 11. (Hence, through the
operation of *į̃* and the loss of
-d-, mod. *supieseis*.)

sopo (pret. 3 of *saber*) learned, was
informed of, **35** 329 *b*; **41** 24; **42**
26. For mod. *supo* cf. *saber*.

sosegad imper. pl. of *sosegar* (V.L.
*sŭbsĕdĭcāre, causative to L. *sub-
sīdēre* ‘cause to rest,’ > **sussedĭ-
care* > **sossedegar* > *sosegar*), tran-
quillize, rest, **48** 14 *b*.

sospecha (L. *sŭspĕctus -um*, with
change of gender, or an abstract
from *sospechar*, L. *suspĕctāre*)
suspicion, **15** 126; **61** 16.

sospirar (L. *sŭspīrāre*) to sigh, **13**
6; **59** 22. (The mod. *suspirar*
shows learned influence in the
restoring of L. *ŭ*.)

sospiraua = *sospirava*, *sospiraba* (cf.
sospirar), **59** 22.

sostenet = *sostened*, imper. of *sostener* (L. *sŭstĭnēre*, V. L. *sŭstĕnēre*), sustain, support, **47** 6.

soterrar (V. L. *sŭbtĕrrare* from *sŭb* and *tĕrra*) to inter, bury, **26** 111 *c*.

sotil (L. *sŭbtīlis -em*) subtle, **50** 509 *b*; *sotil mente* subtly, **30** 10 *c*. (Mod. *sutil* shows learned restoration of L. *ŭ*.)

Soto pr. n., **27** 354 *b*.

Spanna = *Espanna* (the *E* has been omitted here after a vowel. The form could arise most easily in such a combination as *de España > dEspaña > de Spaña*) Spain, **33** 72 *a*.

sperare = *esperaré* (*e* omitted after a vowel, or *le sperare* = *l'esperare*), **20** 1194.

spirital scribal for *espiritual* (*padre sp.* = *padreesp.*; learned word; L. L. *spirit[u]ālis*), spiritual, heavenly, **18** 1102.

Spiritu = *Espíritu* (learned word; L. *Spīrĭtus -um*): *Spiritu Santo* Holy Ghost, **23** 1 *c*; **48** 11 *a*.

sse = *se*, refl. pron. (enclitic to a verb form ending in a vowel; the doubling of *s* indicates that it is to be pronounced as voiceless, and not like usual O. Sp. intervocalic *s*, which was voiced): *fuesse* = *fué* + *se*, **42** 4; cf. similar forms, **42** 19; **46** 23; **47** 17; **61** 20; **62** 7; (after *que* and before verb; really enclitic to *que* although not added to it in writing) *que sse darie*, **43** 17; (added to -*r* of infin.; as -*rs*- properly became -*ss*- in O. Sp.,

the doubling of *s* indicates the necessity of carefully pronouncing both *r* and *s*, which, of course, is voiceless) *mudarssele*, **62** 21.

ssea = *sea* (cf. *ser*; after *que* and really enclitic to it; the *ss* must therefore indicate the voiceless intervocalic nature of *s* here; cf. *sse*), **15** 132.

ssienpre = *sienpre*, *siempre* (the *ss* carried over from cases in which there preceded *siempre* a word related to it syntactically and ending in a vowel, e.g. *lo de siempre*), **62** 15.

'staban = *estaban* (cf. *estar*; the preceding word ends in a vowel), **63** 93 *a*.

strela = *estrela*, *estrella* (perhaps a Latinizing in the *Misterio*; but most of the forms occur also after final vowel of a word connected syntactically with *strela*), **6** 2, 19; **8** 55; *el strela* (but perhaps for *la strela*) **8** 64.

strelero = *estrellero* (formation in -*ero* on *estrella*) star-gazer, astrologer; after a vowel, **7** 37; after a cons. (but meter requires *estrelero*, *estreleros*), **8** 52; **11** 123.

su, sus (poss. adj. before noun) his, her, its, their: before fem. noun, **13** 16; **18** 1103; **19** 1124; **20** 1206, 1220; **26** 107 *b*, 112 *c*, 289 *c*; **27** 358 *a*; **28** 366 *a*; **29** 1 *a*; **32** 19 *a*; **34** 82 *b*; etc., in all about 41 cases in the extracts; add to these the cases of *la su*, *las sus*, **13** 19; **24** 91 *d*, 93 *b*; **26** 112 *d*, 111 *b*; **37** 359 *c*; **45** 23;

47 7, 8 ; **70** LII 4 ; in all, 10 cases, which, with the preceding, give us about 51 examples of the fem. use : before masc. noun, **14** 101 ; **19** 1188 ; **23** 2 *b*, 4 *b* ; **24** 91 *a* ; etc., in all about 45 cases ; add to these the cases of *el su*, *los sus*, **24** 87 *a*, 92 *b* ; **57** 431 *b* ; **59** 6 ; **64** 96 *a*, *d* ; **65** 102 *a* ; in all, 7 cases, which, with the preceding, give us about 52 examples of the masc. use. So that the texts here given afford no evidence as to the preponderance of the one usage over the other. Of the use of *so*, *el so*, etc., appearing only before masc. nouns, the texts present 24 cases, without any exception ; i.e. *so* never stands before a fem. noun. The assumption is that *su* began as a fem. form (L. *sŭam*), and phonetically it would seem that the Sp. *u* (< L. *ŭ*, V. L. *ǫ*) could occur only in the hiatus before *a* (whence **sua* ; cf. *mia* from *mĕam*). *Sŭŭm*, on the other hand, would give *so* ; cf. *so*. For it is likely that in V. L. hiatus, the vowels had an open value before *i* or *u* and a close value before the other vowels ; hence *męam* beside *męum* and *sǫam* beside *sǫum* ; cf. Zauner, *Romanische Sprachwissenschaft*, 2d ed., I, p. 69. A further closing in the hiatus would convert *sǫa* into Sp. *sua*, and this, in the proclitic position, before words beginning with a vowel,

especially *a*, could close ~reduce~ to *su* ; *suaalma* > *su alma* ; cf. *el alma* instead of *la alma*.* Of course all cases of the development of the poss. adj. were subject to the peculiar conditions of their atonic proclitic position.

su (variant of *so* < L. *sŭb* ; it may be a hiatus form) under, **24** 92 *b* ; **32** 19 *b*.

sueldo (L. *sŏlĭdus -um*) coin (of varying value), **27** 357 *b*.

suelo (L. *sŏlum*) ground, **60** 7.

suelto -a p.p. of *soltar* (L. *sŏlūtus*, V. L. **solŭtus*, **sŏltus -a -um*), released, **64** 98 *a*.

suenno = *sueño* (L. *sŏmnum -ium* ' dream ') dream, **45** title ; **46** 6 ; **64** 94 *a*, 96 *b*.

suffrio (pret. 3 of *sofrir*) **26** 108 *d*. (The *i̭* closed the original *o*.)

suma (learned word ; L. *sŭmma*) : *en suma* in brief, **50** 510 *a*.

supiera, supo, cf. *saber*.

suso (L. *sūrsum*, V. L. *sūsum*) above : *de suso* from on high, **60** 23. *< sutyña = su tyña*

suyo poss. pron. in the predicate (L. *sŭum* influenced by *cŭjus* > Sp. *cuyo*), his, **23** 4 *b*.

ɔy = *si* refl. pron., **49** 301 *b* etc.

sy = *si* if, **24** 91 *a*, 96 *c* ; etc. ; *sy quier*, *sy quiere*, *sy quiera* at least, **57** 433 *a* ; **31** 11 *a* ; **57** 429 *b*.

syendo = *siendo* (cf. *ser*), **51** 1664 *c*.

syenpre = *sienpre*, **34** 78 *a* etc.

syeruo = *sieruo*, **50** 510 *c*.

sygro = *sigro* (a dialectal, perhaps Western, form of *siglo* < O. Sp. *sieglo*, a half-learned word, < L.

* So, also, *macc.*
sǫamo > *sg amo* > *su amo* etc.

saeculum) world, **50** 510 *d* ; cf. *seglo*.

syguiente = *siguiente,* participial adj. connected with *seguir* (L. *sequi,* V. L. **sĕquīˢʳe*) following, afterwards, **66** 9.

syn = *sin,* **50** 498 *c* etc.

synificauan = *sinificavan,* mod. *significaban,* impf. 3 pl. of *significar* (learned word; L. *sĭgnĭfĭcāre.* The disappearance of *g* before *n* is a quasi popular trait ; cf. *dino* for *digno*), meant, **59** 6.

t' = *te* (better written *siempret,* as it is really enclitic to the preceding word ; cf. Facsimile of the *Disputa*), **21** 13.

ta' scribal for *tan* before *mal,* which begins with a nasal, **21** 25 ; cf. *tamanno.*

tabardo (origin unknown ; supposed to have relations with L. *tap.ēte* ' tapestry,' etc. The garment might have figures worked on it like those of tapestry) tabard, cloak, **49** 18 *d* ; **57** 429 *d.*

tabla (L. *tabŭla*) plank, board ; pl. draughts, checkers, **41** 11.

tablado (L. *tabŭlātum*) scaffolding, a frame set up for tilting purposes, **41** 10, 15 ; etc.

tado cf. *contado.*

tajar (V. L. *talĭāre* ; cf. L. *talĕa* ' a cutting ') to cut, cut up, **53** 5, 7 ; *tajara* had cut, **53** 13 etc.

tal adj. and pron. (L. *talĭs -em*), such, such a, this, a certain, said, so, such a one, **7** 36 ; **11** 107 ; **32** 21 *a* ; etc. ; so and so, **57** 432 *a* ; *otro tal* such another, **11** 108 ; *tal . . . qual* such as, **24** 94 *d.*

taliento (L. *talĕntum* ' talent,' ' sum of money,' ' treasure ' ; hence in Romance the metaphorical sense of ' mental treasure,' ' intellectual wealth or ability,' and in Sp. ' mental attitude,' ' temperament,' ' disposition ') disposition, **24** 94 *c.* (In mod. Sp. the learned *talento* prevails.)

Tamanno -a = *tamaño -a* (L. *tam + magnus -a -um*) so great, **46** 16.

tan (L. *tam,* or rather, from *tanto,* which in proclitic use shortened to *tant,* and this, by assimilation of its final *t* to the initial cons. of a following word, > *tan*) so, as, **13** 1 ; **17** 1086 ; **21** 9 ; etc. ; (expletive in exclamation) **41** 27.

tanbien = *tambien* (*tan + bien*) as well, also, **22** 37.

tanniendo = mod. *tañendo,* pres. part. of *tañer* (L. *tangĕre,* V. L. **tangĕre,* ' to touch,' ' thrum an instrument,' ' play ') to play on a musical instrument, **34** 82 *c.*

tanto -a (L. *tantus -a -um*) so much, as much, so many a, **19** 1141.

tanto (adv.) so much, as much, **16** 170 ; **42** 15 ; etc. ; *por tanto* therefore, **37** 354 *a* etc.

tardar (L. *tardāre*) to delay, **29** 370 *b* ; *tardan* (cf. *detardar*), **14** 105 ; *tardar* (cf. *detardar*), **20** 1198, 1202.

tarua (cf. *detarua*) **14** 96.

te 2 pers. pron., direct and indirect obj. of verb (L. *tē* ; if *ti* = L. *tibĭ*

were used as an enclitic conj.
pron., it would also, in the final
position, give *te*), thee, to thee,
9 74, 75; **10** 90; etc. (The form
is both proclitic and enclitic in
O. Sp.)

tecum (L.) **51** 1663 *a*.

telo = *te* + *lo*, **46** 22.

temblar (V. L. *trĕmŭlāre; cf. L.
tremulus -a -um, > **trem'lar* >,
by dissimilation of *r* or rather
through the analogy of *tem.er*,
**tem'lar* and, with a *b* produced
in the passage of the speech
organs from *m* to *l*, *temblar*) to
tremble, **62** 21.

temer (L. *tĭmēre*) to fear, **38** 367 *d*;
43 28.

temor (L. *timor*, *tĭmǫrem*) fear, **70**
XLIII 3.

tendal (V. L. *tendalis -em, formed
on V. L. *tenda, abstract from
L. *tĕndĕre*, or V. L. *tendĭta;
[*palus*] *tendalis, or *tenditalis,
'tent pole') tent pole, **19** 1142;
cf. *tienda*.

tender (L. *tendēre*, V. L. *tĕndēre)
to stretch, extend, **17** 182.

tener (L. *tĕnēre*) to have, hold,
keep, consider, **24** 95 *a*; **28**
364 *b*; etc. (*Tienes* < *tĕnes*; *tiene*
< *tĕnet*; *tienen* < *tĕnent* show
the natural diphthongization.
Tengo = L. *tĕnĕo* has a *g* whose
origin is not clear. We should
expect *teño; cf. Ptg. *tenho*.
As the *n* was unpalatalized in
the other five forms of the
pres. indic., a tendency to avoid
the palatalization in the 1 sg.

asserted itself, but it can hardly
be said that palatalized *n*, i.e. *ñ*,
became *n* + a velar stop, *g*. The
g may be borrowed from other
common verbs, *digo*, *hago*, etc.;
the combination *-ngo* exists also
in Sp. verbs from L. *-ngo*, *dis-
tingo*, etc., but they seem hardly
popular enough to have influenced so common and important
a verb as *tener*.) Cf. *terne*, *ternia*,
touo, *touieron*, *touiessedes*, *touieredes*, etc.

tengades = mod. *tengáis* (cf. *tener*),
30 9 *a*: **48** 16 *a*.

tenie, tenien = weakened form of
tenía, *tenian* (cf. *tener*), **31** 11 *c*,
14 *d*, 13 *c*; etc.; cf. *touieredes*,
touo, etc.

tenies = *tenie* + *se*, considered
himself, **30** 7 *d*.

tenjan = *tenían* (cf. *tener*), **27** 358 *d*.

tenjangelo = mod. *tenían* + *se* (not
refl.) + *lo*, **24** 87 *d*.

tenprar = *temprar* (L. *tempĕrare*)
to temper, **31** 14 *a* and *d*.

terçer proclitic and shortened form
of *terçero*, **18** 1113.

terçero -a (V. L. *tertĭarĭus -a -um*,
based on L. *tertius*) third, **29**
370 *b*; **64** 98 *a*; etc.

terçio (learned word; L. *tĕrtĭum*)
third part, third, **58** 440 *b*.

terne (metathesized form of *tenré
< *tener* + [*h*]*e*, *ten*[*e*]*ré*; the
mod. form *tendré* preserves the
stem of *ten.er*) **6** 18.

ternia (metathesized form of *tenria
< *tener* + [*hab*]*ía*, *ten*[*e*]*ria*; cf.
terne) **43** 28; cf. mod. *tendría*.

ternian = *tendrían* (cf. *terne, ternia*), **55** 23.

terra Latinism for *tierra*, **8** 66 etc.

terrenal (V. L. **terrēnālis*, based on L. *terrēnus -a -um*) earthly, **56** 422 *b*.

Terryn (pr. n.) Thierry, **36** 352 *b*. (A French epic hero.)

terzero erroneous for *terçero*, **63** 91 *c*.

tesoro (L. *thēsaurus -um*) treasure, **24** 92 *b*.

ti pers. pron., obj. of prep. (L. *tĭbi*; the form is really analogical to L. *mī, mihi*), thee, to thee, **18** 1102; **21** 12; etc.

tiempo (L. *tempus*, V. L. **tĕmpum*. It has been said that O. Sp. *tiempos* really represents *tĕmpus* and is not originally pl., and that *tiempo* was made from it on the supposition that it was pl. But?) time, **27** 353 *a*; **47** 18.

tienda (V. L. **tĕnda*, abstract from L. *tĕndĕre*, or V. L. **tĕndĭa*) tent, **16** 152; **17** 202; etc.; cf. *tendal*.

tienpo = *tiempo*, **33** 76 *d* etc.

tiento (abstract from *tentar, tiento* < L. *tentare, tĕnto*, 'to handle,' 'touch,' 'attempt,' 'try,' 'essay') essay, method of essay, judgment, prudence, **57** 431 *c*; **58** 438 *d*.

tierra (L. *tĕrra*) earth, region, land, ground, **13** 14; **15** 125; etc.

tiesta (L. *tĕsta* 'pot,' 'shell,' 'skull'; used in Romance, originally as a jocose term, for 'head') head, **13** 13; **21** 22. (In mod. Sp. for 'head' this word

has given way to *cabeza*; in the sense of 'edge and head of barrel staves' it survives; in the learned form *testa* it still denotes 'face,' 'forehead,' 'front' of anything.)

timpo scribal for *tiempo*, **6** 4.

tine scribal for *tiene*, **6** 20.

tio (V. L. **thīus*, Gk. θεῖος) uncle, **42** 31.

tirano (learned word; L. *tyrănnus -um*) tyrant, **69** XIX 1.

tirar (source unknown; it has been ascribed to Germanic *tĕran*, Gothic *tairan*, Eng. 'to tear'; but?) to discharge, fire, **66** I 7 { ... ; *tirad nos alla* get over there! **57** 432 *a*.

tirra scribal for *tierra*, **7** 23 etc.

tiseras pl. (apparently connected with L. *tōnsōrĭus -a -um* 'appertaining to shearing'; cf. L. *ferramenta tonsoria, culter tonsorius*. But great difficulty is presented by the *i* of the first syll. of the Sp. word, to say nothing of its ending. Some analogy or some contamination is to be apprehended; cf. the *i* of Fr. *ciseaux* and Eng. *scissors*. Further difficulty is raised by the mod. *tijeras*, which indicates an earlier *tixeras*), scissors, shears, **53** 4.

to, tos poss. adj. preceding a noun in the masc. (L. *tŭŭm, tŭōs*; cf. for this form the discussion under *so, su*, and *mi*), thy, **21** 20; **22** 27, 31, 35, 36; (with art., cf. *el so, el mio*) los tos **22** 28, 36; cf. *tu*.

tobra metathesized form of *troba*, *trova* (an abstract from the verb *trobar*, *trovar*, 'to compose' verse, etc. The Sp. verb is perhaps a loan-word from the Provençal *trobar* ' to find ' and also 'to invent,' 'compose,' and was introduced into Spain by the Provençal troubadours, being adopted in the poetical and musical sense and not generally used with the sense 'to find.' The ultimate source is a matter of some doubt; cf. V. L. *tropare, from L. *tropus* in the ecclesiastical sense of 'melody,' and L. *tŭrbare*, with metathesis *trŭbare, used as a term of fishing. Grave objections as to phonetic and sense development are to be met in both. In view of the fact that Italian, French, and Provençal all have for *trovare*, *trouver*, and *trobar* the more general sense of 'to find' as the essential one, *tropare seems unlikely. Schuchardt [*Ztschr. f. roman. Philol.* XXVIII. 36, and *Roman. Etymologien*, II] has argued ingeniously for *tŭrbare*, poetical composition, **48** 15 *b*. Cf. *trubada* and *trouauan*.

tod proclitic apocopated form of *todo*: *atod el primer colpe* at the very first, at the outset, **17** 184; **33** 75 *b*; etc.; *con tod aquello* withal, nevertheless, **45** 18.

todavia (*toda* + *via* ' in every way') at all events, at any rate, yet, **64** 97 *c*.

todo -a (L. *tōtus -a -um*) all, every, whole, **6** 8; **7** 40; **13** 81; etc.; (adv. and pron.) *todo* everything, **15** 123; **27** 359 *d*; *del todo, de todo* entirely, **59** 5; **70** LIII *b*; *en todo* wholly, **6** 18 etc.; *con todo* withal, however, **34** 79 *d*; *por todo* in every respect, **24** 94 *d*.

todomal = *todo mal*, **18** 1103.

Toledo (pr. n.) Toledo, **57** 434 *d*.

Tolosa (pr. n.) Toulouse, **35** 328 *a*.

tolosanos (formation in -*ano -a*, L. -*anus -a -um*, on *Tolosa*) men of Toulouse, **37** 357 *a*.

tomar (origin unknown) to take, receive, derive, **9** 70; **20** 1216; **11** 118; **35** 328 *c*; etc.; *tomarse a* + infin., to begin to, **18** 1102; **41** 31.

tomaua = *tomava*, *tomaba* (cf. *tomar*), **17** 185.

tomos = *tomó* + *se* (cf. *tomar*), **18** 1102.

tormento (learned word; L. *tormĕntum*) torment, **25** 101 *b* etc.

tornar (L. *tŏrnāre* ' to turn on a lathe,' whence, perhaps already in popular L., 'to turn' in general) to turn, return, convert, give back, **10** 104; **28** 366 *d*; **29** 369 *c*; etc.; (*tornar a* + infin. gives the idea of repetition with respect to the sense of the infin.) *tornan tiendas a fincar* they again set up the tents, **18** 1101 (cf. mod. *volver á*); *tornarse* to turn, return, become, **13** 2; **18** 1091; **20** 1196; etc. (*Torno, tornas, torne, tornes*, etc., are analogical to the forms accenting the ending.)

tornaua = *tornava, tornaba* (cf. *tornar*), **13** 2.

tornauas = *tornaua* + *se*, he was returning, **20** 1196.

torneo (abstract from *tornear*, V. L. **tornĭdĭare* from L. *tornāre* 'to turn and wheel about in the lists,' 'to tourney') tourney, **34** 83 *a*.

tornos, tornosse = *tornó* + *se* (cf. *tornar*), **18** 1091 ; **61** 20.

torpe (L. *tŭrpis -em*) disgraceful, infamous, awkward, stupid, **49** 490 *b*.

torpedat = *torpedad* (V.L. **tŭrpĭtas,* **tŭrpĭtātem* ; cf. L. *turpitudo*) baseness, stupidity, **53** 4.

Torpyn (pr. n.) Turpin, **36** 352 *c*.

torrnada = *tornada* (n. from p.p. of *tornar*) return, **56** 425 *b*.

torrnado -a = *tornado -a* p.p. of *tornar*, **64** 94 *d*, 101 *d*.

tortola (V. L. **tŭrtŭra*, for L. *tur-tur*, > *tortora* as in Ital., whence, by dissimilation, *tórtola*) turtle-dove, **47** 18.

tost' = *toste* 68 VIII 4 etc. ※

tot = *tod* : *tot siempre* ever and always, **21** 13.

touieredes = *tovieredes*, mod. *tu-viereis*, fut. sbj. 2 pl. of *tener* (the form is analogical to *ovie-redes* from *aver*), **43** 33.

touieron = *tovieron*, mod. *tuvieron* (with the usual closing of *o* > *u* by the *i̯*; cf. *touo* and *tener*), **28** 367 *c*.

touiessedes = *toviessedes*, mod. *tu-vieseis*, impf. sbj. 2 pl. of *tener* (cf. *touieredes*), **43** 30.

toujesse = *toviesse*, mod. *tuviese* (cf. *touiessedes*), **28** 363 *b*.

touo = *tovo* (analogical to *ovo*, < L *habŭit*), whence mod. *tuvo* (through the influence of *tu-vieron*, etc.), pret. 3 of *tener*, **44** 9 ; **46** 25.

toviese (cf. *toujesse*) **33** 75 *d*.

tovo (cf. *touo*) **34** 78 *b* ; **37** 355 *c*.

tovyeres = *tovieres*, mod. *tuvieres* (cf. *touieredes*), **36** 338 *b*.

tovyeron (cf. *touieron*) **37** 357 *a*.

trabaiaron = *trabajaron* (cf. *traba-jar*), **41** 19.

trabajar (V. L. **trabacŭlāre* or **tre-palĭāre* ; cf. *trabajo*) to labor, exert one's self, work, **41** 19; **71** LXXIX 3.

trabajo (possibly a formation on L. *trabs*. *trabem* 'beam'; V.L. **trabacŭlum* [cf. L. *trabalis -e*] 'framework,' i.e. one in which one is confined, 'a hindrance,' 'trouble.' There has been proposed also a V.L. **trepalĭum* [cf. L. *tres* and *palus*], i.e. a torture-frame made of three beams, whence the sense of 'trouble.' The usual Provençal form, *trebalh.s*, favors the latter source, and the V.L. **trabare* 'to catch in with beams,' etc., might have acted on the first syll. to produce the other Romance forms. But ?) trouble, toil, labor, **52** 2 ; **53** 8 ; **56** 423 *b* ; etc.

tractar = mod. *tratar* (learned word ; L. *tractāre*) to treat, **66** 2.

traedes = mod. *traéis* (cf. *traer*), **11** 128.

traer (L. *irahĕre*, V. L. **tragēre* for the Sp. peninsula; **tragĕre* for the other Romance languages. For Sp. **trahēre* would also give *traer*; but the pres. indic. *trago* indicates a present stem with *g*) to bring, carry, have, **6** 20; **14** 91; **15** 126; **24** 96 *d*; etc. (The perf. *traxi* in L. = *trac.si*, i.e. may indicate a stem *trag-* whose *g* unvoiced to *c* before *s*.)

trago (V. L. **trago* for L. *traho*; cf. *traer*) I bring, I have, **61** 14. (Cf. mod. *traigo* and O. Sp. *trayo*; is *traigo* due to a contamination of *trago* and *trayo*?)

traiçion (learned word; L. *tradĭtĭo -ōnem* ‘a giving up,’ whence in Romance ‘a treacherous giving up,’ ‘treachery’) treason, **63** 92 *a* etc.

trainantes pres. part. pl. (perhaps a loan-word from Fr. *trainer*, *trainant*, Provençal *trahinar*, etc. A V. L. **tragīnāre* based on **tragere*, L. *trahĕre*, appears to be the source), trailing, hanging loose, **22** 33. Cf. mod. Sp. *trajinar, trajino, trajín*.

trança (perhaps a loan-word from Fr. *trancher*; cf. Körting, s.v. *trinico*) cuts off, cuts short, **69** XVIII 8. Cf. Sp. *trincar* and *trinchar*.

transido p.p. of *transir* (L. *transīre*), gone by, passed away, dead, **39** 371 *c*.

trapassar (L. *tra(ns)* + *passus -um*, whence V. L. **trāpassāre*) to cross, **47** 12. (In L. already,

trans as a prefix was frequently reduced to *tra-*; cf. *traducere*, *trajicere*, etc.) Cf. mod. Sp. *traspasar* and *traspasante*.

tras (L. *trans*, V. L. **tras*) after, behind, **8** 64; **47** 13.

trasladaçion (half-learned; L. *translatĭo -ōnem*) translation, **66** 1.

trasnochada (n. from p.p. of *trasnochar*) night march, night attack, **19** 1185.

trasnochar (V. L. **tra[n]snoctāre* from L. *trans* and *nox, noctem*) to march by night, make a night attack, **18** 1100.

traspasante part. adj. (from *traspasar*, a variant of *trapasar*, with the fuller V. L. prefix *tras-* < L. *trans-*), piercing, sharp, penetrating, **66** I 8; cf. *trapassar*.

trastornar (V. L. **tra[n]stornare*; cf. *tornar*) turn about, turn over, upset, disturb, **33** 74 *c*.

trastorrnado = *trastornado*, p.p. of *trastornar*, **56** 425 *c*.

tratar (learned word; L. *tractāre*) to treat, plot, scheme, **62** 18, 24.

tratauan = *tratavan, trataban* (cf. *tratar*), **62** 24.

traua (cf. *entraua*) **13** 15.

trauar = *travar*, mod. *trabar* (V. L. **trabāre*, from L. *trabs, trabem*, ‘to catch in with beams,’ ‘to fetter,’ ‘bind’), to bind, catch, **29** 369 *a*; **58** 435 *b*.

travajo = *trabajo*, **36** 350 *b*.

travessar (V. L. **traversare* from L. *traversus* for *transversus*) to cross, **37** 357 *d*.

traxe pret. 1 of *traer* (L. *traxi*), I brought, **68** IX 1 ; cf. mod. *traje*.

traxo (L. *trax.it*) pret. 3 of *traer*, **67** V 4 ; cf. mod. *trajo*.

traycion = *traiçion*, **46** 16.

traye = *traie*, *traía*, weakened impf. of *traer*, **43** 8.

trayo (L. *traho*, V.L. *trago*, attracted to the *i* stems, **tragio > trayo*) I bring, carry, **14** 86.

trebeio = *trebejo* (perhaps an abstract from *trebejar*, V. L. **trĭvĭlĭare* 'to sport' as people do at the crossroads, a common place for rustics to gather in and have games, from L. *trĭvĭum* 'crossroad.' A direct derivation from a V. L. *trĭvĭcŭlum* might be supposed. But?) triviality, sport, trick, jest, **21** 20. (Cf. Ital. *trebbio* 'place where three roads meet,' diversion,' 'fun,' and Eng. *trivial*.)

trecho -a (L. p.p. *tractus -a -um* of *trahĕre*) : *mal trecho* illtreated, **43** 13.

tred (probably a scribal error for *traed*, imper. pl. of *traer*. However, the imper. sg. *trae* in popular pronunciation becomes *traę > tray > trey > tre* ; on this last a new pl. might have been formed by adding *-d*) go, betake yourselves, **15** 142. (Here we see a not infrequent omission of the refl. obj. pron. in the positive imper., *traed* = *traeos* ; cf. *levantad* = *levantaos*.)

tredze (Menéndez Pidal's resolution of the numeral 13 in the *Auto* ; L. *trĕdĕcĭm > *tredeze >* either **treeze* or *tredze*, whence, by absorption of *d* in *z = dz*, *treze*, mod. *trece*) thirteen, **10** 98.

tregua (Germanic *treuwa*, with a treatment of *wa* found often in German words beginning with *wa-* ; cf. German **warda >* Sp. *guarda*, etc.) truce, **45** 9.

tres (L. *trēs*) three, **7** 27 etc.

treuo = *trevo*, pres. 1 of *trever* (L. *trĭbŭĕre*, V. L. **trĭbŭēre* 'to give up,' refl. 'to give one's self up' to a thing, 'to venture' upon a thing) : *me treuo* I dare, **25** 102 *c*. (Cf. mod. *atreverse á*, L. *attrĭbŭĕre + se*, V. L. **attrĭbŭēre + se*.)

treynta (V. L. **trēgĭnta* for L. *trĭgĭntā*, under the influence of *trēs*, *trĕdecim* ; an early loss of *g* and an accent on the *ē* (through the influence of *trĕdĕcim* or of *veínte > véinte*) could produce *trégnta*, i.e. *treynta*, *treinta*) thirty, **31** 18 *c*.

triste (L. *trĭstis -em*) sad, **58** 441 *d* etc.

tristura (*trist-e* + abstract ending *-ura*) sadness, **70** LII 6. (*Tristeza < L. trĭstĭtĭa* has replaced *tristura*.)

trobador (agent noun related to *trobar*; cf. *tobra*) troubadour, poet, **52** 10.

troçir (L. *traducere* ? ; L. *torquere*, V.L. **torcīre* ?) to pass, spend, **24** 91 *c*.

trouauan = *trovavan*, impf. 3 pl. of *trovar* (cf. *tobra*), found, **26** 110 *c*; cf. *trubada*.

trubada (scribal for *trobada*, *trovada*, p.p. of *trovar*) found, discovered, **7** 35. (The sense 'devised,' 'composed' is not impossible here; cf. *trouauan*.)

tu 2 pers. pron., subj. form (L. *tū*), thou, **12** 135 etc.

tu, tus (poss. adj. before noun) thy: before masc. noun, **25** 100 *c*; **49** 299 *b*, 300 *c*; **61** 13, 18; **50** 510 *a*; **64** 94 *c* and *d*, 95 *a* and *d*; accompanied by the def. art., *el tu*, *los tus*, **25** 101 *c*; **46** 6, 7; **48** 13; **51** 1663 *g*; **67** II 8; in all, 16 cases: before fem. noun, **36** 342 *a* and *c*; **61** 15; **64** 98 *b*; **70** LII 8; accompanied by the def. art., *la tu*, **21** 22; **51** 1662 *c* and *f*; in all, 8 cases. Though the cases of the masc. use predominate, the true masc. form was originally *to*, and *tu* was usually at first only fem. It is *tuam*, whence Sp. **tua*, reduced in proclisis to *tu*; cf. the remarks under *su* and *so*; later *tu* was generalized. But might not *to* in hiatus > *tu* ?

tuerto (L. *tŏrtum* from p.p. of *torquēre* 'something twisted,' 'crooked,' 'wrong') wrong, **35** 331 *d*; (or, perhaps, 'twist,' 'turn about') **49** 301 *b*; inscription at the head of a cross, stating the criminal's wrong or crime, **64** 98 *b*.

tuyo poss. pron. (L. *tuus*, *tuum*, influenced by *cujus*, whence Sp. *cuyo*), thy, thine, **49** 300 *d*.

ty = *ti*, **36** 338 *b* etc.

tyene = *tiene* (cf. *tener*), **36** 347 *b*.

tyenes = *tienes* (cf. *tener*), **36** 342 *b*.

tyña = *tiña* (L. *tĭnĕa* 'moth,' 'worm,' hence in Sp. a 'blemish,' 'eaten spot') scab, scurviness, meanness, **50** 499 *c*.

tyra = *tira* (cf. *tirar*) takes off, **50** 497 *b*.

[The O.Sp. scribes often wrote *u* for *v* both in the initial position and within a word.]

ua = *va*, **11** 13.

ual = *val* (cf. *valer*), **7** 33.

ualdra = *valdra* (cf. *valer*), **23** 2 *d*.

uale = *vale* (cf. *valer*), **6** 8.

ualia = *valia* (cf. *valer*), **24** 92 *d*.

ualiesse = *valiesse* (cf. *valer*), **27** 359 *d*.

uara = *vara* (L. *vara* 'crossbar') rod, staff, **43** 3.

uaron = *varon*, **13** 16.

uaso = *vaso*, **25** 102 *d*.

uassallo = *vassallo* (cf. *vasallo*), **44** 17 etc.

uaya = *vaya* (V.L. **vadeat* for L. *vadat*, adopted as pres. sbj. form of *ir*), **24** 96 *a*.

uayades = *vayades* (V.L. **vadĕatĭs*; cf. *uaya*), whence *vayaes* **68** VIII 6, and thence mod. *vaydis*; **14** 89.

uayamos = *vayamos* (V.L. **vadĕāmŭs*; cf. *uaya*), **53** 11.

uazio -a = *vazio -a* (L. *vacīvus -a -um*) empty, **13** 4; **24** 97 *c*; cf. mod. *vacío -a*.

uea = *vea* (L. *vĭdĕam*), pres. sbj. 1 of *veer*, *ver*, **26** 109 *b*.

ueer = *veer* (L. *vĭdēre*), whence, by contraction, *ver* to see: *ueer lo e*

I shall see it, **7** 46. (The full stem *ve-* still appears in mod. Sp. where the ending does not begin with *e*.)

uegada = *vegada* time, **7** 46; **27** 354 *a*.

ueido -a = *veído -a*, a regular p.p. of *veer* (L. *visus* replaced by V. L. **vídĭtum* ; this regular p.p. still appears in the derivative *proveer, proveído* beside *provisto* ; the simple verb has only the strong p.p. *visto*), **6** 3; **7** 30; **8** 62; **10** 100.

uemne (dialect form, showing the stressed development of L. *homo*, *hŏmĭnem* with diphthongization: *hŏmĭnem* > *omne* > *uemne*. In Castilian the word developed in accord with its appearance as an unaccented proclitic, for it had the functions of an indefinite pronoun [cf. Fr. *on*], and the unaccented form was generalized) man, **21** 6; cf. *omne*, *homne*.

uencieron = *vencieron* (cf. *vençer*), **45** 20.

uender = *vender* (L. *vēndĕre*, V. L. **vēndēre*) to sell, **28** 366 *b* etc.

uenga = *venga* (cf. *venir*), **11** 117.

uenides = *venides*, **9** 80.

uenido = *venido* (cf. *venir*), **10** 95 etc.

uenien = *venien* (weakened impf. of *venir*), **31** 14 *a*.

uenjmos = *venimos* (pret. of *venir*), **28** 362 *a*.

uentura = *ventura*, **16** 177 etc.

ueo = *veo* (cf. *veer*, *ver*), **7** 38, 50; etc.

uer (truncated form of *uero*) : *por uer* in truth, **6** 15.

uer, ueremos, uere (cf. *ver*) **7** 27; **8** 64; **13** 16; **24** 95 *a*.

uerano = *verano*, **27** 356 *d*.

ueras = *veras* (substantive use of fem. pl. from L. *vērus -a -um*) : *por ueras* in truth, **12** 136. (The phrase remains in *de veras* ; cf. *de uero*.)

uerdad = *verdad*, **6** 7 ; **7** 45; etc.

uerdadero -a = *verdadero -a*, **23** 3 *c* etc.

uermeio -a = *vermejo -a*, mod. *bermejo -a* (adj. from L. *vermĭcŭlus -um* 'little worm,' 'insect from which vermilion dye is obtained,' 'vermilion'), vermilion, crimson, **14** 88.

uero (L. *vērus -um* ; cf. *ueras*) : *de uero* truly, surely, **7** 28.

uertad scribal for *verdad*, **6** 10, 11 ; **7** 47 ; etc.

uestido -a = *vestido -a* (p.p. of *vestir*, L. *vĕstīre*) dressed, **21** 8.

uez = *vez*, **43** 1 ; **46** 9 ; etc.

uezino -a (cf. *vezino*) **23** 2 *b*.

ui = *vi* (cf. *ver*), **7** 22 etc.

uicto = *victo* (L. *vīctus -um*) food, **25** 105 *b*. (This persists only in the phrase *día y victo*.)

uida = *vida*.

uieio -a = *viejo -a*, **26** 112 *c* etc.

uiene = *viene* (cf. *venir*), **31** 13 *a*.

uieron = *vieron* (cf. *ver*), **43** 15 etc.

uinet scribal for *viene* (cf. *venir*), **6** 19.

uinie = *vinie*, mod. *venía*, impf. of *venir*, **44** 15. (The first *i* is due to the analogy of the pret.

vine, etc.; the ending is the weakened one.)

uinieron = *vinieron* (cf. *venir*), **44** 19.

uiniesen = *viniesen* (cf. *venir*), **44** 17.

uino = *vino* wine, **46** 5 etc.

uio = *vió* (cf. *ver*), **11** 107 etc.

uision = *vision* (L. *vīsĭo -ōnem*; half-learned) vision, **21** 4.

uistes = *vistes*, mod. *visteis* (with an *i* borrowed from the pres.; cf. *veis*), pret. 2 pl. of *ver*, **10** 96.

uita scribal for *vida*, **9** 76.

uiuimos = *vivimos* (cf. *vivir*), **45** 14.

uja = *vía*, **28** 366 *a*.

ujda = *vida*, **26** 289 *c*.

un, una indef. art. and numeral (L. *ūnus -a -um*; the full masc. form *uno* appears occasionally, but, as in mod. Sp., it is usually shortened, because of its proclitic use, to *un*), a, an, one, **21** 3; **8** 55; etc.; (before a fem. word beginning with a vowel, *un* = *una*) *un estrranna manera*, **37** 359 *d*; (*uno* before noun; but in both cases it is erroneous), **6** 8; **7** 39: (pron.) *uno* one, **46** 1, 6; etc.; cf. *vn, vna*.

uo = *vo* (before *lo* and before *l* in dialectal, especially Western, Sp., as in Ptg., *s* may be lost; the case may be a mistake), **12** 136.

uo = *vo*, mod. *voy*, **8** 62.

uoca = *voca, boca* (L. *bŭcca*), mouth, **12** 147.

uoluntad = *voluntad*, **46** 21.

uoluntat (cf. *voluntad*) **24** 87 *c*.

uos = *vos*, 2 pers. pron. pl., used also as sg. of address (L. *vōs*), **8** 52; **40** 14; etc.

uos = *vos*, conj. pron., indirect obj., 2 pers. pl., used also as sg. of address (L. *vōs*), you, to you, for you, **8** 52; **13** 80; **14** 108; **15** 143; etc. (In the enclitic position, after a verb form ending in a vowel, the *v*, already a bilabial spirant in O. Sp., became *u* and this disappeared before the *o*; hence *os*, which was then generalized and used proclitically also.)

uos = *vos*, mod. *vosotros -as*, disjunct. obj. pron., 2 pers. pl., used also as sg. of address; (after a prep.) you, **8** 53; **19** 1128; **42** 14.

uostros (scribal for *vuestros*) your, **9** 81; **11** 128; cf. *uuestro*.

usado -a p.p. of *usar* (L. *ūsāre*), used, wont, practiced, **12** 146; **28** 366 *d*.

uuestro -a = *vuestro -a*, poss. adj. (V. L. **vŏster, vŏstra, vŏstrum*, for L. *vester* under influence of *nŏster*), your, **14** 85; **15** 119; **16** 167; etc.

uuso = *vuso* (scribal error for *vusco*, i.e. *con uuso* = *convusco*) with you, **16** 168. (O. Sp. carried the double combination with the prep. through the 1 and 2 pers. forms of *nos* and *vos*; *con-uusco, convusco*. Why the *o* > *u* is not clear; perhaps the change took place first by way of labialization in *convosco* > *convusco*.)

uynie = *uinie*, **32** 19 *a*.

[Sometimes used, especially in the initial position, for *u*; initially and medially it often stands for *b*.]

va (L. *vadǐt*, reduced in V. L. to
*vat through the analogy of *dat*,
stat, etc.) pres. 3 of *ir* (which
lost in Romance its own sg.
and 3 pl. forms of the pres. indic.,
and supplied them and, for that
matter, the 1 and 2 pl., from L.
vadēre, just as it supplied its
lost preterite forms from *ěsse*),
goes, **19** 1137, 1146; etc.; cf.
ua.

vaca (L. *vacca*) cow, **65** 103 *d*.

vaçia (incorrect or late for *vazio -a*)
65 106 *c*. < C L · vacīvus

vado (L. *vadum*) ford, **37** 358 *a*.

vagar infin. n. (L. *vacāre* 'to have
leisure,' 'be free'), leisure, rest,
slowness : *dar vagar* to be slow
about matters, **65** 108 *b* and *d*.

val (L. *vale*) imper. sg. of *valer*, **39**
370 *d*.

val truncated form of *vale* (L. *valet*),
pres. 3 of *valer*, **57** 432 *d*.

valde (perhaps Arab. *bâtǐl* 'in vain,'
'gratis.' But?) : *en valde* in vain,
to no purpose, **37** 354 *c* ; cf. mod.
balde.

Valdouinos (pr. n.) Baldwin, **36**
352 *a*.

Valençia pr. n., **18** 1097 etc.

valer (L. *valēre*) to avail, help, be
worth, **18** 1096; **38** 361 *d* ; etc. ;
cf. *valo*.

valia = mod. *valía* (abstract in *-ía*
from stem of *valer*) aid, help,
68 XVIII 1.

valien = *valían* (cf. *valer*), **31** 12 *c*.

valiente (L. pres. part. *valens*,
valěntem) valiant, strong, **67**
III 1.

valiessen = *valiesen* (cf. *valer*), **43**
31.

valle (L. *vallis -em*) valley, **47** 1.

vallestero = mod. *ballestero* (agent
noun in *-ero* from *ballesta* 'crossbow,' L. *ballǐsta* 'machine for
hurling missiles') crossbow man,
69 XVIII 3.

valo pres. 1 of *valer* (V. L. **valo*
for L. *valěo*), I am worth, **42** 17.
(The literary form in mod. Sp.
is *valgo*; but *valo* lives in popular
use.)

valor (L. *valor -ōrem*) valor, worth,
esteem, **50** 491 *c* ; **64** 95 *d*.

van (L. *vadunt* ; V. L. **vant* ; cf.
va) go, **20** 1206, 1211 ; etc.

vando (Germanic *band* 'band,'
'bond,' something 'banded' or
'bound' together, 'band,' 'company') band, party, **56** 425 *c*.

vano -a (L. *vanus -a -um*) vain,
empty, **65** 105 *c*.

varon (source not entirely certain ;
said to be L. *baro -ōnem* 'simpleton,' 'blockhead,' 'dull fellow' ;
this seems to have been used in
Carolingian times as a term for
soldiers' servants. Hence, by
successive stages, it is supposed that the sense was gradu-
ally dignified : 'sturdy clown,'
'stout fellow,' 'brave man,'
'nobleman.' In Sp. the noun is
always used in a dignified sense)
man, male, **31** 8 *c* ; **36** 345 *b* ; **59**
13.

vasallo (apparently of Celtic origin; cf. Cymric and Welsh *gwas* 'youth,' 'servant'; the ending *-allo* seems also to be Celtic) servant, vassal, **35** 333 *a* etc.; cf. *uassallo*.

vaso (L. *vasum*) vessel, glass, chalice, **23** 2 *d* etc.

vassalo = *vasallo* and *uassallo* (the *ss* and *ll* are the correct spellings), **13** 20 ; **17** 204 ; etc.

vayaes < *vayades* (cf. *uayades*), **68** VIII 6.

vayamos pres. sbj. 1 pl. of *ir* (V. L. **vadĕamus*), let us go, **17** 208. (In O. Sp. this form could be used in the imperative sense now possessed only by *vamos* < L. *vadāmŭs* >**vaamos* > *vamos*.)

vayan pres. sbj. 3 pl. of *ir* (V.L. **vadeant*), **18** 1107.

vço = *uço* (V.L. **ūstĭum* for L. *ostĭum*) gate, door, **13** 3.

ve imper. sg. of *ir* (L. *vade* > **vae* > **vaɛ* > **vay* > **vey* > *ve*), go thou, **61** 9 etc. (In the imper. pl. the form comes from *īre* : *īte*>*id*.)

ve imper. sg. of *ver*; cf. *vey*.

vedar (L. *vĕtāre*) to forbid, prohibit, **14** 90. (In O. Sp. the pres. tense showed diphthongal forms; cf. *vieda*, **20** 1205 ; now the *e* of the infin. etc. runs through the verb.)

vedes (L. pres. 2 pl. *vĭdētĭs* > *veedes* > *vedes* > **veɛs* > *veis*) you see, **14** 82, 114; **15** 137; **37** 354*d*; **68** IX 2; cf. *ver*.

veedes (cf. *vedes*) **55** 33.

veer (L. *vĭdēre* > **veder* > *veer* > *ver*) to see, **57** 427 *c*.

veet = *veed* (L. imper. pl. *vĭdēte* > **veded* > *veed* > *ved*) see, **41** 27.

vegada (augmented form of L. *vix*, *vĭcem* ; V. L. **vĭcāta*) time, **34** 80 *d* ; **54** 5 ; **57** 433 *a* ; **60** 7 ; **62** 13. (Of the synonymous *vez* and *vegada*, *vez* alone survives.)

vençer (L. *vĭncĕre*, V. L. **vĭncēre*) to conquer, defeat, **37** 355 *a* etc.

vengar (L. *vĭndĭcare* > **vendgar* > *vengar*) to avenge, **35** 329 *c*.

venga, vengan (L. *vĕnĭam, vĕnĭat, vĕnĭant* ; cf. *vengo*, and *tener*) **19** 1122 etc.

vengo (L. *vĕnĭo* ; cf. *tener* for a discussion of the form) pres. 1 of *venir*, **17** 206 etc.

venides (L. *venĭtĭs* > *venides* > *venɩ́ɛs* > *venɩ́ys* > *venɩ́s*) pres. 2 pl. of *venir*, **17** 204.

veniendo (L. *venĭĕndum* ; the stem *ven-*, instead of *veñ-*, is due to *ven-ir* etc.; the *į* closed the first *e* > *i*, hence *viniendo*) pres. part. of *venir*, **62** 19.

veniessen (earlier form of *viniesen*) impf. sbj. of *venir*, **38** 366 *a*.

venir (L. *vĕnīre*) to come, **20** 1189 ; **35** 332 *b* ; etc. Cf. *vengo, venga, veniendo, venides, vernā, vino, viniese*, etc.

venjda = *venida* (noun from fem. p.p. of *venir*, V. L. **venītus -a -um*) advent, coming, **67** III 4.

venje = *venie* = *venía* (cf. *venir*), **49** 298 *b*.

venjr = *venir*, **68** VIII 4.

venjt = *venid* (cf. *venir*), **68** VIII 1.

ventado -a p.p. of *ventar* (perhaps L. *[in]ventāre* 'to come upon,' 'find'; or is it a by-form of *ventear*, based on L. *vĕntus* 'wind,' 'to get the scent of,' 'sniff out'?), found, discovered, **15** 116, 128.

ventana (V. L. **ventana* based on L. *ventus* 'wind,' i.e. 'wind hole,' 'vent') window, grating, **47** 14. (Cf. original probable sense of Eng. *window*, 'wind eye.')

ventanssen scribal error for *ventassen*, impf. sbj. of *ventar*, find, **16** 151; cf. *ventado*.

ventril (L. *ventrilis*) body of a chariot (?), bellyband (this latter is the modern sense), **30** 8 *d*.

ventura (perhaps from *[a]ventura*) hap, luck, fortune: *por ventura* perhaps, perchance, **58** 438 *c*.

venturoso -a (formation in *-oso -a* on *ventura*) fortunate, **30** 7 *d*.

ver (cf. *veer*) to see, **14** 94; **17** 205; **19** 1124; etc. Cf. *vedes*, *veedes*, *veet*, etc., *veriedes*, *vey*, *vi*, *via*, *vie*, *viera*, *vido*.

vera (L. *varĭus -a -um*; cf. *peña*) **49** 17 *b*.

verano (V. L. **verānus -um* from L. *ver*, with change of sense from 'spring' to 'summer') summer, **65** 105 *b*.

verdad (L. *veritās*, *verĭtātem*) truth, **42** 8.

verdadero -a (formation in *-ero -a* on *verdad*) real, true, truthful, **62** 9 etc.

verdat = *verdad*, **53** 15; **62** 23.

verde (L. *vĭrĭdis -em*; V. L. *vĭrdis -em*) green, **65** 105 *b* etc.

vergoñoso -a (formation in *-oso -a* on O. Sp. *vergoña*, *vergüeña* < L. *vĕrēcŭndĭa*) shameful, **51** 1662 *h*.

verguença (abstract from the verb *[a]vergoñar*, V. L. *[ad]verĕcŭndĭāre*, which has analogical *-ue-* in its present tenses, *avergüeño*, etc. Hence came O. Sp. *vergueña* 'shame,' which, through the influence of the large class of verbal abstracts in *-nça*, became *verguença*, mod. *vergüenza*) shame, **58** 438 *b*. (The O. Sp. Glosses have *vergoina*. Was the development *verecundia* > *vergoiña* > *vergüeña*? *Vergoina* may mean *vergoña*.)

veriedes (weak form of *veriades*, whence mod. *veríais*) cond. 2 pl. of *ver*, **16** 170; **19** 114.

vermeia (cf. *uermeio*) **16** 178.

verná (metathesized form of *venra*, fut. 3 of *venir*) will come, **67** II 5. Cf. mod. *tendrá*, and see *terne*, *ternia*.

vestido (L. *vestītus -um*) dress, garment, **30** 4 *b* etc.

vestidura (L. *vestītūra*) garment, raiment, **59** 14.

vey imper. of *ver* (L. *vĭde* > **vede* > **veę* > *vey*, whence mod. *ve*), see thou, **60** 4.

veyen = *veien* (weakened form of *veían*; cf. *ver*), **43** 17.

veyer (perhaps dialect form of *veer*) **30** 7 *d*.

veynte (L. *vĭgĭntī* > V. L. **vigĭnti*, through the closing influence of final *ī*, and then, by dissimilation *vẹginti* > *veínte* and, with a shift of the accent, *véinte*. But?) twenty, **40** 1 and 5.

vez (L. *vix*, *vĭcem*) place, time, **55** 20 etc. Cf. *uez* and *vegada*.

vezino -a (L. *vīcīnus -a -um*, with dissimilation of first *i* from accented *i*) neighbor, fellow, fellow being, inhabitant, occupant, **62** 2 ; **32** 19 *c*.

vi (L. *vīdī*) pret. of *ver*, **57** 432 *c*.

via (= stem of *v-er* + *-ía*, the ending of the impf. 3. The full form *veía* < L. *vĭdēbat*, V. L. **vĭdēat* > *vedia* > *veía*) he saw, **60** 10. (This form occurs in mod. verse.)

via (L. *vĭa*) way, means, **63** 89 *b*.

vianda (perhaps a loan-word from Fr. *viande*, L. ntr. pl. *vīvenda* 'things to be lived upon,' with loss of *v* by dissimilation) viands, food, **54** title.

vida (L. *vīta*) life, **50** 498 *b* etc.

Vidas pr. n., **14** 89 etc.

vidieron pret. 3 pl. of *ver* (with a dialect, and still popular, retention of *d* ; cf. *vieron*, the usual literary Castilian form), they saw, **29** 371 *b*.

vido pret. 3 of *ver* (cf. *vidieron* ; popular *vido* lives on beside literary Castilian *vió*), saw, **53** 7 ; **65** 103 *d*, 104 *b*, 105 *a* and *c*. (Can it be V. L. **vīdŭit*? Cf. O. Sp. *veno* < **venŭit*.)

vie weakened form of *via* (impf. of *ver*), **18** 1096.

vieda (L. *vĕtat* ; cf. *vedar*) forbids, **20** 1205.

viejo -a (V. L. *vĕc'lus -a -um* for L. *vetulus*) old, old man, old woman, **67** III *c* ; *llegar á viejo* to become an old man.

vien = *bien*, **34** 81 *a*.

viento (L. *vĕntus -um*) **57** 431 *d*.

viera (plpf. of *ver*) had seen, **59** 25 ; **60** 9 ; cf. *ver*.

viesso (L. *vĕrsus -um* ; this popular form has given way to the learned *verso*) verse, **55** 30.

vil (L. *vīlis -em*) vile, base, **30** 9 *a* etc.

villa (L. *vĭlla* 'farm,' 'villa,' extended in sense in Romance) town, **41** 23.

vinien = *venían* (cf. *venir*; the first *i* is due to pret. *vine*, etc.), **32** 20 *b*.

viniesse, viniessen = *viniese*, etc. (cf. *venir*), **20** 1190; etc.; **18** 1099; etc.

vinja = *vinia*, *venía* (cf. *vinien*), **26** 106 *b*.

vinjeron = *vinieron* (cf. *venir*), **68** IX 3.

vino (L. *vīnum*) wine, **23** 2 *d* etc.

Virgen (learned word; L. *vĭrgo*, *vĭrgĭnem*) Virgin, **48** 11 *b* etc.

virtuoso -a (learned word; V. L. **vĭrtŭōsus -a -um*) virtuous, **51** 1663 *h*.

visquiessen impf. sbj. 3 pl. of *vivir* (the stem *visqu-* i.e. *visc-* is probably due to the analogy of V. L. **nascŭit* > O. Sp. *nasco* ; cf. O. Sp. *nasquiesse*, etc.), should live, **16** 173.

vistien = *vestían* (the first *i* is due to *viste*, *vistió*, etc. ; cf. *vestir*), **30** 6 *c*.

vivades (L. *vīvātĭs* > *vivades* > **vivaęs* > *viváis*) pres. sbj. 2 pl. of *vivir*, **16** 158.

vivir (L. *vīvĕre*, V. L. **vīvīre*. Observe the retention of *v* after *ī*) to live: cf. *vivades*, *visquiessen*.

vja = *vía* way; *toda vja* still, **50** 1661 *d*.

vjda = *vida*, **66** 4.

vn, vna = *un, una*, a, an, one, **16** 178; **23** 1 *d*; etc.; (pl.) some, **60** 8, 24; etc.; *en vno* together, **14** 100 etc.; *vn* = *vna* (before unaccented *a*-), **17** 182.

vo pres. 1 of *ir* (L. *vado*, V. L. **vao* or **vo* on the analogy of *sto, do*), I go, **58** 437 *b*; **56** 422 *c*. (Did the *y* of mod *voy* arise in cases of inversion: *vo yo* > *voy yo*? Cf. *so* 'I am.')

voluntad (L. *voluntas*, *volŭntātem*; the retention of *ŭ* is not strictly popular) desire, good will, **19** 1139; **62** 5; etc.

voluntat = *voluntad*, **39** 369 *c*.

volutad = *voluntad* (the scribe forgot the nasal dash over the *u*), **16** 149; *de volutad* gladly.

volver (L. *volvĕre*, V. L. *vŏlvēre*) to turn, return, repeat, **34** 83 *a*; **55** 3; etc.

vondat = *bondat*, **39** 369 *b*.

vos 2 pers. pron. pl., subj. of verb; conj. obj., direct and indirect, of verb; obj. of prep. (cf. *uos*), **17** 194; **19** 1130; etc.; **20** 1214; **24** 93 *a*; **31** 11 *a*; etc.; **69** XIX 6.

voz (L. *vox*, *vōcem* > *voz*; pl. *vōces* > *vozes*) voice, shout, **38** 366 *a*; **39** 370 *d*; **47** 11; etc.

vsa = *usa*, pres. 3 of *usar* (cf. *usado*), **48** 14 *d*.

vsaua = *usava, usaba* (cf. *vsa* and *usado*), frequented, **50** 498 *a*.

vsurero = *usurero* (V. L. **ūsūrārĭus -um* from L. *ūsūra*) usurer, **70** LIII 8.

vuen = *buen*, **33** 75 *a*.

vuestro -a (cf. *uuestro*) your, **43** 32; **58** 439 *c* and *d*: pron., *las vuestras* your people, **55** 25.

vy = *vi*, **50** 498 *a*.

vyçio = *viçio*, **36** 350 *d*.

vyda = *vida*, **35** 334 *b*.

vyen = *bien*, **33** 72 *a*.

vyña = *viña* (L. *vīnĕa*) vineyard, **50** 499 *a*.

vyo = *vió*, pret. 3 of *ver*, **39** 368 *b*; **35** 329 *a* (?).

Vyseo = *Viseo* (pr. n.) Viseu, a city in Portugal, **34** 84 *a*.

[In O.Sp. the sign *x* denoted the palatal sibilant sound *š* (i.e., approximately, English *sh*). This later became the velar or guttural aspirate, now written *j* and *g (e,i)*.]

Xerica pr. n., **18** 1092.

xristal scribal for *christal*, i e. *cristal* (perhaps a loan-word, cf. Fr. *cristal* from L. *crystallum*), crystal, of crystal, **30** 3 *d*.

y (cf. *et* and *i*) and, **27** 356 *c*, 358 *c*; **63** 91 *c*; **64** 95 *a*; etc. (The *y* is not common in our texts; its generalized use is rather late.)

y adv. (L. *hīc*), there, in the case, here, **15** 120; **19** 1131, 1141; etc.; **32** 20 *a* etc.; **41** 6 etc. (In mod. Sp. this *y* remains only in *hay* = Fr. *il y a*.)

ya (L. *jam*) now, already, at last, yet, of course, certainly, **14** 114; **15** 137; **16** 155; **25** 104*d*; etc.

yabras = *y*, and, + *abras*, fut. 2 of *aver*, **64** 95*a*.

yago (V. L. **jaco* for L. *jaceo*, pres. 1 of *jacēre*, Sp. *yazer*) I lie, I am, **58** 440*d*.

Yague (L. vocative *Jacŏbe* > ** Yagobe* > ** Yagoue* > ** Yagọe* > *Yague*; cf. *Santi Yague*) St. James, Santiago, **19** 138.

yal = *y*, and, + *al*, **63** 92*c*.

yantar infin. n. (L. *jentāre*, V. L. *jantāre*, 'to breakfast'; in Sp. 'to dine'), dinner, **27** 355*c*; **36** 350*c*.

yaz truncated form of *yaze* (L. *jacet*; cf. *yazer*), lies, is, **48** 14*c*.

yazer (L. *jacēre*) to lie, be, **24** 92*b*; **28** 361*b*; **29** 369*a*; **58** 440*d*; etc. Cf. mod. *yacer*, *yago*, *yazie*. (The verb seems frequent as a mere auxiliary equivalent to the verb 'to be.')

yazie weakened form of *yazia* (cf. *yazer*), **45** 22; **46** 5.

ybierno = *ibierno*, *ivierno* (L. adj. *hībĕrnus -um*, which in V.L. supplanted *hiems*), winter, **27** 356*d*. (Cf. *yvierno* and mod. *invierno* with intrusive *n*.)

yd = *id* (cf. *ir*), **57** 433*b*.

ydes = *ides*, **16** 176.

ydo = *ido* (cf. *ir*), **35** 332*d*.

ye = *le* (?), **65** 138*b*.

yel = *y*, and, + *el*, **63** 91*c*.

yellos = *y*, and, + *ellos*, **65** 108*c*.

yen (= weakened form of impf. ending -*ian*, treated as separable in O. Sp., so that an obj. pron. could intervene between it and the infin. basis of the cond.) : *dar le yen* they would give him, **16** 161.

yen = *y*, and, + *en*, **63** 92*b*.

yent (apocopated form of *yente*) **26** 106*d*.

yente (L. *gens*, *gĕntem* > **yiente* > *yente*) people, race, multitude, **16** 176; **20** 1199; **41** 6; cf. *gente*.

yerro (abstract from the verb *errare* 'to err,' L. *ĕrrāre*, *ĕrro*, etc. The noun comes from the pres. diphthongized stem, *yerro, yerras*, etc.) error, **36** 338*d*; **45** 19; **52** 5.

yncamos (scribal for *inchamos*, pres. sbj. 1 pl. of *enchir* 'to fill'; L. *ĭmplēre*, V.L. **ĭmplīre*) let us fill, **14** 86.

ynojo = *inojo* (L. *gĕnŭcŭlum* for the more usual *genĭcŭlum*, dimin. of *genu* 'knee.' This should give **enojo*; is the *i* due to the constant occurrence of the word in the expression *fincar ynojos*, i.e. to the influence of the *i* of *fincar*?) knee, **60** *7*. (In mod. Sp. *rodilla* has supplanted *hinojo*; yet the phrase *de hinojos* 'on the knees, still lives.)

ynplisyon (ety.? Is it L. *implexio* -*ōnem*, developed in a semi-popular way?) complication of diseases (?), **67** II 7; cf. Notes.

yo (L. *ĕgo*, V.L. **eo*, which in proclitic unaccented position > *yo*) I, **13** 80; **14** 82; etc.

ala

a + ị   daians > lego

　　　　　　　　> beso

　　　　　　　　> hecho

　　　radiu > rayo

ẹ　　　　u

augurium > *agorio > agoiro > agüiro

viginti > viinte / viȩnte

biȩnte